ROOSEVELT'S LOST ALLIANCES

D0208268

ROOSEVELT'S
LOST
ALLIANCES

How Personal Politics Helped Start the Cold War

Frank Costigliola

Princeton University Press
Princeton and Oxford

Copyright © 2012 by Princeton University Press

Published by Princeton University Press, 41 William Street, Princeton, New Jersey 08540
In the United Kingdom: Princeton University Press, 6 Oxford Street, Woodstock, Oxford-
shire OX20 1TW
press.princeton.edu

Jacket photo: Roosevelt recounted that Stalin, on meeting Sarah Churchill at the Tehran
Conference, "leaped to his feet at once," and greeted her "in the most elegant court man-
nerly style." FDR commented, "You see, Stalin has something else in him besides this revo-
lutionist, Bolshevist thing." From right are Churchill, Anthony Eden, Archibald Clark Kerr,
General "Hap" Arnold, FDR, Averell Harriman, Sarah Churchill, Vyacheslav Molotov,
and Stalin. Photo by Evening Standard / Stringer. Courtesy of Hulton Archives / Getty
Images.

All Rights Reserved

Library of Congress Cataloging-in-Publication Data

Costigliola, Frank, 1946–
  Roosevelt's lost alliances : how personal politics helped start the Cold War / Frank
Costigliola.
     p. cm.
  Includes bibliographical references and index.
  ISBN 978-0-691-12129-1 (alk. paper)
  1. World War, 1939–1945—Diplomatic history. 2. United States—Foreign
relations—1933–1945. 3. United States—Foreign relations—1945–1953. 4. United
States—Foreign relations—Soviet Union. 5. Soviet Union—Foreign relations—United
States. 6. United States—Foreign relations—Great Britain. 7. Great Britain—Foreign
relations—United States. 8. Roosevelt, Franklin D. (Franklin Delano), 1882–1945.
9. Stalin, Joseph, 1879–1953. 10. Churchill, Winston, 1874–1965. 11. Cold war—
Diplomatic history. I. Title.
  D748.C67 2012
  940.53'22–dc23   2011025271

British Library Cataloging-in-Publication Data is available

This book has been composed in Sabon text with Impact display
Printed on acid-free paper. ∞
Printed in the United States of America

10 9 8 7 6 5 4 3 2 1

For Diann

Contents

Introduction   1

CHAPTER 1   A Portrait of the Allies as Young Men: Franklin,
            Winston, and Koba   21

CHAPTER 2   From Missy to Molotov: The Women and Men
            Who Sustained the Big Three   58

CHAPTER 3   The Personal Touch: Forming the Alliance,
            January–August 1941   97

CHAPTER 4   Transcending Differences: Eden Goes to Moscow
            and Churchill to Washington, December 1941   141

CHAPTER 5   Creating the "Family Circle": The Tortuous
            Path to Tehran, 1942–43   163

CHAPTER 6   "I've Worked It Out": Roosevelt's Plan to Win
            the Peace and Defy Death, 1944–45   205

CHAPTER 7   The Diplomacy of Trauma: Kennan and His
            Colleagues in Moscow, 1933–46   259

CHAPTER 8   Guns and Kisses in the Kremlin: Ambassadors
            Harriman and Clark Kerr Encounter
            Stalin, 1943–46   291

CHAPTER 9   "Roosevelt's Death Has Changed Everything":
            Truman's First Days, April–June 1945   312

CHAPTER 10 The Lost Alliance: Widespread Anxiety and
            Deepening Ideology, July 1945–March 1946   359

Conclusion and Epilogue   418
Acknowledgments   429

Bibliographical Note   433
Notes   437
Index   523

ROOSEVELT'S LOST ALLIANCES

Introduction

Of all the many books on Allied diplomacy in World War II, Robert E. Sherwood's magisterial *Roosevelt and Hopkins* remains unequaled.[1] Published in 1948, the 962-page tome draws on Sherwood's insider status as a Roosevelt speechwriter and on his discussions with the historical actors. Sherwood was forbidden, however, to use his most explosive interview, the one that assigned blame for the breakup of the Grand Alliance. The interviewee was Anthony Eden, Winston S. Churchill's foreign secretary. In wartime negotiations the top diplomat had loyally supported his chief even when the latter tangled with Franklin D. Roosevelt. Eden stood next in line for prime minster should the Conservatives win the next election. He understood that postwar Britain depended on Washington, where Harry S. Truman served as president. Nevertheless, by August 1946 this habitually restrained aristocrat was so disturbed by the deterioration in relations with Moscow since Roosevelt's death in April 1945 that he let loose. In lamenting the loss of Roosevelt, Eden criticized Churchill and Truman in ways that, if made public, could have crippled his future career. After venting, he insisted on keeping the interview secret. And so it long remained.

To Sherwood, Eden "stated flatly that the deplorable turning point in the whole relationship of the Western Allies with the Soviet Union was caused directly by the death of Roosevelt." The former foreign secretary seemed moved himself as he detailed the emotional valence of FDR's relationship with the Russians. "He spoke at length and with great conviction of the extraordinary ability of Roosevelt to handle the Russian situation and of the overwhelming respect which the Russians had for the President." Decades of practicing realpolitik had attuned Eden to intangibles, such as personality and respect. The

Russians' "respect" for Roosevelt "was for the man himself rather than for the high and powerful position that he held." Eden understood that manner and nuance could tip the balance between success and failure. He was blunt about how Roosevelt differed from others who had dealt with the Russians. "Eden spoke of Roosevelt's infinite subtlety and contrasted him in this respect with Churchill and Truman." Particularly at a critical juncture in history, such as 1945, emotional and personal dynamics could tilt the weightiest matters of international politics. As Eden put it, "had Roosevelt lived and retained his health he would never have permitted the present situation to develop." A professional in the precise measurement of words, he offered a stunning final judgment: Roosevelt's "death, therefore, was a calamity of immeasurable proportions."[2] *Roosevelt's Lost Alliances* reaches a similar conclusion.

Roosevelt's death weakened, perhaps fatally, the prospects for avoiding or at least mitigating the Cold War. FDR was critical to the founding of the Grand Alliance and to keeping it together. He intended the coalition to continue into the postwar era, as did Joseph Stalin. Despite his Marxist-Leninist ideology, the Soviet dictator also identified with Czar Alexander I, who had remained a partner in the Holy Alliance after the victory over Napoleon. Stalin wanted strong confederates to help contain postwar Germany and Japan.[3] Churchill, nervous about the "Great Russian Bear" and the "Great American Buffalo" squeezing the "poor little English donkey," remained more ambivalent about continued Big Three partnership.[4] Just as the wartime alliance depended on Roosevelt, so, too, did Roosevelt rely on a personal alliance of close aides and friends in the White House. Tragically, however, FDR persisted in behaviors that drained this intimate circle. In contrast to Truman and the embittered Soviet experts who would become the new president's principal advisers, the supremely self-confident Roosevelt lavished on Stalin displays of respect that salved the dictator's personal and cultural insecurities, rendering him more amenable to compromise on certain issues.

As the fulcrum of the Grand Alliance, Roosevelt merits primary, but not exclusive, attention.[5] For Churchill and Stalin, as well as for Roosevelt, background, personality, and culture conditioned their emotional beliefs and their interactions with each other. This book examines wartime diplomacy in the context of each leader's family and cultural heritage, formative experiences, and emotional dispositions and sensibilities. Spurred by personal feelings as well as by official responsibilities, Roosevelt and Churchill, and, perhaps, Stalin, too, approached their initial summit meetings as grand adventure. As the terrible strain of the war mounted, these flesh-and-blood titans interacted in ways increasingly conditioned by sickness and exhaustion.

Despite their other differences, the Big Three all sought to appear resolute and manly. Early in the war, each tried to persuade the other two, and the Axis enemies mocking them as weak and decadent, that he possessed the toughness to persevere until victory. Yet all of them, too, in their respective ways, had to live with a gender identity more complex than the conventional norms of masculinity. This complexity also enabled each man to draw from a wider spectrum of behaviors. With a hint of femininity, Roosevelt and Stalin charmed and seduced. Forever boyish, Churchill enthused and effervesced. As the war was drawing to a close, benign impressions of Stalin as seducer were overpowered by frightening reports of the Red Army's rape and pillage.

The functioning of the wartime alliance and the future of the postwar world pivoted on diplomacy inextricably personal and political. It remains impossible, however, to isolate what the precise impact of the "personal" would be on a hypothesized, wholly impersonal "political" interaction—not that such could ever occur among human beings.

The most persuasive evidence for the real-life importance of personal diplomacy was the extraordinary, indeed heroic, efforts made by Roosevelt and Churchill. FDR, aware of his heart disease, risked his life in journeying to far-off Yalta. Defying exhaustion and bouts of pneumonia, Churchill traveled repeatedly to Washington and to Moscow. After negotiating with the Kremlin dictator in October 1944, Churchill found it "extraordinary how many questions yield to discussion and personal talk."[6] Even Stalin, who had not gone abroad since the 1917 Revolution, left the Soviet Union for the Tehran and Potsdam conferences. A telling marker of the shift in Washington's stance after Roosevelt's demise was Truman's telling his staff in late 1945 that he did not intend any further Big Three summit meetings.

The Cold War was not inevitable. Nor did that conflict stem solely from political disputes and the ideological clash between capitalism and communism. Examining how the Grand Alliance operated and then fell apart is prerequisite for understanding how the Cold War formed. The alliance cohered and then collapsed for reasons more contingent, emotional, and cultural than historians have heretofore recognized. If Roosevelt had lived a while longer—indeed, he was trying to manage his health in order to survive—he might have succeeded in bringing about the transition to a postwar world managed by the Big Three. His death and Churchill's electoral defeat three months later disrupted personal and political connections in which all three leaders had invested enormous effort and cautious hope. Neither the men who succeeded these giants, nor the American "Soviet experts" who asserted a more decisive role than they had hitherto been allowed to play, shared Roosevelt's, or even Churchill's, interest in Big Three accord.

The dynamics of the Cold War—the mutually reinforcing pursuit of ambition and fear of threat on the part of the two superpowers—originated in a zero-sum model quite different from that imagined by the Big Three leaders during the war. They had surmised that after the war, their rivalry and differences, though sharp at times, could be corralled by their mutual interest in a stable and peaceful world that would ensure their collective predominance. Their envisioned order would have restricted the liberty of smaller nations in the regional domain of each of the Big Three sheriffs. Roosevelt largely accepted such restrictions in the expectation that they could ease with time. He was amenable to areas of influence as long as they did not become exclusive and closed. The Cold War that actually developed would highlight Soviet injustice in Eastern Europe without doing much to ease the pain. Indeed, perceptive observers, such as the diplomat George F. Kennan, would decades later come to see the Cold War as promoting the repression rather than the liberation of the Soviet Union's empire.

While mobilizing public anger against the Axis, Roosevelt tried to tamp down uproar over issues, such as Poland, that could split the Grand Alliance. At times FDR himself became furious with Stalin. Yet he tried to control such feelings. Churchill and Truman, in contrast, did not or could not exercise such restraint. He also tried harder than Churchill or Truman to build bridges—some of them admittedly shaky—across the cultural divide separating the Americans and British from the Soviets. Though not inclined toward detailed study or abstract concepts, the squire of Hyde Park wielded a razor-sharp emotional intelligence. Masterful in reading personality and in negotiating subtle transactions of pride and respect, he could charm almost anyone. He deployed these skills with surprising success in establishing a bond with Stalin.

The Kremlin chieftain also tried to limit hyperemotional reactions in the alliance and in his own entourage. In January 1945, he instructed fellow Communists: "In relation to bourgeois politicians you have to be careful. They are . . . very touchy and vindictive. You have to keep a handle on your emotions; if emotions lead—you lose."[7] Despite such advice, Stalin himself remained susceptible to anger, revenge, pride, and flattery.

Cultural differences excited emotional reactions and complicated political issues. Insecure pride, craving for respect, anxiety about change, and fear of appearing fearful skewed political perceptions, making political compromises more difficult. Racialized cultural stereotypes of "semi-savage" Soviets and of "conniving" cosmopolitans eager to make "fools" out of Russians hampered the formation of the alliance in 1941 and helped destroy it after the war. John "Jock" Balfour, a British diplomat familiar with both Moscow and Washington, advised a group of influential Americans: "Russia is so different from us historically, politically, and culturally that in many respects she seems almost like another planet."[8] Roosevelt employed personal ties to make such differences appear less alien.

U.S. and British relations with the Soviets played out on two stages with different scenery, performers, and rules—resulting in divergent moods between the two groups of players. At Churchill's 1941–44 conferences with Roosevelt, at the three-way summits of Tehran in 1943 and Yalta in 1945, at Churchill's two conferences with Stalin in Moscow in 1942 and 1944, and at the 1945 Potsdam meeting that included Truman, top leaders emerged from the intense talks convinced they had advanced their personal ties and political agendas. There was something seductive about wheeling and dealing with other men of power. "When Truman returned from Potsdam, he was in a state of advanced euphoria," a top aide later recalled.[9] Feelings of warmth and needs for approval altered perspectives. "I'd like that man to like me," Churchill said after first meeting Stalin.[10] Leaders came away readier to trust each other. Such short-term feelings probably resulted in part from physiological change.[11] Though the pleasant glow from each summit would fade, political progress had usually been gained. A key aspect of Roosevelt's postwar vision was institutionalizing such summits as regular events, in which the three or four "world sheriffs" would gather at some secluded location like the Azores and hash out solutions without the glare of media attention.[12] A master at personal charm, Roosevelt probably expected that such meetings would gradually acculturate participants to the American model.

Far different, however, were the stale and limited roles that the U.S. and British diplomats, military liaison officers, and journalists stationed in Moscow found themselves playing each day. They deeply resented their intense personal isolation. The Kremlin's policy of isolating foreigners from "normal" contacts with Soviet citizens and officials rendered many representatives frustrated, furious, and even disoriented. Feeling especially aggrieved were Kennan and Charles E. "Chip" Bohlen, ambassadors William C. Bullitt and W. Averell Harriman, and the Pentagon liaison to the Red Army, General John R. Deane. Each had intended to strike up personal relations with Russians, immerse himself in Russian culture, and become the interlocutor between Washington and Moscow. The "no-contact" regime thwarted those good intentions. These diplomats and military liaison officials served as the optical nerves of the U.S. and British governments. What they reported from Moscow and what they said on returning home was conditioned by their disappointment, anger, and resentment. Most were skeptical about compromise with a country whose repressive system they had personally experienced.

Colleagues who had not served in Russia tended to defer to the insistent opinion of those with firsthand experience. Moscow-based diplomats expected the contact and freedom that were embedded in their own culture. They had little empathy for the cultural insecurity, military exigencies, and political imperatives of Soviet leaders. Their sense of exceptionalism was always operative, and especially influential once Roosevelt was gone.

Pushing for contact with Soviet citizens constituted the personal element in America's and (to a lesser extent Britain's) traditional foreign policy of the open door, that is, seeking unhampered trade and investment as well as travel and information around the globe. While pursuing this goal, U.S. officials would end up accepting half-measures in much of the world. In Soviet domains, however, the open door policy hooked into not just politics and economics but also gut-level convictions about access, freedom, and information. As Harriman reminded Americans in Moscow, "Anything unknown to us is sinister."[13]

Historiography

For years after 1945, the former diplomats in Moscow helped to enforce not merely a Cold War policy but also a one-sided interpretation of the very history of the conflict. This view blamed the Cold War solely on Soviet aggression and intransigence. In 1949, Edward R. Stettinius Jr., FDR's secretary of state at Yalta, completed a memoir that assigned some of the fault to U.S. policy after Roosevelt's death. Supreme Court Justice Felix Frankfurter, an informal adviser to FDR, applauded Stettinius for having "vindicated the great man who is no longer here to speak for himself."[14] Chip Bohlen, in contrast, sharply disagreed. He warned the retired secretary of state that "all of those" currently (in 1949) managing relations with Moscow concurred that the Cold War had originated wholly "in the character and nature of the Soviet state" and in its ideology. U.S. policy under Truman bore no significant responsibility for tensions, he insisted. Bohlen responded "so frankly" and so vehemently because Stettinius was challenging what had become gospel truth: the Cold War was inevitable and Moscow's fault. Bohlen restated the creed: "Yalta proved the impossibility of expecting agreements with the Soviet Union to provide solutions to the postwar world." He disputed Stettinius's memory that at Yalta "a really solid basis was arrived at which was somehow or other frittered away by mutual suspicion on both sides, etc."[15] By the 1950s, few in the West questioned the prevailing narrative: a largely innocent, well-intentioned United States had reluctantly, indeed bravely, taken up the burden of defending the "Free World" against an aggressive, ideologically driven Soviet Union led by a grasping dictator.[16]

Despite their denunciation of the character and ideology of the Soviet Union, these original Cold Warriors did not assert what some historians would later claim: the supposed madness of Stalin. Bohlen, Kennan, Harriman, and others who had repeatedly seen the dictator up close condemned him as ruthless, brutal, cruel, and calculating—but not as insane.

The historiographical fight over the origins of the Cold War flamed up in the 1960s. Many of the documents published in the *Foreign Relations of the United States* volumes for the war and immediate postwar years undermined the Manichaeism of the orthodox interpretation. William A. Williams's *Tragedy of American Diplomacy* (1959), Walter LaFeber's *America, Russia, and the Cold War, 1945–66* (1967), Gabriel Kolko's *The Politics of War* (1968), and Lloyd C. Gardner's *Architects of Illusion* (1970), among other works, stressed that U.S. leaders were pursuing what they perceived as America's national interest in opening markets and in laying the groundwork for resurgent capitalism around the world, including in Eastern Europe. In another strand of "revisionism," Gar Alperovitz's *Atomic Diplomacy* argued that the Truman administration had dropped the two atomic bombs on Japan, even though Tokyo seemed ready to surrender, in order to intimidate Moscow.[17] The revisionists argued, convincingly, that U.S. policy was far more aggressive than defensive. Such challenges to the orthodox interpretation rankled most policymakers from the 1940s. Harriman labeled Alperovitz's study "an awful book. Horrible book."[18]

In May 1967, Arthur M. Schlesinger Jr. mounted a counteroffensive against the revisionists. A prize-winning historian, adviser to the Kennedys, and champion of the Cold War consensus then fracturing in the Vietnam War, Schlesinger aimed to quash the heresy with an authoritative article in the respected journal *Foreign Affairs*. To assemble the most commanding evidence, Schlesinger held an off-the-record seminar with Harriman and John J. McCloy, assistant secretary of war during World War II and the postwar banker-diplomat dubbed "chairman of the Establishment."[19] Together they would retrace the origins of the Cold War. Harriman, despite his distaste for revisionism and despite his tough line in 1944–46, had by the 1960s become an advocate of reengaging the Soviets. Ever ambitious, the septuagenarian no doubt appreciated that such diplomacy could open fresh vistas for his career as America's most experienced Kremlin negotiator.

Schlesinger focused on getting the former ambassador to Moscow to endorse his, Schlesinger's, pet theory about the origins of the Cold War. This theory lacked relevant sustaining evidence. Yet once assumed as valid, the thesis offered such an unassailable, ideologically and intellectually satisfying explanation for the Cold War that in subsequent decades it would be embraced by some other historians as well. Schlesinger posed a leading question: "When do you think Stalin became irrational?" Harriman: "I don't know." Then, collecting his thoughts, the older man asserted that Stalin, rather than irrational, "was the ablest man that I've ever known." Taken aback, Schlesinger pressed: "Even abler than Churchill, even than Roosevelt? "Yes. Very definitely." The questioner tried again: When did Stalin begin "to lose—to go around mad"? Harriman explained that although the dictator's mental stability had indeed failed, that slippage had occurred only a few years before his death in 1953. Schlesinger would not give up. Harriman just as stubbornly insisted that in 1946, when he had last seen Stalin, the latter was "wholly, wholly" rational.[20] Ruthless—but not irrational or mad. Undaunted, Schlesinger a few months later published in *Foreign Affairs* a widely read essay blaming the Cold War principally on "the intransigence of Leninist ideology, the sinister dynamics of a totalitarian society, and the madness of Stalin."[21]

In the 1970s and '80s, the orthodox-revisionist debate grew more complex as some historians, notably John Lewis Gaddis, argued for a "post-revisionist synthesis." He asserted that "the primary cause of the Cold War was Stalin's own ill-defined ambition, his determination to seek security in such a way as to leave little or none for other actors."

Gaddis did not, however, pick up on Schlesinger's claim of "madness." Rather, he found Stalin "a cagey but insecure opportunist . . . without any long-term strategy or even very much interest in promoting the spread of communism beyond the Soviet sphere."[22] Unconvinced revisionists responded that post-revisionism amounted to "orthodoxy plus archives."[23] Deborah Welch Larson ventured onto new ground with *Origins of Containment: A Psychological Explanation.*[24]

The ending of the Cold War in 1989–91 and the subsequent partial opening of Russian archives enabled the writing of some pathbreaking Stalin biographies. Carefully researched and balanced studies by Robert Service, Simon Sebag Montefiore, and Hiroaki Kuromiya concurred on Stalin's brutality, cruelty, and dark suspiciousness—as well as on the dictator's intelligence, diligence, and sanity, at least until the early 1950s.[25]

Nevertheless, some authors revived Schlesinger's theory that the "madness of Stalin" had made the post-1945 confrontation inevitable. Two influential books combined analysis based on newly opened archival sources with emotional commentary. Vojtech Mastny's *The Cold War and Soviet Insecurity* (1996) asserted that the "insatiable quest for security" that warped Stalin's personality also made accommodation with the West impossible. Alluding to the "possible pathological bent of Stalin's mind" and stressing the "sheer evil of Stalinism," Mastny concluded that the Soviet Union "was not a normal state but one run by a criminal syndicate at the service of a bloody tyrant hungry for power and ready to abuse it."[26] John Lewis Gaddis's *We Now Know* (1997) argued that Stalin had "conflated the requirements of national security with personal security in a completely unprecedented way." With regard to the inevitability of, and responsibility for, the Cold War, Gaddis, in contrast to his earlier scholarship, now saw pathological personality as compelling policy. "Did Stalin therefore seek a Cold War? The question is a little like asking: 'does a fish seek water?'"[27] Much of the problem stemmed from Stalin's "paranoia."[28] It "was Stalin's disposition to wage cold wars: he had done so . . . throughout his life." The dictator's personality required total security only for himself, thereby "depriving everyone else of it." This "made conflict unavoidable," Gaddis concluded. Even if Roosevelt had lived past April 1945, it would not likely "have altered the long-term course of Soviet-American relations."[29]

In 1996, Vladislav Zubok and Constantine Pleshakov published *Inside the Kremlin's Cold War*, a book based on Russian sources. While discussing "Stalin's dark mind," they did not depict the dictator as mad.[30] Instead, they stressed Stalin's effort to balance his postwar imperial and revolutionary aspirations with his desire for continued Big Three collaboration. Zubok, in his 2007 follow-up, *A Failed Empire*, emphasized that until Roosevelt's death, most Moscow officials "believed that U.S.-Soviet cooperation, despite possible problems, would continue after the war."[31]

In the new millennium, arguments over blame and Stalin's supposed madness receded as scholars addressed other concerns, such as North-South issues and the role of ideology. Odd Arne Westad deployed his formidable language skills in producing *The Global Cold War* (2005), an overview of how local conditions around the world frustrated the ideologically driven—and in some ways ideologically parallel—policies of Washington and Moscow.[32] In *For the Soul of Mankind* (2007), a nuanced, finely balanced synthesis, Melvyn P. Leffler drew on a wide range of sources to demonstrate how the pressures of ideology, personality, and international structure sparked the Cold War and then sustained it, notwithstanding repeated opportunities for a settlement. Leffler depicted Stalin in 1945 as "no longer . . . the militant, aggressive revolutionary."[33] Though suspicious and brutal, the dictator sought to sustain the wartime coalition. He often seemed inscrutable, but not insane. Geoffrey Roberts's *Stalin's Wars* (2006), a book deeply grounded in Russian sources, extolled the dictator as "a very effective and highly successful war leader." Echoing Harriman's rejoinder to Schlesinger, Roberts maintained that although Roosevelt and Churchill were "replaceable as warlords . . . Stalin was indispensable." Roberts argued that the dictator "worked hard to make the Grand Alliance a success and wanted to see it continue after the war."[34] Wilson D. Miscamble, the author of *From Roosevelt to Truman* (2007), emphasized what he saw as the continuity between Roosevelt and Truman. In this rendering FDR appears naive and fumbling, while Truman, earnestly trying to pursue good relations with the Soviets, is thwarted by the grasping dictator.[35] Countering Roberts, Jonathan Haslam's *Russia's Cold War* (2011) emphasized the formative influence of Marxist-Leninist ideology from the Revolution to the collapse of the Soviet Union.[36] Jochen Laufer, *Pax Sovietica* (2009), focused on Stalin's postwar designs on Germany.[37]

Disputing the thesis that the "madness of Stalin" rendered the Cold War inevitable does not mean ignoring the dictator's horrific crimes against the peoples of the Soviet Union and neighboring lands. In a succinct analysis of *Stalin's Genocides* (2010), Norman M. Naimark asserted that while a number of factors made Stalin into the person who murdered millions, the primary element remained his "paranoia." "The real Stalin," Naimark reminded us, was a small man "both physically and morally," but he could be "capable" and "self-possessed" as well as "suspicious," "vindictive," and "brutal."[38] Timothy Snyder, in *Bloodlands* (2010), concluded that while both dictators perpetrated genocide in the "bloodlands" between Germany and Russia, Stalin, unlike Hitler, "was able to restrain himself when necessary."[39] That restraint was what Roosevelt counted on in trying to bring the Grand Alliance into the postwar world.

Personality, Emotion, Ideology, and Culture

Although the wartime coalition and the origins of the Cold War have attracted the attention of many gifted historians, *Roosevelt's Lost Alliances* aims to go beyond earlier studies by tracing the political consequences of the relationships, personalities, emotional lives, emotional dispositions, sensibilities, and cultural assumptions of Roosevelt and other key figures.[40] A close-up view of Roosevelt, Churchill, and Stalin is critical to understanding how they interacted to create and sustain Allied unity. Similarly, investigating the inner qualities of Truman, Harriman, and Kennan helps in realizing why they opposed the compromises and the ambiguity that were essential to sustaining the Grand Alliance. The concept of "emotional belief" is useful in exploring how each of these six figures extrapolated—that is, made the leap in logic—from what they knew, to what they wanted to believe.[41]

Emotional beliefs entail arranging the evidence to support a conviction that goes *beyond* that evidence. Examining the assumptions in a statesman's leap in logic can yield evidence of that official's overall perspective and objectives.

Roosevelt's personal background predisposed him to an emotional belief that postwar cooperation was necessary and worth the risk. He had enjoyed a wealthy, privileged, and pampered childhood. He benefited from his charm, good looks, and what became known as "Roosevelt luck." When he had gambled, it had paid off. The former New York governor had defied polio to win six straight elections, including third and fourth terms as president. Service in Woodrow Wilson's administration had left him anxious not to repeat Wilson's failure to win a lasting peace. FDR remained unscarred by the anti-Bolshevism of the 1918–20 Red Scare. He held enormous faith in America's power and future and in himself as a man of destiny. He sensed that his time was limited. Roosevelt bet on Stalin's overwhelming interest in heading off another German invasion. He would die before putting on the table his two high cards, control over the atomic bomb and postwar economic aid.

FDR's effectiveness as president and as keystone of the Grand Alliance depended on his personal alliances with dedicated, live-in aides who entertained him, translated his notions into pragmatic policy, and got results. Harry L. Hopkins and Marguerite "Missy" LeHand (and in earlier years, Louis M. Howe and Thomas G. Corcoran) wore themselves out in trying to cope not only with the extraordinary needs of the "Boss" but also with his possessiveness regarding even their personal lives. By 1944, the very time when Roosevelt faced mounting challenges in managing the war and planning the peace, he had lost the crucial players of his inner circle. FDR became, partly owing to his demanding nature, dangerously isolated.

Churchill's grounding, very different from Roosevelt's, inclined the British leader to an emotional belief that the interests he cared about would be better served by an alliance with Washington against Moscow. He had experienced difficulties during his childhood, and he often clashed with authority figures. Churchill's fondness for things military and naval, his Victorian perspective on imperial rivalry with

Russia, and his fierce anti-Bolshevism in 1918–20 all inclined him against the Kremlin. He had emerged from the political wilderness to become prime minister in May 1940 on the strength of his warning about one evil dictator, Adolf Hitler. Churchill feared that concessions to another dictator, Stalin, especially at the expense of the Poles, thousands of whom had fought alongside British forces, would alienate voters in his July 1945 election campaign. After losing the parliamentary election, Churchill would again seize the stage by sounding an emotional alarm about the "Iron Curtain" and by calling for a renewed alliance with Truman's America.

The destruction wrought by the 1914 and 1941 invasions and the spectacle of Germany's twice standing off most of the world imprinted on Stalin the emotional belief that this irrepressible enemy would strike yet again unless contained by some overpowering coalition. Though he would eventually settle for a ring of satellite nations and the Cold War, he initially preferred an alliance with powerful America and Britain to keep down Germany and Japan. In another emotional belief, Stalin imagined that the Soviets actually could fabricate a Warsaw government that would be simultaneously a "friend" to Moscow, an acceptable solution for the Polish people, and a rampart against another German invasion.

Born Joseph Dzhugashvili, Stalin endured the grimmest childhood. Beaten by his father, a cobbler who according to local rumor had good reason to doubt his paternity, "Soso" grew up surrounded by the authoritarian cultures of family, Orthodox seminary, czarist regime, and Bolshevik Party. Even more than Churchill, Stalin was scarred by the searing emotions of the Russian Revolution. In the 1930s, the dictator's forced collectivization and industrialization exacted a terrible human toll, a cost magnified by his bloody purges against imagined and real rivals. Stalin apparently convinced himself he could postpone or even prevent a German invasion by striking a deal with Hitler in August 1939.

The most consequential emotional belief of Truman's first year as president developed out of his unquestioning faith in America's exceptionalism. He believed the atomic bomb was born of the country's unique engineering and scientific talent, industrial workmanship, and

Yankee "know-how." This combination the Russians could not match, concluded the president. His thinking ignored the explicit advice of atomic scientists and a majority of his own Cabinet. He also ignored those voices in deciding that the safest bet was not in a possible Big Three deal with the Kremlin, but rather in staying ahead in an atomic arms race.

Truman coupled fierce pride with deep insecurity. A bookish boy who had loved school but could not afford college, he had a checkered career in business and farming. He achieved success as an artillery officer in World War I and then as a politician. In 1944, party bosses pushed Senator Truman for vice president. Roosevelt, who kept all his vice presidents at arm's length, regarded Truman as a Senate insider who could help get a peace treaty ratified. Not knowing much about foreign affairs and prone to hasty, emotional judgments, Truman as president proved susceptible to manipulation. Harriman and others exploited his insecurities and his impulse to play the tough guy with Stalin and other rivals.

Harriman's emotional belief, which he pressed on Truman with success and ultimately dire consequences, was that Stalin would back down if pressed hard. Though the dictator gave in on some matters, on most he pushed back even harder. The shoving match would develop into the Cold War. Harriman had grown up in a family with greater wealth but less status than the old-money Roosevelts. Averell inherited from his father, the railroad empire builder E. H. Harriman, a fierce ambition—displayed, for example, by his investment of money and talent to become the fourth-ranked polo player in the nation. As ambassador, he aspired to leverage his position as the crucial American in Moscow into a shot at becoming secretary of state or even president. Repelled by the Soviets' naked repression in Poland and frustrated by his isolation, Harriman by September 1944 was lobbying for a much tougher stance against Moscow.

In 1946–47, Kennan, determined to jolt America out of what he saw as dangerous complacency, used loaded metaphors to create an emotional belief about the Soviet challenge. He went beyond the evidence of Moscow's behavior and ambition, indeed, distorted the picture, so as to depict the Kremlin as a monstrous, existential threat. He warned that the Soviets, while not planning war, aimed in every other way to "penetrate" and disrupt a U.S.-led international order. Though born into a middle-class family in Milwaukee, Kennan came to love the lost world of pre-1917 Russia. He doubted "there could be anyone in the Western world who [had] deeper feelings" for the Russian people than he did.[42] He dreamed of becoming the cultural and/or political mediator between the United States and Russia. Nothing about the Kremlin's repression frustrated Kennan more than the isolation of foreigners from Soviet citizens. Being deprived of contact with Russians facilitated his conclusion that the Soviet government should likewise be contained and isolated. In 1946–47, Kennan helped reframe the issue from whether the United States and the Soviet Union could reach a practical compromise to whether it was realistic and manly to negotiate with a regime impelled by an abhorrent ideology.

Though latent during the war, the ideological conflict between Marxist-Leninism and liberal-democratic capitalism was stoked by Kennan, Stalin, and Churchill in early 1946. Ideology—a condensed, explanatory set of beliefs—reduced the complex global crisis to easily understandable slogans and images, to a contest of good versus evil. At Yalta, Churchill and Stalin had candidly discussed the utility and the danger of whipping up ideological conflict among the masses. Roosevelt nearly always downplayed ideology. As a category of historical analysis, ideology is most usefully understood as one element in the broader realm of culture.[43] Cultural divergences aggravated political issues. As a Soviet diplomat explained it, tensions with the British were "largely due to differences of background and outlook . . . and method." Differences also intruded "in the use of such words as 'democracy' and 'collaboration.'"[44] Dissimilar categories of thought spurred misunderstandings, making political compromise more difficult.

Differences in war circumstance widened the gap between political perspectives. The people of the Soviet Union suffered some twenty-seven million dead. Millions of Ukrainians and other non-Russian nationalities initially welcomed the Germans as liberators. The Americans and British together suffered fewer than a million dead and fought land battles mostly at locations and at times of their choosing. Much of the U.S. contribution came in the form of Lend-Lease, of which eleven billion dollars out of the sixty billion total went to Russia.

Many Red Army soldiers acted on their belief that German atrocities justified extreme vengeance, including the mass rape of German women and pillaging along the route to Berlin.[45] Outrages against German civilians sparked among many Americans and British anger, disgust, and contempt for the Soviets. Cultural and racial prejudice antedated those reports, however. In 1940, British ambassador Stafford Cripps reported on "the universal hymn of hate . . . against the Russians" that sounded "whenever a few Englishmen meet. . . . The whole tradition and bias of the F[oreign] O[ffice] is violently and unreasoningly anti-Russian." Yet even the sympathetic Cripps criticized the Russians' "Asiatic ways, which are not our ways."[46] Notwithstanding the Nazi interlude and all its horrors, for many Americans and British, Germans still figured as racial and cultural kin. The Soviets, in contrast, dwelled outside the pale; indeed they ranked as "barbarians," Harriman told Truman.

Like individuals, nations can exhibit distinctive—though not determining or unambiguous—"emotional dispositions." Culturally and historically conditioned emotional dispositions influence the particular anxieties and imperatives of national leaders. U.S. officials (Roosevelt not included, however) tended to fret over whether others saw them as tough enough. The British, staggering to victory, seemed frantic to assert their authority. The Soviets overcompensated for their status anxiety. These trends and tropes were neither absolute nor exclusive. But like a computer operating system, such tendencies organized more or less inchoate concerns into a pattern of emotionalized political issues.

Russian status anxiety was fed by geography, history, and culture. The Russians, whether viewed as aggressors or as those whom Roosevelt was trying to "get-at," appeared as outlanders. Soviet officials, despite their proud nationalism, appeals to Slavic unity, claims of superiority over the decadent West, and leadership of the world's first Marxist state, nevertheless yearned for respect: to be treated as equals and accepted for who they were. When Roosevelt's emissary, Joseph E. Davies, asked Stalin's henchman, Vyacheslav Molotov, what was needed for real collaboration, the Russian "stressed the necessity for mutual respect."

Davies shot back that another requirement was "mutual trust."[47] The exchange bespoke the legacy of suspicion and cultural difference between the two nations. Trust meant predictive reliability, assurance that the Soviets would reciprocate cooperation, edge toward Western norms, and moderate their geopolitical and ideological ambitions.[48] The Americans and British believed that trust also required the Soviets to permit greater contact and transparency. For the Big Three leaders, fostering trust was a major impetus for going to all the trouble of traveling to a conference. They believed that viewing personality and affect up close could offer crucial clues to a statesman's underlying intent and trustworthiness. In March 1946, Churchill honed in on this key aspect of character. He warned U.S. officials that "the Russians," for reasons of culture or race, lacked "understanding of such words as 'honesty,' 'honor,' 'trust,' and 'truth.'"[49]

The Soviets, concerned about status as well as the imperative of preventing another invasion, reacted vehemently to territorial issues. In dealing with U.S. and British leaders Stalin repeatedly sought recognition of Soviet borders as they stood before the German onslaught in 1941. That boundary included land taken from Poland, Romania, and Finland, and the formerly independent Baltic states of Latvia, Estonia, and Lithuania. From Moscow's viewpoint, that territory (all but Northern Bukovina part of pre–World War I Russia) rightfully belonged to the Soviet Union. The Soviets had taken these lands after their cynical deal with the Nazis in August 1939.

Then in June 1941 the Germans, for the second time in thirty years, hurtled across the flat lands of Poland to pummel Russia. Stalin was adamant about erecting after the war a "friendly" Poland to guard against yet another invasion. In no way did Soviet security concerns justify Stalin's exiling or slaughtering millions after the annexations of 1939–40.[50] Nevertheless, from Moscow's perspective, it seemed insulting to have to wheedle from the Western allies acceptance of Russia's number one war aim, regaining its preinvasion borders and securing against another assault. The Russians resented feeling like supplicants, especially after contributing to victory with the highest costs in blood.

A stunningly frank conversation about the emotional and political impact of this perceived inferior status took place in July 1943 in the Kremlin office of the former ambassador to London, Ivan Maisky, now a vice-minister of foreign affairs.[51] In speaking with the British ambassador, Archibald Clark Kerr, Maisky volunteered that "Russian civilization has always been centuries behind" that of Britain. The Bolshevik Revolution had only widened the gap. Clark Kerr paraphrased the Russian as saying, "We [the British] were sure of ourselves. We knew what we were about." Whatever Britain did "would appear to the rest of mankind to be the right thing. We had in fact a superiority complex and that was our strength. He envied it." In contrast, the Russians "knew that their civilization was callow, that they were only beginners." Turning Marxist dogma on its head, Maisky lamented that the Soviets "did not know the rules of the game." They often did "the wrong thing, not from malice so much as in self-defense." Their "inferiority complex" made "them acutely sensitive and always on the look out for slights." After this startling admission Maisky made his political pitch, suggesting, Clark Kerr reported, that "we" (the British) "should always ask ourselves first whether what we were doing . . . might hurt the feelings of country cousins. . . . We expected them to be grown up and as metropolitan as ourselves. They were not."[52]

Maisky's audacious appeal for empathy might, conceivably, have induced London and Washington to craft policies more attuned to Russian insecurities—and therefore more successful over time. But that would have required an emotional intelligence beyond that of most officials in any government. Russian experts in the British Foreign Office disparaged the "inferiority complex" as an "admirable alibi" for the Soviets "to have their own way." Even the sympathetic Clark Kerr grumbled that Maisky seemed unconcerned about British emotional needs, especially normal contact with Soviet citizens.

Nevertheless, with regard to the substance of Maisky's plaint, "in my heart I felt that he was right," Clark Kerr advised London. "We have not yet let [the Russians] into the club. They are still scrutinized by the hall-porter, stared at by the members, and made to feel that they do not really belong." Meanwhile, Britain went all out "to make the Americans feel at home." Churchill's preference ruled: "We *consult* Washington and we *inform* Moscow." The ambassador warned that the Soviets, "who miss nothing and who refuse to be taken in," would "one day stop wanting to belong to our club and will start one of their own."[53] In the Cold War the Soviets would indeed start their own "club," behind the Iron Curtain.

This book examines how huge policy issues about the very future of the alliance were filtered through highly personal relationships, intense desires and disappointments, and deep flaws of body and personality—all factors presented within the historical context of events. Only by including the overlooked private lives of public statesmen, the emotional stakes of their diplomacy, and the cultural context of their ideology can we arrive at a more holistic picture of how the Allies won World War II and then lost the security they had fought for. Examining the nexus between public and private helps us see the messy way that history really happens.

Chapter 1

A Portrait of the Allies as Young Men
Franklin, Winston, and Koba

In June 1905, twenty-three-year-old Franklin Roosevelt and his twenty-one-year-old bride, Eleanor, the favorite niece of President Theodore Roosevelt, embarked on a European honeymoon. They gravitated to London, Franklin's favorite city and the center of the world's greatest empire. They probably would not have considered vacationing in the backwater of czarist Russia, even if the incipient revolution there had not ignited. The couple were greeted with deference at a fashionable hotel and "ushered into the royal suite."[1] Also accustomed to elite status was a cousin of the Duke of Marlborough, Winston Churchill. Thirty-one years old in 1905, he had already served five years in Parliament. As a soldier for the British Empire he had killed "fanatic Dervishes" in the Sudan and had daringly escaped from a Boer prison in South Africa. He garnered fame and money by writing books about these adventures. He would soon enter the Government as undersecretary of state for the colonies. Roosevelt awaited a less exalted prospect: making up failed courses at Columbia University law school. Despite their differences in achievement, the two privileged cosmopolitans shared membership in a transatlantic elite. Each assumed his nation ranked as world leader. One can imagine them striking up a conversation, perhaps in a shop filled with the naval prints they both loved. It remains difficult, however, to picture either of them chatting with the brutal revolutionary from a remote corner of the Russian Empire who would come to London two years later on quite different business.

A gulf in language, geography, class, and ideology separated Roosevelt and Churchill from Joseph Dzhugashvili, who would later take the name Stalin. Born in 1878, the future dictator came to manhood in rebellious Georgia. Russians despised Georgians as supposed barbarians who spoke a "dog's language."[2] Some geographers placed the province in Asia. Georgians hated dominance by the Russians just as they had earlier hated their Persian overlords. Stalin would later seek autocratic models from both the shahs and the czars. A go-getter who already boasted a record of arrests and escapes, the young revolutionary traveled to London in 1907 to attend the Russian Social Democratic Worker's Party Congress. He eluded czarist police by melting into the London slum quarter favored by Jewish immigrants who had fled Russian pogroms. Decades later, Arthur Bacon, a former errand boy, reminisced that the stranger had tipped him fifty times the going rate. Bacon added, "His favorite treat was toffee. I brought him some every day." Perhaps the generosity stemmed from the provincial's misunderstanding British coinage. Or perhaps Dzhugashvili had cash from the bank robberies in Georgia that he was masterminding for Bolshevik leader Vladimir Lenin.[3] Years later, the dictator would advise a young diplomat bound for London to spend time "in churches listening to the sermons—the best way to learn English."[4]

Despite the difficulty in drawing causal links between early experience and later policymaking, historians can suggest correlations between the cultural and emotional attitudes of the allies as young men and their later ideological and political positions. Throughout their lives, these men behaved as *people* and not just as cool minds separated from actual bodies. In the crucible of 1941, Roosevelt and Churchill forged not only their opposition to the Axis but also cultural kinship and commitment to democratic capitalism into a formidable alliance. By late 1943, however, these elements of mutuality were losing some of their force with Roosevelt. FDR was increasingly put off by Churchill's personality, resistance to dismantling the British

Empire, and resumption of London's traditional maneuvering against Russia. FDR and Stalin, both masters of manipulation and seduction, struck up a personal relationship at Tehran and Yalta. Each hoped personal ties could help bridge their political and cultural differences. While Roosevelt saw Stalin as a potential ally in the future dismantling of European empires, the dictator seemed to appreciate the president's readiness to divide Germany and to approve extracting from the defeated enemy reparations in kind to rebuild the Soviet Union.

Childhood and Youth

Decades before Roosevelt, Churchill, and Stalin became the Big Three, they were children growing up in very different families. The tight embrace of Franklin by his parents, the arms-length distance enforced by Randolph and Jennie Churchill, and the mix of brutality and support shown to "Soso" Dzhugashvili conditioned how those boys matured and how they would interact decades later. Despite the differences in their childhoods, each grew up considering himself a man of destiny. Roosevelt would go through life confident that his heritage, intuition, charm, luck, flexibility, determination, savvy, and good looks would enable him to triumph, eventually, over almost any obstacle. Churchill learned to craft his own world. As a child he stayed close to his affectionate and long-serving nanny, "Mrs. Everest," while adoring his mother and idolizing his father from afar. He was determined to become the accomplished adult with whom his parents would gladly connect. Perhaps in reaction to the pain of his childhood, Stalin used brute force, or the force of his intelligence and magnetic personality, to claw his way to the top. Once there he eliminated even potential rivals.

Also formative for the three were their educational experiences, associations, and love affairs. Roosevelt and Stalin learned to attract people with glamor, guile, flattery, and self-promotion. Churchill developed his extraordinary talent at writing and speaking. In later years Roosevelt and Stalin would remain the seductive actors and Churchill the inexhaustible monologist. These future war leaders had divergent personal experiences with war. Churchill sought out battles in order to write about them for money while also proving his bravery. Roosevelt displayed more ambivalence about combat. Stalin avoided it while scheming day and night to overthrow the czarist system. They would also react in different ways to the Russian Revolution of 1917.

The Churchills and Roosevelts toured Europe as members of the pre–World War I ruling classes. Kaiser Wilhelm II invited Winston to observe German military maneuvers as his guest. The monarch had also welcomed onto his yacht Sara Delano Roosevelt and her nineteen-year-old son, Franklin, who filched a well-chewed pencil from the Kaiser's desk.[5] Quite different was the trip made by Dzhugashvili and the Russian revolutionaries in 1907. Their party congress had originally tried to meet in Copenhagen but was forced to leave after the czarist government pressured Danish authorities. They traveled to Sweden, only again to have to pack their bags for Britain.[6] Dzhugashvili's Marxist ideology and Georgian/Russian national identity prejudiced him against the likes of Roosevelt and Churchill.

Aspects of ideologically tinged cultural difference would later also divide the U.S. president and the British prime minister. FDR prided himself as heir to the antimonarchism of Isaac Roosevelt, a captain in the Revolutionary War. At White House dinners he would needle Churchill by claiming to "remember very clearly that when I was seven or thereabouts . . . my mother took me to England, and we saw Queen Victoria. . . . Why I hated the old woman."[7] Quite different was the boyhood of Churchill. His mother, Jennie Jerome, though born in Brooklyn, New York, had taught her son to adore the queen.

Jennie starred in the sorority of young American women whose dowries were rescuing cash-strapped European nobility. Her father, Leonard Jerome, had risen from upstate New York farm boy to Wall Street speculator. His wealth enabled his wife, Clara, to hobnob with royalty in Paris and London. The Jeromes calculated Jennie's £50,000 dowry as well-spent, as the bridegroom, Lord Randolph Churchill, ranked as the son of a duke and a friend of the Prince of Wales. Leonard boasted about "the greatest match any American had made."[8] The old-money Roosevelts sneered at such commerce and deference. As president, FDR would address royals by their first names, as in "Cousin George" of Britain. A diplomat concluded that Roosevelt delighted in hosting kings and queens because "he considers himself royalty."[9]

Despite Clara Jerome's anguish at the revolutionary overthrow of Emperor Napoleon III in 1871, she remained opportunistic enough to snap up his dinner china at auction. Another American benefiting from Europe's distress was Franklin's father, James Roosevelt. For fifteen dollars he purchased the emperor's sleigh, an elegant conveyance lined with wine-red velvet. Napoleon III had received it as a gift from Czar Alexander II, the ruler when Dzhugashvili was born. In 1881, the czar would be assassinated by revolutionaries. The two bargains hinted at twentieth-century forces that would shape the world of the Big Three: the decline of European monarchy, the rise of radical revolution, and the efforts by rich America to profit from the former while containing the latter.

In contrast to Winston or Joseph, Franklin as a boy was showered, indeed smothered, with loving attention from his parents. Sara Delano, whose wealthy family had arrived with the Pilgrims and claimed descent from William the Conqueror, was tall, beautiful, and twenty-six when she married James Roosevelt, a widower two inches shorter and twice her age. Their only child was born on January 30, 1882. He grew up at Springwood, an estate overlooking the Hudson River about eighty miles north of New York City. Franklin's parents seem never to have spanked him. They encouraged him to assert himself within "proper bounds." After James's first heart attack in 1890, most of the parenting shifted to Sara, who doted on the boy. Whereas Jennie refused to visit Winston at school after he suffered a concussion, Sara refused to stay away after Groton quarantined Franklin because of illness. She recalled that "several times each day I would climb a tall, rickety ladder, and, by seating myself at the top, manage to see into the room and talk" with him.[10] James died in 1900, leaving Sara $300,000, an amount dwarfed by her $1.3 million Delano inheritance.[11] Most of the Delano fortune stemmed from the opium trade and other nineteenth-century business in China, where young Sara had spent two years. The wealthy, still-attractive widow remained a catch. Yet she seems never to have considered remarrying. Instead she devoted herself to her son. Her meddling in Franklin's adult life would aggravate his wife and influence his children—while also saving his marriage and subsidizing his lifestyle. Living to see her adored boy elected president three times, she died in September 1941 amid the world crisis. For the rest of his life FDR wore a black armband.

"My son is a Delano," Sara once claimed. "He is not a Roosevelt at all."[12] Throughout his life FDR used "Algonac," the name of the Delano estate, as a code word signaling "okay." FDR would later tell a relative, "Our branch of Roosevelts hasn't got vitality; mine, such as it is, comes from the Delanos." He described that energy as "a very convenient type because it can be turned on and off at will."[13] As president, FDR would turn the charm on and off to get what he wanted. He worked this manipulation on Churchill. He sought to get close enough to Stalin to do the same.

At eleven, Franklin received his own gun and developed what his mother called "an insatiable interest in shooting" and collecting bird specimens.[14] He sailed the Hudson River and navigated treacherous currents off Campobello Island. He immersed himself in foreign stamps, geography, and history, lifelong interests sparked by stories of the Delanos' business in China. She recounted that he "used to pore over Admiral [Alfred Thayer] Mahan's *History of Sea Power* until he had practically memorized the whole book."[15] What all these interests had in common was Franklin's determination, within the bounds of his mother's control and his father's illness, to secure—as he would try to obtain throughout his life—his independence and his command at the center. Shooting and sailing placed him in charge. Organizing specimens, stamps, and stories about nations, seas, and their past enabled him to construct around himself a meaningful, manageable world.[16]

Young Churchill also crafted a universe centered on himself, but he had to work within a more difficult family. After making and losing several fortunes, Leonard Jerome finished a loser. Randolph and Jennie Churchill also ran short of money. Winston inherited his parents' sense of entitlement to costly travel, champagne, and residences. His financial strategy—"income should be expanded to meet expenditure"—

1.1. Years after this photograph of the young navigator was taken, an observer remarked of Roosevelt that "you could see the jawbones click, the great will in the jawbones." (Reminiscences of Janeway [2003], CUOHRC, 71. Courtesy of FDR Library.)

would not always meet the target.[17] A cousin recalled that "even by the standards of their generation," Winston's parents "were pretty awful."[18] "What a care the boy is," Jennie complained to her erratic husband.[19] Winston's demand for attention also exasperated teachers. Decades later, those demands would also annoy FDR. The schoolboy begged his mother to write. "I have only had one letter from you this term," he lamented one June.[20] Despite such appeals, Jennie did not visit when he had a sports day, a public speech, or a concussion that put him in bed for a week. Reading in the local newspaper that his father had given a speech nearby, Winston wrote, "I was very disappointed but I suppose you were too busy to come."[21]

His parents were busy. A dazzling orator, Randolph championed "Tory Democracy"—an alliance between the aristocracy and the working class—and rose to become chancellor of the exchequer by age thirty-six. He seemed a likely future prime minister. Yet he also endured nervousness and depression, which he tried to soothe by smoking some forty cigarettes a day. He suffered swings in mood, delusions, and partial paralysis. In 1886, he wrecked his political career by abruptly resigning from the Cabinet. He may have been afflicted with a brain tumor. At the time, however, many, including Winston, were informed by doctors that the illness was advanced syphilis.[22] The once rising star flamed out at forty-six.

Winston had tried desperately to get close to his father, "who seemed to own the key to everything or almost everything worth having." But when Winston offered to help his father write letters, "he froze me into stone." Randolph rubbed in the rejection by befriending instead his son's schoolmate. Decades later, the son could still exclaim: "How I should have loved to have that sort of relationship with my father!"[23] It was only on his third try that the future war leader passed the examination for Sandhurst military academy. Randolph, his mind slipping, lashed out. If Winston continued "the idle, useless, unprofitable life you have had during your schooldays, you will become a mere social wastrel . . . and you will degenerate into a shabby unhappy & futile existence."[24] Only the nanny, whom Winston called "Woomany," provided affection. He may have carried these strains into adulthood in the form of his recurring depression, what he called his Black Dog. "When I was young," he later recalled, "the light faded out of the picture. . . . [B]lack depression settled on me." Even as prime minister he still did not "like to stand by the side of a ship and look down into the water. A second's action would end everything."[25]

Churchill also had to cope with having a narcissistic mother who made the most of her extraordinary good looks. She once admitted, "I shall never get used to not being the most beautiful woman in the room."[26] Her son would remain transfixed by that beauty. "My mother always seemed to me a fairy princess: a radiant being of limitless riches and power," he wrote on page four of his autobiography. Even into middle age he held on to his memory of her "in a riding habit, fitting like a skin and often beautifully spotted with mud." He quoted with pride an admirer's description of Jennie's "dark, lithe figure" and "the flashing glory of her eyes." She showed "more of the

1.2. Winston, here shown with Lady Randolph Churchill and his younger brother, Jack, would later write, "My mother always seemed to me a fairy princess: a radiant being of limitless riches and power." (Churchill, *My Early Life*, 4. Courtesy of Corbis.)

panther than of the woman in her look."[27] Jennie deployed this beauty, plus her charisma and intelligence, to promote Randolph's political career. After he died, in Winston's twenty-first year, she mobilized her admirers in behalf of her son's ambitions in publishing and politics. To a mother who needed no reminding, Winston said, "This is a pushing age and we must push with the best." A biographer has commented, "They became the pushiest couple in London, indeed in the empire."[28] Franklin and Sara also operated as a couple but with less Oedipal overtones.

Churchill triumphed over his difficult childhood, just as he would later overcome setbacks in his political career and the existential threat facing Britain in 1940. The youth spurred himself by, first, fixing the memory of an idolized father, then surpassing that paradigm. Even before Randolph died, the son noted with a hint of satisfaction that his father's speeches "were increasingly unsuccessful."[29] Elected to the House of Commons at age twenty-six, he made a point of sitting in his father's former chair. He borrowed his father's style, ambitions, and support of Tory Democracy. One evening in 1947 Winston's daughter asked, "If you had the power to put someone in that chair to join us now, whom would you choose?" "Oh, my father, of course," he replied.[30] The statesman that many considered the greatest Briton ever would die on January 24, 1965, seventy years to the day after his father.

In 1900, Jennie married handsome George Cornwallis-West, who was sixteen days older than Winston. Her third husband would be yet three years younger. One does not have to read Freud to understand the emotional strain placed on Winston by his mother's active sexuality. He channeled those feelings into a safe, even lucrative, direction by penning an autobiographical fantasy-novel.

Savrola explored what Churchill's doctor later called "the inner world of make-believe in which Winston found reality."[31] By force of will and oratory, the hero, Savrola, overthrows a military dictator. He wins not only the leadership of the people but also the love of the despot's wife, Lucile. As Winston was plotting the novel, he described the heroine as "the most beautiful woman in Europe."[32] In a letter to his mother acknowledging Jennie as "the most beautiful woman in the world," he asked for help in portraying "the woman in the novel."[33] Churchill framed the hero's desire for Lucile as an Oedipal tragedy. The "wicked joy" of having Lucile required sinning "against the phenomena of life itself, the stigma of which would cling through death." The hero nevertheless pledges undying love because "no other woman can ever fill the empty space."[34] One wonders to what degree the author was aware of the psychological undertones. Churchill offered another possible insight into his psyche with a passage that likened the trajectory and passions of speech-making to those of sexual intercourse.

> The steam had been rising. . . . All were searching in their minds for something to relieve their feelings. . . . His passions, his emotions, his very soul appeared to be communicated to the seven

thousand people. . . . Then at last he let them go. . . . He raised his
voice in a resonant, powerful, penetrating tone which thrilled the
listeners. . . . Each short sentence was followed by wild cheering.
The excitement of the audience became indescribable. Everyone
was carried away by it. Lucile was borne along, unresisting, by
that strong torrent of enthusiasm; her interests, her objects, her
ambitions, her husband, all were forgotten. His sentences grew
longer. . . . All pointed to an inevitable conclusion. The people
saw it coming, and when the last words fell, they were greeted
with thunders of assent. . . . Every pulse in his body was throb-
bing, every nerve quivering. . . . For five minutes everyone
shouted wildly.[35]

Explicitly linking verbal and sexual energies, Churchill reportedly explained, "The reason I can write so much is that I don't waste my
essence in bed."[36]

With real-life women his own age, however, Winston remained
clumsy. Unlike Stalin or Roosevelt, he had few flirtations before marriage and virtually none afterward. Before Clementine Hozier, whose
biological father may have been one of Jennie's lovers, accepted his
proposal of marriage in 1908, three other women, including the
American actress Ethel Barrymore, turned him down. A relative
judged him "incapable of love. He was in love with his own image—
his reflection in the mirror." His grandmother wrote: "It is clear that
you have not yet attained a knowledge of Women—and it is evident
you have (I am thankful to see) no experience of Love."[37]

Stalin had only limited experience of parental love as a child. The
brutality he suffered from his father probably encouraged, though it
cannot excuse, the horrendous brutality he inflicted against others as
an adult. Joseph, nicknamed "Soso," was born on December 6, 1878
(not on December 21, 1879, as he later claimed) in the village of Gori
to a poor cobbler, Vissarion "Beso" Dzhugashvili, and his wife, Kete-
van, nicknamed "Keke." Both parents had been born serfs. Beso drank
away his earnings. His violence against his wife and son was perhaps
worsened by persistent rumors that Soso's biological father was the
local police chief, a priest, a tavern keeper, or yet another man. The

more Beso bullied the boy, the more the mother favored him. Although Keke also thrashed her son, she showed him love. She grew frantic when he nearly died of the smallpox that left his face deeply pocked. Soso suffered other disfigurements. He was born with two webbed toes on his left foot. Two accidents, one from a runaway horse cart, left his left arm permanently stiff and his legs damaged. Lacking the agility of other boys, he compensated with dirty tactics in wrestling.[38]

Devout Keke helped her bright ten-year-old win a scholarship to the Gori Spiritual School. She saw the priesthood as his path to success. (Decades later, during a rare visit from her son, she asked, "Joseph, what exactly are you now?" He replied, "Well, remember the Tsar? I'm something like a Tsar." Unimpressed, she replied, "You'd have done better to become a priest.")[39]

Soso had a contradictory personality. A tough street fighter, he also impressed his teachers as "very devout" and smart. He would graduate with the highest grades.[40] When cobbler Beso could no longer compete with machine-made shoes, he took a low-paying job in a shoe factory in Tbilisi. He forced Soso to leave school and join him at work. The next few months constituted the future Communist leader's sole experience as an industrial proletarian. At Keke's urging, the priests intervened. Beso allowed his son to return to school. Despite the parental beatings, the adult Stalin would view his father as a victim of capitalism. He adopted his father's name as one of his pseudonyms. To the misery of millions, he also adopted his father's bullying.[41]

Although neither Churchill nor Stalin had enjoyed the security that imbued Roosevelt's childhood, all three emerged as self-centered, charismatic, and fiercely ambitious young men. Churchill articulated a conceit that probably each of them held about himself. "We are all worms. But I really think I am a glow worm."[42]

Schooling

All three had mixed records at school. Roosevelt ranked in the top 20 percent of his class at Groton. He maintained an average slightly above C at Harvard. In his letters home from college he never mentioned the content of his courses. He took mostly history and economics, shying away from philosophy or other abstract thought.[43] "How I hated this school," Churchill later recalled of his first formal education.[44] He followed up at Harrow, where he remained in the bottom form for three years. As he would do at many low points in his life, he turned dross into gold. Abysmal at Latin, he composed essays in English in exchange for another student's translations of his Ovid and Virgil. While stagnating, as he put it, in the lowest form, he snared a school prize for reciting twelve hundred lines of poetry without a mistake.[45] Three years of repeating the basic course under the superb instruction of the prose stylist Robert Somervell endowed the future spellbinder with a magnificent command of the English language. In later decades he would use this facility to secure not only the political heights but also a sizable income from his prolific pen.[46]

The most diligent and most rebellious student was Stalin. Winning a scholarship at the rigorous Tiflis Seminary, sixteen-year-old Soso worked hard to secure straight A grades. He earned pocket money as first tenor in the choir. The seminary was "utterly joyless," remembered another pupil. "Droningly boring—we felt we were in prison."[47] Not only Georgian but even much of Russian literature was banned. Soso and his co-conspirators formed the "Cheap Library" club, whose members circulated forbidden books and surreptitiously read them after lights out. Soso devoured Dostoevsky and Chernyshevsky as well as Russian translations of Hugo, Balzac, Zola, Thackeray, Goethe, and Shakespeare. He could recite Walt Whitman. Zealous as always, he "overdid it and hardly slept at all, looking bleary-eyed and ill," a friend later recalled.[48] He considered becoming a university professor.[49] A writer who changed his life was Alexander Kazbegi. His novel, *The Patricide*, glorified a Georgian bandit-hero called Koba who fought against Russian oppression. An inspired Soso took over the name, insisting that others call him Koba.

While still reading voraciously—he began teaching himself German and English so that he could master *Das Kapital* and other classics in the original—Stalin switched from theology to revolution. He was not alone. "No secular school," another classmate would recall, "produced as many atheists as Tiflis Seminary."[50] A few years before Soso's time, students retaliated against an anti-Georgian rector by running him through with a Georgian sword. Increasingly rude, arrogant, and defiant, Soso/Koba was expelled in May 1899 for refusing to pay his fees or take his examinations.

Even among revolutionaries, many of them middle or upper class and educated at Russian universities, Stalin remained an outsider. His passport classified him as a peasant.[51] In contrast to most Marxist theoreticians, he clung to working-class garb, including a black shirt that signaled his nationality. He wrote exclusively in Georgian until the age of twenty-eight. His lifelong Georgian accent, which grew thicker when he became excited, prompted ridicule. Years of exile in Siberia above the Arctic Circle would be his finishing school. He went out alone on long hunting and fishing trips, using skills he had learned from the native Tunguses, who called him Pockmarked Joseph. Molotov later explained: "A little piece of Siberia remained lodged in Stalin for the rest of his life."[52] Siberian exile under the Soviets would be far ghastlier than anything Pockmarked had endured. The future tyrant read voraciously. He appealed to a friend to send "some English journals. . . . [I]t's for reading since there's nothing in English here and I'm afraid I'm losing all my acquired English skills."[53] Although the dictator had abandoned learning English and Esperanto, he could read ancient Greek and some German and French. From his childhood in multilingual Georgia he knew how to speak Armenian, Azeri, and Russian.[54]

The Marxist never outgrew his Orthodox conditioning. Shortly after the Revolution, Stalin's mother pressed him, "Son, there's none of the tsar's blood on your hands, is there?" No, he swore, making the sign of the cross.[55] At the Tiflis Seminary he had first learned, as he put it, about "surveillance, spying, invasion of inner life, violation of feelings." He would apply those nefarious lessons in creating the Soviet police state. His Bolshevism followed the Orthodox Church in its catechistic language and array of saints and sins. He assumed that all accidents, defeats, and shortfalls resulted from sabotage—"sin"—rather than from innocent error. "One thing the priests teach you," he later recalled, "is to understand what people think."[56] The former

1.3. Dzhugashvili, the Orthodox seminary student, turned Georgian nationalist poet, turned Bolshevik revolutionary would use a mixture of brutality, intelligence, and charm to claw his way to the top. (Courtesy of Corbis.)

choir singer would blasphemously write to a comrade: "Here are some presents for you from God! I am the executor of his will!"[57]

In marked contrast, Roosevelt disliked theorizing about religion, or about anything else. He followed the family tradition by becoming a vestryman of the St. James Episcopal Church in Hyde Park. FDR's son recalled that his father held fast to a "basic, simple, rather unquestioning religious faith." Eleanor later commented about her husband, "I think he actually felt he could ask God for guidance and receive it."[58] Roosevelt nevertheless attended church services only on special occasions. Religion mattered far less to Churchill.

The young men who would mature into warlords each approached war with different past experiences and with distinct masculine identities. One way of comparing Franklin and Winston at the dawn of the twentieth century is to examine them alongside Theodore Roosevelt, an advocate of militant masculinity. Teddy could appear frenetic, enacting his roles as big-game hunter, conservationist, self-proclaimed hero of the war in Cuba, and U.S. president carrying a big stick. He was driven by anxiety that modernizing influences were weakening American manhood, especially for men of the upper and middle classes.[59]

Franklin was at Harvard when Vice President Roosevelt moved into the White House after the assassination of President William McKinley. FDR determined to follow his cousin step-by-step: from Cambridge Square to the New York State legislature, to assistant secretary of the navy, to governor of New York, to president. Just as Winston idolized his father, FDR regarded Theodore Roosevelt as "the greatest man I ever knew."[60] Franklin was so transparent— adopting the great man's pince-nez glasses and peppering his speech with "bully" and "dee-lighted"—that his classmates nicknamed him "Kermit," a mocking reference to Teddy's son.[61] Theodore Roosevelt used his bully pulpit to urge colleges, and the rest of the nation, to adopt a toughening regimen: self-discipline, football, boxing, hunting, and military training. The formula boiled down to a readiness to endure and to inflict pain. Another lifelong mentor of FDR who stressed strenuous athletics was the Reverend Endicott Peabody, headmaster of Groton. "Athletically he was too slight for success," Peabody later recalled of Franklin.[62] At Harvard he remained too willowy for football.

FDR coped with these pressures by forging his strengths into a distinct masculine identity of his own. He earned a Groton school letter not by playing baseball but by managing the team's equipment. At Harvard he pushed hard to become editor of the *Crimson*. He then stressed in editorials that the Harvard football team had to push harder for a winning season. What he decades later called "the greatest disappointment of my life" was getting blackballed from Porcellian, the elite club that had welcomed his father and Teddy. FDR adapted by joining other clubs. With Theodore's sons likely favorites among Republicans, he became, like his father, a Democrat. Whereas Theodore and his sons had rowed in sculling races, FDR sailed tricky currents. Teddy relished the challenge of hiking, literally, a straight course through or over all obstacles. FDR preferred instead circuitous if not devious paths in most aspects of life.

Theodore Roosevelt appeared so fierce in his masculinity that some contemporaries sensed an inner conflict. The publisher William Allen White discerned "the shadow of some inner femininity deeply suppressed." When Teddy first entered politics, some in the press mocked him as another "Oscar Wilde."[63] Years later, an essay by Gore Vidal labeled him "an American sissy." Vidal wrote: "Give a sissy a gun and he will kill everything in sight."[64] Although Franklin liked killing game, he never emulated Theodore's shooting marathons in the American West or in Africa. Perhaps some of the difference between them stemmed from their respective fathers, Theodore Roosevelt Sr. and his cousin, James Roosevelt. Both came of military age during the Civil War. Yet neither participated in their generation's defining martial test. Theodore's father anguished about this for the rest of his life. FDR's father seemed never bothered by his decision.[65]

Teddy Roosevelt felt very differently about Franklin and Winston. He once said of the former, "I'm so fond of that boy, I'd be shot for him."[66] He delighted at the White House wedding of his niece, Eleanor, whom he loved "as if she were my daughter."[67] Churchill sparked an opposite reaction. No stranger to arrogance himself, Theodore fumed after a New York dinner that Churchill had behaved "like a swine. . . . I had to *ask* him to go & say goodbye to his hostess—& to take his cigar out of his mouth when he did so." An observer noted that the two egoists "were too alike" to get along.[68]

War

Churchill and Theodore Roosevelt *were* alike, especially in their ostentatious defiance of death. When war with Spain erupted in 1898, Teddy, eager to join the fray, resigned as assistant secretary of the navy. He assembled his own unit, the Rough Riders, and with his Brooks Brothers–made uniform rushed to Cuba. In the fight for Kettle Hill, Roosevelt rode his horse back and forth, taunting Spanish fire. He was "just reveling in victory and gore," a fellow Rough Rider observed.[69] Only months earlier, cavalryman Churchill was in the Sudan battling Muslim Dervishes, whom he saw as "ugly, sinister brutes . . . the successors of the Saracens." He rode his "grey pony all along the skirmish line where everyone else was lying down in cover." To his mother he later explained: "Foolish perhaps, but I play for high stakes and given an audience there is no act too daring or too noble."[70] Anxious to build his reputation, Churchill regarded fame on the battlefield as "the finest thing on earth."[71] Like Theodore Roosevelt, he understood that voters would elect a hero. Whether to impress a parent, the voting public, or, later, to impress FDR, Churchill would remain the exhibitionist.

When it came to personal killing of the enemy, Churchill experienced what FDR and even Teddy Roosevelt did not. Stalin slaughtered millions through orders to subordinates but, it appears, very few by his own hand. Young Winston's very first memory was as a four-year-old listening with rapt attention to his grandfather "speaking about war and fighting." Afterward, he had "imagined in dreams and day-dreams the . . . thrilling and immense experience to hear the whistle of bullets all around."[72] Dreams came true when he fought "wild tribesmen" on the border between what is today Pakistan and Afghanistan. "The Pathans are strange people," he later explained. "They have all sorts of horrible customs and frightful revenges."[73] He defined the struggle as "civilization face to face with militant Mohammedanism."[74] Civilization had the advantage in weaponry. When a "savage," out of ammunition, threw a stone and "awaited me, brandishing his sword," the Englishman blasted his rifle at close range. "I think I hit 4 men," he recounted.[75] A year later in the Sudan, Churchill "rode up to individuals firing my pistol in their faces and killing several."[76]

In 1915, Churchill, now first lord of the admiralty, confided to a friend on the eve of the Gallipoli campaign: "I *love* this war. I know it's smashing & shattering the lives of thousands every moment—& yet I can't help it—I enjoy every second of it."[77] When that campaign became a bloody disaster, for reasons not all his fault, Churchill was kicked out of the Cabinet. Though already in his forties, he went off to fight in the trenches, an ordeal that FDR and Stalin avoided.

In 1914, as Woodrow Wilson's assistant secretary of the navy, FDR hoped to follow his cousin Theodore by parlaying martial glory into higher office. When war with Mexico threatened, FDR told the press, "I do not want war, but I do not see how we can avoid it. Sooner or later it seems, the United States must go down there and clean up the Mexican political mess. I believe that the best time is right now."[78] He chafed at Wilson's reluctance to battle Germany. Echoing Teddy and conventional views of tough realism, Franklin ridiculed "the soft mush about everlasting peace which so many statesmen are handing out to a gullible public."[79] He crossed the submarine-infested Atlantic and briefly came under fire while visiting the front in 1918.[80]

FDR did not, however, heed Theodore Roosevelt's repeated admonition: "You *must* resign" and go into battle.[81] President Wilson asked FDR to remain at his important post. Regarding himself as more of an expert than his boss, Secretary of the Navy Josephus Daniels, Roosevelt boasted that he was doing the real work in the department. FDR loved commanding, prodding, conniving, and planning. He delighted in the pomp and ceremony of naval command. Yet he also worried about missing out on the testing of his generation. In the end something inside held him back from resigning and risking death in battle, as Theodore had done in 1898 and Churchill in 1915. Perhaps deep down FDR did not really want to hazard more than a visit to the trenches.[82]

He later burnished his war record, just as he exaggerated much about his early life. He insisted that Groton include his name among its war heroes because he had barely escaped "torpedoes and shell and had actual command."[83] As Franklin in later years told and retold the story (and commissioned a painting) of this supposed torpedo attack, the German submarine came ever closer, until he had it circling his ship. In actuality, the reported submarine remained fifty miles away.[84] After he was felled by polio in 1921, Roosevelt would demonstrate ample courage. Yet he continued to shy away from recklessness; indeed as president he would sometimes exercise caution to a fault.

Stalin, too, despite his aggressiveness, shied away from physical danger. Drafted in 1916, he was relieved that boyhood injuries rendered him unfit to serve.[85] In the late 1930s, he tried to avoid war with

Germany. In cables to Roosevelt or Churchill during the war, Stalin repeatedly asserted that he was going to the battlefront or had just returned. He cultivated the image of a military commander daring death. The dictator did learn military strategy after his disastrous decisions early in the war. Yet the man who would celebrate victory by assuming the title "Generalissimo" dared venture to the front only once in the four years of fighting. Even then he stayed safely back from the guns.[86]

While lacking Churchill's courage in face-to-face combat, Stalin sought to command troops. During the Russian civil war, Lenin ordered him to procure grain in southern Russia. He replied, "I need full military powers."[87] Even among Red Army leaders inured to extreme violence, Stalin distinguished himself by risking his troops and terrorizing peasants into surrendering their grain. He torched villages as a lesson. He renewed the draconian traditions of the czarist army in suppressing Georgia. The brutality foreshadowed his purges of the late 1930s. He also incorporated military elements into his identity. He began wearing military-style boots and a simple, collarless tunic. Decades later, as the Red Army was rolling back Nazi armies, he would sport a showy uniform. Despite his orientation toward military and revolutionary struggle, Stalin reminded himself that overreaching invited disaster. A month before the German invasion, he mused, "When Napoleon I conducted war under the slogan liberation from serfdom, he found support, had allies and was successful. When Napoleon I shifted to wars of conquest, he multiplied his enemies and met with defeat."[88] In World War II, the dictator would try to keep the alliance ideologically united under the exculpatory rubric of "antifascism."

Stalin's intelligence, energy, charm, ruthlessness, and prolific pen powered his rise among Lenin's aides. In 1912, he won election to the Bolshevik Central Committee. In 1917, he came in third in the voting, just behind Lenin and Grigori Zinoviev. Nevertheless, the Georgian with the heavy accent worked best in the shadows.[89]

Stalin remained a lifelong writer. Before and during the Revolution he drafted hundreds of political pamphlets. He gained local recognition for his poetry before graduating to revolution. Georgia's ranking poet saluted him as the "young man with the burning eyes."[90] At first Soso/Koba focused on nationalist themes:

> Flower, oh my Georgia!
> Let peace reign in my native land!
> And may you, friends, make renowned
> Our Motherland by study![91]

As he was becoming a revolutionary he wrote:

> When the man driven out by his enemy
> Again becomes worthy of his oppressed country
> And when the sick man, deprived of light,
> Again begins to see sun and moon;
> Then, I, too, oppressed, find the mist of sadness;
> Breaks and lifts and instantly recedes
> And hopes of the good life
> Unfold in my unhappy heart![92]

"Poetry and music," the future mass murderer affirmed, "elevate the spirit."[93] He later explained, "I lost interest writing poetry because it requires . . . a hell of a lot of patience."[94] The dictator would continue, however, to consider himself a man of letters. He took breaks from affairs of state to impose his literary criticism. Although he executed millions of other innocents, he spared some artistic geniuses.[95]

Writing proved another arena in which Churchill, not FDR, matched Theodore Roosevelt. As part of his strenuous life, Theodore wrote a four-volume history of the American West, three biographies, and twenty-nine other volumes, plus some 150,000 letters. Churchill would author forty books. A biographer calculated that in the early twenty-first century Churchill's words still in print numbered over eight million. FDR, in contrast, appeared to suffer from writer's block. He abandoned one attempted novel after two pages, another after four. He researched but wrote little of a projected biography of John Paul Jones. In 1924, recovering from polio and desperate for something to do, he could complete only fourteen pages of a book on the history of the United States. Though Franklin failed as a writer, he excelled at polishing speeches and making the words his own. His

British rival's superiority in this arena bothered FDR, who ordered Harry L. Hopkins on his first visit to Churchill to find out "who writes his stuff." Hopkins dreaded having to tell the "Boss" there was no ghost writer.[96]

Charisma

Roosevelt, Churchill, and Stalin each exploited his charisma. They exercised their theatrical talents in framing issues, arguing persuasively, and flashing nonverbal cues. Roosevelt and Stalin acted. Churchill expostulated. FDR, comfortable with himself and attuned to others, could seduce almost anyone. Churchill, a lifetime friend recalled, "did not charm or try to charm." Instead, he "impressed and often dazzled" with brilliant monologues.[97]

To consider charm in connection with Stalin, who terrorized millions, threatens cognitive dissonance. Nonetheless, "[t]he foundation of Stalin's power in the Party was not fear: it was charm," writes the historian Simon Sebag Montefiore about the period before the Great Terror of 1934–38. Even after the purges, when the dictator "set his mind to charming a man, he was irresistible."[98] Sergo Beria, the son of secret police boss Lavrenty Beria, remembered that Stalin "left each person he spoke to anxious to see him again, with a sense that there was now a bond that linked them forever."[99] Stalin worked at enchanting others; unfortunately, he worked even harder at humiliating them. The tyrant wove a cozy, controlling web. He prescribed the precise hours of sleep for his weary military chief—and then phoned to make sure the man was sleeping. He piled gargantuan, nerve-wracking tasks on his lackeys. If they failed, they could die. Yet he also showed concern for their health and showered them with money, dachas, and even Cadillacs.[100] Uniting Stalin and his comrades was not only ambition but also conviction that harsh brutality would beget a drastically better society.

Stalin's circle resembled a Georgian village, with intermarriage, love affairs, and the sharing of meals, vacations, and child care. An insider later recalled that "Stalin knew everything about his closest comrades—EVERYTHING!"[101] When visiting an associate, he went straight to the man's library and opened the books, looking for telltale notes and turned-down corners.[102] Even after the purges eased in 1938, his disapproval of some detail could mean demotion or disappearance. Adding to others' anxiety was the difficulty of reading his moods. He "was a born actor," Sergo Beria recalled.[103] Lazar Kaganovich, who would die only months before the Soviet Union disintegrated in 1991, remembered him as a "different man at different times. I knew no less than five or six Stalins."[104] He could manipulate a mix of personality traits—modesty, intelligence, and brutality remained his specialties—to secure the desired effect on others, including Roosevelt and Churchill. Yet Stalin could not match Roosevelt in charisma.

Even after polio robbed him of his ability to walk, FDR on being wheeled into a room could "make it his. . . . The *dynamo* was there," an observer marveled.[105] He could project dynamism even when crawling. Eleanor related that "he would get down off his chair" and then position himself "face up, in a sitting position, drawing his body after him" while doing "something to distract you, so that you were never conscious of seeing anything but that wonderful head."[106] People tended to forget his disability. "If he thought that you didn't like him, he'd practically jump over a chair to get you," an official claimed.[107] More than either Stalin or Churchill, Roosevelt liked a broad range of people. And he made sure they liked him. A powerful persuader in his own right, Senator Huey Long told a friend, "'You go in there and see FDR wanting to tear him apart. You come out whistling Dixie.'"[108] Roosevelt bedazzled with his "contagious enthusiasm" and "magnetic personality"—much of it show.[109] He confided to Orson Welles, "You know, Orson, you and I are the two best actors in America."[110] Some saw through him. A White House guest concluded, "he's a magnificent actor, but not magnificent enough to conceal the fact that he's acting."[111]

Roosevelt won over most reporters. Hosting nearly one thousand presidential press conferences, he parried questions with a wordless "twinkle," tilts of the head, huge grins, and precise timing. A journalist recorded that within twenty minutes Roosevelt's "features had expressed amazement, curiosity, mock alarm, genuine interest, worry, rhetorical playing for suspense, sympathy, decision, playfulness, dignity, and surpassing charm." While offering little substance, he gave each questioner "a feeling he had been answered."[112] FDR created intimate circles. He enabled reporters to feel like respected insiders, sharing in the joke that he was not going to reveal much. Yet he might say more the next day, and he remained sympathetic to their needs, often recalling his own reporting for the *Crimson*.

Like Stalin and unlike Roosevelt, Churchill did not regard every new person as a potential convert. At a White House reception, he made no attempt to look in the eye or to speak to those whose hands he was shaking. He walked away "in the middle of some polite remarks that were being made to him."[113] Churchill displayed what may have been Asperger's syndrome.[114] He had difficulty picking up on social cues, reading body language, empathizing, or making small talk. "Though he had vision he appeared to lack antennae," a friend recalled.[115] He often seemed rude, self-absorbed, and obsessive. He seemed "as impervious to atmosphere as a diver in his bell."[116] "Winston," acknowledged his wife, "has always seen things in blinkers."[117] Churchill was no match for Roosevelt or Stalin as a thespian. "His was a face that could not keep a secret," said an associate.[118] No aide claimed to have known five or six Churchills.

Yet Churchill easily outranked Stalin and perhaps Roosevelt as an orator. He theorized, brilliantly, about gaining power through emotional talk. At twenty-two he wrote "The Scaffolding of Rhetoric." The spellbinder "wields a power more durable than that of a great king." Listeners could be transported from "unresponsive silence" to "grudging approval," to "enthusiasm," until they "are convulsed by emotions they are unable to control." Churchill's fictional projection, Savrola, used oratory to win a nation and its most beautiful woman. Emotions could trump reason. Metaphors could mobilize "the standard of the nursery and the heart" against the "powers of reason."[119] This perceptive essay laid out the rhetorical strategies Churchill would deploy to win influence in Parliament, rally Britain in 1940–45, and appeal for confrontation with Russia in 1946. Even in ordinary conversation he often seemed to be speaking according to "Scaffolding."

He impressed guests at a White House dinner with "phrases redolent of the most vigorous period of English literature . . . full of imagery." He himself appeared "exuberant . . . exciting, temperamental."[120]

Sexuality and Gender

Despite their differences in personality, morality, and sensibility, both Roosevelt and Stalin pursued women. "Franklin had to be slapped—hard," remembered Alice Sohier of her ardent Harvard boyfriend.[121] He had many women in his life until the day he died, with most of those relationships entailing an erotic attraction or frisson. The labor expert Anna Rosenberg remembered FDR "as a man who loved women, good-looking women, a flirt."[122] Meeting with female staff, the president, referring to "nice ankles," teased, "I bet none of you girls have ankles like that."[123] It was the sultry actress Jean Harlow who cut FDR's cake at a birthday party in 1937.[124]

Nearly the opposite was Churchill. He maintained "formidable ramparts of indifference . . . to women generally," observed Lord Moran, his doctor.[125] Winston and Clementine had a relationship that was loving but also sustained by her long absences from him. According to their daughter, it was she, not he, who pursued an extramarital affair.[126] One reason for the "formidable ramparts" was that Churchill had been told that his father had gone insane from syphilis. He resolved to expend his energies elsewhere, particularly in talking, writing, and politics.

Stalin, whether hiding from the czarist police or exiled in Siberia, never went long without a female companion. He fathered children out of wedlock. He wrote one teenage lover, "I'm not simply sending a kiss but am kiiissssing you passionately (it's not worth kissing any other way)."[127] Women from throughout the Soviet Union would send the dictator love notes. An insider recalled that in the family of his second wife, Nadya Alliluyeva, all the women "wanted to go to bed with him."[128] His first wife, Ekaterina "Kato" Svanidze, whom he had married in a religious ceremony, had died in 1907 at the age of twenty-two. The grief-stricken husband recalled that she had "softened my heart of stone. She died and with her died my last warm feelings for people."[129] He quickly recouped, at one point stealing a girlfriend from his future foreign minister, Molotov. The latter later explained, "Stalin was quite handsome" with "beautiful dark brown eyes."[130]

Even in Russia, where it was conventional for males to kiss on both cheeks, Stalin was overt in using, or promising, affectionate touch to get what he wanted. After Molotov in the early 1930s succeeded in seizing yet more grain from starving Ukrainians, Stalin responded, "I could cover you with kisses in gratitude."[131] To Lev Kamenev, a leading Bolshevik who would later fall victim in the purges, Stalin wrote: "I give you an Eskimo kiss on the nose. . . . I miss you. . . . There's no one, absolutely no one, to have a heart-to-heart conversation with, damn you."[132] Yet Stalin punished far more than he patted. Nadya had him pegged: "You're a tormentor, that's what you are! You torment your own son, your wife, the whole Russian people!"[133]

In World War II, Roosevelt, Churchill, and Stalin each shone as a strong leader. And yet each throughout his life displayed a masculine identity that varied from the conventional ideal—common in the United States, Britain, and the Soviet Union—that a man should remain cool, calm, collected, mature, and physically vigorous. Thomas "Tommy the Cork" Corcoran, an insider who observed Roosevelt at work and play, later described him as "the most androgynous human being I have ever known in my life."[134] Many of the rich despised FDR as a traitor to his class. It may also be that some people, on a less conscious level, despised him for transgressing gender norms. Even the admirers of Churchill described him as a self-absorbed boy. Stalin suffered a near crippling of his left arm and problems with his legs. More serious in a war commander, the dictator collapsed mentally twice in the first months of the German invasion.

For each of the three leaders, behaviors that were not conventionally masculine enabled a wider repertoire of personal tactics and a broader charismatic appeal. Individual masculine identities traced back to early experiences. With an unknowable degree of intentionality, FDR acted in ways that his contemporaries described as feminine. Theodore Roosevelt's daughter, Alice Longworth, called young

Franklin "feather-duster" because "he pranced around and flut-
tered."[135] Tall and willowy, he was teased about his good looks by
classmates at Groton and Harvard. Navy Secretary Daniels remembered that Roosevelt "always had about him what women would call
glamor and charm." He "had it just like an actress."[136] The author
John Gunther described Roosevelt's "strong streak of the female."[137]
FDR himself boasted about his performance in a newsreel: "That was
the Garbo in me."[138] Greta Garbo projected a sultry toughness, androgynous in her own way. As a schoolboy, Franklin auditioned for
the female lead in the class play, sending home photographs so his
parents could see "what good girls boys make!"[139] As assistant secretary, he began wearing a dark blue naval cape. His mellifluous voice,
patrician air, and nonstop talk and gesture all connoted effeminacy.
Yet FDR's muscular upper torso, developed after he contracted polio,
his visible courage, and his aura of power also denoted masculinity as
it was conventionally understood.[140]

FDR's good looks attracted both men and women.[141] Secretary of
Labor Frances Perkins, perhaps speaking also for herself, related how
presidential kingmaker Louis M. Howe had been drawn to him:
"Louis really fell in love with him because he was so beautiful. His
first view of Franklin Roosevelt was of a beautiful, strong, vigorous,
Greek god-king." Roosevelt seemed to be "kind of from another
world."[142] Daniels recounted his first impression: "I thought he was as
handsome a figure of an attractive young man as I have ever seen . . .
a case of love at first sight."[143]

FDR's undersecretary of state, Sumner Welles, had a sexual orientation that a later generation would term bisexual. He had been a page
at the Roosevelts' wedding. Like Daniels, Welles found FDR "the
most attractive—and the most beautiful young man—he had ever
known." The diplomat usually appeared icily cerebral. Yet when
pressed about his feelings for Roosevelt, he could not come up with a
respectable verbal formulation. Instead he acknowledged impulses
that might prove disturbing if "put into words." He began: "'I will try
to analyze my feelings' and then said, and shook his head, 'No, it can't
be done—I cannot put it into words, even to myself, but it is like a
burning flame.'"[144]

Polio complicated FDR's masculine identity.[145] Compensating for the paralysis of his legs, Roosevelt moved around with his voice and head. Gunther described FDR's face as "almost hyperthyroid, quivering with animation."[146] The tendency toward nonstop gesture and talk worked against prevailing stereotypes of strong, masculine men. On the one hand, FDR's paralysis, which most Americans believed was only lameness, enabled him to display courage. His stumping walks to the rostrum at the 1924 and 1928 Democratic conventions were interpreted as acts of bravery. In a gathering of friends, FDR would crawl backward from room to room, making jokes, his face tilted up and beaming. On the other hand, polio was dreaded as a mysterious physical and perhaps mental crippler.[147] Observers wondered if FDR's paralysis extended to sexual function. Although a medical examination found no sexual impairment, what counted was perception.[148]

While Roosevelt struck some as androgynous, Churchill in some ways behaved like a prepubescent boy—effervescent, easily excited, just as easily downcast, delighting in secrets, eager for adventure, and indifferent to most women. "I love his eternal childhood," enthused his lifelong friend, Violet Bonham Carter.[149] Less enchanted, his chief military adviser, Lord Alanbrooke, found him "temperamental like a film star, and peevish like spoilt child."[150] Like a baby, and similar to Roosevelt and Stalin in their own ways, he loved being in control. Clementine described the "pasha," clapping his hands to signal the servants. He was "never so happy" as when one servant did something for him while another put on his socks.[151] According to a biographer, he displayed "not the calculating seducer's charm but rather the beguiling appeal of a child, expecting affectionate compliance as though by right."[152] Even in meetings with Stalin and Roosevelt, he might dress in a "siren suit." Designed for quick dressing in air raids, these "rompers," some of velvet or silk, resembled what toddlers wear.[153] He liked to don a showy Panama, Stetson, or Australian bush hat. One wonders at the private understanding that led him to treasure the skull cap he got from Stalin.

Churchill delighted in flamboyantly exhibiting himself, whether through passionate oratory, fingers thrust up in the V-salute, or discussing politics in the nude. In the frightening, exciting weeks after Pearl Harbor, Churchill lived in the White House. Together with FDR he charted the future of their alliance. One evening and probably also on a second occasion, Roosevelt and Churchill talked high politics with the latter clad only in a towel draped on his shoulder. Another heady moment of male bonding and political promise occurred in August 1942 in Moscow, where Churchill had ventured into the den of the "ogre" to break the news that the Western allies were reneging on a second front in 1942. After shouting and pouting by both sides, Stalin suddenly invited Churchill and a few intimates to his private apartment. By means of much drinking, eating, and talking until three in the morning, the men got past their anger. Then the prime minister returned to his quarters, stripped down to a skimpy undershirt, and commanded his aides to listen. He burbled until dawn about the wondrous qualities of Stalin and their new friendship. The wonder would evanesce soon after Churchill awoke with a terrible hangover.[154]

In both Washington and Moscow it was Churchill who undressed or stayed unclad, apparently as a way to express his exuberance at the sudden lifting of barriers to personal and political alliance. Why he associated nudity or seminudity with connections to other powerful men remains difficult to answer with assurance.[155] Shedding clothes seemed a vehicle for celebrating individuality and freedom while keeping him the center of attention. Perhaps such a conflux of feelings and behaviors harked back to his earliest years. In general, he felt more relaxed with men than with women. As Pamela Churchill Harriman, Winston's former daughter-in-law, later commented, "Roosevelt liked women; Churchill liked men."[156]

Talking animatedly while undressed is the kind of quirky personal behavior by powerful men that often remains unrecorded by respectful observers and nearly as respectful historians. In this case, the story of the president encountering the naked prime minister in the White House, originally retailed by FDR, has become a beloved chestnut, a colorful detail harnessed to the traditional narrative about Franklin and Winston becoming fast friends during the war. Left out of most accounts, however, is analysis of the pattern of emotional behaviors.

Probably to moderate his swings toward excitement or depression, Churchill dosed himself with small, steady quantities of alcohol and nicotine. Throughout his waking hours he sipped watered-down whiskey and soda. He downed champagne with meals.[157] Hit by a car in Prohibition-era New York, he persuaded the doctor to prescribe whiskey. He went through eight or nine cigars daily, keeping them in his mouth, lighting and relighting them, thereby absorbing nicotine. As one aide observed, "he smoked matches and ate cigars." To get a "lift" before a speech he inhaled pure oxygen.[158] During the war, Churchill would offer Harry Hopkins some of the barbiturate pills upon which he depended.[159]

At the White House the prime minister would nap during the afternoon and stay up late at night. Wearying of these "Winston hours," Roosevelt complained, "I'm nearly dead. I have to talk to the PM all night, and he gets bright ideas in the middle of the night and comes pattering down the hall to my bedroom in his bare feet."[160]

Perhaps one reason for Stalin's cruelty was the gap between the rugged leader he pretended to be and the physically small and cowardly man he remained. Kremlin culture defined masculinity in terms of rational calculation, control over emotions, courage, and physical toughness. Stalin excelled in the first category. At wartime summits, he dazzled nearly everyone with his insight, memory, grasp of details, and readiness to learn more. He was less impressive in other ways, however. A week after the German invasion, the man at the helm suffered a mental collapse. He retreated to his dacha, refusing visitors or calls. Stalin also suffered physical deficiencies—without the compensation of Rooseveltian good looks. Candid observers came away shocked at his shortness, pockmarked face, rotting teeth, paunch, and pigeon-toed gait.[161] He made do with a lame arm and damaged legs. He struck some close observers as "feminine and soft."[162] They noticed his "manicured nails" and "almost a woman's fingers."[163]

Probably owing in part to his physical imperfections, Stalin wanted others to respect him as manly, self-disciplined, and calculating. He framed his identity as not just a member of the proletariat, but as a "hard" or "firm" proletarian.[164] His desire to be tough probably fed his cruelty. Attuned to others' moods, he grew furious when he saw or sensed ridicule. Although Stalin could not match FDR as an actor, he controlled his emotions far more tightly than Churchill could. In terms of rational calculation, the dictator often bested FDR and Churchill, who both tended toward intuition.

The Bolshevik Revolution

In striking contrast to Stalin and Churchill, Roosevelt was not seared by the Bolshevik Revolution, the Russian civil war, and the global turmoil of 1917–21. He retained a somewhat naive confidence that American capitalism and democracy could solve nearly all problems, at least in the United States. In 1919, with 20 percent of American industrial workers on strike, he opined that "if every family owned even a $100 bond of the United States or a legitimate corporation, there would be no talk of bolshevism." His equanimity did not crack even after his family barely escaped a terrorist's bomb. An anarchist placed an explosive device on the doorstep of Woodrow Wilson's attorney general, A. Mitchell Palmer. The bomber destroyed himself, the front half of Palmer's house, and the windows of Roosevelt's house across the street. Franklin and Eleanor were coming home from a party when they heard the blast. Had they arrived a few minutes earlier, they might have been killed. Their son, James, was at home. He later recalled that bits of flesh and blood from the bomber "were on our front steps, and Father had no way of knowing that it was not I who had been blown up." Though "uncommonly unnerved" at the moment, FDR soon recovered his equilibrium.[165] He remained lukewarm to the idea proposed by Wilson and Governor Calvin Coolidge of Massachusetts to use sailors to help suppress the Boston police strike. FDR did oppose bolshevism. Although he argued against firing three socialists who worked for the navy, he favored firing a fourth man who had circulated "literature which advocated the Soviet form of government."[166]

Yet FDR never succumbed to red-baiting. As president in 1933, he would ignore the State Department's objections and end sixteen years of nonrecognition of the Soviet government. In these negotiations FDR insisted to an embarrassed Maxim Litvinov that, regardless of the diplomat's Marxist atheism, he remained what a later generation would term a nice Jewish boy. Suspicious of the State Department's anti-Soviet bias, President Roosevelt would dismantle its Eastern European bureau. That angered Kennan, as did the appointment of Joe Davies as ambassador to Moscow after Bill Bullitt left embittered. Although Davies naively believed that the Kremlin was purging actual traitors, his presence in Moscow also reflected Roosevelt's hunch that the Soviets could prove useful in checking German and Japanese aggression.

Churchill nurtured a visceral hatred of revolutionary Marxism that preceded 1917. In *Savrola*, the hero's most serious competitor was not the military dictator but rather the aggressive, foreign-sounding Marxists, led by "Karl Kreutzer." While agitating for "a community of goods," the revolutionaries really sought "a community of wives"— starting with the president's wife, Lucile.[167] Churchill's fantasy-self battled with the Marxists for the body politic and the body of Lucile. Such association of ideological and sexual struggle may have accounted for the astounding vehemence of his reaction to the Bolshevik Revolution.

By 1919, Churchill was back in the Cabinet as minister of war. His job was to wind down the anti-Soviet intervention in Russia by British military forces, which had joined those of Japan, France, and the United States. He instead, Prime Minister Lloyd George complained, grew "obsessed by Russia." Echoing his Savrola-fantasy, he pledged that if the anti-Bolshevik Whites reached Moscow, he "wanted to go out & help mold the new Russian Constitution."[168] In 1920, as Soviet armies, some under Stalin's command, pushed the Poles back to Warsaw, the war minister turned to rebuilding Germany as a bulwark against communism. Brandishing the slogan, "Kill the Bolshie, Kiss the Hun," he called for "real peace and appeasement" of the recent enemy.[169]

Churchill depicted Bolshevism as a nightmarish violation of order and decency. For all his bravery and swagger, the man remained tightly wound. At home he slept in a draft-proof room kept at a constant 74 degrees. Twice daily he immersed himself in 98-degree bath water.[170] He disliked noise and hated whistling.[171] He stood convinced that "the old ways were good ways."[172] The overthrow of the czar in what he saw as semisavage Russia triggered disgust at perversion, disease, and degeneracy. He compared diplomatic recognition of the Bolshevik government to legalizing sodomy.

Letting the metaphors fly, he depicted revolutionaries as "fungus," "cancer," "plague bacillus," and "barbarism . . . devoured by vermin." They were "enemies of civilization," "deranged and distraught," "subhuman," and eager to "debauch wives and carry off children."[173] Years later when a Soviet trade representative arrived in London, Churchill refused to shake hands with the "hairy baboon."[174] He praised the Italian Fascist, Benito Mussolini, for opposing "the bestial appetite and passions of Leninism."[175] Churchill's language tells us more about his inner demons, determination to persuade, and disdain for the Russian masses than it does about the Bolsheviks, who were not "monsters" but rather humans despite their terrible excesses.

Stalin was an ideologue who believed in violent revolution. As he and other Bolsheviks saw it, Western capitalists had seized much of the world and controlled their workers and colonies through open or masked violence. The Soviets would use whatever violence it took to overthrow that order. Bolshevism fit Stalin's personality. He liked struggle, extremism, planning, domination, and cruelty. He shared the Bolshevik macabre belief that sacrificing millions of human beings was justified in building a new civilization. Yet Stalin could be a pragmatist as well as a raging zealot. On some key issues he tried to moderate Lenin's positions. During and after the Revolution he became the Soviet expert on the nationalities problem. He theorized and then helped launch a Russian-dominated union that allowed some cultural—but not political or economic—autonomy in Georgia and other borderlands.[176]

Stalin's perverse morality derived more from Machiavelli than from Marxism or Orthodoxy. He jotted in the flyleaf of a book:

NB! If a person is

1) strong (spiritually),
2) active,
3) intelligent (or capable),

then he is a *good* person regardless of any other "vices."

1) weakness,
2) laziness,
3) stupidity are the only thing that can be called vices.[177]

His implied standard of goodness was effectiveness. Killing, duplicity, and betrayal were not necessarily bad. But weakness and stupidity were vices. This the-ends-justify-the-means philosophy would yield grievous consequences for domestic and foreign policy.

First, it encouraged the sacrifice of millions in collectivizing agriculture, building industry, and, most egregiously, in the purges of the late 1930s. These values also warranted his seizing the Baltic nations in 1940 and much of Eastern Europe after 1944. Ironically, Stalin's brutality proved countereffective because it crushed spirits and creativity at home and stimulated opposition abroad. It almost led to the conquest of the USSR by Hitler's Germany.

Second, determination not to appear weak or stupid fed into long-standing Russian insecurities about being taking advantage of by supposedly more sophisticated Westerners. In August 1939, Stalin broke off desultory alliance negotiations with London and Paris. "The English and French wanted us for farmhands and at no cost!" he fumed.[178] Determined not to be played for a naïf by these would-be partners, Stalin set himself up for betrayal by Hitler. In 1944–46, the Kremlin chief was so focused on not being deprived of the fruits of victory that he undermined the alliance he wanted to preserve.

The Big Three

The early experiences of Roosevelt, Churchill, and Stalin shaped their respective personalities and perspectives on wartime problems. FDR's unshakable confidence, global perspective, democratic sensibility, sinuous masculinity, instinct for the deal, and relentless pragmatism helped him maneuver the United States into world leadership. Churchill's unbreakable will, imperial view, faith in Tory Democracy, boyish exuberance, ability to accept the inevitable, and irrepressible imagination enabled him to lead Britain to its costly victory. Stalin's intelligence, relentless ambition, provincial resentments, will to dominate, toughness, and unashamed opportunism vaulted the Soviet Union to unprecedented power.

Success invited dangerous even if only half-serious allusions to apotheosis. Stalin characteristically combined near megalomania with a pretense of modesty. Responding to criticism of the cult centered on Stalin as the all-wise leader, he replied with a smile, "What can I do? The people need a god."[179] A political ally listed Churchill's first commandment as "Thou shalt have no other Gods but me."[180] FDR Jr., warned that his father should not be disturbed, knowingly asked, "Is he in his 'I am Jesus—handle me with care' mood?"[181]

Hopkins understood his boss's priorities when he reported after meeting Stalin in 1941 that the latter was "get-atable." Stalin might have said the same thing about Roosevelt. By 1944–45, each of them was working to lure the other into a version of postwar collaboration that would advance his nation's interests, prevent another war, and establish peaceful coexistence for their divergent ideologies. Though he came to greatly admire Stalin, Churchill never could overcome his revulsion against the Bolshevik Revolution. Nor could he forget Britain's imperial rivalry with czarist Russia. In 1941–43, Roosevelt appreciated the prime minister's lectures on the war. By 1944–45, however, Churchill's defense of the British Empire and anti-Bolshevik ideology increasingly grated on Roosevelt.

From her unique vantage point—the Churchill household and the bedroom of Roosevelt's man in London, Averell Harriman—Pamela Churchill Harriman learned about the personal sides of Roosevelt and Churchill. Years later, she claimed that if not for the war, the two leaders would not have become friends. "They had nothing in common. They were not each other's type. They were not amused by the same things. They did not like the same sort of people." She added, "They had a different attitude toward the past. Churchill reveled in tradition. Roosevelt was much more of a pragmatist."[182]

Another perceptive insider, Dorothy Schiff, who spent weekends at Hyde Park with FDR, later recalled his saying that "he definitely favored 'Uncle Joe' [Stalin] and that the two of them ganged up on

Churchill." Schiff recounted Roosevelt's telling her before Yalta, "Uncle Joe and I are meeting; we understand each other. Get along beautifully, speak the same language. [In contrast], Winston is this, that, and the other." She inferred that Roosevelt felt intellectually inferior to Churchill. The president "didn't like Churchill," who "kept him up all night." He told her, "with obvious satisfaction, that . . . in the middle of a long speech he would interrupt Churchill, saying, 'Well, so what, Winston?'"[183] Still another observant woman, Roosevelt's confidante Margaret "Daisy" Suckley, quoted him as saying, "I think that Stalin, [Nationalist Chinese leader] Chiang [Kai-shek] & I can bring Brother Churchill around." Suckley, who was at FDR's side during his last two weeks, reflected a few days after his death, "F. himself did not have too much faith in Stalin, but he thought that he & Stalin looked at things in the same *practical* way, & for that reason, there was much hope that Stalin would follow along."[184]

Churchill would cool toward his transatlantic partner by the end of the war.[185] Though the prime minister had braved many trips during the worst of the war, he pleaded pressing business in not attending FDR's funeral. A few months afterward, Moran marveled that Churchill "seldom seems to allude to [Roosevelt] in his conversation." The doctor concluded, "The war was all they had in common." In contrast, "Stalin's stories, his ways, his habits, [keep] leaking out in Winston's talk; the man has caught his imagination so that the P.M. had looked forward to the meetings in the Kremlin." Despite his fear of Soviet power, Churchill had already anointed Stalin as "one of the great figures in history."[186]

Cultural differences and the emotions they spurred conspired to keep Churchill and Stalin politically apart. In 1944, a British diplomat observed that because Churchill had hoped for relations with Stalin on the "same sort of family basis" as with Roosevelt, the failure of the Kremlin chief to respond was interpreted by the prime minister "as deliberate discourtesy, or worse, and an indication that the Russians had the most sinister designs." Personal desires and disappointments could indeed have dangerous political consequences. The diplomat hoped that Churchill might come to understand that even if Stalin remained "rather formal and correct and not very matey, it [didn't] mean, necessarily, that he wants to stick a knife in your back."[187]

Such cultural differences did not disrupt ties between Churchill and Roosevelt. Moreover, they "had to get on with each other," noted Pamela Churchill Harriman, "and both worked at it."[188] Their relationship operated with less tension in 1941–43, when Roosevelt heeded Churchill's advice, than it did in the last two years, when the president focused on Stalin as the more necessary postwar partner.

A definitive relationship between personal preferences and political ties is difficult to prove, and claiming such causality would oversimplify how elective affinities operate. Still, it remains striking that at the Tehran and Yalta conferences Roosevelt and Stalin each made a point of reaching out to the other emotionally as well as politically. Both believed they had forged personal ties that could mitigate future political wrangles. The dictator and his successors would later reminisce that they had reached an understanding with Roosevelt, despite the underlying ideological differences. And they blamed those who succeeded FDR for betraying that accord.

Roosevelt remained the linchpin of the Grand Alliance. He was the most committed to trying postwar cooperation. In terms of personality and politics, the Big Three depended most on him. Roosevelt in turn depended on a circle of intimate advisers and aides, a circle that, tragically, he himself would undermine.

Chapter 2

From Missy to Molotov

The Women and Men Who Sustained the Big Three

On the night of June 21–22, 1941, two different crises converged, changing the outlook for Roosevelt's presidency. German armies crashed into the Soviet Union. At nearly the same hour, forty-three-year-old Missy LeHand, FDR's closest companion for two decades, was crippled by a stroke followed by a nervous breakdown. Roosevelt faced the challenges of a widened war at the moment when he lost a key member of his circle. Samuel I. Rosenman, a Roosevelt insider and speechwriter since the 1920s, pointed to LeHand as "the one indispensable person around the Executive Mansion and later around the White House."[1] He told Supreme Court justice Felix Frankfurter that she ranked as "one of the five most important people in the U.S."[2]

Indeed, LeHand operated as FDR's personal and political partner. As the New Dealer Raymond Moley put it, "Missy was as close to being a wife as he ever had—or could have."[3] Secretary of the Interior Harold L. Ickes detailed how LeHand's strengths fit Roosevelt's needs. "Missy is really a big woman. She sees the issues that are involved and she is so close to the President that she is in a position to keep him steady at times when he needs advice. The President is the kind of a person who needs help of this sort from someone very close to him."[4]

After LeHand died in July 1944, the *Washington Post* saluted her as "the ablest ... member of the President's inner circle."[5] Frankfurter pointed up the consequences for foreign policy: "Missy's enforced withdrawal is a calamity of world dimensions in view of F. D. R.'s responsibility for world affairs."[6]

That responsibility proved crucial because Roosevelt remained the fulcrum of the Big Three. His relationships with Churchill and Stalin were stronger than their ties with each other. Of the three he displayed the greatest cultural empathy, respect for difference, and emotional restraint—all key to keeping centrifugal forces in check. Examining the personal circle that made Roosevelt an effective president and sustained his health is essential, then, for understanding how the wartime alliance functioned and then fell apart. Important, too, is looking at how Roosevelt, tragically, disrupted the network upon which he depended.

Roosevelt, Churchill, and Stalin were alike in that they all hampered the efforts of those around them. How they treated their key advisers and assistants affected their efficiency as wartime leaders. Counterproductive political behaviors reflected personal habits formed in earlier years.

Roosevelt's Intimate Circle

Missy LeHand exemplified how personal and political influence intersected in a presidency that pivoted on personality. For Roosevelt, who blurred the personal and the political and who often referred to himself as "Father," political influence also hinged on "family." Roosevelt needed a family circle: emotionally committed, multitasking devotees who kept him company, helped him relax, discouraged harebrained schemes, overcame his procrastination by knowing how and when to push, translated his notions into pragmatic policy, and helped maneuver that policy through Congress and the bureaucracy.

In his first years as president, these needs were met superbly by a foursome: LeHand, Louis M. Howe, Thomas G. Corcoran, and Harry L. Hopkins. A fifth, Sumner Welles, had known Roosevelt for decades

2.1. The imperial president. This White House celebration of FDR's fifty-second birthday was probably arranged by amateur dramatist Louis Howe, sitting in the second row, at the right. While Missy LeHand, seated front-row left, and Anna Roosevelt, standing to her father's left, beamed at "Caesar," Eleanor, opposite her daughter, looked straight ahead. (Courtesy of FDR Library.)

and would remain his trusted, hardworking diplomat. Yet the two did not socialize much. Welles maintained a glacial reserve except when he got drunk. Other aides also figured in FDR's presidency, including Rosenman, Ickes, Moley, Rexford Tugwell, Hugh Johnson, James Farley, Felix Frankfurter, Henry Wallace, William Leahy, Frances Perkins, Henry Morgenthau Jr., Robert Jackson, William Douglas, Anna Rosenberg, James Byrnes, and Averell Harriman. Yet none of these (nor figures such as Edwin "Pa" Watson, Steve Early, Ross McIntire, and Marvin McIntyre) quite matched the four in terms of fit, talent, energy, versatility, devotion—and expertise in navigating bureaucratic politics. The foursome of the inner circle all loved Roosevelt and loved wielding power through him. As Corcoran remarked, "the President's people never played for such small stakes as money."[7]

Howe died in 1936. LeHand collapsed in 1941. FDR broke with Corcoran in 1940. Roosevelt was forced to fire Welles in 1943. Hopkins left the White House later that year. No one in this circle was ever effectively replaced. Meanwhile, the burdens of wartime and postwar planning mounted. FDR's isolation allowed his heart disease to go undetected until March 1944; indeed, being alone probably aggravated his condition. A few days before Roosevelt's death, Ickes and the columnist Drew Pearson agreed that quite aside from his health, "the President's situation at the White House is pretty weak. . . . There wasn't anything to hope for from the White House staff as it is at present constituted."[8]

The inner circle broke up for underlying reasons, including Roosevelt's demanding behavior. Franklin had stood at the center of his parents' lives. Relatively immobile because of polio, he maneuvered others to revolve around him. Roosevelt's craving for adoration and companionship drained even those who loved him. His manipulations made administration politics emotional, competitive and unstable. Though LeHand invigorated the group by welcoming Corcoran and Hopkins, no one brought in comparable talent after her stroke.

The team was both strengthened and weakened by FDR's preference for gifted people with some "disability." Facing the prejudices of his time, FDR helped rehabilitate his fellow "polios" through the therapy and public campaigns connected with Warm Springs, Georgia. With regard to himself, Roosevelt engaged in "splendid deception" about the extent of his paralysis rather than challenge prevailing notions about what it meant not to have the ability to walk.[9] With an unknowable degree of conscious intent, Roosevelt chose talented people who defied disability. LeHand was plagued by insecurity and a tendency toward depression. Howe suffered asthma and facial scarring. Hopkins endured near starvation from gastrointestinal problems. Welles drank to excess and desired homosexual acts with men he otherwise disdained. Though not quite a disability, the unrelenting ambition and the no-holds-barred tactics of Corcoran would lead to his banishment from the inner circle. Like FDR, these aides demonstrated that in facing down "disability," one could hone extraordinary ability.

The White House live-ins—LeHand, Howe, and Hopkins—became indispensable by molding their lives to FDR's needs. They shared his work and relaxation. They deftly raised issues while he was sorting stamps or playing cards. Corcoran lobbied for the president during the workday and played the accordion for him in the evening. Receiving such devotion did not stop FDR from turning on those who sinned by putting him second in their personal lives. For years, Howe merely visited his wife. FDR insulted Corcoran to show his disapproval of a new wife. He grew petulant on discovering that LeHand deeply loved William Bullitt. Roosevelt felt betrayed when Hopkins, to salvage his health and marriage, moved out of the White House. FDR's own marriage depended on the two partners leading largely separate lives. After Eleanor discovered Franklin's affair with Lucy Mercer (later Lucy Rutherfurd) in 1918, they stayed married for practical rather than emotional reasons. Rosenman remembered that "when Eleanor was around you could always feel tension of a certain kind."[10]

For most people, Roosevelt's beaming face, upturned cigarette holder, and flattering banter cast a positive glow. Abe Fortas, later a Supreme Court justice, remembered that when FDR wheeled into the Cabinet room, "it was as if a great white light had been turned on."[11] His friend Dorothy Schiff saw him as a "Sun God."[12] Yet while warming others with this radiance, FDR remained ruthlessly self-centered. Ickes concluded that "despite his very pleasant and friendly personality, he is as cold as ice inside."[13] Truman, whom Roosevelt ignored, recalled that "he was the coldest man I ever met. He didn't give a damn personally for me or you or anyone else in the world as far as I could see."[14]

Although Roosevelt rarely displayed deep emotions, he sparked variants of love in his associates. A journalist concluded that "love comes closest to being the discipline of Roosevelt's Praetorian Guard."[15] We get a sense of how this "discipline" worked from a reminiscence of Earl Miller, a former policeman and longtime companion to the Roosevelts. Trying to explain FDR's charm, Miller slid from describing how Lucy Mercer loved him to generalizing how almost everyone "just could not help it": "I know Mercer loved him as so many of us did, every damn secretary in the family did—one just could not help it—it was the magnetism of the man. I was no different than the rest."[16] Roosevelt could also wield the stick. "I don't love you any more," he admonished a resistant aide.[17]

FDR attracted women to help him unwind. In terms of his effectiveness as president, a key criterion was whether his companion of the moment had the capability to assist him in work as well as in relaxation. LeHand could casually broach an item of business while they swam or played cards. Admirers such as Princess Martha of Norway, however, could help only in escape from stress. Miller recalled that "every darn woman Democratic leader in every county kissed him upon greeting."[18] Corcoran, who prided himself as a ladies' man, later remarked, "even I did not like to see so many women kissing you."[19] Visiting Hyde Park, the actress Paulette Goddard, blurted out, "you're so—eligible." FDR shot back, "I'm not! I'm married, among other things." Yet Goddard had picked up the signal. "Well, you're handsome," she replied.[20] Schiff, an heiress in her thirties who owned the *New York Post*, often spent weekends at Hyde Park without her husband.

Decades later, Schiff reflected on FDR's behavior: He "thought probably I had what is called sex appeal. He wanted a companion that he felt fairly comfortable with, and that he could certainly dominate completely, or thought he could." Asked if she had talked about herself, Schiff replied: "Never. Not a word about myself. He couldn't have been less interested in me. He was interested in himself, and having what he thought was this well-dressed young woman, whom he could ramble on to."[21] Such rambling remained a priority. When the actress Katherine Hepburn came for tea, she marveled that "the President seemed to have all the time in the world."[22] The president could afford such recreation as long as he had Howe and others to help with responsibilities.

Louis M. Howe

A struggling journalist when he signed on with FDR in 1912, Howe engineered his election as president in 1932. He grew close with both FDR and Eleanor. Howe coped with disability throughout his life. His asthma and bronchitis, aggravated by smoking, left him wheezing for breath. A boyhood bicycle accident had ground his face into roadside gravel. Thereafter, black-pitted scars disfigured his face. He boasted about being "one of the four ugliest men" in New York.[23] Howe became the prototypical insider: talented and dedicated. He prided himself as the no-man who could veto Franklin's fantasies. He felt free to tell off the man he had promoted. Aides overheard Louis shouting over the telephone: "All right, pig-head. But don't say I didn't warn you. What's that? You're going for a swim? Well, go ahead, damnit, and I hope to God you drown."[24] Nevertheless, Howe loved Roosevelt. An aide who worked for them remembered Howe's "almost insane jealousy" about FDR.[25]

Howe kept the "Boss" in tune with political sentiment around the nation. Eleanor, referring to her husband's disastrous campaign in 1937–38 to "pack" the Supreme Court and purge opposing Democrats in Congress, later wrote that these "political mistakes . . . might have been avoided if Louis Howe had been alive. After Louis's death, Franklin never had a political adviser who would argue with him and still give him unquestioned loyalty."[26]

Nor would Franklin ever again have an aide to help sustain his uneasy marriage with Eleanor. After Howe died, she confided that FDR "is nice to me, but as a person I'm a stranger and I don't want to be anything else."[27] In losing Howe, the president also lost a key liaison with his wife, who might have assisted him after LeHand and Hopkins departed. Instead, the wartime commander-in-chief and the First Lady would go their separate ways. Franklin no longer had patience for the social justice causes that animated Eleanor. She made it a point to leave the White House or Hyde Park soon after Princess Martha arrived.

Eleanor Roosevelt spent much of the war years on long trips bolstering the morale of U.S. servicemen in far-off corners of the globe, including the South Pacific. On Guadalcanal she visited her close friend, Joseph Lash. The gruff commander Admiral William F. "Bull" Halsey later recalled that in military hospitals Eleanor "stopped at every bed, and spoke to every patient. . . . She walked for miles, and she saw patients who were grievously and gruesomely wounded. I marveled at their expressions as she leaned over them. It was a sight I will never forget."[28] Eleanor did not, however, pay such close attention when her husband's health deteriorated in 1944–45.

2.2. In the decades after this 1905 photograph, Franklin and Eleanor Roosevelt would lose the capacity to find such joy in each other. Their daughter later remembered that while "Father loved a relaxed atmosphere with many laughs, Mother could laugh more after Father died." (Anna Roosevelt Halsted, interview with Joseph Lash, November 27, 1967, Lash papers. Courtesy of FDR Library.)

In his last years, FDR probably took heart from the way that Howe had persisted despite his decline in health. Gasping for every breath, Howe could no longer walk. He then wheeled himself around in one of FDR's chairs. Louis remained politically active in the face of death. In 1935, he slipped into a coma under an oxygen tent. Roosevelt readied a train to bring officials to the funeral. Then Howe woke up and said, irritably, "Why in hell doesn't somebody get me a cigarette?"[29] He lived another year. Although the president never replaced this naysaying tactical genius, he still had at his side world-class operators: Corcoran, LeHand, and Hopkins.

Thomas G. Corcoran

A charming, brilliant, high-energy lawyer, Corcoran and his associate, Benjamin V. Cohen, crafted New Deal legislation and lobbied it through Congress. Corcoran recalled that at first, LeHand "arranged that I should arrive for a daily briefing by her and [perhaps] a visit with the President. . . . Gradually, through her pointing out my successes, I was in with the President more often than not."[30] Roosevelt tapped Corcoran's network of contacts throughout Washington, asking, "Tommy, what did you learn today?"[31] LeHand played party politics. She invited "Tommy the Cork" to her parties, where he squeezed out favorites on the accordion while FDR "did most of the singing." Everybody "let [Roosevelt] have the fun of carrying" the tune. "They were lovely parties because everybody had enough glow to get a little bit, shall we say, not indiscreet but . . ."[32] FDR's "great secret was that he could relax," Corcoran remembered. The place where Roosevelt "would be happiest and let go the most and really be carefree, that was at old Joe Kennedy's house."[33] At one such party in June 1935, FDR, Corcoran, LeHand, and a few others motored to Kennedy's Maryland estate, where Missy sometimes spent weekends. Hiding upstairs, a journalist overheard a "very merry" gathering. "The President's laughter rang out over all and was most frequent." The group ate, drank mint juleps, joked, and sang until well after midnight. The president picked up the accordion and "performed creditably."[34] According to Corcoran, they sat "on a lovely terrace with a great big moon" and someone sighed, "Oh God, may the Commies never come." Roosevelt just laughed.[35]

Corcoran was so versatile, connected, and ruthless that Roosevelt ultimately exhausted his usefulness. In 1937–38, the president sent Tommy into battle for the doomed Court packing scheme and the purge in Congress.[36] Expecting that the "Boss" would make him solicitor general or even a Supreme Court justice, Corcoran went all out. His henchmen became known as "Corcoran's OGPU," a reference to Stalin's secret police.[37] Some thought Corcoran capable of murder, literally.[38]

FDR also used Corcoran to "fix" Roosevelt family scandals. The result was to deepen Tommy's reputation for shady dealings. For instance, in the midst of trying to patch up the marriage of FDR's philandering son, James, Corcoran suddenly "had to go to New York to try to quiet a woman who had charged" another son, Elliott, "with assault."[39] Years later, Bernard Baruch, who was close to Eleanor

Roosevelt, recounted what may have been the financial side of this mission: Eleanor "suddenly began to cry," saying "that there was great trouble, and that something had to be done or it would cause Franklin great embarrassment. I then went to my desk and wrote perhaps the largest personal check I've ever written, and I gave it to her."[40] Corcoran remarked that James "made his pile by chiseling, bulldozing, and using his family name."[41] Howe, who parlayed his fame as White House insider into a sizable income, never bothered to file a tax return.[42] In 1939, Hopkins warned that "the President would be lucky if he finished this term without some real scandal involving at least one member of his family."[43] In taking care of such business Corcoran projected an aura of "vulgar mystery," always "ducking in and out of the White house."[44]

Corcoran justified the cover-ups with telling language: the "Empire must go on."[45] He used similar discourse to explain his lobbying against an inquiry into Elliott Roosevelt's financial chicanery: "You realize why I was fighting those hearings so tough. I wasn't fighting for me—I was fighting for the Lawd."[46] Despite his cynicism, Corcoran, like many others, believed in "Franklin D. Roosevelt" as a transcendent cause, like an empire or the Lord. It was a testament to Roosevelt's leadership, agenda, and charisma that he could spark such loyalty. Yet such devotion also fostered the imperial presidency that traced back to this administration. Sending Tommy into gutter fights made him so toxic that Roosevelt by 1940 suspended him from the circle. Unfortunately, Roosevelt never again had at his side an aide who combined Corcoran's energy, versatility, devotion, and brilliance.

Their final break came when Corcoran married against his wishes. In 1940, Corcoran, already resentful because his all-out loyalty had failed to pay off with a prestigious post, decided to defy the "Boss" by marrying Margaret "Peggy" Dowd. Roosevelt had objected because Dowd came from a family that not only lacked money but also had ties to the anti-English Ancient Order of Hibernians. FDR told him, "You can do better" by marrying someone with enough money to fund a run for elective office.[47] When Tommy, ignoring this directive, asked FDR to "receive Peggy and me as newlyweds," Missy arranged the appointment.[48] Arriving at the White House, the couple waited two hours. Finally, Hopkins, Corcoran's old rival, emerged from the Oval Office to say that the "Boss" was too busy to see them.[49] Presidential aides commonly suffer political humiliation in the line of duty. FDR, however, had humiliated Tommy in a most personal way. In an awkward but telling metaphor, Corcoran described the split in terms of marital status: "I could not be as comfortably single-minded as his bachelor-man-at-arms."[50] Corcoran, Howe, Hopkins, and LeHand all stood closest to FDR—and he felt most comfortable with them—as long as they remained actual or virtual "bachelors." Knowing FDR well, LeHand hid from him her true feelings.

Marguerite A. "Missy" LeHand

Perhaps because LeHand was a woman, started out as a secretary, and suffered the destruction of most of her papers, historians have overlooked her importance. From 1921 to 1941, Missy was closer than anyone else to "Effdee," as she alone called him. She complemented FDR in four ways. She met his need for companionship and cared for him, helped him relax, put on a convincing happy face, and took on so many responsibilities that she became in effect his chief-of-staff. With outward cheer, Missy fought melancholy and a tendency toward mental breakdown. FDR's reaction to her collapse indicated in him an empty or shuttered place where many people harbor empathy.

Within a year after FDR contracted polio, he was spending more time with LeHand, who was sixteen years his junior, than with his wife. For instance, from 1925 through 1928, Roosevelt was away from home a total of 116 out of the 208 weeks. Eleanor stayed with him during 4 of those weeks, his mother during 2, and Missy during 110.[51] Throughout much of that time Roosevelt and LeHand were together alone or with just the crew of the houseboat *Larooco*. LeHand shared his pain and small gains as he struggled for mobility and a meaningful life. She later recalled that "there were days on the *Larooco* when it was noon before he could pull himself out of depression and greet his guests wearing his lighthearted facade."[52] In the New York governor's mansion, Missy took the bedroom closest to

FDR's. Eleanor slept in a smaller back room. In the White House, Missy had a suite on the third floor.[53] She worked in the office nearest the Oval Office.

An aide recalled that "when he became President, FDR cut every really personal relationship out of his life except for his love for Missy."[54] When LeHand gave orders, the domestic staff "responded as if it had come from the First Lady. . . . We really had two mistresses," a maid remembered.[55] "Effdee" and Missy spent most weekends together and left dinner parties at the same time. A reporter described her as "an extension of his emotional personality," able to "see the slightest changes in his emotional attitude before they have become apparent to anyone else."[56] LeHand very likely would have noticed FDR's shortness of breath long before his daughter, Anna Roosevelt Boettiger, called in a cardiologist in March 1944.

Were Missy and FDR sexually intimate? They were physically close. On family drives, Missy rather than Eleanor sat next to FDR.[57] She visited FDR in her nightgown and sat on his lap. In dueling memoirs, Elliott Roosevelt argued that there had been a sexual relationship while his brother, Jimmy, disagreed.[58] FDR Jr. told an interviewer that "he was sure there was a physical relationship between FDR and Missy."[59] Given FDR's and Missy's delight at deception, Anna offered the most appropriate answer: "Who could tell?"[60] Roosevelt enjoyed keeping his staff guessing. Rosenman remembered that appointments secretary "Pa [Watson], Steve [Early], and I would get together and ask what the hell's going on with the Roosevelt family?" They "knew the gossip about Missy and FDR and tried to figure out what was the relationship."[61] Some historians have argued that as a proud polio victim, FDR probably would not have risked the vulnerability of sex.[62]

Yet according to Roosevelt's African American servants, who saw him close up and who formed a tight, "backstairs" society, "there was nothing incomplete about FDR's love life." When someone sneered that Herbert "Hoover was dead from the waist up, and Roosevelt was dead from the waist down," FDR's valet snorted, "I'll be damned if he is!"[63] Schiff later recorded that she had asked a doctor at Warm Springs, "Is the President potent?" He replied, "It is only his legs that are paralyzed." She then asked, "How does he manage?" "The French way," came the answer.[64] In historical context, "the French way" referred to oral sex.[65] The physical side of FDR and Missy's relationship may have changed from their years together in the 1920s to later times, when they both found other admirers.

Regardless of whether they had "sex," Missy lavished on "Effdee" the devotion he craved. She listened as he retold stories. She shared his stamps. She sometimes joined the boys on fishing trips. She kept him company in the pool though she hated swimming. When FDR appeared stressed, she would arrange a party. Corcoran remembered that LeHand would "disappear from her desk and come back a few minutes later wearing a lovely gown to make all the President's friends feel right at home."[66] Roosevelt seemed pleased that men in his circle found her alluring—until sometime in 1940–41, when he discovered how much she cared for Bullitt.

In January 1934, during what Missy called "a week filled with happiness," she had fallen in love with William C. Bullitt Jr., the U.S. ambassador to Moscow and then Paris.[67] She visited him when he was home. In hundreds of letters, LeHand revealed an imploring love. "I think of you constantly," she wrote from Hyde Park.[68] "All my love to you, my dear," she pledged in a typical note; "please write to me and please miss me—I miss you so much."[69] She confessed, "I live for your visits."[70] LeHand enticed him with inside information: "Very illuminating cross-currents at this particular time—I wish you were here so I could tell you about them. They cannot be written."[71] Bullitt's feelings for her remain uncertain, in part because of his own complex sexual orientation and in part because he insisted that she burn his intimate letters. For months he did not answer her letters or call. He apparently at one point had suggested marriage. Bullitt used his wealth, hospitality, and bonhomie to assemble a glittering collection of contacts—including Sigmund Freud, with whom he wrote a book on Woodrow Wilson; the families of Joseph Kennedy and Harold Ickes, whom he hosted at his French chateau; European heads of state—and the president's live-in intimate. Knowing that FDR easily felt betrayed, LeHand for years kept secret how much she loved Bullitt.

Like FDR, Missy ranked as a master performer. Raised by a working-class single mother, she adopted the Roosevelts' upper-class manners. Even "her trilling laugh is a soprano echo" of the president's, a reporter noted.[72] She bubbled with energy, "not waiting for the elevator half the time, but just tripping down the stairs."[73] She turned somersaults at a party held at Kennedy's estate.[74] Hopkins's young daughter, Diana, who also lived in the White House, would remember LeHand as "warm and fuzzy and motherly." She added, "Everybody adored Missy."[75] Photographs suggest that LeHand was not, in a conventional sense, beautiful.

But those pictures fail to portray her radiance. A maid remembered that she "could be the most glamorous woman in the room with her chandelier earrings swaying and her blue eyes flashing as she talked. Missy made sure to wear high heels that clicked . . . instead of the low heels and sensible oxfords the First Lady wore." LeHand sported lacy nightgowns as evening wear. The staff noticed that FDR "watched Missy's performance with obvious delight."[76] She acted out various personae. In the world of the Roosevelts, she was known as "Missy," the diminutive coined by young Anna. In letters to Bullitt, however, she clung to a private, pre-Rooseveltian identity as "Marguerite."

Despite her public gaiety, LeHand suffered private melancholy. She had nervous breakdowns in 1927 and 1931. She confessed to Bullitt, "I feel depressed today" or "this is one of my bluest days."[77] In January 1940, she confided that "for months I have been feeling very depressed mentally and physically."[78] She wrote to Roosevelt, "This place is horrible when you are away."[79] Yet LeHand dared not share her darker moments with FDR, who disliked hearing about sadness or sickness. Missy also suffered childlike fears of abandonment. Her alcoholic father had left his family. In a Christmas greeting to the Roosevelts, she appealed: "for all the times I've misbehaved, I hope both you and Mrs. Roosevelt will forgive me—that would be my nicest present."[80] Addressing FDR as "Dear Father," she again sounded like a little girl: "I'm going to be so good when I get back and never get cross or anything."[81] To Bullitt she bared herself: "I am always afraid you will forget about me and I should hate that."[82]

Her anxieties about inadequacy are astonishing in light of her ability and accomplishment. Intelligent, charming, and tactful, LeHand developed from a secretary into a tactical adviser who weighed in on personnel and policy. FDR liked working with such generalists. He tested ideas on her, and she felt free to challenge him. Eugene Meyer, editor of the *Washington Post*, admired her as a "general confidante, listening sympathetically to all sorts of troubles, tactfully giving all sorts of informed and intelligent advice."[83] "She made the Oval Office run like a Swiss watch," Corcoran later remarked.[84] Missy helped Tommy and other talented favorites, such as Hopkins, get closer to the president. Like Howe and Hopkins, she knew how to sidestep FDR's procrastination by alternating work with fun. In 1936, Ickes turned to her, "absolutely certain that she reflects the opinion of the President" with regard to Cabinet politics.[85] By 1939, Ickes, Corcoran, and others took the time to "argue eloquently" with LeHand because she had influence with the president on pending Supreme Court appointments.[86] After war broke out in Europe, she "went after him hammer and tongs on the subject of the War Department" and its ineffectual leader, Harry Woodring.[87] She assisted in drafting Lyndon B. Johnson to run for the Senate.[88]

By intruding herself in politics, however, LeHand risked her personal relationship with FDR, which was already complicated by triangles. By April 1941, she was "caustically" criticizing the president for "doing nothing" to combat noninterventionists, such as Senator Burton K. Wheeler. No longer the adoring secretary, she complained to Ickes: "'We have a leader who won't lead.'"[89] Such criticism echoed what Bullitt was saying, as well as Hopkins (who in 1939 had talked about marrying LeHand.)

April–June 1941 proved a turbulent time for both FDR and Missy. He agonized over how to respond to the undefeated Wehrmacht, which sliced through Yugoslavia and Greece. Suffering with bleeding hemorrhoids and influenza, the president isolated himself from most officials while escaping with the crown princess of Norway.

Roosevelt encouraged the flirtatious, attractive, forty-year-old Martha (whose husband remained in London for most of the war) to rent Pook's Hill, an estate in nearby Bethesda, Maryland.[90] Like Eleanor Roosevelt, Lucy Mercer, and Missy, Princess Martha was tall with blue eyes and brownish hair. FDR's aides referred to her as "the president's girlfriend."[91] Eleanor came to refer to any woman who fussed over her husband as "just another Martha."[92] The president invited

2.3. By dint of her intelligence, personality, and loyalty, Missy LeHand rose from secretary to a de facto chief of staff who "made the Oval Office run like a Swiss watch," an insider noted. (Corcoran, "Rendezvous with Democracy," box 586, Corcoran papers. Courtesy of FDR Library.)

her for long afternoon drives. A reporter described Martha's bursting out the door "in high-heeled slippers and black silk hose. She would race to the car, leap in and off it would go."[93] She joined him on cruises or weekends at Hyde Park. According to the White House butlers, FDR "played kneesies" with Martha under the dinner table. He asked her to call him "dear Godfather." Maids noted "the ardor with which the President kissed Princess Martha at every opportunity" and that he "seemed to eat up" her "little girl act."[94] Even in front of Eleanor, Martha "behaved like an 18-year-old flirt," a friend of the First Lady grumbled. "She says nothing, just giggles and looks adoringly at him. But he seems to like it tremendously."[95]

In the spring of 1941, FDR also began again seeing Lucy Mercer Rutherfurd, who appeared on the White House log as "Mrs. Paul Johnson." On FDR's command, LeHand instructed the switchboard to give priority to Rutherfurd's calls. Missy must have felt jealous and abandoned as FDR turned to the more youthful and elegant Martha and to his lifelong love, Lucy. Schiff, who was often at Hyde Park with FDR and Missy, "didn't envy her."[96] Then the final blow: the triangle of Roosevelt/LeHand/Bullitt blew up after the ambassador returned from France in July 1940.

Bullitt had defied both the president and the secretary of state, Cordell Hull, by lingering in Paris after the German invasion in June. He fancied himself "public enemy number one of the Germans" and declared that he was honor bound to protect the city, somehow.[97] Back in the real world of diplomacy, however, Bullitt was ignoring duty. He disobeyed orders to accompany the fleeing French authorities and influence them toward going into exile in London rather than surrender.[98] Nevertheless, after returning home Bullitt simply assumed he deserved a big promotion. The playwright, politician, and femme fatale Clare Boothe Luce, wife of Time-Life magnate Henry Luce, stepped up her campaign to make the ambassador "President or Secretary of State!!!"[99] Bullitt had LeHand as well as Ickes lobby with the "Great White Father."[100]

Bullitt grew obsessed with replacing or at least unseating Undersecretary of State Sumner Welles, FDR's hard-working confidant in the department. A colleague lauded Welles as "daring, thorough, quick-witted, [and] clear-headed"—all qualities lacking in Secretary of State Hull.[101] On April 21, 1941, Bullitt confronted the president with the true story that on September 17, 1940, Welles while intoxicated had tried five times to solicit homosexual acts from African American porters on the president's train.[102] Bullitt warned that "a criminal like Welles . . . was subject to blackmail by foreign powers." Roosevelt said that he had assigned Welles a permanent bodyguard to prevent further incidents. He refused to fire Welles because he "found it convenient to have him" in the State Department. Both men grew angry.[103]

The spat grew nastier. Furious that Bullitt was airing the Welles scandal all over Washington, FDR revenged himself through torture. If the president had flatly refused to give Bullitt a major job, the latter could have gone on with his life. But that would be letting him off too easily. Instead, the president repeatedly dangled prizes that never quite materialized.[104] As Bullitt recorded, FDR assured him "that of course I could do almost any cabinet job better than the man now in it."[105] The former ambassador traveled to the Middle East on a presidential mission, only to discover once there that he had no clout. FDR encouraged him to run for mayor of Philadelphia and governor of Pennsylvania, then withdrew his support.[106] Harriman, who would quarrel with the president in 1944–45 over getting tough with the Soviets, later reminisced that FDR "always enjoyed other people's discomfort."[107] Seething, Bullitt redoubled efforts to bring down Welles.

FDR humiliated Bullitt for challenging him and because he needed Welles. But perhaps even more infuriating to Roosevelt was his discovery of how much LeHand loved Bullitt. FDR Jr. remembered that "the reason his father would not see Bill was his affair with Missy, which almost reached the point of marriage. FDR did not like that at all." Corcoran, whose personal life FDR had also tried to stifle, later remarked that a marriage with Bullitt "couldn't happen. Missy belonged to the Boss."[108]

In spring 1941, LeHand was squeezed between Roosevelt and Bullitt. She also faced rising responsibilities in a mired presidency. Uncertain how to respond to the German threat and to agitation by the noninterventionists, and feeling physically rotten, FDR sought comfort with Martha and Lucy. Missy suffered insomnia and was "taking opiates," Eleanor reported.[109] Pearson later noted that Missy "took dope."[110] Her equilibrium slipping, LeHand no longer finessed her competition with Eleanor Roosevelt as First Lady.[111]

The crisis climaxed on June 4, 1941. At a White House party, Missy suddenly screamed and dropped to the floor. She had suffered a stroke that paralyzed one side of her body. Eleanor wrote that Missy's "mind went as it does."[112] The following day, FDR visited LeHand for 10 minutes in the morning and 25 minutes in the afternoon. In between, he spent 105 minutes with Lucy, meeting her after a 25-minute session with Secretary of War Henry L. Stimson.[113] Perhaps feeling guilty about LeHand and resisting Stimson's arguments for war, the president sought emotional solace with his lover from the pre-polio years.

Nurses assigned to Missy recorded that she appeared "completely irrational" and "quite depressed." "Screaming, crying, and kicking,"

2.4. Tommy "the Cork" Corcoran later remarked that a marriage with Bullitt, here sitting on the right, "couldn't happen. Missy belonged to the Boss." (Corcoran, "Rendezvous with Democracy," box 587, Corcoran papers. Courtesy of Corbis.)

she was put in bed "by sheer force."[114] Doctors sedated her with morphine. Although the medical attendants did not record what she was screaming, the maids did. Missy called for "Effdee," worrying that he could not get along without her—or that he could. One maid mused, "It's sad to love a man so much."[115] On brief visits Roosevelt would paste on a smile and tell cheery anecdotes. Then he would flash a final grin and wheel himself out. LeHand suffered another stroke the evening of June 21. It was probably a coincidence, but FDR had spent that afternoon with Princess Martha.[116]

Broken in body and mind, LeHand could no longer compartmentalize her life. Although unable to speak, she could write. Anna recalled that Missy penned letters, telling "of this one being in love with her, and that one wanting to marry her."[117] After decades of discretion, Missy was violating the Rooseveltian code of maintaining appearances. As Corcoran had said in reference to another family embarrassment, "the Empire must go on."[118] Anna recounted that "everyone realized that [Missy] could no longer be trusted. . . . Friends and the family drew together to get the letters out of sight, to hush up Missy's lapse."[119] In getting "the letters out of sight," most of LeHand's papers were evidently destroyed. Rosenman, who had been close to Missy, later said that "when she was stricken in 1941, they must have done something with her papers."[120]

LeHand was treated at St. Elizabeth's mental hospital and elsewhere.[121] Eleanor Roosevelt found it "difficult to realize that it is really Missy, she has changed so much."[122] Her voice muscles were paralyzed, enabling her to squeeze out only "yes." After the strokes, FDR was extraordinarily generous in changing his will to provide for LeHand, bequeathing her one-half of his estate. She predeceased him, however. If she knew about the will, she probably found his financial concern no compensation for his apparent coldness. In 1942, LeHand tried to commit suicide by swallowing chicken bones. She then set herself on fire. Finally she was sent to Somerville, Massachusetts, under the care of her sister.[123] Missy's stroke breached FDR's support system.

Losing LeHand diminished Roosevelt's resources for coping with the global crisis. Rosenman later concluded that insofar as "the whole war effort was concerned, this stroke was worse than losing a battle." If Missy had survived in good health, Roosevelt's "own life would have been prolonged."[124] Bullitt, from his skewed perspective, later testified that "it was Missy who gave [FDR] moral character."[125] Pearson may have been alluding to something similar: "In the old days it was Missy LeHand who kept things moving. She would get him in the evening & take up various decisions he had to make and make him make them. Roosevelt is a good procrastinator. She is out now & he has Princess Martha, Harry Hopkins & Pa Watson's gold braid instead . . . a rarefied atmosphere—military, royalty. . . . Missy thought about the plebes."[126]

Harry L. Hopkins

Like Corcoran, Hopkins owed his entrée in part to LeHand. According to Elinor Morgenthau, the wife of the treasury secretary, "Missy LeHand is largely responsible for the intimate position that Harry Hopkins occupies at the White House."[127] At FDR's invitation, Hopkins moved into the White House on May 10, 1940, the day that the Germans invaded France and Churchill became prime minister. He came to dinner and stayed thirty months. With familial intimacy, Harry "could walk into the President's cabin without being announced or even without knocking," Ickes noted jealously.[128] Hopkins taunted his rival, Corcoran: "Remember, Tommy, anything you spend an entire day doing I can undo in ten minutes after supper."[129]

Hopkins displayed in his physical person both ability and disability. Indeed, observers often mentioned in the same breath Harry's achievements and handicaps. Roosevelt explained that because of Hopkins's devotion, "I need that half-man around me."[130] Years later, Robert Sherwood chose that quotation to launch his study, *Roosevelt and Hopkins*. The spectacle of such a fierce personality springing from a frail physique added to Harry's mystique. Ernest Cuneo, a Roosevelt insider (and later the originator of the James Bond thriller, *Thunderball*), described Hopkins as "six feet and a hundred and forty pounds of adrenalin, pure raw guts."[131] Journalists likened him to "an animated piece of shredded wheat."[132] Clare Boothe Luce, who despised Hopkins's liberal politics, marveled that such "intense and ferocious" energy could emanate from his "thin, sloping, caved in chest." Luce also resented Hopkins for jilting her friend, the actress Dorothy Hale, who subsequently committed suicide. Luce wondered "what this man has that a girl can jump out of a window for him."[133] More positive was FDR Jr., who recalled that "Harry could disarm you. He could make you his friend in the first five minutes of a conversation."[134] Hopkins "had this marvelous ability to grow into any new situation, to totally dominate the details of any new problem."[135]

Roosevelt valued Hopkins. First, Hopkins excelled at turning presidential brainstorms into concrete programs. He could lash or bypass the bureaucracy to get results. Second, he became the president's go-between with Churchill, Stalin, and Army Chief of Staff General George C. Marshall. Third, FDR enjoyed relaxing with Harry, who shared his love for cards, jokes, gossip, and attractive women. Like Howe and LeHand (and unlike Eleanor), Harry could sense when the "Boss's" mood permitted broaching a point of business during a poker game or on a Potomac cruise. Finally, Roosevelt seems to have been drawn to Hopkins as a man both empowered and handicapped by his illness. In 1935, as Howe was fading, Roosevelt drew Hopkins closer. In 1938–39, FDR talked about making Hopkins president in 1940. Harry never quite recovered from presidential fever.

But such ambitions were frustrated by illness. In December 1937, Harry entered the Mayo Clinic, where doctors removed much of his stomach. The surgery did not help. He suffered frequent diarrhea, vomiting, and severe pain. At times he dropped a pound a day.[136] Belle Willard Roosevelt, a frequent visitor, noticed that "he is always a different color—sometimes green, sometimes gray—or white—or pink."[137] The diagnosis remained unsure. It now appears that he suffered from intolerance for wheat and from hepatitis B, contracted from blood transfusions. The hepatitis led to cirrhosis of the liver, aggravated by binge drinking. Anna Roosevelt and the White House physician, Ross McIntire, observed the pattern: "Hopkins would keep away from whiskey for long periods and then when the doctors would say that he was better, he would take to whiskey again with the result that he would find himself back in the hospital."[138] Four packs of Lucky Strikes a day did not help. In 1939, with Harry near death, the president summoned the best doctors. They started a regimen of transfusions of blood, plasma, and liver extract. After May 1940, Harry received a psychic boost from the excitement of managing the global crisis from his berth in the White House.

Although Hopkins did not serve as Roosevelt's brain, he did help him think. Frances Perkins observed that "temporarily he [Roosevelt] would have flashes of almost clairvoyant knowledge and understanding of a terrific variety of matters that didn't seem to have any particular relationship to each other. . . . [But] this aptitude for knowing all kinds of diverse things at once in a flash did not stay. It would come and then it would go. It would only stay a minute or two. . . . [H]e couldn't always verbalize on it, but sometimes he could."[139]

In other words, FDR might get the big picture and spark ideas, such as the concept of Lend-Lease, but he was not adept at translating such insight into concrete policies. Hopkins got action. FDR Jr. remembered that Hopkins "worked so well with Father; because Father would say, 'Now Harry, get that God damn thing done.' And Harry would have it done two hours later. And follow up [with] the bureaucracy."[140] Perkins recalled that Hopkins "developed this terrific capacity to . . . relate all sorts of unrelated things to a practical, central focal point, and to go ahead and carry out a project."[141] Churchill famously dubbed him "Lord Root of the Matter." Harry could focus even when tracking myriad details. In the Depression, he ran make-work projects in hundreds of communities. In the war, he watch-dogged the delivery of thousands of Lend-Lease items for the Allies.

General Marshall appreciated that Hopkins both understood the military's needs and could make FDR understand. Contrasting styles separated the buttoned-up military commander from the hedonic former social worker. Nevertheless, Marshall—who avoided going to the White House, refused to allow the president to first-name him, and visited Hyde Park for the first time at FDR's funeral—respected Hopkins. Marshall later recalled that "whenever I hit a tough knot I couldn't handle . . . he and I together would see the president. . . . It required quite a bit of explanation . . . to have the president see" what had to be done.[142] Marshall worried about his partner's excessive working and drinking. One Christmas Eve he wrote: "I pray for the continued improvement in your health, and damn your indiscretions." He hoped "that for once in your life you will be reasonably prudent."[143]

Harry's ill health both hampered and enabled him. Many days he looked "as if he could hardly live," a friend remembered.[144] Eleanor Roosevelt's secretary wondered "whether Harry affects a Louis Howe pose by appearing in pajamas and bath robe and no shave, or whether he is too ill to get dressed."[145] Hospital stays cut him out of the action. Yet even when confined to bed in the Lincoln room, strewn with papers as when Howe had lived there, he could bark orders into the telephone. He could escape reporters while advancing the president's agenda. By excelling in a wartime job despite his illness, Harry garnered respect as a man of courage. Marshall later saluted him as having "more nerve than anyone I had ever seen. If any man sacrificed his life, he did."[146] Harry was so weak "that he had been found crawling up the back stairs at Hyde Park because he wasn't strong enough to walk up."[147] In 1941, Hopkins quietly played up that courage when FDR sent him to assess Churchill and then Stalin.

Despite all his work, Hopkins's clout depended on his propinquity with Roosevelt. He fended off rivals "like a jealous woman," a competitor groused. It meant others "had to play him in a triangle."[148] Anna, who disliked Harry's influence, ruminated on why he remained her father's favorite. She concluded that "the President finds Harry relaxing, and he likes to relax." Like Missy before him, Harry was "getting together people who can give the President a good time." In contrast, Eleanor invited to dinner "reformers," and he "gets no fun out of it." When FDR learned that his wife was also planning a weekend at Hyde Park, he "changed his plans and took Churchill and Hopkins to Shangri La."[149]

Roosevelt and Hopkins both enjoyed what Perkins called "behind-the-barn jokes" where "loud shouts of laughter would rise from the President's study as they competed with each other in what they could tell."[150] They apparently also competed in romantic conquests and in telling about them. In 1938, when Hopkins reportedly became engaged to the brunette New Yorker Dorothy Hale, FDR was spending weekends at Hyde Park with Dorothy Schiff, who had a similar appearance.[151] (During that year, Schiff and Roosevelt split the purchase of a Hyde Park farm on which he built his get-away, Top Cottage, and she later built her own cottage.[152] Schiff explained FDR's plan: "I was to be a sort of back-street wife."[153]) When Hale plunged to her death, FDR, competitive and cold as ever, reportedly told Harry: "I hope you won't let this go to your head; there have been far less handsome men than you who have caused the ladies to commit suicide."[154] The president once startled Lyndon B. Johnson by asking: "Did you ever see a Russian woman naked?" Thrown on the defensive, Johnson replied,

"'No, but then I never have been to Russia.'" Roosevelt then related "what Harry Hopkins, who had just been to Russia, had told him."[155] FDR had also enjoyed such "behind-the-barn" talk with Howe.

But whereas Howe had brought FDR and Eleanor closer together, Hopkins deepened their division. By 1944–45, by which time Harry had moved out, Eleanor had little desire to fill the gap in her husband's network. She felt betrayed by Hopkins, who had started out as her friend and as a reformer. She had favored him for president in 1938–39. She mothered his young daughter, Diana, and arranged to look after her if he should die.[156] Hopkins had crassly cultivated the First Lady. He confided to Jane Ickes, who probably told her friend, Anna Roosevelt, that he had gotten to FDR by focusing on "Mrs. Roosevelt, Missy, the President's mother, and Betsey Roosevelt. It was a waste of time to bother about anyone else."[157] (Betsey Cushing Roosevelt was James Roosevelt's ex-wife and a flirtatious favorite of both FDR and Hopkins.)

Once in the White House, Harry sided with the president and focused only on the war. The former head of the WPA now complained about "those goddamn New Dealers." Missy beamed as Harry was leaving the room: "Isn't he just like Louie Howe?" Eleanor snapped, "No, he isn't at all like Louie Howe."[158] When Perkins suggested that FDR needed his wife and that she should stay around the White House more, Eleanor replied in a hurt tone. "Oh, no, Frances, he doesn't need me any more. . . . He has Harry. . . . He doesn't ask my advice any more. Harry tells him everything he needs to know."[159]

With LeHand's departure and the demands of the war, FDR depended more than ever on Hopkins. Harry recalled "evenings after evenings when Franklin was left entirely alone," except for him.[160] Feeling the strain, Harry escaped some weekends. For FDR, relaxation was limited to stamps, old stories, gossip, poker, fishing, and cocktails, some of them weird concoctions. After years of this routine, Schiff concluded that FDR was "a bore, but his charm hid it."[161]

Though Harry shared more interests with the president than Schiff did, he also grew bored. Hopkins enjoyed socializing with the rich, such as Harriman and John Hertz, who founded the Yellow Cab and Hertz rental companies, and who raced horses. FDR Jr. remembered that "Father used to get very, very upset" if Harry got away for a weekend of horse races and nightclubs. A "jealous" president would "josh him pretty strongly. . . . 'Well, now that you've finished being a playboy around New York are you ready to go back to work?'"[162] One of those weekends, Harriman introduced Hopkins to Louise Macy, the former Paris editor of *Harper's Bazaar*. Macy was "a good looking girl with a determined chin," an observer noted.[163] After a whirlwind courtship splashed in the press, the couple married on July 30, 1942. (Revealing something about himself, Churchill tweaked Hopkins, "You're married to the war. That should satisfy you.")[164]

The new domestic arrangements would turn the White House into a pressure cooker—and cramp Roosevelt's effectiveness as president. FDR simply informed his wife, by telephone, that the newlyweds would be living with them. Three households—that of FDR, Eleanor Roosevelt, and the Hopkinses—would now jostle at 1600 Pennsylvania Avenue.[165] Louise Macy relished the glamor of her new life. Yet she "didn't understand politics; she really didn't understand world affairs," her stepdaughter, Diana Hopkins, later recounted. Nor did Macy appreciate FDR's incessant demands. In a thank-you note from her honeymoon, Louise suggested that the president not send for Harry too soon. The First Lady's secretary groused that despite the limited White House budget, Harry "pays for nothing whatsoever."[166] To support the war, Louise began working in a Washington hospital. Diana remembered, "Mummy would get home from the hospital, and there would be a message that 'the President wants you to go to tea with Princess Martha—now.' No time to get out of the uniform, nothing—and zap, off to Princess Martha's house. Princess Martha would say, 'Louise, why don't you go and see the children.' And so Louie would go and see the children, and the President and Princess Martha would have tea."[167] As the excitement of White House living paled, Louise drank more heavily.

Hopkins was torn between the president and his wife. Rosenman recalled that FDR "wanted someone at the White House whom he could talk to at breakfast, before going to bed; he wanted Harry around."[168] Macy expostulated to her sister, "Can you imagine, Gert, never having breakfast with your own husband?" Gertrude observed that Louise was "jealous of FDR in the intimacy which he shared with Harry." As Harry wasted away, Louise blamed the "Boss." Diana later remembered her stepmother raging, "Roosevelt drove him and drove him and thought maybe he'd get up out of his bed and do something else." Referring to FDR, Louise would ask, "How can you like the man? He killed your father."[169]

Macy aggravated matters by mocking the president and his wife. Rosenman remembered, "We used to have dinner with Harry and Louise, and the latter with a couple of drinks in her would talk about Eleanor in a way that caused me to wish that she would lower her voice."[170] Louise advised friends that "FDR could be very boring in telling the same funny story several times."[171] The Hopkinses exposed the White House to ridicule and charges of corruption by accepting as a wedding gift from Lord Beaverbrook, the British political chieftain, a diamond tiara that Napoleon had given to Josephine. (Louise had the exquisite antique cut into diamond clips.) The president's daughter revealed the details to Pearson, whose column exposed a White House in disarray. Finally, Louise in December 1943 moved the family to a house in Georgetown, "even though this made Harry's work with the President somewhat more difficult."[172]

That proved a tragic understatement. FDR felt abandoned and betrayed, as he had when Corcoran married against his wishes and upon learning of LeHand's dedication to Bullitt. Roosevelt, as his attorney general would later explain, "was very loyal to men who were loyal to him; if they weren't loyal, he cut their throats."[173] FDR was, tragically, also cutting his own throat. In early 1944—the very moment when Roosevelt needed Hopkins's help with the crescendo of the war and postwar planning—the winning team broke apart. Never would FDR and Harry regain their earlier intimacy. For the crucial last sixteen months of Roosevelt's presidency, the circle remained broken. Roosevelt nonetheless, despite deteriorating health and inadequate staff support, continued his struggle to win the war, keep the alliance together, and guide it into the postwar world.

Churchill and Stalin also operated with fading health and support, problems aggravated by their respective behaviors. Churchill's staff recorded the deterioration in the health of their boss. Stalin's subordinates no doubt also noticed their leader's decline but remained more reticent. Keeping a Kremlin diary was one of many offenses punishable by death.

Churchill and His Circle

The very energy and eloquence sparking Churchill's leadership also generated distrust, especially before he became prime minister on May 10, 1940. John "Jock" Colville, who would become the war leader's favorite private secretary, had served his predecessor, Neville Chamberlain. On April 25, Colville disparaged Churchill as given to "verbosity and restlessness" that had proven "ineffective, indeed harmful." Winston's "blasted rhetoric" betrayed a publicist "still thinking of his books." Elevating him to prime minister seemed a "terrible risk." "Everybody here in despair at the prospect," Colville recorded in his diary. Within weeks, however, he found the new PM's "ceaseless industry . . . impressive."[174]

Churchill depended on a trio of long-serving aides, all bachelors: Frederick Lindemann, Brendan Bracken, and Desmond Morton. They lived in No. 10 Downing Street Annex, close by Churchill, worked near him in the underground Cabinet War Rooms, and they often accompanied him on travels. Lindemann, whom Churchill dubbed "the Prof," had, like Churchill, an American mother. A German-educated physicist and an arrogant polymath, Lindemann advised on almost everything, especially new weapons. Churchill mocked but tolerated Lindemann's teetotaling, vegetarian habits. Matching the "Prof" in intelligence was Brendan Bracken who, though born in Ireland and raised in Australia, allowed the rumor to spread that he was Churchill's love child. The unruly redhead ran the ministry of information. Animated and full of witty stories, Bracken proved better than anyone in lifting the PM out of depression. He had known Harry Hopkins for years and played go-between in Harry's crucial January 1941 trip to London. Morton had survived a World War I bullet through the heart to emerge as a key player in British intelligence and military circles. In the 1930s, he fed details about German rearmament to Churchill despite the latter's not being in the Cabinet. After Churchill became prime minister, Morton became his key liaison to the Foreign Office, the Secret Service, and governments in exile.[175]

Churchill's wartime leadership rested also on his magnificent oratory. In inspiring Britons and others to resist Hitler, these speeches also forged phrases that would resonate for centuries. Eloquence that would have seemed exaggerated in ordinary times fit the extraordinary crisis. On June 4, 1940, with a German invasion threatening, the prime minister proclaimed: "We shall fight on the beaches, we shall fight on the landing grounds, we shall fight in the fields and in the streets, we shall fight in the hills; we shall never surrender." Even if Britain were subjugated, the empire and the British fleet "would carry on the struggle, until, in God's good time, the new world, with all its power and might, steps forth to the liberation of the old."

That last sentence signaled to Roosevelt that he, Churchill, would never surrender the British navy to the Germans. Nevertheless, the implied message, made explicit in his secret cables to FDR, was that a post-Churchill government might indeed trade the fleet for easy peace terms. The words also dramatized the duty to rescue the old world—a responsibility most Americans, and probably FDR himself, remained reluctant to assume. After France fell, Churchill urged: "Let us . . . so bear ourselves that if the British Commonwealth and Empire lasts for a thousand years, men will still say, 'This was their finest hour.'"[176] Crafting such oratory—fulfilling the promise of the "Scaffolding of Rhetoric" essay penned as a twenty-three-year-old—served as a catharsis for Churchill himself. In rallying the nation he could also stave off his own depression.

With the PM at his office, "the place was buzzing with atmosphere, with electricity," a secretary later recalled. "When he was away on tour it was dead, dead, dead." Laboring from 8:00 a.m. to 3:00 a.m. and napping in the afternoon, he "made two days out of every one day," noted an aide with awe. He "was a terrific man of action. Nobody was allowed to sit on his bottom. You had to get cracking."[177]

Critics, however, faulted that frenetic activity as often counterproductive. Robert Bruce Lockhart, head of psychological warfare, worried that Churchill, "by sleeping half the afternoon himself and then flogging tired men to work half through the night, is killing more of his countrymen than Germans."[178] Lord Beaverbrook, a friend and rival who aided the PM in various ways including boosting aircraft production, appraised Churchill's judgment as "terrifying—decisions taken at 1:30 a.m.—always bad—People agreed because [they] wanted to go to bed."[179] Even King George VI groused about "one more damned 2 a.m. decision taken by Winston."[180] Unable to nap afternoons, Beaverbrook complained that Churchill's "schedule nearly killed me, almost made me a drunkard, because if you keep these hours you must have stimulants."[181] Lockhart concurred, "Everyone is drinking too much in this war from the P.M. downwards. Brendan [Bracken] lives largely on alcohol; even Anthony [Eden] puts quite a lot away."[182] Moran prescribed sleep aids and stimulants, the "innumerable pills and powders" Colville noticed on his boss's desk.[183] Always ready to dose himself, Churchill heard that Eden had swallowed "a red . . . good stuff" for sleeping on a plane. He grunted: "I took two. I'm a hardened case.[184] Lord Alanbrooke, commander of the Imperial General Staff, expressed the mix of appreciation and apprehension held by many: "God knows where we'd be without him, but God knows where we shall go with him!"[185]

Unlike Roosevelt or Stalin, Churchill delighted in risk. He harked back to his youth, when he reveled in face-to-face combat on the Indian-Afghanistani border and in the Sudan. He believed it best to die in battle "when your blood is up and you feel nothing."[186] Only the intercession of the king kept him away from the beaches during the June 1944 Normandy invasion. Moran observed, "With Winston war is an end in itself rather than a means to an end. It fascinates him, he loves it."[187] He would play games of Chinese checkers as if they were battles in the American Civil War, getting "all involved with the marbles" by pretending they were troops.[188] Inspecting the battlefront in March 1945, Churchill "thrilled" at German sniper fire. When a general insisted he move to safety, he reacted with a look "just like that of a small boy being called away from his sand castles on the beach." Impishness compelled him to halt his convoy so that he could urinate on the Siegfried Line, Germany's defensive barrier. He flashed the same "childish grin of intense satisfaction" after urinating in the Rhine.[189]

Though Churchill demanded highly competent staff, he often seemed "curiously inconsiderate" about their needs, Colville observed. He might keep typists "up until three or four in the morning even when there was no work to do." He thought nothing of holding the Cabinet in session until after "all hope of getting food had passed, because he himself had only to walk upstairs to lunch or dinner. Equally, it never occurred to him to suppose that anybody might be tired or over-worked."[190] Like FDR, Churchill expected aides to sacrifice their family life. When General Hastings "Pug" Ismay, the principal link to the military brass, considered spending one weekend with his family instead of at the PM's country retreat, Chequers, a colleague warned: "You had better be careful. I once did that and was out of favor for weeks."[191]

Several elements accounted for this obtuseness. The war imposed burdens on all. Churchill did not spare himself, but the upper class always had aides at their beck and call. Yet his insensitivity probably also stemmed from his inability to read affect, a lack his friends had long noted. In an admiring biography, Roy Jenkins described Churchill as "not . . . good at bilateral conversation, but with a table he could often be brilliant."[192]

When agitated, the prime minister tended to snap at the first subordinate within reach. Such anger usually passed like a thunderstorm. Nevertheless, the strain of Britain's year without allies sparked such ill-temper that Clementine, in the only known letter that passed between her and her husband in 1940, warned him, "there is a danger of your being generally disliked by your colleagues & subordinates because of your rough sarcastic & overbearing manner—You are supposed to be so contemptuous that presently no ideas—good or bad—will be forthcoming. My Darling Winston—I must confess I have noticed a deterioration in your manner; & you are not so kind as you used to be. . . . You must combine urbanity, kindness and if possible Olympic calm. You won't get the best results by irascibility & rudeness."[193]

Almost as close an observer was Alanbrooke. He admired Churchill as "quite the most wonderful man I have ever met," as someone standing "head and shoulders above all others."[194] Yet he also railed at the impetuous demands to do something, anything almost, to patch the now tattered empire. In summer 1943, Churchill pushed for invading Sumatra in the Dutch East Indies. From there RAF bombers might drive the Japanese from the former British stronghold of Singapore. Informed that the venture violated overall strategy, he reacted "like a peevish child asking for a forbidden toy." Alanbrooke later recalled: The PM "shook his fist in my face, saying, 'I do not want any of your long term projects, they cripple initiative!'"[195] Returning the fury, the military chief snapped a pencil in Churchill's face.[196] He fumed that Churchill "is in a very dangerous condition, most unbalanced, and God knows how we shall finish this war if this goes on."[197] "Pug" Ismay concluded that the PM remained "ignorant of mechanics and organization of war. He did not even know how his own organization worked. Hadn't any idea."[198]

Churchill's health deteriorated under the strain. He suffered at least two heart attacks and two bouts of pneumonia. His "black dog" depression descended, especially after such military setbacks as the surrender of Singapore in February 1942.[199] Eden later recalled that his boss boiled with such fury that it seemed he might die.[200] In July 1943, Lockhart decided that Churchill "had lost his grip. His buoyancy and his capacity for work had gone. His legs had begun to fail him."[201] Colville was shocked to find him "old, tired and very depressed."[202] By March 1944, the war leader appeared in a "desperately tired mood. He seems quite incapable of concentrating for a few minutes." Lockhart and Royal Air Force Marshal Arthur Tedder agreed that "the PM was still the best we had, but he was now a tired and very old man. His brilliance was still visible, but now his peaks were fewer and shorter, and his slumps deeper and longer."[203] Eden and U.S. ambassador John "Gil" Winant agreed "the PM was too old for the peace."[204] Alanbrooke concluded that Churchill "has probably done more for this country than any human being has ever done." Nevertheless, for the good of both Britain and his reputation, "it would be a godsend if he could disappear out of public life."[205]

Like FDR, Churchill could still rebound. A friend noted that he returned from his October 1944 meeting with Stalin looking like "a different being."[206] And, like FDR, he again slumped. On the eve of the February 1945 Yalta conference, the war horse appeared "very old, very meandering in his thoughts and watery about the eyes," Alanbrooke recorded.[207] Both leaders suffered worsening deafness.[208]

Although the war wore out both Churchill and Roosevelt, the former had advantages the latter lacked. The skilled civil servants and private secretaries staffing the prime minister's office outclassed the shoestring, increasingly truncated operation of the White House. Even when ill, Churchill commanded a quantum of energy FDR no longer could muster. Though he could discern others' feelings in ways beyond Churchill's ability, Roosevelt remained the more private man, the one more alone and lonely. Churchill benefited from in-depth backup with Alanbrooke, Ismay, Beaverbrook, Bracken, Eden, Lindemann, and Morton. FDR relied mostly on Hopkins—and after December 1943, on Chief of Staff William Leahy, who did not share Roosevelt's commitment to postwar cooperation with the Soviets. Marshall and Stimson remained more distant from their boss than did Alanbrooke and Ismay from theirs, notwithstanding their fireworks with the PM. The superiority of No. 10 Downing Street over 1600 Pennsylvania Avenue paralleled the advantage in staff planning that would enable the British to dominate Anglo-American conferences in 1941–43.

The Deadly Business of Stalin's "Political Club"

In the decade before the Soviet people faced the German invasion they suffered murderous assaults from their own government. Nearly twenty million Soviet citizens perished from Stalin's policies. The government seized the land of richer peasants, the kulaks, executed some, and exiled the remainder to the Gulag—the archipelago of harsh labor camps in Siberia and the Arctic, where many more died. In the early 1930s, the Kremlin resolved to pay for the imported machinery required for the rapid industrialization of the Five Year Plan by exporting grain. Sinking world prices for food required ever larger sales to obtain the hard currency. Stalin's henchmen ruthlessly seized peasants' last stores of food and seed grain. The resulting political famine killed more than three million in the Ukraine alone. The regime refused mercy even when the starving turned to cannibalism. In the Great Purge of 1937–38, the dictator oversaw the arrest of some 1.6 million Soviet citizens, most on trumped-up charges of treason and sabotage. Seven hundred thousand were executed and the rest exiled. Of the 767 members of the Red Army's high command in 1936, two-thirds had been eliminated by 1941.[209]

The purges swallowed heroes of the Revolution, such as Nikolai Bukharin, Grigori Zinoviev, Lev Kamenev, and Karl Radek. They were brought up on false charges, tortured, humiliated in show trials, and executed.[210] Second-echelon figures in the Politburo also met destruction. Stalin spared, however, most of those who were already in, or who would in 1939 join, his immediate entourage. This group included Vyacheslav Molotov, Lazar Kaganovich, Anastas Mikoyan, Andrei Zhdanov, Nikita Khrushchev, Lavrenty Beria, and Georgy Malenkov. The *vozhd* (Boss) evidently calculated that if his closest associates were charged with spying for the Germans or hatching antirevolutionary plots, it would reflect badly on him. Though sparing the lives of his comrades-in-arms, "Stalin did everything," the historian Oleg V. Khlevniuk has noted, to keep them "in a state of submission, to fill them with fear and deprive them of the slightest trace of independence. He achieved this primarily through actions against their relatives and close associates."[211] The wife of the president of the USSR, Mikhail Kalinin, was sent to a labor camp. (Kalinin compensated by indulging his taste for ballerinas.) Those working for Churchill and Roosevelt had to sacrifice times with family—but not the bodies of family members.

Sergo Beria recalled the dynamics of passion and power. His father and others in the Kremlin circle "had all undergone the same process of evolution regarding Stalin." At the start each had "worshiped him madly," only to grow resentful with how he abused them. "Love did not necessarily turn into hate," Sergo added.[212] Stalin could show latitude for certain hangers-on, such as his incompetent defense commissar, Kliment Voroshilov. Responding to Stalin's "white-hot rage" about the Red Army's deficiencies early in the war, Voroshilov lashed

2.5. Though Stalin abused and even executed close aides, he could also enchant. Toadies such as Voroshilov, shown here on the right, "worshiped him madly," recalled Lavrenty Beria's son. (Sergo Beria, *Beria*, 144–45. Courtesy of Corbis.)

back: "You're the one who annihilated the Old Guard of the army; you had our best generals killed!" He then picked up a platter with a roast suckling pig on it and smashed it on the table.[213] He was fired but escaped further punishment.

Why all the death and repression? Was the dictator a madman with blood lust? Stalin remained a complex person who displayed a wide range of behaviors. An insane person could not have coordinated victory over Hitler's hitherto unbeaten armies. During the war no U.S. or British negotiators described him as mad or erratic. The Kremlin chief defended himself by insisting on a parallel: "Was the English [Queen] Elizabeth really less cruel when she fought to consolidate absolutism in England? How many heads rolled during her reign?" A history buff who regarded himself as successor to the greatest czars, he stressed that the English "honor her by calling her great."[214] Whatever the pretensions to "greatness," the reality on the bloody floor of the infamous Lubianka prison was that Stalin's slaughter vastly multiplied Elizabeth I's.

The more apt parallel was with Hitler. Focused on each other as both model and mortal foe, Stalin and Hitler each perpetrated mass murder in the name of an unrealizable utopia. In addition to the millions killed in the titanic war they fought in 1941–45, the two dictators, acting independently between 1932 and 1945, oversaw the shooting or starving to death of fourteen million noncombatants in the "bloodlands" between Germany and Russia. Stalin did not mimic Hitler, however, in setting up industrial death camps that existed for the sole purpose of killing.[215]

In the morbid mind of Stalin and his defenders, this slaughter was a preemptive strike against rivals for power, who were conspiring with foreign foes. The dictator was willing to imprison or execute tens of thousands of innocents to thwart one real enemy. Khrushchev later recalled the dictum that if a denunciatory report was only "10 per cent true, we should regard the entire report as fact."[216] Premier and later foreign minister Molotov explained that by employing terror "Stalin played it safe." Despite no concrete evidence that, for instance, Marshal Mikhail Tukhachevsky actually was a German agent, he seemed "dangerous" because "we were not sure whether he would stay firmly on our side at a difficult moment." Evidence was not necessary, the henchman insisted, because "there is no smoke without fire."[217]

In later years Stalin would admit to "mistakes" being made in the purges and "many honest people" suffering. Yet he defended the terror as having purged subversives who otherwise, he claimed, would have crippled defenses in the war.[218] The killing did create openings for ambitious, competent young people. Nevertheless, the purges stifled creativity. Decimating the leadership, moreover, aggravated the initial disarray in countering the German invasion. And the purges forever blackened the history of the Soviet experiment.

Stalin called his henchmen the "political club."[219] Membership demanded long hours in the office and longer hours at the dictator's dacha. Running a planned economy, especially in wartime, demanded enormous administrative labor. Efficiency required retooling to meet changing conditions. In November 1940, Stalin railed at his flunkies that he was the only one meeting with cutting-edge aviation experts. "I am out there *by myself*. . . . Look at me: I am capable of learning, reading, keeping up with things every day—why can you not do this? You do not like to learn." His warning grew ominous: If they refused to "learn and relearn," he would "hit the fatsos so hard that you will hear the crack for miles around."[220] Even though the purges dropped off after 1938, terror remained a cudgel with which to beat those who, as Molotov described the crime, "liked to relax."[221]

Helping Stalin to relax came under a different set of rules. Svetlana Alliluyeva described her father's "mixed-up schedule" of sleeping until noon, eating a light meal at 3:00 p.m., and sitting down with the "club" for dinner at ten at night.[222] To a visitor at the dacha it seemed like "a patriarchal family with a crotchety head." Each "would tell the news from his bailiwick . . . what plans he was making."[223] Dinner could drag on until morning. The dictator's toadies staggered "into their offices, exhausted, unshaven, and suffering from headaches and stomachaches." They closed the doors to their offices and snatched some sleep.[224] Like Churchill, Stalin could arrange his schedule so as to stay up much of the night and still get enough sleep. Their subordinates were not so fortunate. Consequently, their efficiency in managing the war suffered.

The mood at dinner could be genial—and bizarre. The dictator wolfed down specialties from the far corners of his realm, at a time when most ordinary people struggled to get enough food. After dinner this former seminarian, who still commanded an excellent voice, enjoyed singing Orthodox hymns. Accompanying him were Molotov on the mandolin and party boss Andrei Zhdanov on the piano.[225] Other times the dictator hovered over an American gramophone, changing records and offering commentary. They watched Hollywood cowboy or gangster films, translated by a hanger-on who knew only pidgin English. (Comedies had been a favorite during the purges.) Stalin delighted in having a servant place a tomato on someone's chair. He never tired of the joke, laughing to tears at the squishing sound of a hapless victim sitting on the seat. Three months before the German invasion, fifteen-year-old Svetlana, who played a game with her father in which she penned him peremptory orders, instructed:

"Eat as much as you like. You can drink, too. I only ask you not to put vegetables or other food on the chairs in the hope that someone will sit on it. It will damage the chairs. As well as the secretaries' clothes."[226]

Stalin liked imposing humiliation with homoerotic overtones. At all-male gatherings he encouraged couples to waltz.[227] Khrushchev later explained that "when Stalin says dance, a wise man dances."[228] Clark Kerr described wartime parties featuring mock slaughter with an unloaded Tommy gun and extended male-on-male hugging and kissing.[229] Such festivities were lubricated by tumblers of vodka, often spiked with pepper. Stalin oversaw the drinking. Yet as he once confided to a German diplomat, he restricted himself to light wine that looked like vodka. In pressing his comrades to lose control of themselves, the *vozhd* got to observe their confessions, humiliation, and infantilism. Men passed out or urinated while sitting at the table. Subordinates pushed each other into the pond at the dacha. He was delighted: "You're like little children!"[230]

The cult of personality he encouraged and the enormous suffering he caused others ironically deepened Stalin's own isolation. Svetlana, whom he alienated when his fierce paternal jealousy could not brook her sexual coming of age, observed her father "feeling lonely. He was so isolated from everyone by this time, so elevated, that he seemed to be living in a vacuum. He hadn't a soul he could talk to."[231] Although he had tortured his second wife, Nadya Alliluyeva, by having affairs and openly flirting with other women (at a banquet he would toss balls of bread at the object of his desire), his grief at her suicide on November 8, 1932, apparently increased with time. Shortly after the war, he told Svetlana that the anniversary of Nadya's death ruined for him the November 7 holiday celebrating the October Revolution. At times he blamed himself: "I was a bad husband. I never had the time to take her to the movies." Mostly, though, he blamed others, such as Nadya's friend and Molotov's wife, Polina. She exerted "a bad influence on Nadya," he charged.[232] He would soon have Polina arrested. Casting about for people to talk to, he began inviting to his dacha boyhood friends from Georgia who had somehow survived the strife for which he bore such responsibility.

World War II produced casualties among leaders as well as soldiers and citizens. Like Roosevelt, Churchill and Stalin persisted in often counterproductive behaviors held over from earlier days. All three drained, alienated, or, in the extreme case of Stalin, killed off those upon whom they depended. The complaint of a British general could have been made about Roosevelt or Stalin as well: "Winston seems to suck the vitality out of his entourage like a leech."[233] The blood did not suffice. Although Roosevelt was the only one of the Big Three to die during the war, the other two were also exhausted by its strains. Despite their bravery, intelligence, and capability, the builders of the Grand Alliance remained flawed giants.

Chapter 3

The Personal Touch

Forming the Alliance, January–August 1941

"This is essentially a young man's war," warned Robert Boothby, a flamboyant, longtime supporter of Churchill. Boothby imagined Nazi military victories as a masculine juggernaut: a "young, virile, dynamic, and violent" force "advancing irresistibly to overthrow a decaying old world."[1] By January 1941, Nazi Germany had swallowed much of Europe and seemed likely to gobble up the Middle East. U-boat attacks on shipping threatened Britain with starvation. Stalin hoped to forestall war by slavishly delivering raw materials to Hitler's Reich. Those hopes were crushed by the German invasion on June 22, 1941. Japan, already controlling much of China, poised to snatch Southeast Asia or Siberia. If Britain, the United States, and the Soviet Union were to halt and eventually destroy German and Japanese aggression, they had to spark a "virile, dynamic" force of their own.

An effective alliance required meeting psychological and cultural challenges along with military, political, and economic ones. Churchill, Stalin, and Roosevelt each had to convince the other two leaders that he was trustworthy, capable, and vigorous; that he commanded enough courage, perseverance, and toughness to defeat a frightening enemy. Yet each deviated in some way from the generalized masculine norm that had come to prevail in all three countries despite differences in their national cultures. According to that norm, top leaders should be brave and able-bodied with a cool demeanor and dependable judgment. Roosevelt, however, could not walk unaided. He appeared unwilling to challenge public opinion in a nation that still shrank from fighting. Churchill had a history of erratic decision making and a reputation as a heavy drinker who careened from excitement to depression. A former bank robber and Bolshevik revolutionary, Stalin had killed off most of his top military and civilian leadership and had then allied with Hitler. Hardly promising material. In terms of relative youth, in 1941, Hitler would turn fifty-two, Benito Mussolini fifty-eight, Roosevelt fifty-nine, Stalin sixty-three, and Churchill sixty-seven.

To triumph in a total war, the would-be allies also had to meet a cultural challenge: crafting an appealing alternative to both the "decaying old world" and the Axis "New Order"—the "Wave of the Future," as Anne Morrow Lindbergh phrased it. In the first eight months of 1941, Roosevelt and Churchill, as well as, remarkably, Stalin, stressed the common cultural values and political aims that set their nations apart from the Nazis. To mobilize whole populations for war, people needed to believe the conflict made sense. The alliance required a structure of meaning and promise even if that structure was rent with contradictions.

As 1941 dawned, the men who would become the Big Three had few grounds for trusting each other. They remained largely strangers. Nevertheless, Roosevelt, Churchill, and, perhaps to a lesser extent, Stalin operated on the belief that the attitudes, feelings, demeanor, and body language displayed by statesmen in face-to-face meetings could reveal inner thoughts and ultimate intentions. International conferences could lead to trust by fostering personal ties and understandings that might then condition future political decisions. Even acrimonious interactions could clarify differences. Of course some meetings were inopportune, complicated policy, aggravated tensions, or dashed hopes.

Despite the differences in their personal backgrounds, each of the three leaders had developed confidence in his interpersonal skills. Roosevelt's talent for charm and guileful maneuver had fueled his rise to the presidency. Churchill could usually sway the room with his rhetoric and marshaling of history, though he often had a tin ear in listening to others. Stalin was a master of charm, feint, and argument. Vast distances and busy schedules, however, made meetings difficult. Roosevelt and Stalin hated flying. Along with the readiest traveler, Churchill, they often became ill after the strains of a long trip. A "summit" meeting could prove risky in terms of prestige and effort. Hence the importance of trusted envoys.

In the first eight months of 1941, five personal missions laid the foundation for the Grand Alliance. In January, Harry Hopkins flew to Britain on a six-week journey to assess Churchill as a person and as a leader. Averell Harriman arrived in London in March as Lend-Lease "Expediter" and as FDR's personal representative to the prime minister. Both Hopkins and Harriman grew close to the Churchill family. Indeed, Harriman, U.S. Ambassador Winant, and famed radio broadcaster (*"This* is London") Edward R. Murrow each developed sexual relations with a member of that family. A key figure in this network was Pamela Churchill, the twenty-one-year-old wife of Randolph Churchill, Winston and Clementine's son. Estranged from her husband within a year of their October 1939 wedding, Pamela Churchill became a central player in an Anglo-American web of friendship, flirtation, sex, and secrets. An analogous Anglo-Soviet or Soviet-American network in Moscow would have been impossible. Instead, the Kremlin-enforced isolation of foreign diplomats and journalists ignited frustration and anger so intense that it would eventually burn through the wartime alliance. Nonetheless, Kremlin culture—and the Georgian predilections of Stalin—mandated lavish hospitality to temporary visitors, such as Roosevelt's envoy, Hopkins. His was the fourth mission, a July flight to Moscow to foster trust and understanding between his boss and the Kremlin *vozhd*. The fifth was the first summit of Roosevelt and Churchill, at the Atlantic Conference off the coast of Newfoundland, for three days beginning Saturday, August 9.

Hopkins and Churchill

Hopkins's mission came amid distrust between Washington and London. In December 1940, Churchill had exploded on learning of plans to send a U.S. battleship to pick up British gold in payment for supplies. He dashed off a telegram complaining of the "sheriff collecting the last assets of a helpless debtor."[2] The telegram remained unsent, however, as Roosevelt soon called for a massive aid program, Lend-Lease, that Congress would pass in March 1941 The PM still fretted about getting help. Roosevelt nursed his own misgivings. In 1940, Ambassador Joseph P. Kennedy had described Churchill as "always sucking on a whiskey bottle." FDR's friend and adviser Sumner Welles rated the "drunken sot" as a "third or fourth-rate man." Roosevelt snickered that Churchill was probably "the best man that England had, even if he was drunk half of the time."[3]

With the few planes and tanks coming off U.S. assembly lines needed for the nation's own defense, the president required reassurances. Could this prime minister live up to the courage of his rhetoric? Was British appeasement really over? Despite his caution in edging America toward war, Roosevelt demanded evidence that London would not surrender. Many Americans worried that Britain could turn over its U.S. weapons to Hitler. Hopkins was to see whether Churchill and his government were trustworthy enough to merit massive aid.[4]

On January 10, Churchill, who choreographed crucial meetings, anxiously awaited Roosevelt's emissary. About his own physical appearance the portly PM could do little. But he could plan how to behave and what to talk about. Hopkins later described the scene: A "rotund," "red-faced" man greeted him speaking with a "mushy voice." A "fat" hand clasped his in a "convincing," manly shake. Then the host smiled and "showed me with obvious pride the photograph of his beautiful daughter-in-law and grandchild."[5] At this critical juncture Churchill was playing to instinct. He was identifying himself as a family man, just like Hopkins and Roosevelt. In ensuing weeks the former American social worker would find himself folded into the Churchill family. It may have been set up that Hopkins would find the daughter-in-law, Pamela Churchill, "delicious," as he later put it. British intelligence no doubt reported on the exploits of this playboy who, despite his delicate health, dated glamorous women, including Paulette Goddard, Charlie Chaplin's ex-wife.

The adrenaline stimulated by deadly bombing and dogfights over London aroused intimacy of various kinds. As significant as the blurring of national interests about which Churchill liked to rhapsodize was the blurring between personal and political relations. Pamela Churchill understood that ties with influential Americans could rescue her country. As she later put it, "As long as [the Americans] weren't in the War it was very precarious. And it was very important—these Americans, who they were; why they were; what they were. The first one was Harry." She added, "Harry knew how to get things done."[6] Pamela had charmed her father-in-law. By quickly producing a male heir, Winston II, she further endeared herself to the prime minister.

With Britain desperate for American help, Pamela took advantage of her surname, social talents, intelligence, and good looks to position herself at the center of a web of contacts. She developed flirtatious friendships with Hopkins and with several reporters. She juggled overlapping love affairs: with Harriman, Murrow, U.S. Army Air Force General Frederick Anderson, and probably others, including British air chief Charles "Peter" Portal—all the while sharing selected confidences with her father-in-law and with his chief rival/supporter, Lord Beaverbrook. She would remember: "It was a terrible war, but if you were the right age ... and in the right place, it was spectacular."[7]

Also on the scene was Harriman's daughter by his first marriage, twenty-three-year-old Kathleen, who worked for *Newsweek* magazine and shared a three-bedroom apartment with Pamela and her father. "During the war there were all sorts of people having affairs with all sorts of people," she later explained.[8] This "mixing up," as Churchill called the various kinds of sharing and intimacy between Americans and Britons, forged political, military, economic, and—not least— emotional ties that would endure for decades. The PM would later boast, "Never did any lover woo his mistress more determinedly than I did Franklin Roosevelt."[9]

Although Roosevelt loved gossip, he also had political reasons for welcoming such intimacy. Especially before Russia was forced into the war, FDR remained unsure about risking ground battle against the Germans. He appeared to believe, like many Americans, that the United States should send supplies to the Allies and have them do the fighting. In the summer of 1941, he ordered military forces to Greenland and then Iceland and thereafter probed the Germans by having the Navy patrol and then convoy Lend-Lease supplies in the Atlantic. Following Japan's occupation of southern Indochina, he approved a cutoff of Tokyo's oil supply. Yet he also seems to have regarded these steps more as a deterrent than as a prelude to war. Roosevelt remained reluctant to incur heavy casualties. (Even after Pearl Harbor, a vestige of that hesitation persisted in his acceptance in 1942–43 of Churchill's arguments against assaulting Germany's stronghold in France.)

In this context it was shrewd for FDR to have Hopkins and Harriman circulate among the British, bond with the Churchills, and encourage them to hold fast. Such personal ties would pressure the president and the American people to do more for Britain. Roosevelt felt comfortable in the eye of the storm. Gusts for and against military intervention enabled him to tack in his own direction, to change course as he wanted. Years later, Harriman remembered that the president tried "in every way he could to strengthen [Britain] so as to prevent America's troops being sent into war. He had a horror of American boys going through what they went through in World War I. He wanted to do everything we could to avoid our having to participate."[10]

Elusive in his own personal relations, Roosevelt probably understood that crafting an alliance entailed a blend of distance and intimacy. Distance in terms of avoiding the shedding of American blood and tears; intimacy in convincing Churchill that Americans would share in the toil and sweat by producing war materiel. A genius at managing impressions, FDR also realized the need to prove the gumption of Americans, especially if they did not enter the fighting. A poignant display of masculine resolve—"guts"—was another reason to send the chronically ill but courageous Hopkins on the long, cold flight to London and then, after the German invasion, on an even more arduous trip to Moscow.

Hopkins had arrived in London on January 9 so exhausted that he could not unfasten his safety belt. He spent his first evening with Murrow. Since the summer of 1940, the former lumberjack with the somber voice had broadcast into American living rooms the stories and sounds of Britons braving German bombing. He helped Americans feel this fight was their fight, that it made sense to ship scarce supplies to Britain. Hopkins confided the two parts of his mission: "I want to get a real understanding of Churchill and of the men whom he sees after midnight." And "I have come here to try to find a way to be a catalytic between two prima donnas."[11] The phrase "prima donnas" alluded, on some level, to the operatic bent of these vocal leaders as well as to the theatrics needed to craft an alliance between a nation at war and another at peace.

The next day, Hopkins, meeting Churchill for the first time, took a punch to gauge the prime minister's mettle. Joe Kennedy, the appeasement-minded ambassador, had reported that the British leader "did not like America, Americans, or Roosevelt." Hopkins repeated the charge to Churchill's face. The PM rose to the bait. He declaimed his fondness for all things American and displayed his telegram congratulating FDR on reelection the previous November. Adept at keeping others off guard, Roosevelt had not deigned to respond to the effusive cable. Churchill then launched into a lecture. Even if the Germans landed a hundred thousand soldiers, "we shall drive them out." Naval blockade and air attacks would cripple the enemy. In a preview of Allied strategic arguments in 1942–44 over tackling Germany head-on, he insisted "this war will never see great forces massed against one another."[12]

Churchill feared ideological differences might intrude. FDR had signaled his faith in the future of the Labor Party by appointing as ambassador John "Gil" Winant, a liberal Republican who had directed the International Labor Organization in Geneva and who already enjoyed warm relations with Labor Party leaders. The president distrusted the PM's love of monarchy and empire. In May 1940, when a German invasion had seemed imminent, Roosevelt had warned His Majesty's Government that if flight proved necessary, it should head for Bermuda, not Canada, "as the American republics would dislike the idea of a monarchy functioning on the American Continent."[13]

After dinner that first day of Hopkins's visit, Churchill launched into a "majestic monologue" about this war for the freedoms of "the humble laborer." Pausing, he asked, "What will the President say to all this?" A performer in his own right, Hopkins held silent for a long minute. In the homespun manner of Ben-Franklin-in-Paris channeled through Will Rogers, he drawled: "I don't think the President will give a damn for all that." A longer pause as the Briton squirmed. "You see, we're only interested in seeing that that godam sonofabitch, Hitler, gets licked." Laughter all round. "At that moment a friendship was cemented," an aide later recalled.[14] Amid the hilarity, Hopkins was hinting that Roosevelt's opposition to territorial empires, whether German or British, trumped his interest in UK domestic reform.

Bedazzled by Churchill, Hopkins expressed his feelings with down-to-earth words that could sway doubters back home. "Jesus Christ! What a man!"[15] To FDR he reported: "*Churchill* is the gov't in every sense of the word—he controls the grand strategy and often the details—labor trusts him—the army, navy, air force are behind him to a man. The politicians and upper crust pretend to like him. I cannot emphasize too strongly that he is the one and only person here with whom you need to have a full meeting of minds. . . . I cannot believe that . . . Churchill dislikes either you or America."[16] Churchill certainly liked Hopkins. As Winston and Clementine's daughter, Mary Soames, remembered, "My father wanted to like [Harry] but also the chemistry was right between them."[17]

The Hopkins sojourn stretched to six weeks. Churchill sought to prove that the British would continue fighting. The emissary assured him that the United States would stand by them. The sixty-seven-year-old prime minister hauled Hopkins around to see the fleet, war factories, and bomb damage. Clambering onto a battleship, Hopkins slipped and would have fallen into the sea if a sailor had not lifted him aboard by the scruff of his neck.[18] Pamela Churchill later recalled that "the greatest thing that Winston and Harry had in common was tremendous courage. That was a quality they each respected."[19] Churchill, under criticism because of military disasters, ostentatiously displayed the American as visible evidence of Roosevelt's ongoing support.

In between the forced marches, Harry luxuriated at Claridge's Hotel. His suite, just like the Lincoln bedroom in the White House, "was always a mess, with papers, some of them highly secret, littered about."[20] Friends worried about his frailty tucked him into bed early. The playboy would sneak out through a back door, nightclubbing through the next morning. He drank. Pamela Churchill remembered that Harry "never seemed to eat anything." She added in a half-finished thought, "he had the scotch—but he never . . ."[21]

The Blitz enabled Churchill to demonstrate his never-say-die courage. On the night before Winant was slated to receive an honorary degree, bombs set the university town of Bristol ablaze. With Hopkins in tow, the PM, adorned in his father's black and gold chancellor's robes, strode "through the flames and ruins" as the wounded were being unearthed. Amid the anguish of an "hysterical woman" and the fainting of the mayor's wife, Churchill appeared as a manly leader, as almost a savior. Military chief Lord Ismay recalled that "it was like a sacrament—they wanted to touch the hem of his garment."[22] The eloquent message: Britain would endure.

Britons warmed to their bedraggled visitor. "You got right under all our skins," one wrote Hopkins.[23] His demeanor suited those culturally inclined to understate emotions. Mary Soames later remembered that Hopkins in his "quite unemotional appearing way, was obviously very moved by England's situation. He seemed to respond to how we all were feeling at that time." That "moved us all very much. We felt very beleaguered then."[24]

Hopkins delivered Lend-Lease for the heart. He promised to report to the president according to the Book of Ruth: "Whither thou goest, I will go; and where thou lodgest, I will lodge: thy people shall be my people, and thy God my God."[25] Then he added, quietly, "Even to the end."[26] An official observed that "everyone cried or felt a throb in his heart. Tears poured from the PM's eyes. Mrs. Churchill cried."[27] As Pamela Churchill remembered, that pledge "went around England like wildfire. That was the clue we had been waiting for."[28] The biblical language resonated with feelings going back to childhood. Ruth, though of a different nation, was promising her mother-in-law union as one people. On the level of realpolitik, Hopkins was suggesting a merger of national interests. FDR would have added, even if only to himself, that he intended to define those joint concerns.[29]

Hopkins also touched hard-boiled newspaper publishers. FBI chief J. Edgar Hoover reported to FDR that Hopkins, looking "lean, shy and untidy," talked at a dinner for the press sponsored by Lord Beaverbrook. "It appeared from facial expressions that all of the guests were quite happy." According to the G-men, the audience was struck by "the very remarkable fact that he combined a very charming but almost shy personality with a very vigorous and dynamic mentality."[30] An editor noted that though they had arrived a bit unnerved by the Blitz, they departed "happy men all; our confidence and our courage had been stimulated by a contact for which Shakespeare, in *Henry V,* had a phrase: 'A little touch of Harry in the night.'"[31]

Others experienced feelings so intense they were difficult to translate into words. An aide, Eric Seal, recounted an evening when Hopkins, "who is a dear," played favorite records on the gramophone. Churchill was "walking about, sometimes dancing a *pas seul*, in time with the music. We all got a bit sentimental & Anglo-American." Seal found it all "very pleasant & satisfying—but difficult to convey in words." This he could articulate: "Everyone present knew & liked each other—it is extraordinary how Hopkins has endeared himself to everyone here he has met."[32] Translating emotions into language is always imprecise. The warmth aroused by Hopkins's charm and empathy, the bonding of these men as Anglo-Americans, may have been particularly difficult to describe without seeming transgressive. Such intimacy would help keep the Anglo-American alliance together even during quarrels over strategy. The contrast lay in ties with the Soviets. Despite the emotional bond with Stalin apparently struck at times by Hopkins, Roosevelt, and Churchill, these ties lacked the cultural glue, the equivalent to the Book of Ruth, *Henry V,* or dance tunes.

Secretary of the Interior Harold Ickes had a point when he sneered that if Roosevelt had sent "a man with the bubonic plague to Churchill," he would have met a warm welcome.[33] Though the prime minister had to give priority to national interest, Clementine enjoyed far greater independence. She would not, for instance, hide from Winston her dislike for FDR. Soames later remembered that although "my mother ... was quite a critical person," Harry had "captivated her quite quickly." As Pamela Churchill put it, "Harry Hopkins was never a stranger in our family; he was always Harry."[34]

How could Hopkins so captivate the Churchill women? He brought hope at a desperate time. He worked at charming them as he had done with the women around FDR. Much of his appeal came from his appearing simultaneously frail and vibrant. Pamela Churchill remembered him as "small, shrunken, sick. He was always cold. Harry never took off his overcoat at Chequers." Decades later she could still envision "the enormous gray overcoat, the battered hat, the battered face." And yet when he talked about something serious "the whole man changed; he became strong."[35] At Chequers he spent hours reading in a bathroom where the heating pipes converged. Hopkins paid Clementine special attention, finding her "the most charming and entertaining of all the people that he had met."[36] When he returned in 1942, she left a rest cure to see him. Once back in the United States where consumer goods could still be found, he sent seventeen-year-old Mary lipstick and nylons. He maintained a flirtatious correspondence with Pamela, relaying FDR's delight at her affair with Harriman. They joked about the many beaux pursuing her and Kathleen Harriman. Pamela teased Harry about some Dorchester Hotel women he had charmed.

Hopkins achieved his goal, as he had put it to Murrow, of understanding Churchill and the people he saw after midnight. He even gained first place in that nocturnal lineup. Roosevelt, "handing himself large bouquets" for having chosen the perfect emissary, boasted at a Cabinet meeting that "the first thing that Churchill asks for when he gets awake in the morning is Harry Hopkins, and Harry is the last one whom he sees at night." FDR understood the importance of personality. He had sent "just the right kind of a human being [to] make the greatest impression on Winston Churchill."[37]

In mid-February 1941, with Hopkins back in Washington, Winant asked: "Are they going to hold out?"[38] Yes, was the answer, but only if America sent supplies. Hopkins also gave a reassuring nod to Harriman, who hoped to run the London-end of Lend-Lease. The "assistant president" intended to oversee the massive program from the Lincoln bedroom. FDR, however, remained the boss. He kept

Harriman hanging. With no call coming from the White House, Averell asked for an appointment.

Harriman in London

On February 18, Harriman was received graciously by the president who "talked to me as if it was mutually understood" that he was going to London as Lend-Lease "Expediter."[39] FDR told him "to recommend everything that you think will be useful to keep the British Isles afloat."[40] The instruction was typical of Roosevelt. As Harriman later explained it, "If you succeeded you were all right; if you made a mistake, you were out on a limb."[41] The president volunteered, "You know, Averell, I am by nature a compromiser."[42] He was also an equivocator, even more so now when he saw no clear path to defeating triumphant Germany. He remained unsure about how far and how fast to push war-averse America. Harriman observed him as "far more humble, less cocksure and more human" than ever before. On March 11, FDR, "just recovering from a cold," appeared "obviously tired and mentally stale"—a condition aggravated by his "unhealthy diet" of "hot water poured over chopped up spinach," spinach souffle, and "three large pancakes with plenty of butter and maple syrup."[43] Though under the thumb of the president, the London-bound aide could escape the tyranny of the White House cook, Henrietta Nesbitt.

William Averell was born in 1891 into the family of E. H. Harriman, the robber baron who had crushed rivals in building a railroad empire. The titan instilled that competitive spirit into his son. He also broadened the boy's horizons with travel to Alaska, Siberia, and Japan and throughout the American West. President Theodore Roosevelt attacked the father as a "malefactor of great wealth" and an "enemy of the republic."[44] That assault fired Averell to restore the family's good name. Another goad was the ostracism he suffered from Yale classmates during World War I, when Averell had elected not to fight but rather try to make money building ships.

William S. Paley, whose drive powered the rise of CBS, admired Harriman as another "very determined man. Once he decided to do something, nothing in the world could stop him, not only from doing it but doing it well."[45] John J. McCloy, who would earn the sobriquet "chairman of the American Establishment," later recalled: "I thought I was working harder than anybody else in [World War II] . . . but Averell would be up later at night than I would. You could call him anytime of the day or night." Harriman sought "a world to conquer." He did not restrict his conquests to business and politics. McCloy remembered "running into him out on the West Coast, and being very impressed with what beautiful women he always had around him."[46] He "had a sort of melancholy personality . . . a little mystery that drove the women mad." Among the millionaire's many girlfriends was Teddy Girard, a "rather spectacular looking cabaret singer," who starred in such productions as *The Cave Girl*.[47] A neighbor remarked that Harriman also played "very serious croquet. It wasn't just for fun, it was for blood."[48]

Such drive did not insure against humiliation. Harriman would ultimately fail in his ambition to become secretary of state or president, in part because he tended to mumble, stammer, and ramble when speaking in public. The journalist Charles Collingwood, whom he later hired as speech coach, found him "practically inarticulate."[49] Another aide concluded: "He couldn't say it, he couldn't analyze it, but he had intuitions that were very sound." His second wife, Marie Whitney Harriman, "treated him like the village idiot."[50] When he first arrived in London, American correspondents dismissed him as "Roosevelt's tame rich man." FDR, after all, collected lapsed Republicans. Franklin Jr. was probably echoing family lore when he explained the social gulf between "the old Hudson River families" and the "nouveau" Harrimans with their estate on the western bank of the river. "The east side was always the most respectable side."[51] Kathleen would later remark that her father and FDR had not been childhood friends. Indeed, "Ave didn't have a very close relationship with Roosevelt at all."[52]

It was Hopkins's love of night life that got Harriman into the Roosevelt circle. McCloy recalled that "Harry liked the fleshpots of life, and Averell could give them to him." In addition to picking up the tab at nightclubs, Harriman subsidized the fancy hotels and travel of

Hopkins, who otherwise "couldn't rub one nickel against another."[53] There was probably a bit of truth in the jeer of a Washington fixer that "in order to send a message to Churchill . . . you always had to find Hopkins someplace in a hotel room with a babe and . . . a case of whiskey."[54] In 1938, the "tame rich man" had earned points by assuring a Senate committee that Hopkins, despite his reputation as a spend-tax-and-elect New Dealer, would indeed make an ideal secretary of commerce. Roosevelt probably saw Harriman as an energetic problem solver who could fit in with British society while watch-dogging the president's interests. Ironically, by 1944–45, Harriman would develop an agenda that threatened FDR's postwar aims.

On March 15, Harriman landed after a hop-scotching Clipper trip on the Washington-Bermuda-Azores-Lisbon-Bristol-London route. He later recalled, "I was very excited, feeling like a country boy plopped right into the center of the war."[55] An enthusiast of air travel as his father had been with rail, he envisaged nonstop planes to London as vehicles for U.S. cultural influence. He urged Hopkins to make such service a "super priority" so as to "create an atmosphere and understanding [of the United States] that is completely lacking in London."[56] He would later attempt to tie Moscow into an east-west air network.

Churchill dedicated himself to cultivating Harriman, as he had done with Hopkins. He invited him to (staged) Cabinet meetings and offered some secret intelligence. The two enjoyed staying up late playing bezique, a fashionable card game. They proved a well-matched pair. As Kathleen Harriman later recalled, "Churchill liked to talk, and Averell was a ready audience while they were shuffling" cards.[57] (FDR, in contrast, would grow annoyed at the PM's constant buzz.) Kathleen would answer the telephone at 11:00 p.m. to hear, "'If the ambassador doesn't have anything to do, maybe we could run through the pack.'"[58] In this relaxed setting they could discuss policy. Each impressed the other with his courage. Churchill responded to German air raids by leading his cronies, tin hats on head, up on the roof to watch the bombs and antiaircraft fire. This struck Averell, "who was no coward . . . as really very remarkable."[59] Next day, the American, "for morale purposes," would tour the bomb damage.[60] While valuing

U.S. support, the prime minister chafed at the president's caution. Harriman agreed, even questioning the manliness of FDR's policy. He complained to his wife: "Hasn't the country any pride? Are we to continue to hide behind the skirts of these poor British women who are holding up the civil defense here?"[61]

As FDR probably intended, Harriman went native, spending seven of his first eight weekends at Chequers with the PM and key advisers. Soames remembered, "Papa was very intent that Averell should sort of understand all the personalities involved."[62] The American came to understand in particular the personality of Clementine, who survived by taking long vacations from her difficult husband and by seeking close ties beyond her family. "I went to Chequers even when Averell didn't," Kathleen remembered; "Mrs. Churchill told me she was my surrogate mother."[63]

Clementine asked Averell's help with an intimate family problem: persuading her seventeen-year-old daughter, Mary, to break off her premature marriage engagement. Clementine "wasn't getting any support from Papa," Mary later remembered. And so despite the "horribly cold weekend," Averell and the young woman "walked round and round and round" the gardens as he talked with her in a fatherly way. Whether in political or personal matters, "it was like family," concluded Mary, who did end the engagement.[64] Averell would often invite Clementine to dinner and to the theater. Their shared passion, however, was croquet, in which each figured as a "ferocious competitor." She stood unbeaten until Harriman "absolutely thrashed her."[65] Like Hopkins, Harriman helped smooth relations between Clementine and Winston. Perhaps that added to the latter's eagerness to keep these Americans close. Hopkins and Harriman both gave the Churchills gifts of goods that were no longer available in Britain, such as citrus fruit, silk stockings, Havana cigars, and Virginia hams.

Though Churchill also cultivated Ambassador Winant, they never grew close. In appointing Harriman as Lend-Lease czar, Roosevelt was following his usual practice of setting up rival fiefdoms that he could manipulate. Harriman's direct line to the president cut out the ambassador as well as Secretary of State Hull. The affronts mounted to the point where Churchill warned Harriman: "We'll have to be more careful."[66] Nevertheless, Winant's pattern of missing appointments and misplacing documents made it easy for Harriman to run bureaucratic circles around him. Nor was the unhappily married ambassador adept in romance. The Churchills' daughter Sarah, an actress who had inherited her father's red hair and dramatic flair, escaped her unhappy marriage by living for a time with Averell and Kathleen. Winant apparently first pursued Kathleen, who later recalled that he "was a big problem in my life. The reporters would tell him, Mr. Ambassador, you leave Kathy alone."[67] Winant then fell in love with Sarah, who later ended their affair. Despite his depression and heavy drinking, the ambassador was beloved by Londoners. He would walk streets after an air raid, empathizing with the suffering.[68]

In matters lighthearted and serious, small and large, personal and political; during night and day, weekday and weekend, "the whole aim of that time," John Colville remembered, "was to incorporate as much as possible our American friends in what we were doing."[69] Such intimacy afforded a pattern of consultation: ongoing opportunities to clarify differences, clear up misunderstandings, and work out compromises. Both Harriman and Hopkins—as well as General John Dill, head of the British Joint Staff Mission in Washington and a close friend of General Marshall—greased the Roosevelt-Churchill relationship. They prenegotiated agreements, headed off angry telegrams, and smoothed over personality conflicts. In blurring some elements of national rivalry, they helped create a special relationship. These go-betweens could not, however, do more than work around the edges of major strategic differences, particularly America's refusal to enter the war—until Pearl Harbor changed everything—and the 1942–43 quarrel over when and where to attack the Germans.

Pamela Churchill's Network

As Harriman was leaving for London, Hopkins offered the tip that Pamela Churchill had more information than anyone in England.[70] Kathleen later remarked that Pamela shone brightly as not only "the apple of Churchill's eye," but also as "the apple of Harry Hopkins's eye, too. Everybody loved Pam. She was in on everything , and it was a good way to find out what the Prime Minister was about." She also "got to know all the press people."[71] What's more, millions of Americans came to see her as an appealing symbol of Churchillian Britain.

Soon after Churchill showed Pamela's picture to Hopkins, a similar photograph appeared on the cover of *Life*. In an age before television, many of the images that fixed in the American mind originated in this weekly pictorial magazine. One can extrapolate the reception of the photograph from the pattern of *Life* covers. In the weeks before and after Pamela's picture appeared, covers featured actress Katherine Hepburn, a woman in a bathing suit, a starlet in a low-cut gown, a brave American soldier, menacing Nazis, and Churchill's ambassador, Lord Halifax.[72] Dedicated to making money and to helping Britain, publisher Henry Luce peddled cheesecake and Churchill. Auburn-haired, blue-eyed Pamela provided both. Her picture was captioned "pretty mother" with her son, who had a "Churchill mouth." In a subsequent issue the editors chose to publish a letter praising the "symbolical loveliness" of the cover, "the most beautiful you have ever printed."[73]

No doubt Harriman looked forward to meeting this smart woman who could supply the information and contacts he needed, and whose transatlantic reputation as a beauty probably aroused his competitive instinct. When they first met in late March 1941, the forty-nine-year-old appeared to the twenty-one-year-old as "the most beautiful man I ever met." She later recounted, "He was marvelous, absolutely marvelous-looking with his raven black hair."[74] The aura of his power and money no doubt enhanced his good looks. As Pamela later recalled it, "Harry had set the stage" for her and Averell getting together.[75]

As Colville wryly observed, there soon "started a very special relationship between Averell and Mrs. Randolph Churchill."[76] On the night of April 16, the Luftwaffe pounded London in the heaviest attack of the war. Averell and Pamela both happened to live in the Hotel Dorchester, a steel and concrete structure that, particularly in its lower floors, offered better bomb blast protection than other buildings. An antiaircraft battery nearby offered another plus. As the bombs hit

3.1. On greeting Harry Hopkins for the first time, Winston Churchill showed him "with obvious pride the photograph of his beautiful daughter-in-law and grandchild." A similar picture soon appeared on the cover of *Life* magazine. Pamela Digby Churchill would position herself at the center of an Anglo-American network of sex and secret information. (Sherwood, *Roosevelt and Hopkins*, 238. Courtesy of Camera Press.)

closer, a party on an upper floor scattered, and the duo retreated to his private quarters. As Harriman would later explain, "There was nothing like a blitz to get something going."[77] Pamela would later send Averell a letter disputing a passage in a book on the bombing. The author claimed "that the Wednesday night of April 16th 1941 was the worst night anyone has ever spent." She penned: "I take another view!"[78] The morning after, Colville spotted the lovers walking arm in arm inspecting the damage. At Chequers one of them would scuttle through dark hallways to the other's bedroom. In mid-May, Averell brought over his daughter, Kathleen, a graduate of Bennington College, which had a reputation of producing worldly young women. "Kath" and "Pam" quickly became best friends, sharing clothes and secrets. Pamela appreciated her new friend "as a good alibi."[79] Kathleen in turn admired her as "one of the wisest young girls I've ever met—knows everything about everything, political and otherwise."[80] When Averell secured larger quarters in the Dorchester, Pamela "moved right along with us," Kathleen later remembered."[81]

Did Winston and Clementine Churchill know of this affair? It remains difficult to believe that the prime minister, who loved secrets and who received reports from his superb intelligence service, was not apprised of this turn in the life of the American astride Britain's lifeline. Some aides, such as Colville, would later try to protect reputations by denying that the PM would permit adultery under his roof. But Colville also described Pamela's parties at which, despite wartime rationing, "you would have a five or six course dinner . . . foods which you didn't normally see. . . . And I do remember thinking to myself . . . Averell takes good care of his girlfriend."[82] Clementine had only to peek at the names in the guest book at Chequers. Kathleen recalled, "Pamela was always very careful" not to sign it when Averell was also there for the weekend. She added that "Randolph didn't know about it for ages."[83] Stationed in Cairo, the husband grew fond of Harriman when Averell inspected the Middle East on behalf of the British and U.S. governments. Randolph wrote that Averell "has definitely become my favorite American."[84] With the United States still aloof from the fighting, the love affair must have seemed to the PM a godsend for further "mixing up." Frederick Lindemann (now Lord Cherwell), who advised Churchill on many matters, liked to say, "We must never forget that man is polygamous. Woman is monogamous."[85] It seems probable that the father of the cuckolded son did not allow himself to "know" what was known by the leader fighting for his nation.

Despite vast differences in their relative experience and power, the young mother and the thrice-elected president both ranked as world-class jugglers, seducers, and manipulators. FDR, who loved salacious gossip, "got a big kick out of" hearing about the affair.[86] Ever competitive, he probably also enjoyed the notion of his man in London bedding his ally/rival's daughter-in-law. In a letter to FDR, Pamela Churchill confided that she had placed the signed picture he had sent her next to that of her father-in-law, and that two-year-old Winston "calls both photographs Grandpapa!"[87] She probably sensed that FDR, who appropriated the most distant kin as "family" and who liked the prerogatives of "Father," would be delighted to learn that the PM now had to share his status as grandfather. She made sure the president knew she was honoring his photograph. She might even have embellished the toddler's purported response.

Pamela Churchill adroitly managed multiple paternal ties, love affairs, and flirtations. The links afforded personal and financial freedom. She operated like many men of power. Her comment that Hopkins "wasn't quite a pinup," while Harriman was "beautiful" sounded, in terms of conventional sex roles, more masculine than feminine. Indeed, she displayed a streak of androgyny. According to a biographer, "one of the more provocative aspects" of her personality was "her mixture of masculinity and femininity." Being a "gutsy girl" probably enhanced her sex appeal.[88] An American correspondent recalled that "Pamela was a great beauty, a gorgeous woman. Every man in London was attracted by her, not only Harriman and Murrow but a lot of correspondents. She was honey drawing flies."[89]

She would later recall, "I suddenly became very American and spent most of my time with Americans."[90] While seeing Harriman, she also pursued a serious affair with Murrow, sometimes sitting by his side as he broadcast to America. She became lovers with another married man, General Frederick Anderson, a commander of the U.S. Army Air Force. And then there were the flings with Time-Life publisher Henry Luce, psychological warfare officer William Paley, and playboy and OSS operative Jock Whitney. "Pam liked to go around with men, and she liked sex and she was attractive and they liked her," explained an American journalist who knew her well. "She said no to some and yes to some. . . . It was the mood of the time."[91] Paley remembered the atmosphere of wartime London as "a romantic place, very romantic.

Because of the urgency ... the normal barriers to having an affair with somebody were thrown to the winds."[92] The journalist Harrison Salisbury recalled that "sex hung in the London air like the fog."[93]

Pillow talk made this sexuality politically significant. Sex can both express and give rise to intimacy and trust. Such feelings can have political consequences even if they remain, as was the case in wartime London, conditional and circumstantial because of competing allegiances. Indeed, the essence of what Hopkins, Harriman, and Pamela Churchill tried to do was to blur the distinctions between loyalty to Washington and loyalty to London. Those sleeping around were also loosening the link between intimacy and trust with a bed partner, and sexual fidelity to that person.

A master at this game, Pamela Churchill became a back channel for communication. Information she gleaned from Lend-Lease representative Harriman could assist Beaverbrook in ramping up production of aircraft. To facilitate Pamela's affair with Averell, Beaverbrook subsidized her wardrobe and provided a live-in nurse at Cherkley, his estate, to care for Winston II. He appreciated that she also brought air general Anderson to Cherkley. The tie with Anderson dovetailed with her flirtation (and perhaps more) with RAF Chief of Air Staff Charles "Peter" Portal. (The latter was so smitten that he would send her a thirty-page missive from the Yalta Conference "because I love you so much & feel I must do something when I can't talk to you in person." He added, "I simply *must* see you very soon after I get back.")[94] A reporter later explained that "these relationships were solid politics. The Americans believed in precision bombing and the British believed in area bombing. Winston used Pamela to plant these ideas on the American generals. Churchill would question her on what she believed General Fred Anderson's position was.... Pam and I would trade information constantly."[95] Such information probably also found its way into Murrow's radio broadcasts, listened to by millions of Americans.

Outranking all other ties, however, was her link to "Papa." The prime minister would phone late at night and send an armored car to fetch her for bezique and hours of gossip. "The phone would ring, and Pamela would come in and say, 'I have to go now. He's calling me now.'"[96] Earlier in the war, when Pamela was living at No. 10 Downing Street, Clementine had a private section in the improvised bomb shelter but Winston and Pamela shared a bunk bed. When she divorced Randolph in late 1945, her father-in-law would side with her. FDR had done the same when his son, James, split from Betsey Cushing, who had not hidden her own preference for "Father."

Intimacy juiced the flow of money as well as information. Harriman paid Pamela Churchill a monthly allowance. He also covered the rent on the luxury apartment she rented after he left to become ambassador to Moscow in 1943. (In 1971, when Pamela and Averell married, his banker called to ask whether the allowance—long since forgotten by Harriman—was still to be paid to the new Mrs. Harriman.) Beaverbrook and Jock Whitney also gave her generous subsidies. After Pamela and Randolph divorced in 1945, her father reportedly remarked after a visit, "It is absolutely amazing. I don't know how she manages this marvelous apartment when I only give her 400 pounds a year."[97]

Pamela Churchill's agenda mixed personal and patriotic elements. She decided what information to share or withhold, and how to spin it. As a Washington kingmaker would later observe, "Pamela likes power. A lot of us do."[98] Precisely what she told to whom will probably never be known. Talking, not writing, was her métier. Told by Luce about his diary, she expostulated: "Oh, what a Goddam bore! Imagine! If something exciting happened during the day, the last thing you want to do is write it down."[99] Anything written down could fall into the wrong hands. Always discrete, she believed "it is better to be dull than dangerous."[100] She once tellingly penned Kathleen, "There is so much to tell you that one can't write about."[101]

Roosevelt Hemmed In

Even as Hopkins, Harriman, the Churchills, and the people around them developed the intimacy that Sherwood called a "common-law marriage," Roosevelt faced seemingly intractable problems.[102] More than 80 percent of Americans opposed entering what seemed to many a lost war. Seared into his memory was the unraveling of Woodrow Wilson's administration after he lost the public's confidence in 1919–20. Roosevelt himself fell ill. He was threatened with the loss of Sumner Welles. He did lose his closest partner, Missy LeHand. On Easter Sunday, April 13, Russia signed a pact with Japan. That same day Germans captured Belgrade after only a week of Yugoslav resistance. As the Germans rolled on into Greece, the British again retreated. A spectacular airborne assault captured Crete. Ship losses from U-boats multiplied threefold. A coup in Baghdad replaced the pro-British monarchy with a pro-German junta.

Hitler seemed invincible. Would he next pounce on Russia, Britain, or Turkey? Or would he lunge across Spain and North Africa toward the Azores, Dakar—and Brazil? Some U.S. military attachés openly admired German prowess. An assistant secretary of state recorded the global consensus that the British "are licked. We hear it from South America, from the Far East, from West Africa. . . . The Turks act that way—so do the Russians—the Finns even are turning, the Swedes are impressed, the Japs are convinced." He concluded: "I am very depressed."[103]

Roosevelt's antidote to depression was water. As a youth he had had sailed the Hudson and navigated around Campobello. Trying to recover from polio, he found solace on the houseboat or at Warm Springs. In water he could still walk. He remained proud of his service as assistant secretary of the navy. As president he relaxed on fishing cruises. He enjoyed viewing naval ships and collecting naval prints. He micromanaged "my Navy" while entrusting the army to Marshall and Stimson. He valued warships as flexible instruments of power that he could shift between the Atlantic and the Pacific.

Yet now, in the spring of 1941, his naval options were limited by an insufficient fleet. Spurred by Secretary of the Navy Frank Knox, Stimson, Ickes, Hopkins, the British, and his own inclinations, FDR ordered the Atlantic fleet to patrol more aggressively. That required more ships. Stimson and Knox urged transferring much of the Pacific fleet to the Atlantic. Yet the president agreed with Hull on retaining most of the Pacific fleet at Pearl Harbor to deter Japan, never realizing that a deterrent could become a target. Moreover, he worried about public uproar if the Germans attacked U.S. ships convoying British supplies, a risk he had promised to avoid during the Lend-Lease debate.[104]

Characteristically, FDR tacked. In a May 27 fireside chat declaring an unlimited national emergency, he announced that "all additional measures necessary to deliver [Lend-Lease] goods will be taken." Meeting with reporters the next day, however, he pooh-poohed the very notion of such additional measures: "No, no, no. No. You are just letting your imagination run away with you."[105] Hopkins, who boasted that he understood Roosevelt, was aghast.[106] Pivoting yet again, FDR a few hours before this press conference told Halifax that he was thinking about occupying, and extending naval patrols to Iceland, more than halfway across the Atlantic.

Daunted, Roosevelt in April and May "spent a great deal of time in bed and rarely went to the office," Sherwood remembered. The White House doctor, Ross T. McIntire, failed to detect potentially catastrophic anemia. A problem, possibly bleeding hemorrhoids, reduced the hemoglobin in his blood to less than one-third the normal level. Over the next months he received at least eight blood transfusions.[107] Missy opined, "he's suffering most of all from sheer exasperation."[108] Bullitt spread vicious rumors that Welles was likely being blackmailed by the enemy, and that the "President showed moral deterioration."[109] Roosevelt, who had a history of nightmares, dreamt that "a squadron of German planes had passed over Hyde Park," forcing him to hide in "a bomb-proof cave two hundred feet" down.[110]

The harried commander in chief sought diversion with Princess Martha and with Lucy Mercer Rutherfurd. From April until August 1941, FDR spent part or all of fifteen days with the princess.[111] She was often, though not always, accompanied by her young children and by her lady-in-waiting.[112] The attention to the princess could not have escaped Missy. She may have been the one who spurred Hopkins to warn the Norwegian king about the supposed view among the American people "that the Crown Princess should go to the Middle West where the Norwegians live."[113] A vicious cycle developed, with FDR turning to other women as Missy became more stressed by his behavior, her responsibilities, and her ailments, which she aggravated by taking opiates. She got so keyed up over FDR's May 27 address to the nation that she "vomited violently," a friend reported.[114] Missy's stress probably helped induce the strokes that crippled her on June 4 and June 21, 1941.

Hopkins's Mission to Moscow

At nearly the same instant as Missy's second stroke, the Germans lunged at the Soviet Union in Operation BARBAROSSA. Roosevelt had lost his Girl Friday. Yet if the Soviets could stay in the fight, he would have gained a way to hobble Hitler's armies. Defying expert opinion, the president pushed for sending Russia war supplies. The State Department took the opportunity to denounce godless communism while mustering little sympathy. Churchill pledged support, remarking that if Hitler invaded hell, he would say a good word for the devil. Former Soviet foreign minister Maxim Litvinov later recounted that Churchill's declaration eased fears "that the British fleet was steaming up the North Sea for a joint attack with Hitler on Leningrad."[115] Though not about to join Hitler, most Americans and British detested the Bolsheviks' atheism, purges, subversion, renunciation of czarist debts, and abolition of private property. According to prevailing notions of so-called national and racial character, the harsh climate, vast plains, and "Mongol" heritage of the Russians kept them backward and governed by instinct and emotion rather than reason.[116]

Such assumptions colored the views of U.S. Ambassador Laurence Steinhardt, a political appointee esteemed in the State Department. Five days before the German invasion, he urged a set of principles similar to what Washington would later adopt during the Cold War. The Russians, like "all primitive peoples," lacked "ethical or moral considerations." Russian "psychology recognizes only firmness, power and force, and reflects primitive instincts entirely devoid of the restraints of civilization." Therefore Washington need not reason or compromise. Indeed, efforts at "friendly cooperation" would be misunderstood as "evidence of weakness." He allowed no room for ambivalence or complexity: The Soviets "must be dealt with on this basis and on this basis alone."[117]

Steinhardt felt "fortified" in these views after talking with Hitler's ambassador, who confided that the Kremlin behaved better "when the violence of the German [political] campaign against the Soviet Union was at its height." Cultural congruence made it seem natural for this American, though he was Jewish, to find the German view compatible. Steinhardt even argued that Moscow, not Berlin, was responsible for the European war.[118] Four years later, as Germany lay in ruins, cultural affinities would again make it easy for many Americans and British to sympathize with the defeated enemy rather than with the vengeful Soviets. The ambassador's hostility had been aggravated by his isolation. Only a day before sending this telegram, he wailed: "I am confined in this concentration camp without a breath of fresh air."[119]

FDR remained skeptical of such vitriol; after all, he did not have to live in Moscow. Even he, however, described Stalin as having manners "of a deeply Oriental European kind."[120] Roosevelt and Hopkins probably realized that prevailing assumptions about racial and cultural difference required that an alliance with the Soviet Union be sold to the U.S. public—and, on some level, sold even to themselves—as grounded in compatible values. The Grand Alliance could not be just a pact with the devil. One day into the new war, Stimson advised Roosevelt: "Germany will be thoroughly occupied in beating Russia for a minimum of one month and a possible maximum of three months."[121] Almost no one in the War Department doubted a German triumph. Ivan Yeaton, the U.S. military attaché in Moscow who got much of his information from his German and Japanese friends, reported that "the Germans will go through the Red Army like a knife through butter."[122] On June 30, the war secretary tried to buck up the president, telling him that "if he would lead, the whole country would follow." But FDR remained ill and depressed, probably in part over losing Missy. He replied "in a rather weary and tired voice that he . . . had no pep."[123]

While the Soviet ambassador Constantine Oumansky labeled Stimson as "arrogant and hostile," the latter despised the Russian, who was disliked by many, as "slick and unscrupulous." In meetings in Washington, they quarreled over the conditions for U.S. military aid.

The dispute highlighted a cultural difference that would eventually undermine the Grand Alliance. Pushing for what he called "friendly contact," an exasperated Stimson charged: "You are blindfolding us—our military attaché is not permitted into the theater of military operations." What Americans and British regarded as normal—moving about and associating freely—struck the Russians as unjustified, disrespectful prying. Offended, Oumansky reported that Stimson was "hitting us on the nose," trying to "penetrate into our affairs," "doubting whether we would be able to use the American arms." As the Soviets fought on despite massive losses, Stimson's antagonism softened. Indeed, he began to "Americanize" the new allies. As he saw it, partisans battling behind German lines were "acquiring the old frontier methods" pioneered by "our American forefathers."[124]

In late July, FDR asked Hopkins to get a firsthand sense of Stalin as he had done with Churchill. Could the Red Army, decimated by purges and barely able to defeat Finland in the Winter War of 1939–40, hold out against the unbeaten Wehrmacht? Would Stalin make a separate peace? Could this "oriental" Bolshevik align with the Western democracies? Stalin also had questions. Would his new allies, so recently hostile, contest his possession of the Eastern European territories he had seized in 1939–40? Would the Americans keep their promise regarding aid? What was Washington's attitude toward Tokyo's designs on Siberia? Could Roosevelt overrule the anti-Soviets in the U.S. State and War Departments? Were the Americans brave enough to take on the Germans? Regarding the last issue, Steinhardt did not inspire. He "talked about nothing except the need to save his property" and escape, reported Cripps, the British ambassador.[125]

Hopkins, however, did display courage on the flights to Archangel and Moscow. On July 28, he took off from Scotland in a seaplane piloted by RAF captain David McKinley. The flight around the northern tip of Scandinavia lasted more than twenty hours. McKinley lost his way for a time. The plane made an easy target by flying in perpetual daylight off the coast of German-held Norway. It was "damned uncomfortable," an officer later recalled. It was also cold, particularly for Hopkins whose flying suit did not fit. A too large hat, borrowed from Churchill, kept sliding down his face. Hopkins injected himself with plasma and liver extract, telling the crew, "This is where my energy comes from."[126] In Archangel, Soviet officials, probably apprised of their guest's roving eye, assigned as interpreter "an attractive-looking Russian woman."[127] Authorities laid out the customary four-hour feast.

In later describing the meal to Americans, Hopkins tried to bridge the cultural gap. The food had an "Iowa flavor, what with the fresh vegetables, butter, greens." Regarding drink, "vodka has authority." It could "tear you apart. The thing to do is to spread a chunk of bread (and good bread it was) with caviar, and, while you are swallowing that, bolt your vodka. Don't play with the stuff."[128] Vodka could certainly tear apart Harry's truncated and re-stitched gastrointestinal tract. He did not know that the "good bread" could also play havoc because of his apparent intolerance for wheat, which was diagnosed only after his death. The flight to Moscow passed over solid forest for four hours. The emissary took heart, wrongly, that German tanks could never smash such a barrier. He landed appearing "very frail, weak, pale."[129] Determined to join the upcoming Atlantic Conference of Churchill and Roosevelt, he had only three days before the grueling return flight.

As the dictator's interpreter later recalled, Stalin "understood psychology." He had "to persuade, convince Harry Hopkins that we would continue to fight."[130] He began by stressing not military cooperation but rather cultural values: "the necessity of . . . a minimum moral standard between all nations." Nazi leaders "knew no such minimum moral standard" and therefore represented "an anti-social force in the present world." The Germans casually made and broke treaties. "Nations must fulfill their treaty obligations or international society could not exist." Stalin's emphasis on honoring treaties dovetailed with the repeated efforts he would make in 1941–45 to nail down U.S. and British endorsement of Russia's preinvasion borders. Without such agreements, the Kremlin chief would have been freer to take what he wanted. But he preferred certainty and international order. Because Americans also favored living up to treaties, he said, "our views coincide."[131]

Stalin added that no matter how different the regimes of neighboring states were from each other, these states had to live side by side and cooperate in economic and other spheres. Hitler's "antisocial" attitudes threatened "the coexistence of states."[132] The dictator was evidently thinking about the "coexistence" of powerful states, given that he had recently swallowed up his small neighbors, Latvia, Lithuania, and Estonia. Hopkins was impressed that Stalin stressed help over the long term. "Give us anti-aircraft guns and the aluminum [for making planes] and we can fight for three or four years." As their first talk ended, Stalin said, "You are our guest; you have but to command."[133] They agreed to meet early the following evening—the middle of the day for Stalin, who rose at noon and worked or partied until dawn. In a separate talk with Molotov, Hopkins assured the worried foreign minister that Washington "does not want Japan to penetrate to Siberia."[134] Roosevelt, viewing Germany as the main foe, hoped that Japan might be contained without a conflict.

Hopkins observed the whipsaw effect of the Kremlin's favoring guests while infuriating foreign residents. He invited Steinhardt to spend the night in the luxurious bomb shelter, stocked with "champagne, caviar, chocolates, and cigarettes," that Stalin had thoughtfully provided. When the ambassador complained, "no bomb shelter had ever been placed at *my* disposal," Hopkins "laughed heartily."[135] His delight at the diplomat's anguish may have been heightened by a strange coincidence. Early one morning in October 1938, Harry's former girlfriend, the actress Dorothy Hale, had leaped from the window of her Manhattan apartment. The previous afternoon she had thrown a party for Steinhardt.[136]

Stalin posed for the American public. He welcomed *Life* photographer Margaret Bourke-White, then in Moscow with her husband, the novelist Erskine Caldwell. Caldwell was broadcasting on the war from Moscow, as Murrow was doing from London. Though Bourke-White had "imagined Stalin as a person of super-human size," she found him "little, gray, flat-chested, with bad posture." Five feet five inches in height herself, she judged him shorter. "As I crawled on my hands and knees from one low camera angle to another," the dictator "started to laugh." She captured the smile. Unlike others who had amused him by crawling, she emerged triumphant.[137]

Hopkins returned the next day for a three-hour talk. Despite the staggering defeats, Stalin remained optimistic about the long run.

Scoffing at British and U.S. caution, he explained that he was "anxious to have as many of his divisions as possible in contact with the enemy, because then the troops learn that Germans can be killed and are not supermen."[138] The two men agreed on a meeting of supply experts in Moscow in October. The desperate dictator invited "American troops on any part of the Russian front under the complete command of the American Army."[139]

After talking about troops and weapons, Stalin steered back to emotions and morality. Roosevelt should realize that "Hitler's greatest weakness was found in the vast number of oppressed people who hated Hitler and the immoral ways of his Government." The "moral strength" to resist could arise "from only one source, and that was the United States." The apostle of Marxist-Leninism "repeatedly said that the President of the United States had more influence with the common people of the world today than any other force."[140] Though it would be easy to dismiss the words of a brutal dictator about international moral standards, FDR and Hopkins were more designing than naive. They hoped that such talk just might develop into a silken cord drawing the Soviets toward a more Western system of values.

In between talking with Stalin, Hopkins sparred with Yeaton, the U.S. military attaché. They rehearsed themes that would become central to the Cold War: resentment of the Soviets, favoring Germany over Russia, and dismissing Soviet interests. Yeaton despised Moscow as "truly the most depressing post, city and country on earth."[141] He boasted about his "very fixed and violent opinions" shared with his German and Japanese friends.[142] FDR's strategy of arming the Soviets against the Nazis dismayed him. He did not relish a German defeat. Indeed, even British military attachés in Moscow rooted for the Germans against the Soviets. "A Russian defeat fills them with joy," officials back in London complained.[143] Yeaton urged that Lend-Lease be made contingent on the Soviets' giving officials like him information and freedom of movement. Hopkins replied "with a cold, flat *NO*." As he and Roosevelt saw it, the Soviets would be killing Germans by the millions; that was payment enough. At that point, Yeaton later recalled, "I lost my temper."[144] Though Yeaton and Steinhardt were soon removed from Moscow, the argument would continue for decades. Their replacements would also bridle at the imposed isolation. Postwar critics would mistakenly explain Lend-Lease not as a strategy for defeating Hitler while saving American lives but rather as appeasement by men too cowardly and weak to stand up to Stalin.[145]

Months later, Hopkins cast about for some way to "sell" the dictator to average Americans. How to emphasize the determination and courage while countering distrust of the bloody, "Asiatic" Bolsheviks? He opted, in effect, for a discourse of rational masculinity. He described Stalin as the kind of taciturn, practical, sincere tough guy Americans admired. Writing about Stalin in a popular magazine, Hopkins recalled, "Not once did he repeat himself. He talked as he knew his troops were shooting—straight and hard. . . . He's built close to the ground, like a football coach's dream of a tackle. . . . He looked straight into my eyes." The hands were "as hard as his mind." (Other observers had noted the dictator's soft hands and manicured nails.) He wasted no "gesture or mannerism." Using a figure of speech that would become world-famous in Kennan's 1946–47 call for containment, Hopkins, with a very different purpose, compared Stalin to "a perfectly co-ordinated machine, an intelligent machine." In keeping with notions of a primitive national character, Hopkins depicted emotions as signals of basic intentions. Stalin's "smile was more friendly" when mentioning "the President of the United States." Speaking "of Hitler his manner was more eloquent than his words. . . . His body grew tense." The underlying message was of a Grand Alliance founded on concrete interests and compatible feelings. Hopkins concluded by challenging readers to surmount their fears of racial, ideological, and cultural difference: "Put your prejudices aside. Whom would you want" across the narrow Bering Strait, Stalin or Hitler?[146]

Atlantic Conference

On August 1, Hopkins left Moscow to rendezvous with Churchill, about to board the battleship *Prince of Wales* for Newfoundland and a meeting with Roosevelt. Somehow the emissary left his life-sustaining injections in Moscow. He boarded the seaplane in Archangel "critically ill" and with "great blue circles under his eyes," Captain McKinley later reported. The plane—laden with caviar, vodka, and "a large quantity of platinum"—dodged antiaircraft fire and landed in rough seas off Scotland. The pitching plane risked smashing into the waiting naval launch. Hopkins had to clamber atop the hull of the plane and leap across the water into the arms of seamen on board the ship. His luggage was tossed after him. Observers feared that the exhausted man might die that night. Though bravery had become routine in the RAF, McKinley was struck by Hopkins's "unbelievable courage" and "unparalleled devotion to duty."[147] FDR no doubt sensed that such gumption boosted American credibility in war-wracked London and Moscow.

Roosevelt saw the Atlantic Conference as an opportunity to demonstrate his own courage and determination while assessing Churchill's. To the PM's disappointment, the meeting would remain a get-together, not a war conference to agree on joint strategy. In limiting the conference to theatrics and personal diplomacy, Roosevelt hemmed in the military and naval advisers accompanying him. He knew that U.S. officers could not match the detailed plans of the well-prepared British. Churchill, meanwhile, aimed "to get the Americans into the war."[148] He indulged in wishful thinking, confiding to the queen before sailing: "I do not think our friend would have asked me to go so far for what must be a meeting of world-wide importance unless he had in mind some further forward step."[149] Yet FDR had in mind only smaller steps, such as extending naval patrols to Iceland and the Azores and increasing aid to Russia.

While each leader saw an opportunity to sway the other, a British Roosevelt-watcher judged the PM as unequal to the challenge. He expected "meetings *a deux* in which all sorts of rainbows will be woven, and when it is over no one will know quite what has passed. No one . . . except F.D.R., for he is a consummate politician, and far more slippery than" Churchill.[150] Despite the rivalries and differences, the prime minister and the president each saw the meeting as an occasion to display his manly resolve and their common values. Both regarded theatrics and personal bonding as vital in constructing an alliance.

Roosevelt and Churchill were also alike in approaching the conference as boys setting off on an adventure. Walter Thompson, the PM's bodyguard, recorded that as departure neared, Churchill "grew more and more intense—actually boyish."[151] Another aide found him "like a boy who's been let out of school suddenly."[152] He sported a blue "siren suit," making him appear like a "Teddy Bear." H. V. Morton, a journalist aboard, described Churchill as "boyish; and not a very good little boy either." His "naughtiness" included adopting as his trademark gesture two fingers thrust upward, a double entendre, because it "has not always meant V for Victory."[153] On the train to the dock he instructed "the Prof" to calculate how much champagne he, Churchill, had drunk over the decades. How many railroad coaches would that fill? Told that it would take only one end of one coach, he was "very put out and disappointed," Thompson noted.[154]

Churchill inspected every corner of the *Prince of Wales*, especially its scars from the recent battle with the *Bismarck*. Some aides worried that Hitler's navy might attack. Although Churchill welcomed a fight, he knew that the ULTRA code-breakers could decipher radio instructions to prowling U-boats. The *Prince of Wales* could steer clear of submarines.[155] A military aide, Ian Jacob, observed that Churchill "seems quite content to forget about what is going on elsewhere and simply to enjoy himself."[156] An "almost fanatically clean person," he "bathed with gusto and frequency . . . using half the Atlantic," or so Thompson recorded.[157] He viewed for the fifth time his favorite movie, *That Hamilton Woman*, about the glorious victory over Napoleon's navy. Dabbing away tears, he "was completely absorbed in the story," like children "who wish themselves into picture-books," Morton observed.[158]

The prime minister nevertheless worried whether the president "will like me."[159] He pressed Hopkins: "What sort of a man was Roosevelt? What actually did he think?"[160] The American later remarked, "You'd have thought Winston was being carried up into the heavens to meet God!"[161] While not deluding himself that he was that exalted, FDR appreciated that the Briton was crossing the Atlantic to meet him. Roosevelt had underscored this superiority in selecting, over London objections, a meeting site at Argentia, Newfoundland, where the U.S. Navy was building "this new base of ours—one of the eight I got last August in exchange for the 50 destroyers."[162]

Churchill was not the only "boy" off on a secret adventure. Roosevelt confided to his friend "Daisy" Suckley, "Even at my ripe old age I feel a thrill in making a get-away—especially from the American press."[163] In one the few memoirs FDR dictated during his presidency, he detailed "the delightful story" of how he fooled the press, the public, and even the Secret Service. He had switched with a look-alike, complete with up-tilted cigarette holder, "pretending to be the President" on a fishing trip off Cape Cod.[164] Elliott Roosevelt observed that his father "enjoyed himself thoroughly, much as a twelve-year-old boy playing cops-and-robbers."[165] Though such secrecy was justified to protect against U-boats, it did not account for keeping in the dark the secretaries of war and state, not to mention the First Lady.[166] Since boyhood Roosevelt had loved secrets. Secrecy helped keep the levers of power in his hands. Such behavior probably also stemmed from his boyish delight at getting others to squirm a bit. For added fun en route to Argentia, he spent a day speed-boating around Buzzards Bay near Cape Cod with Princess Martha of Norway and her young daughters.[167] FDR balanced his boyish fun with near-royal prerogative. The commander in chief not only arranged for his sons, Army Air Force officer Elliott and naval officer FDR Jr., to join him at Argentia, but also claimed that the reunion was pure coincidence. He would ignore the subsequent public uproar.[168]

Despite an "extremely cold and violent wind" blowing across the deck of the *Prince of Wales*, Churchill spent hours directing rehearsals for the planned religious service. With stand-ins for the leaders, the PM "stood apart, criticizing and frequently stopping the proceedings." The production was complicated by Roosevelt's paralysis. Churchill expected that FDR would stand still as British officers filed past him.[169] Jacob explained, "all this procedure is necessary because the President is unable to walk sufficiently far."[170] Roosevelt would delight in smashing that assumption.

The Americans also challenged British assumptions about a key question: What time zone prevailed in Placentia Bay? That question flowed from the issue of which nation was sovereign over this U.S.

base on British territory. The *Prince of Wales* had reset its clocks to arrive on schedule according to Newfoundland time.[171] The Americans kept to Washington time, which ran ninety minutes later. As the British vessel glided majestically toward Roosevelt's ship, the *Augusta*, precisely at the agreed hour of 9:00 a.m. on Saturday, August 9, the gap became embarrassing. The huge warship had to lumber around and put out to sea. The incident underscored precisely who was running the show. The loss of face "infuriated Winston. He banged about the decks, hunting a target for his wrath."[172] Ninety minutes later, as the *Prince of Wales* again steamed toward the *Augusta*, the morning mist suddenly cleared, revealing a harbor filled with U.S. warships crowded with cheering sailors and displaying the Stars and Stripes. Churchill was relieved by both the welcome and the flags. According to navy protocol, flying the U.S. flag signaled that the ships were in a foreign port—and that the Americans considered their ninety-nine-year lease on Argentia only temporary.[173] To counter the advantage of the British in expertise, Roosevelt kept them in the dark as to schedule. The day before the meetings began, Jacob fretted, "the programme is quite unknown at present."[174] Finally the British were informed that most meetings would take place on FDR's ship and on his schedule.[175]

Still unsettled were weightier issues, such as how to allocate war materiel and establish war aims. Overarching all was the difference in perspective between those fighting for their lives and empire, and those remaining at peace and regarding empires as old-fashioned. A U.S.-based British official warned, "FDR has only one clear idea about the peace and that is that America shall emerge ... as the strongest Power in the world."[176] A fresh surge of Axis victories overshadowed the get-together. Elliott Roosevelt remembered his father's worry that "the Nazis are riding high these days. Masters of Europe."[177]

Hitler and Mussolini had seized center stage, dominating even the discourse about top-level meetings. In referring to the Atlantic conclave, chroniclers could not avoid the arresting image of "the Dictators stepping from their armoured trains in the Brenner Pass."[178] General "Hap" Arnold recorded that "Marshall told us of our 'Brenner Pass' conference ahead."[179] Halifax wished Churchill "a new and better Brenner."[180] The challenge facing U.S. and British leaders was to fashion a democratic "Brenner" and democratic courage.

Hopkins transferred aboard the *Augusta* early the first morning, finding "all of the Americans, including the President, excited. All of them wanted to know about Churchill."[181] FDR asked, "Are you all right? You look a little tired." "The Russians are confident," Hopkins blurted out as Roosevelt, Marshall, Arnold, Admiral Ernest King, Welles, Harriman, and the president's sons, Elliott and Franklin Jr., gathered around. An officer recorded that Hopkins was "so sick that he was having blood transfusions all during the conference."[182] Anxious that the two "prima donnas" get along, he nevertheless dragged himself to meetings and meals. At 11:00 a.m., Churchill and his advisers came aboard. Bands saluted with the "The Star Spangled Banner" and "God Save the King." The prime minister, sporting a semi–naval blue uniform, bowed slightly and presented a letter from King George VI. The president, wearing a light brown Palm Beach suit, stood straight with his arm on Elliott's bent elbow. Appearances hid how heavily FDR was leaning on his son. (Roosevelt's sons had lifted weights to build up the strength to support their father.) Though serious, neither scowled like the dictators. Instead, they erupted in smiles and handshakes; Churchill produced a cigar and Roosevelt his cigarette holder. The president in his wheelchair gave a tour of his ship. Aides paired up with counterparts for informal talks.[183] The spectacle of the unspectacular contrasted with the pomp of the Axis dictators.

The only sour note came when the PM failed to remember that he had met Assistant Navy Secretary Roosevelt at a London dinner in 1918. Roosevelt believed he had been snubbed by this "stinker." Whether it was attributable to lack of ability or interest, the affect or even the presence of others often failed to register with Churchill. Perhaps he never really "looked" at the offended visitor. Whereas the prime minister could be oblivious, the president could rarely forgive. At subsequent summits he would exact revenge by needling Winston. But not now. Instead he turned on the charm. Roosevelt later told Daisy that his new friend "is a tremendously vital person." He added, "I like him—& lunching alone broke the ice both ways." Ever the Hudson River aristocrat, Roosevelt likened this scion of the Duke of Marlborough to the half-Italian/half-Jewish "Mayor [Fiorello] La-

3.2. Roosevelt talking to Churchill at the Atlantic Conference. FDR's hand gripped the rail to help him stand upright. The president would also lean on the arm of his son Elliot, who was waiting nearby. (Courtesy of FDR Library.)

Guardia. Don't tell him I said so!"[184] Churchill's adviser, Alexander Cadogan, undersecretary of the Foreign Office, dropped his usual caustic tone to applaud FDR's "great, and natural, charm."[185]

The president asked his guest to talk on the war. He wanted to assess the fabled oratory. He also wanted his military aides to hear the arguments for assaulting only the peripheries of German-occupied Europe. Most U.S. generals preferred instead building a mass army, landing across the Channel, and marching to Berlin.[186] Air chief Arnold dismissed the British strategy as "always hoping for a break—a miracle."[187] The one detailed account of Churchill's talk appears in the 1946 memoir by Elliott Roosevelt. Although based, it seems, on wartime notes, the book is also marred by Anglophobia and exaggeration. Yet even Elliott was impressed. The PM reared back in his chair, shifting his cigar "from cheek to cheek and always at a jaunty angle, he hunched his shoulders forward like a bull, his hands slashed the air expressively, his eyes flashed. . . . He held us enthralled even when we were inclined to disagree with him."[188] Churchill urged bombing Germany into submission while holding on to the seas, the Middle East, and the empire. He appealed for a joint warning to Japan not to move deeper into Southeast Asia.[189] U.S. military officers fumed at Churchill's apparent desire that "100% of all planes produced in U.S. go to Britain."[190] Privately the British compared Americans wanting to hold on to their weapons to "reluctant bathers" standing around with no "thoughts of how to get rid of the sharks."[191] Elliott probably exaggerated by depicting the prime minister as "pleading" for U.S. entry into the war.[192] When FDR interrupted to ask about the Russians, Churchill, with "an edge of contempt in his voice," shot back that the Russians would collapse.[193] More evidence for this attitude would appear in Cadogan's diary. Munching on the caviar Hopkins had brought back, the PM grunted, "it was very good to have such caviar, even though it meant fighting with the Russians to get it."[194] Regardless of his specific intent, the remark had multiple meanings, all of them prophetic.

FDR said he wanted a declaration of war aims, particularly a reaffirmation of support for political self-determination and open door access to raw materials and markets. These tenets appealed to many ordinary Americans and to people in Congress as well as to Hull and Welles. President Wilson had inspired millions by eloquently promoting these ideals. It would be political suicide for Roosevelt to publicly abandon these goals. Nevertheless, he would readily dilute, postpone, or ignore this Wilsonian ideology in order to clinch a deal, whether with Churchill in 1941 or with Stalin in 1943–45. Churchill feared that a declaration of war aims would be divisive. He changed his mind, however, after he realized that Roosevelt refused to commit to war. A declaration of war aims was the most the British leader could get.[195] Concern that Hitler would soon launch a "peace offensive" also impelled action.

Negotiations over the eight articles of the Atlantic Charter occupied Welles and Cadogan, with Roosevelt and Churchill weighing in on occasion. Hopkins brokered a deal on the most troublesome issue, article four. Hull and Welles wanted to use Lend-Lease as a lever to take apart the imperial preference system, the trade and financial rules that had welded the British Empire into an inward-oriented economic bloc. Though initially a free-trader, Churchill resisted this assault on a system that had helped Britain emerge from the Depression. As finally agreed, article four pledged nondiscrimination in postwar trade—with, however, an escape clause that would negate the promise. The first through third articles championed democratic governance and no territorial changes without consent of the people affected. Though aimed primarily at Hitler's empire, these provisions could also challenge the protective barrier and imperial booty Stalin had seized in Eastern Europe in 1939–40. Whether the self-determination promised in the charter included the British Empire would remain contentious throughout the war. While Churchill later assured Parliament that self-determination did not apply to the empire, Roosevelt told reporters that it applied to all humanity. Other articles urged disarmament of the aggressors and freedom of the seas.[196]

Roosevelt did not schedule formal talks between the U.S. and British chiefs of staff until only a few hours before the end of the conference. Though Churchill's staffer Ian Jacob fumed about the hours "entirely wasted," FDR did not want the military planning for a war that most Americans hoped to avoid.[197] The conclave remained "disorganized," Jacob complained. "Quite often the person you wanted to talk to quitted a ship just as you arrived on board."[198]

Liquor probably heightened the confusion. Though the U.S. Navy forbade alcohol among seamen, it supplied plenty of food and cigarettes. His Majesty's Navy dispensed rum. An officer observed, "The American Navy visits the British Navy in order to get a drink, and the British Navy visits the American Navy in order to get something to eat."[199] Skilled at the poignant gesture, Roosevelt, aware that many British sailors had not seen an orange in two years—ordered the *Augusta* to pack 1,950 gift boxes. Each contained two hundred cigarettes, fruit, cheese, and a card that read: "The Commander-in-Chief, United States Navy, Sends Greetings and Best Wishes. Franklin D. Roosevelt, President of the United States."[200] British sailors got the boxes on Saturday afternoon, timing that would boost enthusiasm for the climax of the conference, the religious service the following morning.[201]

Frances Perkins, who had known FDR, Churchill, and Hopkins since the 1910s, later commented that in view of his agnostic background, "it seemed just nonsense to Churchill to sing hymns in Argentia on Sunday morning."[202] Roosevelt, in contrast, "had the kind of religious faith that a child has. It was very simple, very regular, very uncomplicated." Hopkins envied Roosevelt for his "complete faith in God, that God was guiding him."[203] Francis Biddle, who had also known FDR for decades, explained that Roosevelt was "religious but not pious. He knew he was a man." (Biddle added that Woodrow Wilson "was never sure whether he was a man or God.")[204] Churchill realized that a joint service could underscore common elements in Anglo-American culture. With the help of Hopkins, whose mother had been religious, they selected the prayers and hymns, including FDR's favorite, "Eternal Father, Strong to Save." Churchill's secretary recorded that his boss vetted the prayers, "which I had to read to him while he dried after his bath."[205] FDR knew them by heart.

Sunday, August 10, dawned the only sunny day of the conference. Waiting for the president on the *Prince of Wales*, Churchill bustled about, "moving a chair an inch one way or another and pulling out the folds of the Union Jack."[206] Roosevelt sent word that he would walk, not just stand as Churchill had expected. In contrast to the dictators, and to Churchill, FDR wore a civilian suit. On this, his only visit to the British ship, he walked aboard "leaning on a stick and linking his [other] arm" with his son Elliot. Jacob observed, "It is a very great effort for the President to walk, and it took him a long time to get from the gangway to his chair." On the one hand, FDR was trying to obscure what was obvious: "His legs are evidently rather wasted and he has not much control over them."[207] On the other hand, he was demonstrating that he *could* walk, despite the jibes of the dictators and despite the considerate though patronizing assumptions of Churchill. FDR wanted the British to judge him—and the nation he led—as courageous and fit. The walk also seemed, an aide observed, "a sort of marriage service."[208]

Once Roosevelt reached the afterdeck, the couple sat side by side. Behind the president and the prime minister stood hundreds of U.S. and British sailors and higher-ups. Churchill would later describe "the symbolism of the Union Jack and the Stars and Stripes draped side by side on the pulpit, the American and British chaplains sharing in the reading of the prayers; the highest naval, military and air officers . . . grouped together behind the President and me; the close-packed ranks of British and American sailors, completely intermingled, sharing the same books and joining fervently together in the prayers and hymns familiar to both."[209] Probably many felt a lump in the throat. Morton was moved by "a situation that was almost intolerable in its uncalculated emotionalism."[210] The genius of this planned emotionalism was that it could appear "uncalculated." Moving pictures show Churchill wiping away tears, FDR beaming. While the PM kept his head down and spectacles on as he read the hymns, the president held head high and mouth open as he sang.[211] Elliott remembered his father explaining after the ceremony: "It was our keynote." That alone "would have cemented us. 'Onward, Christian Soldiers.' We *are*, and we *will* go on, with God's help."[212]

But "go" where? And how far? FDR valued the service because it fed a sense of common values, themes that Hopkins had emphasized in London and, in a more limited way, in Moscow. Churchill, however, had hoped for a military alliance. More symbolism than substance, the Atlantic Conference helped set the stage for, but it did not create, a functioning alliance. The two nations were still courting and wooing. Getting them to move in synchrony remained difficult. As a gesture, FDR had his namesake son sail aboard one of the U.S. destroyers accompanying the *Prince of Wales* to Iceland. In the first hours of this voyage, the U.S. vessel twice missed "by a narrow squeak" colliding with the British battleship.[213]

Assessing the conference, Oliver Harvey, Eden's assistant, appreciated that the Americans "have the goods" London needed and that most shared British ideals. He concluded, "We can manage the Americans. They are children, simple, naif, yet suspicious." Eden corrected him: "I would not regard Roosevelt as either simple or naif."[214]

FDR dared not commit the United States to fighting when majority sentiment opposed war. To be sure, the 203–202 Congressional vote extending the draft for eighteen months understated support for a mass army.[215] A large majority in Congress stood ready to renew the

3.3. Churchill lecturing at the Atlantic Conference. Later in the war, Roosevelt would tire of such monologues. (Courtesy of FDR Library.)

draft for twelve months. Nevertheless, even in the navy, peace sentiment ruled. At Argentia Jacob felt "sick" that none of the many Americans coming aboard for drinks inquired about the recent scrape with the *Bismarck*. "Not a single American officer has shown the slightest keenness to be in the war on our side," he despaired. "The Americans appear to be living in a different world from ourselves."[216] FDR stage-managed the Atlantic Conference with precisely that goal: keeping the United States in a "different world" from wartime Britain, at least until a German or Japanese attack would crush antiwar sentiment.

At this perilous point in the war, with the Nazis appearing nearly invincible and most Americans reluctant to fight even as they increasingly opposed Hitler, FDR demonstrated how perseverance could trump paralysis. In returning to politics after being struck by polio, he had insisted on "walking" at the 1924 and 1928 Democratic conventions in order to get across the message that he could get things done despite his handicap. Attuned to emotional reactions, he probably understood that the spectacle of his intense effort could sway onlookers. An observer recalled how Roosevelt's "slow procession became extremely impressive." People seemed "hypnotized. . . . An audience of strangers had become a group of friends."[217] His "walking" along the deck of the *Prince of Wales* probably had a similar, cohering effect on those watching him. Although the "virile, dynamic, and violent" force of the Axis frightened Boothby, the demonstrated grit of Roosevelt, Hopkins, Churchill, and Stalin, none of whom quite fit the conventional masculine ideal, coincided with wartime shifts in gendered notions of wartime bravery. Attacks on women, children, and other civilians were expanding what people understood by courage and heroism.

Despite his fortitude, Roosevelt remained uncertain about how to respond to the international crisis. He was constrained by divisions at home and by too few ships, weapons, and troops. He also suffered the loss of Missy LeHand and his own illness. His mother would die within three weeks. Unsure about America's eventual role in the fighting, he nevertheless determined to aid the nations already battling the Axis. In the 1930s, he had assembled the New Deal as a bricolage of often contradictory ideas, programs, and slogans directed toward a sweeping goal. The alliance with the British and the Soviets was similarly pasted together with conflicting politics and cultures. FDR understood that with both ventures people had to believe the framework made sense. It all boiled down to the need for structures of meaning and promise even if the construction was ad hoc and in part an illusion.

Hopkins proved an ideal emissary. For all his wisecracking cynicism and playboy habits, he was a true believer, whether in creating Depression-era jobs or the wartime alliance. He imbued FDR's intuitive vision with substance and drive. His low-key intensity and his empathy enhanced his effectiveness as FDR's representative. He gained entrée to the Churchill family and to other influential Britons. Stalin would remember Hopkins as the first American to whom he had spoken "*po dushe*," from the soul.[218] His bravery in flying to Moscow despite his illness appealed to the Soviets, who were themselves on the ropes. If Washington or London had somehow answered Stalin's appeal for U.S. and British troops, the history of the war and of subsequent decades might have taken a different turn. What an admirer saw as Harriman's "total ferocious dedication" and "very firm convictions" made him effective as Roosevelt's point man with Churchill.[219] His hand on the Lend-Lease spigot made him "the most important American in London," as Pamela Churchill surely appreciated.[220] Her network of lovers, friends, and patrons enabled intimate communications and a variety of liaisons between Americans and Britons. So did the personal ties of Hopkins and Harriman. These personal and political relationships would be put to the test after the Japanese attack on Pearl Harbor when the Americans and British became, finally, fighting allies.

Chapter 4

Transcending Differences

Eden Goes to Moscow and Churchill to Washington, December 1941

Roosevelt and Stalin each seemed shocked and shamed at failing to protect his nation. Secretary of Labor Perkins observed that Roosevelt on December 7 talked to the hastily assembled Cabinet "without looking up or looking at anyone. (Most unusual because even in bad times he usually talks & looks at someone.)" He admitted a "very confused story coming in. Navy didn't know exactly what or how." Pressed on the failure in U.S. intelligence, he repeated, "We don't know."[1] A bit later, Senator Tom Connally of Texas banged his fist on the table demanding, "How did it happen that our warships were caught like tame ducks in Pearl Harbor?" He seemed to feel that the nation's manhood had been exposed and found wanting. "How did they catch us with our pants down?" With bowed head FDR muttered, "I don't know, Tom. I just don't know."[2]

Even more devastating was the blitzkrieg launched against the Soviet Union on June 22, 1941. A stunned Stalin temporarily abdicated to Foreign Minister Molotov, who, prone to stutter, was forced to explain the war in a radio address. Pulling himself together, the dictator worked nearly nonstop for a week. Then on June 29, with accelerating losses of troops, tanks, planes, and territory, he fell apart. He retreated to his dacha, refusing contact. An aide later explained that though "we were all depressed . . . Stalin was very depressed."[3] The *vozhd* despaired, "Everything's lost. I give up. Lenin founded our state and we've fucked it up. Lenin left us a great heritage and we his successors have shitted it all up."[4]

Despite the massive scale of World War II, its direction was shaped by the behaviors, assumptions, and decisions of a few leaders. Roosevelt, Stalin, and Churchill studied each other for clues as to underlying intent and future action. Each ranked as a master at swaying others with his personality and understanding. Immediately after Pearl Harbor, Churchill determined to make his influence felt in Washington. He arrived on December 21 and stayed three weeks. On December 15, Foreign Secretary Anthony Eden, who had negotiated in Moscow in 1935, returned there for talks with Stalin. Even though booming German guns could be heard within the Kremlin, Stalin focused on the postwar territorial settlement. He wanted his new allies to accept the Soviet annexations of 1939–40.

Pearl Harbor and Barbarossa

Pearl Harbor stunned Americans. After hearing from the president, Eleanor Roosevelt confided to a friend, "No one really knew what had happened at Hawaii. No boat had escaped damage. Fleet crippled."[5] Because authorities in the Philippines had inexplicably kept their B-17s parked on airfields in tight formation, the planes had been easy targets for Japanese bombers. From her White House window, a secretary observed rows of "armed soldiers with steel helmets. . . . We are almost literally surrounded with a ring of steel."[6] Roosevelt, Corcoran later recalled, felt hit by a "second polio strike."[7]

As he had done in 1921, FDR fought back. The attack freed him of indecision. On December 8, he delivered his eloquent "day of infamy" speech, asking Congress to declare war on Japan. The next evening he spoke to the nation in a fireside chat and "looked relieved—as if a load was off his mind at last," a White House guest observed.[8] Later that night, speechwriter Sam Rosenman found FDR in the Oval Office sorting stamps. Though appearing "deeply worried . . . there was no trace of panic." Rosenman believed it significant that he "was all alone. If Missy had been well, she would have been sitting up with him in the study that night. She always did so in times of great stress."[9] LeHand had called the White House the evening after Pearl Harbor. Paralyzed by her stroke, she struggled to ask for her beloved "Effdee." Roosevelt said he was too busy to talk with her. He failed to call her back afterward. Nor did he call her on Christmas Day, though he knew she was expecting to hear from him.[10]

Stalin and his nation suffered worse. Whereas the Americans endured the loss of 2,403 men and eight battleships damaged or sunk at Pearl Harbor, the Soviets lost 319 Red Army units and two-thirds of its military supply dumps in the first weeks of the German onslaught.[11] Though breached, the Pacific and Atlantic moats still held. No such barriers stopped the Germans from slicing through Belorussia and the Ukraine. For months Stalin had dismissed as disinformation both American and British warnings of imminent invasion. He had convinced himself that he had another year or two to prepare.[12] He could not accept that Hitler had betrayed him. He even forbade counterattacks in the first hours. He blamed a supposed conspiracy within the Wehrmacht. "Hitler surely doesn't know about it," he kept saying.[13] While Secretary of State Cordell Hull lambasted the Japanese ambassador with Tennessee hill country curses, Molotov stuttered to the German ambassador, "Surely we haven't deserved that."[14]

Stalin may have withdrawn to his dacha in part to test the loyalty of his lackeys. He probably wanted to demonstrate that he was indispensable. He needed a new beginning on a war that had started disastrously. After a few days, his aides meekly sought him out. He resumed leadership, heading the new defense council. In a July 3 nationwide address, he appealed to "Brothers and Sisters" and to Russian nationalism, and promised victory. Significantly, he downplayed communist ideology. Four weeks later, he would impress Hopkins with his determination to resist the Germans. He may have tried to send a peace feeler to Hitler, which got nowhere.[15]

In mid-October 1941, with the Germans only fifteen miles from Moscow, Stalin suffered yet another collapse. Order was breaking down. Unchecked mobs looted shops, empty apartments, and the British embassy. "People were dumping communist literature and portraits of the party leaders," a Muscovite later recalled. "All of Moscow seemed to be streaming out somewhere."[16] As elites fled the capital, their cars stuffed with valuables, workers stopped the vehicles to beat and rob the occupants. In one incident, "six cars were thrown into a ravine," the NKVD (secret police) reported.[17] "White flags were hung on some of the houses of the collective farmers." On the radio a patriotic Soviet tune was cut off mid-stanza, replaced by the "Horst Wessel Lied," the infamous marching song of the German SS.[18] Stalin could not decide whether to order a general evacuation of Moscow. "What shall we do?" the dictator sputtered. "What shall we do?"[19] He called a top general, crying: "Comrade Stalin's not a traitor. Comrade Stalin's an honorable man."[20] He ordered diplomats and many officials to leave for Kuibyshev, six hundred miles to the east. Yet he hesitated to abandon the capital. He had a special train prepared, packed with his library and other possessions. Four American-built DC-3 planes also stood ready.[21]

The dictator decided to stay. In front of his aides he staged a didactic drama with Valentina "Valechka" Istomina. A shrewd, pretty former peasant, Valechka had devoted herself since the late 1930s to managing Stalin's household and keeping him company. Years later, Molotov, pressed about whether Valechka had "served as [Stalin's] wife," offered sacred precedents: Engels had "lived with his housekeeper"; "Lenin had an affair."[22] As Valechka served dinner one evening, Stalin suddenly asked her, "Are you preparing to leave Moscow?" "Comrade Stalin," she replied in peasant idiom, "Moscow is our Mother, our home. It should be defended." "That's how the Muscovites talk!" the dictator pointedly instructed his henchmen.[23] He relied also on other informants. His spy in Tokyo, Richard Sorge, reported that Japan intended to move south rather than attack Siberia. That freed up four hundred thousand fresh troops to rescue Moscow. Russia's traditional ally, winter, also harassed the thinly clad invaders. General Georgi Zhukov promised to hold the capital.[24]

To signal renewed control, Stalin cracked down on looters and staged the traditional November 7 military parade to commemorate the Revolution. Troops marched through Red Square on their way to the front. With snow thwarting German air raids, the former seminarian proclaimed, "God is on the side of the Bolsheviks."[25] By the time Eden arrived in mid-December, the tide had turned enough to revive self-confidence. Stalin pushed for a wartime and postwar alliance with the British and their acceptance of the Soviets' pre–June 1941 western borders.

Churchill and Stalin

Though trying to cooperate in the current war, the prime minister and the dictator could not forget their enmity in a previous one. In 1918–19, Churchill had championed Allied intervention. Both recalled a British slaughter in the Caucasus during the Russian civil war from which Stalin's longtime aide, Anastas Mikoyan, emerged as the only survivor. Moreover, British reluctance to take on the German army sustained Stalin's darkest suspicions. "In essence the English government is helping the Hitlerites by its passive policy of waiting," the dictator feared. "What do they want? It seems they want us to be weakened."[26] In late September, Beaverbrook and Averell Harriman met with Stalin in Moscow. After heated discussion, they hammered out a delivery schedule for war supplies. Once back in London, Beaverbrook hectored Churchill for not doing enough to aid the only nation actually fighting the Germans. Eden and his assistant, Oliver Harvey, worried that Churchill was again showing "very evident signs of anti-Bolshevik sentiment." Labor Party ministers in the Government were "as prejudiced as the PM against the Soviets because of their hatred and fear of the Communists at home."[27]

Sending Stalin troops, a large trove of weapons, or giving him the second front he demanded all presented enormous difficulties. Instead, Churchill dictated grandiloquent telegrams praising "the grand resistance" of the Russian armies, their "wonderful fight," and their "remarkable victories."[28] Eden and Harvey deplored this "sentimental and florid" language. Flowery, unmanly words would "have the worst effect on Stalin," who would "think guff no substitute for guns."[29] In

November, Stalin's anger boiled over when the British refused to declare war on Romania, Hungary, and Finland—all German allies that had invaded Russia. This "situation is intolerable," he warned Churchill in a scathing telegram.[30] The latter refused to reply. A week later, the Kremlin boss, desperate for an alliance, came close to apologizing.

Putting aside the emotionless norm of diplomatic language, Stalin pleaded that he could not "overcome certain personal feelings." He "felt himself hurt." His nation "was in a humiliating position." The British refusal cast "a depressing effect on the minds of my people."[31] Regardless of his actual sincerity, Stalin made a show of exposing his feelings. He departed from the cool rationality he usually displayed. Perhaps the gesture moved Churchill. The latter responded with a two-part proposal that also referred to emotional ties. He would send Eden to discuss an alliance. Commenting that his "personal correspondence" with Roosevelt had led "to a very solid understanding," Churchill reached out: "My only desire is to work on equal terms of comradeship and confidence with you. Our intention is to fight the war, in alliance with you and in constant consultation with you." Conflicting ideologies need not get in the way.[32] The PM's offer fit the pro-Soviet thinking held by some in the Foreign Office.[33]

Veteran analyst Orme Sargent argued, "we should have a Volga Charter as a counterpart to the Atlantic Charter."[34] The Atlantic Charter had reaffirmed Woodrow Wilson's principles of democratic self-determination and open-door trade and investment, tenets that challenged the British and the Soviet empires. Eden and Harvey valued a Volga Charter as a check to Roosevelt, "a headstrong man who means to monopolize the limelight at the Peace but whose political ideas are still those of 20 years' ago." A pact with Russia seemed practical: "Russia is fighting the war and America is not."[35] Eden and Harvey disparaged the Atlantic Charter as "a terribly woolly document full of all the old cliches of the League of Nations period."[36] The very words of their criticism, however, underscored their familiarity with the principles in that document. London officials had experience in working around or through the Americans. Back in August, Churchill had asked Alexander Cadogan in the Foreign Office to work with

Welles in drafting a charter that would assuage the Americans' Wilsonian impulses while safeguarding Britain's imperial interests.

Quite different was Cadogan's experience in late November when he sat down to draft a "Volga Charter." The words would not flow. An accord with Moscow lacked the cultural familiarity afforded by old clichés, even if they might be "terribly woolly." The workhorse grew "bored" with this task. He jotted in his diary, "I can't get on with it." Aboard the *Prince of Wales*, he had been able to "sit down and write straight out something that makes some sort of sense—like the Atlantic Charter." But the Volga Charter, despite its military utility, did not make "sense." He found himself "niggling about and altering phrases." His decades as a draftsman proved useless in writing a set of joint principles with the Soviets. "I lose sight of the whole thing, and get lost."[37] Though ideology remained an obvious point of divergence, Cadogan did not even mention that problem. Instead he instead appeared uneasy with having to bridge cultural differences that included and went beyond ideology.

Missions to Moscow and Washington

Unaware of Japanese aircraft carriers secretly steaming toward Hawaii, Cadogan, Eden, and Harvey set off to meet Stalin. Churchill would soon arrive in Washington. The backdrop of these visits included a series of embarrassing British military setbacks. The advance against the Germans in Libya stalled in late November. Then Japanese planes sank the pride of His Majesty's Navy, the *Repulse* and the *Prince of Wales*. Britain's naval presence in the Indian and Pacific Oceans would never recover. Hong Kong surrendered on Christmas Day.

Despite these blows, British leaders remained steadfast in the belief that they stood at the center of world civilization. For all their wealth and potential, the Americans seemed provincial and disorganized. The Soviets appeared backward and alien. Churchill believed that he and Roosevelt could safely thwart Stalin's primary war aim, reestablishing the Soviets' preinvasion borders. The PM was also confident he could outmaneuver the Americans.

Parallel entries in the diary of Harvey, who stood close to Eden, and in the journal of Cadogan, who often echoed Churchill, illustrated how prejudice could warp understanding. After they landed in Russia on December 12, Cadogan saw all manner of deficiency and strangeness; Harvey interpreted the same evidence as quaint difference. Describing the welcoming officials, Cadogan remarked, "We suffered from an influx of Russians," including "Frogface." He found it "odd" that the landscape appeared attractive. Perceptions of strangeness dominated. Russia possessed an "eerie beauty" that was "fairy-like."[38] The two shared a compartment on the train to Moscow. Harvey wrote, "We climbed into a very warm and comfortable looking old-fashioned sleeping car. . . . All plush and silk curtains and tassels, just like a nineteenth century drawing room," while his colleague complained, "I have to double up with O. Harvey in a cramped and antediluvian sleeping compartment. . . . Water (cold) runs hopefully for 2 seconds and then relapses into a thick and completely black fluid."[39] Later, in Moscow, Harvey reported: "We've been allotted magnificent rooms—like an old-fashioned French hotel." Cadogan's assessment was: "Hotel old-fashioned. . . . Bathroom with a tap that squirts water impartially into the basin and on to the operator."[40]

As they prepared for meetings with Stalin, the outlook was radically altered by Pearl Harbor. A few months earlier, Cadogan had despaired, "How exactly we are going to *win* this war, I shd. like someone to explain." Deepening his gloom was evidence that RAF *"bombing does NOT affect German morale."*[41]

On the evening of December 7, Winston sat down to dinner with Pamela Churchill, Averell and Kathleen Harriman, and "Gil" Winant. Averell recalled that Churchill, looking "tired and depressed," sat resting "his head in his hands."[42] When the radio announced the attack, the PM jumped to his feet, announcing, "We shall declare war on Japan." Winant, who probably realized that a precipitous declaration would feed isolationists' suspicions of a British plot, pulled him back, saying: "Good God, you can't declare war on a radio announcement."[43] A telephone call to FDR soon confirmed the destruction in Hawaii. For Churchill, and for Nationalist leader Jiang Jieshi, a path toward victory had suddenly opened. As FDR put it, "We're all in the same boat now."[44] Churchill recalled that Harriman and Winant reacted with "exaltation—in fact they very nearly danced for joy."[45] The prime minister "got so excited that he began to lisp," Moran recorded.[46]

Churchill announced he would go to Washington. He feared that vengeful Americans might abandon the Europe-first strategy reaffirmed at the Atlantic Conference. FDR tried to hold him off. He did not want the PM barging in, particularly with military and naval affairs in such disarray. Nor did he relish having a seasoned warlord upstage him. By December 10, however, Roosevelt, suspecting that Germany would soon declare war, assented. The British Cabinet reacted with dismay that the prime minister would risk submarine-infested waters while his number two man remained in far off Russia. Harvey fumed, "Really the P. M. is a lunatic: He gets in such a state of excitement."[47] Undaunted, Churchill on December 12 boarded the *Duke of York*, sister ship of the lost *Prince of Wales*. He brought along more than eighty military and political advisers. He effervesced nearly nonstop, or so it seemed to colleagues kept in close quarters by stormy seas. He "feasts on the sound of his adjectives," Moran grumbled. They all waited "for the chance to slip off to bed, leaving Winston still talking to those who have hesitated to get up and go."[48]

Churchill used plenty of nouns and verbs in dictating three lengthy memoranda on war strategy. "The Atlantic Front" argued for securing northwest Africa in 1942. Anglo-American forces should invade this French-held territory, reinforce the British fighting in Libya, and secure the southern shore of the Mediterranean. He advocated sending supplies, but not troops, to Russia. "The Pacific Front" aimed to satisfy the Yanks' itch for revenge without diverting much from the Atlantic Front. The memorandum "1943" looked toward defeating Germany through bombing and blockade, peripheral landings, and assistance to local uprisings. The strategy left the destruction of the Wehrmacht mostly to the Russians. The Anglo-Americans would focus on naval and air warfare, secure the British Empire's Mediterranean lifeline, and avoid heavy casualties.[49] Once the *Duke of York* docked at Hampton Roads, Virginia, Churchill insisted on hurrying to Washington by air. He appeared "like a child in his impatience to meet the President."[50]

As Eden and Churchill neared their respective destinations, each saw evidence that once-isolated Britain had gained a mighty ally. Soviet soldiers manning antiaircraft guns in open-air cars attached to Eden's train seemed inured to the cold. They "had icicles hanging from their eye-lids, but seemed quite cheerful!" Cadogan recorded.[51] Although such toughness gave comfort in late 1941, it would appear dangerous in 1945, when evidence of such endurance would reinvigorate stereotypes of insensate "Asiatics." As Churchill and his party approached Washington, they beheld "the amazing spectacle of a whole city all lighted up." The lights roused "a sense of security" and promised "freedom, hope, strength."[52] (The illumination would soon be extinguished. German U-boats had a field day sinking ships outlined by city lights up and down the East Coast.)

While valuing the latent strength of the Americans, many of the British also patronized them as provincials. A letter from Clementine, probably reflecting her husband's view, referred to the "drama in which you are playing the principal—or rather it seems—the only part." She hoped that after he returned home, "the fervor you have aroused may not die down."[53] If the PM shared such assumptions of superiority, he also understood he had to hide them. In thinking it necessary to order his staff to treat the president "with ultra respect," Churchill may have revealed his own condescension.[54]

British military officers outclassed their U.S. counterparts. Roosevelt shied away from discussing strategy with his military chiefs and offered them little direction. Even at this conference, code-named AR-CADIA, he kept them in the dark. Often Churchill's aides knew more about FDR's thoughts than the Americans did. U.S. forces still operated according to structures little changed since 1903. War Secretary Stimson griped that he could not counter British plans unless his department developed its own. The British in effect colonized U.S. power.[55] The Americans organized a more independent Army Air Force so that it could coordinate with the Royal Air Force. Washington established the Joint Chiefs of Staff, reporting directly to the president, to match the British schema and to enable formation of the Combined Chiefs of Staff (CCS). Despite British protests, Roosevelt insisted that the CCS operate from Washington.[56]

Some close to Churchill interpreted Washington's loose organization as evidence of a general societal deficiency. Lt. Colonel Ian Jacob, an adviser to the prime minister on military planning, was born at Quetta, in what is today western Pakistan. Like many imperial officials, Jacob developed an eye for cultural differences. He believed the values, attitudes, and practices of a people, whether Pashtuns or Americans, conditioned their economic, political, and military behaviors. Bountiful America delighted him. He found the beds in Washington's Wardman Hotel "a dream, and the plumbing all one could want." Having escaped the strict rationing of home, he and his colleagues wolfed down eggs, oranges, and butter—while also fearing "we should become the fat, pasty-faced, double-chinned people who seem so prevalent in America."[57]

Jacob viewed the U.S. government as almost tribal. While the British government ran "like a motor car," the "American Government is not a machine at all." The perceived backwardness of Washington prompted images that apparently recollected Quetta. The president acted like "a patriarch with a rather unruly flock." Lacking trained ministers, he relied on "sheep dogs," such as Hopkins. Compared to Churchill, Roosevelt "is a child in military affairs" unable to "grasp how backward his country is in its war preparations." He saw FDR as leading "a most simple life." The Oval Office appeared "full of junk. Half-opened parcels, souvenirs, books, papers, knick-knacks . . . lie about everywhere." Working in that environment "would drive an orderly minded man, or a woman, mad."

Much like Cadogan in Moscow, Jacob revealed his own cultural prejudices in leaping from minor details to major conclusion: FDR's office typified "the general lack of organization in the American Government."[58] Nevertheless, the Americans, despite all their deficiencies, remained cousins. The Russians, in contrast, were not family.

Churchill and Roosevelt

"We live here as a big family, in the greatest intimacy and informality," Churchill boasted from the White House.[59] He apparently assumed the British would hold on to the masculine authority in this household. Reminded after Pearl Harbor of the need to consider American preferences, Churchill, "with a wicked leer in his eye, said: 'Oh! That is the way we talked to her while we were wooing her, now that she is in the harem we talk to her quite differently!'"[60] The president's inability to walk prompted more such thinking. He later recalled wheeling Roosevelt to the elevator "as a mark of respect, and thinking also of Sir Walter Raleigh spreading his cloak before Queen Elizabeth."[61] In this imagined drama, Churchill, who loved monarchy, performed as the gallant empire builder while Roosevelt played the great queen who had safeguarded the realm from the Continental aggressor. Churchill described Roosevelt as "majestic and statuesque." This depiction puzzled Moran, who, seeing FDR for the first time, remarked that though he had a large head, "he has no legs to speak of since his paralysis."[62]

The PM proved a maestro at playing the emotions in his address to a joint session of Congress on December 26, 1941. In this nationwide broadcast he spoke movingly of his American mother, Jennie Jerome, "whose memory I cherish across the vale of years." He used wit to deflate anti-British sentiment, remarking, "If my father had been American and my mother British, instead of the other way round, I might have got here on my own." He then reaffirmed his primary, paternal heritage: "I am a child of the House of Commons. I was brought up in my father's house to believe in democracy." After gently chiding Americans for not supporting British diplomacy in the interwar years, Churchill reached out to them on the basis of shared racism. Questioning the sanity of the Japanese, he asked with scorn: "What kind of a people do they think *we* are?" An observer recorded that listeners "erupted, the first sound of blood lust I have heard in the war." Tearing up, Churchill concluded, "I shall always remember how each Fourth of July my Mother would always wave an American flag before my eyes."[63]

The performance worked. This was "the most highly dramatic and exciting event I have ever seen staged," a Washington veteran enthused.[64] Senators and representatives jumped up, cheering and flashing the V-sign. Dropping his usual reserve, Supreme Court Chief Justice Harlan Stone raised his arm in a return V-salute.[65] Ickes, who rarely enthused about anyone other than himself, pronounced Churchill "the greatest orator in the world."[66] FDR, however, remained unwilling to concede that superlative. He first congratulated, then admonished his guest. Referring to the crack about prewar policy, he cautioned: "You skated on thin ice three different times in your speech, but you didn't break through."[67]

The excitement may have affected Churchill's heart. That night as he struggled to open a stuck window in his room, he suddenly "was short of breath," he told Moran the next morning. "I had a dull pain over my heart. It went down my left arm." The doctor diagnosed a mild heart attack. Yet he could reveal this dire news neither to his patient nor to anyone else, as the prescribed treatment was six weeks in bed. "This at a moment when America has just come into the war, and there is no one but Winston to take her by the hand." Deciding he knew the best for his patient and that the latter knew the best for America, he said, "There is nothing serious." The following evening the PM again suffered shortness of breath. "There seems to be no air," he complained as he opened the car window.[68]

Churchill's gifted oratory figured as only one expression of his delight at performing. He loved wearing costumes, whether his zipped-up "rompers," assorted naval uniforms, ten-gallon Mexican hat, or his pink dragon dressing gown.[69] Thronged by well-wishers in Ottawa in late December 1941, he flashed his cigar, lofted his hat with a cane, and enthusiastically gave the V-sign, "like a ten-year old," observed the Canadian prime minister.[70]

He also liked padding around nude before other men. After a naked Churchill welcomed FDR into his White House guest room, the latter chuckled to Grace Tully, his secretary: "You know, Grace, He's pink and white all over."[71] Versions of this story would become a staple of the World War II canon. Probably the most dependable account comes from the diary of Jacob, who spoke to an eyewitness, a "Mr. Jones," who affected "a most peculiarly pompous and over-correct way of speaking." The incident roused in the aide "a state of intense

excitement, with difficulty suppressed." Jones was waiting in the hall-
way as Churchill bathed. FDR wheeled up to him.

> "Good morning. Is your Prime Minister up yet?"
> "Well, Sir, it is within my knowledge that the Prime Minister
> is at the present moment in his bath."
> "Good, then open the door."
> Jones flung open the bathroom door to admit the President,
> and there was the Prime Minister standing completely naked on
> the bath mat.
> "Don't mind me," said the President, as the Prime Minister
> grabbed a towel, and the door closed.[72]

In Jones's account, Roosevelt pushed the encounter. As Hopkins
told the story, a surprised Roosevelt "started to apologize and made
as if to leave, but Churchill protested it was quite all right. 'The Prime
Minister of Great Britain,' he said, 'has nothing to conceal from the
President of the United States.'"[73] At dinner soon afterward, Churchill
could not resist describing his recent bath, when he was "lying back
and kicking [his] legs in the air like at birth."[74] The allusion was obvious to those in the know.

Evidence suggests more than one meeting with Churchill nude or
nearly so. Jacob recorded that what Jones witnessed occurred "quite
early on during our visit," which began on December 22. FDR, in
contrast, told Daisy Suckley that he had viewed the PM "without a
stitch on" when barging into his room the day before the January 1
United Nations Declaration.[75] Without specifying a date, a secretary,
Patrick Kinna, recalled that Roosevelt entered the bedroom while a
"completely naked" Churchill was dictating to him.[76] The PM's bodyguard, Thompson, recounted an incident from the first evening in the
White House. Churchill, holding a drink in one hand and a cigar in
the other, paced around his bedroom, naked because of the stuffiness
from the central heating. When FDR knocked, Thompson opened the
door at his boss's request. As Roosevelt turned away, Churchill, looking "innocently down at his dramatic nudity," said, "'Come on in,
Franklin. We're quite alone.'" Then "Churchill posed briefly and ludi-
crously before the President," said he had nothing to hide, and "tossed

a Turkish towel over a shoulder." They talked for an hour, with Churchill pacing about though not covering himself further.[77] Odd as it may have been, such nudity likely fostered a sense of intimacy and trust as they discussed intelligence secrets and atomic research. This combination of high politics and homoerotic frisson fed the "excitement" that prompted Moran to double Churchill's usual dose of barbiturate sleeping pills.[78]

In 1946, Churchill would deny to Sherwood, then researching *Roosevelt and Hopkins,* that he had appeared nude with the president. At the time, however, he had boasted about the political promise of the incident. Ambassador Halifax reported that the PM "has got onto the most intimate terms with the president, who visits him in his bedroom at any hour and, as Winston says, is the only head of State whom he, Winston, has ever received in the nude!"[79] Halifax cabled the news to Moscow, where Eden after contentious negotiations had to endure the more exhausting ritual of Kremlin-style male bonding.

Eden and Stalin

Though the Germans had penetrated the Moscow suburbs, Stalin surprised Eden by focusing on the map of Europe after victory. He demanded the Soviet borders of June 1941. "That is really what the whole war is about," he insisted, and "I would like to know whether our ally, Great Britain, supports us in regaining these Western frontiers." He favored a division of Europe into British and Soviet spheres of influence. It was "absolutely necessary" to detach the industrial Ruhr from the Reich, impose reparations in kind, and take other steps to "ensure that Germany would be permanently weakened." He suggested British bases along the coasts of France, Belgium, Norway, and Denmark. The Soviets would set up bases in Romania and Finland. The United States had no place in this conception of Europe. Eden responded that His Majesty's Government was not ready to accept any shifts in prewar borders. He added that the Americans stood firmly opposed to such changes. Stalin replied sarcastically, he "had believed your Government to have more freedom of action." The lines seemed drawn. "It now looks as if the [Atlantic] Charter was directed against the U.S.S.R." From Washington, Churchill ordered Eden to hold firm.[80]

When Eden offered a general declaration on alliance instead of a concrete treaty, Stalin replied, "a declaration I regard as algebra, but an agreement as practical arithmetic. . . . I prefer practical arithmetic." The metaphor spoke to cultural as well as to political differences. With "arithmetic," the Russians, who had a history of hostility with neighboring states, could simply add up the areas they would control. "Algebra" suggested more complicated calculations of power. Open door principles, as contained in the Atlantic Charter, accorded with the experience of the Americans and the British, who had built informal empires. (In the late nineteenth century London had switched to more formal control.) Unlike the Soviets, the British and Americans could generally count on the support of smaller neighbors.

Concluding that Eden would not budge, Stalin finally yielded. He agreed to a military alliance and to an airy political declaration that remained silent on postwar boundaries. There would be no Volga Charter. Though Roosevelt and Churchill had succeeded in putting off the demand for recognizing the Soviets' prewar borders, a persistent Stalin would return to this issue again and again.

With the deal struck, the dictator hosted a surprise 10:00 p.m. banquet in Catherine the Great's throne room. Harvey marveled at the vaulted ceiling and the "magnificent malachite with white marble pillars."[81] The contrarian Cadogan recoiled at the "rather gaudy suite."[82] "Stalin came padding in, very like a kindly bear," Harvey observed. He "walked quietly around among us all shaking hands." In contrast to the strutting Axis dictators, Stalin underplayed emotions in a way the British appreciated. "There is nothing striking about him except his extreme simplicity and quietness."[83] Despite the shortages suffered by most Russians, the dictator pressed on his guests what Eden described as an "embarrassingly sumptuous" display that included "an unhappy little white suckling pig which looked up with its black caper eye."[84] The British had already eaten dinner. No matter. Soviet custom pitted the generosity of the host against the endurance of the guest. As Molotov later put it, "Russians like to make people drunk."[85]

Stalin proposed the first of thirty-six toasts, many with "Russian whiskey"—vodka laced with chilies—"which is like fire."[86] Marshal Semen Timoshenko staggered even before the toasting began. Looking embarrassed, Stalin asked Eden, "Do your generals ever get drunk?"[87] After further boozing, the dictator adopted a more positive perspective: "The better my generals are, the more drunk they get!"[88] Marshal Kliment Voroshilov collapsed onto Stalin's lap. Timoshenko "got so drunk he was stretched out on the floor heavily asleep," Eden later recalled. "Nearly everyone" was inebriated.[89] It was now the morning of December 21, the dictator's official birthday.

Stalin tried getting closer to Eden by damning others. He blamed the August 1939 Soviet-German pact on Molotov. He mocked Roosevelt's impulsive suggestion of holding military conferences in Moscow, Chungking, and Singapore.[90] The party dragged on until 5:00 a.m., a reasonable hour for the dictator, who slept until noon. Finally they "were able to say good-bye to Stalin and get away—what a party! We were all dead this morning," Harvey scrawled. "I slept until 12, A[nthony] E[den] till 3. No work done."[91] Once back in London, Eden and Harvey urged recognizing the boundaries that existed before June 22, 1941. Stalin seemed "very straight, direct, and reasonable," altogether "quite a nice gentlemanly fellow."[92] Cadogan, in contrast, agreed with Churchill on resisting "Stalin's demands."[93]

Roosevelt and Global Strategy

On December 21, the day before Churchill's arrival and, coincidentally, the day of Stalin's party, the president finally discussed war strategy with his military advisers. Beyond reaffirming a Europe-first strategy and sending warships to the Pacific to stem the Japanese advance, Roosevelt still lacked a comprehensive plan.[94] Churchill, however, had detailed blueprints, which became the basis for the AR-CADIA discussions. Churchill pushed Operation GYMNAST, the invasion of northwest Africa. U.S. army chief General Marshall objected to shoring up the British Empire rather than confronting the Wehrmacht. Roosevelt proved more receptive to the prime minister. The geographer-president worried about a German leap from northwest Africa to West Africa and then across the Atlantic to the South American bulge. He sought a battlefield where U.S. troops could test themselves against the Germans with minimal risk.

The president also worried that preparing an assault on German-held France would take so long that pressure would build for first revenging Pearl Harbor. The Americans ended up endorsing most of Churchill's memoranda dictated on the *Duke of York*. Though short on plans, the Americans were projected to surpass the British in weapons and soldiers. This disparity of forces led Churchill to accept basing the Combined Chiefs of Staff in Washington. After some resistance the British also went along with Marshall's plan for a unified command over the armed forces of both nations in each theater of war. To sweeten the pill, the Americans urged as the first supreme commander a British general, Archibald Wavell, for the newly created American-British-Dutch-Australian (ABDA) theater. Churchill understood that this was probably a poison pill, because the Japanese had already invaded Malaya and the Philippines and were sweeping aside weak defenses in most of that vast area.[95]

Roosevelt valued the visit of the flamboyant PM as an opportunity to sell the new alliance to the American people. He encouraged Churchill to be Churchill in addressing Congress. The two leaders lit the White House Christmas tree. At a joint press conference, Roosevelt asked his guest to stand on a chair so reporters could get the impact of the dramatic gestures and heroic phrases. Yet Roosevelt also realized that other issues portended conflict with this Victorian imperialist determined to hold on to the empire. Impressed that the Soviets were driving the Germans back from Moscow, FDR and Hopkins were also thinking about closer ties with Stalin.

FDR heeded the warnings of Pearl S. Buck, the novelist and China expert, that "more basic than Chinese antagonism to Japan was [the] colored races' antagonism to white." He believed "we would have to compel England to give Dominion status to India" and "get more equal rights for Negroes here."[96] Throughout the war he would stress "the importance of turning the Chinese away from anti–white race attitudes."[97] In heading off a united front by "the colored races," FDR probably counted the Georgian-born dictator, whom he called "an oriental gentleman," as a potential ally. Roosevelt appreciated that the Soviet Union sprawled across Asia.

At the very moment when Eden was reminding Stalin of U.S. opposition to the Soviets' preinvasion borders, the president pitched for closer relations with the Kremlin chief. Dangling the lure of "joint operations," FDR cabled on December 16: "I should like very much to see you and talk it over personally." With a summit not possible immediately, he suggested conferences in Chungking, Singapore, and Moscow. These meetings should devise strategy for military action in each theater by December 20, two days before Churchill was due in Washington. FDR's proposal stalled for several reasons, not least for his failure, as Stalin put it, to "indicate the aims of the conferences."[98] The dictator nonetheless probably appreciated the gesture. He worried that the shaky alliance might fall apart. As the PM was steaming across the Atlantic, Stalin directed his intelligence chief in Washington to "[s]ee to it that Churchill and the Americans do not conclude a separate peace with Hitler and that they don't jointly move against the Soviet Union."[99]

Though amateurish, Roosevelt's proposed three conferences hinted at the postwar strategy he would pursue in 1943–45: lining up with Russia and perhaps a revitalized China against old-fashioned European colonialism. According to this schema, ambassador to London Winant, with his close ties to the Labor Party, might help inspire reform in post-victory, post-Churchill Britain. FDR was trying to think past the proto–Cold War that had frozen relations with the Soviets after 1917. He remained the intuitive pragmatist with a record of overcoming the odds. His wife discerned "a certain gambling spirit in him."[100]

He had reason to feel lucky. Observers remarked on instance after instance of "Roosevelt weather"—smiling skies that encouraged the large voter turnouts that contributed to his electoral victories. Former attorney general Robert Jackson recounted that on cruises FDR usually caught the biggest fish. In poker games, "the President, as usual, went way down and in the last four hands came back. It seemed to be his luck for there was no discernible difference in his technique between the early and late evening. It must have been just that unde-finable thing known as Roosevelt luck."[101]

Despite the energy generated by Churchill's visit, Russia, not Brit-ain, remained the principal ally battling Hitler's armies. On New Year's Eve, Churchill's train was still en route from Ottawa as a party gathered at the White House. Hopkins "pooh-poohed" the "common cultural and political traditions with England" he had lauded in push-ing for aid to Britain. Probably reflecting his talks with FDR, the "as-sistant president" ruminated about a possibility that would haunt Washington for the next six decades: a communist Europe. Though "many people feared that if Russia reached Berlin, all Europe would go communist, he didn't care." His view reflected Rooseveltian opti-mism and rejection of red-baiting. "If we feared Europe would go communist, that only betrayed our own insecurity about [the] vitality of our own system. Either we could adjust to a communist Europe or we weren't worth surviving." Hopkins believed that postwar Europe "would get the economics of communism but accompanied with civil liberties because the terrific pressure of capitalist encirclement would have been lifted."[102] Though Hopkins was naive about the liberating effect, at least in the short run, of ending capitalist encirclement, any inclination to pursue that experiment would be abandoned after Roo-sevelt's death.

Churchill-fatigue may have sparked some of the sympathy toward the other ally. Like the PM's aides, FDR found the effervescence wear-ing. Not yet accustomed to napping in the afternoon, Roosevelt was worn out by the late hours. For years Clementine had escaped on solo vacations or rest cures. Hopkins decided it was too exhausting to have Churchill visit more than twice a year. Barely four hours after their last talk over drinks at three in the morning, a barefoot Winston padded in, asking him, "Have you done anything about what we were discussing last night?"[103] Halifax confessed to difficulty in following his pattern of talk, which called to mind a water bird "jumping from stone to stone." Like other observers, the ambassador was struck by Churchill's inability to read and adjust to the emotions of others. "The faults that people find with him arise entirely from overwhelm-ing self-centeredness, which with all his gifts of imagination make him quite impervious to other people's feelings."[104] After sitting next to the great man, one of Eleanor's friends remarked, "I didn't open my mouth. Didn't have to. The language poured out of him."[105]

Eleanor, whose father and brother had died of alcoholism, resented the liquid requirements of the visitor. She later recalled, "We had to have, in his room," scotch, "and then you found that the White House, which ordinarily served American champagne, must have French champagne of a special vintage. And in addition to that you must remember to have brandy after dinner." Such indulgence, she insisted, "were not part of the life of any American."[106] The liberal First Lady clashed with the Victorian imperialist on many matters, from Churchill's opposition to the Republicans in the Spanish Civil War to his belief that women, except in wartime, should stay at home. She probably saw him as a dangerous influence on her husband. One day she glanced into the Map Room where the two leaders talked animatedly about the shifting pins representing troops and ships. "They looked like two little boys playing soldier," she recalled. "They seemed to be having a wonderful time, too wonderful in fact. It made me a little sad somehow."[107]

FDR enjoyed playing soldier and statesman with Churchill and admired his unquenchable energy and persistence. In a crowded elevator the two gazed only at each other.[108] Roosevelt committed to the alliance with Britain. He greeted the prime minister with a toast that "has been in my head and on my heart for a long time—now it is on the tip of my tongue—"TO THE COMMON CAUSE."[109] Continuing the religious instruction of Argentia, FDR brought the PM to church with him on Christmas Day. "It's good for Winston to sing hymns with the Methodies."[110]

Yet Roosevelt also needled him in ways small and large. During a service at Mount Vernon, he relished the irony of the king's first minister kneeling in George Washington's church. He knew that Churchill hated mixed drinks, preferring instead scotch with soda and ice. FDR persisted nevertheless in handing him cocktails with pineapple juice, raw egg, or other exotic ingredients. Winston dumped them down the toilet or onto the potted plants. He had greater difficulty escaping Rooseveltian denunciations of his beloved empire. Shortly before his departure on January 14, Churchill sat at the dinner table as Roosevelt pontificated. "It's in the American tradition, this distrust, this dislike and even hatred of Britain—the Revolution, you know, and 1812; and India and the Boer War, and all that. As a country, we're opposed to imperialism—we can't stomach it." Glancing at the annoyed veteran of the Boer War, FDR added, "That's what my friend over there doesn't understand."[111] Though the anti-imperialism was genuine, the outburst was also calculated to keep his rival/ally on the defensive. Mike Reilly, the president's bodyguard, later recalled that both Roosevelt and Churchill were performers. The Secret Service agents "who had to arrange their exits and their entrances found we were working for a pair of master showmen, who were determined that no scenes would be stolen by the other."[112]

With Washington still reeling from the Japanese assault, Churchill and his staff leveraged their superior military expertise and organization. In these December 1941–January 1942 talks they succeeded in enlisting U.S. power while masking their condescension. Bidding for trust with FDR, Churchill revealed himself in the nude while talking high-level politics. Though receptive to much of the prime minister's agenda, the president and his family tired of their guest's hyperkinetic behavior and his defense of the British Empire.

On the other front, long-standing Anglo-Russian rivalries and prejudices, reinforced by the Bolshevik Revolution, doomed the creation of a "Volga Charter" to balance the Atlantic Charter. The parallel experiences and diverging interpretations of Harvey and Cadogan demonstrated how stereotypes could color what diplomats saw. Though Eden argued the brief demanded by Churchill and Roosevelt, he left Moscow impressed with the moderation of both Soviet aims and Stalin's personality. Despite his opposition to those war aims, Roosevelt hoped to enlist Stalin in his vision of a postwar world free of colonies and "race war." Meanwhile, the Kremlin boss desperately sought much-needed aid against the Wehrmacht. The intertwined issues of the second front and the postwar world would figure at the center of relations among the Big Three in 1942–43.

Creating the "Family Circle"
The Tortuous Path to Tehran, 1942–43

As relations with Moscow soured in early 1943, Roosevelt blamed Stalin's "feeling of loneliness."[1] The remark was typically Roosevelt: at once simplistic and insightful. The president, who himself could often appear as "loneliest man in the world," often cast political problems in personal terms.[2] When Stalin, fuming at the delayed second front and the stalled Anglo-American offensive in North Africa, refused to attend the January 1943 summit at Casablanca, FDR did not give up on face-to-face persuasion. He wanted General Marshall to go to Moscow and assure Stalin that Washington and London would pursue the total defeat of Nazi Germany. The emissary should also invite the dictator to a Big Three meeting in Nome, Alaska.[3] Roosevelt also proposed cozier summits that excluded Churchill. None of these meetings ever took place. Stalin icily questioned "the purpose" of Marshall's would-be mission, grumbling that "my colleagues are upset."[4] The tension between Stalin's resistance to personal contact and FDR's resolve to "get-at" him fixed the boundaries of Allied diplomacy in 1942–43. Complicating the politics were culturally and emotionally inflected issues of trust and respect.

Roosevelt understood that the Soviets were fighting a lonely war. In mid-1943 in Sicily, the Americans and British tangled with 2 German divisions while the Red Army struggled against 180 divisions along a huge front stretching from Leningrad to the Caucasus. By late 1943, the Red Army had inflicted more than 90 percent of German losses. Stalin fumed that the Allies were trying to bleed Russia white. Roosevelt feared the Soviets might surrender or negotiate a separate peace. He believed that "the whole question of whether we win or lose the war depends upon the Russians." He told an adviser, "I would rather lose New Zealand, Australia or anything else than have the Russians collapse."[5] The importance of Moscow for winning the war and for securing postwar cooperation gradually convinced him to accept Stalin's aim of restoring the preinvasion Soviet border. In December 1941, he had vetoed Eden's endorsement of those boundaries. By April 1942, he privately allowed that he would not mind if Russia took "quite a chunk of territory."[6] Much of the American and British public, however, detested these 1939–40 seizures as Hitler-like violations of the Atlantic Charter. The Soviets self-righteously defended their reclaiming of lands lost during World War I and the Revolution.

Some far-sighted British officials tried to head off postwar trouble. Harvey warned that "once the war stops, passions will be unloosed." He pinpointed the Soviet-Polish border as the most dangerous area. Poland "loathes Russia and, like another Italy, regards herself as the equal of the Great Powers. Her political fecklessness is notorious."[7] Some Poles hoped to annex Lithuania. Most probably resented Moscow's claim to the 1919 Curzon line, which had allocated to Russia territory that Poland had defiantly snatched away by defeating the Red Army in 1921. Stalin, as a front commander in that war, had shared in the humiliation. His revenge and desire for dominance in Poland were not sated when he seized the borderland in 1939. The following year the dictator ordered the slaughter of some twenty-two thousand Polish officers at Katyn. Harvey understood that hatreds boiling up from this "bloodland" could ignite far-reaching cultural and ideological battles.[8] "Poland is quite capable of defying Russia and appealing to Christendom." That would explode "European and American unity, fanning in every country afresh the flames of ideology."[9]

Roosevelt and Churchill believed that personal diplomacy might forestall such disasters. At face-to-face meetings statesmen could persuade, clarify attitudes, heal rifts, and discern whether the other fellow was trustworthy. After the November–December 1943 Tehran summit, Stalin would agree. Meetings were also occasions for giving and getting respect. In order to reach Tehran, Roosevelt, who hated flying, made the second presidential flight. (The first was his trip to Casablanca.) Churchill endured yet another arduous journey. And Stalin left the Soviet Union for the first time since seizing power. Conferences in far-off places left leaders exhausted and ill. Personal diplomacy also proved emotionally draining. The jealous politics of three's-a-crowd permeated Big Three meetings and telegrams.

Ideology, which remained muted during the war, accounted for only part of the spectrum of cultural differences separating the Allies. The Americans and British each prided themselves as superior in character and civilization to the other. Perceived difference between them paled, however, in comparison with judgments of the Soviets as "primitive" and partly "Asiatic." Bullitt referred to Stalin and his government as the "descendants of Genghis Khan."[10] Whereas Churchill often openly despised the Russians, Roosevelt's bonhomie masked a subtly condescending attitude; indeed this was his attitude toward almost everyone. Stalin and Foreign Minister Molotov suspected "sophisticated" Westerners were trying to cheat them out of the spoils of war after contributing themselves only the minimum to defeat the Germans.

Molotov's Mission to London and Washington

As Hitler's 1942 spring offensive slashed toward Stalingrad and the Caucasus oil fields, Stalin sent Molotov in May–June on a diplomatic mission to London, Washington, and back to London. The visit forced Roosevelt to face a dilemma. He appreciated that a second front in 1942, that is, an invasion of German-held France, would ease Stalin's "loneliness," keep the Soviets in the war, and lessen domestic pressures to focus on avenging Pearl Harbor. Yet an ill-prepared assault against Hitler's fortress could sacrifice hundreds of thousands of troops, as the failed commando raid on Dieppe in August 1942 later demonstrated. Moreover, the venture depended on the British, as so few U.S. soldiers were yet available. Roosevelt also still hoped, somehow, to win over Stalin while not recognizing his 1939–40 grabs of territory. That concession would outrage many Americans and violate the Atlantic Charter. FDR tried to sidestep the Eastern European border issue by having Stalin focus instead on postwar global cooperation by the Big Three.

With this perspective, FDR disparaged Anglo-Soviet negotiations on the pre–June 1941 border as "provincial." In March 1942 he airily told Churchill, "I think I can personally handle Stalin better than either your Foreign Office or my State Department. Stalin hates the guts of all your top people. He thinks he likes me better, and I hope he will continue to do so."[11] At the president's request, Harriman in February had asked Ivan Maisky, the Soviet ambassador to London, "whether it would be possible to arrange a meeting between Roosevelt and Stalin" to eliminate "the distrust between the USA and the USSR, as well as between the USSR and England."[12] Harriman explained that "the President and the Prime Minister had become personally intimate, this intimacy and confidence had come down to the lower levels" of officials, and that Roosevelt wanted to knit similar ties with Stalin.[13] Again in April, Roosevelt reached out while suggesting that the two leaders "spend a few days together next summer near our common border off Alaska." In cozy seclusion they could reach "a meeting of minds in personal conversation." He dangled "a very important military proposal . . . to relieve" the Red Army. "I need your advice" on "the strategic course of our common military action." Unimpressed, Stalin put off such a get together. And, in contrast to FDR's proposed exclusion of the British, Stalin affirmed, "it goes without saying that Molotov will also go to London."[14]

On May 20, 1942, Molotov landed in Britain after a perilous flight across German territory. The Nazis were driving deep into central Russia. Days earlier, a plane carrying Molotov's advance secretary and some Britons had mysteriously caught fire in midair.[15] Molotov told Churchill he had risked the trip because of the "importance of the [second front] question raised by Roosevelt."[16] The PM replied that such an invasion would have to wait until 1943. Soviet armies might not hold out until 1943, Molotov retorted. U.S. objections to the pre–June 1941 border stalled negotiations for an Anglo-Soviet treaty.[17] A discouraged Molotov cabled his boss, "the British do not seem to want to meet us half-way."[18] Then Eden, backed by the Americans, recast the Anglo-Soviet treaty. He offered a twenty-year alliance against Germany. The new treaty ignored the border issue. The unstated premise was that Britain would not try to eject its ally from regained territory.

Stalin seized on the long-term alliance as "important." Nearly engulfed by the second German invasion of his lifetime, he welcomed this guarantee against a third. He also pivoted from seeking the approval of Washington and London for Soviet ambitions to securing those ambitions unilaterally. Eden's formula "is not bad, perhaps, for it gives us a free hand. . . . The security of our frontiers . . . will be decided by force."[19] Instead of telling Winant about Stalin's shift, Molotov stressed that because the new treaty "had been approved by Roosevelt, the Soviet Government would consider it carefully." "This was a definite concession," the ambassador crowed to Roosevelt.[20] FDR mistakenly congratulated himself on having reversed Soviet policy.

Many saw Molotov as a dour workaholic. Lenin had supposedly dubbed him "Comrade Filing Cabinet."[21] He would be the only man in history to shake hands with Lenin, Stalin, Hitler, Roosevelt, and Churchill. His stubbornness in Cold War negotiations would earn him the sobriquet "Mr. No." Yet this die-hard Stalinist, who survived into the era of Mikhail Gorbachev and Ronald Reagan, was not two-dimensional. Before the Revolution he had played the mandolin in restaurants to earn pocket money.[22] He saw diplomacy as entailing not just policies but also "moods."[23] A frugal servant of the "proletarian state," he wore the same drab outfits year after year. Yet he understood the political import of sartorial style, especially to Britons and Americans, who assumed they set the standard for modern civilization. And so as the Russian landed in Britain, Eden found him "in cracking form, all smiles and in a smart brown suit—very different to the usual Molotov."[24] He did, however, revert to form by including in his baggage Russian sausage, dark bread, and a pistol, which he kept under his pillow.

On reaching Washington, he was apparently feeling, in terms of geography and culture, very far from home. In making small talk, he repeated that his journey was "unusual," and along "unusual paths."[25] Hopkins found "it was pretty difficult to break the ice," but not because of "any lack of cordiality and pleasantness on the part of Molotov."[26] Rather, "Roosevelt was unusually uncomfortable, and his style was cramped."[27] Joking later with his friend and Dutchess County neighbor, Daisy Suckley, FDR half-seriously imagined his guest as an exotic Asian: he "comes from Shangri-La and speaks nothing but Mongolian." According to reports, he "is *not* very pleasant, and *never smiles*."[28] Roosevelt took up the challenge to get a smile. He seated Molotov "beside him on the sofa" and—always competitive with Churchill—coyly asked whether he "had enjoyed himself as much in London." Resisting the charm, the envoy replied, yes, that indeed "he had been very agreeably treated." Apparently unfamiliar with the PM's usual post-midnight hours, Molotov boasted that "one evening Mr. Churchill had kept him up talking until 2 a.m."[29]

In competing with Churchill, Roosevelt enjoyed a cultural edge: better plumbing. In his fastidiousness Molotov resembled Cadogan in December 1941, and other visitors to the Soviet Union, who regarded bathroom facilities as signifiers of respect and advanced civilization. Decades later, a resentful Molotov still fumed that at Churchill's estate "there was a bathroom but with no shower." At "Roosevelt's place," however, "everything was as it should be. He had a bathroom with a shower, too."[30] FDR also bested Churchill in dirty jokes. The Russian remained "frozen" until the president "gave him a lot of liquor to drink, then told him an off-color story." Molotov laughed and became "quite human."[31] They put ideological differences aside by sharing in anti-Semitism. Hopkins and Roosevelt explained that Russian Communists had a bad name because American Communists were "disgruntled, frustrated, ineffectual, and vociferous people—including a comparatively high proportion of distinctly unsympathetic Jews." The Russian nodded affably "that there were Communists and

Communists." The trio then agreed on "the distinction between 'Jews' and 'Kikes.'" Hopkins handled a delicate matter by arranging, at Molotov's request, for "one of the girls he brought over as secretaries be permitted to come" to his room in the White House, possibly to take dictation.[32]

Though claiming to be an "ardent supporter" of a second front in 1942, FDR remained ambivalent.[33] As Molotov tried to pin down a "straight answer," Roosevelt left himself wiggle room: "This is our hope. This is our wish."[34] Even General Marshall's unambiguous "Yes" about a second front came in response to an ambiguous query from FDR: Was the United States "preparing a second front"?[35] "Preparing" did not mean delivering. Moreover, "it all depended on the British," Roosevelt warned, as most of the troops would be theirs.[36] Stalin saw some value in the hedged promise. He seems to have considered the game to be more like chess than checkers. Even the appearance of Allied unity could bolster the morale of his hard-pressed people. Molotov later recalled that the unfulfilled pledge made it easier to argue for Lend-Lease aid.[37]

In 1940–41, the president had talked publicly about remaining at peace even as he brought the nation to the brink of war. Similarly, in 1941–45 he talked publicly about an Atlantic Charter peace of self-determination for small nations even as his own thinking evolved toward what he described to Molotov as "peace by dictation."[38] He waited for the proper psychological moment to sell this reality to the American people. He also sought to keep his options open. Tragically, he would never find the moment or the strategy for fully leveling with the American public about his more practical postwar design.

FDR did, however, lay out this design to Molotov. For a transitional period of two to three decades, the United States, Great Britain, the Soviet Union, and, if it unified, China would "act as the policemen of the world." "All other nations save the Big Four should be disarmed." Roosevelt specified not just Germany, Japan, and France, but also Russia's traditionally hostile neighbors, Poland and Turkey. Molotov responded "warmly" to the proposal that "if any nation menaced the peace, it could be blockaded and then, if still recalcitrant, bombed."[39] FDR sought to entice Stalin as a partner by positioning Churchill as the outlier. He said that at Argentia, the prime minister had "had no definite plans" for postwar organization, only another League of Nations, which FDR regarded as a failed concept.[40] Dismissing Britain's "old balance of power theory," he repeated that a "police force" would secure the peace.[41] "Churchill would have to accept this proposal, if the USA and the USSR insisted on it."[42] Reading Molotov's cable, Stalin enthused about this "absolutely sound" design. He agreed that "it would be impossible" to keep the peace without such a "united military force" of the four. "We can do well without" the military power of "Poland, Turkey, and other States." Molotov should tell Roosevelt that he was "absolutely right" and he would be "fully supported by the Soviet Government."[43] In laying out his Four Policemen theory, the president was bidding for Stalin's trust. The plan offered respect to the Soviets as a global partner and as the cop on the beat in Eastern Europe.

Ever the independent thinker, Eleanor Roosevelt pinpointed problems with such a scheme. She asked, "Do you think you could ever sell that to the American people?" Further, "You have more faith in human nature than I have. Even Anglo-Saxon races will become drunk with power and will use this power to bring economic pressure on the smaller nations."[44]

Undeterred, FDR invited Soviet participation in two further long-range projects: dismantling the colonial empires and heading off a "race" war. He believed "there were, all over the world, many islands and colonial possessions which ought, for our own safety, to be taken away from weak nations." That meant not only Japan's Pacific islands, but also perhaps "islands now held by the British." Trusteeships overseen by three to five nations, including the Soviet Union, could prepare colonies for gradual autonomy.[45] As the joke about speaking "only Mongolian" suggested, the president imagined Molotov and other Soviets as part-Asian. Hopkins concurred that "bringing the Russians [and the Chinese] in as equal partners" was vital because "the days of the policy of the 'white man's burden' are over."[46] Ideally, the managerial responsibilities of trusteeships could channel Soviet and Chinese energies toward evolution rather than revolution.[47] Participation in international projects might also relieve the Soviets' "loneliness."

Whether imposed by hostile capitalists or enforced by zealous police, Soviet isolation remained the cultural antithesis of the open economic, political, and social relations that Americans and, to a lesser extent, Britons regarded as normal. U.S. officials believed that improved relations would flow from more open connections and communications—traffic of various kinds. Roosevelt and Hull stressed the "extreme importance" of commercial and military air links via Washington-Basra-Moscow and Alaska-Siberia.[48] Stalin quickly agreed to the military air routes. Cornering Molotov at the Soviet embassy, Vice President Henry Wallace rhapsodized about plans to open travel with auto and air routes "from Buenos Aires through Canada to Alaska and across Siberia and Russia to Europe with branches into China and India." The Russian allowed that such links would develop "in our lifetime."[49]

Molotov tried to escape for a few days into the openness of New York City. On May 30, he notified the *vozhd*: "Three or four days are needed to check the plane's engines. I shall spend this time visiting New York." A different story, however, was told by the American mechanic inspecting the plane: Aside from a blown tire, "everything else about the ship is O.K."[50] It appears the workaholic was trying to squeeze in a vacation, even at the cost of lying to a boss who had few qualms about executing unsatisfactory employees. He told Roosevelt, "I want to go up to New York. . . . I wish you would take these secret service men off my trail." "Have a good time," boomed FDR, who reduced the detail to one agent.[51] Years later Stalin would use Molotov's fling to trump up charges of betrayal. FDR gave "Comrade Filing Cabinet" a showy, even sensuous gift: a large photograph of himself, elegantly framed in green silk, and inscribed in violet ink: "To my friend Vyacheslav Molotov from Franklin Roosevelt, May 30, 1942." The photograph would remain a prized Molotov possession through four decades of the Cold War.[52]

After flying back to London, Molotov tried retailing FDR's vision. The Russian described the president as "completely sympathetic to the idea of opening the second front in 1942." "Roosevelt agreed with me," he emphasized.[53] When he mentioned FDR's talk about sacrificing 120,000 troops in a lunge at France, Churchill "interrupted me in great excitement," exclaiming that he would never risk another Dunkirk, "no matter who recommended" it. The PM disparaged the notion of disarming all but the Four Policemen as "simply impracticable." Not surprisingly, he "utterly opposed" trusteeships. Although careful not to disparage the president as a person, Churchill dismissed his ideas as a "complete fiasco." He pounded home that "it is impossible to bring about the second front this year." For such an assault in 1943, however, he promised "colossal preparations."[54]

In Moscow, Molotov described Churchill as "a grand personality." They had "quickly found common language" and had spoken "not only on political but also nonpolitical questions." The president had impressed with "his intellect, talent, and courtesy. Roosevelt was attractive." They had reached a "mutual understanding"; Roosevelt had "done everything necessary for improving our relations with the United States of America."[55]

Once Molotov departed from London, Churchill flew to Washington to squelch plans for a second front in 1942. Roosevelt was proving slipperier than he had expected. FDR gave nearly everyone the impression he agreed with them. An observer described his emotional energy: "There was a warmth about the man that made you believe that he was trying to help. He was trying to go your way."[56] The personality of this juggler helped him keep many balls in the air. He built up U.S. forces in Britain for an eventual second front—or for a quick cross-Channel landing if the Germans or the Soviets collapsed. Unlike Stalin, who frostily declined Roosevelt's invitation, Churchill leapt at high-level contact.[57] It is a telling detail that the weekend after their talks, Roosevelt and Molotov both traveled to New York, but separately—the envoy to the City and the president to Hyde Park with Princess Martha. Roosevelt and Churchill, in contrast, met at Hyde Park to do business while relaxing. Despite his differences and annoyance with Churchill, Roosevelt felt comfortable with him. These cultural cousins might indeed have met at a London print shop back in 1905. Daisy observed the "real friendship & understanding between F.D.R. and Churchill. F.D.R.'s manner was easy and intimate—entirely *natural*."[58]

Political and military developments also bolstered Churchill's effort to "mix up" the interests of the two nations. Despite Roosevelt's appreciation of the Red Army and Marshall's complaint that Mediterranean operations acted as a "suction pump" that drained resources from the buildup for the second front, both men recognized realities. A sacrificial landing in France would boost Hitler's confidence and the average American's desire for revenge against Japan. Roosevelt did want to bloody his troops against the Germans—but somewhere safer. In June 1942, Britain's abject surrender at Tobruk in Libya to a smaller German-Italian force underscored the need for an Anglo-American invasion of North Africa. This became Operation GYMNAST (later named TORCH). Churchill learned of the embarrassing defeat while in the Oval Office. Roosevelt offered immediate sympathy. "What can we do to help?" He promised three hundred new Sherman tanks, diverted from still underequipped U.S. forces. Such generosity did not assuage Churchill's humiliation. He moaned to Moran, "I am ashamed."[59] He later admitted to Maisky, "The Germans wage war better than we do. . . . Also we lack the 'Russian spirit': die but don't surrender!"[60]

Roosevelt concluded that the psychology and vitality of the British were in decline. He told Wallace that "the British were beginning to develop an inferiority complex." FDR believed that the "United States and Russia are young powers, and England is an old tired power. . . in second place behind the United States, Russia and China."[61] Because the British had transferred to America most of their atomic research effort, FDR promised to share with them future developments in this project, code-named TUBE ALLOYS. Like Roosevelt's pledge to Molotov of a second front, this pledge remained vague and was not honored until much later.

Churchill in Moscow

Temperament, culture, and history brewed volatile emotions between Churchill and Stalin. In July, with the Wehrmacht nearing Stalingrad, the latter appealed desperately for a landing in France. Believing that personal diplomacy could cushion his refusal, the prime minister flew to Moscow. His attitude was reflected in Clementine's reference to "your visit to the Ogre in his Den."[62] Roosevelt sent along Harriman as his representative. Between August 12 and 16, the visitors stayed in Stalin's hideout. What Harriman described as a "comfortable" dacha with "simple furniture," Cadogan found "really rather vulgar!"[63] On the first day of talks, the PM informed the dictator what the latter already knew from his spies and diplomats: Britain and America would not launch a frontal assault on Hitler's Europe in 1942. Stalin tartly responded that "he who does not want to risk will never win the war." He taunted, "You don't have to be scared of the Germans."[64] Stalin grew visibly "glummer." His mood then picked up as Churchill detailed the relentless bombing of workers' housing.[65] Harriman reported that "between the two of them they soon destroyed most of the important industrial cities of Germany."[66]

Churchill then extolled the impending invasion of North Africa. TORCH promised to expel the Germans, secure the Mediterranean, and pressure Italy. The master of metaphor drew a crocodile and then illustrated how the Allies would "attack the soft belly" of the beast. The description was more graphic than geographic, as it ignored the toughness of advancing through mountainous Italy. The prospect of the assault nonetheless aroused Stalin to "a high pitch." The former seminarian declared, "'May God help this enterprise to succeed.'"[67] While tracking Stalin's moods in his notes, the British secretary remained silent about Churchill's. The disparity reflected three apparent assumptions. First, the expressed feelings of Stalin might clue his intentions and convictions. Second, the leader of His Majesty's Government should always remain cool and calm, at least in the official record. Third, emotions were deemed most telling in less civilized people.

In actuality, however, the feelings of both leaders swung wildly. Churchill emerged from his first talk with Stalin saying, "I'd like that man to like me."[68] Complicating that desire were not just political and cultural differences, but also a hunger for respect and a readiness to retaliate with humiliation when that appetite remained unsatisfied.

Back at the dacha, an ebullient Churchill boasted that Stalin amounted to "just a peasant, whom he, Winston, knew exactly how to tackle."[69] Reminded that the room was likely bugged, he bellowed, "The Russians, I have been told, are not human beings at all. They are lower in the scale of nature than the orang-outang. Now then, let them take that down and translate it into Russian."[70] Even discounting the hyperbole and spite, the insult aimed at Russian sensitivity about being regarded as "primitive." Unlike FDR, who had escaped the hatred flowing from the Bolshevik Revolution, Churchill and Stalin remain scarred by it.

Amidst the Kremlin haze of endless toasts, Churchill, putting on his "most twinkling" face, said, "I hope that Mr. Stalin has forgiven me for my past." Stalin, molded by both the seminary and Siberia, gruffly answered: "Who am I to forgive? Only God can forgive." At that point Churchill's happy face "switched off," Clark Kerr observed. The PM rejoined that he had been honest in his hostility. Stalin shot back, "Yes, and I respect open enmity, but not broken commitments from Allies."[71] A British general concluded that Stalin's anger reflected "what the Dictaphone, doubtless concealed in their quarters, had recorded."[72] The dictator lashed out about getting only "remnants" in supplies and about British timidity against the enemy.[73] Churchill's "manners deteriorated." He stormed out. Stalin bolted out of his chair. On gimpy legs he began "trotting in order to keep up with the P.M.'s petulant stride, and talking all the way."[74]

The next day, August 15, witnessed more extreme swings. Even Cadogan voiced surprise at "the violence and depth of the resentment that [Churchill] had worked up." He "was like the bull in the ring maddened by the pricks of the picador."[75] In a cable to the War Cabinet, the PM recounted the dictator's nastiest stab as the slur about "our being too much afraid of fighting the Germans."[76] But he also appeared personally hurt and humiliated. "Stalin did not want to talk to me." Fury bleeding over into disgust, he imagined that "the food was filthy."[77] He petulantly decided to depart without seeing Stalin again. Clark Kerr worried that such a deliberate insult, coming on top of the postponed second front, might goad the temperamental Georgian into another deal with Germany.

Marching up and down the garden of the dacha with "a preposterous ten gallon hat on his head," Churchill kept muttering, "the man has insulted me," and "from now on he will have to fight his battles alone." The ambassador eventually salved his leader's pride by reminding him that while he ranked as "an aristocrat," Soviet leaders came "straight from the plough or the lathe." He must "swallow his pride if only to save young [British] lives." Without the Russians, who would kill Germans? "But I am not a submissive man," he protested.[78] After hours of verbal massage, Clark Kerr got his boss to give Stalin another chance. The dictator had also spent much of the day in pouting. Aides finally set up another meeting.

This time it turned into what Churchill's aide remembered as a "love feast" in the dictator's apartment, lasting over seven hours and ending at 3:00 a.m., shortly before the prime minister departed.[79] Stalin, Churchill, Molotov, Cadogan, and their two interpreters drank bottle after bottle and feasted on enough food, including a suckling pig, "to feed thirty people." The PM relished being "taken into the family" as he met Svetlana, the "red-headed, well-favored" daughter.[80] Churchill and Stalin bonded at another's expense. Churchill, who had apparently heard the story from Roosevelt, tattled that Molotov had faked engine trouble in order to "visit to New York entirely by himself." As the foreign minister stuttered about the need for repairs, Stalin interjected, "It was not to New York he went. He went to Chicago where the other gangsters live."[81] Churchill asked about the kulaks, whom Stalin had starved and exiled. It was "much worse" than even the war, the Kremlin chief admitted. "Ten millions of them. But we had to do it to mechanize our agriculture. What is one generation?"[82] Mesmerized by the sudden intimacy, the PM did not bristle at the brutal rationalization.

Churchill returned to the dacha ecstatic. He lay on the sofa and called for Clark Kerr and Moran. Kicking his legs in the air, he exclaimed, "What a pleasure it was to work with that great man." As he undressed he told them, "Don't go. I want to talk to you." He was apparently trying to prolong the glow by recounting the encounter in another intimate setting. Indulging in what Clark Kerr labeled "exhibitionism," Churchill, cigar in mouth, stripped down to "his skimpy undershirt," from which his "penis and a pair of crinkled, creamy buttocks protruded." He burbled on about "Stalin this, and Stalin that." His *au naturel* monologue on men and war matched his nude or nearly nude discussions in the home of another man of power, Roosevelt. Jacob recorded that even after the boozy elation had given way to a hangover, "the Prime Minister really felt that he had established with Stalin a personal relationship of the same kind as he had already built up with President Roosevelt."[83] Molotov reported that Stalin's intimate meeting had fostered "close personal rapport with the guest."[84]

The get-together illustrated the potential dynamics of meeting in pairs. Three would have been a crowd. Harriman had even seized a moment with Stalin to press the "great importance" of a bilateral meeting with Roosevelt.[85] The PM's comment to Jacob that his relationship with Stalin was "of the same kind" as his tie with the president suggests that Churchill's "special relationship" with Roosevelt was not totally sui generis. (Notably, only a day after FDR's death, Churchill would offer Truman the same "intimate comradeship" that supposedly had taken years to forge with Roosevelt.)[86] Although the quarreling and reconciliation of the PM and the dictator sparked male bonding, the excitement dissipated, as it did after other wartime summits. Lingering resentment from the time of the Revolution, traditional Anglo-Russian imperial rivalry, and Churchill's racial stereotyping eroded most of the good feeling. But not all. At subsequent summits and even after the Cold War broke out, Churchill would again and again return to the belief that he and Stalin, man-to-man, could reach a political settlement.[87]

Even if Churchill's promise in Moscow of a second front in 1943 actually came about, Roosevelt faced a range of thorny problems. He disliked using U.S. forces to rescue the British Empire. He had to "get-at" Stalin personally in order to convince him that the United States was trustworthy in terms of joining the battle against Germany. He also hoped to enlist the Soviets in the war against Japan. He needed to reconcile the Kremlin's territorial claims with the American public's expectations of a peace based on political self-determination. He had to head off the nightmare of Stalin's getting fed up and negotiating a separate peace with Hitler. Roosevelt's closest aides were diminishing in number and in strength. Hopkins's precarious health limited what he could do. Harry's wedding to Louise Macy in July 1942 added the complication of three households vying for control in the White House. Meanwhile, Welles came under all-out assault from Bullitt and Hull.

Roosevelt also faced some new implications of his old struggle with paralysis. Given Stalin's reluctance to travel far beyond the Soviet Union, FDR had to fly in order to wield his charm. Plane trips could be agonizing because his paralyzed legs did not brace him in a wind-buffeted plane. Moreover, his lifetime terror was fire, and he had little chance of escaping a burning plane.[88] As Sherwood wrote, it was "generally assumed that the President's infirmity made it impossible for him to travel such great distances."[89] As Stalin told Harriman in August 1942, "It is the President's health that should concern us."[90] Nevertheless, the dictator would resist leaving the Soviet Union.

Casablanca and Marrakech, January 1943

After the TORCH landings in North Africa on November 8, 1942, decision making grew pressing. FDR favored meeting at an oasis in North Africa, explaining, "I don't like mosquitoes." Churchill pressed for U.S. military advisers to stop off first in London. Still hoping the Soviet chief might attend, FDR put Churchill off. "I do not want to give Stalin the impression that we are settling everything between ourselves before we meet him." In Rooseveltian form, he added, "you and I understand each other so well that prior conferences between us are unnecessary."[91] To Daisy, he confided a different rationale. He outlined his program for "an international police force" run by the Big Four, disarmament for others, and gradual independence for colonies. He predicted, "Stalin will understand this plan better than Churchill."[92] On December 5, the Soviet leader cabled that the ongoing battle of Stalingrad prevented his leaving for even a single day.

Undaunted, FDR expected the trip to Africa to "do me personally an enormous amount of good."[93] Boyish spirit abounded. Roosevelt cabled Churchill that he was taking the code name Don Quixote. Hopkins would be Sancho Panza. Moran observed that neither FDR nor Churchill "has ever grown up."[94] In preparing for their adventure, the president and his aide spent New Year's Eve watching a new romance, *Casablanca*. The air trip marked the first time any president had flown so far, and FDR's first flight since 1932.

Roosevelt and Churchill met at Anfa, outside the Moroccan city of Casablanca, from January 14 to 23, 1943. Discussions focused on where to send forces after clearing the Germans and Italians from North Africa. Complicating that decision were shortages of landing craft, sinkings by U-boats, the promise to Stalin of a cross-channel invasion in 1943, Churchill's horror of repeating the slaughter of 1914–18, and quarreling among the Americans. Marshall favored a second front to tackle the Germans head on and honor the pledge to Stalin. He faulted the British as "extremely fearful of any direct action against the continent until a decided crack in the German efficiency and morale."[95] Some U.S. brass wanted to focus on the Mediterranean and Pacific theaters.

Roosevelt remained uncertain. Alanbrooke charged that "Marshall has got practically no strategic vision."[96] As at previous conferences, British unity and superior staff work prevailed. A U.S. Army planner noted bitterly, "We came, we listened and we were conquered."[97] Roosevelt ended up concurring with Churchill that in 1943 they would invade Sicily, build up forces in Britain for a second front late in the year or in 1944, and supply the Soviets and operations in the Pacific. If the Germans or the Russians suddenly cracked, forces in Britain would leap onto the Continent. The PM hoped to hit the Germans from other points in the Mediterranean. He would then drive up through the Balkans, possibly cutting off the westward advance of the Red Army.

Casablanca became famous for two further developments. First was Churchill's and Roosevelt's brokering of a shaky accord between rival French generals, Henri Giraud and Charles de Gaulle. Second was FDR's statement at a joint press conference that the Allies would fight until the "unconditional surrender" of the Axis. Although unconditional surrender had won a nod from the PM and the War Cabinet,

5.1. FDR cutting birthday cake aboard plane en route to the January 1943 Casablanca conference. Hopkins sits opposite the "Boss"; Admiral William Leahy is to his right. (Courtesy of FDR Library.)

it countered centuries of British preference for a balance of power. A draconian peace would destroy German and Japanese capability to balance the Soviets. Indeed, within months of Casablanca, British postwar planners were proposing to arm the Germans against the Russians. Such plans would surely infuriate Stalin, whose spies riddled the Foreign Office.

Roosevelt's espousal of a draconian peace reflected his bid for Stalin's trust and his acquiescence to Soviet preeminence in Eastern and Central Europe. The policy also aimed at heading off a feared separate peace between Berlin and Moscow. On January 24, the president spoke to the fifty newsmen sitting on the grass outside his villa. He framed "unconditional surrender," with all its international consequences, as homespun American. He recalled the "old story—we had a General called U.S. Grant . . . he was called 'Unconditional Surrender' Grant."[98] Roosevelt appreciated that harsh terms could quiet complaints about the post-TORCH deal with the Vichyite Admiral François Darlan to secure a quick French surrender. No more such trafficking with the enemy.

Churchill and Roosevelt each regarded closer ties as a means of influence. The prime minister assured journalists that he and the president were "in this [war] as friends and partners."[99] Roosevelt enthused that the military leaders of the two nations have been "in intimate touch; they have lived in the same hotel. Each man has become a definite personal friend of his opposite number."[100] Jacob explained, "British and Americans met round the bar, went for walks down to the beach together, and sat about in each other's rooms in the evenings. Mutual respect and understanding ripen in such surroundings, especially when the weather is lovely, the accommodation is good, and good food and drink and smokes are unlimited and free."[101] The Soviets also sought "mutual respect" with their Allies. Yet the Kremlin's closed-door political culture, coupled with the language barrier, stifled informal contact and the satisfaction of shared esteem.

The president and the PM enjoyed luxurious, indeed sensual, quarters. At first, Churchill's villa lacked sufficient hot water for his bath. "The end of the world had come," Jacob wryly observed.[102] Meanwhile, FDR in his villa delighted in the "most beautiful bedroom he ever had, and the most beautiful bed."[103] His room had belonged to a "very feminine French lady. Plenty of drapes, plenty of frills."[104] He quipped to his body guard, "Mike, what did you do with the madame and the red curtains?"[105] Nearby was a library filled with pornography.[106]

Just as FDR had tried to lure Stalin to a secluded getaway, Churchill invited Roosevelt. After the conference, a 150-mile trek by automobile brought them to the ancient city of Marrakech, a favorite getaway for the prime minister. They stayed at Flower Villa as guests of U.S. Vice Consul Kenneth Pendar. Even the president's official log gushed about this "most beautiful" villa, set in a Garden of Eden and "furnished in splendor befitting a Sultan."[107]

When Churchill suggested climbing the tower of the villa for the magnificent view of the snow-covered Atlas Mountains, FDR readily agreed. Two of his men made a chair with their arms and carried him up the sixty steps, "his legs dangling like the limbs of a ventriloquist's dummy, limp and flaccid," Moran recorded. The setting sun lit the snowy mountains with a pink glow. Churchill murmured, "It's the most lovely spot in the whole world."[108] Also moved was Roosevelt, who later described the view as "the most breath-takingly beautiful he had ever seen."[109] As the temperature sank, Churchill spread a coat over Roosevelt's shoulders. FDR interpreted his paralysis as impelling not pity but rather homage. That evening he stretched out on the couch, and as Pendar approached, he smiled and said, "I am the Pasha, you may kiss my hand."

He regaled the dinner party with his knowledge of the Arabic world, including "the conflict of Koranic law with our type of modern life."[110] Ignoring Churchill's discomfort, he recalled his advice to the sultan of Morocco to assert independence from his French colonial masters. He ignored the PM's bid for a confidential discussion. Harriman later recalled, "Roosevelt rather liked the idea that he did not have to go through with this talk. He always enjoyed other people's discomfort."[111] Perhaps because Churchill had won on strategic matters, Roosevelt felt compelled to assert personal dominance. Or perhaps he was thinking more and more about the colonial issue. In any case, while calling Churchill "Winston," FDR allowed the latter to address him as "Mr. President." Roosevelt tried to control even their goodbye. "Now, Winston, don't you get up in the morning to see me off. I'll be wheeled into your room to kiss you goodbye."[112]

Nonetheless, the next morning Churchill—arrayed in black velvet slippers monogrammed "W.C.," a blue air marshal's cap, and a bathrobe patterned with red dragons—accompanied FDR to the airport. As the president's plane took off, Churchill took Pendar's arm, saying, "If anything should happen to that man, I couldn't stand it. He is the truest friend; he has the farthest vision; he is the greatest man I've ever known."[113] Churchill reclimbed the tower, trying to capture on canvas the view and the intimacy with Roosevelt.

Churchill seemed passionate about both friendship and empire. He interrupted the painting, which he would give to Roosevelt, to vow, "I shall, with the last drop of energy I have in me, defend His Majesty's Empire" from "dismemberment."[114] A few months later, Daisy Suckley observed that the PM "*adores* the P[resident], loves him, as a man, looks up to him, defers to him, leans on him."[115]

Roosevelt increasingly detested colonialism. As his plane refueled in Bathurst, British West Africa, he fumed at the failure to develop "this awful, pestiferous hole." He later described the "crowds of semi-dressed natives—thatched huts—great poverty and emaciation."[116] Elliott recalled that when reminded that the Europeans did have legal title to their colonies, FDR exploded: "'I'm talking about another war, Elliott,' Father cried, his voice suddenly sharp. 'I'm talking about what will happen to our world, if after *this* war we allow millions of people to slide back into the same semi-slavery!'"[117] Once, as FDR was sorting some stamps, Churchill asked where they were from. "One of your colonies." "Which one?" "One of your last. You won't have them very much longer, you know."[118] After returning to Washington, Roosevelt lectured reporters that centuries of colonial rule had not resulted in "very much progress."[119] He apprehended colonized peoples as potentially dangerous, even in their sexuality. FDR told a senator "about native women in Africa, their tits, how long it took men to get over gonorrhea."[120] He himself had caught a disease, or believed he had. To Churchill he groused, "I think I picked up sleeping sickness or Gambia fever or some kindred bug in that hell-hole of yours called Bathurst. It laid me low." Then, softening his tone, he inquired about the PM's health.[121]

Travel exacted a heavy toll. The strains of the summit had lowered the resistance of Churchill, who grew "quite seriously ill with pneumonia."[122] Afterward he remained "thinner and older looking."[123] Even before Bathurst, FDR had suffered "a bad cough and look[ed] very worn."[124] Flying disturbed his sinuses and his balance. "I *don't* like flying!" he told newsmen after returning. "The more I do of it, the less I like it."[125] (He had logged 17,989 miles, with nearly 107 hours in the air.)[126]

FDR also paid an emotional cost. In Morocco he reviewed U.S. troops who "were headed up for the front fairly soon." The sight brought Roosevelt, who rarely cried, "closer to having tears in my eyes than at any other time."[127] After witnessing the slaughter of 1918, he never again glorified war. (Shown a picture of a surgical operation, he had "turned it over quickly and said he couldn't bear to look at it.")[128] Wartime leadership proved a killing job in part because Roosevelt could not look away from the suffering and death resulting from his orders, however necessary.

Roosevelt's insistence on unconditional surrender spoke to Soviet fears that Washington and London might make a separate peace with Berlin. Only days before FDR's statement, Maisky wrote in his diary that America remained the "weakest link" in the unity of the Big Three. He agreed with former prime minister David Lloyd George that "the USA hopes to seize (de facto or perhaps de jure) . . . French Africa, the Dutch Indies, and possibly Australia." While securing this "Great American Empire," the Americans might never, the Russian feared, commit enough resources to launch a second front in Europe. Worse, a conservative Republican might beat Roosevelt in the next election.[129]

Postwar Planning and the Battle over Welles

In the hectic months from Casablanca in January 1943 to the election in November 1944, Roosevelt would devote himself to building a strong link with Stalin, preparing the American people for the realities demanded by a Three (or Four) Policemen peace, and winning reelection. Regarding the "Great American Empire," he aimed not for de jure colonialism, which he detested, but rather a mostly open, postcolonial world that would welcome U.S. business and values. Insofar as average Americans thought about foreign policy, they favored the self-determination of small nations over the interests of powerful states, unless, of course, U.S. interests were at stake. Four months before Pearl Harbor, Roosevelt had pitched the Atlantic Charter to this sentiment. Uncertain whether America would ever enter the fighting, he had used the charter to justify a de facto alliance with Britain.

For the rest of his presidency, he would struggle to fit the square peg of the Four Policemen approach into the round hole of the Atlantic Charter. Having witnessed President Wilson's debacle in 1919–20, FDR concluded that his predecessor "had committed the unforgivable sin of not preparing" American opinion. "History would not forgive" Wilson "for his bungling of the League of Nations—allowing it to become a political issue." Failure had stemmed also from the president's "illness. Wilson had a stroke in Paris," Roosevelt told newsmen.[130] FDR decided that Wilson had erred in miring discussion of the League in fights over specific articles. He, in contrast, determined to stick with the big picture. Roosevelt breezed to journalists, "Well, as to details, I have no idea, it isn't worth talking about."[131]

On the toughest detail, the Soviets' pre–June 1941 border, Roosevelt began publicly backpedaling from the charter's pledge of self-determination. In March 1943, after Bullitt publicly demanded that Moscow live up to the code, Hopkins informed a journalist that the president opposed using that "stick . . . to beat Russia. When Russia signed the Charter, nobody told her that this meant she would have to give up [the] Baltic States and Bessarabia, etc. . . . We have to be realistic if we are going to have any peace at all."[132] Referring to the Atlantic Charter, Roosevelt in July 1943 told reporters that "common sense" dictated treating such moral principles as "a long-range thing."[133] In September, he disparaged Wilson's precedent, charging that "people are awfully . . . immature" in expecting "an immediate peace conference" or "a great treaty signed." Instead, he alerted, "there will be a transition period."[134]

Gradual change over a period of years would enable flexible diplomacy. Roosevelt predicted, "the victors will maintain the peace during that transition period, and they will try out things." They would police their respective beats, "meeting, watching, ready to maintain peace by force if necessary."[135] Even if the president expected, as he later told Churchill and Stalin, U.S. troops to withdraw from Germany within two years after victory, Russia and Britain would guard Europe while Americans patrolled the Western Hemisphere, parts of Asia, and much of the sea. To prepare for this responsibility Roosevelt was overseeing construction of the world's largest navy and air force and a global network of air and naval bases.

Roosevelt's occasional drum beats did not, however, amount to an all-out campaign to educate the America public. Welles remained confident that the "Boss" would make "speeches to the country when the

time comes. He had an astounding sense of timing for such matters."[136] But Roosevelt never would find the right time or the energy
for such a blitz. Frances Perkins, who had observed him for decades,
pointed to another problem, FDR's difficulty in turning his "flashes of
almost clairvoyant knowledge and understanding of a terrific variety
of matters that didn't seem to have any particular relationship to each
other" into practical policies.[137]

Hubris seduced the thrice-elected president into assuming that he,
Hopkins, and Welles could take on postwar planning while also running the war. A result was that the State and War Departments pursued their own planning, often at odds with Roosevelt's vision.[138] A
month after Casablanca, Hopkins confided to the journalist Raymond
Clapper what Roosevelt was saying "during evening talks." The
"Boss" had waxed "extremely confident of himself"—perhaps over-
confident.[139] Hopkins, however, believed Roosevelt needed help. So
far, the president was "discussing many details of postwar, but putting
nothing on paper and nothing seems to be crystallizing."[140] With his
inner circle nearly drained, FDR was turning yet again to his live-in
aide. Clapper observed, that "Hopkins [is] obviously being pulled
deeply into post-war planning as a hand-holder for Roosevelt, but
[he] himself seems to feel some hesitation about breaking away from
military stuff which he has now mastered . . . whereas post-war would
require whole new field of reading and personal contacts."[141] No
wonder Harry hesitated. Daisy described him as "sick—white, blue
around the eyes, with red spots on his cheek bones."[142]

The frailty of Harry Hopkins magnified the tragedy of Sumner
Welles. The Argentine ambassador marveled, "What an amazing
grasp of many things Sumner has. He is so concrete, so exact." Hull,
in contrast, "is always vague, so full of ideals, and in the sky somewhere."[143] Welles's ability and glacial bearing led an insider to conclude that he was "*the* Department; the dictator . . . undisputed and
supreme."[144] FDR relied on Welles more than on Hull for planning a
United Nations organization that would allow for the dominance of
the Big Three (or Four).[145] These responsibilities proved exhausting.

Mathilde Welles noted in her journal the "trying, nerve-wracking
days," and nights when her husband, telephoned by the president or

5.2. Hopkins and W. Averell Harriman at the Tehran conference. Within a month, the Hopkins family would move out of the White House, and Harry would enter the hospital for a long stay that failed to repair his health. (Courtesy of FDR Library.)

the State Department "would dress hurriedly and dash into town, sometimes well after 2 a.m." The tightly wound workaholic sought release through binge drinking. Late one night, Mathilde left him a despairing note: "Why do you have to go to stag dinners and Mr. Hull doesn't. . . . You are killing my love for you. I know you cannot stop drinking."[146]

In 1943, just as postwar planning was becoming critical, Welles suffered all-out assault from Bullitt and Hull. The attackers were driven to fury by Roosevelt-inflicted humiliations and by their own homophobia. The president dangled before Bullitt top posts that never quite materialized. He bypassed Hull for Welles. Bullitt wanted Welles's job. Hull wanted to wreck Welles's authority. FDR Jr. and Tommy Corcoran believed Roosevelt, in addition to faulting the former ambassador for failing to stay with the fleeing French government in 1940, was exacting vengeance for Bullitt's years-long affair with Missy LeHand.

Hull wailed that he "knew nothing whatsoever about the President's thoughts on major issues of foreign policy."[147] Indeed, FDR treated him like a "mummy," to be kept in a museum case until brought out to get a peace treaty ratified by the Senate.[148] Hull ranted that "the President was going crazy"; he "was increasingly surrounded by crazy men whose whole idea was to rebuild every country except America."[149] He pleaded to Roosevelt about Welles, "For God's sake, get rid of this degenerate!" FDR, by the standards of his time, was not homophobic. He replied that Welles did good work, adding, cryptically, "Napoleon was a degenerate too."[150] Bullitt asserted that youthful homosexuality explained FDR's loyalty to Welles. He asserted, falsely, that the two "had been extremely intimate when Welles was a small boy and the President was an older boy, and Welles spent most of his summers at Campobello in the President's mother's house."[151] Ironically, Bullitt himself had lived with his aide, Carmel Offie, who had a record of arrests for soliciting homosexual sex.

Another irony was that while Hull resented Welles's work, the secretary lacked the energy to do much himself. The Mexican ambassador complained that Hull "is always 'preaching' and never has a clear or practical knowledge of our problems"; in contrast, "Sumner does."[152] The secretary of state had spent much of the previous two years in Florida recuperating from tuberculosis.[153]

Caught in the cross fire was Courtney Letts de Espil, the glamorous, U.S.-born wife of the Argentine ambassador. She had befriended both Mathilde Welles and Frances Hull. (A Roosevelt favorite, de Espil found herself gazing at this "truly handsome" president and fantasizing that he could "have been loved by, and have been in love with, a beautiful woman.")[154] Mathilde Welles confided to de Espil that Hull seemed on the brink of "mental breakdown. . . . He can't sleep and paces the floor all night."[155] Frances Hull, speaking of Welles, countered: "It is *that man*, Courtney." That "beast . . . does the most terrible things to my husband. That is why he was ill [and] why I haven't been well."[156] Though torn, de Espil pinpointed the major "tragedy" as the jettisoning of Welles, who commanded more knowledge in "the tip of his finger than the whole rest of the [State] department put together."[157]

In 1943, the Hulls and Bullitt escalated their attack. Frances Hull actually asked Bullitt, "'Won't you shoot that man for me?'"[158] The secretary of state warned the president, "Every time that a Senator sees Welles and thinks of his degeneracy, he gets mad." Ratifying a peace treaty "would be impossible" with that man in office.[159] Goaded, the president staged a showdown with Bullitt in the Oval Office. He began with the accusation that "[y]ou have ruined Welles's reputation and his life." In response, Bullitt staunchly claimed that Welles was shaping "policies for which you are asking our soldiers to die. . . . Every one of those soldiers, if he knew what Welles was, would spit on him." FDR countered, "What if he does behave that way when he has been drinking? Your talking about Welles has been unchristian." "Balls," Bullitt shot back.[160] Roosevelt "was raving after Bullitt left his office," a stenographer remembered, "raving!" Roosevelt raged that while Welles would go to heaven, Bullitt, who had "destroyed a fellow human being, would be sent to Hell."[161]

Bullitt went public with ugly insinuations that would in the 1950s be amplified by Senator Joseph McCarthy. He smeared efforts to get along with the Soviets as evidencing a deficiency in manliness, heterosexuality, and vigor. To a reporter for *Time* Bullitt said Welles, because of his homosexual indiscretions, was being blackmailed into "playing the Russians' hand." The president was "almost abasing" himself in seeking to meet with Stalin. Roosevelt relied on Hopkins, who, as a social worker, "is used to giving things away to . . . make people love you." With innuendo about a craven desire to be loved, Bullitt charged that "all [Stalin] had to do with Harry was slap him on the back, and he had him." Switching to a metaphor of debility, he warned that "Harry's imbecilic" policies only rendered the Russians "more hostile."[162] Stories about Welles's indiscretion circled the country.[163]

The boxed-in president dared not risk repeating Wilson's fiasco in the Senate. In August 1943, he reluctantly asked Welles to resign.[164] Yet Roosevelt was famous for exacting vengeance. On September 9, in what may have been the result of a White House–inspired sting, FBI director J. Edgar Hoover received a report that "Carmel Offie, Secretary to William C. Bullitt, was picked up in Lafayette Park by the police for being a pervert."[165] However sweet his revenge, the president still had to handle the crisis over Poland without Welles and, after December 1943, without Hopkins.

In 1944–45, the Soviets' brutal domination of Poland would spark moral revulsion in Britain and America, undermining the wartime alliance. Before then, however, many in London and Washington regarded the Russian-Polish quarrel as an ancient struggle, with authoritarians and avarice on both sides, that threatened more war. A British official in Washington asked, "Can you wonder that the Russians are getting a little cagey when it is so obvious that leading Polish politicians are only waiting their time in order to turn the Polish Army against the Russians?"[166] The Polish prime minister-in-exile in London advised Harriman "that the only thing that will settle Polish relations with the Soviet Union will be a war between the Soviet Union and the United States and Great Britain, with the latter countries on Poland's side."[167] When told about the ambition for "a port on the Black Sea for Poland," Welles replied that "the Poles were the most impossible people in the world to deal with except, perhaps, the Rumanians." Disdainful also of the ambitious French general, Charles de Gaulle, he and Roosevelt did not "believe that any of the governments-in-exile should be pitchforked into any European countries after the war." Liberated nations would instead be occupied by "disinterested forces, like troops from Arkansas," then hold plebiscites.[168] Welles criticized the landholding elites dominating the London Polish government, who opposed reforms. "That is the real issue," he argued.[169] Roosevelt grumbled that he was "tired of hearing about 'national honor' from little nations."[170] The exiled government was mobilizing voters in U.S. states "with large Polish populations," Winant reported.[171] Hopkins noted that "close to a million dollars a year are being spent for propaganda in this country. The Polish propaganda booklets are handsome, done on very fine paper, despite the shortage."[172]

Shortly before Tehran, FDR emphasized to a British guest, Lieutenant Miles, that he would not choose Poland over Russia. The president probably intended the blunt talk to reach Churchill and Eden, who did read the transcript.[173] And perhaps Stalin read it, too, courtesy of his spies in the Foreign Office. Roosevelt mocked Churchill for contesting the Soviets in the Balkans, questioning the region's significance. When "Winston asks me about his sphere of influence in the Balkans, I tell him, now don't let's have another headache there." The British would never get "a penny out of" it. Regarding the London Polish government, FDR said, "I am sick and tired of these people. The Polish Ambassador came to see me a while ago about this question. (The President here mimicked the Ambassador). 'Please Mr. President . . . etc., etc.' I said, do you think [the Russians] will just stop to please you, or us for that matter? Do you expect us and Great Britain to declare war on Joe Stalin if they cross your previous frontier?" "What is more," Roosevelt added, "I'm not sure that a fair plebiscite, if there ever was such a thing, would not show that those eastern provinces would not prefer to go back to Russia. Yes, I really think those 1941 frontiers are as just as any." While FDR believed that Lvov "should go to Poland," the "rest of the area was Russian first, and all those Baltic republics are as good as Russian." The "President had quite made up his mind on these problems."

By late 1943, Roosevelt looked to the Four Policemen as the practical, desirable postwar arrangement. The Atlantic Charter, in contrast, figured as window dressing and a long-term ideal. He told Miles: "You can't invoke high moral principles where high moral principles do not exist. In international politics they don't always apply, unfortunately, and our job is to win the war." Yet the charter could keep the "public sold on" an active postwar policy.[174] And, Roosevelt being Roosevelt, he preferred keeping his options open.

He pushed this two-sided strategy at the Moscow foreign ministers conference in October, and at his summit with Stalin and Churchill, November 28– December 1. To Moscow he sent Hull, who signed the Four-Nation Declaration, which advocated an international organization open to all nations.[175] Despite his shaky health, Hull, pleased at finally attending a major Allied conference, stepped onto an airplane for the first time. Word on the diplomatic cocktail circuit was that many were "betting he will never come back alive."[176]

Roosevelt persisted in trying to get-at Stalin in a meeting face-to-face. In May, he had former ambassador Davies deliver to Stalin a handwritten invitation. Though Davies served as an errand boy and reporter, he never wielded the clout of Hopkins or Welles. He was tapped for this mission because he had preserved good relations with the Soviets even through the ghastly purge trials. In Washington he socialized with Soviet representatives. The letter to Stalin proposed "a meeting of the minds"—without Churchill—"either on your side or my side of Bering Straits." FDR believed his charm could work best in "some place remote."[177] He even suggested a private code for further communication.

On June 3, Davies reported that in eleven hours of talk he had chipped away at Stalin's suspicions. The dictator had concluded that delays in the second front were intentional and that Roosevelt supported "the classic British foreign policy of walling Russia in, closing the Dardanelles, and building a countervailing balance of power against Russia."[178] He expected "reciprocity and respect" from allies. Despite his favoring postwar cooperation, he would go it alone if necessary to secure the June 1941 border and "friendly" governments in Poland, Finland, and Romania. "Democracy" in those nations "could be of the British or United States type," Stalin explained. These neighbors could have a "defense pact with the Soviet Union and with each other, and with the Western nations as well." His only requirement, he repeated, was governments genuinely not "hostile to Russia."[179] Many in Britain and in America also believed, or hoped, that compromises could be struck in postwar Poland and neighboring states making possible governments that were genuinely independent and "friendly" to Russia. Stalin told Davies, "Your President is a great man. I will be very glad to meet with him." With regard to a conference in Siberia, the Kremlin boss, making a show of apparent empathy, said, "No. The President has difficulty in walking, as I understand. It is difficult for me, physically, to come by air, but I will be glad to meet him at Nome or Fairbanks, whichever he prefers. This will make it easier for him."[180]

Within days, however, Stalin was probably cursing the very notion of a cozy meeting. He learned that at the May 1943 TRIDENT meeting, the prime minister for the third time since mid-1942 had convinced the president to postpone the second front. Marshall was also furious. After the July invasion of Sicily, Anglo-American armies would invade the Italian boot. Roosevelt did, however, wrest a commitment to launch the second front on May 1, 1944. When Churchill initially resisted even that date, FDR told the "spoiled boy" to "shut up."[181] Stalin angrily cancelled the Nome meeting without bothering with Roosevelt's secret code. Posing as the only war leader with the mud of battle on his boots, he claimed, "I have frequently to go to the different parts of the front."[182] In reality, he ventured forth only once, and then to a quiet sector. Even the possibility of an exclusive Roosevelt-Stalin meeting threatened Churchill. The future was "loaded with danger," he warned FDR. "The only hope is the intimacy and friendship which has been established between us and between our high staffs."[183]

After getting Roosevelt to agree to meet in Cairo before the Big Three Tehran summit, the PM cast it as Casablanca redux. Invoking the memory of Marrakech, he enthused about the "beautiful villa" near the Sphinx and the "very interesting excursions into the desert which we could make together."[184] FDR accepted, though he jinxed the intimacy by also inviting Generalissimo and Madame (the "Missimo") Jiang Jieshi.

Tehran

At Tehran FDR finally got his chance to "get-at" Stalin. Hopkins explained that "Roosevelt could say things to Stalin which . . . the President would not allow anyone else to say for him."[185] More of a talker than a writer and a keeper of secrets, Roosevelt left few diary fragments. Yet what he called his "Odyssey" so excited him that he simply had to record it. As a boy, he had written an award-winning essay in Latin. Traveling to Tehran, he again imagined himself as "the hardy

Trojan whose name I used to take at Groton." He expected that he, like Aeneas, could triumph with wit, charm, and other power.[186] His "Rome," would be a peaceful postwar order open to expanding U.S. influence and gradual colonial independence, all secured by cooperation among the Four Policemen. Such self-assurance, even self-delusion, was dangerous in anyone commanding a nation as powerful as the United States. Yet Roosevelt moderated his confidence with his flexibility in means.

In the months before Tehran, the Red Army won smashing victories, retaking Kharkov, Smolensk, and Kiev. Kremlin fashion shifted further from proletarian to imperial. Red Army officers sported gold braid and epaulets reminiscent of czarist times. Stalin, who had gained weight and had greyed under the strain, decided his simple tunic no longer sufficed. Sergo Beria recalled that the *vozhd* kept altering uniforms in seeking something "impressive without being ostentatious."[187]

Stalin and Molotov went all out in demonstrating their friendliness at the October 1943 Moscow foreign ministers conference.[188] Before Hull could even ask, Stalin offered to join the war against Japan after Germany's defeat. Harriman cabled FDR that Molotov "showed increasing enjoyment in being a full member with the British and ourselves."[189] Hull returned from Moscow seeing few barriers to cooperation. He even declared that "any American having Stalin's personality and approach might well reach high public office."[190]

From Moscow, Eden seemed genuinely touched by Stalin's readiness to make the three-way alliance much tighter. He urged Churchill to drop objections to full-fledged participation by Soviet officers in a meeting of the Anglo-American Combined Chiefs of Staff. Stalin and Molotov "really have shown a desire to understand our problems." Now was the time, Eden pleaded; "nothing of this kind has ever been offered us before." Opportunity beckoned. If you were in Moscow, "you would soon have the Russians eating out of your hand." Referring to Soviet sensibilities, Eden emphasized how "essential" it was that "the Russians should not feel that they have been deliberately left out." Churchill, however, remained cold to deeper three-way collaboration. A limited triple conference was acceptable. But admitting what he termed "an irresponsible Russian observer" to a meeting on "purely Anglo-American operations would be most injurious," the PM insisted.[191]

In contrast to Churchill, Roosevelt contoured his diplomacy so as to fit the emotional disposition of the Russians. The aplomb of the Hudson River aristocrat freed him from the anxiety of having to assess every interaction for maximum prestige. Stalin's refusal to journey farther than Tehran required FDR to travel some six thousand miles. Roosevelt commented that Russia had grown so "strong, that she can impose her will, & must be treated *at least* as an equal." Years later, when Truman and every other Cold War president confronted such arrogance, they would bristle and respond with counterdemands. Looking deeper, however, Roosevelt saw that Stalin "may be too anxious to prove his point. . . . Stalin suffered from an inferiority complex."[192] The president calculated that playing up to the former revolutionary's craving for respect could reap substantive gains. As Hopkins would remark at Tehran, FDR "had spent his life managing men."[193] The columnist Walter Lippmann later explained that "Roosevelt was a cynical man. . . . [W]hat he thought he could do was outwit Stalin."[194]

FDR's "Odyssey" did prove an adventure. The president avoided another transatlantic flight by boarding the battleship *USS Iowa*, commanded by his former naval aide, Admiral John L. McCrea. During a drill, an escort ship accidentally fired a torpedo at the *Iowa*. McCrea recorded that as he ordered "Right full rudder—all engines ahead full" and the ship swerved, Roosevelt flung out his arm to grab hold.[195] His powerful upper body could not have stabilized him in an airplane. After a conference with Churchill and the Jiangs in Cairo, Roosevelt on November 27 took off for Tehran. Flying over "bare looking" terrain, he focused briefly on the smoldering conflict between Jews and Arabs. "I *don't want* Palestine as my homeland," he jotted in his diary.[196] (In addition to dozens of mystery novels such as *The Trapper of Rat River*, he had brought along travel guides about the Middle East.)[197]

At the U.S. legation, which lay four miles from the British and Soviet embassies and the conference site, Roosevelt heard that German agents were plotting assassination. Traveling across the city could prove deadly. Stalin invited him into the Soviet embassy while he shifted to a smaller building nearby. The president "enjoyed the cloak-and-dagger adventure," naval aide William M. Rigdon later recalled.[198] Roosevelt later explained that moving to the embassy of the Soviets "was a small thing to do to please them. . . . If we could woo them in this way, perhaps it was the cheapest thing we could do." He added, "It was a matter of exhibiting my trust in them, my complete confidence in them. And it did please them. No question about it."[199]

One reason it pleased the Soviets was that they had bugged Roosevelt's quarters.[200] Just as FDR had tried to lure the Kremlin chief to Alaska, and Churchill had enticed the president to Marrakech, now Stalin was seeking close relations—Kremlin style. He assigned young Beria to transcribe everything FDR and his associates said. Breaking his routine, he rose early to pose "very detailed questions about Roosevelt's conversations." Attitudes seemed important: he demanded to know "how Roosevelt said something—even what his intonation was."[201] Little wonder that Lord Alanbrooke judged Stalin the most prepared leader of the three.[202] U.S. officials expected to find "*all* rooms and places of tete-a-tetes wired for recordings."[203] FDR reacted to this invasion of privacy, which could be interpreted as a sign of disrespect, differently than the PM had in August 1942. Back then an incensed Churchill had bellowed into the walls that Russians ranked lower than apes. FDR apparently seized the chance to build trust. Beria got "the impression that sometimes Roosevelt quite simply said things [into the microphones] he couldn't say to Stalin officially. That he conveyed a whole lot of information to him which it was impossible to convey at a state level."[204]

Even as he declined Churchill's invitation for a private lunch, the president welcomed the Soviet leader to his quarters. "With a most engaging grin on his face," Stalin ambled over to Roosevelt, who, sitting in his wheelchair, said, "I am glad to see you. I have tried for a long time to bring this about." The former bank robber "burst into a very gay laugh," taking the "blame for the delay in this meeting." Mike Reilly observed that however brutal, "he is certainly not dour. In fact, he laughed almost as much as the Boss."[205]

5.3. FDR and Stalin at the Tehran conference. (Courtesy of FDR Library.)

Roosevelt suggested they utilize their proximity to confer "more frequently in completely informal and different circumstances."[206] Rigdon later described such meetings. Stalin and his interpreter, V. N. Pavlov, stopped by unannounced for chats. The dictator, who could lavish extraordinary courtesy on favorites—including some he later had executed—would ask Roosevelt, did he need anything? Was he comfortable? He explained the "Russian knickknacks on the desk FDR was using . . . all the while smiling and showing great deference for his guest." Each was showing the other respect. The Georgian "showed genuine liking for Roosevelt," Rigdon would recall.[207]

Unedited movie footage of the conference shows Roosevelt and Stalin at times talking with no interpreters visible.[208] (In his Siberian exile Stalin had worked at learning English.) They seem to have developed a measure of rapport and trust. Charles E. "Chip" Bohlen, Roosevelt's interpreter, was not, as he would claim in his memoir, "present at every meeting that Roosevelt had with Stalin at Teheran."[209]

Indeed, Roosevelt always operated so as to reserve to himself the full story, whether it concerned diplomacy, domestic politics, or diagnosing his illness. Regardless of what was resolved in these chats, both men understood that small talk, gestures, and displays of affect could influence attitudes and signal political intent. Determined to like each other, they probably did.

On November 28, Roosevelt opened the conference by welcoming the Soviets "to the family circle." Churchill commented, "this was the greatest concentration of power that the world has ever seen." Picking up on the theme of family, Stalin first acknowledged their "fraternal meeting," then said, "Let us get down to business."[210]

The Kremlin chief insisted that OVERLORD, the cross-Channel invasion of France by spring 1944, remained "the most important" priority. He disparaged operations in the Mediterranean, "even the occupation of Rome," as "not really important."[211] Haunted by the bloody battlefields of 1914–18, Churchill struggled against the U.S.-Soviet accord on OVERLORD. Might not the second front lead to more such slaughter? He also sought to shore up imperial interests by retaking islands in the eastern Mediterranean, securing Greece, and contesting Russian control of the Balkans. Roosevelt, despite some initial wavering that was probably for effect, backed the Soviets on the second front, as did Marshall. In return, Stalin offered the Americans another second front: against Japan after Germany surrendered. Trying to undermine the U.S.-Soviet entente, Churchill confided to Stalin that the real obstacle to a second front in France came from the Americans. They were hoarding landing craft for the Pacific. The dictator cut him off, warning if spring 1944 passed without a landing in France, "a feeling of isolation might develop in the Red Army."[212] The PM acquiesced to the invasion while remaining skeptical.

How was the conference going, Moran asked his boss. "A bloody lot has gone wrong," he barked.[213] Raw movie footage captures a beaming Roosevelt gesturing with hands or head, while a nervous Churchill taps his foot or chair. More than one film shows the prime minister sitting in a chair shorter than those of Stalin and FDR.[214] Hopkins reported, "[T]he President knows now that Stalin is 'get-atable' and that we are going to get along fine in the future." Moran recorded, "Harry kept repeating the word 'get-atable.'"[215] Cadogan interpreted the disagreement with Churchill as a failing. "In his amateurish way, [Roosevelt] had said a lot of indiscreet and awkward things."[216] Cadogan looked down his nose at Stalin, remarking that he "does *not* look well in his Marshal's uniform."[217]

How to deal with defeated Germany became the second major issue at the conference. Roosevelt and Stalin argued for breaking up the Reich and keeping the parts weak. Churchill urged softer treatment for non-Prussian provinces. The Soviet leader responded that although the Germans had taken forty years after 1871 to launch another war, they had halved that time after 1918. He feared they would attack again within fifteen or twenty years. He betrayed admiration and dread toward "these very able and talented people," who had "burst into Russian homes, killed Russian women, etc."[218]

Differences on postwar Germany also erupted over dinner. Bohlen later recalled that Stalin, "in a quasi-jocular fashion," insisted that fifty thousand German military officers "must be killed."[219] Churchill, the butt of the dictator's teasing all evening, denounced "such butchery in cold blood." Getting red in the face, he declared, "I would rather be taken out now and shot than so disgrace my country." Roosevelt piled on with another bad joke, suggesting a "compromise. Not 50,000 but only 49,000 should be shot."[220] Churchill stormed out. In a replay of their Kremlin spat, Stalin rushed after him. The dictator put his hands on Winston's shoulders, Clark Kerr later recounted, "grinning broadly and eagerly declaring" that it was only a joke.[221] Then, a "convivial embrace. The P.M. and Stalin stood with their hands on each other's shoulders, looking into each other's eyes. The last thing I saw of them was Stalin with his arm round the P.M."[222]

The joking revealed serious differences. To Stalin, who had executed twenty-two thousand Polish officers at Katyn, killing fifty thousand from a nation that had slaughtered millions of Soviets and that might attack again, seemed sensible. To Churchill, those German officers could tilt toward Britain in the postwar struggle for power. Looking into Stalin's eyes did not reassure. The blowup foreshadowed the conflict between Roosevelt's desire to get along with Stalin-as-Policeman and the geopolitical, historical, and cultural differences that would make it easy to depict Stalin's realpolitik as criminal. The president would later inform his Cabinet that he had "had a rather hard time with Churchill all the way."[223]

Roosevelt and Stalin also clashed with Churchill over colonial empire. The president needled the PM by stressing, "I want to do away with the word 'Reich' [empire] in any language."[224] He affirmed that he "was 100% in agreement with Marshal Stalin ... that France should not get back Indochina." He grumbled that "after 100 years of French rule in Indochina, the inhabitants were worse off than they had been before." They favored setting up trusteeships, which would prepare colonies "for independence within ... 20 to 30 years." Regarding India, where Churchill had fought against rebellious Pashtun tribesmen, Roosevelt suggested "reform from the bottom, somewhat on the Soviet line." FDR was apparently signaling that he would not allow the bogey of Bolshevism to wreck postwar cooperation. In replying, the Bolshevik sounded more like a technical expert on revolution than a zealous revolutionary. India presented a "complicated" situation, "with different levels of culture and the absence or relationship in the castes. He added that reform from the bottom would mean revolution."[225]

Stalin remained wary of revolutions not under his control. He challenged Roosevelt's insistence that China, wracked by civil war and Japanese occupation, merited inclusion in the Big Four. Roosevelt saw the partly "Asiatic" Soviets as more useful than the British in staving off a global conflict based on race (or what would later be called a "clash of civilizations"). Moran observed that "to the President, China means four hundred million people who are going to count in the world of tomorrow, but Winston thinks only of the colour of their skin."[226] Roosevelt, who sought bases on Formosa, regarded China as vital in terms of its strategic location as well as its racial makeup.[227]

Although Stalin focused on the land and Roosevelt mostly on the sea and air, they concurred on the concept of "strategic strong points." As the president recalled saying, "If there is to be a world police force, there will have to be police stations at strategic points." Stalin replied, "You will want Dakar, will you not?"[228] Under enemy control, that

French-owned territory on the West African bulge could threaten the Western Hemisphere. The dictator said the Allies should "control certain strong physical points either within Germany, along German borders, or even farther away." The same "applied in the case of Japan."[229]

Here, then, was the rough outline of a Four Policemen peace. Germany would be invaded from east and west, divided, and prevented from making war. Russia would join in defeating and policing Japan. Britain and China would police their respective beats. Trusteeships would facilitate gradual decolonization while soothing the pride of losers, such as France, by blurring sovereignty over colonies and strategic locations. In off-the-cuff remarks to U.S. troops after Tehran, Roosevelt underscored his readiness to share the burdens of the policeman approach. "Even if we have to keep peace by force for a while, we are going to do it." He hastened to add, "that does not mean that you are going to have to stay overseas all your lives."[230]

Regardless of Roosevelt's intentions, his vision remained undeveloped. How would the Big Four actually get control over and set up the trustee territories and the "strategic strong points"? How could U.S. and British leaders reconcile their publics to Soviet domination of Eastern Europe? The closer the Allies came to victory, the less leverage FDR had. By postponing decisions, he left decisions to events and to those who followed. No detailed plan also meant that the bureaucracies would go their own way.

As Tehran wound down, Hopkins, Eden, and Molotov discussed organizing "strategic strong points" on the basis of the Four Policemen. The Soviets appreciated that their hold over Poland might be easier to justify in an international regime in which other allies also held crucial territories. Molotov suggested that the French Tunisian port of Bizerte "should be controlled by Great Britain to ensure control of the Mediterranean." Eden replied, a bit evasively, that the French should "make . . . some strategic points available to the United Nations." Drawing a parallel with the Atlantic bases leased to the United States in 1940, he did not find such arrangements "a question of pride." Unresolved, however, was the difference between the unilateral control that the Soviets understood, and the United Nations fig leaf that the British and Americans envisioned. Hopkins asked, how could we "know what would be the strategic points" until "we knew the potential enemies"?[231] A credible alliance needed a credible threat. He reported Roosevelt's worry that "this control question" might "start each of the three powers arming against the others."[232]

The president probably also worried that the Anglo-American monopoly on research for an atomic bomb could spark its own race. Trying to minimize even the British share of this deal, Roosevelt seems to have expected that he could, at some dramatic moment, play the aces of the atomic bomb and postwar aid to win the game.

At Tehran, Hopkins had posed another issue: On what basis could the victors justify taking these strategic points? Occupying territories belonging to the defeated enemy would be the easy part. By referring to strong points "located in friendly territory," Hopkins alluded to the explosive issue of reconciling Poles to Russian dominance. Neither Molotov nor Eden said much in answer. He put this "most important postwar" issue off to the future.[233] It never was settled. Weariness and impending bad weather shortened the conference. "All remaining discussion must be crammed into today," Cadogan noted on December 1.[234] Unresolved in the context of the Four Policemen, these serious issues—strategic bases, useful threats, and the sovereignty of small nations—would later resurface in the context of the NATO and Warsaw Pact alliance systems.

Poland remained a source of U.S.-Soviet discord. At Tehran, Roosevelt explained to Stalin that while "personally he agreed" with the pre–June 1941 border, he would like to see the Soviets take a bit less from Poland. Moreover, owing to the 1944 election and the sentiments of Polish-Americans, he could not publicly endorse any arrangement with regard to Poland. Stalin said he understood.[235] Was this guarded statement Roosevelt's only assurance regarding Eastern Europe? Stalin and Molotov would later refer to a more specific commitment. FDR may have been more forthcoming in the private chats not within earshot of Bohlen. A month after Tehran, Bullitt received a report of Roosevelt's acknowledging that he had listed for the Russians the "countries they could take over and control completely as their sphere—so completely that the United States could from this moment on have no further policies with regard to them—Rumania,

Bulgaria, Bukovina, Eastern Poland, Lithuania, Estonia, Latvia, and Finland."[236] A Soviet spy in New York even reported that Roosevelt favored "the establishment of good relations with the USSR" in part because he was "very worried about the position of the English after the war and wish[ed] to use the USSR as a barrier to the reinforcement of [English] influence in Europe, especially in the Balkans."[237] Regardless of Roosevelt's readiness to accommodate Moscow, however, he had to contend with American public opinion—which was aroused by Polish propaganda, electoral politicking, humanitarian concerns, and his own pandering to expectations of an idealistic peace.

Roosevelt miscalculated in thinking that Stalin would help defuse that challenge by blurring the contradictions between the Four Policemen approach and the Atlantic Charter. The Kremlin boss remained cold to the plea for plebiscites in the former Baltic states. When Stalin reiterated that these nations had long belonged to Russia, FDR replied that the American people "neither knew nor understood." The dictator's response pinpointed a dangerous lacuna in the Roosevelt preparation for the postwar world. The American people "should be informed and some propaganda work should be done."[238] FDR fatally overestimated his time and capability for swaying the American people. Even more unfortunate, Stalin ignored advice from Litvinov and others about the dangers of antagonizing public opinion in the democracies.

Although Tehran drew a sketch for postwar cooperation, the meeting and its follow-up were limited by problems of health and energy. Stalin appeared "exhausted and for that reason not in the best of humor."[239] Churchill arrived after the long trip with a head cold. "He is not fit and not in the best of moods," observed Alanbrooke.[240] The PM went downhill. Dwelling on "how inadequate" British power seemed, he sank into "black depression," saying, "I want to sleep for billions of years." To Moran, who supplied his barbiturates and other drugs, he begged, "Can't you give me something so that I won't feel so exhausted?"[241] Afterward, he suffered another bout of severe pneumonia. FDR was "keyed up" before leaving Washington. Though excited about meeting Stalin, he dreaded going "to Tehran, which is full of disease" and lay across mountains requiring a high-altitude flight.[242] During the conference, Roosevelt suddenly "turned green and great drops of sweat began to bead off his face; he put a shaky hand to his forehead."[243] He would never regain full vigor. Earl Miller, a body guard and family friend, later wrote that the "Boss" "contracted an intestinal bug." He added that "most of the Secret Service was ill most of the time while [in Tehran]—water, food or whatever."[244] After returning to the States, FDR came down with influenza. In March 1944, he would be diagnosed with congestive heart failure.

Hopkins's health also deteriorated. He came away from Tehran joking about "the last of that Russian champagne I had to take in a prone position."[245] On January 1, 1944, barely a week after angering FDR by moving out of the White House, Harry entered the hospital. He would emerge months later a changed man, no longer Roosevelt's sidekick or all-purpose fixer.

Before that disruption, however, Hopkins described a future that would never be, a world spared the Cold War. He told naval officers aboard the *Iowa* that Stalin "and the President took to each other beautifully." Both were "plain spoken men," who did not bother with "diplomatic language." He added, "we got plenty of that at Casablanca. Churchill is a past master" at hedging. Contrasting the British with the Russian leader, Hopkins emphasized that with the latter, "I heard more *plain talk*. What [Stalin] wants after the war—and some small nations aren't going to like it a bit—is to set up certain 'strong points'—that's what he called them—in Europe, controlled, land, sea, and in the air by Russia and England and us. I'd say he is willing to trust us more than he is England. Yes, we got along swell with 'Uncle Joe.'"[246] A quite different conclusion was reached by Churchill, who was fretting, "We've got to do something with these bloody Russians."[247] Roosevelt assumed that he, as a man of destiny, could mediate between Churchill and Stalin while overseeing the transition to a peaceful postwar world. FDR did not realize that after Tehran he would have only sixteen months in which to make his vision a reality.

Chapter 6

"I've Worked It Out"
Roosevelt's Plan to Win the Peace and Defy Death, 1944–45

Hours after Roosevelt's death on April 12, 1945, Harriman found Stalin "obviously deeply distressed at the news." The dictator "greeted me in silence and stood holding my hand for about 30 seconds before asking me to sit down."[1] At three o'clock that morning, Molotov had rushed to the embassy. Kathleen Harriman reported that Molotov, forsaking his habitual demeanor as "an impersonal, cold man," had "that night showed good instincts—Averell said that he was much upset—shocked."[2] The ambassador had "never heard Molotov talk so earnestly" as he did in stressing the importance of Roosevelt's policies.[3] "All Moscow is shattered," Harriman cabled Eleanor Roosevelt.[4] Kathleen observed red flags with black borders hanging throughout the capital. The British embassy reported Kremlin "anxiety lest anti-Soviet elements in the United States might now have a stronger influence on American policy."[5] Mingling with Muscovites, U.S. diplomat Elbridge Durbrow overheard "real consternation by the man on the street."[6] The pervasive grief reflected a gut-level understanding: Roosevelt had been really serious about promoting cooperation.

In 1944–45, FDR did work hard to lay the groundwork for a postwar alliance that included Stalin. Roosevelt had decided that the

Three Policemen (or four, with China) offered a more realistic basis for international order than the Wilsonian principles of the Atlantic Charter. Roosevelt and Stalin both believed they had forged a personal and political bond at Tehran. The president boasted of the dictator's warning a Polish visitor, "the President is my friend, we will always understand each other."[7] Whatever the actual depth of their friendship, it could ease but not eliminate geopolitical problems. Another limitation was bodily. Wartime leadership proved a punishing job. Although Churchill's pneumonia recurred and Stalin visibly aged, Roosevelt's health deteriorated the most.

The Big Three also suffered hubris. Churchill boasted that together they commanded thirty million soldiers, "the greatest concentration of power that the world had ever seen."[8] "Power corrupts," an aide sneered. Another official found the warlords growing "more and more arbitrary and unaccountable." The PM seemed "really as demented as the President."[9] A friendly journalist was appalled at FDR's "almost arrogant casualness" in anointing himself "destiny's appointed agent."[10] Absolute power had bloodied the rule of Stalin. His personality and experience left him clueless about how to translate military triumphs into foreign influence without counterproductive repression. Despite their success against the Axis, each of the three was flummoxed by challenges at home, resurgent nationalism abroad, and the limits of personality and body.

Health Problems

When Harry and Louise Hopkins moved out of the White House in December 1943, FDR felt abandoned and betrayed. Rosenman recalled that "a coolness developed then between Harry and FDR."[11] Relations grew colder after Hopkins, perhaps from celebrating the night before, collapsed on New Year's Day and then remained in the hospital until summer 1944. In a presidency that pivoted on proximity, Harry, now outside the inner circle, became exposed to bureaucratic attack. Rumor circulated that he had grown too partial to Churchill. No longer flippant in attitude about his health, he confided to his eldest son, Robert, "it has been difficult for me to bounce back this time."[12] Then he was crushed by news of another son's death in the Pacific.[13]

Facing his own mortality, Hopkins grew desperate and even more cynical. It had never been easy to serve FDR, who expected much, rarely said thanks, and teased mercilessly. Harry instructed an aide sorting his papers, "I want the whole story known," including his "very ambitious" political aspirations.[14] In 1938–39, he had prepared to run for president or vice president, expecting FDR's support.[15] Bitten by the presidential bug, Hopkins entertained fantasies even about the 1944 election, Corcoran later recalled.[16] Having given his all to the "Boss," Hopkins concluded, sadly, "there were few selfless people, and no great people were selfless."[17] The man who loved gambling at cards now tossed in his remaining chips. Doctors remained "really hesitant about pushing Harry into more surgery." Yet they went along because "he seemed so anxious that something be done." Plagued by blurry vision, swollen legs, red toes, hair loss, and painful diarrhea, he bet on a lifesaving operation. He wisecracked in the operating room, "Open me up. Maybe you will find the answer to the fourth term, or maybe not!" General Marshall saluted his "cold nerve and great courage."[18] Bravery notwithstanding, the surgery on March 29 achieved little. In July he emerged from the hospital more reckless about himself and about his relations with FDR. He gave in to hedonism, periodically savaging his system with alcohol and rich food.

Roosevelt responded to illness far differently. He cut down on alcohol, food, cigarettes, and work. "I have a terrible pile in my basket," he wrote to Hopkins, "but most of the stuff has answered itself anyway."[19] In contrast to Harry's risk taking, FDR doggedly "kept the rules," as he put it.[20] Determined to survive, he changed his lifestyle. His resolve hardened. As he struggled up from his wheelchair, "you could see the jawbones click, the great will in the jawbones," an insider observed.[21]

Nonetheless, Roosevelt did weaken in 1944–45. Controversy continues as to the precise diagnosis. He certainly had heart disease, including hypertension. Since at least 1938, he had suffered periodic nonconvulsive seizures that robbed him of consciousness. Perkins remembered "the oncoming of a kind of glassy eye" and a dropped jaw. He might faint. "It would be momentary. It would be very brief, and he'd be back again."[22] Circumstantial evidence indicates that a pigmented lesion above his left eyebrow might possibly have been deadly melanoma cancer that later metastasized to his abdomen and brain.[23] Roosevelt came back from Tehran with a bronchial infection, severe cough, and maybe an intestinal bug.[24] Daisy Suckley observed that he "looked & felt tired" and "sounds depressed." He complained, "I am feeling 'no good'—don't want to do anything & want to sleep all the time."[25]

He also endured medical incompetence. Ross McIntire, the White House physician, was a respiratory specialist who probably never gave the president a comprehensive examination. (McIntire may well have later destroyed the president's medical records to hide his negligence.)[26] Eleanor paid little attention to anyone's health—mere "physiology," she told their daughter, Anna.[27] She often criticized FDR's naps as "indulging himself."[28] White House maids remembered that Missy used to fuss over her "Effdee's" pains. LeHand's stroke, Corcoran's departure, and the pressures of the war ended the boisterous parties where FDR's voice and laughter had boomed and where he might squeeze out a tune on Tommy's accordion. In earlier years, LeHand had joined him in the swimming pool. Such diversion, companionship, and mild exercise would have lowered his stress and probably his blood pressure. Missy probably would have noticed that he now huffed with the slightest exertion. Daisy and his old flame, Lucy Mercer Rutherfurd, did notice but dared not make waves. Finally, his daughter, Anna Boettiger, insisted that McIntire bring in a specialist.

When Lieutenant Commander Howard G. Bruenn, a cardiologist, examined Roosevelt on March 27, 1944, he took alarm. The president suffered from hypertension and cardiac failure of the left ventricle. Heavy smoking had inflicted chronic obstructive pulmonary disease, resulting in a persistent cough, shortness of breath, and intermittent confusion and drowsiness.[29] Bruenn prescribed digitalis, which in two weeks reduced the size of the heart. He also administered phenobarbital "as a brake on excessive activity as well as a cushion against emotional trauma."[30] The barbiturate also mitigated seizures.[31] The doctor put the patient, who weighed 188 pounds, concentrated in his upper torso, on a diet. He urged the president to reduce work, cigarettes, and alcohol and get more sleep and mild exercise. Despite his habitual resistance to "experts," FDR followed Bruenn's advice. He insisted on losing weight, even after he had dropped to 165 and looked haggard.[32] He cut down on his beloved cocktails. He smoked fewer cigarettes; "luckily, they still taste rotten."[33]

With rumors buzzing about his health and the November election impending, FDR on April 7 invited a friendly journalist, Marquis Childs, for an Oval Office interview. In response to a question about the burdens of a fourth term, FDR laid out his strategy for survival. "I've worked it out. . . . You see, I don't work so hard any more. I've got this thing simplified. People are doing their jobs. It isn't necessary for me to do so much. . . . I've cut down the night work. . . . After lunch I take a nap on that sofa over there."[34] Although the regimen followed Bruenn's advice, one element did not compute. By 1944, most of the "people doing their jobs" possessed neither high capability nor commitment to the ideas FDR had outlined at Tehran. Childs noticed "the man's curious aloneness."[35] Given FDR's craving for company, loneliness probably raised his blood pressure. Bruenn, who examined him nearly every day, recorded his "return to more normal levels when relaxed and at ease."[36] Particularly relaxing for him was seeing his old love, Lucy.[37]

The Big Three Solution

With Hopkins out and his own energy down, the great communicator faltered in shaping public opinion. Roosevelt had delivered fireside chats every 2.8 months, on average, from December 1941 to January 1944, but he gave only two in the remainder of 1944, both at the time of the D-Day invasion of June 6. His relative silence matched the September 1939–December 1941 period, when he had cut the talks to an average of one every 5.4 months.[38] In 1940–41, he was maneuvering a conflict-averse nation closer to war. In 1944–45, he was seeking to moderate Soviet war aims and nudge the American people toward accepting a peace based more on Big Three cooperation than on Atlantic Charter universalism. He knew that public antipathy to big power deals had helped sink Senate approval of Wilson's peace.

In both 1940–41 and in 1944–45, FDR tried to shape opinion and events while reserving his options. In this second period, however, no transformational, Pearl Harbor–like event occurred to provide the wind at his back as he navigated. Nor did he have Hopkins, LeHand, or Welles to advise, help him relax, and counter his procrastination. Although domestic affairs czar James F. Byrnes aspired to becoming an operator of the Tommy Corcoran class, "Jimmy" could not match Tommy in contacts or in loyalty. Speechwriters Sam Rosenman and Robert Sherwood also lacked the savvy and ruthlessness of Hopkins and Corcoran. Admiral William Leahy offered tough-minded competence while remaining unsympathetic to Roosevelt's readiness to accommodate Stalin's war aims.

Left on his own, FDR reverted to old ways. He had described the maneuver in 1940, when African Americans were pressing for integration in the armed forces. The army would create divisions with segregated white and black battalions. In the confusion of war, the men would inevitably mix. "We sort of back into" progress, Roosevelt explained.[39] Years earlier, the polio victim had "backed into" rooms by crawling backward while diverting onlookers with banter. Faced with the anti-interventionist sentiment of 1940–41, he had backed into the conflict while talking about aid to the Allies and defense of the hemisphere.

Now, in 1944–45, he was trying to back into Big Three governance, which would entail Soviet dominance in Eastern Europe, while downplaying the principles of the Atlantic Charter. Those ideals, reaffirmed in the January 1942 United Nation Declaration, barred territorial changes not in "accord with the freely expressed wishes of the people concerned." Reincarnating the principle of national self-determination championed by Wilson, the document promised "the right of all peoples to choose the form of government under which they will live."[40] Roosevelt played to widening support for an international organization while sidestepping sentiment for a one-nation, one-vote setup. He wanted most of the power in the United Nations organization to reside not in the General Assembly but rather in the Security Council, run by the big powers. The Three (or Four) Policemen would guard strategic locations, contain Germany and Japan, discipline small nations, promote global prosperity, and, in the post-Churchill era, shepherd colonies toward gradual independence.

To get across this complex, realpolitik message, Roosevelt worked through pet journalists. He confided to Childs that if he tried to specify the Polish boundary, the Russians "might not agree. Then what could I do?" He recalled telling Stalin at Tehran, "'We're not going to go to war with you over Poland.'"[41] Despite his caution in Europe, Roosevelt aspired to remake the colonial world, where "the white man is more and more in disfavor." Without "positive steps," such as trusteeships and gradual self-government, European and American influence would be "pushed out completely." Churchill vehemently objected to such change. Roosevelt had told him at Tehran that "after all, there were three votes against one, and he had better look out. He didn't like that at all." Impressed by the anti-imperialist fervor, Childs asked, "Why can't you tell people something of all this?" Roosevelt responded that with D-Day approaching, he dared not risk a rumpus with Britain.[42] A public row would also damage congressional support for postwar collaboration. An overburdened Roosevelt lacked the energy and trusted staff to develop an actual program for phasing out colonialism. Private talk was cheap. He needed to have talked more with the public.

FDR did encourage the State Department to convene a conference at Dumbarton Oaks in Washington to plan the United Nations organization. When the conference stalemated over voting procedures, he terminated it, saying he would take up the issue with Stalin.[43]

Though not risking an all-out publicity campaign for the Big Three approach, FDR in talking with reporters consistently pushed the policemen idea as practical while panning the charter as unrealistic. He did not even mention the Atlantic Charter to Childs or to *Saturday Evening Post* writer Forrest Davis, who interviewed him twice. The British embassy reported that FDR vetted the resulting stories.[44] Resistant State Department veterans were instructed regarding Davis's articles, "You'd better memorize [them] because that's the Bible."[45] Roosevelt urged "flexibility rather than adherence to rigid doctrine." He desired to "extemporize in harmony with developing events, and not against them."[46]

Given the Red Army's sweep toward Berlin, "flexibility" in response to "developing events" meant accepting Soviet control in Eastern Europe. Inflexible principles had destroyed Wilson's dream. Queried at a press conference about another Fourteen Points, Wilson's program in 1918–19, the pragmatist rejoined, "Oh, No—Oh, No. Things like points, well, are principles." Did he, like Wilson, feel frustrated by "a little group of willful men" in Congress? A grinning FDR replied, "No, I never have. . . . I don't hate people."[47] Unmoved by that famous grin, many Republicans were already agitating against foreign entanglements undertaken at distant conferences.

FDR took his stand in the kitchen. He offered the "visual illustration" of the Big Three at Tehran discussing "fifty-seven varieties" of proposals. Just as folks in Kansas or California might sample Heinz brand relishes, Roosevelt, Churchill, and Stalin had tested various plans. "Chewing over the ideas with the utmost frankness, [in] a proceeding spiced" by mild disagreements, the three gained "valuable insights into one another's minds, intentions, and limitations."[48] This normalizing discourse invited readers of the *Saturday Evening Post* to imagine the Big Three as people just like them, trying to understand each other and solve problems. Roosevelt was saying, in effect, that an activist policy did not mean getting mixed up with border fights, extreme ideologies, or strange people. The imaginary of fifty-seven varieties was deceptive—and potentially powerful, just like the paradigm-shifting metaphor of borrowing a neighbor's garden hose that Roosevelt had used to popularize Lend-Lease. By 1944–45, however, the president lacked the energy and the gifted staff to alchemize an image into concrete policy.

While aiming for accord with Moscow, Roosevelt remained alive to the dangers. Communist revolutionary fervor "may have run down. But" there was no guarantee. He acknowledged to Davis that Stalin might revive "the imperialistic thrust" of czarist Russia.[49] When Daisy Suckley lauded his understanding with Stalin, FDR "smiled & said he keeps his fingers crossed."[50] Whatever Stalin had in mind, he, like Roosevelt, would leave no detailed plan.

Top Soviet diplomats were, however, planning for the postwar. Significantly, they were mostly assuming postwar cooperation with Washington and London. Former ambassador to Washington Litvinov and former ambassador to London Maisky, now back in Moscow as planners, had survived Stalin's purges. Andrei Gromyko, the wartime emissary to the United States, shone as a rising star. All three understood the deadly peril in displeasing the *vozhd*. Though writing separately in 1944–45, they reached overlapping conclusions. Each must have believed his recommendation accorded with what Stalin and Molotov were thinking.[51]

They sketched postwar aims in terms not of world domination or revolution but rather of peace, national security, and continued collaboration with the wartime allies. Security meant keeping Germany and Japan down, regaining the June 1941 borders plus the Kurile islands and South Sakhalin in the Far East, obtaining transit rights across Iran and bases in Romania and Finland, and ensuring friendly though not necessarily communist governments on the Soviet periphery. Regarding Britain and the United States, "our cooperation with these countries is an absolute necessity," Maisky affirmed.[52]

Gromyko rooted for Roosevelt in the November 1944 vote. The "election of a Republican for President would be very damaging for Soviet-American relations." He nevertheless anticipated that sometime in the future the Republicans would win. In keeping with Marxist-Leninist ideology, he analyzed the "ruling class's position toward the USSR," that is, the likely U.S. policy regardless of which party ran Washington. Even under the Republicans, the two nations would likely "collaborate on advancing their interests." They shared an interest in controlling Germany and Japan, supporting antifascist, "democratic" governments in Western Europe, and expanding trade. Gromyko extolled the potential for exchanging Soviet raw materials for sophisticated machinery: "the ability of the United States to turn scientific advances into products is amazing."

Just as amazing was the trio's downplaying of ideological conflict. They knew that other diplomats had been executed for ideological "treason." Maisky and Gromyko did not argue against proletarian revolution or the sovietizing of liberated nations. Nevertheless, they warned that the Americans and British would find such developments "threatening." They evidenced little enthusiasm for spreading communism, which could destroy the alliance against resurgent Germany.[53] Maisky predicted that, absent revolution, there were "no grounds to expect that relations between the USSR, on the one hand, and the USA and England, on the other, would be bad."[54] Like many Western officials, they expected a leftist tide to sweep across the postwar world. FDR seemed unconcerned with that tide engulfing Eastern Europe. A State Department official explained "that the President did not want us to interfere in Balkan affairs; that was the understanding reached" at Tehran.[55]

If Roosevelt had lived, this "understanding" might have allowed diverse paths leftward. Even Stalin, who had helped destroy the German Social Democrats in the early 1930s, seemed open to a broader view. He lectured a Balkan Communist leader: "We have to forget the idea that the victory of socialism could be realized only through a Soviet rule. It could be presented by some other political systems—for example by a democracy, a parliamentary republic, and even by a constitutional monarchy."[56] Stalin regarded collaboration with the Americans and British as not antithetical, at least in the short run, to the rise of socialism in Europe.[57]

To be sure, the dictator's long-term ideological goals did seriously challenge capitalism. Nevertheless, those aspirations might have become—absent a militarized Cold War—co-opted, muted, or diverted over time. Such, after all, has been the fate of all millennial projects. In contrast to his rival Leon Trotsky, Stalin remained patient about world revolution.

Their Marxist ideology misled the diplomats into overestimating the lure of Soviet markets while ignoring cultural affinities among the Americans, British, and Germans. Gromyko also misjudged in expecting Soviet prestige to rise as capitalist economies sank into postwar depression. Evidently confident that he remained within mainstream Kremlin thought, the ambitious diplomat concluded, "In spite of possible difficulties, which from time to time may emerge in our relations with the United States, the necessary conditions are clearly present for a continuation of cooperation between our two countries."[58] Gromyko completed this analysis only two weeks before the August 1944 Warsaw uprising. Despite his warning that sympathy for the Poles made "anti-Soviet attacks unavoidable" in Congress, he failed to anticipate the explosive force of that volatile sentiment.

Poland

Polish issues ensnared each of the Big Three. Roosevelt needed the votes of six million Polish Americans, most of them sympathetic to the government-in-exile in London. Many lived in Michigan, the home of the senior Republican on the Senate Foreign Relations Committee, Arthur H. Vandenberg, who could thwart ratification of a peace treaty.

The history buff in the Kremlin could not forgive the Poles' occupation of Moscow centuries earlier. He steamed over his failure to prevent their triumph over the Red Army in 1921. He also resented any insinuation that Catholic Poland, culturally identified with the West, condescended to Russia. "The Poles liked to think that the Russians were good fighters but that they were fools" who could be cheated out of "the spoils" of war. Well, "the Poles would find out who were the fools."[59] The dictator understood that only a Warsaw government bound in "friendship" with Moscow would forestall revenge for the Katyn murders of 1940. Stalin pleaded with Harriman, "Why can't the President leave Poland to us? Doesn't he realize that this is the invasion route?"[60]

The British had gone to war over Warsaw's independence. More than 115,000 Polish troops battled alongside their forces. Polish fliers with the RAF reigned as "the glamor boys of England," a journalist noted. "As for the women," one of those fliers boasted, "one just cannot shake them off."[61] George A. Hill, the British Special Operations Executive agent in Russia trying to collaborate with the secret police, the NKVD, worried that "the Polish element in S.O.E. is far too strong, and their hatred of the U.S.S.R. tends to dominate the councils."[62] The

Poles were so popular that Parliament would protest "appeasement" of Russia at Warsaw's expense.[63] The British ambassador to the exiled government, Owen O'Malley, framed the alternatives as "abetting a murder" by "selling the corpse of Poland to Russia," or asserting anticommunist "moral authority."[64]

Despite his sympathy for the Poles, Churchill agreed with Stalin and Roosevelt that the big nations should discipline the smaller ones. In February 1944, he warned that if Prime Minister Stanisław Mikołajczyk refused to drop the Russophobes from his London-based exiled government, he and Stalin would "make the best bargain we could for our clients."[65] Churchill even applauded the Curzon line, adding that Poles should welcome the compensatory German territory as "a fair, healthy and wholesome offer." Refusal would "only make the Russians more angry and drive them to the solution of a puppet Government in Warsaw."[66]

Churchill nonetheless blamed the Russians when they clashed with the Poles. The Red Army in 1944–45 was advancing into a confusing battleground. The Polish Home Army (*Armia Krajowa* or AK), linked with the London exiles and supplied by British air drops, switched from combating Germans to fighting Russians and pro-Soviet Poles. Most but not all in the AK hated the Soviets. Red Army commanders also varied in how they treated the AK. Churchill and Eden ignored this complexity when they dismissed as "quite untrue" Kremlin charges that pro-Soviet Poles were "attacked, tortured, and shot" by the AK.[67] Churchill reached the dangerous conclusion that Soviet accusations against Poles amounted to disrespect for Britons. The Russians believed "we will put up with anything," he sputtered.[68]

Insulted, Churchill responded with hyperbole about a Manichean struggle. "I fear that very great evil may come upon the world. This time at any rate we and the Americans will be heavily armed. The Russians are drunk with victory and there is no length they may not go."[69] He saw Russians not as fellow policemen but rather as lawbreakers. Walter Lippmann, with his extensive network of informants, saw things differently.[70] Many Poles, "even before they are liberated from the Nazis, conceive themselves as the spearhead of a hostile coalition against the Soviet Union."[71]

Roosevelt hoped to stifle such hostility, at least until after his reelection. In May, he told Harriman "that he didn't care whether the countries bordering Russia became communized."[72] FDR encouraged Stanislaus Orlemanski, a left-leaning Massachusetts priest, and Oskar Lange, a politically connected University of Chicago economist, to mediate between Soviets and Poles. In January 1944, Lange, after discussion with U.S. officials, advised the Soviets to nurture a broad-based, pro-Moscow government that could win American support and supersede the London exiles.

Stalin seemed receptive.[73] In talking with Orlemanski, Stalin promoted Slavic unity to help contain postwar Germany. Surely Poles were "tired of serving as a corridor" for invasions into Russia. The dictator apparently did not assume that primacy in Poland required an East-West fault line. He stressed that "Poland would also be allied with the Western countries—Britain and France."[74] In May 1944, when Soviet repression and AK resistance were both escalating, Stalin told Lange he favored a Three Policemen solution. He downplayed the idea of communism in Poland where "there is no initiative for collectivization." Indeed, "we are holding [the leftists] back from radicalism." Like Lippmann, he blamed "some circles in England [who] desire a fight between the Poles and the Russians." He favored instead a "unified government of Poles living in England, America, and Russia."[75]

Stalin detailed "his Bolshevik view" on the promising outlook for postwar cooperation. U.S. and British bombers were destroying German and Japanese economic competition. American and British capitalists would continue to influence their respective governments. Consequently, "it is no accident that England and America are united with Russia" against Germany. "This alliance was not caused by opportunism, but is long-term." Poles should "understand that [only] in alliance with Russia, England, and America could they defend themselves." Russia needed "a strong Poland with an army. This is not a game."[76]

The Kremlin boss spoke in much the same terms to Polish Communists and to others. At a Kremlin reception for the Soviet-dominated Lublin Committee, he warned that "for Poland it won't be enough to have an alliance only with one state." The postwar German danger mandated "an agreement of four states: Poland—the Soviet Union—England—America."[77] He said the same to Mikołajczyk in August.[78] In December, he told French leader Charles de Gaulle that history had proven that neither France and Russia, "nor any other two countries are strong enough to stay on top of Germany." Containment required "a solid entente among the Soviet Union, France, Great Britain, and America."[79]

Overestimating his ability to shape events, Stalin sought to square the circle: to secure a neighbor not only friendly to Moscow, but also independent, vital, and "democratic." He emphasized "that *it must be Poland itself which closes the passageway.*" Poland could not "be strong if it is not democratic. We have an interest in a strong Poland."[80] Even as late as March 1945 he warned the Communist Władysław Gomułka not to "renounce an alliance with England and America—the people would not understand that."[81]

Churchill, Roosevelt, and Stalin sought, respectively, to broker, finesse, or impose a Three Policemen solution. Their efforts were swamped by emotional reactions to the Warsaw uprising that began on August 1 and lasted until October 2. Harvey despaired as the street battle "magnified into the acid test of Soviet-Polish-Russian relations."[82]

Overly eager Poles saw their hour of delivery. The Germans seemed spent. The Red Army seemed ready to vault the Vistula into Warsaw. Soviet broadcasts urged revolt. AK patriots rose up, expecting to own the capital before the Red Army arrived. The Germans, however, sent in reinforcements. As brave street fighters begged for aid, the Nazis killed over two hundred thousand, more than would die in the atomic bombing of Hiroshima and Nagasaki.[83] Though the Red Army did need to pause, it probably could have taken Warsaw by late August. Yet Stalin refused to rescue those who interpreted Polish "independence" as total independence from the Kremlin.[84] The Soviets brought on themselves a public relations disaster in the West.

The uprising was the centerpiece of Operation Tempest, a countrywide effort to seize control as the Germans retreated. Ingenious AK fighters traded homemade vodka for ammunition from German and Soviet soldiers. Nevertheless their only successful uprising occurred in

Radom, where they had coordinated with the Red Army.[85] According to an internal Soviet report, the Polish resistance killed forty-two Red Army soldiers and police agents in two months.[86] Armed resistance would soon engulf much of western Poland.[87] Heightening Moscow's alarm were the one hundred thousand anti-Soviet guerrillas fighting in neighboring Ukraine. The Germans had aided the Ukrainians, and the British and Americans would do likewise after the war.[88] Some evidence indicates that the British Special Operations Executive had parachuted U.S.-trained Poles into Warsaw.[89] Polish pilots in the RAF flew near-suicidal aid missions from Bari in southern Italy, to Warsaw, and back. On August 29, the British air chief reported "that out of the last 9 sorties to Warsaw only one succeeded." Even ardent Polish patriots began reporting "technical troubles" preventing takeoff. Undeterred, the exiled government pushed for more aid missions.[90] U.S. B-17s dropped 1,300 containers, of which only one-third reached the defenders, now restricted to a narrow perimeter. Stalin, possibly worried about his standing with even pro-Soviet Poles, ordered some air drops. But the Warsaw fighters were crushed.

The Warsaw crucible forged proto–Cold War attitudes. Moralized judgments fused political issues into an intractable lump. Once again Churchill reacted to insult by talking about military force. Only surging forces in Western Europe would secure "some respect for what we say."[91] Moran observed that the PM, riveted on Poland, and on Greece, where the British were fighting against leftists, "never talks of Hitler these days; he is always harping on the dangers of Communism. He dreams of the Red Army spreading like a cancer from one country to another. It has become an obsession, and he seems to think of little else."[92]

Empathy for the Warsaw fighters was only one reason for Harriman's deeply personal interest in Russian-dominated Poland and the adjacent area. The ambassador had sunk his heart into Washington's project—excitingly successful for a while—of setting up three U.S. air bases in the Ukraine. He pushed hard to get Soviet permission for U.S. and British planes dropping supplies to the Warsaw fighters to refuel at these bases. In early 1945, he urged yet another operation in Soviet-occupied territory. Backed for a while by Roosevelt, Harriman proposed that U.S. planes based in the Ukraine be allowed to search for and then evacuate the thousands of liberated American and British POWs wandering through Poland. To Harriman's rage, Stalin vetoed both plans. (The Soviets did assist with ground evacuation of the POWs.) Harriman had still another personal concern. His nephew, a descendant of the last king of Poland, was fighting in the Polish army.[93]

In an incendiary telegram Harriman warned Washington that the Soviets "expect that they can force their will on us and all countries."[94] By seeing domination of Poland as equivalent to domination of the United States, he offered an incontrovertible, even if hyperbolic, argument for confrontation. It proved tragic that the Russians' fixation on their most vulnerable border hit Harriman so hard, and that he reacted by insisting that Soviet control of Poland endangered critical U.S. interests, indeed America's very freedom of action. Whereas Roosevelt resisted Harriman's alarmism, Truman would make it a centerpiece of U.S. policy.

Harriman's sharp tone probably also echoed the whipsawed emotions of his right-hand man, George Kennan, who in July 1944 had returned to Moscow after a seven-year absence.[95] Kennan had not lost his passion for Russia, which seemed "poignantly familiar and significant . . . as though I had lived here in childhood. I react intensely to everything I see and hear." Mingling with ordinary Russians, soaking in "their tremendous, pulsating warmth and vitality" imbued Kennan with "an indescribable sort of satisfaction." He mused, "I would rather be sent to Siberia among" Russians "than to live in Park Avenue among our own stuffy folk." Such longing made it "harder than ever to swallow . . . that I must always remain a distrusted outsider." For the forty-year-old diplomat this forced isolation from the Russian people meant that "the peak of life . . . was definitely passed."[96] Kennan's personal resentments would sharpen his call in 1945–47 that the Soviet Union itself be isolated through a policy of containment.

In another foretaste of the Cold War, Poland erupted into an election issue. FDR's Republican opponent, Thomas E. Dewey, marched in the Pulaski Day parade. He charged that the president's "personal secret diplomacy" was betraying Poland.[97] The British embassy reported the "large pro-Russian wave" in U.S. opinion shifting toward "an attitude compounded of somewhat uneasy suspense and guilty conscience."[98] Poles were "filling Christendom with their anti-Soviet cries," Harvey noted anxiously.[99]

Roosevelt tried to quiet things down. He urged Stalin to "think of world opinion." The Kremlin chief instead exploded with a rant against "power-seeking criminals."[100] Polish issues were complicated, FDR cautioned reporters. "I suppose I know as much about that particular thing as any American, and I don't know enough to talk about it."[101]

The dictator, however, decided that he now knew enough to harden his position. In October he told the group he controlled, the Lublin Poles, that "to admit the London emigres to participate in exercising power in Poland might have made sense during the August talks with Mikołajczyk" if the latter had accepted the Curzon line and Lublin's radical reforms. "Since that time, Mikołajczyk had rejected all this" while the AK engaged in "sabotage and . . . murders." Churchill, at this very moment in Moscow negotiating his "percentages" deal for dividing the Balkans, failed to get the London Poles to bend. As Władysław Gomułka later told it, it was the October impasse that sparked Stalin's "basic decision" to bypass the London exiles in creating the provisional Polish government.[102]

Nevertheless, Stalin still saw postwar Big Three cooperation as the most powerful guarantee against renewed German aggression. In his November 1944 speech celebrating the anniversary of the Revolution—a high-profile address analogous to the U.S. president's annual message to Congress—the dictator assured the Soviet people that "the alliance between the U.S.S.R., Great Britain and the United States of America is founded not on casual, transitory considerations, but on vital and lasting interests." Regarding Germany's likely revival in a couple of decades, there was "only one means . . . to preclude further aggression": establishing a world organization, which would "be effective if the great Powers . . . continue to act in a spirit of unanimity and accord."[103]

Roosevelt's Limits

In the effort to sutain that accord, Roosevelt could marshal only limited energy and creativity. He juggled rest and work. He could no longer settle issues while eating with LeHand or playing poker with Hopkins. When Harold Ickes asked Anna Boettiger who was advising her father, she, "throwing her hands into the air, said, 'I don't know; no one.'"[104] FDR never fully forgave Hopkins for moving out of the White House, and the latter no longer seemed interested in giving his all to translate Roosevelt's Tehran ideas into concrete policy. Sour, sick, and suspecting that his wife was cheating on him, Hopkins asked Hoover to assign FBI agents to follow his wife and tap her phone calls. Roosevelt icily ignored Hopkins in the run up to the September 1944 summit at Quebec and Hyde Park.[105] Clementine Churchill, along for the trip, lamented, "Harry seems to have quite dropped out of the picture. Now it seems that the intimacy has ended, and I cannot but feel that this is a disaster to the Anglo-American relationship."

Never a fan of the president, she remarked that despite "his genius," he could not focus "on the war for more than 4 hours a day, which is not really enough when one is a supreme war lord."[106] Although FDR did tire, he also feigned inattention. He ignored Churchill's plan to retake Singapore. He opposed extending Lend-Lease without a pledge to open the British Empire to global trade and investment. Pressed on all sides, the prime minister exploded, "What do you want me to do? Get on my hind legs and beg like Fala?"[107]

Roosevelt did renew their atomic alliance by initialing the Hyde Park aide mémoire of September 18.[108] The previous month he had listened to the Danish scientist Niels Bohr warn of an atomic arms race unless the Soviets were brought into the atomic fold.[109] Bohr's mission to Roosevelt was in fact choreographed by Churchill's principal atomic advisers: John Anderson, head of the British program; Lord Cherwell, the prime minister's science adviser; and Lord Halifax, the ambassador to Washington. They hoped to sidestep their chief's opposition to a nuclear control agreement that would include the Russians. The prime minister's adamancy stemmed not so much from his prescience about the power of the still-untested weapon but rather from his appreciation of atomic cooperation as a vehicle for further "mixing up" the scientific and military establishments of Britain and the United States. Anderson, Cherwell, and Halifax worried that developing and then using the bomb without any agreement with Moscow would invite an arms race. They coached Bohr on how to overcome his "philosophical vagueness of expression" and "inarticulate whisper" so as to convince Roosevelt, who in turn might bring Churchill around.[110] The prime minister, however, ended up persuading or at least overpowering the president. Roosevelt, perhaps too tired to have another row with Churchill, acceded to the latter's dismissal of Bohr as a meddler. Nevertheless, Roosevelt held up his sleeve the cards of atomic energy and reconstruction aid. Whether they would turn out to be aces would depend on whether the bomb actually exploded and on whether Congress came across with money. He tried to keep options open by procrastinating, juggling alternatives, and backing into situations. Despite Churchill's opposition, FDR in ensuing months inched toward telling the Russians about the atomic project. He preserved flexibility by inserting into the Hyde Park agreement hedging language: the weapon "might perhaps, after mature consideration, be used against the Japanese."[111]

Secretary of War Henry L. Stimson had informed FDR that workers on the Manhattan Project sympathetic to Moscow were "already getting information about vital secrets and sending them to Russia."[112] While agreeing to precautions, Roosevelt did not seem to find such spying alarming. Perhaps he was tacitly permitting a back-channel trickle of atomic information, just as he had reportedly talked into the microphones at Tehran.[113]

Whether the Big Three could stay together in the postwar era depended in large part on whether they could agree on how to treat defeated Germany. Like the Russians, and in contrast to the British, Roosevelt anticipated a harsh peace. He informed Stimson that "every person in Germany should realize that this time Germany is a defeated nation. I do not want them to starve to death but . . . they should be fed three times a day with soup from Army soup kitchens." Above all, "the fact that they are a defeated nation . . . must be so

impressed upon them that they will hesitate to start a new war."[114]
Treasury Secretary Henry Morgenthau shared FDR's belief that Germany's victims, not the defeated enemy, deserved priority in American relief and in distributing the resources still in Germany. In his various plans submitted to Roosevelt, Morgenthau never, despite what some critics charged, seriously proposed deindustrializing Germany so that it became a helpless "potato patch." Rather, like Roosevelt, he favored restructuring and decartelizing the German economy so as to encourage light industry. Dismantled plants could be sent to devastated neighbors, especially the Soviet Union, as "restitution" for war damages.[115]

Despite Roosevelt's strong sentiments, policy toward postwar Germany remained confused and contested by conflicting groups in the War, Treasury, and State Departments. The administration eventually settled on a compromise plan, J[oint]C[hiefs of]S[taff] 1067.[116] With the presidency often on autopilot, departments and agencies followed, as in this incident, their different bureaucratic inclinations. FDR's habit of waiting until he "had to" make decisions often meant that the bureaucracy or (ultimately) Truman decided.

Before her June 1941 stroke, Missy LeHand had checked such drift. She reinvigorated the circle with new advisers, such as Corcoran and Hopkins. She regulated the flow of visitors and paper to the president. She aided "Effdee" in balancing work and fun. She cared for him, kept him company, and worked around his procrastination. No one had ever replaced her. On July 29, 1944, she grew agitated after seeing in a newsreel how much weight FDR had lost. The next day a stroke killed her. Ickes mourned "the greatest loss that the President has suffered since he came here."[117]

At the moment of her death, FDR was touring facilities in the eastern Pacific. On the trip he edged closer to his military chief of staff, Admiral Leahy, and his cardiologist, Dr. Bruenn. Roosevelt routed all key information through himself. His health care proved no exception. In their thirteen months together, FDR never talked to Bruenn about his heart or even indicated he knew the doctor was a cardiologist. He checked his blood pressure independently with his physical therapist, George Fox. FDR did talk about his "ticker" problem—but with Daisy, Lucy, and his daughter, not with Bruenn or McIntire.[118] As with war production or work relief, he assigned competing aides to overlapping jobs.

He also folded the doctor into his circle. Bruenn helped the patient relax: "Gin rummy again!" the doctor noted in his diary. In Hawaii, they enjoyed the "Hula-Hula girl. Beautiful!!!" Talking with the president day and night and with the brass at meals, Bruenn began sprinkling his medical diary with political and military concerns.[119] He was developing into one of the "Boss's" generalists. Although a Republican, he also fell for the charm, telling Suckley, "You realize that like all people who work with this man—I love him. If he told me to jump out of the window, I would do it, without hesitation."[120]

Bruenn kept watch as the president pushed his limits. In Bremerton, Washington, he spoke from the deck of a destroyer on a windy day while standing in heavy braces that no longer fit since he had dropped so much weight. He continued speaking even through fifteen minutes of severe chest distress from angina. "I had a helluva pain," he told Bruenn afterward. The doctor found no residual damage.[121] FDR also went the extra mile at a hospital for amputees on Oahu. In earlier years he had shrunk from hearing about a son's illness. "He hates the sight of blood," Eleanor once remarked.[122] Now he wheeled past the beds, talking one by one with the young men who would have to learn, as he had, how to become differently able. He appeared close to tears.

Weeks later, angered by Dewey's attacks on "tired old men," FDR threw himself into the presidential campaign. Despite the pain, he practiced "walking" again, as he had aboard the *Prince of Wales*. "I never saw such a display of guts," Rosenman later testified. Yet the effort proved too much, and he had to sit while giving his rousing "Fala" speech to the Teamsters.[123] On October 21, he braved the tail end of a hurricane, campaigning for four hours in an open car. The previous day he had warned reporters about the "rain, and a fifty-mile gale in New York, which is not cheerful."[124] At least a million New Yorkers turned out to see the apparently fit president. Though grizzled, he seemed a survivor, a contrast to the robust Wendell Willkie, his 1940 opponent, who had died two weeks earlier. (Roosevelt would go on to win the November 8 election by a solid 53 percent to 46 percent margin.)[125] Bruenn recorded that despite FDR's "prolonged exposure" and "intense activity" in the rain, his "B.P. levels have been, if anything, lower than before."[126] His pressure jumped, however, as he watched his predecessor suffer a stroke in the movie *Wilson*. "By God, that's not going to happen to me!" he cried. His pressure again soared fifty points after Eleanor prodded him about one of her causes.[127]

In the six months before Yalta, Roosevelt's health and appearance seesawed. He complained to Suckley and Bruenn about feeling "low" and "logy." He groaned about back, stomach, and tooth pains. If he did have melanoma, the deadly cancer was spreading. Because of the clogged sinuses in his nose he had to spend "about a ½ hour almost every evening, getting it cleared out." He fretted that his heart "muscles are deteriorating, and they don't know why." Daisy alternately despaired that "he gets so tired-looking and grey," then cheered that he "looks 100% better after a rest." Despite the ups and downs, "his mind is wonderfully active and interested in everything."[128]

All three leaders were growing dead tired. FDR complained that Churchill "exhausted him. Kept him up all night."[129] The Russian dictator grumbled "that his health was beginning to fail him. Any change from the climate of Moscow now upset him." He had needed two weeks to recover from the air trip to Tehran. When Clark Kerr proposed a meeting in Scotland, Stalin responded, "It took a man with the health of the Prime Minister—that desperate fellow—to stand these journeys. He [Stalin] could not."[130] Eyeing Churchill en route to Quebec, Eden "was shocked at his appearance." Winant reported that "each journey has taken its toll" on the PM.[131] When someone described the three leaders as the Holy Trinity, Stalin quipped, "If that is so, Churchill must be the Holy Ghost. He flies around so much."[132]

Roosevelt pondered what might follow if the three of them died. In Britain "Eden would be the only possible successor, though by no means possessing the desirable qualities." Losing Stalin "would be very grave, as Russia would either break up" or Molotov, with his narrower vision, would take over. "In either case a Russian menace to Europe is out." His third vice president seemed able enough, but no

Roosevelt: "Truman has certain qualities which are not to be despised. He is colorless—he has no vision." Nevertheless, "his integrity is beyond question."[133] Roosevelt had picked him "because Truman will make the least trouble for me."[134]

FDR determined to survive. He stubbornly believed that although vice presidents were expendable, he was not. As a Washington fixer put it, "Roosevelt ran out of time, or he'd have had as many vice-presidents as Henry VIII had wives."[135]

Sidestepping the Atlantic Charter

Despite differing perspectives, all three leaders saw that the rigidity of the Atlantic Charter could wreck cooperation. As Lippmann observed, the principles were "perfectly valid" and "perfectly irrelevant."[136] The document offered no guidance for establishing preelection governments. Nor could it settle border disputes in mixed ethnic territories. Both the British in Greece and the Russians in Poland violated the principles. The charter envisioned not a world run by three or four policemen but rather a parliament of nations, an ideal many ordinary Americans found appealing. Lippmann discerned the deception: Roosevelt's top officials "have taken the position, or to be more accurate, they have allowed the American public to think it was our position" that the postwar world would look to the UN "General Assembly, where one-nation, one-vote ruled."[137]

In October at the TOLSTOY Conference in Moscow, Churchill and Stalin ignored the charter as they divided the Balkans. The British would dominate Greece; the Soviets Romania, Bulgaria, and Hungary. They would share Yugoslavia. The prime minister again ignored the principles when he ordered the British military to treat antimonarchist Greeks as a conquered people. He urged the Polish exiles to make a "great gift" to Russia of the territory east of the Curzon line.[138] Churchill made matters worse by claiming that all this accorded with the charter. Parliamentary critics asked whether he had ever read the document. Although Hull's successor, Edward R. Stettinius Jr., condemned British intervention in Greece and Italy, he also endorsed the "mutual agreement" foisted on the Poles. On December 19, the *New York Times* warned, "This is not the way border problems were to be settled under the terms of the Atlantic Charter. This is isolationism. It engenders isolationism in others."[139]

Roosevelt, however, rebelled at having to choose between "isolationism" and the charter, neither of which allowed the big power deals necessary for a realistic peace. At a White House meeting he bluntly told key senators "that the Russians had the power in Eastern Europe, that it was obviously impossible to have a break with them and that, therefore, the only practicable course was to use what influence we had to ameliorate the situation."[140]

The afternoon after the *New York Times* editorial, FDR treated reporters to some vaudeville-type storytelling. He disparaged the Atlantic Charter as a haphazard compilation. Queried about Churchill's heresy, he volunteered, "Nobody ever signed" the document. "There isn't any copy . . . so far as I know. I haven't got one." The so-called guide amounted to only a "scribbled thing" with a "great many corrections," some in "Churchill's handwriting, some in [mine]," scrawled on "scraps of paper." He allowed that Allied representatives had signed the Declaration of the United Nations, based on the charter, in a ceremony on January 1, 1942. He then minimized the seriousness of that document, too. The declaration was mistakenly left in a State Department safe, "so there was nothing to sign." Though he had intended to write "out in longhand some very simple words," his pen "didn't have any ink in it," and he had to borrow a pen. He joked, "probably, in time, they will find some documents and signature." Thrown off balance, a reporter queried about the charter, "The spirit is still there, sir?" FDR offered only: "We all agreed on it, that's all I know. It isn't considered signed by us both." Asked whether he wished there were an official copy, he replied, "No, except from the point of view of sightseers in Washington."

The juggler then tried tossing the charter upstairs. He depicted its principles as relevant to long-term progress rather than immediate diplomacy. "The Atlantic Charter stands as an objective," he affirmed, a segment of the upward curve "over these thousands of years," like the Ten Commandments or Christianity.[141] Just before leaving for

Yalta, he again commented on the Ten Commandments. "Perfectly good principles" were "very often interpreted differently in individual cases." Revealing his sophisticated understanding of geopolitical and cultural issues as well as "reality," Roosevelt explained that precisely because principles could be interpreted differently, "the existing facts in relation to this particular valley, or that particular town, or that particular minority group, will vary from one case to the other."[142]

Despite his understanding and his attempts at education, Roosevelt failed to launch a vigorous public relations campaign for the Three Policemen approach. He did not meet his own standard, "to explain to the individual man on the street—in three letter words."[143] He could muster neither the physical strength nor the support from aides. He was probably also hedging his bets in case Stalin proved aggressive. He dared not alienate international-minded Wilsonian idealists. Nor would he repeat Wilson's mistake of jumping ahead of public opinion.

One of the many who failed to discern this tack was Kennan, who believed that the president was catering "slavishly and minutely" to the "American [public's] fondness for dealing [in] high moral principles."[144] FDR was instead trying to back into a realistic policy. He gambled on enough time and luck to secure a Three Policeman transition to an eventual multilateral world order. Summing up his approach, he told reporters, "You do the best you can. . . . You do the best you can."[145] No Moses he. His points got lost in the bulrushes. He could neither square the circle nor part the Red Sea. FDR remained a frail human.

Despite his own frailty, Hopkins had reentered the scene in October. Opportunity came on the eve of Churchill's meeting with Stalin. The president was preparing to send a telegram absolving himself from any deal on Eastern Europe. Significantly, it was the State Department Russian expert "Chip" Bohlen who brought the issue to Hopkins and guided his reaction. Hopkins warned FDR that Churchill, having just come from Quebec, would claim to be speaking on the president's behalf. At Harry's urging, FDR sent Stalin a quite different message: "There is in this global war literally no question, either military or political, in which the United States is not engaged."[146] Stalin probably wondered precisely how the United States might "engage" in Eastern Europe. Limited U.S. ambitions in his backyard did not necessarily portend conflict, however, because Stalin preferred, as he repeatedly stated, not a rigid division of Europe but rather a Big Three alliance to contain Germany and a Poland allied with both Russia and Western nations. Moreover, to Harriman's dismay, Roosevelt "consistently shows very little interest in Eastern European matters except as they affect sentiment in America."[147]

In contrast to happier days when the president and his friend mixed work with meals, stories, and cards, Hopkins from September 1944 to April 1945 dined with FDR on only two days. He no longer went along to Hyde Park or Warm Springs.[148] Resentments among FDR, Harry, and Louise Hopkins (who mocked Roosevelt as "nutty about some fool dog") kept relations cool.[149] Yet Hopkins remained the one insightful problem solver who could complement the "Boss's" mode of thinking.

The emptying circle created space for Bohlen. His family tree included a Civil War general, the Krupp arms czars of Germany, and the wealthy Thayers of Philadelphia. The handsome, intelligent forty-year-old boasted a Kremlin-tested capacity to hold his liquor. Harry and FDR enjoyed having the charmer around.[150] He had interpreted for Roosevelt at Tehran and for Hull at Moscow. Perhaps because of Bohlen's ties with Bullitt, the First Lady never trusted this rising star. After Stettinius became secretary of state on December 1, 1944, Bohlen, who kept his job as director of the Eastern European division of the State Department, worked out of a White House office with Hopkins.[151] The Bohlens vacationed in Maine with Louise Hopkins's sister and her husband. Isaiah Berlin, who reported on the American scene for the British embassy, also befriended Bohlen. Berlin alerted London that Bohlen "is very genuinely a key man just now." He stood "well disposed towards us, and things can obviously be said to him which cannot be said at a higher level quite so easily."[152] The Berlin-Bohlen connection provided Churchill with another link to Hopkins. In a Christmas greeting to Churchill, Harry affirmed his pride at getting "attacked by some of my countrymen as your good friend."[153] FDR, in contrast was telling a cousin, apropos of Churchill, that while he appreciated the English, "you had to be rude to them—and honest—and laugh at them."[154]

Bohlen's rise brought the sensibility of Moscow-soured diplomats like Bullitt back into the White House. Berlin discerned his friend's emotional ambivalence: Bohlen appeared "still pretty touchy about Russia, like everyone who has sat there, particularly with Bullitt, but is thoroughly excited about the President's 'Great Design' for a real permanent alliance."[155] By tapping Bohlen's expertise on Russia, Hopkins expected to enhance his own influence with the President. Yet Hopkins was also tapping into the State Department's deep-seated skepticism of the Kremlin. A friend remembered that Harry "took a fancy to Bohlen," believing he was "entirely different from anybody else in the State Department. . . . Well, actually Bohlen wasn't that different."[156] Indeed Harry's protégé may well have encouraged Stettinius to elevate conservative, anti-Soviet department stalwarts, such as James Dunn and Joseph Grew. These officials were now ensconced in positions that would enable them to help change U.S. policy under Truman.[157]

Bohlen later recalled that American condemnation of ham-fisted British intervention in Greece and Italy in December 1944 had plunged Churchill, already exhausted, into "a terribly dangerous and explosive mood." Ties "between the White House and Downing Street were more strained than they had ever been before." On January 21, 1945, Hopkins and Bohlen flew to London on a pre-Yalta mission to soothe the PM. Enduring Churchill's "volcanic explosions" of "wrath" brought the two Americans closer together.[158]

"Chip is tremendous, and at the moment we are sharing quarters," Harry informed Louise. "We have become fast friends, and I admire him ever so much."[159] Hopkins, who in December 1941 had professed indifference if much of Europe went communist, was now tutored by Bohlen on "the importance of the ideological factor in Soviet thinking."[160] In Paris, Hopkins tried without success to mollify Charles de Gaulle, who was incensed at not being invited to Yalta. A further sign of distance from FDR was Harry's dining amiably with Bullitt's longtime companion, Carmel Offie.[161] Harriman, another Roosevelt critic, also ate with Hopkins, "and they were clearly very close."[162] Then it was on to a villa outside Naples, where Hopkins ravaged his gastro-intestinal system by overindulging.

Yalta

Roosevelt meanwhile carefully alternated work with rest. He could still rise to challenge. Though appearing gray and fatigued on January 19, he "looked much better" at his fourth inauguration, the next day, Frances Perkins observed.[163] He stood "there, straight and vigorous, thin but with good color."[164] Bruenn recorded that his patient, wearing leg braces for the first time since Bremerton, was "in excellent spirits and mood." His "general condition is essentially unchanged. . . . [N]o cardiac symptoms. . . . Blood pressure levels tending to be a little lower." Worrisome, however, was the loss of appetite, a side effect of digitalis and perhaps also his heart disease.[165] He had also lost the boyish enthusiasm of his "Odyssey" to Tehran. "He doesn't relish this trip at all," Suckley recorded before Yalta. "Thinks it will be very wearing, & feels that he will have to be so much on the alert, in his conversations with Uncle Joe & W. S. C." Especially with the PM present, "the conversations will last interminably & will involve very complicated questions."[166]

Aboard the heavy cruiser USS *Quincy*, Roosevelt reached the Mediterranean island of Malta the morning of February 2, expecting help from Hopkins. Harry, however, suffered "continuous dysentery."[167] He joked that he had been "all right until he saw the Pope."[168] Stettinius told Anna Boettiger a different story: "Harry has been drinking far too much." Hopkins had already angered the "Boss" by grandstanding with the press.[169] Naval aide Admiral Wilson Brown feared the publicity might tempt the Germans to attempt assassination of the Allied leaders. That evening Harry knocked on Anna's cabin door and "demanded a drink." When she turned her back, he "stole my one bottle of scotch."[170] Advised to eat only bland cereal, "the fool had 2 huge helpings of caviar, cabbage soup with sour cream & then his cereal," Kathleen Harriman recorded.[171] Brown fumed that Hopkins showed "no more sense than a child in caring for his own health or the health of Franklin Roosevelt."[172]

Roosevelt's grueling schedule on February 2—his only day on Malta before the flight to the Crimea—made him look worse, especially to those who had not seen him in months. Anna, who had assumed Missy's gatekeeper role, pleaded with Churchill. "I wanted Father to have a little restful time to himself." While "the P.M. had had a 1½ hour nap, FDR had been going strong since 9:30 without a break," she groused. Fourteen hours of work that day raised his blood pressure.[173] Roosevelt did manage to fend off Churchill's plea for a tête-à-tête about the "Bear," as Eden put it.[174] Their brief meeting entailed instead "much teasing and joking . . . about the unsigned Atlantic Charter." Then the prime minister "went off on a very serious vein" about "freedom from international fear." Adopting what would become the antitotalitarian discourse of the Cold War, he pointed to the "many countries" where people were "being ruled by Gestapo, for example." Growing "very emotional," Churchill vowed, "'As long as blood flows from my veins, I will stand for'" this freedom. Roosevelt vaguely promised "very careful study."[175] He did not intend to break with Stalin over Eastern Europe.

Near midnight the president was whisked up the elevator of his new plane, the *Sacred Cow*. Ninety C-54s, with some seven hundred U.S. and British officials aboard, created a racket gunning their engines. Brown recalled that no one aboard the *Sacred Cow* slept "because a plane took off alongside us every ten minutes until we left" at 3:30 a.m. Even then the noise, vibration, and pitching of the aircraft did not permit much rest. "The President was already a tired man when we arrived at Saki air field," Brown later recounted. That arrival started what the latter—a robust man who would live for many years—called "one of the most tiring days I have ever experienced."[176] They endured a five-hour, freezing auto trip from Saki to Yalta over curving roads with no retaining walls. Every fifty feet stood a soldier, many of them young women. FDR slept part of the way. Upon awakening, he was stunned at the destruction. "The sight of it now made him want to exact an eye for an eye from the Germans."[177]

As usual, Roosevelt bounced back. On February 6, Cadogan acknowledged that FDR "looks rather better."[178] Bohlen, who again interpreted for the president, remembered that while his "physical state

6.1. Roosevelt apparently glaring at Churchill, February 1945. (Courtesy of FDR Library.)

was certainly not up to normal, his mental and psychological state was certainly not affected." He remained "mentally sharp" and "effective."[179] Valentin Berezhkov, one of Stalin's interpreters, testified years later that "everybody who watched [FDR] said that in spite of his frail appearance, his mental potential was high." He emphasized, "those who say that Roosevelt did not quite grasp what was going on in Yalta are wrong. Stalin treated Roosevelt with great esteem."[180] Kathleen Harriman would remember, "I was horrified at the way he looked but there was nothing wrong with him mentally."[181] Bruenn recorded in his diary: Roosevelt "has worked very hard" at Yalta, often having "no time to take his afternoon rest."

On February 8, an "emotionally disturbing" session on Poland induced an alternating weak and strong pulse (*pulsus alternans*), indicating an impaired left ventricle. The cardiologist ordered no visitors before noon and an hour's nap in the afternoon. Two days later the *pulsus alternans* disappeared, and the patient's spirits rose. He was

6.2. FDR at Yalta could look terrible. Yet aside from the British officials upset about his policies, most observers affirmed that his mind remained sharp. (Courtesy of FDR Library.)

"eating well—delights in Russian food."[182] The doctor later recalled that at Yalta Roosevelt's "mental clarity was truly remarkable." His "recollection of detail" outshone "associates ten and twenty years younger than himself."[183] FDR reported to Daisy, "I either work or sleep!"—it was the survival plan he had outlined to Childs.[184]

Heart disease did not account for all his symptoms. The intermittent slack jaw, blank stare, hand tremor, and forgetfulness probably stemmed from encephalopathy (reduced supply of oxygen to the brain) that resulted from heart and obstructive pulmonary disease, as well as the phenobarbital.[185] Patients with low-grade encephalopathy often do better when facing challenges.[186] Recurring difficulty in signing his name originated from the polio, which had mildly affected his right hand and sometimes acted up.[187] Despite all these physical problems, Roosevelt remained mentally fit.

What did limit the president was his need for rest, a diminished circle of close associates, and partial deafness. In dealing with the first problem, his handlers aggravated the second. Anna fretted that her father "gets all wound up, seems to thoroughly enjoy it all, but wants too many people around, and then won't go to bed early enough." The upshot was that "he doesn't sleep well." With Bruenn she worked to "keep the unnecessary people out of his room and to steer the necessary ones in."[188] Making this distinction required tricky political judgments. Roosevelt could tap Stettinius, Bohlen, Leahy, Harriman, Byrnes, and others for advice.

Yet tragically he lacked anyone both committed to his postwar vision and gifted with the brilliance and energy to translate it into concrete proposals. Anna lamented, "the only practical guy here, on our side, who is smart is Jimmy B[yrnes]. But he is not 100% loyal to the Boss." As for Hopkins, he "is a complete d-fool about his health; doesn't think straight when he is not well; and so can't be counted on."[189] Harry, who dropped considerable weight at Yalta, mostly stayed in bed except for plenary meetings.[190] FDR kept the increasingly anti-Soviet Harriman off to the side. At plenary sessions, Portal reported to Pamela Churchill, "poor Averell was frozen out into the back row, whereas Archie Clark Kerr got a seat at the table."[191]

Roosevelt's saddest, most dangerous failing as wartime leader was that he never—for reasons of privacy, inertia, or lack of opportunity—opened himself and his inner circle to anyone talented and trustworthy enough to replace Howe, Corcoran, LeHand, Welles, or Hopkins. While the "Boss" worked, most of "his immediate party just sit on their fannies and play gin rummy," Anna griped.[192] Churchill interpreted FDR's political agenda as incapacity: "He won't take any interest in what we are trying to do.[193]

Churchill was himself showing wear and tear. His "work has deteriorated a lot in the last few months," and he tended to obsess, on "Greece, for example," his private secretary told Moran.[194] The PM's 102.5-degree temperature threatened another bout of pneumonia.[195] He had "a grey look about his gills which I hadn't seen before," the doctor worried.[196] On February 8, FDR's tough day, Cadogan disparaged Churchill as a "silly old man," who had "plunged into a long harangue" while "knowing nothing whatsoever of what he was talking about."[197] An impatient Roosevelt snapped, "Yes, I *am* tired! So would you if you had spent the last five years pushing Winston uphill in a wheelbarrow."[198] After the conference, Stettinius described "a

6.3. At Yalta, Roosevelt sidelined his increasingly anti-Soviet ambassador, Harriman. Sitting clockwise from center right: Churchill, Archibald Clark Kerr, Stalin, interpreter Pavlov, Ivan Maisky, Andrei Gromyko, Leahy, Edward Stettinius, Roosevelt, "Chip" Bohlen. Anthony Eden is standing behind Churchill. (Courtesy of FDR Library.)

change in Churchill, who apparently has grown older and more eccentric during the past year, and who was very erratic at Yalta."[199]

Stalin outshone the other two. Though appearing "greatly over-exhausted" afterward, he had remained sharp at the conference.[200] Even Cadogan acknowledged, Stalin "*is* a great man, and shows up very impressively against the background of the other two ageing statesmen."[201]

Yalta appeared to Cadogan as a muddle, in part because "the Great Men don't know what they're talking about."[202] Shaping outcomes were not only exhaustion, illness, and aging, but also confusion, misunderstanding, and trauma. "This place is still rather a madhouse," another participant observed.[203] Uncut movie footage reveals the disorder that later generations would not see in the famous photographs and official transcripts.[204] Those transcripts probably miss many of the discrepancies in what was said, translated, and understood. In giving Roosevelt an "accurate picture" of a previous conference, Harriman made a rare admission of a probably not-so-rare occurrence. Often both Stalin and Churchill "were talking at the same time and not always on the same subject." In "attempting to translate what was being said," the interpreters only added to the din.[205] Faulty hearing, mistranslations, and cognitive dissonance all undercut the veracity of official transcripts of conversations. This gold standard did not in fact always accurately measure what had been said.

All the more important, then, was the emotional context of diplomacy. The British relied on the supposed superiority of their diplomacy to redress their relative deficiency in power. On the eve of the conference, a plane carrying a dozen key Foreign Office officials crashed into the Mediterranean. The accident threw Churchill into "a discouraged state of mind," Kathleen Harriman observed.[206] Mourning the death of his "most intimate companion," British military chief Alanbrooke "found it extremely difficult to concentrate." "The thought of dear old Barney" Charlesworth continued to haunt him. Alanbrooke acknowledged, "This conference has been a nightmare with his loss hanging over me the whole time."[207] Such trauma did not "determine" this or that policy, but it did probably intensify British anxiety about slipping behind the emerging giants. Coolness between Hopkins and Roosevelt also hampered British influence.

The first night at Yalta, Harry, "in a stew," insisted to Anna that "FDR *must* see Churchill in the morning for a long meeting to dope out" how they would direct the conference. Churchill, Eden, and probably Bohlen had been pressing this case to Hopkins. Roosevelt, however, preferred to meet privately with Stalin first, then see Churchill. When Anna explained that her father would not risk the Russians' distrust, Hopkins countered with "insulting remarks to the effect that after all, FDR had asked for this job and that now, whether he liked it or not, he had to do the work."[208] In physical agony—his antidysentery medicine no longer worked—Hopkins seemed goaded also by resentment. His slap that "after all, FDR had asked for this job" evidenced an astonishing eruption of ego. After years of sacrifice for the president, he, Harry, whose brains and drive had lifted Roosevelt into greatness, would never get "this job" for himself. He would never satisfy his urge "to dominate, rule, and give orders—not take them," that his psychoanalyst had noted a decade earlier.[209]

In terms of policy, Hopkins was arguing for what would become standard procedure in the Cold War. According to his logic, the only way Roosevelt could act responsibly—"do the work," as he put it—was to exclude the Russians by agreeing with Churchill on "some pre-arrangements before the Conference started."[210] As the British appreciated, on most issues "Hopkins is a valuable ally."[211]

By journeying so far to meet with Stalin, Churchill and Roosevelt were, according to diplomatic custom, paying the dictator great respect. Sublimely self-confident, FDR, had little compunction about this homage or about his own physical discomfort if he could secure his postwar aims. Kathleen Harriman, who observed the conference up close, later reflected that Stalin seemed to "realize that Roosevelt had shortened his life in order to come meet with him because he cared so much about the future of the world."[212] Other Americans, however, seethed at the perceived humiliation. The Pentagon's liaison to the Red Army, General John R. Deane, later testified that "no single event of the war irritated me more than seeing the President of the United States lifted from wheel chair, to ship, to shore ... in order to go halfway around the world as the only possible means of meeting J. V. Stalin."[213] The latter, while unwilling to sacrifice his own health, did respond to Roosevelt's show of respect. He arranged for the Americans to live in the conference headquarters, the fifty-room summer home of the czar, Livadia Palace, while he resided six miles away. It was probably no accident that the British were placed ten miles distant.

The Germans had left Livadia a shambles. More than fifteen hundred rail cars were sent to Yalta with building materials, furniture, food, and workers. A shop was set up to produce marble for the floors, which had to be smooth enough for FDR's wheelchair. Lavrenty Beria, head of the secret police, ordered maximum hospitality. Kathleen Harriman, who arrived early with her father to advise on preparations, observed that the staff "have set and un-set the table 3 or 4 times a day for the past week—experimenting with glassware and china effects. Rugs have been laid and relaid and pictures hung and rehung."[214]

The Soviets were probably trying to get right these markers of bourgeois culture. Kathleen, however, saw different criteria: "the Soviets just couldn't make up their minds which oriental colors looked best."[215] A request for lemon peel for cocktails yielded a tree loaded with lemons planted in the hall. Churchill had at his disposal "buckets of Caucasian champagne" and an ever-full decanter of vodka in his room.[216] The eagerness of the staff to please the guests—and avoid exile to Beria's gulag—blended with apparent resentment at the imperiousness of the foreigners. In a possibly apocryphal story, a workman recounted that Kathleen had pointed to the sea to indicate the desired color for the president's bathroom. As the color of the sea kept changing, she ordered the walls repainted seven times.[217] A. D. Beschastnov, commander of security in Livadia, reported that his men "felt bad about the expensive furniture we had brought from Moscow." The Americans, "lacking inhibitions," sprawled out, "putting their feet on priceless engraved tables."[218]

Also getting things ready was Sergo Beria, who had spied for Stalin at Tehran. His surveillance team bugged Livadia and the surrounding gardens with directional microphones effective at up to two hundred meters. They even bugged the Lend-Lease jeep transporting Roosevelt after his plane landed. The younger Beria later recounted listening as Churchill, walking beside the vehicle, "tried to take up certain questions, but Roosevelt cut him short."[219] Stalin was also briefed with reams of secret U.S. and British documents copied by his network of spies. Especially valuable moles were Guy Burgess, who had burrowed deep into the Foreign Office, and Donald Maclean, first secretary of the British embassy in Washington.[220] Roosevelt's staff was alert to spying from all quarters. Referring to the preliminary meeting with the British as well as the three-way summit, a memorandum directed: "Assume *all* rooms and places of tête-à-tête are wired for recording. This applies to Malta as well as Yalta."[221]

The Kremlin apparently cared more about espionage than it did about sanitation. Although the Soviets claimed they had de-loused the palace, the Americans were attacked by "creepy-crawly creatures," as an itchy Anna recorded. The lice could spread typhus. Exterminators from the USS *Catoctin* spread DDT "by the gallon."[222] Decades later, medical experts would warn that short-term effects of excessive exposure to DDT can include tremors, facial numbness, and loss of perception.[223] The pesticide may have aggravated the medical problems of FDR and others.

As with Molotov's stay at Chequers and at the White House, toilets and bathing facilities were seen as cultural markers. U.S. Army Air Force General Laurence Kuter recalled that "excepting only the war, the bathrooms were the most generally discussed subject at the Crimean conference."[224] Only Roosevelt and Churchill had private baths. At 7:30 a.m. one could "see three field-marshals queuing for a bucket."[225] More startling were "chambermaids [who] nonchalantly bustled in and out of bathrooms without the faintest concern as to who was there or what he was doing."[226] Alger Hiss, a State Department official later convicted of perjury in connection with charges of spying for the Soviets, recalled that during breaks Stalin "stood in the lavatory line with his aides and the rest of us lesser fry while Churchill was taken to Stettinius's suite and Roosevelt went to his own."[227]

Many Americans and Britons did not bother hiding their sense of superiority. Having ordered an American-style breakfast, Admiral Leahy received instead "a tray laden with such delicacies as caviar." He "let out a bellow" and lambasted the waiter for "speaking no known language," ordering him to get "his wares out of here!" The humor in what Anna called a "light story" also belittled Russians.[228] The phrase "his wares" suggested a peddler rather than a professional server. Leahy's shouting on Russian territory that Russian was "no known language" expressed the kind of contempt that infuriated Stalin. That Anna found the episode amusing reflected her upper-class privilege and Western bias. Even Roosevelt irritated Stalin by confiding, "We always call you Uncle Joe." The dictator did not see this as just a term of endearment, as FDR implied.[229] The Russified Georgian sensed, rightly, that "Uncle Joe," "U. J.," and "Joe" signaled, as did "the Bear," condescension. As the dictator had probably gleaned from his spies, U.S. and British telegrams and letters sometimes juxtaposed the moniker "Uncle Joe" with references to "the President" and "the Prime Minister."

Nevertheless, Stalin, in contrast to his customary harshness, seemed genuinely to care for Roosevelt. After leaving the president's room, he reportedly stopped, turned to Molotov and Gromyko, asking, "Why did nature have to punish him so? Is he any worse than other people?" Gromyko was astonished because the dictator "rarely bestowed his sympathy on anyone from another social system." Beria marveled "how full of consideration he is where Roosevelt is concerned, when, as a rule, he is dreadfully rude."[230] Brown later recalled that Stalin "deferred to [Roosevelt] and his whole expression softened when he addressed the President directly."[231] Kathleen Harriman remembered that Stalin "really admired Roosevelt and had great respect for him."[232] Indeed, Moran and Churchill complained that on issue after issue, "Stalin made it plain at once that if this was the President's wish, he would accept it."[233]

Even when lecturing communist acolytes about the nefarious capitalists, the Kremlin boss had distinguished between Churchill, who would "slip a kopeck out your pocket," and Roosevelt, who "is not like that. He dips in his hand only for bigger coins. But Churchill? Churchill—even for a kopeck."[234] In the depth of the Cold War, the dictator would laud FDR as "a great statesman, a clever, educated, far-sighted and liberal leader who prolonged the life of capitalism."[235]

At Yalta, Stalin and Roosevelt tightened the bonds knit at Tehran. The American revisited the macabre "joke" that had earlier incensed Churchill. Remarking that the destruction in the Crimea had rendered him "more bloodthirsty," he "hoped that Marshal Stalin would again propose a toast to the execution of 50,000 officers of the German Army." The Kremlin chief emphasized, as he had to Hopkins in July 1941, that the civilizational/racial divide lay not between East and West, but between the Germans and the rest. "The Germans were savages and seemed to hate with a sadistic hatred the creative work of human beings." Roosevelt agreed. They chatted until the start of the first plenary session, at 5:00 p.m. on February 4.[236]

The eight-day conference entailed tough, exhausting diplomacy among powerful nations. Such serious effort to hammer out compromises would be largely abandoned in the Cold War. The Soviets bargained from a strong position. While the Red Army battled 45 miles from Berlin, Allied forces remained on the far side of the Rhine, 250 miles away.[237] With the atom bomb still untested and the United States likely facing heavy casualties in the projected invasion of Japan, the Americans needed the Red Army to tie down Japanese troops in Manchuria and China. The Soviets occupied most of Poland, giving them the upper hand in the most contentious issue during the conference. The Americans and British also held cards, however. By repeatedly praising Lend-Lease, Stalin signaled his desire for postwar credits and equipment. While leaning toward Roosevelt, the dictator also valued the understandings reached with Churchill in Moscow the previous October. Indeed, on the first day of Yalta he met with the prime minister before seeing the president.[238] He understood that opposition from Washington and London could magnify his problems in securing a Poland strong enough to guard the gate and friendly enough to wish to do so. Above all, the Kremlin chief wanted the Big Three to contain postwar Germany, thereby forestalling another terrible invasion. During feel-good toasts, it was usually Stalin who most often emphasized "our duty to see . . . that our relations in peacetime should be as strong as they had been in war."[239]

Although subsequently controversial, the easiest agreements concerned East Asia. Stalin clarified his pledge to enter the war against Japan within three months of Germany's surrender. In return, the Soviets would get southern Sakhalin, the Kurile Islands, and rights in China lost in Russia's 1904–5 war with Japan. Roosevelt pledged to secure the agreement of Nationalist Chinese leader Jiang Jieshi, and Stalin promised to sign a treaty with Jiang—thereby containing Mao Zedong and the Communist Chinese.[240] As island-hopping across the central Pacific met fierce Japanese resistance, U.S. military planners eyed possible bomber bases on Soviet territory. Referring to "intensive bombing" that could "destroy Japan," Roosevelt confided to Stalin that "he hoped that it would not be necessary actually to invade the Japanese islands and [that he] would do so only if absolutely necessary." Stalin responded by offering two bases in the Soviet Maritime Provinces with more to come later.[241]

In terms of Germany, Yalta finalized plans for division into four military zones, with the French sector to be carved out of U.S. and

British areas. Berlin, in the middle of the Soviet zone, would also be cut in four. Stalin stressed that a real peace required permanently dismembering Germany. Though Roosevelt at Tehran had urged a partition, he and Hopkins had not followed through with detailed planning. Their failure eventually allowed the resistance in the State Department and in London to prevail. For more than a year, the UK Post-Hostilities Planning group had been discussing rearming Germans against postwar Soviet expansion. Yalta yielded no concrete agreement on permanent dismemberment, only on the military zones of occupation.[242]

Determined that Germany help repair the destruction it had wrought, the Soviets proposed $20 billion of reparations in kind (machinery, other goods, and labor), of which they would get half. While Churchill opposed setting a fixed amount, Roosevelt agreed on $20 billion as the basis for discussion by the Reparations Commission that would meet in Moscow.[243] FDR, who in the early 1920s had speculated in depreciating German currency, opposed a repeat of U.S. loans to finance reparations. Nor did he want Germans to starve. "We want Germany to live but not to have a higher standard of living than that of the U.S.S.R."

This last point marked a divergence—crucial in its cultural, economic, and political implications—between Roosevelt and postwar U.S. officials. For more than a century, highly productive Germany had enjoyed a living standard higher than Russia's. The Germans had used their industrial and war-making prowess to devastate a huge swath of the Soviet Union. Roosevelt believed that Germany's "manpower and factories" should help repair that damage, even if reparations reduced the German standard of living to the Soviet level.[244] In contrast, Roosevelt's successors sympathized with the former enemy because of ethnic and cultural (including ideological) affinities, and because they saw Germany's economic revival as key to rebuilding Western Europe and containing the Soviets.

The president was abandoned by advisers when it came to forging United Nations trusteeships to shepherd colonies toward eventual self-government. His traveling in Africa had strengthened his disgust. "For every dollar that the British have put into Gambia," he had told reporters, "they have taken out ten. The natives are five thousand years back of us. Disease is rampant, absolutely."[245] Worry that he had contracted "sleeping-sickness of some sort" fed his belief that colonial backwardness threatened global sickness and possible race war.[246] He envisioned UN inspection committees mobilizing "pitiless publicity" to spur economic development, health advances, and self-government. To African American reporters, Roosevelt had declared it "a grand thing if we had a committee of the United Nations come [to the American South] and make a report on us. Why not?"[247] He was harking back to his first years in politics, when reformers, including his settlement-worker wife, were trying to uplift the poor. Roosevelt's progressive vision was opposed by the State Department, the Foreign Office, and Churchill.[248] In contrast to earlier battles in which Hopkins had sidestepped or bulldozed the bureaucracy, the former social worker now consorted with FDR's opponents.[249]

Unable to flesh out his framework, Roosevelt wearily acquiesced to a State Department proposal for France to regain Indochina and for limiting trusteeships to former League of Nations mandates, Axis colonies, and colonies voluntarily placed in the new program.[250] Though this amounted to only a shadow of the original plan, Churchill exploded. Even the toned-down minutes report him protesting "with great vigor." He regarded the imperial domain as, literally, a body politic threatened with unwanted penetration. Never would he "consent to forty or fifty nations thrusting interfering fingers into the life's existence of the British Empire."[251] He asked how Stalin "would feel" if forced to internationalize the Crimea as a summer resort. In his half-serious response, the Soviet leader opted not for a spa with freely associating vacationers but rather for "the Crimea as a place to be used for meetings of the three powers.[252]

Even absent the Cold War, Big Three meetings in the Crimea or anywhere else probably still would have confronted Polish aspirations for independence. Decades later, Molotov would complain, "the Poles never calm down. . . . They are always on one's neck."[253] At Yalta, Polish issues sparked nearly eighteen thousand words of argument.[254] Though still formally recognizing the London exiles, Churchill and Roosevelt resented their refusal to compromise with Stalin in

1944. Roosevelt publicly downplayed the controversy. Yet in November, in response to queries about whether the exiles had offered fresh proposals, he had fulminated to reporters: "For about three years. Nothing new. No."[255]

With the Soviets controlling Poland, it was Roosevelt and Churchill who had to broach that thorny issue. For those watching Poland—and especially for Stalin, Harriman, and Churchill—the makeup of its government and the location of its borders seemed a geopolitical imperative. But Poland involved still more. Many geopolitical issues could be settled long term with a well-balanced, coldly calculated deal. The fate of Poland, however, remained an explosive issue because it touched core emotional beliefs, cultural assumptions, and historical legacies, in Britain and America as well as in Russia.

After Churchill at Yalta stressed Britain's interest in Poland as a matter of "honor," Stalin called for a recess. He returned vehement. This was "not only of a question of honor for Russia, but one of life and death." Twice in thirty years Germany had marched into Russia through Poland. "Since it was impossible by the force of Russian armies alone to close" this gate, Russia needed "to have Poland independent, strong, and democratic." Stalin's reiteration of this formula to very different audiences suggests that he believed it. Yet forging a vibrant, independent ally out of a nation with many grievances against Russia would prove a task beyond Stalin's crude politics. When Roosevelt and Churchill suggested that Russia modify the Curzon line so that Poland could retain Lvov and adjacent oil fields, Stalin reminded them that in 1920 "Curzon and [Georges] Clemenceau fixed this line." Again rising from his chair, he angrily asked how could he be "less Russian" than they.

Despite such agitation, the Kremlin boss reaffirmed "that Poland should maintain friendly relations not only with the Soviet Union but with the other Allies."[256] In the end, the Big Three agreed to the Curzon line with minor adjustments (but not Lvov) in Poland's favor. They postponed a decision on how far west to fix the Polish border with Germany. Although Roosevelt had joined Churchill on these issues, the dictator attacked mostly the PM, in an apparent bid to preserve his entente with the president. In another nod to Roosevelt, Stalin accepted the U.S. voting formula (retaining the Great Power veto but limiting it to decisions and not to discussions) in the UN Security Council, the postwar embodiment of the Policemen.[257]

The makeup of the Polish government proved a rancorous issue. On January 1, 1945, Stalin, ignoring Roosevelt's plea, had unilaterally recognized the Lublin committee as the provisional government. With little bargaining power, the Western allies signaled they would settle for elections free from overt Soviet interference. On February 8, after torturous discussion, Roosevelt passed the issue to the foreign ministers. He wheeled back to his room with a roller-coaster pulse, frightening both Bruenn and Anna. On the 9th, he tried to wrap things up by proposing, vaguely, "some gesture" to show Polish-Americans "that the United States was in some way involved with the question of freedom of elections." He had never cared much about Poland beyond how it affected U.S. opinion. He was now asking Stalin to camouflage what would become Soviet domination. Roosevelt evidently believed that if Poland were to achieve actual democracy, such progress would have to come by embracing the Russians and slowly backing into freedom.[258]

With regard to Polish elections, FDR offered an analogy focused on appearance more than achievement. "It should be like Caesar's wife. I did not know her but they said she was pure." Stalin countered, "they said that about her but in fact she had her sins." The exchange suggests that both men were cynics—and ladies' men in their day. Yet they diverged in that whereas the Hyde Park aristocrat relied on seducing voters, the former bank robber insisted that the election could not avoid sinning. Perhaps annoyed, the president reiterated his concern with political fallout. "I don't want the Poles to be able to question the Polish elections." This was a matter not just "of principle but of practical politics." At this point, Roosevelt, probably worn out, suggested leaving the details to the foreign ministers.[259]

Before adjourning, however, Roosevelt mustered the energy to reestablish relations with Stalin at Churchill's expense. The Declaration on Liberated Europe pledged consultation, though not action, in response to violations of self-determination. Taken at face value, it gave the illusory image that Yalta was following the principles of the

Atlantic Charter. Roosevelt, however, kept the declaration toothless and separate from the Security Council, wherein lay the major power of the projected UN. Stalin and Molotov valued the declaration as a means to discredit their opponents in Eastern Europe as "fascist."[260] Churchill, worried that the Americans and Soviets—along with colonials aspiring for independence—would try to wedge apart the British Empire, reaffirmed that self-determination "did not apply" to His Majesty's realm. His very next sentence, however, illustrated the difficulty of championing both democracy and empire: "As far as the British Empire was concerned the principles already applied." He added that he had explained all this when Wendell Willkie had visited England. "Was that what killed him?" Roosevelt jabbed.[261]

The final, vague agreement on Poland provided for broadening the existing, Soviet-dominated government: "The Provisional Government which is now functioning in Poland should therefore be reorganized on a broader, democratic basis with the inclusion of democratic leaders from Poland itself and from Poles abroad."[262] In return for a largely free hand in Poland, Stalin accepted the American formula for voting in the UN. He dropped his earlier demands that the big power veto in the Security Council apply not only to action but also to talking about an issue. He abandoned also the request for membership in the General Assembly for all sixteen Soviet republics—only fair, the dictator had argued with a straight face, to counter London's locked-in support from its dominions and Washington's from Latin America.[263] Stalin settled for three votes for the Russian, Ukrainian, and Belorussian Soviet Republics.

After a week of hard bargaining, each side emerged satisfied, indeed aglow. FDR compared the "atmosphere at this dinner" to "that of a family."[264] Hopkins noted to Roosevelt that "the Russians have given in so much at this conference that I don't think we should let them down."[265] Maisky celebrated a different conclusion: "The decisions of the conference were 75 per cent our decisions."[266] Even Churchill, who had "been in a vile mood throughout the Conference, irritable and bad-tempered," felt afterward "very pleased with the decisions we have gained."[267] He concluded that "all personal relations are excellent."[268] Cadogan allowed, "I have never known the Russians so easy and accommodating. In particular Joe has been extremely good."[269] In a letter to Pamela Churchill, British air chief Charles Portal sighed, "I do hate being so far away from you XXXX." He then confided, "We are all becoming very pro-Russian, as they really do seem to be nice people, kind & sincere, clean-looking . . . and with absolutely no 'bounce' or arrogance. . . . I am absolutely certain that we shall *have* to make friends with them, and that we shan't find it difficult."[270] Meanwhile Stalin reportedly remarked, "Let's hope nothing happens to [Roosevelt]. We shall never do business again with anyone like him."[271] Robert Hopkins, who photographed the conference, observed "a kind of euphoria among the principals and members of all three delegations for all that was accomplished during the conference."[272]

Though evanescent, this bonding and catharsis resulted from serious diplomacy and shared work, not just from sentimental toasts. Working together had forged a measure of trust. Afterward Churchill remarked, "Poor Neville Chamberlain believed he could trust Hitler. He was wrong. But I do not think I am wrong about Stalin."[273] Nevertheless, the PM still worried that Russian predominance in Poland would "raise a dreadful outcry" in Britain.[274] At the final banquet tongues were loosened by the forty-five toasts. Churchill frankly warned, "We are going to have an Election quite soon in England and I shall have to speak very harshly about the Communists." But "[t]he Communists are good boys," Stalin offered. "We are against them and we shall have to make our case," the PM insisted, "You know we have two parties in England." To which Stalin promptly rejoined, "One party was a great convenience to a leader of a state." While respecting the prime minister as a wartime leader, Roosevelt nudged him to step aside: "Mr. Churchill has been perhaps of even greater service when he was not in the government since he had forced the people to think."[275]

Despite his electoral worries, the PM enjoyed the most post-Yalta maneuvering room. The dictator believed Russia absolutely needed a "friendly" Poland. The president determined to cooperate with Russia. Churchill, however, could and—with ultimately dire consequences—did back away from the ambiguous deal on the Polish government. By overstating the Soviets' Yalta obligation to broaden the Lublin government, he set up them up to be viewed as unlikely alliance partners by the public in Britain and America.

Churchill—goaded by Stalin's crackdown in Poland and Romania (where the Russians were not, as the dictator had expected, welcomed as liberators), the wrenching stories of POWs liberated in Poland, his desire to pry Roosevelt from Stalin, and, not least, his need to win British voters—increasingly framed issues on the emotional basis of solidarity among the Western democracies. To Eden he explained, "every effort must be made to reach complete understandings with the United States, and Poland is an extremely good hook."[276] In a speech on February 27, he stressed that the "totalitarian" and "Communist" Soviets were obliged to live up to the Declaration on Liberated Europe.[277] Anti-Yalta protests by Poles in Britain and in the United States added to the chorus.[278] Clark Kerr later confided to Lippmann that Churchill had ordered a tougher stand on Poland. By March 6, Molotov was also taking a more intransigent line regarding broadening the Lublin regime.[279]

Even before Churchill's maneuver hemmed in Roosevelt, the latter pondered how to get the American people to accept necessary big power deals. FDR had Byrnes leave Yalta early so as to mold first reactions. At a Washington press conference, the point man credited the president's leadership with securing an "eventually" democratic Poland and sound voting procedures in the UN. He conveyed a Rooseveltian message that allowed listeners to draw whatever conclusion they preferred. Byrnes appealed to Wilsonian sentiment with stress on the Declaration on Liberated Europe and a nod toward the Atlantic Charter. Yet he also indicated how the policemen might discipline other nations. With the Big Three "in concert in liberated areas, it was hoped that political factions that might resort to violence or appeals to some outside power for support would be deterred."[280]

Four years earlier, Roosevelt and Hopkins had figured out how to sell Lend-Lease while aboard the USS *Tuscaloosa*. Now FDR needed Harry's talents in crafting a more difficult pitch. The voyage home on the *Quincy*—broken by FDR's delivering an anticolonial message to the royalty of Saudi Arabia, Ethiopia, and Morocco—afforded the chance to relax, recoup, and write a report to Congress. Hopkins, however, again disappointed. After Yalta, Harry, already "completely played out, stayed up all night playing poker and then took to his bed," Admiral Brown recalled.[281] He holed up in his cabin until the *Quincy* docked at Algiers. Then he disembarked to fly home with Bohlen. Already mourning his fun-loving sidekick, "Pa" Watson, who had died suddenly aboard ship, FDR griped, "Why did Harry have to get sick on me?" Harry's son, Robert, later recalled that "the President was good and mad, so much so that he didn't actually say good-bye."[282] Roosevelt lapsed into procrastination. Speechwriter Sam Rosenman would later complain that he "couldn't get him to work. . . . He would sit up on the top deck with his daughter Anna most of the day."[283] Determined to rest and uncertain how to explain Yalta, he dawdled. Desperate, Rosenman cobbled together a memorandum by Bohlen and phrases from Leahy and Anna Boettiger.

Roosevelt did rouse himself, however, to disparage both Churchill and the charter. He lambasted the PM's "mid-Victorian" opposition to ending colonialism. When newsmen aboard pointed out that this stance "seems to undercut the Atlantic Charter," FDR could have clinched his argument by affirming that, yes, the British Empire did violate these principles. Instead, he took the chance to dismiss the charter as just "a beautiful idea." When "it was drawn up, the situation was that England was about to lose the war. They needed help, and it gave it to them." He then dropped the subject. Implied lesson: Don't look to the Atlantic Charter as a practical guide for the postwar world.[284]

The president procrastinated until the very moment he sat down before Congress on March 1. He then departed from his prepared text with lengthy, significant improvisations.[285] Aside from the statement that he was sitting in order to avoid "having to carry about ten pounds of steel" braces, the most enduring line was actually a distortion—a legacy of drafting by Bohlen, Leahy, and Rosenman, and a contradiction of what FDR had told newsmen days before aboard the *Quincy*. He probably kept the line in the speech to disarm critics. As usual, Roosevelt was approaching the challenge by backing into it. He told Congress that Yalta "spell[s] the end of the system of unilateral action, exclusive alliances, spheres of influence, balances of power, and all the other expedients which have been tried for centuries—and have failed." In actuality, however, Yalta had fostered tacit balance of power deals for a Soviet sphere in Eastern Europe, a British sphere in Western Europe and in the empire, and a U.S. sphere in Latin America, Japan, and perhaps China. How open those spheres would be remained uncertain.

An inelegant collage of contradictions, the report on Yalta nonetheless ranks as one of Roosevelt's most ambitious speeches. In articulating his less mediated thoughts, FDR more accurately depicted the ambiguity, ambivalence, and accommodations of Yalta. Lippmann caught the big picture. "Not for a long time, if ever before, has he talked so easily with the Congress and the people, rather than to them, and down to them."[286] The president warned that despite the power of the United States, the nation could not dictate the peace. He tried to lower expectations. He ad-libbed a qualifier to his claim about the end of spheres of influence so that it began, Yalta "ought to spell" the end rather than "it spell[s]" the end. A world order based on the Atlantic Charter would develop only gradually. The peace "cannot be, what some people think, a structure of complete perfection at first." In talking about "interim governments," he added to the written text that free elections would only come "thereafter."

To a nation accustomed to simplifying foreign issues and universalizing the American experience, Roosevelt ad-libbed that postwar issues were "very special problems. We over here find it difficult to understand the ramifications of many of these problems in foreign lands, but we are trying to." In a long addition, he instructed Americans on Russia's case for Poland's new borders. Alluding to the dispute between Lublin and London Poles, he said that the government in Warsaw would not immediately, but rather "ultimately" be selected by the Polish people. Yalta "was a compromise," he stressed. To give a sense of how the Soviets felt, he described the Germans' "terrible destruction" in the Crimea. Speaking seven weeks before President Truman would say that the Russians could go to hell if they objected to America's program, Roosevelt emphasized "give-and-take compromise. The United States will not always have its way a hundred percent—

nor will Russia nor Great Britain. We shall not always have ideal answers to complicated international problems, even though we are determined continuously to strive toward that ideal." Roosevelt—who considered himself the first diva while complaining about the "many prima donnas in this world"—was tragically remiss in not explaining all this nuance and complexity to his parochial vice president.[287]

He evidently believed he had time, that he could "work it out" with his health. To be sure, he tired easily, his appetite flagged, and his appearance fluctuated. Yet as Anna observed after Yalta, he was "standing up under it all extremely well."[288] Daisy Suckley rejoiced "that F[ranklin] looks so much better than anyone can expect—his color is good & his blood pressure is pretty good.[289] Lippmann, who before the election had called FDR a tired old man, agreed that he had returned "manifestly" in "good health and much refreshed."[290] On March 1, Bruenn recorded: "Patient has rested well. Cough has disappeared. No cardiac symptoms."[291] But wasn't FDR's death imminent?

A Contingent Death

Nearly all histories of Roosevelt's last year track an irresistible story line: Great Leader Dies on Eve of Triumph. Pervasive cultural memories—of Moses dying as he approached the Promised Land and of Abraham Lincoln being assassinated just after the Confederacy surrendered—add emotional resonance to this grand narrative. Accounts of Roosevelt's demise have clinched the sentimental script.

The drama of the fallen war hero seduces us into underplaying the contingency of Roosevelt's death weeks before V-E Day. FDR continued his strategy for cheating death—and for cheating those who calculated on his dying in office. Believing he was a man of destiny, he did not prepare any of his vice presidents. Roosevelt may well have been deluding himself about his own mortality. But he also had before him the examples of Howe and Hopkins, who had performed long after others had given them up for dead; his father, who survived a decade after his heart attack and died at seventy-two; and his mother, who thrived until the age of eighty-six.

Iconic images of FDR fit into two categories. There is the beaming face and up-tilted cigarette holder of a man so bursting with energy that his disability seems vanquished, along with fear itself. Then there is the image associated with 1944–45: a shrunken figure whose haggard face, slack jaw, and shaking hands portend collapse. Like most polarities, however, these stereotypes simplify a more complex situation. Consider these observations by the president's supporters:

> January 11: "He looked a good deal more worn and tired. . . . His color was bad and . . . he showed the effect of nerves in that his hands were not quite steady."[292]
>
> February 14: "I really was shocked when I saw his face—he looked almost ghastly."[293]
>
> February 28: "He looked tired and he seemed to lack fighting vigor or the buoyancy that has always characterized him."[294]
>
> May 25: "He still looked tired. I wonder if he is going to have the physical stamina to lead us during these next critical years, for upon physical stamina depends the will and the ability to lead. I find that many people are beginning to have doubts about his health."[295]
>
> August 4: "He has paid a heavy toll during these past four years. His face is heavily lined and inclined to be gaunt. . . . He is punch drunk from the punishment that he has suffered recently."[296]
>
> December 6: "He looked badly and he seemed listless. I wondered whether or not his trouble was spiritual or physical. . . . He seemed to have the appearance of a man who had more or less given up.[297]

The above descriptions date not from 1944–45 but rather from 1933, 1938, 1935, 1941, and 1937. Until the end, FDR amazed others with his capacity to rebound.

Moreover, he could look better in person than in photographs. After the return from Yalta, a White House aide peered at Roosevelt up close. She wrote to her mother: "I know this will be hard to believe, if you have seen the recent pictures of him, but he looked simply wonderful—in radiant health!" Secret Service men back from Yalta "were astonished" to read in the newspapers "that he was not well while over there—they all said he was in fine health and spirits."[298]

The juggler continued to loft an astonishing number of balls. Consider, for instance, his schedule on March 13, 1945, a day when longtime aide Leon Henderson took fright at the president's "decline in energy."[299] Later that day Canadian Prime Minister William Mackenzie King found FDR "a very tired man . . . hardly in shape to cope with problems."[300] Despite his appearance, Roosevelt was putting in a long workday. He first conferred with delegates to the April UN conference in San Francisco. Then he met with Stimson and Leahy to discuss the negotiations in Berne about a possible separate surrender of German forces in Italy.[301] Though the war secretary often vented in his diary criticism about Roosevelt's performance, he on this day made no such complaint.[302] After four additional appointments, the president napped. Then Henderson on German affairs. During a ninety-minute press conference he fielded questions on Yalta, the St. Lawrence seaway, the San Francisco conference, New York City politics, UN voting procedure, the Moscow Reparations Commission, Romania, Austria, Italy, and nighttime baseball.[303] He wrapped up the day at a three-hour dinner with the Boettigers, Mackenzie King, and Lucy Rutherfurd, who had been introduced to the prime minister as "a relative of the President."[304] The next day he had a detailed discussion with Stimson on the atomic bomb and a three-hour dinner alone with Lucy.[305]

Tackling all this remained difficult. Much was neglected. And yet on issue number one—overall cooperation with Moscow—Roosevelt stayed largely on course. He did not permit Stalin's fury at the separate surrender negotiations at Berne to derail collaboration. He resented Soviet callousness toward U.S. POWs in Poland. An aide would remember him boiling over: "Averell is right." Stalin "has broken every one of the promises he made at Yalta."[306] He allowed Leahy and Bohlen to draft tougher telegrams regarding Poland. Nevertheless, even these messages recognized the primacy of the pro-Soviet Lublin Poles to a degree that neither Churchill nor Harriman and Truman would accept.[307] Above all, Roosevelt kept his head and resisted pressure from Churchill and Harriman to break with Stalin.[308] He looked forward instead to convening the Security Council in a cozy getaway, possibly the Azores. He himself wrote the last telegram sent the PM before his death. "I would minimize the general Soviet problem as much as possible. . . . We must be firm, however, and our course thus far is correct."[309]

Though FDR at Yalta had allowed Churchill to dissuade him from informing Stalin about the atomic bomb, he now appeared to change his mind.[310] On March 9, he told Mackenzie King, a junior partner in the project, "the time had come to tell [the Russians] how far the developments had gone," even though "Churchill was opposed to doing this."[311] The president predicted victory over Germany by late April and over Japan "possibly three months" later. He expected the new weapon "would be in shape by August," when the Soviets were slated to enter the war. Rather than racing to get Tokyo's surrender so as to shut out the Soviets, he intended the three jointly to "be responsible for order in Germany and Japan for a number of years." He seemed undecided whether to use the bomb for demonstration or destruction. "The main difficulty" remained "just how to have the material used."[312]

Despite failing energy, Roosevelt remained prescient and in command. Yet he was also working too late into the night. While his blood pressure trended lower, he was growing exhausted, Bruenn worried. By late March he looked "very badly. Color is poor (grey). Very tired."[313] Nevertheless, within days of arriving at Warm Springs on March 30, FDR showed "decided improvement."[314] His blood pressure levels, however, fluctuated. With rest and four adoring women in attendance—Daisy, his cousin Laura Delano, Lucy, and Lucy's portraitist friend, Elizabeth Shoumatoff—he gained ground. By April 10, he was eating double helpings, and his face had regained color. He was taking it easy while also working through baskets of papers. Then, on Thursday, April 12, he was signing documents when he suddenly bent forward. Daisy later recorded that as she went over to him, "he looked at me with his forehead furrowed in pain and tried to smile." He said, "I have a terrific pain in the back of my head."[315] Roosevelt lost consciousness and died at 3:30 p.m.

Although not surprised, Bruenn categorized the stroke as "a bolt out of the blue."[316] He diagnosed a subarachnoid hemorrhage, which is the rupture of a blood vessel just outside the brain that allows blood to

6.4. Portrait by Elizabeth Shoumatoff done shortly before Roosevelt's death. (Courtesy of FDR Library.)

press into the cranial cavity. A "subarachnoid hemorrhage is most often caused by abnormalities of the arteries called cerebral aneurysms." These aneurysms "may develop from birth or in childhood and grow very slowly." Such hemorrhages "can occur at any age, including teenagers and young adults."[317] In sum, while FDR's hypertension and other heart problems heightened the risk of a hemorrhage, the fatal stroke could have occurred years earlier, years later, or not at all. He might have survived into the postwar era. If he had had more time, he might well have "worked it out."

For all his prescience FDR had difficulty mustering the energy and assistance to translate his vision into concrete postwar policies. All three leaders overestimated their reach. Sadly for Roosevelt and Hopkins, personal estrangement jinxed their political cooperation. The president lacked the daring, the drive, and—most important, the hectoring that someone like Hopkins or LeHand could provide—for an all-out campaign to persuade the American people that a Three Policemen alternative promised a safer peace than the Atlantic Charter. He delivered no paradigm-changing fireside chats. Yet he tried to educate key reporters. His report on Yalta, especially the spontaneous sections, did advance public education. And he expected the San Francisco conference, which he planned to attend, to do more. Yalta demonstrated the will of the Big Three to compromise enough to preserve overall collaboration. Those compromises aroused opposition that might—or might not—have prevailed had Roosevelt lived through his fourth term. After Yalta, Maisky noted with satisfaction, "Cooperation among the 'Big Three' is now very close, and Germany will not fare well either during the war or after it."[318] Fear of resurgent Germany and Japan ranked as Stalin's number one reason for pursuing a postwar alliance.

Pitted against Churchill and his own State and War Departments, Roosevelt was almost alone in his readiness to choose the culturally different, politically difficult Soviets over the Germans, who in defeat would regain the appeal of Anglo-Saxon kin. As the Soviets perhaps sensed when they urged an autopsy to rule out poison, the death of Roosevelt removed their best hope for a continuing alliance. His replacement by an inexperienced and insecure new president would allow full scope for the influence of State Department officials, many of them fiercely resentful of the Soviet Union because of the personal and professional frustrations they had suffered in Moscow.

The Diplomacy of Trauma

Kennan and His Colleagues in Moscow, 1933–46

Shortly after arriving in Moscow as the first U.S. ambassador since the Russian Revolution, William C. Bullitt kissed with Stalin. The occasion was a Kremlin banquet on December 20, 1933 that combined initiation, seduction, and diplomacy. "Everyone . . . got into the mood of a college fraternity banquet, and discretion was conspicuous by its absence," Bullitt later blithely reported to Roosevelt. Commissar for Foreign Affairs Maxim Litvinov whispered to the delighted American, "Do you realize that everyone at this table has completely forgotten that anyone is here except the members of the inner gang?" Bullitt recorded that as he was leaving, Stalin "took my head in his two hands and gave me a large kiss! I swallowed my astonishment, and, when he turned up his face for a return kiss, I delivered it." Bullitt's young assistant, George F. Kennan, recalled that the ambassador was so "thrilled" by his "evening with Stalin and the inner circle" that he woke Kennan up, and sat on the latter's bed dictating an account of the events—and thereby shared them in another intimate male-to-male setting.[1]

Thirteen years afterward, by which time Bullitt had become fiercely anticommunist, his remembered intensity powered a different narrative. Speaking as someone who had been seduced and betrayed, Bullitt remarked that "these Bolsheviks are charming people." He could not resist mentioning that "Stalin at one time was very affectionate toward me." Indeed, the dictator "kissed me full on the mouth." This time Bullitt did not mention the return kiss. Instead he spat out, "What a horrible experience that was!" He then compared the Soviets to an "amoeba, sending out pseudopods, surrounding" others.[2] He apparently had felt engulfed, an experience at first exciting, then frightening.

Bullitt, Kennan, Charles "Chip" Bohlen, Elbridge Durbrow, and Loy Henderson would never forget the honeymoon of 1933–34, when Stalin, hoping for aid against Japan, had allowed American diplomats to associate freely with Kremlin officials, literary lions, and Bolshoi ballerinas. The lost paradise of those pre-purge years would forever haunt these future Cold Warriors. After Roosevelt's death, resentful "Soviet experts," such as Averell Harriman and Kennan, previously kept at arm's length, would shape how a neophyte president and his advisers made sense of the confusing issues arising from the end of the war.

Although working from different assumptions, the Soviets and the Americans/British each wanted their nationals to infiltrate the other's society. Each side tightened defenses against what it perceived as contaminating intrusion. The Americans and British, in keeping with the general openness of their cultures, believed it only "normal" to associate freely with Soviet citizens. Many regarded making friends and establishing contacts as crucial to an individual's satisfaction and to their nation's expanding influence. Contact between individuals seemed requisite to trust between nations.

The Soviet government, in contrast, feared such free association as threatening its control of information, hold on its citizens, and very survival. Self-conscious about their relative economic and cultural backwardness, Moscow leaders worried that contact with foreigners would expose the superior standards prevailing outside the "workers' paradise." A British official groused that after three years in Moscow, he "had never been inside a Russian house or flat." The Royal Air Force's liaison in Moscow did "not even know where . . . the Russian

Air Ministry works."[3] In keeping with such obsessive privacy, the Kremlin regarded as "spying" an exchange of information or ideas that Westerners regarded as innocent and normal. Article 58 (4) of the Soviet penal code criminalized unauthorized or unnecessary contact with foreigners. While imprisoning or exiling Soviet citizens who associated with foreign "spies," the Kremlin dispatched battalions of secret agents to recruit Americans and Britons as spies.

Isolating foreigners embittered the "experts" who shaped how the Soviet Union was perceived in the outside world. Stalin even joked about the harshness of the system. Celebrating the signing of the Franco-Soviet treaty of December 1944, the dictator turned to the *Narkomindel* interpreter, saying with a chuckle, "You seem to get on very well with these foreigners: We shall have to send you to Siberia." The young man blanched. The dictator smiled, assuring him, "Well, it won't happen this time." A London official penciled on the report, "Beastly."[4] During the war years, the secret police (OGPU, later called the NKVD, still later the KGB) eased up on but did not end the ban on contact. After interrogating the friends and lovers of foreigners, the secret police might arrest these Soviet citizens, exile them to Siberia, free them with a warning, or make them inform on their foreign associates. On the very night in 1937 that Durbrow, the U.S. diplomat, departed Moscow, the secret police arrested his longtime girlfriend, Vera.

Authorities tended to crack down when diplomatic relations soured.[5] Foreigners could feel played like a yo-yo. Harriman's secretary, Robert K. Meiklejohn, commented that "when Stalin is mad at you everybody from the doorman to the bus conductor is mad at you."[6] The head of the British naval mission reported that "as far as our personal relations are concerned, the curve rises after a visit such as the P.M.'s or Eden's or after the signing of an agreement or treaty. But when nothing material follows these incidents such as second fronts, or convoys are stopped . . . then the curve falls steeply."[7]

Ordinary Russians braved contact because of curiosity, love, friendship, desire for stockings, eagerness to talk English—or at the direction of the secret police. Some started out as informants or began informing after threatened. Sometimes officially conflicting loyalties did not actually conflict. Llewellyn "Tommy" Thompson, who decades later would become John F. Kennedy's ambassador to Moscow, cultivated a "close wartime liaison with a member of the Moscow ballet," an aide recalled. The woman and her police connection "provided a pipeline through which [Thompson] could try out and receive suggestions that could not safely have been made officially."[8] Such convenient coziness remained the exception.

Geoffrey Wilson, a Russian analyst in the Foreign Office, pointed to the fallout from the "appalling isolation" of diplomats and journalists. "In all too many cases" their "whole attitude toward Russia is determined by the bitterness to which this [isolation] gives rise. Such bitterness] is quickly sensed by the Russians and greatly resented." The Russians were to blame for the vicious cycle. Nevertheless, London's policy was skewed, Wilson worried, because experts on Russia found it difficult to retain "their capacity for balanced judgment."[9] In short, just as the political became personal, so could the personal become political—with disastrous consequences for diplomacy.

The right to associate with locals figured as the personal corollary to the Open Door policy, a traditional U.S. and, to a lesser extent, British tenet. The logic of the open door entailed not just the prerogative to develop economic opportunities but also the right of individuals to move around, explore the environment, meet people, and build influence. The Kremlin's restrictions on contact violated emotionally resonant norms of individual opportunity and freedom. Americans and British regarded informal, personal contacts across borders as a means toward security. Their nations had a history of expansion through informal contact backed by state power, and both had a standard of living that outclassed that of the Soviet Union. Although U.S. and British officials remained wary of Communists proselytizing their own populations, they regarded a relatively open flow of people as an arena in which they could compete to advantage.

To the Russian government, however, whether under the czars or the commissars, the free competition of open contact threatened security. Like their czarist predecessors, the Soviets resented uncontrolled contact with foreigners "as so much grit in the machine of government."[10] Litvinov confided to a U.S. journalist that he had tried to make Stalin understand the importance of cultivating foreign journalists. "But it's no use." The dictator and his cronies persisted in believing that in the West "the government makes public opinion and that the government can make policy regardless of what the press says." Kremlin officials were "creating unnecessary difficulties for themselves."[11]

Intensity

U.S. and British responses to Russia were shot through with intensity. Near the end of his life, Durbrow reflected on why so many diplomats had turned 180 degrees, from eagerly anticipating close ties with the Soviets to bitterly opposing such cooperation. "The best way to talk about it," he decided, was to think of "a disappointed lover." "It's the disappointed lover," he reaffirmed after further thought.[12] Others also arrived at this analogy. In a novel based on his work in the Moscow embassy, Sam Spewack wrote that U.S. diplomats "came with love, and left with fury."[13] Harriman in 1953 explained the entire Cold War as originating in Bullitt's failed mediation in 1919. Conflict began "when Wilson did not support Bill Bullitt's idea of making love to Lenin."[14] The choice of words here is striking. The discourse of falling in love or of making love suggests that, on one level, key American diplomats regarded this giant, distant country with its very different traditions and ideology as an exoticized object of desire. In their quest for intimacy they risked vulnerability. No wonder they reacted with fury when feeling scorned.

The prize-winning *New York Times* journalist Harrison Salisbury remembered that colleagues married to Russian women "were living on the edge of catastrophe all the time."[15] As another American, Henry Shapiro, put it, "I was never sure whether [my wife] would be arrested. She was in danger because of me, primarily, married to a foreigner."[16] Salisbury later recounted that the Russian wife of a British diplomat never left the embassy because she was wanted by the secret police. One day her brother called. Their mother was deathly ill and was begging to see her. Friends warned of a trap, but the woman insisted. Salisbury related that the wife was "taken in a British car by a British embassy attaché to the rendezvous point—they got out of the car, and a [Soviet] car whizzed up and she was grabbed and forced into the car—while the English watched, unable to interfere—and that was the last they saw of her." Four decades later, Salisbury again waxed furious in telling the story. Everyone "was outraged by this goddamn thing as any human being would be but the journalists and diplomats with Russian wives—to whom it might also happen, well, I mean, Jesus Christ—you can IMAGINE what it did to them! Aaah!"[17] What leaps out of the page here is the screaming-out-loud intensity of the anger by the people on the scene, by the diplomats and reporters in Moscow, and by Salisbury, even many years later.

Kennan, who observed these agonies, nonetheless retained a life-long love affair with Russian culture. He enjoyed melting into a Russian crowd or savoring the old Russia at an untouched monastery. He felt happiest when "I could have the sense of Russia all about me, and could give myself, momentarily, the illusion that I was part of it." His involvement had the insistence of a physical need. He wrote of his "consuming curiosity to know it in the flesh," of his returning to Russia "like a thirsting man on a stream of clear water." In a "flashback," he remembered, "I drink it all in, love it intensely, and feel myself for a time an inhabitant of that older Russia."[18]

In December 1933, he and Bullitt had received a warm welcome as Washington's envoys. It seemed a time of infinite promise. The Soviet famine was ending, and rightist figures such as Nicolai Bukharin were reappearing. Stalin reassured a party congress that "there is nothing more to prove and, it seems, no one to fight."[19] For embassy officials, Moscow was "immensely exciting." Kennan remembered 1933–34 as the "high point of [his] life . . . in comradeship, in gaiety, in intensity of experience." He threw himself into investigations of the Soviet economy, research for a biography of the poet-dramatist Anton Chekhov, and all-night parties of "endless talk, in the Russian manner." He escaped from what he called the "social discipline of the Western world" into a "true Boheme" of journalists and others. "I loved it. I felt at home with these people," enthused Kennan, who rarely felt at home in U.S. society. In turn, Soviet officials were "delighted by young

7.1. In a "flashback" decades later, George F. Kennan recalled that at a time of "immensely exciting days" he had stood next to William C. Bullitt as the ambassador presented his "credentials to the titular head of the Soviet state—old Daddy Kalinin, as we used to call him." (Kennan, *At a Century's Ending*, 33. Courtesy of the Seeley G. Mudd Manuscript Library, Princeton University.)

Kennan," Bullitt reported. Soviet president Mikhail Kalinin "kindly" told the junior diplomat that the books about Siberia written by his elder cousin, another George Kennan, had been "the bible of the early Bolsheviks."[20]

With Bohlen, who would also become an architect of the Cold War, Kennan began "a lifelong intellectual intimacy . . . unique in its scope and intensity." Kennan hoped that he, Bohlen, and other smart young diplomats, "able to wield the pen as skillfully as the tea-cup," would develop an American critique "much stronger and more effective than that of the Paris émigré crowd."[21]

Although Kennan's published memoirs emphasize distaste for the Soviet government, his unpublished writings reveal more ambiguity. In 1938, he described the commissars he had met in 1933 as "unforgettable" and macho-masculine: "strong-nerved, lean, ruthlessly competent"—not "paunchy and flabby like their bourgeois counterparts abroad." Although Kennan never subscribed to Marxism, he affirmed that he and his colleagues had "read a good deal of our Marx and Lenin. We had thrilled to the exploits of John Reed, to the tales of the Revolution." In 1933–34, Kennan found it hard to hold himself back from involvement in Russian society, to only "witness with detachment the spectacle of a generation of young Russians engaged with the realities of life."[22] During these early years Bohlen enthused about "young Russians . . . with a lack of self consciousness [*sic*] that is amazing. They really are in a great many ways a new type of human being."[23] Although a conservative, Kennan did not champion the marketplace. Instead he sympathized with the project of building a rational society with a group ethic. Kennan's villains were the "political bosses," such as Stalin, who had betrayed revolutionary idealism, and the fanatical Bolsheviks, who carried revolution to excess.

By December 1934, Kennan was becoming "too fascinated by Russia." Losing the balance between his duties and his engagement with Russian society, he felt that "Moscow had me somewhat on the run." Kennan confessed to Charles Thayer, a friend at the embassy, that he chafed under the "restrictions of a diplomatic status," particularly "the compulsion to political inactivity, self-restraint and objectivity." In revealing language, Kennan worried that he would "end up at an early age mentally, physically and emotionally sterile."[24] What Kennan called his "nervous strain" built until December 12, 1934, exactly a year after his arrival in Moscow, when he collapsed under an attack of duodenal ulcers. His colleague Loy Henderson and sister Jeanette believed that the ulcers were at least partly psychosomatic. Kennan himself distinguished between his "physical symptoms" and their underlying "'causes,'" and his doctor diagnosed "severe physical and nervous strain after service in Russia." "Something had snapped," Kennan recalled, and he felt "relief, that this was the end."[25]

In 1933–34, Kennan was not the only American diplomat with intense experiences during what they later remembered as the honeymoon period of Soviet-American relations.[26] Many developed relationships with Russian women at a time when the Soviet women's liberation movement had not yet suffered the repression of the mid- and late 1930s.[27]

Bullitt encouraged the fraternity-like atmosphere by handpicking the forty men of his staff with the assumption that "there is absolutely nothing for a woman to do here." "There were usually two or three ballerinas running around the Embassy," Bohlen remembered; "the ballerinas were given free run of the diplomatic corps, and many temporary liaisons were formed." Soviet authorities encouraged such liaisons for information, while Bullitt "constantly urged us to mix with the Russians." Bohlen left no doubt as to the kind of "mixing" when he added that, "as a bachelor, I eagerly carried out his instructions."[28]

Thayer, who would later become Bohlen's brother-in-law, wrote in his diary that the ballerina and fervent Communist Irena Charnodskaya had taken "the trio of B[ullitt] B[ohlen] and myself by storm." Their relationship apparently focused not just on physical heterosexuality, but also on homosociality among the "trio" based on their shared possession of and fascination with an exotic woman. Thayer recounted, "we simply cannot keep our hands off her. She has become an acquisition of the Embassy and . . . sleep[s] in some vacant room which the three of us carefully lock together and then fight violently as to who will keep the key. . . . What an embassy!" Bohlen, who had had considerable experience as a playboy, wrote that "I have never had more fun or interest in my whole life. . . . [T]his Embassy . . . is like no other Embassy in the world."[29]

Much of this "fun" in 1933–34 came from the opportunity casually to cross boundaries of ideology, class, sexuality, rank, convention, and nationality—crossings that would at other times and places figure as serious transgressions. Bohlen wrote that "everything is topsy-turvy and the most amazing things happen, which could only happen here." Bullitt palled around with his "boys"; Charnodskaya wrote the ambassador's speech for a newsreel; street urchins shouted "Your health Comrade Bullitt!" as he sped through Moscow; a veteran of the International Workers of the World regaled embassy officials with tales of life inside U.S. prisons.[30] Counselor of the embassy John C. Wiley went "snooping around . . . to get the lowdown" on "Stalin's N.E.P. (New Erotic Policy!)" on homosexuality.[31]

The more enjoyment "the new boys in town," as Bohlen put it, had in 1933–34, the more they would feel assaulted—personally, professionally, and politically—when Stalin shut down contact with foreigners and denied the Americans the privileges they had so intensely enjoyed. They regarded Stalin's efforts to isolate the Soviet people as a kind of aggression against them, and this sentiment contributed to what became their visceral anticommunism. For Kennan, who would wistfully remember the "numerous, curious and friendly company of Russian guests," including Bukharin and Karl Radek, who filled the embassy drawing rooms, Stalin's repression left those rooms, and a vital aspect of his life, "emptier and emptier."[32]

Kennan also witnessed the brief exuberance and long resentment of Bullitt. Stalin initially agreed to the ambassador's plan for Monticello in Moscow—an embassy modeled on Thomas Jefferson's home on a choice fifteen-acre site overlooking the Moscow River. Kliment Voroshilov, commissar for defense, agreed to attend, with the chiefs of the Red Army, a U.S. embassy dinner. Bohlen noted with pride that "no other Embassy in Russia has ever been able to get them to come." Once again the exuberance of American and Russian officials produced a bonding—on the basis of shared planning and interests, exclusivity, alcohol, ribaldry, physical contact, and homosocial attraction—the intensity of which would aggravate the bitterness of later estrangement. Voroshilov and Bullitt also agreed that the ambassador would import equipment for polo and instruct the Soviet cavalry in that aristocratic sport.

Thayer wrote in his diary that as the drinking escalated, a U.S. official "put on a very good show with dirty American words which I had to translate for V[oroshilov]." As the party ended, "the Ambassador and V[oroshilov] danced together some sort of a medley of Caucasian and American fox-trot ending with the usual sweet kiss toasts being drunk on all sides." Immediately after describing this dancing and the "sweet kiss toasts," Thayer noted that "V[oroshilov] is one of the most attractive persons I have ever met. He . . . looks exactly like . . . [a] cherub. . . . [A]bout fifteen—very nice looking, bright and good humoured—everyone is crazy about him." Bohlen also underscored the edge toward homoeroticism with his comment that Voroshilov's attendance "shows how they are making eyes at us."[33]

The purges that began after the murder of Leningrad party boss Sergei Kirov in December 1934 and that ran until 1938 horrified Americans in the embassy. With the continued impasse over repayment of czarist debts and the wrangling over the U.S. Communist Party's participation at the 1935 Comintern meeting in Moscow, both Bullitt's hope of becoming the essential go-between in a cordial U.S.-Soviet relationship and Stalin's and Voroshilov's desire for aid against Japan were largely frustrated. For Bullitt the disappointment turned to resentment, and perhaps to a degree it did for Stalin too.

When Kennan in November 1935 returned to Moscow after nearly a year of recuperation and diplomatic work in Vienna, he initially thought that his "life had begun once more." This life, however, entailed a more repressive regime, for both political and personal reasons. In 1937, Kennan reported to Washington that "the great majority of those Soviet citizens who have had . . . extensive social or official relations with diplomats during the past few years have now disappeared. . . . [T]hey have been intimidated, arrested, exiled, or executed." Thayer wrote that "I even dream of friends being arrested." Significantly, Kennan's official report concluded not with the Soviet effort to insulate citizens from foreign influence nor with the government's fear of foreign intrigue, but rather with the aspect that hurt Kennan personally, the policy of destroying "any prestige and popularity which foreign envoys might otherwise enjoy in the eyes of the Soviet public." In the late 1930s, someone in the State Department pulled from the files the December 1933 letter in which Bullitt had listed his Soviet friends. Whoever it was penciled next to almost every name: "Purged in 1936," "Shot in 1937," or "Purged in 1937—probably shot." Kennan would remember that the purges "imprint[ed] on my political judgment"—that is, his judgment on matters far beyond Soviet domestic policy, and for years thereafter.[34]

Meanwhile, the "fun" in the embassy had produced a backlash. In a ten-page memorandum, State Department personnel chief Wilbur Carr confronted Bullitt with complaints of drunkenness among embassy officials, of "pawing women," and of Bullitt's behavior in ignoring Madame Litvinov while turning over his "entire cellar of wines to the ballet girls of the Bolshoi Theater." Scapegoating his subordinates, Bullitt himself complained that relationships in the embassy had gotten out of hand and, worse, had cut him out. He complained that although Thayer had started out as a "reliable" assistant, "he then developed an intense intimacy with Bohlen and fell completely under Bohlen's domination. Bohlen, on his side, seemed attached to Thayer with an almost violent affection." Neither Bohlen nor Thayer would withhold Bullitt's confidences from the other and now, "leakages" were running "in all directions." Having lost control over his "boys," the vindictive Bullitt had Bohlen removed from Moscow.[35]

With such crackdowns, Kennan resolved to rein in his involvement with Russia for the sake of his career. In 1938, he wrote that a diplomat "must never abandon [his] reserve, either in life or in literature." Yet while making this pledge, he could not refrain from alluding, in an unpublished memoir, to intense relationships: "I have not told of the furtive, clandestine bonds of intimacy and affection which nevertheless arose in the forbidden no-man's land of personal relations between the Soviet world and ours. I have not told of the demoralization and tragedy often inflicted on western lives and marriages through this strange environment." "Furtive," "clandestine," and "forbidden" suggested extramarital sexuality, and Kennan's reference in the next sentence to the "demoralization and tragedy" suffered by marriages reinforced the reference. He blamed the "demoralization and tragedy" in Western lives on the abnormal no-contact regime imposed by the Kremlin.[36]

In December 1940, FBI director Hoover reported to the president that an investigation had revealed it "practically impossible for a single man to live a normal life while attached to the Embassy at Moscow." Unable to obtain "normal female companionship" because of Kremlin restrictions on contact, many embassy men turned "to a group of Soviet prostitutes" who reported to the secret police. By pretending they could not understand English, the women encouraged the men to talk shop. "Their knowledge of what is going on in diplomatic circles is described as being amazing." Other men "find a 'love life' among themselves," even engaging "in sexual perversion in the

Code Room of the Embassy." The FBI agent had witnessed men "in passionate embraces and kisses." Unable "to lead normal lives," at least two employees verged on "nervous breakdown." The investigator detailed how safes and code books were left open while the officer in charge sauntered out of the room. Wads of secret cables scheduled for burning in the basement furnace were ignited and then left unattended. Only the Soviet employees, who "loiter in the basement," knew whether the thick bundles had burned thoroughly. The file room had become a gathering place "because it is a source of interesting reading matter. Communications marked strictly confidential are considered choice reading." The clerk in charge drank and associated with prostitutes. Officials smuggled gold, currency, and rugs through the diplomatic pouch and bought luxury goods with the proceeds.[37] The investigation stemmed from an urgent request by the U.S. military attaché in Moscow, Ivan Yeaton, for an FBI "expert on homosexuality."[38] Even after the crackdown subsequent to Hoover's report, Yeaton continued his homophobic campaign.

In October 1941, Brigadier General Philip Faymonville arrived in Moscow as military adviser to the Lend-Lease mission. Faymonville had learned Russian as an officer during the Siberian intervention of 1919–20. As military attaché in the 1930s, he had made a show of respecting Russians, and it had paid off. A British diplomat who disliked Faymonville nonetheless acknowledged that the general "did get around a bit more than most of his colleagues, no doubt because of his confiding air of liking his job, which contrasted with the obvious distaste for it displayed by most 'capitalist' military attaches."[39] Like Hopkins and Roosevelt, Faymonville believed that by killing Germans, the Red Army was making ample payment for Lend-Lease. In contrast, Ambassador William H. Standley (who served in 1942–43) and most other military attachés indignantly maintained that the Soviets should prove their gratitude by allowing greater personal and professional contact and exchange of military information. This policy dispute, Soviet favoritism toward Faymonville, and the latter's direct access to Hopkins infuriated Standley, Yeaton, and the latter's successor, Joseph A. "Mike" Michela. The ambassador assailed Faymonville: "You are not worthy of wearing the uniform you have on."

"You mean that I am a traitor." "That's just about what I mean." Michela chimed in that "Faymonville is emotionally involved in the interest of the USSR and this operates against US interests. I am not speaking to him any more."[40]

General George C. Marshall ordered a military investigation. Informants described Faymonville as dedicated to Washington's alliance with Moscow, "excessively enthusiastic about music," and "entirely disinterested in women." The combination triggered suspicions, fanned by Yeaton and Michela, that Faymonville was a homosexual being blackmailed by the Soviets. Sleuthing in the United States and among Americans in Russia yielded, however, no such evidence.[41] Nevertheless, those critical of Roosevelt's policy continued to smear Faymonville as a compromised "pervert." Deciding on a clean sweep, Marshall ordered both Faymonville and Michela back home. In October 1943, General Deane, accompanying newly appointed Ambassador Harriman, was sent to Moscow as the new Pentagon liaison to the Red Army.

Meanwhile, in response to Anglo-American criticism during the 1939–40 Soviet war against Finland, the secret police had tightened the no-contact regime. Then they eased up a bit as the German threat mounted. Some arrested during the worst of the purges, like Durbrow's Vera, came home. In May 1941, she met with Thayer, who was still at the American Embassy.

Vera told him that back in 1937, with Durbrow departing, she had expected arrest. She had "'sold her silk dresses and stockings and bought a few warm garments.'" She and other prisoners endured hardship in a lumber camp just south of the Arctic Circle. Yet the "'relative liberty . . . seemed like real freedom.'" Eventually, "'they allowed me to join the camp theatrical group where I worked until my release.'" Though robbed of three years, Vera had apparently adjusted. She did not regret her affair with the Durbrow; rather "she had enjoyed [those] four years more than any others in her life." Nor did she dwell on the government's oppression. "The times were bad," she shrugged.[42]

Laurence Steinhardt, the anxious ambassador Hopkins would encounter in his July 1941 visit, interpreted Thayer's verbatim record in ways that fed his own stereotype of "the Russian." Despite their admirable "resilience," these people displayed a "complete lack of any real concept of justice." Steinhardt was flabbergasted that "her only resentment is toward her former" lover. Thayer's account, however, indicated no such resentment; indeed she expressed "few regrets." Seeing the case through his own jaundiced perspective, the ambassador found it astonishing that "she has no feelings of revenge . . . toward the fanatical judges . . . and the regime."[43]

Durbrow, who would encounter Vera again when he returned to Moscow in 1945, would in later decades cite her fate as proof of the iniquity of the Soviets. He judged them as worse than the Nazis, who at least had allowed scope for private property and private lives. He recalled that officials from the U.S. embassies in Moscow and Berlin "used to get in awful arguments . . . whether Hitler was the worse dictator or Stalin. The Moscow boys always won." Stalin "made Hitler look like a little kindergarten kid."[44] Durbrow's personal feelings colored—not determined but colored—his attitude for decades. Anger and contempt toward the Soviets would inform his work in heading the State Department's Eastern European bureau, in encouraging Harriman's hard-line stance in interpreting the Yalta accords on Poland, in spurring Kennan to write the long telegram, in replacing Kennan as number two in the embassy in 1946, and, appropriately enough, in cementing ties to Ngo Dinh Diem's South Vietnam while ambassador there in the 1950s.[45]

Disorientation and Depression

The isolation of foreign diplomats and journalists and their resulting unhappiness sparked disorientation, depression, and desire for revenge. Like Kennan, the British interpreter A. H. Birse had cultivated an "almost passionate interest in the life and fate of ordinary Russian people."[46] Yet his wartime work at the British Military Mission in Moscow kept him "cooped up . . . in restricted surroundings, with little or no normal intercourse with local people," all the while being "treated with suspicion and indifference."[47] (Although Birse saw such suspicion as unjustified, F.O. officials in London believed the War

Office was "using the supply question as an excuse for getting information for information's sake," which "annoys the Russians considerably."[48]) Birse felt "driven to the verge of lunacy." He later recounted the widespread psychological disorientation. There was "a specialist ... whose nerves broke down after months of inactivity. He was not the only one. The majority of us gradually lost our sense of proportion." They suffered "depression and frustration," "jaded nerves," and the threat of "collective insanity." Kremlin restrictions had created a "diseased atmosphere."[49] Birse, whose Scottish family had lived in pre-Revolutionary Russia, felt that "everything now was out of focus. It seemed unreal, almost like a bad dream, to be meeting Russians and yet not to be able to speak frankly and to be cold-shouldered."[50]

Paul Winterton described how he and other correspondents in Moscow "have become pretty frayed. We feel dejected and frustrated. Sometimes, inevitably, we become savagely angry."[51] Upset about censorship and restrictions on travel and interviews, he exploded, "We're so browned off now that we don't care about anything—even common politeness." He closed this letter, "X&_?:%)&- ... Yours on the brink of insanity."[52] Another American journalist, named Fleming, furious at the censor's penciling out most of his news story, "tore up the cable and threw it into Mr. Okhov's face." He was summarily expelled from the country. When the Association of Anglo-American Correspondents protested, Soviet officials—operating in a proto–Cold War, tit-for-tat mode—justified their response: "We acted in exactly the same way as Mr. Fleming did."[53]

Back in 1936, Bullitt had reported that "a considerable number of the chiefs of mission have collapsed in one way or another. The Polish Ambassador has had a complete nervous breakdown and the British Ambassador did not seem far from one."[54] In 1940, Steinhardt acknowledged that "the strain of this place is terrific. Just being bottled up in Moscow for three or four consecutive months is enough to get on anyone's nerves."[55] He confided that life in Russia had "on several occasions" driven him into "periods of depression." He blamed his "mental agony" on the Russians' "Oriental" "race" and on their being forbidden to "associate with any foreigners, particularly the diplomats."[56]

Steinhardt's response foreshadowed the Cold War. He enthused to another diplomat, "I have found that [retaliation] works magnificently—the results thus far have been a hundred per cent and 'believe me' I am an expert retaliator."[57] American correspondents joked that Steinhardt's expertise lay elsewhere: "As an ambassador, he's the best vice-consul the United States can have."[58]

Even the usually buoyant Kathleen Harriman was deflated by the gloom and the sensory deprivation. She later remembered, "In the Soviet Union—unlike London—you were knocking your head against the wall every day, nobody smiled on the streets. . . . There was no exhilaration." The embassy often ran out of fresh food, "and we had spam, spam, spam and potatoes." The weather did not help. "We had been there three or four months, and it was the second day that the sun had shone. It was a dreary, depressing time." Returning to New York City on a holiday felt "like having that extra half a martini, you were in continual elation." Kathleen later recounted that her father's publicity man, the playwright Sam Spewack, "got terribly depressed, really very, very depressed, and he started drinking. He wasn't the only one—it just got you down." What bothered him most was that he had come "over expecting to get to know the intelligentsia, and he never did. He couldn't get to see anybody."[59]

Yeaton also bemoaned his fate in "truly the most depressing post, city and country on earth." Living in this "prison camp . . . does things to one's outlook and judgment that are not healthy."[60] He nevertheless proudly stuck to that judgment. "I naturally have some very fixed and violent opinions."[61] Of political significance was his fixed opinion, buttressed by German propaganda, that the Red Army could not resist the Wehrmacht, and therefore did not merit U.S. aid in 1941. Henry Shapiro later recalled Yeaton after the invasion pointing up to two planes in the sky. "You see those planes, Henry? That's all that's left of the Soviet Air Force. I suggest that you get yourself an Iranian visa and be ready to leave; you'll have to run any minute."[62] After Hopkins's July 1941 trip to Moscow exposed this egregious defeatism, Yeaton was parked in a desk job in Washington. Years later, he acknowledged that what "brought me to the edge of a nervous breakdown" was the conclusion by the War Department that he and Michela "had become psychological and/or emotional over the whole Soviet question." He admitted, "all Mike's trouble was psychological."[63]

Michela held a psychological/racial picture of the Russians' "national character." He believed their "mixture of Nordic and Mongolian blood" produced an "Asiatic" character and a "resigned and almost stupid attitude of the people." This affliction ensured that they would "yield readily to brute force and are helpless without it." As the hitherto unbeaten Wehrmacht massed on Soviet borders, Michela drew two conclusions. First, the Soviets "cannot possibly compete with high powered, efficient competitors." Second, it was necessary for Americans to show these "Asiatics" who was boss. Negotiations "must be accompanied with a forceful, decisive, blunt and almost rude, and in appropriate cases even contemptuous personal demeanor, which will indicate that business is meant. *Any other approach will be interpreted as a weakness.*[64] Like many Cold Warriors after him, Michela argued that the Soviets would despise and even become disappointed at any readiness to help or compromise. The iron dictum: Humiliate the Soviets or be humiliated by them. Though the proto–Cold War views of Yeaton and Michela were eclipsed by the necessity of keeping the Soviets as allies, they would reemerge by the end of the war.

By that point, officers of the British Naval Mission had reached similar conclusions about their "suspicious and semi-civilized ally." Their final report seethed. As individuals they had suffered "personal insults and humiliations." As Navy men they had to put up with "clumsy duplicity and professional incompetence." And as representatives of Britain, they had encountered "downright treachery." Their conclusion did not bode well for postwar cooperation: "If you make an agreement with the Russians, you hand them a stick with which to beat you."[65]

Contact from the Soviet Perspective

For the Kremlin, having allies meant risking what they saw as cultural pollution and political subversion. Soviet sailors bound for U.S. ports to pick up Lend-Lease materiel were handed a list of prohibitions. In addition to avoiding taverns and houses of prostitution, sailors were not to accept gifts, read U.S. newspapers, make friends, or talk with Russians living in America. Further, "upon your return don't discuss what you have seen or heard in the United States."[66] As the counterattacking Red Army advanced beyond Soviet territory, *Pravda* warned about "strange circumstances"—in other words, alien culture. Worried that Soviet citizens might succumb, the newspaper instructed: "Abroad, the Soviet man very often finds himself in an atmosphere of private property and profit, speculation, predatory instincts, prostitution, and disrespect for man. Not one drop of this filth must sully the Soviet man."[67]

Pravda had cause to worry. "Soviet man" seemed eager to try Western ways. And some Allied officials were eager to instruct him. In reporting from liberated Romania, British Air Vice Marshal Stevenson sounded like a proud teacher. He wrote that his Soviet colleagues, including General S. Vinogradov, "lose no time in learning Western customs and manners." Soviet generals "and their wives, having got over their first shock of Western social contacts are becoming accustomed to our ways and now copy not only things we do but how we do them." The wives "are now well dressed, giving some attention to Western foibles [such] as clothes and permanent waves." At an "English five o'clock tea" hosted by the Romanian royal family, the Soviet generals "enjoyed themselves" and "kissed the Queen Mother's hand for the first time, which was affecting." Soviet generals visited the British and exchanged gifts around a Christmas tree. Stevenson looked forward to having more British wives in Bucharest, which "would help Russian wives acclimatize themselves more easily." He reported that "Vinogradov asked frequently when they are to arrive."[68]

Neither Stevenson nor Vinogradov mentioned how the British and Romanians might acclimatize themselves to Russian customs. Even if one discounts missionary zeal and self-puffery, the appeal of Western culture seems palpable. No doubt it also appeared that way to the Soviet secret police when they began cracking down in Bucharest.

While restricting informal contact, Soviet officials pursued their own transnational customs: lavish Kremlin banquets and elaborately choreographed, brief visits by foreigners. The writer John Hersey got the intended point. "The best way to come here: Get famous and invited. They really open up in that case." He envied the visiting playwright, Lillian Hellman, for having "already seen [Sergei] Eisenstein, the great movie director, whom I've been trying to see for two months!"[69]

Westerners did not realize how even formal contact could strain the Soviet system. Ambassador Litvinov's secretary explained why her government shied away from granting visas. "Russia is not like America," she said. "When any foreigner goes to Moscow, it takes at least four people to follow him around and see to his food, visits, etc."[70] While one Soviet tradition mandated lavish hospitality for guests, a related custom required monitoring their every move. Most Soviet officials worked into the night, squeezed into crowded apartments, and survived on meager food allotments. For people ever-anxious to prove their system's alleged superiority, Soviet backwardness had to be hidden from foreigners who were quick to interpret difference as primitiveness. As a U.S. general concluded, "'What can you do, anyway, with a people without sanitation?'"[71]

As long as Roosevelt remained at the helm, unhappiness in the Moscow embassy and anti-Soviet attitudes in the State and War Departments had only limited impact on overall policy. More ambivalent than Roosevelt about the Russians and about a postwar alliance, Churchill permitted the War Office and the interagency Post-Hostilities Planning Staff to spin elaborate scenarios with Russia as the next enemy.

Soviet Spying and American Response

By spurring the alliance with Moscow and the flow of Lend-Lease, Roosevelt also, ironically, opened the United States to increased Soviet spying. When the extent of that espionage became apparent in late 1945 and early 1946, the resulting fury would bolster the arguments of Harriman, Kennan, and others about shifting from cooperation to confrontation. During the war, Roosevelt directed the FBI to focus on taking down German and Japanese spy rings, not those of the Soviets. This is not to say that FDR was indifferent to such spying; rather, it remained a low priority. He sought to forestall a public outcry that could disrupt the alliance. One consequence of the stepped-up traffic of people and goods was a marked increase in the number of messages transmitted between Moscow and the Soviet consulate in New York City. Apparently on its own initiative, the FBI in 1943 began to tap these communications. Not decoded until the late 1940s and not made public until a half-century later, these "VENONA" decrypts offer a stunning view of Soviet espionage in the United States.[72]

To facilitate the flow of $11 billion in Lend-Lease supplies, thousands of Soviet technical personnel came to work the United States. Not content with authorized transfers of technology, the Soviets proceeded to steal industrial and political secrets. Spy masters lured scores, if not hundreds, of Americans (and Britons), many of them members or sympathizers of the Communist Party, to provide industrial blueprints, State Department memoranda, and other secret information. Some informants were paid. The aptly named *Enormoz* program enlisted several scientists and technicians in the United States, Britain, and Canada to pass information regarding the atomic bomb. That intelligence would prove crucial when the Soviets, in response to Hiroshima, put their own bomb program on a crash schedule. The vast expansion of the war industry made it easy for Communists and sympathizers to get key jobs in industry. With the Soviet Union as an ally, many could tell themselves that they were not being disloyal to America; rather they were aiding the common effort against the Nazis.

A few influential U.S. officials—including Lawrence Duggan and Alger Hiss in the State Department, Lauchlin Currie in the White House, Harry Dexter White in Treasury, and Duncan Lee in the Office of Strategic Services—passed secret documents or discussed their contents with Soviet spy masters. The so-called Cambridge Five moled their way into the most sensitive jobs in the British government. Their inexcusable actions betrayed their countries. Why did they do it?

Consider, for instance, Duggan. Like many other well-educated left-wingers, he had joined the Communist Party in the late 1930s. The

Soviet Union was then trumpeting its stalwart opposition to Nazi Germany, while the democracies seemed intent on appeasement. (Communism in America and Britain would never recover from the shock of the August 1939 Nazi-Soviet pact.) He was promoted by the State Department to head the Latin American division at roughly the same time he was designated agent "19" by Soviet spy masters.

Duggan never lost his ambivalence. Russia under the purges seemed to him "a distant, incomprehensible nightmare." The Soviets corralled him by insisting, as one agent argued in a six-hour talk in July 1937, that "all American liberals would have to decide once and for all whether they will stand for socialism and progress, or cross over into the fascist and reactionary camp." Duggan replied, "Let's continue our work together."[73] He regularly handed over batches of State Department cables, sixty pages one time, one hundred another. Some revealed what Bullitt and others were saying about the Soviets. Duggan's doubts were reinforced by fear as the FBI began wiretapping, and as suspicion rose in the State Department. During the war years, his handlers complained about "the skimpiness of his information." He "sympathizes with us," it was reported to Moscow, "but at the same time, he is an American patriot through and through." While spying for the Soviets, he did not cease "putting into practice America's influence on its neighbors."[74] In 1944, he left the State Department and cut off ties with the Soviets. What Duggan had attempted—to be "at the same time" loyal to both Moscow and Washington—had always been naive and misguided. The Cold War would make it impossible. In 1948, the Soviets were pressing him to revive ties just as the FBI and the House Un-American Activities Committee were investigating him. Wracked by the strain, Duggan, on December 20, jumped to his death from a sixteenth-floor office window.[75]

U.S. officials tried two responses to the Soviet espionage. The first, which would prevail after the defections in late 1945 of Soviet code expert Igor Gouzenko in Canada and KGB courier Elizabeth Bentley, was the Cold War pattern of sensational publicity, prosecution, and barricading against contact with the offender. In an ironic turn, Cold War America would crouch down to the Kremlin's position of regarding association with persons from the other side as contaminating and transgressive. Promoting a cooler, more open, and confident alternative was Roosevelt's chief spy master, William J. "Wild Bill" Donovan. A brash empire builder, Donovan in 1942 assembled the Office of Strategic Services (OSS), the predecessor of the CIA, to face off against German and Japanese spying.[76] Donovan's Big Three strategy of allying with the British Special Operations Executive (SOE) and the Soviet NKVD (the People's Commissariat for Internal Affairs—the secret police—who also carried out spying operations in foreign countries) was aimed also at his upstart agency's most serious rivals—the FBI, State Department, and U.S. military and naval intelligence. A thick FBI file on Donovan detailed his willingness to hire leftists, the alleged "boondoggling" atmosphere in his office, and, most egregious, his reported interest in replacing Hoover as director or having him fired.[77]

Donovan's response to the Soviets' inveterate spying paralleled in some ways Churchill's tactic of influencing the Americans—"mixing up" with them. With FDR's approval, Donovan in late December 1943 flew to Moscow to knit institutional ties. He wanted the OSS to set up an office in Moscow and the NKVD to do the same in Washington. The Soviets invited him to a meeting within hours of his arrival. Donovan made his pitch to Pavel Fitin, head of the foreign intelligence section, and Gaik Ovakimyan, whose flawless English reflected his years as New York station chief. The OSS would consult and cooperate with regard to sabotage against Germans facilities, information on bombing targets, and exchange of technology. Donovan offered to share newly developed "bombs out of plastic in the form of slices of bread." The OSS could "insert" Soviets agents into France and western Germany by air drops in return for aid to U.S. agents in the Balkans.[78] Perhaps unbeknownst to the Soviets, Donovan had already set up a small-scale spy ring led by R. E. McCurdy, an engineering executive who was supervising the erecting of six oil refineries given to the Soviets under Lend-Lease. OSS operatives in Afghanistan, China, and Iran would receive McCurdy's radioed reports.[79]

When Ovakimyan at 2:00 a.m. on January 5, 1944, called the embassy with the news that Stalin had approved the NKVD-OSS exchange, Donovan "persistently requested" a meeting that very night. He brought along Colonel John H. F. Haskell, slated to head the OSS office in Moscow. Haskell, in civilian life a banker and the vice president of the New York Stock Exchange, also ranked as the son of General William N. Haskell, who had directed the American Relief Administration's food relief program in Russia after World War I. Talking until 4:00 a.m., "Wild Bill" zeroed in on U.S.-Soviet cooperation to force Bulgaria out of the war.

According to the Russian record, Donovan was "emphasizing that the British are gradually leaving Yugoslavia and Greece, and the Americans' positions in those countries are simultaneously growing stronger." Ambition in the Balkans accounted for part of the "reason for the Americans' interest in cooperating with us." Harriman—this was months before he would become embittered by Stalin's refusal to aid the Warsaw uprising—reported that "the Soviets want us to take the initiative in connection with Bulgaria but we can count on their cooperation and assistance."

Eager to engage his new friends, Donovan urged the NKVD to "speed up" sending its mission to Washington. He promised to show off OSS facilities.[80] (An inveterate womanizer, "Wild Bill" had brought other lures as well. "It was an absolute riot," Kathleen Harriman would later recall; "he came over with all these lipsticks and stockings and perfumes to corrupt the young ladies."[81]) Later that day, the Soviets introduced Andrey Graur, a veteran spy who would head up the Washington contingent of six NKVD officers and their wives. To wrap up this productive day, Harriman suggested watching the rousing movie *Yankee Doodle Dandy*.[82]

Regardless of Donovan's enthusiasm and ambition, the Soviets would never have accepted more than a short-term U.S. "initiative" in Bulgaria or elsewhere in Eastern Europe. No doubt, too, Stalin probably expected his veteran spies to run circles around American neophytes. Nevertheless, the immediate prospects for mixing up seemed promising. In March 1944, the NKVD passed to the OSS a detailed intelligence report on Bulgaria that impressed Deane and Harriman as "evidence of considerable effort and a full cooperative spirit."[83] Like Roosevelt, they remained confident that in the hurly-burly of cultural exchange and political competition the United States held the advantage in what, decades later, would become known as soft power.

Hoover, however, bristled at this apparent bureaucratic and national threat. He warned the White House that permitting a NKVD office in Washington would enable Soviet "penetration into the official secrets of various government agencies." It would prove worse than "the very trying experiences" of "attempting to keep the British Intelligence Service within some legitimate or, at least, limited field of operation."[84] The FBI chief warned that unless Roosevelt and Donovan backed down, there would be "an unfavorable public reaction," in other words, a leak to the press and to the Republicans in an election year. After procrastinating, the president on March 29—coincidentally, two days after his cardiologist had reached a dire diagnosis—decided to halt the initiative for "the moment." FDR admitted that "the predominant factor in my decision was the domestic political situation."[85]

On hearing of the FBI's "blackmail," Donovan exploded that Hoover was "a fool. . . . If he doesn't think the NKVD [already] has its own representatives in the US, he is deeply mistaken." In terms of spy-vs.-spy competition Donovan preferred a proactive stance. "If the NKVD is going to have its representatives in the US—whether we like it or not—it will be better if their official mission is in the US, in order to have a chance to monitor their activities."[86] Ironically, Donovan's close aide, Duncan Lee, was already such a "representative." Like Duggan, Lee had joined the Communist Party in the late 1930s. While considering himself a loyal American, he passed secret information to Moscow, most significantly the names of OSS officials suspected of being Soviet sources or sympathizers.[87]

In protesting FDR's backtracking, Harriman reiterated U.S. aims in Russia, objectives that he would continue pursuing in 1944–45 despite Washington's retreat from the NKVD-OSS deal and despite fractious conditions in areas under Soviet sway. He reminded the president that "[f]or the past two and a half years, we have been unsuccessfully trying to penetrate sources of Soviet information and to get on a basis of mutual exchange and confidence. We have penetrated here for the first time one intelligence branch. . . . [T]his will be the opening wedge to far greater intimacy in other branches, if pursued." The Soviets were showing "cooperative spirit and good faith," a prerequisite for the three U.S. bases planned for the Ukraine. "Since we are now asking that over 1,000 men be permitted to enter the Soviet Union in connection with our air operations, I do not know how I can explain satisfactorily to Molotov or Stalin why these few Soviet officials should not be allowed to enter the United States." Harriman feared "an adverse effect" on U.S. ambitions to have "much larger forces" operating in the Soviet Union, particularly in proposed air bases aimed at Japan.[88]

Lee's Communist sympathies may have influenced his boss. With an air of proprietary pride, the aide reported that Donovan "regards Stalin as the smartest person heading any govt. today."[89] Quite apart from Lee, however, Donovan prized the NKVD as an ally against both the Axis and his domestic rivals. He kept the Soviets informed of feelers from Germans seeking separate negotiations.[90] In March 1945, plans to bring the Soviets into the OSS's Berne negotiations with the Germans would be scotched by Harriman, now embittered by the Soviets' naked control in Poland. Donovan understood that Hoover and Adolf Berle of the State Department planned to eliminate the OSS after the war and have the FBI take control of overseas operations. Trying to outflank U.S. naval and military intelligence, Donovan believed "the Russians have valuable information about Japan that he'd like to have, so he [Donovan] is prepared to make concessions to the Russians." As Lee informed Moscow, Donovan "keeps saying that the president and his advisers did a very foolish thing by rejecting his original plan" for mixing up with the NKVD. "There are more than 1,000 Soviet people in the US who work in Washington and who probably are doing work for the NKVD."[91]

Years later, Harriman's anti-Soviet secretary, Meiklejohn, affirmed that Donovan's deal "would have helped us because the Soviet spies were in the United States anyway."[92] Despite mounting tensions between other U.S. and Soviet agencies, the OSS and the NKVD would cooperate until August 1945. Donovan's last message to Fitin relayed Hitler's dental chart, obtained from the Führer's dentist and necessary for identifying the burned corpse the Russians had found in the ruined Reichskanzlei.[93]

A Big Three Military Committee?

Impressed with the enormous success of D-day on June 6, 1944, Stalin suggested, in effect, mixing up the military establishments of the Big Three. At a meeting with Harriman and Deane on June 28, Stalin grandiloquently praised the landing in France as "an unheard of achievement, the magnitude of which had never been undertaken in the history of warfare." Deane recounted that the dictator "then surprised" them "by suggesting . . . a combined military staff should be set up."[94] As with the proposed NKVD-OSS deal, the Soviets welcomed tighter ties as long they retained control over the means and extent of their participation.

A few weeks later, Moscow postwar planner and former ambassador to Washington Litvinov published an article calling for a tripartite military commission to foster closer wartime and postwar links.[95] Soviet officials urged Americans to pay attention to the article. This was the kind of Big Three venture FDR and Hopkins had encouraged at Tehran.[96] Litvinov, who in the 1930s had worked for collective security through the League of Nations, complained to an American journalist, "You know, we have never been accepted in European councils on a basis of equality. We were always outsiders."[97]

In response to the Soviet bid for intensified interaction, Foreign Office analysts in London noted approvingly that military conversations and staff talks "would go a long way to increase Soviet confidence in us." Refusing to participate would "make the Russians still more mistrustful." The talks could educate the Soviets about "our vital interests in Middle Eastern oil and communication in the Eastern Mediterranean." In return the British would "have to recognize Russian vital interests in Eastern Europe." (In fact, Churchill and Stalin would outline such a deal in their October 1944 talks in Moscow.) Such contact also appealed as "a means both of keeping us together with the Soviets and enabling us to watch more closely the trend of their policy."[98]

Much as Donovan saw the NKVD as a possible ally against his domestic rivals, the Foreign Office seized on the tripartite military commission as a weapon "for our counterattack against the Chiefs of Staff and their wild acolytes in the P[ost-] H[ostilities] P[lanning] S[taff]." This British interagency group, dominated by military and navy brass—some of them probably influenced by the infuriating experiences of their liaison officers in Moscow—looked askance at postwar cooperation with the Kremlin. Instead they expected, as worried Foreign Office analysts put it, to enlist "the man-power and resources of north-west Germany in an eventual war against the Russians." Some PHPS papers were quite explicit that "a hostile Russia is one of our basic assumptions."[99] In July 1944, military chief Marshal Alanbrooke urged making Germany into "an ally to meet [the] Russian threat of 20 years hence." Looking beyond the still-raging war, he argued, "we must from now on regard Germany in a very different light. Germany is no longer the dominating power of Europe. Russia is." The Soviet threat figured as also a cultural/racial one, because, "unfortunately, Russia is not entirely European." The aim was to "foster Germany, gradually build her up, and bring her into a federation of Western Europe. Unfortunately this must be done under the cloak of a holy alliance between England, Russia and America."[100]

With journalists already catching wind of such views, word would get to the Soviet Embassy. Indeed, Stalin was no doubt already informed by the "Cambridge Five" and by other moles deep inside the British government . Some in the Foreign Office feared that their government's "military will make inevitable the very danger they are trying to avoid." The situation, as one analyst warned, could get "completely out of hand."[101]

Suspicion, contempt, and resentment did get out of hand, dooming the proposed commission and undermining the possibility of longterm cooperation. The group was to consist of General Deane, General Brocas Burrows (his British counterpart), and a senior Soviet officer. In London and in Moscow, Burrows had vented his contempt for the Soviets on racial and cultural grounds. Stalin fumed that "General Burrows had no respect for [Soviet] leaders or for the army. And they had none for him." Meeting with Harriman and Clark Kerr on September 23, Stalin explained, "it was not a question of praising the Red Army. The Red Army had many faults." Rather, "Burrows looked upon their people as savages. That hurt them." Stung, the dictator repeated the word "savages."[102] Many top-level British military officers spoke similarly. The Foreign Office feared that with joint military groups being set up to administer liberated territory, such open contempt by British officers would prove explosive. Personalities mattered: "It is on the conduct and general attitude of our personnel in these organizations that the Russians will base their views about our policy, just as our policy towards the Russians will be greatly influenced by the same considerations."[103]

Churchill, who often expressed his own underlying contempt for the Soviets, did not intervene in behalf of the tripartite proposal. With the PM's knowledge, military adviser Lord Ismay used Stalin's vetoing of Burrows as an excuse to abort the commission. Christopher Warner, a Russian expert in the Foreign Office, deplored the indifference of the War Office to Stalin's "feel[ing] that we had deliberately evaded the proposal because we did not like the idea of closer contacts on military matters." Moreover, "dropping the matter when the ball is on our side of the net" handed "the Russians a ready-made excuse for evading any proposals" for such collaboration in the future.[104]

Talk with allies was essential if they were to remain allies. The British diplomat Frank K. Roberts noted that history had shown that "alliances which do not provide for military staff talks are entirely useless and break down."[105] Given the cultural differences and rivalries, talk was all the more needed to ease suspicions and prevent drifting apart. In planning for the next war, military staffs made assumptions about who the enemy would be. No doubt Stalin had pushed the tripartite military commission hoping to secure allies against another German invasion. But British military planners looked to side with Germans against the Russian colossus. No wonder they "evaded" military talks. What could they talk about with the Russians? As Gladwyn Jebb, a Foreign Office European expert and future architect of the Western alliance caustically observed, "it was rather difficult to see what could come under discussion here except defence against each other."[106] Although the Soviets' isolation of foreign representatives and their mania for spying goaded Americans and Britons into seeing the alliance as a wartime expedience, so too did U.S. and British rebuffs of Soviet invitations to mix up.

Cold War Consequences

Such petty and profound slights, many aggravated by cultural difference, pointed up the vital need for leaders at the top to hold on to a broad perspective and to set a standard that would percolate downward. Although getting along was difficult, allowing the alliance to break up could prove deadly. Despite their blinding pride, British naval officials still discerned how cultural differences could charge relations. Heated feelings could blur the vital distinction between personal and national agendas. "British integrity and efficiency and Russian ignorance and inefficiency do not mix. When in contact they produce on the British side impatience, exasperation and even arrogance; while in the Russian mind there is a desperate resolve to cover deficiencies by lies and obstruction. . . . The great object is to 'save face,' and to trip this arrogant foreigner, who is seeking to assert his superiority."[107]

Although Americans did not doubt their own cultural superiority over the Russians, they also worried about exposure to unnatural behaviors hatched in the Kremlin or in its shadow. Stories about liaisons with Bolshoi ballerinas, homosexuals kissing in the code room, and other sexual/political transgressions would circulate for decades. They would feed into the Cold War feeling that ties with the Soviets were by nature subversive, "perverted," and un-American.

A problem with the spurned Soviet specialists who turned angry, even those who, like Thayer, were later witch-hunted, is that they helped set the standard narrative for interpreting Cold War origins. Even after revisionism, Cold War orthodoxy would keep coming back to the Russian experts' judgments, especially Kennan's. But that was like relying on the participants in a series of bad marriages to be the best judge of why those relationships failed. They were too involved personally to render fair judgments.

Memories of service in Moscow reflected the frantic intensity of experiences there. Thayer recalled that in 1933–34 "we came hoping to find something new—some sincere attempt to find a solution to many problems." He acknowledged that with the failure of that idealistic quest, "it is we who have changed most." Thayer sorely missed "the madness of '34," the "not entirely sane existence we led before with Mrs. and mistresses all together in an alcoholic haze, [which] has given way to solid husbands with stolid wives." Now one could associate with "ballerinas" only in "clandestine meetings." He concluded his lament about the restrictions: "It's almost enough to turn you pansy (there are plenty of partners in the diplomatic corps)."[108] Ironically, during the Lavender Scare of the early 1950s, Thayer would himself be ousted from the State Department on charges of being a *"high class homosexual."*[109]

Followers of Senator Joseph McCarthy and others attacking the supposed "twenty years of treason" of the Roosevelt-Truman administrations would focus on the alleged connection between "underground" communism and "underground" homosexuality." Alger Hiss, a Harvard-educated rising star in the Roosevelt State Department who played a small role at Yalta, would be accused of spying for the Soviets by a former Communist and self-confessed homosexual. Hiss's conviction for perjury (revelations decades later would indicate that he had indeed passed documents to the Soviets) seemed to bear out anxieties that America stood vulnerable to a dangerous mix of political and sexual "perversion."[110]

Many people would blame the Cold War on Roosevelt, the supposed "sick man at Yalta." According to their emotional beliefs, FDR's paralyzed legs, liberal politics, and naïveté had rendered him susceptible to conniving homosexuals, too-powerful women, and sickly men. With U.S. policy in the hands of "weaklings," Stalin had grabbed Eastern Europe. Yeaton, venting his homophobia and misogyny, would later explain that a "powerful" lobby, directed by *"MRS F. D. R.*, give or take a Harry Hopkins," had cleared the way for "perverts."[111] "Phil [Faymonville] was GAY and was trapped by the NKVD."[112] Durbrow subscribed to such emotional beliefs. He explained that running foreign policy during the war were "Mrs. Roosevelt. FDR."[113]

Bohlen, who would be appointed ambassador to Moscow in 1953, was in 1951 asked by a State Department official what was appropriate in terms of socializing with Soviet officials. Bohlen erupted with a warning against "the spectacle of American and Soviet diplomats with arms around each other in whoopee parties." The seemingly innocuous question had evidently triggered memories of actual "whoopee parties." Though abhorring the methods and agenda of the McCarthyites, Bohlen shared their opposition to "any dangerous intimacy" with Cold War enemies. Bohlen was now helping limit contact even though such restrictions, far more brutally enforced by Soviet secret police, had anguished him and his colleagues in Moscow. Inasmuch as some social interactions remained unavoidable, the veteran diplomat prescribed careful, heterosexual control: social relations with Soviet officials had to be "normal" and "handled with common sense and reason."[114] The Cold War drastically narrowed what was acceptable personal or political behavior.

Guns and Kisses in the Kremlin

Ambassadors Harriman and Clark Kerr Encounter Stalin, 1943–46

What the Russian-born British journalist Alexander Werth tagged as the wildest Kremlin party since 1917 lasted through the night of November 7–8, 1943. The "extremely sumptuous and extremely drunken" affair "sparkled with jewels, furs, gold braid, and celebrities," he recalled.[1] The last included Averell Harriman, his daughter Kathleen, and Archibald Clark Kerr. Following his bent and Soviet custom, the host, Foreign Minister Molotov, tried to get the envoys embarrassingly drunk. The festivities marked the anniversary of the Bolshevik Revolution and the liberation of Kiev. In a speech earlier that day, Stalin had warmly thanked Washington and London for sending war supplies. The dictator "praised the fighting in Italy as 'not the Second Front but . . . something like the Second Front . . . which is now not so far away.'"[2] It was a heady moment: the October foreign ministers conference in Moscow had proven surprisingly cordial, and the Tehran summit was scheduled in a few weeks. The Big Three seemed on the road to postwar cooperation.

Heightening the anticipation were signs that the Kremlin was easing up on ideology and control. Historians will never know for sure whether these developments were solely wartime expedients or buds that might have blossomed absent the freeze that followed the collapse of the wartime alliance. When Clark Kerr asked Stalin why the huge photographs of Marx and Engels over his desk had been banished to a far corner (and replaced by oil portraits of victorious Russian generals), the dictator, referring to the founders of communist ideology, remarked, well, "after all, they weren't Russians."[3] The November 7 party signaled a further possible shift. For diplomats and journalists, a major source of frustration and anger was their forced isolation from Soviet citizens. Now, however, Kathleen noted with surprise, even "wives of officials . . . artists, writers, etc. [had gotten] invited to an official function and were allowed to mingle freely with foreigners."[4]

She was also struck by the "dazzling" effect of the new uniforms worn by Molotov and other foreign ministry officials: black with gold buttons, gold braid, and lavish decorations denoting rank. The new attire evoked an ambiance more Ruritanian than proletarian. Kathleen alluded to the insecure vanity of her hosts while expressing her own condescension: "Each little individual Soviet was as proud as a little boy, all dressed up in his new Christmas present fireman's suit." After Molotov had downed enough vodka, his pride and vulnerability poked through. He demanded of her why "I'd been the only one not to compliment his uniform! Because I didn't like it?" She commented that "the only [Westerner] not to look insignificant next to a Russian" in uniform was Clark Kerr, with his "big KCB red and blue ribbon worn . . . across his chest and stomach."[5]

The drunken revelry peeled back the curtain from emotions, attitudes, and cultural differences that would make postwar collaboration difficult though not impossible. Both Harriman and Clark Kerr had determined to become key interlocutors between Stalin and their respective governments. Both regarded service in Moscow as a springboard. Clark Kerr aimed for the top post in the foreign service, ambassador to Washington. Harriman was shooting for secretary of state or even president of the United States. The two ambassadors and their staffs, joined by the Canadian, Australian, and French legations, often worked and socialized together. Kennan, number two in the U.S. Embassy, befriended his British counterpart, Frank K. Roberts.

Despite this special relationship, however, Harriman and Clark Kerr differed radically on how to interpret and how to respond to the Soviets' growing domination in Eastern Europe in 1944–46. Harriman might have taken a pointer from what his daughter had discerned—the mood of the "little boy all dressed up in his . . . fireman's suit," of Molotov fishing for a compliment. The budding Cold Warrior might have dealt more productively with the Russians had he possessed the perspicacity and emotional self-control to realize the extent to which self-absorbed, insecure pride shaped Soviet attitudes and actions. While Kathleen's condescension positioned herself—and the United States—as the superior adult, that attitude also afforded emotional space for enduring Russian arrogance without suffering humiliation. In contrast to Harriman, Clark Kerr advised patience with "the incorrigible inferiority complex plus cockahoopness which afflict the Russians."[6]

With consequences that became disastrous after Roosevelt's death, Harriman responded with anger, disgust, and contempt to the Russians' brutal domination of Poland. These volatile feelings fostered not patience but rather outrage. In a series of telegrams beginning in September 1944, Harriman depicted the Russians as a "bully" who had to be confronted—and who would back down when confronted. Harriman's attitude meshed more closely with Churchill and with Truman, while Clark Kerr was more in tune with Roosevelt.

The November 1943 party also highlighted the Kremlin ritual of male bonding wherein the ambassadors were subjected to a drinking contest. Molotov invited Harriman and Clark Kerr into a "secluded" room and seated them with "the three toughest drinkers": trade expert Anastas Mikoyan, military intelligence chief Aleksandr Cherbakov, and Aleksandr Korneichuk, the playwright and later Ukrainian "foreign minister."[7] All three had jobs that could make them interlocutors in postwar relations, especially if the alliance held together. Kathleen observed that with "bottoms-up" toasts in vodka, "it's hard to cheat . . . as you have to turn the glass upside down at the end of it and the drops of liquor that fall out are, according to the Russian custom, drops of misfortune you wish on the person you are drinking with." Exempt from such pressure, the young woman found it all "quite genial and at times very funny."[8] Her father had prepared by stuffing down bread with lots of butter to sop up the alcohol. He explained, "This is what I had before I was initiated into [the Yale secret society Skull and] Bones."[9] Clark Kerr described the scene: "Brotherly love began to manifest itself in a cascade of kisses from Korneichuk, and the party boomed on."[10]

Archibald Clark Kerr

Many hours and bottles later, "Mikoyan had fled, Korneichuk had been taken away, and Cherbakov was dozing in his corner"—this according to Clark Kerr. Molotov, still drinking and playing host, had to be propped up by stalwarts on his right and left. He thumped the ambassador on the chest, exclaiming: "Kerr is all right. He's the sort of chap we like. If he was one of us he would be a partisan." The manly poke and comradely praise, the honorary guerrilla status—all this gratified the ambitious ambassador, who wanted his boss, Eden, to appreciate the closeness that he had achieved.[11] By including Clark Kerr as "one of us," the professorial-looking Molotov was imagining that he himself ranked as a tough partisan. Then the honored guest rose to give a toast, reached for a table to steady himself, "missed it, and fell flat on his face at Molotov's feet," with "plates and glasses clattering down on top of him" and cutting his forehead.[12] Kathleen told her father, "let's get the hell out of here" while he could still stand. She later reported, "Averell did himself up proud, because the one thing the Soviets apparently appreciate is a guy who'll drink with them and be able to keep the pace and not show any effect. All the Moscow Americans were very pleased."[13]

Kathleen's comment indicated that in late 1943 the Anglo-American community in Moscow categorized competitive, marathon drinking as normal and civilized, even if somewhat bizarre and juvenile. Within a year, however, a growing number of Allied officials, irritated at matters small and large, would interpret these customs as further evidence that the Soviets were unsuitable as postwar partners. In December 1944, General Deane wrote to General Marshall: "I have sat at

8.1. Kremlin banquet table laden with food and drink. Many Americans and Britons found the late hours, endless food, and mandatory drinking of Kremlin banquets personally assaulting, even disgusting. (Courtesy of Small Library, University of Virginia.)

innumerable Russian banquets and become gradually nauseated by Russian food, vodka, and protestations of friendship."[14]

Clark Kerr's report that "brotherly love began to manifest itself in a cascade of kisses from Korneichuk" bears further examination. The ambassador explained that "when Russians get tight they become very affectionate." They showed "very warm hearts." While Clark Kerr made a point of including apparently homosocial encounters in his dispatches to London, Harriman and other diplomats did not, as the archival record indicates, do so. Did the others not have such experiences? Did they not dare report them? Did they not find them relevant? Diplomats could shape perceptions of a far-off land by what they included and omitted from the narratives in their messages.

Thomas Brimelow, Clark Kerr's wartime secretary, would years later recall how his boss, following up a conversation at the foreign ministry, would "get out his quill pen and turn Molotov's stilted jargon into readable and slightly idiosyncratic English. It was quite an education on how to draft telegrams."[15] It is telling that Brimelow, who made this statement after his own distinguished career as an ambassador, interpreted Clark Kerr's shaping a narrative—his "turn[ing] Molotov's stilted jargon into readable ... English"—as neither unusual nor as a distortion of the record, but rather as "quite an education on how to draft telegrams." Communications to the Foreign Office, like other historical evidence, were "turned," as on a lathe. Informal reports were also shaped. In recalling her years in Moscow, Kathleen said matter-of-factly, "You always tried to write letters making things sound a little less dreary than they were."[16]

Clark Kerr crafted his own story. Over the years the British government entrusted him with ever more responsibility. He was appointed ambassador to China in 1938, to Russia in 1942, and to the United States in 1946.[17] Top London officials trusted him. Hugh Dalton ranked him as "the best of our diplomats."[18] Cynthia Jebb, privy to Foreign Office gossip through her husband, Gladwyn, snapped back that "Clark Kerr dyed his hair, [and] mis-stated his age in *Who's Who*. Although he wore a kilt and talked about his 'place' in Scotland, he was really an Australian and his 'place' only a bungalow by the roadside." She went on with "malicious allegations about his intimate life and the unfortunate little Chilean whom he had married when in South America but had been separated from for a number of years."[19] The snide charges were accurate.

Nevertheless, because Clark Kerr put on such a good act, the image approached reality. He did appear youthful, Scottish, and married to his wife, who, to be sure, stayed in New York. The British crown, recognizing his service and his home at Inverchapel in the Highlands, did elevate this Australian-born commoner to Baron Inverchapel in 1946. U.S. and British reporters, who appreciated his bonhomie and willingness to talk, half-seriously promoted Clark Kerr as "first President of the World Government."[20]

In 1944–45, Clark Kerr apparently believed that a similar alchemy—by which an image approached and helped bring closer the desired circumstance—might help moderate Soviet behavior, soothe resentments between the British and the Soviets, and narrow their cultural gulf. Displaying his flair for instructive metaphor, he aimed at making Soviet behavior appear more acceptable by drawing analogies to the behavior of nonthreatening inferiors familiar to the British elite. In August 1944, he depicted the easily affronted Soviets as being "as sensitive of their reputation as is a prostitute who has married into the peerage."[21] In March 1945, he portrayed the brusque Russians as "a wet retriever puppy in somebody else's drawing room, shaking herself and swishing her tail in adolescent disregard for all except herself."[22] He would reassure his colleagues about British superiority while also persuading them that patience with Moscow was not equivalent to humiliating appeasement. Once reaffirmed in their own status, British officials might process their anger, fear, and resentment toward the Russians into less explosive feelings, such as condescension—or so he hoped.

Discerning of others' emotions, Clark Kerr was often blunt about his own. A colleague remembered his "obsession about sex."[23] Like many upper-class Britons of his generation, Clark Kerr did not subscribe to a strict hetero-homosexual binarism.[24] He had sexual relations with both men and women, although he evidently preferred men. He amassed a world-class collection of erotica and risqué stories. Yet he was neither promiscuous nor careless. There is no available evidence that the Soviet secret police or anyone else succeeded at or even tried to blackmail him. Nevertheless, others faulted him for his predilections. Many years later, Kathleen Harriman asserted that "Churchill hated Clark Kerr." She herself had objected to him as "fag number one. . . . Anything he said always came out lewd." She had detailed to her father "what a terrible man he was." To which Averell replied, "Stop telling me this; I have to get along with this person."[25]

Kathleen's slur notwithstanding, Clark Kerr liked playing the tough guy. Over six feet tall, muscular from daily workouts, and sporting a broken nose, he looked like a boxer. He swam the turbulent Yangtze, walked the hills of Chongqing with Jiang Jieshi, and refused to move the British Embassy out of the line of fire of Japanese bombing. On meeting Ernest Hemingway in China, he reportedly commented, "*Tough*? Why, I'm tougher than he is!"[26] He claimed that while he liked the company of his NKVD escort, a surefire way of getting rid of them "was to take them to a hospital to see an operation. His four had followed him once and all four fainted at the goings on."[27] The ambassador constructed his masculinity in ways that a later age would term homoerotic, camp, and misogynist. John Hersey, a writer for *Time* and *Life*, said talking with him was like conversing with a "combination of Mark Twain, Churchill, and Jesus Christ."[28] Hersey also remembered Clark Kerr as "mischievous. . . . This was the secret of his success in China and . . . in the Soviet Union."[29] The ambassador feminized his fellow diplomats as members of "an anti-Soviet sewing bee . . . that girlish Swede waggling his buttocks . . . the scented Afghan . . . the chatter[ing] Greek . . . the yelling . . . Mexican, and [the Turkish minister] Mr. Mustapha Kunt."[30]

While belittling his colleagues, Clark Kerr played up to Stalin as a fellow tough guy. The dictator—who remained sensitive about his short height, webbed toes, and lame left arm—enjoyed man-to-man talk. In March 1942, shortly after arriving in Moscow, the ambassador met with Stalin for two and a half hours. Like others seeing the dictator for the first time, he "had expected something big and burly. But I saw . . . a little, slim, bent, grey man with a large head and immense white hands." He limply shook "my hand, look[ing], almost furtively, at my shoulder and not at my face." Then German planes began bombing Moscow. Invited into the "dugout" under the Kremlin, Clark Kerr aimed to "break the ice." One way to become close to a second person was to exclude a third "other."

Noting that Stalin was smoking his long, curved pipe, the ambassador responded to Molotov's offer of a cigarette by commenting that "all good people smoke a pipe" and by taking out three pipes of his own. Then Stalin's

> tobacco and mine were brought out and sniffed by two practised noses, rolled in the palm of the hand and teased with finger tips. All this was accompanied by much talk on a technical level far beyond the reach of the cigarette smoker, Molotov, whose cigarette lay neglected. Inevitably my tobacco went into Stalin's pipe and his into mine. Common and really solid ground had been

reached. It was by no means unimportant! And so, through a cloud of friendly reek, the long talk began.

By exchanging, sniffing, talking about, and inhaling a pleasurable substance, Clark Kerr and Stalin shared a sensuous intimacy while creating their own atmosphere or "reek."[31] He reported to Eden that "Rogue No. 1, has now seduced rogue No. 2 with a present of pipe tobacco." Key to the seduction was the exclusion of a feminized other, the cigarette smoker Molotov. The two tough guys were "chuckling all the more shamelessly because of the governessy presence" of Molotov.[32] (As Stalin smoked a cigarette at the Tehran conference, Clark Kerr turned to him suddenly and said, "It's sissy to smoke cigarettes." Stalin stubbed it out and lit his pipe.)[33]

Years later in Washington, Clark Kerr was asked what he had talked about in that air-raid shelter. "There was only one thing to discuss—SEX."[34] His cable to London detailed their discussion of international issues, "democracy and its weaknesses, love, the way of handling (1) wives and (2) women in general, China . . . and the private habits of Chiang Kai Shek (about which [Stalin] had some queer ideas . . .)."[35] By talking about "handling" women, the men emphasized their masculine control. The discussion of Stalin's "queer ideas" about Chiang's "private habits" afforded a titillating discussion of intimate practices without either man having to reveal details about himself. Stalin no doubt knew about the ambassador's sexual preference, and on some level he may have wanted to verbally explore that exotic territory.

The intimate interlude was followed by months of what Clark Kerr dreaded, "the isolation which is imposed on us."[36] The social deprivation helps explain why there never developed a coterie of "Russia hands" comparable to the "China hands"—Sinophile diplomats who cherished memories of China and their service there and who lobbied for good relations. In Chongqing his "house was always full of Chinese, bursting with useful and stimulating talk, and, often as not, of roars of laughter." In Moscow, however, "there has been nothing but . . . silence."[37]

In September 1942, Wendell Willkie, the 1940 Republican presidential candidate, visited Moscow on his "one world" tour. The "doors" of the diplomats' "cages . . . opened" for another Kremlin bash, Clark Kerr reported. While drinking after dinner, Mikoyan and Voroshilov "threw their arms and legs around me in a two-sided affectionate embrace," he later recounted. "I passed the next hour being hugged" as the three dissolved into the "shapeless mass that was the ex-People's Commissar of Defence, the People's Commissar of Defence, and the British Ambassador." The men agreed to "go together to Stalingrad and try our luck with the Germans." Stalin watched the hugging and joined in the banter.

As they argued about how best to shoot a Tommy gun, someone thrust an unloaded weapon into the ambassador's hands. "I welcomed it because it was a means of escape from the huggings of my neighbours. . . . Shooting from the hip . . . I raked the bellies of Stalin, Molotov, and Willkie. This produced much scorn." The Russians exclaimed that a Tommy gun should be put to the shoulder and sighted like a rifle. "It was snatched from my hands by Voroshilov, who . . . shot me dead. Then Stalin seized it and fairly decimated his guests. This he seemed to enjoy immensely. . . . He picked off [not for the first time] nearly all the members of his Government." The shouting and shooting "went on until hardly anyone in the room remained alive."[38]

The shooting and the hugging acted out a homosocial ritual that blended aggression and affection, guns and kisses. Lest Eden or Churchill criticize him for sinking into a "shapeless mass" in front of Stalin, the diplomat emphasized his own agency: he "had managed to retain some control"; he sought "escape from the huggings of my neighbours"; and he had shot first. Sustaining this narrative of control was particularly important for someone whose masculinity could be attacked because of his sexual proclivities. A narrative of control was also essential for building closer ties while avoiding charges he was "appeasing" the Soviets. Although the dictator did not himself hug Clark Kerr, his Soviet underlings probably thought he would enjoy watching it, given that they did so for an hour in front of him. Both comradely and controlling, the physical contact was analogous to other edgy, intrusive Kremlin entertainments, such as the thirty-plus toasts at banquets.

W. Averell Harriman

Harriman was wound far more tightly than Clark Kerr. He relaxed not by letting go but rather by chopping wood. Kathleen later recalled that her father was "not thrilled about going to Moscow" as ambassador.[39] In London he had enjoyed a dense social network that included his friendship with Winston Churchill and his romance with Pamela Churchill. An associate later recalled that Harriman "thought he was going to deal with Stalin as he had with Churchill. He was just going to spend weekends at Stalin's dacha. And it was going to be 'Joe' and 'Ave' and so on."[40] Such intimacy never blossomed, though Harriman did talk frequently with Stalin. In terms of social contact with other Soviets, Meiklejohn remembered, there was none "except for [those] specially authorized by the NKVD, and they were all spies. Days would go by without an appointment with anybody." Anywhere Harriman went, the four NKVD men waiting outside the embassy would follow. This was not all bad, as "you could always borrow a cigarette, and you never got lost." The Russians gawked at the spectacle of the ambassador of the United States venturing out to the front yard of Spaso to play "volleyball with newspaper reporters and ballerinas."[41] Harriman did not report on, and probably did not participate in, the homosocial experiences in the Kremlin that Clark Kerr described.

Nevertheless, Harriman sought close personal relations with Molotov and Stalin. Arriving as ambassador in October 1943, he pledged to Molotov that he stood "available to him to be of whatever use I could in any matters." He used the words "intimacy" or "intimate relations" five times in emphasizing his desire to "know not only him but other Commissars . . . as well as the military."[42] Although Molotov's version of this conversation is otherwise lacking in emotion, it conveys Harriman's assurance that the Soviets could "completely rely on him"; they could get from him "any information," including possibilities for postwar reconstruction aid; and he would respond "with total straightforwardness and in all sincerity."[43] The ambassador wrote to FDR, I wish "I could speak Russian as I think I could get on an intimate basis with several of the commissars, all of whom have been extremely friendly and gone out of their way to show their satisfaction with me in this job."[44]

The ambassador showed off to Molotov his four-engine, B-24 bomber on loan from the U.S. War Department. The plane signified Harriman's ambition to make a mark in Moscow while remaining linked to Washington. It also symbolized the U.S. technological lead in long-range aviation. Pentagon military planners hoped that the lure of getting such aircraft would induce Stalin to agree to U.S. air bases in the Ukraine and, later, bases in the Soviet Far East and a postwar civil air accord. The air-travel enthusiast reached out to Molotov, saying, "I hoped he and I would be able to make a trip together . . . and for that reason I had two bunks put in the plane, one of which would be for me and one for him."[45]

Bunking close by and sharing meals and other experiences as they traveled would foster shared memories and understandings to which Harriman could appeal in some future negotiation, thereby securing his position as interlocutor between Washington and Moscow. Or so Harriman thought. Molotov would never accept the invitation.

Deane, in the very first sentence of his memoir about Moscow, recalled his initial mood: "I was eager, hopeful, confident, and happy."[46] At a Kremlin banquet a few days later, he toasted to a future meeting of the victorious Allies in Berlin. To his "amazement," Stalin ambled "around the entire table to drink a separate toast with me."[47] Another diplomat observed that in the meantime, Harriman, "eager to muscle in wherever he can, had hurried along the other side of the table with beaker in hand. But on his offering to join in the fun, U[ncle] J[oe] curtly remarked that his glass was empty and turned away."[48] Sounding like Bullitt after his first banquet with Stalin, Harriman boasted to Roosevelt that the atmosphere was "genuine, genial and intimate. The conversation . . . was free and uninhibited with plenty of humor about past misunderstandings. Stalin appeared to enjoy himself as much as anyone else." Deane's salute "stole the show. . . . Stalin paid him alone the high honor" of a man-to-man toast.[49] Harriman wanted Roosevelt to appreciate the "intimacy" already achieved.

In February 1944—that is, four months before the air bases were set up in the Ukraine and six months before Stalin refused to aid the Warsaw uprising—Deane stressed to Soviet officials the "inevitability and desirability of a close rapprochement and cooperation between the USSR and the US after the war." According to the Soviet record, Deane argued that the cultural parallels between the two nations trumped the ideological divergences. Both adhered to "peace-loving traditions" and faith in science and technology. Moreover, "We and you have so much in common in our character, habits, and objectives." Neither, he assumed, sought foreign territories or colonies. That concord positioned Washington and Moscow against London. "The British Empire contains so many insoluble contradictions. Therefore it won't be easy for Great Britain to cooperate with the other Great Powers during the postwar period," he predicted.[50] Presumably Deane believed what he said. His statements fit what Roosevelt was saying privately, though the latter had no illusions about postwar cooperation as inevitable. Although the president would largely stick to this agenda, the general would become embittered. After the war, Deane would fantasize about titling the memoir of his Moscow years "Two Years with the Bastards."[51]

From Moscow, Clark Kerr reported that Harriman put "his whole heart" into his work, was "forever troubled by the importance of being important," and viewed his success there as a possible stepping stone to the presidency. The Briton detected an underlying insecurity that rendered his American counterpart "so eager to impress, so concerned to beget and to nurse a personal prestige that does not by nature dwell in him."[52] He was "a champion bum sucker," Clark Kerr decided.[53]

Ever ambitious, Harriman considered shunting aside even Roosevelt. In a much-crossed-out, eventually discarded section of a telegram, he tried to explain the "danger" and "misunderstanding" that could arise from direct communication between Roosevelt and Stalin.[54] Harriman cultivated Admiral Leahy, head of the Joint Chiefs of Staff, and FDR's military adviser, as his inside man in the White House. In an attempted end run around the president, Harriman asked Leahy to relay to him any messages Roosevelt received from Stalin.[55]

Harriman's hopes of becoming the key interlocutor with the Kremlin were crushed along with the brave resisters in Warsaw. Stalin prohibited U.S. or British planes bearing relief to land at the Poltava base in the Ukraine. Kennan later pinpointed this as the moment for a "political showdown with the Soviet leaders." Harriman was so "shattered by the experience" that he suffered what Kathleen referred to as a near nervous breakdown.[56] Making Stalin's veto especially frustrating was that Poltava was a hard-won *American* air base.

Behind Soviet Lines

Almost everything about that "little patch of America in the middle of the Ukraine," as its commander called it, sparked intense feelings.[57] Deane was "interested in nothing" but those bases, Clark Kerr reported.[58] Kathleen later remembered the "heartaches in getting it established."[59] Opened in June 1944 for shuttle bombing of German targets, Poltava and smaller facilities at Mirgorod and Piryatin seemed a wedge for possibly opening the Soviet Union—to Far Eastern air bases against Japan, postwar civil air agreements, and other contact. Deane and Harriman flew to Poltava to greet the first mission. After taking off from southern Italy and bombing enemy targets in Hungary, 130 Flying Fortresses and 70 bombers—silvery planes, flying in formation and silhouetted against a dark sky—landed deep in the Soviet Union.

Deane experienced "a thrill beyond description" because the planes "epitomized American power, the skill of American industry and labor, the efficiency of American operations, and the courage of American youth."[60] He expected these glittering symbols of America to excite the admiration and respect of the Soviets. Averell himself had never "been so thrilled by anything," Kathleen observed.[61] Such strong feelings were reflected perhaps in the final military code name, FRANTIC. As the original name, BASEBALL, suggested, the project dovetailed with plans for a U.S.-led, postwar global system of air bases and civil air agreements.

8.2. An all-American crew of fliers and mechanics at Poltava with their Ukrainian girlfriends. (Courtesy of National Archives.)

On these bases, cultural exchange took off almost immediately. U.S. fliers and local technicians developed their own patois, and "after only a few weeks, some of the most amazing types of conversations could be heard between Russians and Americans," an Army history noted.[62] With Ukrainians sporting GI shirts and Americans displaying Ukrainian fur hats, it was hard to "tell an American officer from a civilian," a Soviet official complained.[63] Copies of *Life* and *Yank*, permitted on the condition that they remain on base, soon circulated in nearby villages. Like Harriman and other top officials who invested emotions analogous to romantic "love" in their missions to Moscow, lower-level Americans at the bases nursed "a strange fascination for the Russian mission and a feeling ... that its significance was far greater than its reputation."[64]

Such investment of feeling led to disappointment, especially as the secret police regarded informal contact as contamination. A visitor to the base observed that Americans "dated civilian girls, and plenty of them."[65] Nevertheless, the "main gripe" of the GIs was "interference by the Secret Political Police (NKVD) with their dates with girls." Jealous Red Army soldiers helped enforce this "interference." Undeterred, some of the GIs started "keeping Lugers in girl friends' houses just in case."[66] Cultural insecurity probably spurred the Soviet objections to closer contact. A Ukrainian explained that during the two-year German occupation, she and other young women had seen that "the Germans were much more cultured and civilized than the Russians, [and] if these girls were allowed to see that the Americans were even more cultured and civilized than the Russians in their way of living, they obviously would prefer the Americans to the Russians."[67] From the Kremlin's perspective, unrestricted contact was also worrisome because of the anti-Soviet guerrillas fighting not far away.[68] Uncomfortable with the implications of Americans buzzing around the Ukraine, Stalin by late summer 1944 began throttling operations at the bases.

In February–March 1945, Poltava figured in another operation that poked at Soviet control while tugging at American and British hearts: evacuating from Poland seven thousand U.S. and U.K. POWs liberated from German camps by the Red Army and three hundred airmen who had bailed out or crash-landed.[69] Some bomber crews landed near Soviet troops, who, taking them for Germans, kept shooting until convinced by shouts of "Amerikanski!" and "Roosevelt!" Because of Kremlin dictates, the Soviets tended to regard all POWS as more likely cowards than heroes. They expected these Americans and Britons to hitchhike and forage (that is, pillage), much as the Red Army did. (A few ex-POWs even clambered aboard the gun-carriers and tanks, joining the Red Army.)[70]

Some Soviet officers offered the strangers a meal, a ride, and medical care. Others enthused about Lend-Lease trucks and offered vodka—"and what vodka! It tasted like Ethyl alcohol," recounted a former POW.[71] Still others were not so friendly. "The majority of them were drunk," a GI reported, "and they wanted to shoot me because I couldn't speak Russian but finally compromised by relieving me of a $125 Elgin watch."[72] The Soviets told the ex-POWS to hitchhike to concentration points in central Poland, where they would be transported in boxcars to the port of Odessa, from which nearly all were evacuated by V-E day.

Americans—who have mythicized and ennobled war captives since the days of Mary Rowlandson and the Indians—were appalled at such callousness. Harriman and Deane planned for U.S. planes based at Poltava to criss-cross Poland evacuating ex-POWS directly. Roosevelt urged Stalin to comply. Such rescue flights would give Poltava a new rationale, as German retreats had ended the need for shuttle bombing. The dictator refused, further infuriating Harriman and Deane.

The Kremlin boss undoubtedly saw the rescue plan as further meddling in his sphere. As he knew or suspected, British Special Operations was already smuggling anti-Soviet agents in and out of Poland disguised as ex-POWs.[73] Harriman and Deane were pressing for a new air base in Soviet-occupied Hungary. Though he had come to resent the Soviets, Admiral Ernest Archer of the British military mission was appalled at London's brazenness in getting into Soviet-occupied Poland. His government had "kept at the Russians for months until eventually permission was given to inspect an acoustic torpedo" from a U-250 boat at Gdynia. He added that "it came as something of a shock to hear from the [inspection] party that the visit was really only paid for political reasons, as plenty of information had become available from other sources. The same, I imagine, is true of many other desired visits or facilities, such as bomb damage assessment and the like."[74] Although such intelligence efforts were dwarfed by Soviet operations in Britain and America, a cloak-and-dagger contest was already under way.

Emotional thinking linked oppression of Poland and oppression of Americans and Britons. As Deane's aide put it, "the Soviet attitude toward liberated American prisoners is the same as the Soviet attitude toward the countries they have liberated. Prisoners are spoils of war. . . . They may be robbed, starved, and abused—and no one has the right to question such treatment."[75] Deane would recall the quashing of the air rescue as "my darkest days in Russia."[76]

Soviet brutality induced individual U.S. and British soldiers to repudiate the alliance. British intelligence reported that ex-POWs "would like to have a crack at the Russians. Practically all made clear that the Russians were the crudest barbarians, who devoured everything like locusts."[77] One such former POW was staying with a Polish family who "could not do enough for me." One night he was wakened by screams. "It was 'Mama! Mama!' It was a young girl of 17 screaming her heart out. . . . I got out of bed and saw a Russian soldier tearing the clothes off the girl and then raping her. . . . The people of the house turned around and said to me, 'You have seen for yourself tonight an example of your Russian comrades.' . . . I told them that the Russians were no comrades of mine."[78] A GI reported with contempt that "Russians include rape as an integral part of total war. Raping German women is patriotic, raping Polish women is good clean fun."[79]

Poles and Ukrainians desperately worried about Soviet repression clutched at these strangers as possible saviors. Poles expressed to the fliers stranded in their village hope that the bomber crew would become "a permanent force stationed there, an advanced echelon of a large American force that was to come liberate them."[80] In the western Ukraine, a village leader presented a U.S. pilot with "a very beautiful girl of about 17–18 years of age," promising him, "if you stay here long enough, I'm going to marry you to her."[81] To honor two dead airmen, a Polish village staged an elaborate funeral complete with a U.S. flag made the previous night by women who had painstakingly cut out and sewn each of the stars and stripes.[82] Those staying in a poor Polish home were typically "treated with a good meal, the best that they had yet been given, clean beds with clean sheets."[83]

In these contested lands even clean sheets could be political. A U.S. airman concluded that the apparent Polish "culture" of "cleanliness" and "orderly fashion" demonstrated "that a democracy of the highest order had at one time prevailed in the country."[84] Other Americans, however, who had joined the Russians in toasting "to Stalin and Roosevelt using de-icing fluid and gasoline as the beverage," concluded, despite their having also stayed in Polish homes, "that the Poles are trying to promote a war between the Russians and the Americans in the hopes of furthering their own ends."[85]

The emotional drama of the liberated POWs, the struggle to keep Poltava open, and the dire fate of Polish independence were affecting her father, Kathleen worried. "Averell is very busy—what with Poland, P[risoners of] W[ar]. . . . The house is full of running feet, voices, and phones ringing all night long—up until dawn."[86] Harriman and Deane read wrenching testimony from repatriated POWs and airmen. When Stalin turned down the Poltava rescue mission, the ambassador let loose on Roosevelt: "I am outraged."[87] He warned the "Boss" that when word of the POW story got out "there will be great and lasting resentment on the part of the American people."[88] Though also angry that Stalin refused to allow the air evacuation of ex-POWs, FDR rebuffed Harriman's plea to escalate the dispute. While the president remained focused on the big picture of postwar collaboration, the Americans and Britons in Moscow grew ever more frustrated and angry.

Their worsening mood was recorded in a detailed diary. With Spaso House so difficult to heat in the frigid Moscow winter, a kerosene stove was rigged up in the top-floor bedroom of Meiklejohn. He jotted in the diary, "My room is very comfortable now," and it has become "the usual gathering place in the evening."[89] In March 1945, Richard Rossbach, an ex-POW connected to the Morgenthau and Lehman families in New York, regaled those clustered around the stove with lurid descriptions of the Red Army. Commenting that he "had a much better time with the Germans than with our allies," he described Soviet forces as operating under "primitive and chaotic conditions. . . . Their men live like animals, forage off the countryside for their food . . . and fight in a semi-drunken state maintained by a generous ration of vodka." While Soviet soldiers robbed Americans of their watches at gunpoint, Poles "always welcomed and cared for our men as best they could."[90]

The cultural and incipiently political lines of division seemed obvious: affinities between Americans and Poles and even Germans, in contrast to enmity between Americans and Soviets. "Primitive," "chaotic," and animal-like men, who stole for sustenance and robbed allies, appeared not as postwar partners but as a horde to be contained or fought. Kremlin bosses whose "generous ration of vodka" fueled soldiers' "semi-drunken state" seemed themselves bereft of judgment and a sense of limits. Americans and British reacted with understandable disgust as they saw Soviet soldiers raping, looting, and defecating without restraint. Rossbach and others reported that "rapes are constantly occurring." Common were "cases of thirty or forty Soviet soldiers raping one woman and then killing her."[91] Searing stories habituated embassy officials to referring to the Soviets as "animal-like people" even when talking about such mundane matters as overcrowded trains.[92] Seeing the cultural difference as a racial one, Kennan advised a reporter that Stalin had a "deeply suspicious, dark, Asiatic mind. He had a genius for power in the true Asiatic way."[93] As Harriman operated in this poisonous atmosphere, he was actually undercutting the alliance.

When the Russians in March 1945 asked to be included in the Berne negotiations for the surrender of German forces in Italy, Harriman, backed by Deane, urged Washington to refuse. Their arguments resonated with a logic that would prevail in the Cold War. Not only would admitting the Soviets "gain no . . . goodwill"; the gesture would be interpreted in the Kremlin as "a sign of weakness" and spur further "demands."[94] Years later, Harriman admitted that exclusion from the Berne talks "terrified" and infuriated the Soviets, who feared a separate peace on the entire Western front would leave them alone against the Germans. "I was amazed at the emotion that was showed by the Russians at that time," he would recall.[95]

Meanwhile, Roosevelt, seeking to end the spat over Berne, cabled Stalin: "In any event, there must not be mutual distrust, and minor misunderstandings of this character should not arise in the future."[96] Instead of delivering the telegram, Harriman, astoundingly, tried to change it. He urged the president to eliminate the word "minor" because "the misunderstanding appeared to me to be of a major character."[97] FDR insisted, "I do not wish to delete the word 'minor' as it is my desire to consider the . . . misunderstanding a minor incident."[98] Two aspects here bear emphasis. First, Roosevelt understood that a dispute he considered minor might remain so, and a dispute he considered major would become so. Second, an angry Harriman was so intent on "toughening" U.S. policy that he jeopardized his ties to the president.

Denied permission to come to Washington, Harriman, fuming, wrote an extraordinary telegram on April 10. He made the emotionally explosive, difficult-to-dislodge argument that the policy of cooperating with Stalin had "been influenced by a sense of fear." Charging that a policy was influenced by fear was to delegitimize that stance. The draft of this telegram reveals how Harriman was trying to smear Roosevelt's policy by describing it as based on cowardly fear—even though he had little proof of such emotion. He was initially unsure how to argue this far-fetched proposition. Exactly what did the United States fear? In the draft, he first wrote that U.S. decisions "have been influenced by a sense of fear of the Soviet Union." He evidently then decided, however, that it would be difficult to convince the president that he, Roosevelt, feared the Soviet Union. So Harriman scratched out "fear of the Soviet Union," and wrote the vaguer formulation "fear of it." Then he crossed that out and settled for the still vaguer, but even harder to refute, formulation that decisions were "influenced by a sense of fear on our part." Harriman then repeated the word "fear" five times by representing policy concerns as cowardly "fears."[99] He used the word "insult" five times in detailing the "almost daily," "outrageous" indignities he was suffering in Moscow.[100]

Two days later, FDR died. Harriman's status quickly soared from insubordinate ambassador to Soviet expert. The unfortunate contingency of Roosevelt's death unleashed those bent on changing U.S. policy. Alice Acheson, whose husband, Dean, would later assign Harriman many an arduous task, recalled that Averell "had enormous energy . . . getting people interested and following it up. Going around to lunches, dinners, cocktail parties, receptions, and lectures. Every kind of thing. . . . He seemed to have no limit to his energy."[101] Finally free of Rooseveltian restraint, Harriman rushed to Washington to lobby nearly everyone from the president on down. He insisted, incorrectly as it would turn out, that Stalin would back down if pressed hard. The struggle shifted from guns and kisses in Moscow to influencing Truman in Washington.

"Roosevelt's Death Has Changed Everything"

Truman's First Days, April–June 1945

Anxious to shape Truman's views before the president met with Molotov, Averell Harriman on April 17, 1945 embarked on what Robert Meiklejohn dubbed an "'around-the-world' race."[1] His plane hopscotched westward, landing in Washington forty-nine hours later, seven hours off the previous record. "You must have taken all the short cuts," an admirer wrote.[2] Flying eastward, Molotov took days longer. The Soviet Union lacked the navigation aids needed for nighttime flying. U.S. superiority in the air was also reflected in the Russian's taking an American plane piloted by an American crew. Harriman was demonstrating that air travel could bring Washington and Moscow together—or enable an attack. In the hubbub of the ambassador's departure, Soviet authorities neglected to check passports. Ever mindful of the personal contact issue, the Americans rued the missed chance to smuggle out some Russian wives.[3] Agitated, with a tic in his eye, Harriman appeared to Elbridge Durbrow "just steaming."[4] He had ceased believing that unconditional surrender, that is the total defeat of the German and Japanese governments, "was a good policy."[5] Referring to Russia, Meiklejohn believed that Roosevelt's policy had let "a Frankenstein [monster] loose upon Europe. . . .

Until that Frankenstein is disposed of, there will be no peace in the world."[6]

Also aboard was Archibald Clark Kerr, who observed that over the previous year Harriman had careened from "high elation" to the deepest melancholia. . . . His melancholia had turned into something like hate, and he was determined to advise his government to waste no more time on the effort to understand and to cooperate with the Russians."[7]

Even if Roosevelt had lived, the ending of the war in Europe, particularly because it came so suddenly, probably would have heightened tensions.[8] With Truman, however, came changed personalities and perceptions that further aggravated those tensions and, in turn, exacerbated suspicions in Moscow. The most lasting change from Roosevelt to Truman was in the emotional tenor of attitudes and discourses. Although U.S.-Soviet political relations cooled, warmed, and then cooled again in the year following FDR's death, the discursive breakthroughs pushed by Harriman and George Kennan endured. After Harriman's April 20–23 talks with Truman and Washington officials and his briefing of leading journalists on May 1, it became more permissible and habitual to talk about the Soviets not as fellow world policemen as Roosevelt had most often depicted them, but rather as international criminals.

Truman as President

Harriman found a ready listener in Truman. The ambassador criticized Roosevelt's policy as born out of "fear" of the Soviets. This specious argument touched a nerve with the insecure new president, anxious to demonstrate that he was big enough for the job and feared neither Stalin nor anyone else.[9] A few weeks after FDR's death, Truman banged his fist on the table, declaring: "We have to get tough with the Russians. . . . We've got to teach them how to behave."[10] He never moved far from this assumption.

"We are waking up to the fact that Roosevelt's death has changed everything," Churchill's doctor concluded.[11] The prime minister welcomed the change. Indeed, he went so far as to ask British military planners, many of whom already considered Russia an enemy, to submit a contingency plan to attack the Soviet Union that very year. Also waking up to the shock was Roosevelt's old guard, who had excluded the vice president from decision making. Truman's "retribution was swift and ruthless," a Washington insider later recalled.[12]

Truman learned the presidency on the run. He faced the challenges of the atomic bomb, the sudden peace, postwar turbulence from "Korea to Timbuktoo," and painful conversion to a peacetime economy.[13] In the November 1946 election, widespread discontent would wipe out the Democrats' majority in Congress for the first time since 1930. That mood seemed likely to defeat Truman in 1948. His come-from-behind win that year would secure his place in the pantheon of American democratic ideology: the plucky, no-nonsense common man who had made good. This everyman would remain the only U.S. president of the twentieth century not to attend college. Though Truman had excelled in high school, his father's soured financial speculations forced the youth to get a job instead. From childhood on, Harry read voraciously, especially historical biography. He wanted to know how men become great.

He believed that individual leaders, not forces, shaped history. "Ancient History is one of the most interesting of all courses," he wrote his daughter, Margaret. "By it you find out why a lot of things happen today. But you must study it on the basis of the biographies of the men and women who lived it."[14] As president, he pushed his authority to the limit. Believing the executive branch should shape public and congressional opinion, he showed little patience for disagreement. In 1950, he would plunge into the Korean War without a congressional vote. He also drew from his reading simple, black-and-white lessons that ill-served him in dealing with the ambiguities of foreign relations. Though the autodidact considered himself an expert on history, historian George F. Mowry found that of all the presidents from Warren G. Harding to John F. Kennedy, Harding and Truman were "the most inexact" in their references to historical examples.[15]

In contrast to his predecessor, this president bustled with plenty of energy. He modeled himself after his father, who had "worked from daylight to dark, all the time." He had applied that ethic in the Senate, particularly as head of the committee investigating war contracts. He earned a reputation for earnest diligence. He advised his daughter, "It takes work and more work to accomplish anything—and your dad knows it better than anyone. It's been my policy to do every job assigned to me just a little better than anyone else has done it."[16]

Doing the job better than FDR posed a challenge, particular in the eyes of average Americans. In a July 1945 poll, 61 percent of respondents picked Roosevelt as the greatest American ever. Despite the flush of sympathy for Truman, he garnered only 3 percent in that tally.[17] Undaunted, the new president believed he could best FDR as an administrator. Roosevelt had tangled lines of authority so as to keep control in his own hands. Truman assigned his aides sole jurisdiction over their jobs. The clear lines also enabled subordinates, such as Harriman and, later, Dean Acheson, to manipulate him by playing to his numerous prejudices and delicate ego. The man from Independence took pride in being the "buck-stops-here" leader. But that assertive attitude sacrificed careful deliberation. At a time when Truman still counted Henry Wallace as a supporter, the latter observed that the president "seemed eager to make decisions of every kind with the greatest promptness. Everything he said was decisive. It almost seemed as though he was eager to decide in advance of thinking."[18]

Truman's desire to appear as the intrepid decision maker was probably rooted in his early years. At about five years of age he had to wear glasses with thick lens. "Four eyes" Harry was excluded from rough-and-tumble games. "That's hard on a boy," he later recalled. "It makes him lonely, and it gives him an inferiority complex, and he has a hard time overcoming it." He acknowledged that he had not been popular. "The popular boys were the ones who were good at games and had big, tight fists. I was never like that. Without my glasses I was blind as a bat, and to tell the truth, I was kind of a sissy. If there was any danger of getting into a fight, I always ran."[19] Nonetheless, he would vow not to run from a fight with the Kremlin, especially after Harriman told him that Roosevelt's policy was based on fear of the Soviets.

Truman placed women on a pedestal. He framed the danger in World War I as a domestic as well as foreign threat. "Just think what he'd [the kaiser] do to our great country and our beautiful women if he only could."[20] He appeared in awe of his wife, Bess, the only woman he had ever courted. In July 1945, en route to the Potsdam summit conference, he wrote to her in a tone that a later generation might term passive-aggressive. "I'm sorry if I've done something to make you unhappy. All I've ever tried to do is make you pleased with me and the world. I'm very much afraid I've failed miserably."[21] As president, Truman, unlike Roosevelt, excluded women from his political inner circle. According to a biographer, "he never felt comfortable working with them and thought their presence inhibited free discussion."[22]

Reflecting on the repercussions of FDR's death, Secretary of War Stimson predicted a postwar "period of great confusion," when Roosevelt's "great foresight and keenness of vision" would be missed.[23] Truman would react to that confusion by simplifying issues and making snap decisions.[24] While Roosevelt had reveled in the ambiguity of issues, Truman required clear-cut answers. Like many Americans, the Missourian remained skeptical of foreigners and hostile toward Bolshevism. When Litvinov in December 1941 had appealed for an alliance, Truman had opined that the Russians were "as untrustworthy as Hitler and Al Capone."[25] He lacked his predecessor's appreciation of the Soviets' history-changing role in demolishing the German war machine.

FDR expected a long postwar transition during which Americans would have to tolerate spheres of influence in Eastern Europe and other departures from the Wilsonian principles of the Atlantic Charter. Tragically uninstructed by Roosevelt, Truman was neither temperamentally nor intellectually inclined toward such patience. Eleven days after becoming president, he dismissed previous dealings with Stalin as "a one way street [that] could not continue; it was now or never."[26] Eleanor Roosevelt urged Truman to lighten up. The Russians are "like us. They enjoy a practical joke, rough-house play. . . . That was where Franklin usually won out because if you know where to laugh and when to look upon things as too absurd to take seriously, the other person is ashamed to carry through even if he was serious about it."[27]

Even hard-boiled Chief of Staff William Leahy appreciated the potential clout in Roosevelt's light touch. After the funeral in Hyde Park, Frances Perkins traveled back to Washington with Leahy, who had drafted several of the tougher telegrams to Stalin in March and April. In ensuing years, she would think often of what Leahy, looking "very, very sad and depressed" had told her. "'This is the most terrible thing that could have happened from the point of view of the peace of the world. . . . If only [Roosevelt] could have been spared just one year more . . . many things that are going to trouble us I think would not have troubled us.'" Roosevelt had a "'sort of high handed, happy way of carrying [the Soviets] along with him before they had a chance to say "no" or renege, and getting a commitment while they were sort of enjoying him.'" At Yalta, FDR had lifted the Soviets "'above the level of their ordinary situation, so that in a kind of atmosphere of happiness and good will, they had perhaps gone further than they knew. Only one year more,'" the admiral reportedly said, "shaking his head."[28]

Lacking Roosevelt's touch or confidence, Truman relied on advice from Harriman, James Byrnes, Joseph Davies, and Harry Hopkins. Harriman and Byrnes agreed on the need for a tougher policy toward the Soviets. Davies argued against confrontation, and his advice actually prevailed for a while in late May, when even Harriman and Bohlen worried that relations with Moscow were falling off the cliff. Hopkins, on the outs with Roosevelt since December 1943 and especially since Yalta, stewed with resentment that did not improve his already precarious health. FDR apparently did not consult his former friend when tensions with Stalin mounted in March. Adding to his stress was suspicion that his wife, Louise, was having an affair—with a woman as it would turn out. Hopkins asked Hoover to have agents tail Louise. He also had the FBI tap his home phone. Like Meiklejohn's diary of conversations around the kerosene heater in Spaso House, the fortuitous Hopkins telephone transcripts trace the evolution of foreign policy views quite different from those of Franklin Roosevelt.

After taking his oath as president at 7:09 p.m. on April 12, 1945, Truman looked around the room and asked, "Where's Harry

Hopkins?"[29] The new president needed a crash course in foreign policy. He afterward complained that FDR "never did talk to me confidentially about the war, or about foreign affairs or what he had in mind for the peace after the war."[30] The man Truman wanted a briefing from languished at the Mayo Clinic, sinking in body and spirit— "so low he's a goner," feared Louise.[31] Though FDR had discussed his heart disease with Daisy Suckley and Lucy Rutherfurd, he had not confided in Harry.[32] It was not the White House staff or the Roosevelt family that informed the former live-in friend of the death, but rather Chip Bohlen. Hopkins defied his doctors and rushed to Washington to pay his respects.

Hopkins also paid homage to the new president. When Ambassador Lord Halifax commiserated that the death must be a "shock to Harry," Louise replied that despite the trauma to the country, "Harry takes things like that very well."[33] Much of his melancholy actually stemmed from his fall from power. Roosevelt had obliged, however, by keeping his perennially cash-short former aide on the government payroll. Truman's ascendancy opened a path to renewed influence. Then again, the new boss might cut off his salary. "You know we could be out overnight," Louise worried to a friend. She joked that if her husband was fired, they could not even drink their problems away because "we won't be able to afford the booze." Even Harry's twelve-year-old daughter, Diana, fretted, "What is to become of us?"[34]

Hopkins was delighted, then, when Truman called on the 13th to invite him for a long chat the next morning. The heady elixir of the White House worked some of the magic that it had in May 1940, when he had moved into the Lincoln bedroom. Describing her husband after the meeting, Louise enthused, "Every inch of that man is better. . . . Not only in color and looks, but in enthusiasm and interest."[35]

Most Roosevelt insiders had difficulty accepting Truman as president. "I know he is decent," allowed the secretary of the interior and professional curmudgeon Harold Ickes, "but can anyone mention any other attributes?"[36] Hopkins, in contrast, found the new boss "a wonderful person."[37] In subsequent days FDR's former Mr. Fix-it conferred with Bohlen and with the ambassadors of Britain and China.

He apparently did not, however, meet with the Soviet ambassador. As for booze, he "hasn't had a sip. He doesn't miss it," Louise exulted.[38]

More than illness, rivalry and emotion limited the comeback. Years later, Harriman confirmed that Truman "didn't like Hopkins."[39] Byrnes, who flew to Truman's side hours after FDR died, faulted Hopkins for allegedly having soured Roosevelt on his, Byrnes's, nomination as vice president in 1944. Long Truman's mentor in the Senate, Byrnes would not tolerate such competition in the new administration. The first full day of the new administration someone from the White House—perhaps Byrnes or Truman himself—informed the British Embassy that Churchill should "not take up matters with Harry Hopkins as in the past." Churchill should instead go "direct [sic] with President Truman and not bypass him."[40] Hopkins hit back. No doubt echoing her husband, Louise mocked Byrnes (soon to be appointed secretary of state) for "acting like a perfect moron" by strutting about as "presidential adviser."[41] Even before Roosevelt was laid into the ground, she complained, Byrnes was angling for position. So was her husband—who lost out. Truman would soon relegate Harry Hopkins to the role of elder statesman: excluded from the inner circle but nevertheless tapped for advice and for one last critical mission to Moscow. It was not this demotion, however, that was responsible for the administration's shift away from Roosevelt's priority of collaboration with the Soviets. Hopkins in fact endorsed the change in tone and focus spearheaded by Harriman.

Harriman's Impact

Harriman was spurred by not only his own anger and ambition but also by the pent-up resentments of Kennan, Deane, Durbrow, Bohlen, Meiklejohn, and their journalist friends from Moscow. Not many in that grousing group possessed the patience or insights of a Clark Kerr. The ambassador's April–May visit marked the merging of two strands of U.S. policy that had operated separately since Hopkins's 1941 mission to Stalin. In talking with officials and people in Congress and in the press, Harriman claimed expertise as the nation's top

"Soviet expert." He insisted that it was not just permissible, but also responsible, realistic, normal, and tough-minded to regard the Soviets as more foe than friend. Roosevelt had resisted this line, and he likely would have continued fighting it.

Voices in the administration still favoring collaboration with the Soviets included General Marshall, Stimson, Wallace, Ickes, State Department public affairs chief Archibald MacLeish, and Lend-Lease executive Oscar Cox; influential figures outside that group who also supported this approach included Walter Lippmann and Eleanor Roosevelt. Postwar turbulence and confusion—and the Soviets' domineering behavior in Poland and elsewhere—made it difficult to argue for a calm, self-confident policy based on the Big Three. Harriman won out in part because of what a collaborator called his "total ferocious dedication."[42] He could be "absolutely single-minded," future CIA director Richard Helms remarked. Determination sometimes led to distortion. Harriman "will exaggerate things, and know that he exaggerates them." When called on it, he would justify himself, saying, "Well, yes, perhaps, but you know, I feel very strongly about so and so."[43]

With his on-the-scene authority, Harriman lobbied hard for the view that the Soviets' insistence on the primacy of the pro-Moscow Lublin Poles violated the Yalta agreement. That accord was certainly ambiguous. Nevertheless, five firsthand American and British witnesses, four of them otherwise unsympathetic toward Moscow, independently acknowledged that the Russians had the stronger case when they insisted that Yalta provided for retaining the Lublin government and merely adding other Polish elements. In the first days after the summit, Clark Kerr remained behind with Churchill while Harriman and Bohlen flew to Moscow, where they rendezvoused with the hardliner Durbrow. "Durby" had been sent by the State Department to back up Harriman in the negotiations with Molotov and Clark Kerr to implement the Yalta agreement on Poland. Clark Kerr later confided to Lippmann that a higher authority—Churchill himself, most likely—had "overruled" his judgment and had "asked for an interpretation of the Crimean agreement which made the problem insoluble." (Lippmann added, "I know also on unimpeachable au-

9.1. After the Soviets refused to aid the August 1944 Warsaw uprising, Harriman and Stalin grew increasingly estranged. To the left of Harriman is Bohlen. (Courtesy of Library of Congress.)

thority that President Roosevelt was attempting to mediate.")[44] Another stick in the spokes came from the Americans in Moscow. Years later, Harriman privately acknowledged that following Yalta, he and Bohlen "wanted to hit hard, right away." Impelling them was the conviction that "this Polish agreement has got to be negotiated a second time."[45] According to Durbrow's recollection, the aim of the second go-around was a deal that would take back most of Roosevelt's and Churchill's concessions to Stalin at Yalta. As Durbrow put it, "we wrote the instructions out before . . . they went to Yalta." He repeated, "our original drafts" predated the summit conference.[46] In sum, Harriman, Bohlen, and Durbrow, like Clark Kerr with his arm twisted, were trying to revise the Yalta agreement on Poland.

A few weeks later, the British diplomat Frank Roberts, who later testified, "I had been educated by the Poles in London," and who would write his own "long telegram," arrived in Moscow. He reported that the accord as signed at Yalta "was interpreted not only by the Russians but also by . . . independent and by no means pro-Russian journalists here as being a Russian victory in the sense that we, for the first time, completely ignored the Polish Government in London and went some way towards recognition" of the Lublin regime. "In so far as we want a new deal, and, in fact, the elimination or subordination of the [Lublin] group, we are fighting for something which the Russians . . . are not prepared to concede."[47] A final witness was Jimmy Byrnes, who had been at Yalta. In June 1945, he acknowledged "that there was no question as to what the spirit of the agreement was. There was no intent that a new government was to be created independent of the Lublin government. The basis was to be the Lublin government."[48]

Taken together, this testimony indicates that Stalin could rightfully feel that the Americans and British were going back on their concessions regarding the issue that, along with the future of Germany, seemed most vital to postwar Soviet security. Though there would be many other issues forming and then intensifying the Cold War, it was over Poland that the Grand Alliance ran aground.

Harriman years later acknowledged that the dictator had still further reason for disappointment with regard to Poland. "Much to Stalin's surprise and chagrin, he found that the Red Army was accepted not as a liberating force" in Poland or Romania. Instead, "they were looked upon as a new invading force. And that hurt the Russians. That was an awfully, awfully upsetting thing for them to accept." The Soviet-supported Lublin group would lose any free elections.[49]

What Clark Kerr characterized as Harriman's "hate" influenced four discourse-changing conversations in Washington and in San Francisco. First he spoke with Truman alone, thereafter with Truman and other advisers, and then the president confronted Molotov. A week later, the ambassador briefed journalists at the San Francisco conference.

Meeting with the new president on April 20, Harriman tossed the fear-bomb. He said that FDR's policy had rested on shameful fear. Proud and insecure, Truman quickly interjected that "he was not in any sense afraid of the Russians." Harriman then undercut the rationale for the alliance by presenting as a fatal contradiction that which Roosevelt had regarded as a fact of life. During the postwar transition Moscow would seek both cooperation with its allies and dominance over its neighbors. The ambassador made still another alarmist claim: the Soviets lacked any sense of limits. Therefore getting along with Russia would require the United States to endure a humiliating passivity. He concluded with a flatly wrong prediction. Because the Kremlin "did not wish to break with the United States . . . we had nothing to lose by standing firm."[50]

Roosevelt, understanding that cultural differences could doom the alliance, always played them down. Harriman played them up. Indeed, he inflated them. To Truman, who liked reading about Genghis Khan, he repeated the kerosene-stove comment that the armies rolling back the Nazis amounted to a "barbarian invasion of Europe." Bohlen liked the zing. His minutes paraphrased the rest of the conversation; this was the only phrase to appear in quotation marks.[51] General John Deane meanwhile was making similar arguments to Pentagon officials.[52] Perceptions of cultural difference sparked in Truman another analogy. "The Russians were like people from across the tracks whose manners were very bad," he would tell Wallace.[53]

On April 23, the president canvassed advisers before meeting with Molotov. He set the tone by declaring that the Russians "could go to hell" if they did not attend the impending San Francisco conference. Harriman and Deane reconceptualized the problem of the Soviet domination of Poland so as to directly and morally involve the United States. "The real issue," Harriman insisted, "was whether we were to be a party to a program of Soviet domination of Poland."[54] According to this provocative formulation, unless Washington escalated Poland into a crisis, U.S. leaders themselves would become "a party" to Moscow's brutal domination—perpetrators rather than bystanders. In other words, Washington had to assume responsibility for freedom up to the very border of its victorious, touchy, and insistent ally. Or else Polish blood would stain American hands. Such dangerous reasoning greased the slide from the Atlantic Charter to the Cold War.

In the meeting with Truman's advisers Deane's insinuation was equally explosive: "If we were afraid of the Russians, we would get nowhere." Washington had to act in order to regain Moscow's respect. Charges of being afraid were an effective slur: easy to make, difficult to disprove. Once someone raised the issue of fear, it became harder to argue against confronting the Russians. Even readier to scuttle the alliance was Secretary of the Navy James Forrestal, who argued that if the Russians did not retreat, "we had better have a showdown with them now than later." Leahy, who had stood at Roosevelt's side at Yalta, informed the group that the agreement on Poland "was susceptible to two interpretations." Nevertheless, he also insisted on "a free and independent Poland."[55]

In keeping with the customary discourse of official minutes, Bohlen's record flattened the emotional tone of the talk. The meeting was actually, however, very emotional, as a participant soon informed Felix Frankfurter. There was "much 'banging of fists' on the table in arguing that it was 'high time' to take a 'tough line' with Russia." Harsh talk was "the only language the Russians could understand." Stalin had sent an "insulting" note to Roosevelt.[56] Such masculine, tough-guy renderings implicitly faulted the late president. Almost in caricature they were implying that the wheelchair-bound Roosevelt may have been unwilling or unable to stand up to the Russians, but the new leadership was eager to prove its grit and avenge America's honor.

Only Stimson and Marshall sounded caution. Stimson worried that emotional thinking was distorting perceptions of national interest. He had noted in his diary that Harriman and Deane "have been suffering personally from the Russians' behavior on minor matters." "Influenced by their past bad treatment," they were arguing "for strong words by [the] President."[57] Stimson did not see U.S. vital interests as extending deep into Eastern Europe, especially given that "25 years ago all of Poland had been Russian."[58] Truman, however, ignored Stimson's skepticism. After the meeting ended, the president asked Secretary of State Stettinius, Bohlen, and anti-Soviet State Department veteran James Dunn to remain. Having decided to press the Russians, the rookie requested talking points for his meeting with the Soviet minister.[59]

Molotov was meanwhile lunching with Davies, whom he regarded as the friendly ambassador from the 1930s. The Russian acknowledged that the president's death weighed as "a great loss and an irreparable one." His government "had had full confidence in Roosevelt." After Tehran and Yalta, "Stalin and Roosevelt understood each other." Despite post-Yalta tensions, Stalin had believed that "any difference could always be adjusted through mutual discussions and tolerance, for there was a will to achieve cooperation." Now, however, fears were mounting that the new president lacked a will to cooperate. Stalin worried that Truman "was not familiar with all these matters and their background." Such "background" included personal understandings. Molotov had come to America as a tribute to Roosevelt and to assess the new president. Uncertainties were mounting because of the sudden folding of the Germans. His government sought peace, but it also expected "understanding, respect, and cooperation."

Davies replied with cautionary warnings. He stressed the "sentimentalism which attached to the Poles." Many of Truman's advisers were critical of Moscow. Eden was in Washington pressing Churchill's views. Roosevelt's successor would be fair, Davies assured. Yet he also predicted that "if there were trouble" with Truman, it "would be due to the fact that he would rely on others." He "strongly urged" Molotov to "specifically ask the President" not to commit himself on the issue of the Polish government "until he has heard all the facts and the Soviet point of view." A longtime poker crony of Truman, Davies feared "the principal danger . . . would come from a 'snap judgment.'"[60]

In meeting with Molotov, Truman lectured rather than listened. Their encounter followed two days of exhausting diplomacy aimed at getting the Russian to back away from what Truman later called forcing "this puppet government upon the United States and England."[61] Two days earlier, Stalin had poked the Allies in the eye by signing a treaty with that Polish regime. Echoing Harriman's provocative formulation, the president warned that America "could not agree to be a party" to Soviet domination of Poland.

Molotov tried to make two points about how the Big Three had functioned. First, despite their differences, "the three Governments had been able to find a common language and decide questions by agreement." Second, they "had dealt as equal parties, and there had been no case where one or two of the three had attempted to impose their will on another." Truman repeated that the Yalta agreement on Poland was clear cut. He seemed undeterred by Leahy's admission that Yalta was open to two interpretations. He probably did not know, and may not have cared about, the views of Clark Kerr and Roberts. It remains a puzzle precisely what Byrnes did and did not tell Truman about Yalta. In any case, the president insisted that the Russians were violating the agreement. Molotov rejoined that unlike the other Allies, they had stuck by Yalta. Moreover, Poland loomed on their border, and they would not tolerate anti-Russians in Warsaw. Truman interrupted that there was no use discussing that further. When Molotov brought up the Far Eastern war, where the Red Army would be needed, Truman cut him off, saying, "That will be all, Mr. Molotov."[62] Durbrow, who observed the Russian leave, would later recall, "I've never seen a man come out more ashen in my life."[63] Afterward, Truman bragged, "I gave it to him straight. I let him have it. It was straight one-two to the jaw." Yet the champ remained insecure. "Did I do right?" he asked.[64]

As Davies had feared, his friend had reached a "snap judgment" after refusing to consider the Russian viewpoint. The shortened discussion hurt Truman himself, as he needed all the foreign policy experience he could get, and Molotov channeled Stalin. Notwithstanding Truman's pledge to stick with Yalta, the tone and attitude of the U.S. government had changed. Upon hearing of the heated exchange, morale at the State Department "began to soar," recalled the hardliner Loy Henderson.[65] Ironically, Harriman, who had pushed the "fear" thesis as a way of prodding Washington, would later "regret that Truman went at it so hard because his behavior gave Molotov an excuse to tell Stalin that the Roosevelt policy was being abandoned. . . . I think it was a mistake."[66]

Bohlen would recall the conversation as, quite literally, a discursive break—"probably the first sharp words uttered during the war by an American President to a high Soviet official."[67] Memories of an exciting event endure. Decades later Bohlen could still exclaim, "How I enjoyed translating Truman's sentences!" Perhaps on some level he also enjoyed avenging what he and other young American diplomats had lost in the post-1934 purges. Rather than editing the emotions out of his minutes, Bohlen highlighted them. He probably realized that his new boss would fancy a record of himself talking tough. The fast-rising diplomat influenced all three April 20–23 conversations. He crafted the official minutes, spoke at the second meeting, and along with Dunn he wrote the talking points for the conversation with Molotov and the follow-up to Stalin. Harriman later praised Bohlen as "a man of decision [who] took great initiative with me, the President, and the Secretary."[68]

Sensing that the Truman-Molotov dustup could prove pivotal, Bohlen and Stettinius sought Hopkins's approval. Louise told a friend that "the minute they finish with Molotov, they end up at this house, and they have a long talk about what's what." Apparently, Hopkins approved. Louise said, "Truman really and truly stood up for the United States today with Molotov, which is good, I think." Her words "really and truly" suggested that her husband, whom she reflexively followed on such issues, endorsed Truman's forcefulness. "Stood up for the United States" implied criticism of FDR's past policy, as had the discussion among Truman's advisers earlier that afternoon. The ambivalence of the phrase "which is good, I think," may indicate that while Harry endorsed the tough tone, the change remained surprising. Or perhaps Louise lagged behind Harry in adjusting to the new disposition.

Molotov muted the tone of the meeting in his report to Stalin. Reportedly he tried to avoid Stalin's scapegoating him by downplaying the rancor.[69] Decades later he bristled on recalling how Truman "began talking with me in such an imperious tone!" The former mandolin minstrel admitted that the president played the piano "not badly." But "he was far from having Roosevelt's intellect. A big difference."[70] Accustomed to the calibrated hospitality of Stalin's court, Molotov must have noticed the new chill. Truman admitted that the guest received "no military honors" at the airport.[71] Nor did he have a welcoming dinner. Though described as "tightly wrapped," "Mr. No" liked a good time.[72] He probably reflected on the shift from May 1942, when he had stayed at the White House, dining, drinking, and talking at length with the president. Attitudes and policies had clearly changed. Hitler's suicide and V-E Day were still weeks away.

Grappling with Cultural Difference

An explosive blend of pride, anxiety, and resentment accelerated that change. The Big Three countries had all sacrificed—but differently. Each regarded its contribution as the key to victory. The British had fought the longest and for a frightful year all alone. The Soviets had suffered the most blood and damage and had waited three years for the second front. The Americans had donated tens of billions of dollars in supplies while massing forces in different theaters on opposite sides of the globe. With victory, expectations of gratitude and respect spiked. As Sherwood put it, "it is difficult not to be an eagle-screaming, flag-waving chauvinist."[73] Molotov pounded his chest while exclaiming, "I am proud, proud, I tell you, to be the foreign minister of this great country."[74] A U.S. official observed that many of the Red Army soldiers on Moscow's boulevards looked like "a boxer walking down Broadway after he has won the world's championship."[75] Kennan saw incipient pathology. The Soviets seemed "proud almost to the point of hysteria."[76]

Swollen pride impelled each of the Big Three nations to expect from the others displays of gratitude and respect. And each was quick to see the other's strutting as a signal of disrespect and aggression. Resentments mounted as the Soviets repressed Polish independence and the British suppressed Greek leftists. Irritation at the Allies contributed to the U.S. decision, later partly rescinded, to suddenly shut the spigot on Lend-Lease.

Such feelings were expressed according to each nation's emotional disposition. Many Americans looked at a match-up with the Russians as a trial of manly courage. Harriman pitched his arguments to Truman on the premise that Roosevelt's policy rested on fear. Truman responded that he was not afraid of the Russians. The man whom many contemporaries described as "little" bragged that he had figuratively punched out Stalin's emissary, who had literally turned white. The banging of fists on the table, the impatience for tough talk, and the alleged need to recoup from a dying, half-paralyzed president all signified a need to assert—and to get the Soviets to respect—the vigor and virility of the new team. In translating into words their anxieties about the Soviet Union, Americans chose figures of speech related to gender or to associated categories of health, strength, and integrity (in the sense of wholeness.)

The Soviets' brutal intrusion into Eastern Europe made them seem threatening in many ways. The mass rapes underscored the violation of sexual borders. Positive aspects of the intensely manly image of the Red Army were enhanced by its to-hell-and-back victory over the most aggressive and heretofore invincible army in the world. Perhaps the failed attempts to open up Soviet society left U.S. and British diplomats feeling personally vulnerable because of their own openness. The gendering of the Soviets as a hypermasculine foe bent on "penetrating" with force, ideology, and propaganda would become central to the American Cold War imaginary.

Victory spurred Soviet leaders to ponder the meaning of the cultural differences brought into relief by wartime contact. With a convert's zeal, the Georgian-born dictator stressed pride in Russia. He hated the taunts of British military representative Brocas Burrows and others that the Soviets remained "savages."[77] Soviet cultural chauvinism would grow savage indeed as the Cold War worsened. Even during the alliance years Stalin resisted aping the West. Yet he also devoted enormous effort to spying on the Americans and British and copying their weapons and industrial designs. A similar love/hate, dependent/independent pattern had characterized his drive to industrialize under the Five-Year Plans.

Before the Cold War polarized nearly everything, even Stalin could acknowledge some lag in Russian culture. When Finns asked about his postwar agenda for the Soviet Union, he replied, "first to make the people more human and less like beasts by stilling their animal passions, their fears and lusts."[78] At Potsdam, he volunteered that Soviet generals "still lack breeding, and their manners are bad. Our people have a long way to go."[79] Although Stalin's technical knowledge outshone Churchill's or Roosevelt's, in the elevated circles of their summits, he remained a cobbler's son. Arthur Birse later recalled a British dinner where the Kremlin boss "sat uncomfortably on the edge of his chair [and] looked with anxiety at the display of different-sized knives and forks before him." He finally turned to the interpreter, saying, "'This is a fine collection of cutlery! It is a problem which to use. You will have to tell me, and also when I can begin to eat."[80] Many in Washington and London interpreted cultural difference with the Russians as evidence of Western superiority. As Harriman snidely put it, if the Soviets "expect really to play a part in world affairs," they had "to learn to stop eating with their knives."[81] Perhaps class consciousness had impelled the former Bolshevik bank robber, who liked watching Hollywood movies, to bolt out of his chair at Tehran as Churchill's daughter, the actress Sarah Churchill, approached. According to Roosevelt, Stalin bent down to kiss her hand.[82] Churchill seemed to play on Soviet concerns about cultural difference when he warned the dictator not to ignore "the divergences . . . about matters which you may think are small but which are symbolic of the way the English-speaking democracies look at life."[83]

Hints at a possibly more inclusive perspective faded as the dictator gave up on collaboration. In November 1945, he would scold Molotov for approving publication of a speech by Churchill praising Russia and Stalin. He would demand instead "hard struggle" against "servility towards foreigners," whose praise "only jars me." By 1946, he would be spurring Andrei Zhdanov's attack on those "cringing before philistine foreign literature." Ideologically correct patriots were creating a culture "a hundred times higher and better than any bourgeois system."[84] The campaign to make the Soviet people "more human" was finished.

In eight separate interviews done late in life, Molotov boasted that he and Stalin had escaped the humiliation of being made "fools" by the West.[85] (Seven times he detailed how careful he and Stalin had been to stick to territorial "limits.")[86] A photograph of the Potsdam conference sparked memories of Stalin's fuming that while Russians "fight magnificently," they "never get their due." It "was my main task as minister of foreign affairs to see that we would not be cheated," Molotov stressed.[87] He kept repeating: "It was hard to fool us."[88] "Fools" merited not respect, but rather contempt. Fools lacked the intellectual and cultural capital to hold on to what they had earned. The proletariat was "cheated" by those who wrote the rules and knew

9.2. Americans and British tended to see the Red Army as brave but primitive and partly "Asiatic." The original caption on the photograph reads, "These are the Russians." It was taken on an OSS mission to Romania in late 1944 to evacuate downed U.S. fliers. (Courtesy of National Archives.)

how to manipulate them. He feared sophisticated Westerners could steal at the conference table what Russians had died for on the battlefield. Molotov would later remember Roosevelt as expecting the Russians to "come groveling" for help after Lend-Lease.[89] In May 1945, after Washington interrupted Lend-Lease, he warned Gromyko, "Do not barge in with pitiful requests."[90] Adamant about not looking—or being—fooled, cheated, or otherwise disrespected, the Soviets behaved in ways that struck Americans and British as arrogant, grasping, and lacking in respect.

The Soviets tried fitfully to head off sensationalism that could derail collaboration. In March 1945, a group of Soviet editors and foreign ministry officials attended a lunch hosted by the London *Times*. A Soviet editor affiliated with *Trud* stressed, "the last thing the Russians wanted was 'exotic' reporting on Russia." He "kept on repeating his objections to 'exoticism.'" By *exoticism* he seemed to mean exaggerating and making a spectacle out of either the good or the bad in Russia.

Groping toward a concept that scholars decades later would term *orientalism*, the Soviet editors urged "giv[ing] a picture of Russia as she [really] is."[91] Similarly, when Stalin in September 1945 was asked what he would advise Americans, he replied, "Just judge the Soviet Union objectively. Do not either praise us or scold us. Just know us and judge us as we are and base your estimate of us upon facts and not rumors."[92] It remains unclear to what extent self-deception prevented Stalin from seeing the contradiction between this invitation to "know us" and the strict isolation his secret police imposed on foreigners trying to do just that.

Another bid for acceptance of difference came from Konstantin Koukin, counselor of the embassy in London. He told Russian expert Christopher Warner that rising tensions stemmed from "differences of background and outlook and differences in the use of such words as 'democracy' and 'collaboration.'" Both sides should tolerate such divergence while translating each system of values into the other. Apparently acting on instructions, he cited Greece. The British should not "talk about democracy, free elections, etc.; to do so made his Government wonder what we were really getting at." The example demonstrated the Soviets' grievous failure to understand the emotional and cultural resonance of "democracy" in Britain and America. Nevertheless, repression of the popular Greek leftists did contradict Britain's own discourse on democracy. Koukin could say little when Warner complained about the cultural difference that most upset Westerners. Secretiveness and isolation of foreigners were "not at all what we expected or understood from Allies."[93] Withal, the Foreign Office found this "opening up . . . encouraging."[94] Alluding to the cultural blinders of his own colleagues, Geoffrey Wilson joked, "It's too bad that Stalin and Molotov were not at Eton & Harrow."[95]

While the *Trud* editor and Koukin argued for understanding on the basis of cultural equality, Alexandra Kollontay appealed for empathy. In early April, Kollontay—a hero of the Bolshevik Revolution, a feminist theorist, and the ambassador to Sweden—told Clark Kerr and Harriman that the "Russians are at about the same stage of mental development as [the British] were in the age of [Oliver] Cromwell."

Here was the notion that the life cycle of a nation paralleled that of a person. The Russians were just like the British, only three hundred years younger. She described Soviet leaders as not aggressive men but rather as insecure, unaware adolescents: "naive, clumsy, and blundering. . . . They have no idea of when or why they give offense." Yet they easily took offense. Flushed with victory, "they want the world to feel their strength and to pat them on the back for their success." To those in London and Washington who feared the Soviets as a rising menace, Kollontay advised, "They are children, and must be treated as such." Deep down Kremlin leaders knew "that they must cooperate." Until the adolescents outgrew their "unruliness," the British had to "practice patience and more patience."[96]

Ivan Maisky appealed for patience on the basis of sympathy. This approach was riskier. He was depicting the Russians not as younger kin but rather as different in psychology. Clark Kerr warned Maisky that Churchill and Eden were growing "much puzzled and irritated." Maisky replied by reminding him of their discussion in 1943, when he had frankly acknowledged the Russians' "sense of inferiority" and consequent "touchiness." Now he "pleaded for still greater patience and understanding." He alluded to the spheres-of-interest outlined at the wartime summits. "Our real interests clashed in no part of the world."[97]

Impatience in London

Anthony Eden and Alexander Cadogan had run out of patience, however. They ordered the ambassador to "rub it into [Maisky] again" that they had already shown forbearance for "the peculiarities of Russian mentality." This last phrase illustrated the slippery slope of condescension. Kollontay, Maisky, and Clark Kerr argued that London should allow the Russians slack because of their supposed immaturity or insecurity. It proved dangerously easy, however, to slide from that premise to the soon-to-be-promulgated argument of Kennan and Roberts that Soviet mental pathology made collaboration impossible.

London officials already depicted Maisky's bid for sympathy as evidence of Russian mental problems. And where, they asked, was Moscow's patience for British concerns?[98]

Wanting to "rub it into" the Russians reflected sharp anger. Many in the War Office already viewed Russia as an enemy. Now in April 1945 some in the Foreign Office were also pushing to reverse alignments. Undersecretary of State Orme G. "Moley" Sargent depicted the wartime pact as a "state of paralysis." Because Britain had needed the Red Army to defeat the Wehrmacht, it had acted defensively. Now, however, the Anglo-Americans commanded the skies, and their armies were slicing through Germany. They could well end up holding the whip hand. "Given the Russian character," cooperation appeared unlikely. The British should now "show our resentment" and push for "a show-down." Sargent acknowledged that it would prove "easy to strike a bargain" dividing Europe, as indeed Churchill had done with Stalin in October 1944. He opposed such a deal, however, because it abdicated "our right as a Great Power to be concerned with the affairs of the whole of Europe." He enunciated what would become an article of faith in the Cold War: compromising with the Soviets only confused them. To "propitiate Stalin . . . when we are strong would surely appear to him as a cunning manoeuvre intended to put him off his guard. He is much more likely to understand it if we insist on a show-down." He offered a prediction as ill-judged as Harriman's promise that Stalin would back down once confronted. Nothing, he insisted, could be worse than "the present state of uncertainty and drift."[99] Sargent preferred instead the political and psychological certainty of having an irreconcilable rival. Now that Hitler was nearly defeated, evil Stalin could replace him.

The Russians, impelled by their own arrogance and insecurities, heightened the anxiety of others. In early April, Stalin announced that not Molotov but only a lower-level official would attend the San Francisco conference. (He relented after April 12 as a gesture to the new president. The dictator also wanted Molotov to take Truman's measure.) The Soviets arrested sixteen Polish leaders who had gone to Moscow to negotiate. Endorsing Sargent's call for a showdown, Cadogan cried, "We can't go on like this." If the Russians won on

Poland, "we shall have lost all our bearings."[100] Also on edge, the heretofore conciliatory Eden wrote, "I agree, emphatically."[101]

On April 25, 1945, Roberts, who was already close with Kennan, laid out for London the arguments that the American diplomat would make famous through his long telegram in February 1946 and his "Mr. X" article in July 1947. First, Roberts disagreed with those who feared Russia would press issues to the point of war. Second, he also dismissed Clark Kerr's argument that "Russia would soon settle down into a normal and well-behaved member of the family of nations." He rejected the possibility that "normal" political conduct could emerge from a state run by "orthodox Marxists" with their "totalitarian practices." Third, he depicted Soviet policy as hatched by shadowy others, beyond the reach of diplomacy or Big Three deal making. Though Stalin had appeared to FDR as "get-atable," that perception seemed irrelevant, because Moscow was "controlled by the tough, tricky and untrustworthy personalities who comprise the Politburo." Furious at being deprived of close, regular contact with such important "personalities," embassy officials like Roberts and Kennan were now exacting their revenge. Fourth, London and Washington had to "show [the Soviets] that there is a limit beyond which they cannot safely go." Such limits would become known as containment. Fifth, the corollary, with regard to Europe, was building up "the better and—with the support of the outside world—the stronger half." Sixth, he reiterated the view, as argued by Arnold Toynbee in his popular histories of civilization, that a society needed challenges to remain vigorous. Confronting the Soviets would invigorate Western society. Finally, Roberts depicted the Kremlin's "hard-headed realists" as aggressively masculine. The response had to be similarly "tough and realistic."[102]

Churchill did not need Roberts's alarm. In London he gave Soviet ambassador Fedor Gousev such a "brisk talking to" that the minutes dared not specify "the forceful words which the Prime Minister used." A "very irritated" PM vented his "anxieties and dissatisfactions" with "sharpness," "vigour," and "still more vigour." Nearly a year before his famed "Iron Curtain" speech in Missouri, he deplored the "iron screen across Europe, from Lübeck to Trieste." When Gousev "murmured something" in response, "he was swept away." Churchill defined the crisis in Eastern Europe as not just Russian dominance of the area, but also as efforts to "shut if off from the rest of the world." Like diplomats in Moscow, he regarded no-contact as a central issue. "Why could not the Russians content themselves with the Curzon Line and let us have a look at what was happening West of it?" The PM interpreted bullying in Eastern Europe as disrespect for Britain. He led proud people who refused to accept "being treated as if they were of no account in the after-war world." They "still counted for something and they refused to be pushed about." He would hit back with a military display. He would "postpone the demobilisation of the Royal Air Force."[103]

Like Truman's April 23 tough talk with Molotov, Churchill's May 18 dressing down of Gousev signaled a discursive break. The Soviets replied in kind. Gousev reported to Stalin that the PM spoke "with great irritation and open venom. We are dealing with an unprincipled adventurer: he feels more at home in wartime than in peacetime."[104] The emotion-infused images, arguments, and notions of the Cold War were gelling.

Four days after he scolded Gousev, Churchill was handed "Operation Unthinkable," a contingency plan for attacking Russia on July 1, 1945. He had requested his military planners to blueprint a war that could "impose upon Russia the will of the United States and the British Empire," especially regarding "a square deal for Poland." Twenty-nine pages detailed the gargantuan hurdles to defeating the Soviet Union. British military chiefs shrank from attempting a venture that had destroyed the Wehrmacht. Not totally dissuaded, Churchill ordered further planning for what, "I hope, is still a highly improbable event." "Unthinkable" proved not so unthinkable. The study would become the first document in a Cold War–era file of contingency plans for war.

"Unthinkable" also pointed up the military salience of Poland. As Stalin feared, the British expected to "have full assistance from the Polish armed forces." Initially this meant Polish forces already in the West. But a long war would recruit other Poles. The plan also envisioned, as the Post-Hostilities Planning Staff had laid out since 1943, enlisting Germans. The Ministry of Defence titled the file: "Russia. Threat to Western Civilization."[105] Stalin did not have to suffer from paranoia to fear such a plan completed only two weeks after V-E Day.

Moscow picked up on the mood underlying "Unthinkable." The staff at the newspaper *Tass* feared "the rest of the world is turning against us; our enemies in Britain and America are already talking about going to war with us."[106] The *vozhd* no doubt got a copy of the plan from his spies, who riddled the U.S. and British governments. One agent in particular, Donald Maclean, enjoyed access to PHPS plans as the liaison between the British government's military and its embassy in Washington.

San Francisco Conference

To head off such destructive tendencies, FDR had planned the conference at San Francisco to mobilize mass support for Big Three cooperation. Unfortunately, however, the gap between Roosevelt's strategy for the conference and what Truman and his advisers pursued only widened the breach in the alliance.

"No one ever accused Franklin Roosevelt of having a single-track mind," wrote reporter Anne O'Hare McCormick, "but for once he hardly deviated from his subject." In late March, Roosevelt had explained that the conference scheduled to open on April 25 promised a "rendezvous" with destiny. He seemed to her not sick but only weary. He was anxious to strike "while the forge of war was still hot enough to fuse the nations together." Issues such as Poland could not be allowed to wreck the alliance. "'We can't afford to let disappointment over specific solutions pull us back.'" He determined to succeed where Wilson had failed. He meant to bring together isolationist-minded Americans and suspicious Soviets. The showman chose San Francisco to highlight America's Pacific battlefield and global interests. He intended to rally support for his postwar vision by speaking eloquently about America's own struggle for unity after 1776.[107]

Roosevelt envisioned the gathering of forty-six nations as more a public advertisement than a diplomatic arena. He sought to reconcile in the mind of a fireside chat listener the idealism of the Atlantic Charter with the realpolitik of the Four Policemen. Lippmann regarded FDR as a "wonderful finagler." The trickster hoped once again to come up with the right mix of inspiration, politicking, and artifice. As Lippmann also noticed, Roosevelt "*loved* to take a complicated thing which involved a certain amount of deception—hornswoggling of people—and somehow get it done."[108] Reconciling a peace settlement acceptable to the American public, the aspirations of each of the Big Three, and the swirl of other national interests was an especially "complicated thing." Popular nationalistic uprisings from Greece to Indochina added to the difficulty. Roosevelt said he understood such "ebbs and flows of popular feeling."

The finagler sensed that with the ebbing of the war emergency, the Big Three could no longer simply ignore the wishes of the smaller nations. The "'appointed moment'" had arrived to deflect popular pressures and hedge bets on Big Three accord by tapping the moral authority of democratic governance. At San Francisco the three-way condominium would "be divested of some of its power, *at least ostensibly*, by giving a voice and a *feeling* of responsibility to smaller nations."[109] The appearance of such power sharing was more important than the reality. As Lippmann explained, in peacetime the great powers "cannot command. They can only lead." And so they were asking the smaller nations "for their consent and for their collaboration" during the transition, which might last a generation.[110] Throwing off fatigue, FDR grew "vehement" in explaining his plan to McCormick. If he had lived, his catchword—"a democratic organization of the world"— would have become the Rooseveltian slogan at San Francisco.[111]

Roosevelt selected delegates geared more toward publicity than diplomacy. Republicans included Senator Arthur Vandenberg; former Minnesota governor Harold Stassen, popular with soldiers; and John Foster Dulles, Thomas Dewey's would-be secretary of state. From the Democratic aisle he tapped Senate Foreign Relations Committee chair Tom Connally of Texas and two other legislators. To attract the support of women, he included the internationalist Virginia Gildersleeve of Barnard College. From his hospital bed Hull was enlisted as honorary adviser. On one key point Roosevelt did miscalculate, however.

Ominously, that error came at the juncture of Soviet-American relations and congressional politics. He dallied until late March before revealing his Yalta agreement to admit the Ukrainian and Byelorussian republics as members of the General Assembly. Though the Soviets were eager for the United States to also enjoy three votes, many Americans found the deal offensive because it was secret and it violated the one-nation, one-vote principle.[112] Roosevelt aimed the public diplomacy at San Francisco to erect an appealing United Nations structure "that would be there, for all men to see.[113]

Four days after FDR died, Oscar Cox, a well-connected Roosevelt loyalist and a source for Lippmann, reviewed the deceased president's thinking. Picking up on Roosevelt's analogy between 1945 and the 1780s, Cox likened San Francisco to the Constitutional convention. The conference should stick to broad articles that could readily be "ratified and adopted by the Congress." This would not be the peace conference. He warned against trying to settle difficult issues in the glare of public debate.[114] Echoing another principle of FDR, he emphasized that "friendly relationships between the US and the USSR" were "basically necessary" for world peace.[115] Stettinius, however, without FDR to guide him, veered away from this plan. He listened instead to Harriman, Bohlen, Dunn, and Nelson Rockefeller of the State Department as well as to Senators Vandenberg and Connally.[116] They saw San Francisco in a different and dangerous way, as the arena for a showy victory over Molotov.

The conference pivoted between the alliance and the nascent Cold War. The nominal issues—whether and how to admit Argentina, whose profascist government had declared war on Germany only after the March 1 deadline set at Yalta; Poland, whose increasingly Soviet-dominated regime was not recognized by the Americans and British; Ukraine and Byelorussia, whose independence remained a fiction; and voting procedures in the UN—all entailed mind-numbing, anger-sparking technicalities.

Boiled down, however, the issue was whether the UN would operate primarily through cooperation by the Big Five (now including China and France) of the Security Council or through the big powers lobbying in the one-nation, one-vote General Assembly. Roosevelt had envisioned the assembly meeting only once a year to let "the smaller powers ... blow off steam." He advised reporters that the General Assembly "is not really of any great importance. It is an investigatory body only."[117] Harriman, in stark contrast, warned Truman that Washington "could not accept" that "the Security Council should dominate the Assembly." Harriman would later remember assuring Stettinius, "if the Russians walked out, we could have [a] United Nations of more like-minded nations."[118] The State Department felt confident of winning the race for votes thanks to Roosevelt's Good Neighbor policy in Latin America, wartime business ties there, and the successful politicking of Rockefeller at the recent Pan-American conference in Mexico City.

The microgeographics of the meeting in San Francisco pointed up the shift since Tehran and Yalta. At those summits, the Russians and Americans had arranged to live close together, with the British at a distance. Proximity had facilitated informal talks between FDR and Stalin. At San Francisco, however, "the British and the Americans delegations [were] cheek by jowl on the top of Nob Hill with the Russians half a mile away," a reporter noted.[119]

While calling for unity among the great powers, the Soviets foolishly antagonized with their brutality in Poland. They continued holding the sixteen Polish leaders, some of them slated to have joined the expanded Warsaw government.[120] To the Kremlin, such naked repression appeared justified by the weakness of their Warsaw puppets, continued partisan fighting, and the possibility of Poland's again becoming the keystone of an anti-Soviet bloc. To others, the arrests seemed inexcusable. Even "Stone Ass" squirmed. "I have never seen Molotov look so uncomfortable," Eden noted.[121]

At first Molotov and Stalin seemed unsure how to assess the situation at San Francisco. Were the Big Three still a unit? Were Washington and London now more foe than ally? Could they be played against each other? Could the Soviet Union operate successfully in the UN? How could someone from a closed society deal with public diplomacy? The Soviet response proved surprisingly flexible.

Molotov's behavior suggests that he and Stalin realized, in effect, that crossing certain cultural boundaries could keep political rivalries fluid. Then Moscow could wheel and deal with both Washington and London. According to Western diplomatic practice, conferences are chaired by the host nation. This meant that Stettinius would chair the gathering. At the first meeting, Molotov proposed instead the Soviet practice of a presidium, a group chairmanship in which the Big Four (including China) would take turns leading the conference. That would have limited U.S. influence and set a precedent for other UN positions. A suspicious Vandenberg picked up on the cultural implications. He objected to the scheme as "sort of a 'Soviet' of Chairmen."[122] Under this arrangement, none of the Big Four could have been cast outside the leadership. Lippmann observed that Molotov, "here for serious work" was trying to adapt the UN to Soviet cultural practices.[123] Truman, however, dismissed the presidium as "absurd."[124] A young journalist, John F. Kennedy, charged that the Soviets' focus on this "comparatively small question" betrayed ambition to "write their own terms on the big ones."[125] Outgunned, Molotov accepted Eden's face-saving proposal of four nominal chairs headed by Stettinius as president.

When Stettinius demanded an immediate vote on seating quasi-fascist Argentina but not Poland, Molotov urged further negotiation. The Russian quoted from Roosevelt's and Hull's 1944 attacks on the pro-Nazi government in Buenos Aires. Backed by Latin American votes, Stettinius insisted that diplomacy was exhausted. (Such impatience with drawn-out negotiations marked another cultural difference. Harriman would later reflect that he had not really understood how much the Soviets "enjoyed arguments" and "a long time thrashing things out.")[126] Though heated, the issue of Argentina did not break on an East-versus-West basis. Paul Henri Spaak of Belgium, who years later would become a NATO stalwart, spoke for Europeans in urging continued talk. Truman had earlier opposed admitting Argentina. Now, however, he applauded the news that "we had a public showdown" with Molotov. In getting tough with the Russians, Truman was recasting America's ideological orientation away from the anti-fascism that had united the Big Three. He now favored allowing into the UN a western hemisphere neighbor that had not hidden its sympathy with Nazi Germany.

Stettinius boasted, "we gave him a good licking, a good public licking."[127] The Russian responded, "Now I understand what you mean by voting here at the conference. The United States really has twenty-two votes."[128] Lippmann ominously concluded that "the death of Roosevelt has had a profound effect on this conference." FDR had envisioned a limited agenda: erecting a structure that could appeal to the Senate and to world opinion. "Nothing was further from the original intention" than public showdowns over difficult issues. With Truman leaning toward the British, "the loss of Roosevelt has upset the delicate balance within the councils of the Big Three."[129]

Bested in the voting, the Bolshevik tried his hand at another American institution. Facing five hundred journalists in a packed room, Molotov "smiles, beams all around, gestures disarmingly, and answers right to the point—when he wants to," observed a *New York Times* reporter. His three press conferences "would do credit to Franklin D. Roosevelt."[130] Adviser to presidents Isaiah Bowman marveled that the usually dour Russian spoke "with a zest and abandon that represented something new in international affairs." Much as U.S. officials aimed to do in other countries, Molotov "spoke over the heads of American leaders to the American people."[131] The door on acculturation had cracked open. If Molotov "was doing his bit to 'Sovietize' the thinking of millions of Americans," the *Times* recognized, he was also "becoming 'Americanized' himself." Even if he was "merely 'putting on an act,'" that, too, was in the American grain.[132] The mustachioed, bespectacled "Molotov does look like the late T[heodore] R[oosevelt], doesn't he?" an observed remarked."[133] On a Sunday drive around the San Francisco Bay area, Stalin's henchman sighed, "What we could do if we controlled this country!"[134] Such testing of cultural borders would be forbidden and forgotten in the Cold War.

But a Cold War atmosphere did not yet control. Americans gagged at embracing the pro-fascists in Buenos Aires. Even Harry Hopkins's son believed "that Molotov had a point about Argentina.[135] Many Americans wanted to keep Russia as an ally. In softening, "Stone Ass" had proven seductive. Even the notion of Russians as aggressively hypermasculine was perhaps not wholly negative. The society maven Elsa Maxwell—dubbed the "hostess with the mostest" and later a

Republican-appointed ambassador to Belgium—saw the Soviets as a "bunch of magnificent he-men."[136] Much of the U.S. press echoed *Time* in finding Stettinius's "straight power game" on Argentina "as amoral as Russia's game in eastern Europe." Lippmann warned that "in the hands of men who lack experience and wisdom and are impatient and not objective," the UN may "destroy diplomacy."[137] The State Department responded to this criticism with a public relations counterattack.[138]

On May 1, Harriman called in a dozen top journalists. He startled them by warning, "On long range politics there is an irreconcilable difference" between the Soviet Union and the Western allies. He made his pitch with the same emotional words that had circulated around Meiklejohn's heater. Kennan would employ a similar rhetorical strategy in 1946–47. The ambassador blamed everything on the Kremlin's "Marxian penetration." The phrase suggested assault that was simultaneously ideological, political, and sexual. The trope caught fire. The first question posed by a journalist asked the difference "between Russian policy of penetration as you put it and Nazi policy." Repeating the word "penetrate," Harriman answered that the Soviets probably did not intend military aggression. Other journalists also picked up on "penetration." The ambassador went on to charge that Molotov's bid for a presidium signaled intent to "dominate" the UN as well as Eastern Europe. Like Roberts and Kennan, he blamed a shadowy group of Kremlin insiders for supposedly talking Stalin out of cooperation.[139]

Harriman's alternative to Roosevelt's policy was naked dollar diplomacy. Moscow needed a loan, because even the best Soviet living conditions were "no better than the standard of the slums of America." Washington could dole out the money only in small increments and in return for political concessions.[140] He predicted, incorrectly, that the Russians would buckle. But until then it was necessary to scare the public about the Kremlin so as to ease the pressure on Washington to compromise.

While some bought this scare-argument, others reacted with fury. Lippmann and Raymond Swing, a popular radio announcer, stormed out of Harriman's briefing in protest. Queried "has our policy changed since Roosevelt?," Harriman nervously backtracked. The journalist retorted: "But it is obvious there IS A CHANGE." The ambassador grew "extremely annoyed" when reporters charged he had followed Churchill's hard line with regard to specific Poles to add to the Warsaw government. He left the room with a parting shot: "The Russians won't live up to their agreements."[141] Ironically, at dinner a few hours later Harriman would hear Molotov contend that "the four Major Powers" should again operate on the basis of "unanimity with respect to all major questions."[142] Reports circulated that the Russians had urged replacing Harriman because he had supposedly become another Bill Bullitt.

Bohlen grew "very bitter" at the Rooseveltian diehards.[143] The latter included Anna Roosevelt Boettiger, who remained unsympathetic to Truman's explanation that he was just listening to his advisers. Boettiger, whose assistance to her father at Yalta had bordered on diplomacy, concluded that in terms of "holding relationships with Russia on a constructive and stable basis," Truman "has not done well."[144] Eleanor Roosevelt, too, would soon be "talking with unbelievable hostility" against Truman's stance toward the Soviets.[145]

After Harriman's talks in April and May, it became more customary to refer to the Soviets not as fellow world policemen as Roosevelt had often depicted them, but rather as international criminals. This discursive attack on the alliance persisted even when political relations warmed, as they did on and off for the remainder of 1945. Truman never made a splashy statement to stem the trend. Parallel changes were propelled by Churchill and others in London. Anti-Soviet stalwarts in the State Department and other hard-liners, such Forrestal, did not need Harriman to turn them against FDR's priority of getting along with Moscow.

The ambassador had his greatest impact on Truman, particularly in claiming that Roosevelt's policy had reflected cowardly "fear" of the Soviets. This argument pushed an emotional button with the insecure new president, anxious to show he feared neither Stalin nor his new job. For all Truman's public praise of Roosevelt, he liked to think that he was in certain respects a better president because he could and did act decisively. Harriman was not alone in driving the shift in words, tone, attitude, and policy. Yet he voiced the authority of firsthand experience in dealing with Stalin.

Fanning fears proved easier than quieting them. Donald Nelson, a wartime production administrator who had found Stalin eager to expand trade, now feared war. Nelson "put the responsibility chiefly on Averell Harriman."[146] Assistant Secretary of State Dean Acheson faulted his friend's attitude and tactics. "Averell is very ferocious about the Rouskis. . . . He seems in favor of any stick to beat them with." Nevertheless, Acheson accepted the ambassador's argument that the Russians "are behaving badly."[147] Although Harriman and his cohort sought not armed conflict but rather a calibrated policy of containing Russia and building alliances in the West, their pushing for a tougher stance fed public fears of war.

Lunching at the State Department with Bohlen and public affairs officer Archibald MacLeish, Raymond Swing charged that recent decisions toward Russia "would never have been taken had Mr. Roosevelt lived." The changed policy seemed focused on "toughness" and "scoring points against the Russians." MacLeish observed that the broadcaster, usually "a man of judgment and reserve," spoke with "force, and even emotion" about the danger of war. At San Francisco, U.S. delegates were reportedly opining, within earshot of the Soviets, that "we will have to fight Russia."[148] Acheson noted the "great gloom over the imminence of World War III."[149] Alarmed, MacLeish made a national broadcast that challenged Harriman's emotionalism and assumptions. He doubted an "inevitable conflict of interest with the Russians."

Invoking Roosevelt's assurance that "the only thing we have to fear is fear itself," he found "nothing real, nothing logical" in exaggerated suspicions. Instead, the "logic" of geography and national interests united the two nations. Like FDR, he downplayed ideological and other cultural differences. They had similar identities as "young, strong, self-confident" countries that aimed, "even in dissimilar ways at betterment of the lot of their own peoples and not at the conquest of the earth."[150] Though rhetorically powerful, MacLeish's speech was buried on page nineteen of the *New York Times*. Not MacLeish or Davies but rather Truman, Byrnes, and Harriman drove U.S. policy.

Truman alternated between doubt he could fill FDR's shoes and confidence he could walk a better path. He appraised Roosevelt as "the greatest politician and statesman in the world, but the poorest administrator." He aimed to "straighten the Administration out."[151] Worried about his inexperience in foreign affairs, he scrambled to clarify his predecessor's commitments. (Roosevelt, in contrast, believed ambiguity was often crucial.) Harriman and the State Department pushed a clear-cut policy that fit Truman's predilection for tough guy, no-nonsense solutions. The president was also bolstered by Stimson's briefing on April 25 that the War Department was developing "the most terrible weapon ever known in human history, one bomb of which could destroy a whole city."[152] Byrnes had assured him that this "bomb might well put us in a position to dictate our own terms at the end of the war"—presumably to both Japan and Russia.[153]

Other considerations, however, pushed the president toward mending fences. He needed to soothe the war talk roiling the public. He could be blamed for the collapse of the alliance. What if the atomic bomb failed to explode or pack the punch to force Tokyo's surrender? He might still need Soviet help against Japan.

Davies challenged the Harriman-Bohlen thesis. On May 13, he and Frankfurter commiserated about "the grave deterioration in diplomatic relations since Roosevelt dropped out of the picture."[154] Davies then telephoned Truman. The president invited him to the White House. It was Mother's Day, and the guest met ninety-three-year-old "Mama." "Bright as a squirrel," she had come to Washington "'to see that Harry was started right.'" As the men settled down to talk, the part-time diplomat detailed Roosevelt's efforts to reach out to Stalin. He explained Soviet grievances over the delayed second front and the abrupt cancellation of Lend-Lease after V-E day. Advice from State Department experts was "conditioned [by] their hostility toward the Soviets." At one point Truman, referring to a Soviet concession, asked incredulously, "Molotov did that as a gesture to Roosevelt?" He insisted that the Russian had gone "out to San Francisco to make trouble." Davies disputed the charge, adding that the foreign minister "went white when the President told him about his attitude on Poland." He showed Truman a recent letter from Molotov arguing that renewing the "personal contact of the heads of our governments" could prove "extremely positive."[155] Taking a page from FDR's playbook, Truman affirmed that he did intend to meet Stalin—alone and before he met Churchill.

Only two days after Davies's visit, however, Truman listened as Bohlen urged him to meet with Churchill rather than Stalin before the next Big Three summit. Bohlen countered Davies's thesis by assuring that such "'ganging up'" against the Soviets was not dangerous, as Stalin already accepted "that Great Britain and America would be very close together." Indeed, a show of Anglo-American collaboration could "make Stalin more reasonable."[156] This was Harriman's dangerous thesis: pressure the Soviets and they would back down. A week later, Truman decided to postpone any summit until mid-July, that is, after the scheduled testing of the atomic bomb. If the bomb were indeed powerful, he could negotiate with a stronger hand.[157]

Truman understood that this delay risked the alliance. He begged Davies to fly to Moscow to soothe Stalin. The would-be fixer, citing his delicate health, declined. Meanwhile, Bohlen and Harriman, worried that tensions were escalating out of control, urged sending Hopkins instead. The president, whose dislike of Hopkins was fanned by Byrnes, responded, "No, I don't want to do that."[158] Finally, he relented. Finding Churchill "nearly as exasperating" as Stalin, Truman worried about the PM's eagerness to confront the Russians.[159] He persuaded Davies to go to London, which required a much shorter flight, to get the PM to agree to a Truman-Stalin parley before the Big Three conclave.[160]

The Davies Mission to London and the Hopkins Mission to Moscow

Shortly before Davies arrived on May 26, Churchill's doctor found his patient fretting about the July 5 general election. Unable to accept that his years of "arbitrary powers" could actually end, the prime minister was trying to reassure himself that "universal . . . gratitude" would surely trump the allure of Labor's social welfare programs.[161]

Davies observed that Churchill was "terribly concerned" that a prior meeting between Truman and Stalin would undermine his appeal to voters as a key international player. With "emotional, heated" protests, the PM insisted instead on a tripartite summit, preferably in June, early enough to help him in the election. When he accused Truman of planning a sneaky "deal" with Stalin, Davies angrily got up to leave. Calming down, Churchill then apologized. For years, Kennan and other diplomats had mocked Davies as a rich dilettante too fatuous to appreciate their expertise. As U.S. ambassador he had foolishly glossed over the horrors of the Moscow purge trials.

Nevertheless Davies could have a discerning eye, as Roosevelt had appreciated. Davies saw that underlying Churchill's "tired, nervous, and vehement" demeanor abided a "clear-headed," "overpowering personality." The torrent of words and feelings remained focused. "There is always a strong, mental control and reserve behind his emotionalism."[162] He aimed those feelings at the Russians. The once-uncompromising foe of the Nazis now questioned the elimination of Hitler. Churchill insisted that "he could have made peace with Hitler at any time."[163] He had acceded to unconditional surrender only because Roosevelt had insisted. The PM's "monologue berating the Russians" reminded Davies of "listening to Goebbels, Goering and Hitler." Emotions aside, the diatribe fit the calculus of Operation Unthinkable: deploy German territory and troops against Russia. Churchill urged that U.S. forces stay fast in territory east of the agreed-upon zonal borders. Going far beyond Harriman's hard line, he gave the "impression . . . that he advocated a showdown . . . even though it meant conflict of Soviet forces with British forces and ours."[164]

Appalled, Davies tried to soothe Churchill's "emotionalism." "There was no need for loss of self-respect on either side," he reassured. Like FDR, he feared that ideological and political rigidity could wreck cooperation. Situations had to "be kept fluid." Davies could be obtuse and self-important. Nevertheless, he, like FDR, grasped that "the simple facts" were rarely simple. He warned that "it was not the facts, so much as the interpretation of the facts" that could destroy the alliance."[165] Churchill regarded Davies's Rooseveltian ideas as, literally, disgusting. He sniffed to aides that "he needed a bath in order to get rid of the ooze and slime."[166] He warned the president that he would not attend any summit preceded by a private Truman-Stalin meeting.

Churchill was not alone in his prejudices. To work with the Red Army after the war, the Foreign Office observed, the War Office had appointed one general with "pretty strong Czarist associations," another who had rooted for a German victory over the Bolsheviks in 1941, and a third "who would be the last to deny that he is strongly anti-Soviet."[167] In Moscow for a goodwill visit, U.S. General Dwight D. Eisenhower, who still favored Roosevelt's policy, was growing "very upset," he confided to Clark Kerr. Ike believed the Russians were sincere in charging that British generals were going out of their way to jinx cooperation in occupied Berlin. He explained that "the gist of [Soviet] complaints was apparently personalities, not policies."[168] Eisenhower also tackled Harriman: "You're wrong, Averell. We're going to get along with the Russians."[169]

Meanwhile, Hopkins on May 25 arrived in Moscow. Harriman and Bohlen had gone along to assist with diplomacy, Louise to monitor Harry's health. Though the messenger to Stalin was Roosevelt's former adviser, the message was largely Truman's. Hopkins and Stalin did renew personal ties. The American recounted that while FDR had clearly been tired, his death had come as a surprise. The Georgian compared the president to the father of the Bolshevik Revolution, who "had also died of a cerebral hemorrhage." They reminisced about 1941, when they had pledged unity against the seemingly unstoppable Germans. When Hopkins jokingly asked whether Molotov had "recovered from the battle of San Francisco," the latter downplayed the fight as "merely arguments."[170] Six talks over ten days covered the gamut of issues. They concurred on holding the Big Three summit in July, not in June as Churchill had wanted. Stalin reaffirmed that Russia would enter the war against Japan by August 8, as long as China agreed to the Yalta concessions. They agreed on a trusteeship for Korea.

Once again, however, the makeup of Poland's government loomed as a deal-breaker. Hopkins displayed none of the histrionics that Churchill vented at Davies. Yet he, like the PM, advanced arguments that would become Cold War principles. He insisted that Poland tested the entire U.S-Soviet relationship, and that the Soviets had to permit Western-style democracy to prevail there as elsewhere. These ideologically grounded, cut-and-dried assertions reflected more the focus of Truman, Harriman, and Bohlen than the fluid policy of Roosevelt.

According to Bohlen's notes, Hopkins told Stalin "very forcefully . . . that our whole relationship was threatened by the impasse of Poland." He repeated the warning three times, stressing "that Poland was only a symbol."[171] Washington had no material interests there. Compromising about a symbol, however, was more difficult than dividing up trade or influence. In battling the Axis, harsh necessities had fostered workable arrangements, such as Lend-Lease and the bombing lines separating Allied air forces. The Cold War would, instead, celebrate irreconcilable symbols.

While FDR had striven to keep differences specific and manageable, Hopkins put into play "the entire structure of world cooperation and relations with the Soviet Union." All could be "destroyed" because public opinion had soured on the Soviets as a result of their oppressive behavior toward Poland.[172] This was exaggeration. Though anxious about Poland and about a possible war, public opinion also blamed the State Department, especially for the rancor at San Francisco. Many of those in the know blamed Harriman. According to polls in late May, 72 percent of Americans still favored cooperation with Moscow.[173]

Claiming that the public directed U.S. policy, Hopkins insisted that Poland had to be seen in terms of America's universalist ideology. Even in nations "geographically far from our borders . . . there were certain fundamental rights which, when infringed upon or denied, caused concern in the United States." Bohlen may have been grinning to himself as he recorded Hopkins telling the dictator, "There must be the right of freedom of speech . . . right of assembly, right of movement and the right to worship. All political parties, except the fascist party . . . should be permitted the free use of the press, radio, meetings and other facilities of political expression; all citizens should have the right of public trial . . . and the right of habeas corpus."[174]

For Western democracy, these rights were core values. For the *vozhd*, allowing such rights to prevail could have dire geopolitical consequences, namely losing control of Poland, not to mention the Ukraine and Russia itself. Despite assurances that Washington "aggressively opposed" another cordon sanitaire, the dictator feared that such a fence would arise from British (and perhaps American) machinations and from the ancient hostility of Russia's neighbors.

The Kremlin boss did not take up Hopkins's ideological challenge. Instead, he tried, in the spirit of the alliance, to downplay ideological conflict. "Any talk of an intention to Sovietize Poland was stupid." Poles opposed collective farms. "The Soviet system was not exportable."[175] Regardless of whether Stalin totally believed this assurance, his agents and toadies possessed few political and economic tools other than the Soviet system. Repression through the secret police and control of the economy would prove well adapted to creating "friendly" governments and repressing popular resistance. (Just days after this conversation, Red Cross officials would report "that a good part of the Polish underground army that fought the Germans is still underground fighting the Soviets.")[176] The dictator repeated the cultural/strategic thesis he had argued to Hopkins in 1941 and to FDR at the summits. It was the Germans, not the Russians, who stood on the wrong side of the gulf between civilization and barbarism. The invasions that Russia had suffered "were not warfare but were like the incursions of the Huns."[177]

In response to Hopkins's lecture on political rights, the Kremlin boss affirmed, "These principles of democracy are well known and would find no objection on the part of the Soviet Government." He then, however, listed caveats. Such freedoms could be applied only in peacetime "and even then with certain limitations" to thwart "fascists." He cited the all-out opposition of the Orthodox Church during the Revolution. "What could the Soviet Government do," shrugged the old Bolshevik, but "declare war on the church?"[178] Stalin's arguments were self-serving, casuistic, and to some extent dishonest. Still, he was trying to steer away from ideological impasse. He sought to blur the concept "democratic" sufficiently so as to give postwar cooperation a chance.

Roosevelt had believed that the ideological divide could be finessed in a gradual postwar transition. He had alluded to halfway measures in his on-board press conference after Yalta and in the ad-libbed portions of his address to Congress. Ambiguous, "common language," as Molotov had phrased it to Truman, exacted a moral cost: sacrificing legitimate democratic aspirations in Poland and elsewhere. That was the price, however, that Washington would actually pay in ensuing decades as it supported brutal right-wing dictatorships as part of the "Free World." In the end, getting tough did not roll back the Iron Curtain as Harriman and Sargent had promised. Instead it spurred the Soviets to tighten their grip on satellites. Ironically, it was the diplomacy of détente that eventually undermined the Soviet system. In demonstrating their toughness, the so-called wise men sealed the loss of Eastern Europe, which some of them blamed on FDR. Stalin's complaints against Washington all revolved around respect, including respect for Russia's geostrategic imperatives in Poland and elsewhere. This remained an emotional valence Americans unfortunately neglected. The Truman administration might have gotten further with Stalin had it addressed the dictator's apparent emotional needs, as Roosevelt had tried to do.

Stalin waved his own list of Yalta violations: admitting profascist Argentina into the UN, allowing France onto the Big Three Reparations Commission, antagonism toward the Soviet-dominated Warsaw government, and delay in dividing the German navy and merchant fleet. These amounted to "an insult to the Soviet Union," "an attempt to humiliate the Russians." Lend-Lease had ended in a "scornful and abrupt manner." Airing a gripe that Molotov would emphasize decades later, Stalin said that Russians were "regarded as fools, which was a mistake the West frequently made." Americans valued them only as cannon fodder against the Wehrmacht. Attitudes had "perceptibly cooled once it became obvious that Germany was defeated. . . . [T]he Russians were no longer needed." Although a ruthless player of power politics, the Kremlin chief felt, or claimed he felt, used. Despite their offensiveness, the victorious Soviets easily took offense. As Kollontay also observed, they expected to be patted on the back even when they were unruly.[179]

One wonders how Harriman reacted on hearing his thesis knocked down. Since September 1944, he had maintained that the Soviets would retreat if pressed hard. He had objected, however, to the turn-around and unloading of Lend-Lease ships shortly after V-E day as too blunt an instrument. He wanted economic aid conditioned on Moscow's political concessions or military moves against Japan. Stalin warned, however, that any attempt to "soften them up ... was a fundamental mistake." If "the Russians were approached frankly on a friendly basis, much could be done." But "reprisals in any form would bring about the exact opposite effect."[180] This warning proved sadly prophetic of behavior on both sides. Even as he faulted Washington for disrespect, the Kremlin boss volunteered that "the United States had more reason to be a world power than any other state." That included the right "to participate in the Polish question"—as a backer of Moscow, of course.

Although America's colossal power could check the Soviets, it might also help secure Stalin's primary goal: staving off renewed Axis aggression. The world wars "had shown that without United States intervention Germany could not have been defeated."[181] Despite the Soviet triumph, Stalin remained awed by the almost supernatural foe: "The Germans had built an entire underground city under Berlin. . . . It was impossible to imagine what they had accomplished."[182] Though his troops had found what appeared to be Hitler's charred remains, he believed, or feigned to believe, that the Führer and other top Nazis had escaped, perhaps by submarine to Japan.[183] The specter of German revenge would haunt Soviet leaders throughout the Cold War.

FDR's former right-hand man regaled a party in Kennan's apartment with stories of the supposedly "confused state" of Roosevelt's administration going back to the New Deal. "Various advisors [were] forever persuading the President to follow diametrically opposite courses of action."[184] While working with Hopkins, Kennan developed "a great admiration for him."[185] Their tie pointed up the swift triumph of the anti-Soviet stalwarts after Roosevelt's death. Kennan, still close with Bullitt, warned that any compromise with Russia would prove worthless, because Moscow violated deals "in the most barefaced fashion."[186] The following year Kennan would spell out his alternative to compromise: containment.

Sounding as if they had been warming themselves around Meikle-john's kerosene heater, Louise and Kathleen described the officials at a Kremlin banquet. Most were "the big fat sinister type with pig eyes and pince nez." Louise "classified them as the 'unhappy pansies.' The terrifying thing is visualizing them as ever cooperating with foreign-ers."[187] Such thinking helped propel political conclusions. Disgusting, animal-like, "sinister" types unable to cooperate had to be contained.

If Hopkins's mission to Moscow was not to be his last job in gov-ernment, he had to prove himself. Harriman reported to Truman: "Harry did a first rate job in presenting your views and in explaining the most important matters, particularly Poland." The ambassador also lauded Bohlen, "whose presence was, as usual, most helpful." Hopkins would, nonetheless, remain just a messenger boy unless he secured a deal. That required switching from Wilsonian principles to Rooseveltian compromise. On June 1, he assured Stalin that Washing-ton did not want to see "anyone connected" with the present London Polish government "involved in the new Provisional Government of Poland." Though urging mercy toward the sixteen arrested Poles, he did not insist. Seizing the opening, Stalin agreed to allow a few inde-pendent Poles, including former prime minister Mikołajczyk, to join the Warsaw government. He grumbled that he still "did not intend to have the British manage the affairs of Poland," which was "exactly what they want to do." Hopkins urged Truman and Churchill to ac-cede. The dictator sweetened things by agreeing that the veto in the Security Council should pertain only to action, not to discussion.

This last-minute dealing replicated the Yalta pattern of Soviet con-cessions on the UN in return for U.S. acquiescence on Poland.[188] On hearing the news, Vandenberg crowed, "America Wins!"[189] "We may get a peace yet," Truman exulted. "Hopkins has done a good job in Moscow."[190] All this made it easier to recognize the Soviet-dominated Warsaw government on July 5. Hopkins brought back a thank you from Stalin: four kilograms of the choicest caviar.[191]

Once home, Louise exulted to a friend that Harry "has gained 8 lbs. and is looking well and feeling grand."[192] Truman concurred: "Hop-kins is looking better than when he left here."[193] Challenge and excite-ment had yet again invigorated the old warhorse. (Also invigorated was Louise's persistent admirer, Bess Johnson. A mutual friend told Louise, "she's been driving around your house probably 5,000 times.")[194] Despite his success, Harry could not, however, surmount the opposition of his rival. Probably forced out by Byrnes, he resigned from government service on July 5, two days after the latter became secretary of state.

Diplomacy quenched the post–April 12 crisis ignited by the inherited Polish dispute, Truman's insecurity, and Harriman's incendiary advice. But plenty of tinder remained. As to whether the fix done in Moscow would hold, Hopkins believed "only time will tell." Of one thing he was sure, however: "They had never seen a gal like Louie in that part of the world in many a long year."[195]

Reparations and the Atomic Bomb

The Russians directed the Hopkins's flight westward so that they could witness the devastation. "One could see it all plainly," Louise later wrote in *Harper's Bazaar*, "the foxholes, trenches, and destruction."[196] Indeed, the Nazi invasion had wreaked terrible damage. More than 1,700 cities, 71,000 villages, 31,000 industrial enterprises, 40,000 miles of railroad track, 56,000 miles of road, and 90,000 bridges were destroyed. The Germans killed or stole some 180 million livestock animals.[197] As many as 27 million Soviet civilians and soldiers perished. While Stalin's deportations and refusal to permit surrender accounted for some of deaths, the enemy inflicted by far the most. To rebuild their own country while delaying the enemy's revival, the Soviets determined to extract from Germany reparations in the form of factories, locomotives, labor, and anything else movable.

At Yalta, FDR, who remained in favor of being tough with the Germans even after he toned down Morgenthau's plans, had agreed to $20 billion as the basis for reparations, with half going to the Soviet Union. Roosevelt appointed experts, headed by the economist Isador Lubin, to attend the Allied Commission on Reparations in Moscow. FDR instructed Lubin, a Roosevelt loyalist, to settle reparations in a practical manner and report directly to him.[198] Their departure for Moscow stalled, however, when Roosevelt died.

Truman demoted Lubin to technical adviser and put in charge Edwin W. Pauley, an oil mogul and Democratic Party treasurer, who had helped engineer his nomination as vice president. Lubin remembered Truman's explaining, "I want somebody as head of the delegation who can throw his weight around."[199] Byrnes informed Lubin that after this job, "there won't be any place in this administration for people like you."[200] Pauley added to the commission personal friends and headed for Moscow aiming for a "stand-off with the Soviet Union on reparations."[201] This stance fit what Pauley remembered as "a very major difference in the attitude of President Roosevelt and that of President Truman toward the designs of the Soviet Union."[202]

Intent on beating out Byrnes for the job of secretary of state, Pauley wanted to show that he could out-trade the Russians.[203] Richard Scandrett, a Republican Wall Street lawyer, adviser to conservative Senator Robert Taft, and one of Lubin's original experts, observed that Pauley had his staff in Moscow "racking their brains to conjure up something that could be taken home physically by the U.S. as reparations—gold, 'scientific know how' ... or 'Hitler's private train.'"[204] Scandrett noted that Pauley's friends, lacking technical expertise to calculate reparations, tried instead to "renegotiate the Yalta agreements." The "prevailing attitude ... ranged from irritation to contempt and unconcealed antagonism toward the Soviets." The "atmosphere ... was indeed horrible ... members of the delegation selling old clothes to the Soviets ... open name calling—sneering." The Soviets, already grabbing what they could from their zone in Germany, allowed the commission to fizzle. Meeting Truman at Potsdam, Pauley could offer only "complaints about the Soviet attitude."[205] This bungling of a chance to reach a reparations agreement covering all of Germany proved a major step in the Cold War division of that nation.[206]

The pace of anxiety-provoking change would accelerate with the testing of the atomic bomb on July 16 and the destruction of Hiroshima on August 6. It was coincidental but also telling that on June 6, the day Hopkins wrapped up negotiations with Stalin, Stimson reported to Truman the recommendations of the Interim Committee regarding informing Moscow and London about the bomb. A week before, Byrnes, speaking for the president, had vetoed the idea pushed by General Marshall and several of the scientists to invite Moscow to join an international control commission. Marshall had even suggested asking Soviet scientists to witness the first atomic test.[207] Now Stimson, who himself was torn between dread of an atomic race and desire to play this "royal straight flush," pleased Truman by assuring him that if either the British or the Russians at the upcoming summit broached the question of sharing, the Americans would "decline to take them in as partners." If the British brought up Churchill's Hyde Park memorandum with Roosevelt, which had pledged such partnership, the Americans would merely "give them such information as they [already] know" and promise to talk later. With regard to the Russians, the "quid pro quo . . . for our taking them into partnership" would be "the settlement of the Polish, Rumanian, Yugoslavian, and Manchurian problems."[208]

Truman, Byrnes, and Stimson regarded a quick Japanese defeat as the primary reason to shock the world with the destructive power of the atomic bomb. Yet they also saw playing this "master card" with the Russians as a significant bonus. Churchill was blunter. At Potsdam he enthused about the new Anglo-American option for threatening the Kremlin: "If [the Soviets] insist on doing this or that, well we can just blow out Moscow, then Stalingrad, then Kiev, then Kuibyshev, [and] Kharkov."[209] Stalin, however, would not cave so easily. He would instead race to develop (and steal the secrets for) his own bomb.[210]

Another long-term question was how to organize postwar relations: Big Three collaboration or politicking with smaller nations? Stalin and FDR had agreed that being small did not make a country virtuous. Indeed, small countries had instigated many troubles, the dictator reminded Hopkins.[211] Truman, in contrast, valued having the "confidence of the *smaller* nations." Neither Russia nor Britain had that trust. "We have," the president noted with misguided satisfaction.[212]

To Americans, and especially to the former senator, democratic coalition building appeared natural. In ensuing years, Washington would construct the "Free World" coalition of smaller nations. But the "confidence" of those nations would rarely be given as freely as Americans liked to think. Already at San Francisco, Stettinius had strong-armed the Belgians, who opposed big power control of the Security Council. After dangling the carrot of economic aid, the secretary warned that "Belgium and the United States are drifting apart." Alarmed, the Belgian delegate asked plaintively whether he "should now speak in favor of something which he had been opposed to." The American advised that abstaining would suffice.[213] The Soviets, of course, had more brutal methods of persuasion.

In the weeks after Roosevelt died, U.S. policy pivoted from trying to get along with the Soviets to emphasizing differences with them. Embittered by his disappointments and frustrations in Moscow, Harriman, bolstered by Kennan, Bohlen, and Durbrow, helped shift policy and opinion toward denigrating the Soviet Union and Big Three cooperation. Harriman's argument that Roosevelt's policy toward Russia had been based on fear fed into Truman's anxiety about appearing fearful or not up to the job. The president tried to assure himself, "I'm not afraid of Russia."[214] While wanting to get along with the Soviets, Truman expected good relations on his terms. He reverted easily to his original premise: "the Soviets only understand the 'tough method.'"[215]

When it came to continuing the alliance, Stalin appeared more committed than either Truman or Churchill. Even Bohlen concluded from the Hopkins mission that "Stalin has shown genuine desire for continued co-operation."[216] Bohlen's "one major deduction" was the Russians' "feeling of weakness." The Soviets seemed daunted by the challenge of running "half [of] Europe whilst at the same time reconstructing the very great devastation" at home.[217] Stalin needed the Big Three alliance. The coalition might well have survived if FDR had lived longer. A key question is how the juggler would have handled atomic diplomacy. That issue would bare Truman's most basic assumptions and accelerate the plunge toward the Cold War.

The Lost Alliance

Widespread Anxiety and Deepening Ideology, July 1945–March 1946

"Today has been an historical one," wrote Truman in his diary on July 16, 1945, on the eve of the Potsdam conference.[1] That day's events and experiences would prove even more significant than he could realize. A lasting impression, a missed opportunity, and a huge fireball would shape history for decades to come. Truman began the day conferring with Churchill. He then motored to the former Nazi capital whose dazed inhabitants struck him as sympathetic victims. That evening he dropped a carefully arranged meeting with Stalin in order to discuss with his advisers the successful test in New Mexico of the world's first atomic bomb. Stalin overreacted to the cancellation. Truman's "historical day" did not include a special, possibly ice-breaking meeting with the leader who would become his Cold War antagonist. The bomb got in the way. Pride then magnified the tiff. The bomb and pride would continue to intertwine in ways that would thwart efforts by key Truman advisers to stave off an atomic arms race with Big Three collaboration.

Although Truman had determined to resist Churchill's forceful monologues, he ended up sharing much of the latter's dislike and distrust for the Soviets. He was probably sincere in telling Davies, "Joe,

I am trying my best to save peace and follow out Roosevelt's plans."[2] Truman, however, lacked a full understanding or appreciation of FDR's plans for a Big Three–led postwar transition. Nor did he possess the patient and confident temperament necessary to deal with the Soviets, whose brusque behavior stemmed from a mix of pride and insecurity. With unquestioned faith in the United States as a uniquely moral force, he expected that agreements would be on American terms 85 percent of the time. Soviet brutality reinforced Truman's self-righteousness. By March 1946, the president would find himself sharing the stage with Churchill in Fulton, Missouri, as the former prime minister delivered an anti-Soviet ideological manifesto. Churchill followed in the paths of Stalin and Kennan, who had both issued their own ideological declarations in February 1946. To populations already anxious over postwar turbulence, these emotion-evoking proclamations jolted and stunned like "electric shocks."[3] Despite their initial resistance, officials and ordinary citizens would line up in this charged atmosphere, like magnetic filings, along an ideological divide. Ideology promised simple, clear-cut answers to complex, puzzling issues. Anxiety, ideology, and the bomb would prove crucial in forming the Cold War by early 1946.

Potsdam

In arranging his July 16 meeting with the prime minister, the neophyte resolved not to be overawed by the great man. Truman specified 11:00 a.m., compelling Churchill to rise earlier than he had in a decade, his daughter marveled. "I'd been up for four and one half hours," the president crowed. Churchill appeared "most charming and very clever"—but "clever in the English not the Kentucky sense." The distinction underscored Truman's "I'm from Missouri" determination to look all horses in the mouth. The former farmer snickered at Churchill's "hooey about how great my country is and how he loved Roosevelt and how he intended to love me, etc. etc."[4] Despite such skepticism, Truman generally followed the advice of Harriman, Leahy, and Byrnes—as well as Churchill. Since becoming president he had been pivoting away from his predecessor's preferred stance as mediator between London and Moscow.

At the Potsdam conference Truman interpreted the ruined capital as "Hitler's folly. He overreached himself by trying to take in too much territory. He had no morals." He would come to regard Stalin as almost as bad. Like many Americans and British, the president regarded "the deluded Hitlerian populace" not so much as accomplices but rather forlorn "old men, old women, children." Unsympathetic to the Soviet expectations of reparations in goods and labor, he criticized the Russians for having "kidnaped" Germans into slave labor and for having "looted every house left standing."[5] Chief of Staff Leahy similarly empathized not with Russian allies but rather with these "highly cultured and proud people who are racial kinsmen." He detected no "vindictiveness or revenge" on the part of his fellow Americans.[6] Meanwhile Harriman, the ranking "Soviet expert" of the group, was referring to the Russians as "those barbarians."[7]

Harriman was hearing from Meiklejohn about local horrors. Typical was "a Russian soldier pursuing a German woman down the street with drawn pistol, catching her, and dragging her into a nearby building." Red Army soldiers entered houses, "raped the women right where they were . . . cut up the rugs and destroyed the furniture wantonly, and refused to use the toilets, but relieved themselves wherever they happened to be, on the beds or in the living room." Agitating for a tough line against the Soviets, the ambassador no doubt passed these stories on to Truman, who believed in keeping women on a pedestal. (Or in the case of actress Lauren Bacall, sitting atop his piano.) The Soviets' predilection for not using latrines also assaulted sensibilities. At Tempelhof airport it was "impossible to move in any room . . . without wading through piles of human excreta. . . . The Soviets must practically live in it."[8] Those assailed by the stench likely felt disgust. It would seem only natural to contain or destroy that which appeared disgusting or horrible. A friend of Churchill depicted Soviet soldiers as "savage children—wearing wrist-watches up to their shoulders in rows—filling their pockets with alarm-clocks which terrify *them* when they go off—raping right & left & mistaking lavatories for shower-baths so that they put their heads in them & then pull the plug!"[9]

Pride in American achievements made it easier to downplay the military prowess of such "savage children." Driving into Berlin that first day, Truman inspected "Hell on Wheels," the U.S. Second Armored Division. GIs and their tanks stretched as far as the eye could see. "This is the most powerful land force I have ever seen," ventured sailor Leahy. "I do not see how anybody could stop them if they really wanted to go somewhere." "Nobody has stopped them yet!" the division commander boasted.[10] Despite such patriotic pride, Truman remained anxious that "machines are ahead of morals." He may have been brooding about the planned test that day in New Mexico of a terrible new weapon. "Maybe when we bore too deeply into the planet there'll [be] a reckoning—who knows?"[11]

Meanwhile, Davies, at Truman's request, was negotiating with Stalin's aide, Andrey Vyshinsky, to set up a preconference meeting. Vyshinsky confided that "the death of President Roosevelt had disturbed them greatly" because "Stalin and his leaders had complete confidence in Roosevelt's" commitment to "understanding & mutual respect & reciprocity." They had less confidence in Truman. Perhaps for that reason Stalin was eager to meet with him before the conference began. Despite his preoccupation with prestige, the Kremlin chief would waive the protocol that elevated him as host in the Soviet zone. He offered to call on the president, at 9:00 that very evening. Davies, worried that Churchill might already be getting his hooks into Truman, eagerly agreed.

Davies then left for the president's house. Truman appeared "tired, worried and irritated over something." He abruptly announced he would not see Stalin that evening. Davies protested that "this might be construed as a rebuff to Stalin's exceptional friendly 'gesture,'" especially as Truman had asked for the meeting. No matter. Davies, dismayed, left to tell Vyshinsky, who turned as "cold as ice." Meanwhile, Stimson and Marshall arrived and took the president aside. They described an astonishingly powerful atomic explosion. This "has taken a great load off my mind," Truman responded. He was now eager to meet with Stalin that evening. Davies gamely drove yet again to Vyshinsky's residence. Probably offended by the earlier rebuff, the touchy *vozhd* now refused. The American and Soviet chiefs had passed each other in the night.[12]

More significant than what was actually agreed to or not agreed to at Potsdam was the attitude that Truman would take away regarding future summits. Issues that remained conflicted or only papered over could potentially be settled or finessed at subsequent meetings. Roosevelt had believed that regular, intimate gatherings of the Big Three (or Four) leaders, preferably in isolated locations such as the Azores, would constitute the beating heart of their informal corporality, overseeing the transition to lasting peace and, he hoped, an open world order. Truman manned up to the challenge of the summit and even enjoyed it, but he never fully overcame his initial impulse: "I hate to go."[13] His mood contrasted sharply with the boyish excitement of Churchill and Roosevelt embarking for their first summits. Yet Truman was not burdened with the fatigue that had made Roosevelt apprehensive about the arduous trek to Yalta.

Though snide, Clark Kerr captured the shift in style from Roosevelt to Truman. "The brilliance, the glory, the color, the glib showmanship and with all this, the prestige, the cocksureness and the obliquity . . . were departed. Here were now drabness, bewilderment and an acute sense of inferiority, which were painful to watch, as they brooded over the new President under the quiet and practiced, if somewhat puzzled, gaze of Joseph Stalin." The ambassador also discerned the qualities that would make Truman a beloved president. He was "endearing and disarming in his utter simplicity and modesty." Truman, who in the 1920s had owned a men's clothing store, appeared meticulous about most everything, including "his daily careful matching of shirt, tie, and handkerchief."[14]

Truman, understandably nervous about going one-on-one with two fabled war leaders, approached the challenge with both self-doubt and self-assertion. He bragged to Bess, "I gave them an earful," then admitted, "I was so scared." A couple days later, "I reared up on my hind legs and told 'em where to get off and they got off." To Clark Kerr, Truman's tough talk sounded more like "little presidential splutterings." The Missourian concluded that Stalin "seems to like it when I hit him with a hammer." Truman was always ready to go home. After the second day of the two-week conference, he concluded, "I've gotten what I came for"—Stalin's reaffirmed promise to enter the war against Japan.[15] On the fourth day, he confided to Bess, "I'm sick of

10.1. Harry S. Truman at Potsdam looking both self-satisfied and a bit insecure. Sitting from left: Prime Minister Clement Attlee, the president, and Stalin. Standing from left: Leahy, Foreign Secretary Bevin, and Secretary of State James F. Byrnes, gripping Molotov's arm. (Courtesy of Library of Congress.)

the whole business." Talking with her made him so homesick that "I spent the day after the call trying to think up reasons why I should bust up the conference and go home."[16] The personal could indeed be political!

Truman never appreciated that diplomacy required talk, even extended talk. From the start he displayed impatience for "more action and few words."[17] He boasted, "there were three proposals and I banged them through in short order," adding, "I am not going to stay around this terrible place all summer just to listen to speeches."[18] A week into it, he reported "we have accomplished a very great deal in spite of all the talk." He evidently imagined the gathering not as a talkfest but rather as a poker game, in which more than minimal speech was distracting and likely deceiving. At the start he worried whether "things were going according to Hoyle or not." As it wrapped up, he concluded, with reference to the atomic bomb, Stalin "doesn't know it but I have an ace in the hole and another one showing—so unless he has threes or two pair (and I know he has not) we are sitting all right."[19] In fact, the ace in the hole would become a deadly joker.

Despite his impatience with talk, Truman was to a degree seduced by summitry. Following his first meeting with the Soviet leader, he decided, "I can deal with Stalin. He is honest—but smart as hell." After the Kremlin boss "talked to me confidentially at the dinner," Truman came to believe "things will be all right in most instances." Sounding not so different from FDR, he did not see it as a crisis that on "some things we won't and can't agree." He believed a relationship had been established.[20] Years later Truman, like Bullitt, would grow indignant when recalling the evidently painful memory of feeling lured in and then betrayed. He recounted that the Potsdam accords were "broken as soon as the unconscionable Russian Dictator returned to Moscow! And I liked the little son of a bitch." Truman had been labeled "little" so often that the word never lost its sting. Introducing the subject of height in a discussion of foreign policy, he claimed that Stalin "was a good six inches shorter than I am and even Churchill was only three inches taller than Joe! Yet I was the little man in stature and intellect! So the press said."[21]

The two most difficult diplomatic issues at Potsdam, the atomic bomb and the future of Germany, would drive the Cold War for nearly a half-century afterward. Nevertheless, the question of what and when to tell the Russians about the atomic bomb, and whether to share it with them remained largely sub rosa at the conference. Assistant Secretary of War McCloy observed that after receiving a detailed report on the weapon's astounding force, Truman and Churchill "went to the next meeting like little boys with a big red apple secreted on their persons."[22] Their secretive, boyish clubbishness and excitement seems analogous to the mood displayed by Roosevelt and Churchill en route to the 1941 Atlantic Conference. Both moments were potential turning points. In 1941, the two leaders had each reached out in personal and political ways to form a creative alliance. None of the three rose to that challenge in July 1945. Truman casually mentioned the weapon to Stalin without offering any details. Remaining outwardly calm, the Kremlin chief said he hoped it would be used against Japan.

Thanks to his spies, Stalin knew far more than he let on. Nonetheless, upon learning details of the destruction at Hiroshima on August 6, the dictator would be shocked. His daughter Svetlana recalled that he turned silent, retreated to his room, and became ill.[23] The atomic bomb "has shaken the whole world," he would soon tell aides. "The balance has been destroyed."[24] He ordered a crash program. Atomic scientists should "ask for whatever you like. You won't be refused."[25] Many in Moscow interpreted Hiroshima as the imposition of "atomic blackmail."[26] The journalist Alexander Werth reported the "acutely depressing effect on everybody." The painfully won victory seemed "as good as wasted'"[27]

While the issue of the atomic bomb hovered below the surface, discussion of Germany, particularly reparations, dominated the conference. The issue went to the heart of a dilemma the United States had faced since World War I. As Wilson's adviser, Colonel Edward M. House had put it, should America choose Russia or Germany? The Russians were allies in two world wars, but the Germans figured as ethnic, cultural, and (aside from the Nazi era) ideological kin, and they operated the powerhouse of the European economy. Reparations had implications for political relations between Germany and the victors, the postwar standard of living in those nations, and whether the Allies would together govern the former enemy or fall out over the spoils. For Russians, reparations figured in emotional and symbolic ways. As Davies, who remained close with Soviet officials, related, reparations "touched the core of their fear that the West would use Germany to attack them."[28] As Stalin no doubt knew from his spy network, British and some American military planners envisioned mobilizing German industry and manpower against the Soviet Union.

Should Germans or Russians enjoy the higher postwar standard of living? At Yalta, Roosevelt had opined that Germany, which had perpetrated terrible destruction, should not be permitted to regain its prewar standard until it had paid reparations in existing machinery, ongoing production, and labor. He had agreed to $20 billion in reparations as the basis for discussion, with the Soviets to get half the eventual total. Polls in late April 1945 showed that the American people, by an 82 percent to 11 percent margin, approved using German labor, presumably unpaid, to rebuild Russia.[29] Echoing FDR at Yalta, Ivan Maisky at Potsdam argued, "We must visualize quite another Germany whose level will be that of middle Europe which is very much lower." Molotov chimed in that "if anyone had to suffer and be punished, it should be the aggressor and "not the ally who had already suffered more to defeat him than any of the allies."[30]

U.S. negotiators responded that payment for imports had to take precedence over payment of reparations. They believed that Germany first needed to import food and raw materials in order to survive; only then would it become able to export, especially coal.[31] Maisky countered that the Germans had manipulated the Allies after World War I to get out of paying reparations. Once they realized imports trumped reparations, "they will try to prove that without very considerable imports they can't live and can't export."[32]

Reparations also galvanized emotions among Americans, but for different reasons. Truman remembered the rancor of the 1920s and '30s. U.S. private loans to Germany had helped finance reparations to the Allies, who had used some of that money to pay their World War I debts to Washington. The whole structure collapsed in the early 1930s, aggravating economic and political tensions that had deepened the Depression and fostered the rise of Hitler.[33] Truman's mantra at Potsdam was, "Santa Claus is dead." America would never again "pay reparations, feed the world, and get nothing for it but a nose thumbing."[34] Encouraging the president to play down Russian claims for reparations were Harriman and Pauley. Harriman still believed that dollar diplomacy, in the form of political conditions on a U.S. loan to Moscow, could loosen the Kremlin's grip on Eastern Europe. Getting significant reparations would lessen the need for a loan. Pauley, later praised by Truman as almost "the only hard boiled, hard hitting anti-Russian around," argued, on the basis of his committee's superficial study, that the $20 billion figure from Yalta was impractical.[35]

The Soviets were also to blame. They had undermined their argument for Allied unity by acting unilaterally to give Poland a large slice of German territory, reaching westward to the Oder and Neisse Rivers. This border had been proposed but not finally approved at Yalta. The territorial cession, which included valuable coal mines in Silesia, reduced the resources with which Germany could pay for reparations or imports. More important, the unilateral move angered Americans and Britons. Truman himself resented this "Bolsheviki land grab."[36]

Backing up Truman was the State Department. Unlike Roosevelt, the State Department chose Germany over Russia, in part because Germany, and in particular its coal exports, seemed key to reviving the European economy and to securing U.S. exports in the long term. The State and War Departments also worried that economic misery would boost the appeal of Communists, already the largest parties in France and Italy. If Communists won elections there and elsewhere, they could strike up close economic and political relations with Moscow, possibly excluding the United States and Britain. Once planners abandoned the notion of Big Three cooperation as the first principle of the postwar era, every accretion of power to one side seemed like a potential threat to the other.

Back in December 1941, Harry Hopkins had believed the American model possessed enough appeal and the United States enough resilience to weather large-scale Communist wins in Europe. Despite having triumphed in a global war since then, U.S. leaders no longer commanded such confidence. Even Hopkins had swung around to the Wilsonian position of wanting to promote American values and institutions nearly everywhere, including "in Poland [and] Greece." Sounding very different from Roosevelt in 1944–45, Hopkins in September 1945 would declare that U.S. interests "throughout the world are jeopardized by the advent of any kind of totalitarian government whatever its name or label."[37]

The day before the conference ended on August 1, Truman wrote to Bess, "the whole difficulty is reparations. Of course the Russians are naturally looters." He recognized that they "have been looted by Germans and you can hardly blame them for their attitude."[38] Byrnes, whom Stalin would call the most honest horse thief he had ever met, pushed through a compromise over reparations that allowed them to go home but would prove illogical and unworkable. The Americans and British granted de facto recognition of the Oder-Neisse border. Each of the four powers would take reparations from its own zone. The bulk of German industry, however, lay in the west, principally in the Ruhr Valley in the British zone. To compensate, the Russians would be entitled to 25 percent of surplus equipment from the three western zones—but how much would be deemed "surplus" would be decided solely by the Americans, British, and French. In operation this scheme would deepen the division of Germany along zonal lines. Zonal reparations conflicted with other provisions of the Potsdam agreements aimed at treating Germany as a whole.

The logical and practical inconsistencies of, first, making both reparations and imports a first charge on German earnings from exports and, second, removing reparations on a zonal basis while dealing with Germany as a whole, would in coming years spark rivalry, frustration, anger, and the Cold War. In little more than a decade, atomic-armed armies would be eyeballing each other along the border between East and West Germany. This outcome brought to fruition the Kremlin's deepest fear: the richest, most productive western portion of Germany unified into a strong state, allied with atomic-armed America, and adamant against officially accepting the territorial losses imposed by Russia, Poland, and Czechoslovakia.

Heading off an Atomic Arms Race

The demonstrated destructive power of the first atomic explosions—over the New Mexico desert on July 16, over Hiroshima on August 6, and over Nagasaki on August 9—shocked leading members of the Truman administration into trying to head off an atomic arms race. McCloy feared the bomb might "augur the destruction of modern civilization."[39] Acheson, the usually unflappable assistant secretary of state, felt "too weary to try to figure things out."[40] Stimson and McCloy struggled with the "moral aspects" of this "primordial weapon." They concluded that regardless of "the wickedness of Russia," the "atom itself, not the Russians posed the central problem."[41]

As he approached his ninth decade, Stimson ranked as a statesman who could take the long view and acknowledge previous errors. The destruction at Hiroshima impelled him to backtrack from his plan to bet America's "royal straight flush" against Russia in atomic poker. Horror at the prospect of another war focused his thinking. He gave the highest priority to preventing an atomic arms race. Despite a conservatism so deep that he still idolized former President William Howard Taft, the crusty old warhorse experienced an epiphany.[42]

On September 12, he handed Truman a memorandum stressing that relations with the Russians were "virtually dominated by the problem of the atomic bomb." It was "most important" to approach them directly. London also could not be ignored. But the issue of controlling atomic weapons had to be discussed with Moscow on a big power basis. He might have added that this was the Rooseveltian approach. A proposal threaded through a thicket of smaller nations in the UN would get tangled and torn. The United States should offer to halt work on the bomb in return for the Russians and British agreeing likewise. Washington could pledge to impound its bombs. The three should concur on no use unless all agreed. The key point was building trust through step-by-step sharing of atomic information.[43]

Stimson proved prescient. He warned that tying atomic issues to other issues, a strategy that decades later became known as "linkage," would fail. Soviet repression would ease through engagement, not pressure. An atomic "armament race of a rather desperate character" loomed, he stressed. Washington's atomic monopoly was spurring Moscow's spying, about which he had warned FDR. Indeed, on that very day the FBI alerted the White House about a spy caught in Canada.[44] He cited the scientists' testimony that the Soviets would certainly get the bomb. Would Moscow then consider itself an ally or an enemy? Stimson grasped that "the old custom of secrecy and nationalistic military superiority" had to give way to "saving civilization."[45]

Disputing Byrnes, the war secretary cautioned against "having this weapon rather ostentatiously on our hip."[46] The sheriff's hip-holstered pistol had subdued bad guys in the mythic West. Yet hanging onto it now would encourage the Soviets to become outlaws. Truman nevertheless clung to the frontier model. Asked in a Cabinet meeting, "Why [is it] necessary to police [the] world?" He replied, "You must have a marshal ... have to have a sheriff."[47] Stimson, who grew up in the nineteenth century and who still exercised on horseback, proposed a more advanced code. "The chief lesson I have learned in a long life: The only way you can make a man trustworthy is to trust him; and the surest way to make him untrustworthy is to distrust him and show your distrust."[48] That lesson required vision broader than Truman could muster.

Limiting the president were his staff and his own personality.[49] Budget director Harold Smith marveled at finding "Truman more disorganized than FDR."[50] Smith had assumed that "Truman's natural inclination for order would make him superior in this respect." But "inadequate staff preparation" led to "messes." From the British Embassy, Isaiah Berlin observed the president surrounding himself with "respectable, unfrightening hacks." (Although Matthew J. Connelly, Charles G. Ross, and Harry Vaughan might have qualified as "hacks," Truman would also appoint highly capable officials, notably Acheson, Marshall, and Clark Clifford.) Truman's crisp demeanor operated on "such a minute scale, such a Dutch interior," as to reduce all situations to the same "general principles."[51] Though loyal to the president, McCloy characterized his decisions on the bomb as "not distinguished at all." He seemed "not Lincolnesque," but rather "common ... a simple man, prone to make up his mind quickly and decisively, perhaps too quickly."[52] The Truman administration appeared "very chaotic," McCloy told Stettinius. "The whole atmosphere at the top did not have the high tone either from the standpoint of personalities or program that it did a year ago."[53]

What Truman called "a stormy Cabinet meeting" took up the proposal that Stimson had outlined in his memorandum on September 21, Stimson's seventy-eighth birthday and last day in office.[54] The old wise man pointed out, "We do not have a secret to give away—the secret will give itself away." At stake was the safety of the world. A majority in the Cabinet, including acting secretary of state Acheson, incoming war secretary Robert Patterson, and liberal lion and commerce secretary Wallace, agreed. As Acheson put it, "there was no alternative." They simply had to parlay the wispy secret into a solid agreement.[55]

Only four dissented outright.⁵⁶ Navy Secretary Forrestal, Attorney General Tom Clark, and Truman's poker buddies—Secretary of the Treasury Fred Vinson and Secretary of Agriculture Clinton P. Anderson—disputed the scientists. America, with its exceptional heritage and unequalled might could damn well shape the atomic future, they insisted. Washington did not have to "give" away the bomb. That word categorized the proposal as another liberal "giveaway" to ungrateful allies or, worse, as craven appeasement of an aggressor. The notion of a unitary "secret" reified the scientific, engineering, and production discoveries into a single formula that supposedly could be locked in a vault. Regarding the secret as an American possession ignored the crucial work done in the United States by the British, Canadian, German, French, Danish, and Hungarian scientists who had produced the "world bomb."⁵⁷

Forrestal argued that the Russians, like the Japanese, "are essentially oriental in their thinking." Sharing scientific information was trying to "buy their understanding and sympathy. We tried that once with Hitler. There are no returns on appeasement."⁵⁸ His analogies linked the Soviets to both defeated enemies. The Hitler/Munich allusion remained easy to assert and difficult to refute. How to prove that Stalin lacked Hitler's appetite? Or that one concession would lead to further demands rather than a solid deal? The phrase "oriental in their thinking" racialized the Soviets as "Asiatic" others—as treacherous non-Westerners, "barbarians" as Harriman had put it, liable to inflict another Pearl Harbor. The attorney general complained about Soviet spying. Anderson warned the insecure president that abandoning the secret would wreck public confidence in his leadership.⁵⁹ Unsure what to do, Truman asked for written responses to Stimson's proposal.

Even as the responses were being drafted, untrue reports precipitated a suddenly public discussion. Someone, most likely Forrestal and/or his allies, leaked a fabricated account of the Cabinet meeting. The *New York Times* headlined: "Wallace Plan to Share Bomb Data as Peace Insurance." The story omitted Stimson's authorship. Wallace's supposedly "ardent advocacy" evoked the stereotype of emotional leftists panting to sell out to Russia.⁶⁰ Forrestal's responsibility is suggested by parallel language in his diary: Wallace was "completely, everlastingly and wholeheartedly in favor of giving it to the Russians."[61] The minutes of the meeting reveal no such gushing.[62] Forrestal alerted navy brass that civilians favored "turning Atomic Power over to Russia."[63] In a stunning falsification, the newspaper story portrayed Stimson as wanting to turn the issue over to a world organization. In actuality, Stimson had urged talks with Russia.[64]

Also in the headlines the day after the Cabinet meeting was the blitz in the nation's media capital by General Leslie R. Groves, military manager of the Manhattan project. Five thousand listened to him at City Hall in New York. A luncheon at the Waldorf Astoria open to reporters ensured further publicity. He wrapped up the day with a press conference. Groves stressed that the bomb could and should remain an "American secret." No sharing "until all of the other nations of the world are as anxious for peace as we are." Raising the bar still higher, he added, "and by 'anxious for peace,' I mean in the heart and not by a . . . treaty which they do not intend to honor." Meanwhile, the bomb "could be used as a diplomatic bargaining point."[65]

But could the secret be kept? Here Groves, who had listed his ten years of engineering school as "the equivalent of about two Ph.D.s," disputed the scientists over the essence of the "secret."[66] More important than "science and theory" was hands-on, distinctly American "know-how." "No one but the men who built" the weapon could "know its complexity and the almost impossibly close tolerances required." Why, then, worry about the Russians obtaining the bomb? The essential component was not uranium, physics, or engineering but rather the "teamwork, the intense enthusiasm and the skill of American workmen."[67] The argument appealed because it rested not on unpleasant facts but rather on the reassuring ideology of American exceptionalism.

Nevertheless, a majority of the Cabinet echoed Stimson in their written responses. Despite his later prominence as architect of the struggle with Russia, Acheson in September 1945 could not "see why the basic interests of the two nations should conflict." Secrecy appeared "both futile and dangerous." The logic seemed inescapable: "The advantage of being ahead in such a race is nothing compared with not having the race." He empathized that the Kremlin "must and will exert every energy" to acquire bombs. Rejecting Forrestal's conceit of America as "trustee for the world," Acheson saw this as meaning "nothing more to the Russian mind than an outright policy of exclusion." Why invite "the added complication of fifty or more countries"? The Soviets should be approached directly. The man who would later prove masterful at manipulating American opinion urged Truman to lose no time in publicizing "the opinions of the scientists." Forrestal and Groves had already struck. Russian suspicions were mounting. The president should consult with the British, start talking with the Soviets, and explain it all to Congress.[68]

While Stimson's allies felt horror at atomic warfare, those opposed were galvanized by suspicion of foreigners, scientists, and rational argument. Contending that the partially "Asiatic" Soviets could not catch up, Anderson quoted Rudyard Kipling's imperial verse:

> They copied all they could follow, but they couldn't
> copy my mind
> So I left them sweating and stealing a year and a half
> behind.[69]

Forrestal denied that the bomb mandated a revolution in international relations. He cited the Romans' ability to "counteract Hannibal's use of elephants."[70] Vinson also believed "the historical argument is stronger than the logical argument." Echoing Groves, Anderson reasoned that despite mastering the "cold science" of the bomb, the Russians remained incapable of using the "know-how" to produce it. Though the Soviets boasted factories, they had needed Lend-Lease trucks and planes. The key lay not in the "mechanical formula," which could be turned over to the Russians—or stolen—but rather "the genius to apply these laws."[71]

Faith in exceptionalism ran deep in American culture. As the Nobel Prize physicist James Franck perceived, an eternal secret was as alluring as "the movies and the funny papers."[72] Vinson reminded that even though the Germans had made "great developments, the simple fact remains that they did not come up with the atomic bomb, and we did." Margaret Truman remembered "Papa Vin" as her father's closest adviser. Truman elevated him to Chief Justice of the Supreme Court and favored him for president in 1952.[73]

Vinson believed that the vigor of the nation depended on keeping this "secret." The 1921 Washington conference had sunk America's spirit along with its battleships, he charged. Interwar Americans had afterward suffered "apathy and listlessness." According to this melodrama of degeneration, national fitness required possessing powerful instruments of destruction. Vinson's warnings harked back to Theodore Roosevelt's warning that wealthy nations tended to "go soft" without war. "We must be a military nation," Truman affirmed to the Cabinet only weeks after the Japanese surrender.[74]

But would a triumphalist-minded American public have tolerated giving up the "secret"? In ensuing years the administration's publicity campaigns would overcome serious opposition to a loan to Britain, aid to Greece and Turkey, interim aid to Europe, and the Marshall Plan. Polling in September 1945 showed that as long as the atomic issue was framed in terms of "the secret," Americans by 85 percent to 12 percent favored holding on to the prize. Yet only 13 percent believed the secret could be kept, and 56 percent believed Russia would get the bomb within five years. More than 80 percent feared the next world war would go atomic. Nearly half looked to a scientific miracle to protect them. Absent that deus ex machina, the outlook looked grim.

Despite uncertainty about how, precisely, to avoid an atomic race, Americans preferred that solution. If the "secret" was not dangled as an option, most favored international controls. Asked whether "our country should rely more on our own ability to make better atomic bombs . . . or on the ability of the world organization to prevent any country, including our own, from ever using such bombs," Americans inclined toward international control by 48 percent to 43 percent. A nearly three-to-one margin favored the major nations getting "together to agree that atomic bombs should never be used as a war weapon." In early 1946, a 56 percent to 13 percent majority opted for a UN law requiring all nations, including the United States, to destroy its atomic weapons. An astounding three-quarters of Americans approved allowing international atomic inspectors to "search any property in any country" including the United States.[75] The FBI's warning to Truman that the bomb had become "the Number One project of Soviet espionage" rendered scientific sharing trickier to justify.[76] The administration nevertheless could have used the widespread desire for international agreement as a springboard. The spying might even have been cited as demonstrating the need for a regime-changing agreement.

Truman ended up siding with the minority that opposed Stimson. He spent the weekend after the September 21 Cabinet meeting with friends, probably including Anderson. The following Monday he paraphrased Anderson's argument stressing know-how. Whether it was atomic bombs or automobiles, other nations could not "make them equal to the United States, " the president asserted.[77]

What would Roosevelt have done? Two veteran observers, British ambassador Halifax and *Foreign Affairs* editor Hamilton Fish Armstrong, concurred that "F.D.R. would have used the bomb in some imaginative way to improve our relations with Soviet Russia." Halifax added that "Churchill would have then exclaimed: 'What! Give the secret to those bloody Bolsheviks? Never!'"[78] That protest could not, however, have blocked a determined Roosevelt. Frankfurter criticized "Truman's failure to show as much imagination in turning the atomic bomb to advantage as F.D.R. would have shown." The new president was instead hunkering down with a "Maginot Line" psychology.[79]

On October 8, Truman picked a down-home setting to announce a policy based on the ideology of American exceptionalism. Standing on the porch of a fishing lodge at Reelfoot Lake near Tiptonville, Tennessee, he scuttled Stimson's proposal without even mentioning it. He repeated the term *know-how* seven times. Reporters picked up on the words, as did the ensuing *New York Times* headline. Scientific knowledge had become irrelevant to international control, he asserted, because other nations "all know that, anyway." Far different was "the know-how of putting that knowledge practically to work." "That is our secret." "Know-how" had spawned America's unique aviation and automobile industries. Asked whether other nations could produce a bomb if they got this Yankee magic, Truman replied, "I don't think they could do it, anyway." Pressed, "Is anybody in position to use that know-how, if we offered it to them?" he repeated his faith: "No. That is the best answer."[80]

A few weeks later, he asked J. Robert Oppenheimer how long it would take the Russians to get a bomb. The atomic scientist replied he did not know. Truman said he knew: "Never."[81] A friend asked the president, "What it amounts to is this. That the armaments race is on, is that right?" Yes, Truman answered, but "we would stay ahead." He appeared "smiling and gracious" with the attitude of "a man who has made up his mind and was supremely confident of the correctness of the decision."[82] In 1957, Truman would assert that the Russians had no hydrogen bomb, though they had in fact exploded such a weapon in 1953. He explained, "After all, they're Russians. They're basically peasants. They're not Americans. They can't hope to achieve the technology we've achieved."[83]

Such certainty did not purge guilt about Hiroshima. In their October 1945 meeting, Oppenheimer confessed, "Mr. President, I feel I have blood on my hands." Afterward Truman fumed, "Blood on his hands, dammit, he hasn't half as much blood on his hand as I have. You just don't go around bellyaching about it." He ordered, "I don't want to see that son-of-a-bitch in this office ever again."[84] Decades later, as Truman lay dying, former attorney general Clark came to visit. Doctors ordered him to stay only five minutes. Yet he lingered nearly an hour as Truman tried to justify his decisions on the bomb.[85]

Stalin likely knew about the debate over Stimson's proposal. His agents had only to read the newspapers to learn of the so-called Wallace plan. A British diplomat noted that the Kremlin chief stood "too proud to ask for the 'Know-How.'"[86] But perhaps he was not above hinting. To junketing Florida Senator Claude Pepper, Stalin emphasized that "common interest" had "brought the two nations very close together" during the war. Russia, he added, "was very greatly indebted to the United States" for Lend-Lease. Now, however, the "tie which has held us together no longer exists and we shall have to find a new basis for our close relations in the future." Pressed on what that new basis might be, the former seminarian intoned, "'Christ said, seek and ye shall find.'"[87] Even if Stalin was referring to economic ties and control over Germany, such engagement might have encouraged atomic ties as well. Edward C. Carter, a left-leaning, nongovernmental organization official, had developed good contacts with Soviet authorities. He returned from Moscow reporting that "after the President made his Reelfoot Lake statement, the whole attitude in Russia changed."[88]

The London and Moscow Conferences

The failed London Foreign Ministers conference (September 11–October 2, 1945) probably hardened Truman against Stimson's proposal. After three weeks of squabbling, it folded without even a face-saving communiqué. At this first conclave of the atomic era both sides jockeyed for power and status.[89] Byrnes believed that the bomb, which he jokingly told Molotov sat in his "hip pocket," could win diplomatic concessions.[90] Molotov determined to prove him wrong. The American found the Soviets were "stubborn, obstinate, and they don't scare."[91] Wrangles ensued over peace treaties with Romania, Bulgaria, and Italy; the control set up in Japan; and the Soviet bid for a trusteeship in the former Italian colony of Libya. (Despite U.S. agreement in principle in San Francisco to such a trusteeship, Americans now seconded British opposition to a possible Soviet naval base in the Mediterranean. Byrnes also fantasized that once ensconced in Libya, the Soviets could lunge thousands of miles across the Sahara desert to seize the uranium-rich Belgian Congo.) When Byrnes proposed a Big Three pact guaranteeing German demilitarization for twenty-five years, Stalin ordered Molotov to demand an anti-Japan treaty as well. The American declined. Though difficult, these issues paled before a procedural question that was actually substantive, and so basic that it deadlocked the meeting.

Roosevelt and Stalin had favored restricting wartime decisions to the Big Three (or Four). That was also how they conceptualized the immediate postwar order, despite the window dressing of the UN General Assembly. Potsdam specified that France and China could participate in decisions regarding peace treaties only with those nations with which they had been at war. When the London conference opened, however, Molotov, with Stalin's approval, accepted an Anglo-American request that China and France participate in the discussions (but not the decisions) regarding all the treaties. That proved the wedge for Big Five decision making, with France and China siding with the Anglo-Americans. Molotov charged that Byrnes had veered away from Roosevelt's course when "the relations between the Soviet Union and the United States had been quite different."[92] Stalin rued that "the whole Roosevelt entourage [has fallen] out of favor."[93]

Contributing to the fiasco was Byrnes's dislike for mixing with foreigners or even his own advisers. The secretary of state sailed into the conclave convinced he could "play better by ear than anyone else can play from a written score." John Foster Dulles, the Republican foreign policy expert and a consultant at London, complained that Byrnes "was the only head of any delegation who didn't do any entertaining of any sort, didn't pay any calls, and received as few as he could possibly manage." Instead, he and a buddy who had never left the country before would "sit around late in the evening and drink and gossip, and [sing] Irish songs." Asked who ranked as the better secretary of state, Dulles remarked that "Stettinius knew what he didn't know, while Byrnes doesn't know what he doesn't know."[94] Former secretary Hull faulted Byrnes for refusing to "face the fact that [foreign policy] couldn't be dealt with offhand."[95]

On September 21, coincidentally the day of the key Cabinet meeting, Stalin blew up. He ordered Molotov to take back the concession. Frank Roberts observed from Moscow that "Soviet foreign policy has since Tehran been based upon Big Three co-operation." The London deadlock was "sincerely attributed here to the apparent Anglo-American departure from this fundamental principle."[96] Part of the problem was cultural. Unused to the wheeling-dealing of large democratic legislatures, the Soviets found only small settings "flexible and satisfying."[97]

Status-driven anxiety sharpened antagonisms. When Foreign Secretary Ernest Bevin warned that relations were sliding to where "we had found ourselves with Hitler," Molotov erupted. "Hitler had looked on the U.S.S.R. as an inferior country." Russians regarded "themselves as good as anyone else." They refused to be treated "as an inferior race."

He reiterated Stalin's June plaint to Hopkins. "During the war we had argued but we had managed to come to terms." Then "the Soviet Union was needed." Now the British "had seemed to change their attitude. Was that because [they] no longer needed the Soviet Union?" Bevin grumbled that it was the British who were "treated as inferiors by both the Russians and the Americans."[98]

Stalin could measure respect with the precision of a diamond dealer. Blaming Molotov for accepting the Big Five formula, he lurched from the comradely *ty* form of *you* to the coldly formal *Vy*. Despite the tensions at London, he still, significantly, referred to the United States and Britain as "allies." He ranted like someone insulted but hanging on to a tattered relationship. To Molotov he railed against the "people who call themselves our Allies." They showed "no elementary feeling of respect towards their ally." He warned, "The Allies are pressing on you to break your will."[99] He retaliated with his own insults: cancelling Marshal Zhukov's visit to America and calling home the Soviet representative on the allied commission in Japan. He interpreted as "desecration" rumors in the diplomatic community and in the foreign press that he was not really vacationing on the Black Sea. According to various false reports he was deposed, paralyzed, or had run off with a beautiful Georgian princess.[100] He even criticized Soviet publication of Churchill's speech, which *praised* him. Such press stories signified only "servility before foreign figures," he fumed, repeating the word *servility* twice more.[101]

The British had their own reasons to feel insulted. At the insistence of Prime Minister Clement Attlee, whose Labor government had swept into power when Churchill was defeated in the July 1945 parliamentary election, Truman agreed to an Anglo-American-Canadian atomic summit in early November. Unenthused about sharing or about another meeting with foreigners, the president did little to prepare. He planned to kill time with a visit to Arlington Cemetery and a cruise down the Potomac. An aide joked that the yacht "might run aground and that would take up the evening."[102] Time aboard the *Sequoia* was wasted listening to "interminable stories," so the British groused. Atomic issues were restricted to ninety minutes. They agreed on keeping "know-how" secret.[103] Some London officials questioned

Attlee's "boosting the bomb" when Washington insisted "it's 100% a U.S. affair, nobody else knows about how to make it & nobody else (including the British) are going to. Seems to make us look rather silly."[104] Indeed, only months after pledging "full and effective cooperation," Truman denied that the agreement applied to "engineering and operational assistance," that is, to know-how.[105] In November, Britons were polled on whether they felt more or less friendly toward the United States as compared with a year earlier. Significantly, 35 percent answered less friendly, 9 percent more. By comparison, 19 percent felt less warmly toward the Soviets, 16 percent more.[106]

The Grand Alliance was not the only entity wearing out. "The war broke me," cried the exhausted *vozhd*. He retreated to a boyhood haunt, semitropical Abkhazia on the Black Sea.[107] For two months he indulged himself by puttering in the garden, reading secret police reports, reminiscing with old friends, and tormenting Molotov by cable.[108] Into this idyll he welcomed Harriman, sent to ascertain the dictator's health and post-London mood.

Stalin complained about Soviet humiliation in Japan, where, as Walter Lippmann had observed, General Douglas MacArthur's absolute control made U.S. objections to Soviet domination in Eastern Europe look "ridiculous."[109] Back in August, Harriman had informed the Russians that they would be excluded from sharing in the administration of defeated Japan. Molotov grew "so angry, he stuttered and sputtered more than" ever before.[110] Now Stalin proposed a spheres-of-influence deal. Washington would set up an Allied Control Commission. "General MacArthur should be the permanent Chairman and have the final voice as in the case of the Soviet Commander in Rumania." While dropping the bid to share in the occupation of Japan, Stalin resented that his representative was being treated "'like a piece of furniture' . . . neither informed nor consulted." It violated "the dignity of the Soviet Union to be thus treated as a satellite state instead of as an ally." He repeated: "The Soviet Union would not be a satellite of the United States in the Far East or elsewhere." Despite these "blunt remarks," the Kremlin boss "has never discussed matters in a more calm and open manner," reported Harriman. He "could not have been more friendly to me personally."[111]

Stalin said resignedly that if Washington wanted to control Japan, far better "for us to step aside and let you act as you wish and we will not interfere." Russia might then turn "isolationist . . . as the United States had done" in the 1920s. He added that U.S. isolationism had proven a mistake. Harriman later told Roberts that the dictator "spoke very calmly without any hint of blackmail."[112] Stalin seemed to believe the Soviet Union could go its own way without unleashing a cold war. Separate spheres would indeed violate the Atlantic Charter and the Wilsonian dream of a single, open world. Yet a measure of separateness accorded with actuality. It was the pattern that FDR and Stalin had anticipated as the basis for collaboration in the postwar transition. It would turn out that separateness could operate on the basis of collaboration or cold war.

The inadvertently revealing conclusion in Harriman's report points up how culturally divergent emotional dispositions could intersect in ways that undermined the alliance. "It is my feeling that [Stalin] wants to work things out with us but is inordinately suspicious of our every move that we are trying to put something over on him."[113] Here was Harriman, trumpeter of the "barbarian invasion of Europe" and of "irreconcilable differences," acknowledging that the Kremlin boss preferred a deal. Stalin's suspicion was certainly on trigger alert. But by labeling that anxiety "inordinate," the ambassador was dismissing the need or the possibility of mitigating it.

Even Hopkins, who had supported a tougher stance after Roosevelt's death, now worried that Truman's policy was becoming too extreme. He was not "too happy about the way the atom bomb is being handled. In fact I think we are doing almost everything we can to break with Russia, which seems to unnecessary to me."[114] Roberts, who agreed with Harriman and Kennan on getting tough, nevertheless recognized that Soviet distrust stemmed largely from specific policy changes in Washington and London. "Soviet suspicions, which had decreased as a result of Big Three collaboration during the war," had flared up "since we and the Americans embarked upon a vigorous policy in Eastern Europe, followed by unilateral American action in the Far East, and . . . preference for wide international cooperation instead of the Big Three procedure favored by the Russians. All this

[made] the Kremlin regret [the departures of] Roosevelt and Churchill."[115] The Americans and British might have achieved greater success at less cost had they considered that Stalin focused on concrete gains, yes, but also, as he told Harriman, on avoiding being made the fool who had "something [put] over on him."

The Black Sea tête-à-tête illustrated Roosevelt's thesis that frequent top-level meetings could cobble together personal relations, clarify differences, and counter demonizing. Roosevelt hoped regular summits could institutionalize rapport. Leaders, including Truman, emerged aglow from the wartime summits, even if that feeling faded. Lippmann concluded from the wreckage at London that "the basic issues of power and influence can be dealt with only by the chiefs of state."[116] Truman disagreed. Though proud of his performance at Potsdam, he did not relish a return engagement. Byrnes told Dulles that the president "didn't plan to attend any more meetings abroad."[117] Sharply reversing Roosevelt's concept of the UN as run by the Big Three or Four, Truman believed that if the world organization "works as it should, there shouldn't be any reason for a Big Three conference."[118] Part of the president's reluctance stemmed from his preoccupation with the terrible inflation, shortages, and unemployment plaguing the nation. Only 9 percent of Americans deemed foreign policy the nation's worst problem.[119] For the moment Truman left it largely to Byrnes.

The once-scrappy South Carolinian had departed London "extremely nervous, tired out," and daunted by the "failure of his first mission on his own."[120] He and Truman feared that unless Moscow joined the proposed international atomic commission, "we can just kiss off" the UN.[121] The renewed effort at a deal with Moscow may also have received a boost from Clark Kerr's analysis of the "strange psychological effect of the atomic bomb" in making Soviet leaders feel insecure. The ambassador warned that getting anywhere with the Soviets required approaching them through the Big Three, not the Big Five or the General Assembly. By November, Byrnes was actively working to rekindle diplomacy.[122]

The result was Roosevelt redux. Byrnes proposed a Big Three foreign ministers conference in Moscow where the decision-making dictator would be on hand. Paraphrasing FDR, Byrnes reasoned that regular meetings "were valuable in themselves." When Bevin threatened to boycott, Byrnes said he would go anyway.[123] The secretary removed the bomb from his hip and placed it on the negotiating table. In a national broadcast he revived aspects of Stimson's proposal. While Tiptonville had denigrated scientific sharing, he advocated such exchange as a step toward international control. Unfortunately, public and congressional sentiment had hardened since September. The London debacle, the Gouzenko spy case in Canada, and grandstanding about America's "sacred trust" and exceptionalist "know-how" had pushed opinion toward unilateralist solutions. Lippmann feared the international atmosphere had been "poisoned" by the U.S. atomic monopoly.[124]

Trying to placate both Congress and his boss, Byrnes pledged to safeguard the "know-how." Yet he also signaled Moscow. Naked atomic diplomacy violated U.S. traditions, he assured. Washington had tried to stay out of the two world wars and would not launch a third. He also edged closer to the Rooseveltian position of equidistance between Moscow and London by lashing out at British imperial trade restrictions.

The upcoming meeting "put a completely fresh complexion on the whole situation," Litvinov sighed with relief. "Now we were out of the dark valley."[125] Despite the chorus at home against "appeasement," Byrnes aimed at deals to secure peace—and his own crowning as peacemaker. He would appeal to the Russians' "pride and prejudice."[126] He would disprove Lippmann's sneer that in Washington "there is no navigator, there is no helmsman, and the captain is not setting the course."[127]

Although letting Byrnes take the helm at Moscow, Captain Truman also heeded the warnings of Senator Vandenberg who, a reporter observed, opposed giving "the Russians—those barbarians—even the telephone number of plutonium."[128] Vandenberg linked the atomic issue to the contact issue. He opposed any atomic sharing until the Soviet Union ended the practice of "hermetically sealing herself" off from Western contacts.[129] Truman's reflexive response to complexity was to simplify issues. He now charged that his deal-making secretary of state had degenerated into a conniver.[130]

Byrnes probably wished he could navigate when his C-47 got lost in a blizzard on the flight from Berlin to Moscow. Nearly out of gas, the plane skimmed treetops searching for familiar farmhouses. Bohlen, State Department counselor (and Tommy Corcoran's former collaborator) Ben Cohen, and Harvard president and scientist James B. Conant were also on board. Awaiting them were Kennan and Harriman, both skeptical about renewing Big Three diplomacy. Kennan saw a portent in Byrnes's arrival. After the plane descended from a blur lacking any "distinction between sky and snow," the South Carolinian, wearing "a light coat and no overshoes," stood in the deep snow speaking into a howling wind.[131] Meanwhile, Stalin returned to Moscow fit and rested, thereby scotching rumors that he had succumbed to either illness or the Georgian princess. Queried by Byrnes on what he had been doing on holiday, the old charmer replied, "Reading your speeches."[132]

The U.S.-Soviet negotiations in Moscow proved more productive than any between Yalta and the 1963 atomic test ban accord. Byrnes accepted the pro-Soviet governments in Romania and Bulgaria with a fig leaf of broader popular inclusion. The Soviets, in turn, acceded to U.S. dominance in Japan. They headed off a confrontation between their troops in China but could not defuse the civil war there. Stalin, who had signed a comprehensive treaty with the anti-Communist Nationalists in August, predicted that "if the Chinese people became convinced that Chiang Kai-Shek was depending on foreign troops, he would lose his influence." Focusing on respect, the dictator promised "no objection if the United States wished to leave its troops" in northern China, but he "would merely like to be told about it."[133] Though skeptical about agreement, Byrnes had listed atomic weapons first on the agenda. Molotov downgraded it to third.

Yet Stalin stood ready to deal. When Molotov at a raucous banquet began joking that Conant had a bomb in his "waist-coat pocket," the *vozhd* cut him off, saying the bomb was "too serious a matter to joke about," and "we must work together to see that this great invention is used for peaceful ends." Conant reported that "much to everyone's surprise the Russians did not argue or talk back" about the U.S. proposal for sharing information in stages. They insisted only that the international Atomic Energy Commission report not to the UN General Assembly but to the Security Council, where Moscow enjoyed veto power.[134]

Byrnes's Rooseveltian deal making elicited Kennan's zealous opposition. Even before the secretary arrived, Kennan found himself "thoroughly enraged" over Soviet-American relations and his apparent impotence at redirecting them.[135] He resented the "insulting, total isolation" of diplomats as well as Washington's seeming indifference to both those indignities and his policy recommendations. Lack of contact rendered normal diplomacy "impossible," he fumed for the umpteenth time.[136] He and the other diplomats empathized as Bevin grew "furious" at Byrnes and his compromises. Kennan despised his boss as a naïf seeking "*an* agreement" to curry favor from what Kennan mistakenly believed was a still pro-Soviet American public. In contrast, Molotov, "eyes flashing," a cigarette dangling from his mouth, bet like the "passionate poker player who knows he has a royal flush."

Kennan acted on his anger by helping to sabotage Byrnes's diplomacy. Veteran diplomats H. Freeman "Doc" Matthews of the State Department and Alexander Cadogan of the Foreign Office already disliked the Soviets. Yet even they blanched when briefed by the Moscow crew. Kennan recorded that "Matthews looked so crestfallen at the things that he had heard from Roberts and myself I felt sorry for him." They likewise "shook Cadogan's composure." Kennan was testing the shock-strategy that would make his February 22 "long telegram" a blockbuster. He was frank about his technique. "In the introduction of newcomers to the realities of the Soviet Union there are always two processes; the first, which is to reveal what these realities are and the second, which is to help the newcomer to adjust himself to the shock."[137] In abetting this adjustment, the ambitious diplomat proffered his own prescription. He would contain the Soviets rather than cooperating or fighting with them.

Bohlen and Harriman also undercut Byrnes. While Kennan and Roberts shock-talked Mathews and Cadogan, Bohlen "apologized" to the British for Byrnes's reaching out to the Soviets. Harriman went further, dismissing these initiatives as "mistakes" borne of "inexperience." In an astounding arrogation of authority recalling his attempted overruling of Roosevelt's conciliatory cable to Stalin, Harriman assured the British that Byrnes's actions "did not reflect any policy of the Administration." Repairing relations with the Russians amounted to a failed "experiment. . . . The U.S. Government was absolutely solid with [London] on essentials."[138]

Freed of the opposition from Byrnes's subordinates and his boss, the December talks just might have slowed down or even stopped the slide toward the Cold War. Moscow newspapers celebrated the "reestablishment of Three Power unity and the necessity for Three Power consultation on world problems." Despite "reactionary elements abroad," collaboration with "the two great western democracies . . . has been strengthened and the new year opens hopefully."[139] Roberts reported that regarding the bomb, "the Russians now seem to be in a happier frame of mind." Gone was "the acute sense of grievance which has marked their attitude in recent months."[140]

The conference wrapped up at 3:30 a.m. on December 27. Byrnes felt "dead tired; all of us were."[141] Only hours later the sixty-six-year-old took off on the grueling flight to Washington. He arrived exhausted but satisfied. Yet all his efforts soon came to naught. Also exhausted was Truman's patience. Even before Moscow, he was complaining about having "to read the newspapers to get the U.S. foreign policy."[142] He had given the secretary full rein in London. But Moscow was different. Byrnes was buying agreement with concessions when many at home condemned such "appeasement." In Moscow he had not done enough to keep informed the former junior senator whom he still called "Harry." Imprudently, Byrnes planned a broadcast to the nation even before briefing Truman.

The president felt assailed on all fronts. Families blamed him for meat shortages. GIs impatient to get home rioted in Manila. Truman was mocked as the "poor perplexed little man of the White House," Isaiah Berlin reported.[143] Whispers circulated of "resignation."[144] Even Bess, furious that her husband made it back to Independence only on Christmas Day, treated him like "something the cat dragged in." He felt knocked off his perch as "a No. 1 man in the world."[145] Truman's insecurity heightened his sensitivity to criticism that his secretary of state had become an appeaser.

10.2. Months after Truman became president, Byrnes still called him "Harry." Tired of Byrnes's condescension and responding to political pressures, Truman repudiated Byrnes's Rooseveltian diplomacy at the December 1945 foreign ministers conference in Moscow. (Courtesy of Library of Congress.)

Despite long hours at his Oval Office desk, Truman remained short on perspective and patience. He simplified the disputes over Iran, Turkey, and Manchuria into cookie-cutter cases of Soviet aggression. He discerned neither the complex history nor the agency of local actors. Compromise solutions to these crises remained possible. But Truman had become fed up with ambiguity and compromise. Even his aged mother urged him to "get tough with someone."[146] On January 5, 1946, he bluntly told Byrnes that policy was changing. "I'm tired babying [the] Soviets." Rather than horse trade, Washington would now use "an iron fist and strong language."[147] The bite did not yet match the bark. Nevertheless, the conversation marked what Robert Messer, the historian of the Byrnes-Truman relationship, called the president's "personal declaration of the cold war."[148] A politician to the core, the South Carolinian bowed to the wind, starting with the subsequent crisis in Iran.

Sliding toward the Cold War

In 1907 and again in 1942, Iran had been divided into a Russian sphere in the north and a British zone in the south. During the war Americans upgraded the railroads so as to transport Lend-Lease to Russia. They also negotiated oil concessions. At the Tehran summit the Big Three agreed to evacuate troops within six months after the war. The Nazi lunge toward the Caucasus oil fields had focused the Kremlin's attention on the "struggle for oil." Stalin reminded his oil minister that tanks would be useless if a future enemy cut off oil supplies. The minister concluded they needed "much, much oil."[149] Aiming for oil and status at least equal to that of the British and Americans, the Soviets pressed for an oil concession in northern Iran. Late in 1944, the U.S. and British embassies advised Tehran to refuse the Soviet request. Iranians hoped Washington could check the Russians and the British. Stung, the Soviets violated a Big Three agreement by delaying withdrawal of their troops. They pressured Tehran by encouraging the pro-Communist Tudeh Party and separatist movements in the Azerbaijani and Kurdish areas of northern Iran. Stalin vetoed, however, the Tudeh's ambition to transform Iran into a wellspring of the global anticolonial struggle. He still aimed minimally for an oil concession and equal status.

Then Iran in January 1946 brought the issue of Soviet troops before the UN General Assembly meeting in London. Angry debate erupted. Molotov was dismayed to find that "nobody supported us."[150] With tensions rising also over Korea and Manchuria, an excited Truman announced that "we were going to war with Russia."[151] He acted on an earlier decision to send to the eastern Mediterranean a naval task force including the USS *Missouri*. Soviet archival documents clarify that Moscow withdrew not because of the naval force but because Tehran finally approved an oil concession. Soviet forces pulled out on May 9, 1946, after which Tehran reneged on the deal. Washington mistakenly concluded that getting tough worked.[152] Stalin also erred in not understanding how much his hardball tactics were angering U.S. and British opinion.

When Harriman's replacement, Walter Bedell Smith, arrived in Moscow in early April 1946, he asked, "How far is Russia going to go?" Stalin replied, "the Soviets demanded a base in the Dardanelles."[153] This was the narrow waterway linking the Black Sea with the Mediterranean and the seas beyond. The choke hold was, according to the Montreux Convention of 1936, controlled by Turkey, which had sympathized with Germany for most of the war. At Tehran and Yalta, the Americans and British had voiced support for revising Montreux in Russia's favor. Churchill had said he wanted to see Russian ships sailing the seven seas. At Potsdam, Truman had pushed for internationalizing waterways passing through several nations, but not the Dardanelles, which ran through only one. In 1945–46, Moscow sent diplomatic notes to Ankara requesting base rights. These were the very months when Washington was pressing for bases in Iceland, Greenland, North Africa, and Asia, even from reluctant governments. The furor in Washington exaggerated the danger to Turkey. To Clark Kerr, "Stalin spoke with the greatest contempt of the Turks as cowards and intriguers. But he stated categorically that there would be no military action against Turkey."[154] The U.S. Joint Chiefs of Staff concluded that "Soviet pressure in the Middle East" was defensive, with "its primary objective the protection of the vital Ploesti, Kharkov and Baku areas." Pentagon contingency plans, however, were already envisioning an attack against the Soviet Union through Turkey.[155]

In August 1945, Stalin had signed a treaty that recognized Nationalist leader Jiang Jieshi, the rival of Communist leader Mao Zedong, as the primary leader of China. The *vozhd* aimed at keeping China weak and divided. The Soviets pursued a warlord policy, helping Mao take over Japanese weapons and then insisting his troops leave some Manchurian cities. A shocked follower of Mao questioned the coldbloodedness. "The army of one Communist party using tanks to drive out the army of another Communist party?"[156] Such blindness to ideology grew increasingly difficult, however. A milestone of sorts was reached when U.S. Ambassador to China Patrick Hurley, who, according to his staff suffered from mental delusions, resigned in November 1945. Hurley charged that communists in the State Department were undermining him and Jiang Jieshi. Truman responded by blaming "parlor pinks" and by imposing Manichean explanations on the ambiguous situation in China as well as those in Turkey and Iran.

Despite the surge in "us-versus-them" ideology by early 1946, Moscow, unlike Washington and London, still preferred deal making. In late January, Harriman visited Japan, where he and MacArthur traded stories of Soviet iniquity. The general, Harriman reported, made "the extremely astute observation that what Stalin really wanted was [a] military alliance extended into the peace." The dictator sought to "continue the same type of relationship that existed during the war, which left each side to carry out their own operations to attain their individual objectives."[157] In early February, Byrnes, by then on board with Truman's get-tough policy, confided to Forrestal that the Soviets "were always eager" to confer. "They would like to discuss stability and peace with the United States alone" or with Britain as a third. Nevertheless, he had "discontinued the practice of having private meetings with the Russians."[158]

Stalin complained to Clark Kerr that Britain did not "treat the Russians as allies. All he wanted was to be trusted and treated as an ally." Was Stalin sincere? Although the dictator was a skilled actor, the ambassador was skilled at reading emotions. He reported that the "grievance seemed genuine and was brought out very emphatically"[159] The Soviet transcript of this conversation also reveals the *vozhd* sounding personally aggrieved: "Nobody obliges Bevin to love the Soviet Union—he can even hate the Soviet Union—but it is necessary to restrain yourself."[160]

However sincere, the old Bolshevik remained a committed Marxist-Leninist. He believed the future belonged to his brand of socialism. Stalin's apparently preferred strategy in Eastern Europe was to encourage local communists to spearhead broad coalitions that could win and hold power without resorting to dictatorship or help from the Red Army. This "national front" strategy depended on reasonably good relations with Washington and London, so that opposition parties in Eastern Europe would tend to cooperate with rather than defy leftist coalitions. Continuing the wartime coalition was also key to heading off a dangerous resurgence of Germany and Japan. If the national front strategy had succeeded, much of Eastern Europe might have adopted popular leftist governments assuaging Soviet security and ideological concerns. In the immediate aftermath of the war, discerning Eastern Europeans believed that the degree of Soviet control in their countries was not fixed but rather open-ended. The Finnish solution might indeed have prevailed more widely. What jinxed this development was the brutality of the Soviet occupation, which antagonized millions in Eastern and Central Europe, and deteriorating relations with Washington and London, which gave Stalin no economic or political incentives to refrain from the repression that came so naturally to him.[161] Though ready to concede Eastern Europe to the Soviets, Roosevelt had hoped that in the difficult postwar transition, Big Three meetings could induce Soviet restraint. Truman wanted no such get-togethers.

Even when Roosevelt was around, Stalin had undermined the alliance with his merciless, obstinate, and narrow-minded policies. He did not relieve the social isolation that embittered foreign diplomats and journalists, that is, the influential people who shaped outside perceptions of the Soviet Union. He waited far too long before reining in the atrocities committed by Red Army soldiers. He ignored Roosevelt's plea to paper over annexation of the Baltic states with Mississippi-style "elections." He treated liberated U.S. and British POWs callously. He did not muzzle the vociferously anticapitalist Soviet press. On February 9, 1946, he gave a major speech that insulted Washington and London by failing to mention Lend-Lease, the Western front, or the ships ferrying supplies through icy, submarine-infested waters. His aggressive espionage also antagonized. After his August 1939 pact with Hitler, Stalin had reversed on a dime years of anti-Nazi propaganda. Little wonder he remained deaf to the warnings of Litvinov and Maisky against angering U.S. and British opinion. He needlessly and, yes, foolishly, made it easy for Harriman and others to push for confrontation.

In his last days at the Moscow Embassy, Harriman lectured Americans on the contrasting reactions to Byrnes's horse trading. "Russians are satisfied with the Moscow Conference. They had been concerned over the break and were worried about where it would end." In Washington, however, Byrnes was slapped down because "he wasn't aggressive enough." Harriman saw such criticism as "a good thing as it will make greater pressure against further acceptance of Russian actions." Complacent public opinion remained a challenge, he admitted. The American people needed to be shocked into accepting that "there is no settlement with Russia and that this is a continuing thing." Once the public was disciplined, Washington could call the shots. "England is so weak she must follow our leadership. She will do anything that we insist."[162] Harriman's teaching would have a rippling effect.

Plans for postwar economic collaboration through a U.S. loan to be repaid with Soviet raw materials were going nowhere. In September, Stalin had asked why there had been no reply to the Soviets' January 1945 request for a $6 billion loan. He again dangled the prospect of Russia's "boundless" import market, saying it would be "suicidal" not to convert to a peacetime economy.[163] As Harriman and Kennan had urged, the loan was made contingent on political concessions in Eastern Europe, which the Soviets refused. Moscow was also backing away from cooperation with the International Monetary Fund and the World Bank, institutions that Washington hoped would foster a vibrant capitalist economy.[164]

Confrontation was winning out just as Harry Hopkins was losing his final battle. He died on January 29, 1946. Though Hopkins in his last year had adopted much of Bohlen's hard-line perspective, the former "assistant president" remained a symbol of Big Three deal making. Over dinner a subdued Ambassador Gromyko confided to Stettinius that he found "very strange" the "complete change" in Washington officials since FDR's death. Himself a former Hopkins protégé, Stettinius contrasted the "real reaction of distress and sympathy on the part of Gromyko over Hopkins's illness" with the "rather cold reaction from men like Churchill, Harriman, and Bohlen, all of whom were devoted friends of Hopkins."[165] Much seemed topsy-turvy.

Indeed, the whole world appeared "bewildered, baffled, and breathless," Churchill wrote to Truman in January.[166] Dizzying change appeared on every front: the devastation of the war, the suddenness of the peace, the disappearance of Roosevelt and Churchill, the bomb, economic dislocation, wrangling over Eastern Europe, revelation of Soviet spying, colonial unrest, the London debacle, the repudiated Moscow talks, and crises over Iran, Turkey, and Manchuria.[167] Uncertainties plagued even the victor nations. What were the lessons of the war? What was their postwar role and identity? What had happened to the alliance? Was the wartime ally now an enemy? Did a more terrible war loom? What had the atomic bomb wrought? How best to respond to the postwar crisis?

Ideological Manifestos: Stalin, Churchill, and Kennan

Though many proffered answers, the most enduring voices came from Stalin, Churchill, and Kennan. During February and March, each of them stamped events with his overarching, attention-grabbing explanation. "How should our victory over the enemies be interpreted?" Stalin queried before instructing the Soviet people in his February 9 election address. In his "Iron Curtain" speech on March 5, Churchill promised "the facts as I see them." "Nothing but the whole truth would do," Kennan later wrote in justifying the "long telegram" he sent the State Department on February 22.[168]

Each of the three manifestos was simplified, comprehensive, and culturally resonant—in a word, ideological. Ideology offered easy-to-grasp answers and reaffirmed cultural norms. While the dictator could command attention, the former prime minister and the diplomat used emotional rhetoric and imagery to attract notice. Each eruption set off an international tidal wave. Yet each proclamation also reflected inner, even personal, aspirations. Such inner motivations would remain masked or ignored as the manifestos were deployed in the emerging Cold War. The emotional and ideological nature of these declarations made it dangerously easy for others to extrapolate conclusions more extreme than their authors probably intended. In contrast to the long telegram, Churchill's Fulton speech was populated with actual persons, places, and events. Nevertheless, those two statements were alike in exploiting worries and then offering a simplified, in some ways reassuring, message. Stalin's election speech was similarly ideological. The dictator failed to give adequate credit to the Allies, or even to the Red Army, in winning the war. Still, he refrained from demonizing or even attacking the U.S. and British governments. The foil against which he projected the Soviet Union's shining success was a critical "foreign press." While Churchill and Kennan fed anxieties in order mobilize support for, respectively, a special relationship, and a revitalized America and Western Europe, Stalin stoked pride and a bit of fear to justify continued Communist rule.

Despite his autocratic power, the Kremlin chief faced massive problems at home. Many non-Russian nationalities had welcomed Nazi invaders. A million captured Red Army soldiers had sided with the Germans. Other millions had flocked to the Communist Party without ideological indoctrination. Many hoped the victorious military would check the Communist Party. Soldiers had marveled at luxuries, such as wooden floors, common outside the "workers' paradise." The Kremlin added to its woes by swallowing non-Russian territories. Kennan reported "genuine concern in Moscow over lack of enthusiasm for [the] Soviet system in newly acquired areas."[169] An avid reader of history, Stalin knew that nationalist dissent had undermined czarist rule. Army officers exposed to the outside world had revolted after the Napoleonic wars. Soviet citizens expected a better life. The dictator did not have to be paranoid to worry. Even had the Big Three stayed together, he probably would have tightened control. U.S. and British opposition in Eastern Europe made Communism even more important as a tool of power.

Nevertheless—and this is a key point—Stalin apparently did not believe that his emphasis on ideology mandated a cold war. He emphasized to Harriman that ideologies "related only to the internal policies." With "respect to foreign affairs it seemed to him that the two countries could find common ground. The United States would arrange their internal life according to their desires. The Soviet people would do the same."[170]

To "arrange" that "internal life" Stalin had to persuade his people that their victory sprang primarily not from love for Mother Russia nor from the valor of the Red Army but rather from Communist ideology. According to this narrative, the terrible sacrifices inflicted by Stalin's collectivization, industrialization, and purges had proven his foresight. To foster this myth Party officials choreographed a pageant: the election for the Supreme Soviet, the first since 1937. Observers marveled at the "gigantic campaign of ideological re-indoctrination . . . through all the resources of the press, radio, cinema."[171] "Countless banners and slogans" boosted the February 10 election as "a major public holiday."[172] Foreigners understandably ridiculed "voting" without a choice of candidates. Soviet leaders, however, participated in their civic sacraments piously. Nominal President Kalinin explained that "our elections act as a universal review" by the rank and file.[173] The campaign would "rally our people still closer," Molotov enthused.[174] The hoopla culminated with the *vozhd*'s speech, "New Five-Year Plan for Russia."

The structure of this seventy-seven-paragraph manifesto points up its complex message. The first five paragraphs underscored Stalin's Marxist bona fides by blaming "monopoly capitalism" for the two world wars. The next five moderated that ideology by shifting the category of analysis from economic to political systems. In contrast to the "Fascist States" that had crushed "bourgeois democratic liberties" was the victorious "anti-Fascist coalition of the Soviet Union, the United States of America, Great Britain and other freedom-loving countries." Because of that lineup, the second world war differed "radically" from the first. Then followed fifty-two paragraphs of the core thesis. It was the Communist Party—Stalinism—that had enabled the Red Army to win and the multinational state to hold together. The argument made military power subsidiary. There followed five paragraphs detailing a future upsurge in heavy industrial and consumer production and in scientific development that by implication included the atomic bomb. He wrapped up with eight paragraphs extolling the organization of the Party.[175]

In America the speech sparked exaggerated reactions. Forrestal and Supreme Court Justice William O. Douglas saw a "Declaration of World War III."[176] Not understanding the Kremlin's aim to reshape memory of past sacrifices, Lippmann titled his column, "Stalin Chooses Military Power." He informed readers, "there is no mystery now about the central purpose of the Soviet Union." The essay fed into the popular myth that America's global empire arose solely in defense. "Now that Stalin has made the decision to make military power his first objective, we are forced to make a corresponding decision," namely, to "reinforce, rebuild and modernize the industrial power of Western Europe" while helping develop Asia and the Middle East. Americans could succeed only "if we have the moral energy," that is, the righteousness and drive.[177] Kennan in his long telegram would similarly follow up his scary depiction of Kremlin intentions by recommending not a militarized competition but rather building up a U.S.-led Western community. Apprehension at the speech probably also stemmed from Stalin's de facto declaration of economic independence. U.S. leaders, particularly Harriman, had confidently assumed that the Soviets' need for an American loan would keep them on a short leash. Stalin instead announced an economic race.

The *New York Times* headline, "Stalin Sets a Huge Output near Ours in 5-Year Plan," glossed over the overwhelming lead the United States would still command. While Stalin called for Soviet steel production of sixty million tons in 1960, the United States had reached ninety million tons in 1944. (The body of the article did mention that the Soviet goals were for 1960.) The *Times* story focused on Stalin's economic aims and his blaming the wars on capitalism. It ignored the core of the speech exhorting pride in the Communist system.[178]

In the first, hard-line Marxist section, Stalin described the two world wars as "the inevitable result" of the "uneven development of capitalist countries" that resorted to armed force to secure raw materials and markets.[179] That claim stung. As a British Embassy official observed, with capitalism "still the nearest thing to a universal religion in the United States, Americans resented "denunciation of so

cherished a creed."[180] One did not have to denounce capitalism, however, to note that Germany in World War I and the Axis in World War
II had gone to war to gain resources, territory, and markets. Stalin did
not regard war between capitalist and communist nations as inevitable. In a world where capitalist nations demonstrably did clash,
prudence dictated that Moscow defend itself from another invasion
while advancing its interests. Such commonsense principles of foreign
relations reflected little that was uniquely Marxist. The implications
of Stalin's analysis of capitalism and war fit rather with his comment
to Harriman that Russia would isolate itself if Big Three collaboration died.

Stalin churlishly referred to the Alliance without even mentioning
Lend-Lease. Acknowledging foreign aid did not fit his thesis that
Communism had secured victory. Americans and Britons understand-
ably resented this omission and his neglect of the UN. Nevertheless,
this distortion came in the context of his focus on the domestic scene.
He did not even mention Moscow's new "allies" in Eastern Europe.
After the speech, Moscow radio stressed in an English broadcast the
Soviet desire to make the UN "truly effective."[181] The implication was
a UN run by the big powers.

Curiously, Americans passed over the core of the speech wherein
Stalin invested most effort. In contrast to his laconic recitation of
Marxist dogma, he waxed loquacious about how industrialization
had taken only thirteen years. To him the appalling cost in destroyed
lives and environments meant little. What counted was preserving the
Stalinist system. It had skirted collapse. The dictator had ignored
warnings before the invasion and had incurred military disasters afterward. Many non-Communists and non-Russian nationalities had
seized on the war as an opportunity to escape. For reasons of pride
and politics, Stalin sought to harness the undeniable fact of victory to
two shakier propositions. First, that victory had proven the Soviet
social system the most efficient in the world. Second, that the triumph
had demonstrated the Soviet Union's permanence as a multinational state. This was what "victory means," he insisted. He peppered
his remarks with so many affirmations—such as "everybody now
recognizes"—as to signal insecurity.[182]

Nine times in six consecutive sentences he hammered home that the Soviet Union would not break up like Austria-Hungary. (His prediction would hold true for merely forty-five years.) In trying to recast actual ethnic rebellion as a myth of national solidarity, the Kremlin chief had little to work with other than ideological dogma. He argued that the Soviet system ensured "fraternal collaboration between the peoples of our state." Barely six months after victory he was downplaying the Red Army. He mocked "swell-headedness." Victory was owed primarily to the Communists. For twenty-five statistic-laden paragraphs, he droned on about breathtaking leaps in steel, oil, cotton, and arms production under the Five-Year plans. He took proprietary pride in the progress from the czar's world war, when "one rifle was issued for every three soldiers." The speech carried foreign implications by celebrating the Soviet system as a model for the world. Yet in all these many paragraphs he said nary a word about exporting the model.

After justifying his past rule, he turned to the future. He mentioned, first, that "the rationing system will be abolished, special attention will be focused on expanding the production of goods for mass consumption, on raising the standard of life of the working people." Even though true-believing Communists packed the audience, these points drew the most applause. In view of Western reactions that the speech signaled another war, it is striking that Stalin featured, first, not heavy industry nor military production but rather consumer products. The second priority was science, which implied developing an atomic bomb. Two weeks earlier he had told the head of the Soviet project to spare no expense in getting a bomb quickly. Third were plans for a "new mighty upsurge" of the economy, a threefold increase in heavy industry over prewar levels. This would require three or more Five-Year plans. "Only under such conditions"—that is, with the rise in living standards, science, and heavy industry—"will our country be insured against any eventuality."[183]

Did "any eventuality" signal aggression? The British Embassy interpreted the Russian word to mean "hazards," "accidents," or "contingencies." That did not necessarily mean war, let alone aggressive war. In view of the recent Russian experience of invasion in the two world wars, intervention in the civil war, and the shock of Hiroshima, preparing for any eventuality seems more precautionary than belligerent. Isaiah Berlin, just returned from Moscow, believed that "Stalin would be surprised" that his speech "was so alarming."[184] Even Roberts, usually quick to criticize the Kremlin, acknowledged the "special attention to consumer goods and improving standard of living." In fact, Stalin was demobilizing much of the Red Army, reducing its numbers from 11.3 million in May 1945 to 2.8 million in 1947.[185]

In sum, Stalin's manifesto focused on reshaping the memory of prewar and wartime experiences so as to legitimate both the Communist Party's future rule and further sacrifices in rebuilding the nation. Yet even wholesale myth making could not alter memory of sacrifices for, above all, Mother Russia. It remained the "Great Patriotic War." Nevertheless, in ensuing decades as the great future of true Communism receded into cynical platitudes, memory of the war as the "great past" did legitimate the Soviet system. Observers would later note that the USSR itself lasted only as long as the World War II generation.

The shoving grew rougher in the month between the manifestos of Stalin and Churchill. Harriman stayed in Washington to advise on "our policy toward Soviet Russia."[186] Truman ordered Byrnes "to stiffen up and try for the next three months not to make any compromises."[187] The latter soon inveighed against Soviet domination in Bulgaria, Romania, Albania, and Austria. He ventured deeper into the Iran crisis while shoring up Italy. He loaded up a prospective $1 billion credit to Russia with enough political conditions to sink it. He and Truman in effect scuttled the atomic accord reached in Moscow by choosing Bernard Baruch as delegate to the UN Atomic Energy Commission. Baruch lacked sympathy for the State Department's Acheson-Lilienthal plan, a watered-down version of the Stimson proposal for atomic sharing by stages. The New Deal veteran David Lilienthal lamented, "We need a man who is young, vigorous, not vain, and whom the Russians would feel isn't out simply to put them in a hole, not really caring about international cooperation. Baruch has none of these qualifications."[188] Baruch stripped from the proposal the great powers' veto power. That doomed any chance of Soviet acceptance.

The veto power in the UN Security Council enshrined the first principle of the Big Three: no one of the three could coerce another. Byrnes hacked away at the provision. "The mere legal veto" did not trump the "moral obligation to act in accordance" with the United Nations Charter, he asserted in a major speech. The charter remained a vague document, affording wide scope for self-appointed "moral obligations." Driving his point home, Byrnes affirmed, "Veto or no veto," America would intervene in crucial issues.[189]

A steady drumbeat assailed the Soviets. On February 26, Baruch followed up a visit to Churchill with a speech blasting the Kremlin. Vandenberg weighed in on the 27th, Byrnes on the 28th, John Foster Dulles on March 1, and Joseph Kennedy on March 3.[190] Meanwhile, Truman ordered into the Black Sea straits the battleship *Missouri* in order to return the ashes of the Turkish ambassador. Only months earlier Japan had surrendered aboard this symbol of U.S. military might.[191]

Stalin also threw punches. He pushed crudely in Iran, the Dardanelles, Manchuria, and elsewhere. He ordered one of his henchman, Andrei Zhdanov, to mobilize a xenophobic campaign against foreign culture. The dictator's preoccupation with respect for himself, his nation, and his system mushroomed to bizarre proportions. What became known as the *Zhdanovshchina* movement drew also on Slavophilism and traditional Russian suspicions of the West. The result further closed off the Soviet Union from Western influence while heightening the antagonism of those like Kennan who longed to partake in Russian culture.[192]

While the *vozhd* focused on justifying his system, the former prime minister aimed at reviving his spirits and the Anglo-American alliance. "Shame" gnawed at Churchill that his "wonderful years" had ended in humiliation at the polls.[193] Clementine confided that they were constantly fighting because "he is so unhappy & that makes him very difficult."[194] He admitted, "I am very depressed." He remained "out of a job, looking for something to do, anything to keep his mind away from the past," his doctor worried. There were "flies buzzing round this old decaying carcass," Churchill grumbled; he had to find "something to keep them away."[195] Also humiliating was pressure from party bosses to step down as leader of the Conservatives. Bulldog-defiant, he would hang on, a friend observed, "till he becomes Prime Minister on earth or Defence Minister in Heaven."[196]

Rescue came from what had always saved him. Razzle-dazzle oratory had fueled the rise of his fantasy-hero *Savrola* and his real-life career. A game-changing speech would defy detractors. He would resuscitate the tie to America by pumping the Soviet threat. Churchill seized on an invitation from Westminster College in Fulton, Missouri. An alumnus, Harry Vaughan, who happened to be Truman's military aide, had secured a promise from the president to introduce the speaker. The spectacle of Truman and Churchill appearing together in a town of 6,500 in the heartland guaranteed global attention.

In contrast to Stalin, who downplayed immediate war, Churchill highlighted the danger. Britain was "going to have a war with Russia," he predicted.[197] Sounding that alarm could restore his authority, as it had done in the late 1930s. Closer ties with Washington remained London's best hope for averting a conflict or for winning it. The ex-PM also appreciated the dollars-and-cents aspect. The British loan bill in Congress faced tough sledding. Americans by a 60 percent to 27 percent margin opposed the lending. (These were also the precise poll numbers for a possible loan to Russia, which the administration had not proposed.) Even among the minority of Americans favoring the loan, only one out of sixteen cited the need for London as an ally.[198] By emphasizing the "Soviet threat" Britain could tap support while escaping U.S. tutelage. Diplomat Ben Cohen reported that London "was almost hysterical in refusing to accept the fact that now it wasn't even a 'Secondary Power.'"[199]

From the British Embassy in Washington, Isaiah Berlin observed that Stalin's speech had rendered "a considerable service to us."[200] Others in the Foreign Office agreed "that when Soviet-U.S. relations are bad, our own press in America is correspondingly improved. So while the Loan hangs in the balance and ... we need American support in Persia, Palestine & over India, this critical Soviet line may at least be turned to some account."[201] The day after Stalin's manifesto Churchill talked about his upcoming speech with Truman and

Leahy. They waxed "enthusiastic" about "full military collaboration" with Britain.[202]

While Stalin claimed that ideology had banished ethnic discord, Churchill argued for ideology based on racial unity. In a series of lectures he promoted the ideology of freedom as "the joint inheritance of the English speaking world." Only months after the German defeat he lauded "the great Bismarck" for recognizing the common language of Americans and Britons as "the most important fact in the world."[203]

Before the Virginia Assembly, founded as an offshoot of Parliament in 1619, he waxed lyrical about the Magna Carta, Shakespeare, "and even George Washington."[204] In categorizing nations according to the ideology of freedom, the Victorian imperialist ran up against Americans' distaste for formal empire. His determination to hang on to the colonies had irritated Roosevelt, and 56 percent of Americans agreed that the British ranked as "oppressors." Of those concerned about India, an eight-to-one margin favored immediate independence.[205] Churchill tried to fudge the issue of independence by referring to "our great self-governing Empire."[206] He realized that playing up Moscow's new empire in Eastern Europe might get London off the hook.

As Churchill and Truman drank brandy, joked, and played poker on the train out of Washington, some twenty-five thousand visitors, including a flock of reporters, packed the town. The *Daily Sun-Gazette* gloried in Fulton's "Biggest Day in History." No longer depressed, Churchill looked "cherubic, pink-cheeked, and very fit." The master of ceremonies, Westminster College president Franc "Bullet" McCluer, won *Time* magazine's accolade as a "whirlwind of energy and salesmanship. . . . Never had Bullet shot so high." McCluer tried not to let the balloons, flags, and bands get out of hand. "This is a serious lecture, not a football game," he instructed. In homage to Churchill's love of beef, a twenty-seven pound roast was prepared for the dinner following the speech. Lunch featured the wellspring of local pride, Callaway County hickory-smoked ham. The churchwomen serving lunch were not disappointed. "In this ham," Churchill assured them, "the pig has reached its highest form of evolution."[207]

His speech appealed to another kind of pride, and then to anxiety. The United States had reached "the pinnacle of world power," he began. But danger threatened. His rhetoric seemed intent on heightening unease. He emphasized "this sad and breathless moment," "these anxious and baffling times," this "still agitated, and ununited world." "Beware, I say; time may be short." "You must feel anxiety." With atomic war, "the Stone Age may return." Echoing Harriman's warning about a "barbarian invasion," he warned that "Christian civilization" lay imperiled. (Truman amplified the apocalyptic mood by advising reporters that two alternatives loomed: "complete destruction" or "the greatest age in history.")[208]

Back in the world of actual diplomacy, compromises and contradictions remained unavoidable. Churchill himself had haggled with Stalin over the Balkans in October 1944. The speaker in Fulton—unlike Roosevelt reporting to Congress on Yalta—did not try to educate Americans about such complexity. To the contrary, he used his authority to advocate "grand simplicity" in deciding what he insisted were "high and simple causes." While pushing for "fraternal association" between "kindred systems of society," he condemned tyranny outside the family circle. He intimated a later rollback of Soviet power: "It is not our duty at this time when difficulties are so numerous to interfere forcibly in the internal affairs of countries which we have not conquered in war." In the meantime, "let us preach what we practice—let us practice what we preach." Given the rise of leftist movements around the globe, he dared not champion untrammeled capitalism. Moreover, he hoped Britain's imperial economic system could resist U.S. assault. Far safer was championing the free association of individuals, which could open other doors. "Above all we welcome constant, frequent and growing contacts between the Russian people and our own people."

Churchill cloaked himself with the authority of a prophet: "Last time I saw it all coming." The phrase "last time" played on fears of Soviets as Nazi-like. To undercut charges he was warmongering, he stressed that the Soviets did not want war and that they deserved security from invasion. He proposed extending the 1942 Anglo-Soviet treaty from twenty to fifty years. Yet he also encouraged anxiety of an unknowable, alien force. Twice he warned of the "indefinite expansion" of the Soviets and Communism.[209] Vague, unlimited expansion seemed nightmarish. In the arena of concrete diplomacy, however, Stalin's claims had changed little since he had talked with Eden in December 1941. Despite the dictator's ideological campaign at home and manipulation of Communist assets abroad, he was in early 1946 still reining in would-be revolutionaries in France, Italy, and China.[210]

With much still in flux, Europe was not yet divided between East and West. Largely free elections in Hungary and Czechoslovakia had or would take place. Finland maintained a cautious independence. Western troops occupied three out of four zones in Berlin and Vienna. Soviet writ was not absolute even in Poland. Such ambiguity was lost in Churchill's magnificent cadence. An already divided Europe was a "fact," he instructed. "Our difficulties and dangers will not be removed by closing our eyes to them." His most memorable words marched across history and geography, drawing alliterative force with their sweep from T's to B's: "From Stettin in the Baltic to Trieste in the Adriatic, an iron curtain has descended across the Continent. Behind that line lie all the capitals of the ancient states of Central and Eastern Europe. Warsaw, Berlin, Prague, Vienna, Budapest, Belgrade, Bucharest and Sofia." The ideology of freedom had apparently wiped away British repression. "Athens alone—Greece with its immortal glories—is free to decide its future."

Sensationalizing the Soviet threat primed the pitch for a "special relationship." An exclusive atomic partnership with America held out the only sane alternative to the "criminal madness" of sharing the "secret." Churchillian rhetoric twisted the equipoise of the Big Three into something inherently weak and implicitly unmasculine: "a quivering, precarious balance of power." He urged instead an "overwhelming assurance of security." Unfortunately, however, such preponderance of power ensured a cold war or worse unless the Soviets knuckled under.

Respect remained a touchy matter, whether in the context of the Grand Alliance or the Cold War. Churchill made a dangerous argument that would be repeated by Kennan and others: Only a tough stance was appreciated by the Russians. "There is nothing they admire so much as strength and there is nothing for which they have less respect than for weakness, especially military weakness."[211] With Stalin's explicit blessing, the historian Eugeni Tarle shot back: "Up to now those who tried to 'show strength' to the Russian people have always and without exception lost in this undertaking."[212]

The Soviets, unfortunately, pursued the same dangerous tactic. They believed that by having enough strength to spark the other side's fear and humiliation, they would gain security and respect. In the "election" campaign, Georgi Malenkov urged strengthening the armed forces so that "friends will respect us."[213] Lazar Kaganovich, a comrade of Stalin who would die only months before the demise of the Soviet Union, agreed. "The weak one is always beaten and abused, while the strong one is feared and respected."[214]

Truman predicted that Churchill's message "would do nothing but good, though it would make a stir."[215] To aides and reporters he denied having read the speech beforehand—though that claim apparently hung on his having seen only "a mimeographed reproduction."[216] The publicity gratified Churchill, confident that he had delivered the "most important speech of my career."[217] Sixty-eight percent of Americans polled knew about "C-T Day"—and they rejected military cooperation with Britain by a two-to-one margin.[218] Truman then made a show of distancing himself from the unpopular measure. Eleanor Roosevelt reportedly told Churchill to his face that he was "desecrating the ideals for which my husband gave his life."[219] Perhaps it also struck her that the former prime minister in his speech had failed even to mention FDR.

The discursive shift toward the Cold War steamed along. At the Achesons' dinner party, "Mrs. Acheson spoke in lyrical terms" about the speech, Wallace recorded in his diary. Also present were Richard Casey, the Australian minister; the Bohlens; and the Lippmanns. "Casey spoke of the Russians as being beasts." The spread of Spaso House stove-talk made advocacy for the Grand Alliance seem transgressive. When Wallace urged reviving the Big Three, Casey "interjected very brusquely, 'We might as well talk about a trip to the moon.'" "Bohlen made fun of the idea" that the Soviets felt encircled by U.S. and British bases. Wallace concluded that "Bohlen, Acheson, and Casey all think that the United States and England should run the risk of immediate war with Russia by taking a very hard-boiled stand and being willing to use force."[220]

Although "Operation Unthinkable" had warned of the obstacles in smashing Russia, that was before Hiroshima. Churchill probably expected to avoid war. But he had warned Lord Moran it would come. And his eloquence licensed many on both sides of the "Iron Curtain" to plan for, and push to the brink of, war. Some evidence suggests a darker reading of his intentions. After Fulton, Lippmann urged "trying to make a peace" rather than "merely preparing for war." He pointed up the contradiction between the ideology of freedom and insistence on colonial rule.[221] Angry at the criticism of his father, Randolph Churchill invited Lippmann to lunch. Clearly drunk, he blurted out, "We'll show you. We'll show you. . . . We dragged you into two wars, and we'll drag you into the third." Lippmann remembered the talk as "undoubtedly reflecting *something* of the old man—who never would have said anything like that."[222]

Although Stalin railed against Churchill, especially when playing the tough guy to subordinates, he retained some respect for his old foe and comrade. In the July 1945 British election, the Soviets had preferred Churchill because he was a known quantity and because Labor figured as a competitor for the left wing. When Churchill lost, Molotov "went white." "What does it mean?" he had demanded of Moran. "What will happen?"[223] The *vozhd* also valued the former prime minister as a foil against Bevin and Attlee. To Clark Kerr in late January he made "extremely cordial" references to Churchill and Eden, adding that "he would probably have come to London under the Conservatives, under Churchill, but he would not go there under the present government."[224] Such personal feelings probably sharpened his response to Fulton.

In an interview on March 13 in *Tass*, Stalin sounded like someone betrayed. His anger zeroed in on personal affronts, on Churchill's "discourtesy and tactless[ness]." Speaking as if the alliance were still viable, he condemned the speech as "dangerous" because it would "sow the seeds of dissension among the Allied States and impede their collaboration." Imputation of inferiority drove him to fury. Sounding like Hitler, Churchill had hatched a "race theory" that "only English-speaking nations are full-fledged nations." Like the Nazis, he "call[ed] for war on the USSR." Lingering humiliation from Hitler's betrayal probably swelled this rage. How could Churchill attack as "'expansive tendencies'" the Soviets' goal of securing friendly neighbors?

With phrasing suggesting outrage directed at a fellow player rather than an out-and-out enemy, he called criticism of the new Polish-German frontier "plainly cheating." He appealed to the authority of the Big Three at Potsdam. "It was not only the Russians, but the British and Americans as well, that voted for the decision." Only in conclusion did the diatribe appeal to the Marxist "law of historical development." That ideology would triumph over anti-Communist "Don-Quixotery," he crowed.[225] Meanwhile Tarle, with Stalin's approval, disputed Churchill's assertion that the determining factor in postwar relations was "irreconcilable ideologies."[226] Speaking "very strongly" to the new U.S. ambassador in early April, the Kremlin boss deplored Fulton as "an unwarranted attack on himself and the USSR." Russia "is not stupid," he felt compelled to say.[227] Open fighting between the remaining Big Two sparked "hysterical reactions by the Soviet public," Roberts reported. "All available bread was being bought up."[228] Soviet authorities stepped in to reassure that neither side intended war. Churchill publicly agreed. Nevertheless, "the hysteria on both sides" persisted, a close observer worried.[229]

U.S. officials absorbing the Fulton speech were hit with another whammy on the same day. On March 5, the State Department circulated to U.S. diplomats around the world Kennan's 5,540-word telegram dispatched on February 22. The logic, rhetoric, and imagery of this emotionally gripping manifesto would do much to define the Cold War.

A letter Kennan sent to friends in the State Department on January 21 reveals the personal frustrations underlying the long telegram written a month later. For all his "authority, objectivity, and courage" regarding Soviet affairs, he had garnered little influence on U.S. policy. Fault only began with deficiencies at the top (read: Byrnes at Moscow) and with the limits on career diplomats. More basic were the public's "lack of understanding of the realities" of world affairs and the "general deficiencies of our governmental system." Kennan, who would acknowledge feeling more at home in the eighteenth than in the twentieth century, saw the fundamental problem as the very nature of U.S. society. Unless he could somehow springboard out of his "subordinate position," he would probably resign and "try to influence public opinion at home along the lines of my own convictions."[230]

Kennan looked to Bullitt, with whom he, like Bohlen, had remained close, as someone who might assist in this new venture. He often stayed at the former ambassador's home when in Washington. While finding in American society "much to disturb a thoughtful person," the scholarly diplomat counted his former boss among "the very few who could understand" such problems.[231] Those problems began with the excessive individualism and commercialization of U.S. society. In 1938, Kennan had mused on "the truly wonderful fashion" in which Americans responded to flood or war. He would "welcome almost any social cataclysm, however painful, and however costly, that would carry away something of this stuffy individualism and force" a rebuilding of community.[232]

To U.S. foreign service officers in Portugal in June 1944, he had warned of "a very cruel test." He said nothing about a Soviet threat. Rather he worried that women working in factories and workers spoiled by high wages were corrupting traditional American values. He predicted to fellow diplomats—in his eyes, a disinterested elite— that they might have to "take a prominent part" in solving "some of the really crucial internal problems." Trying to dramatize his appeal for domestic reform, he first wrote the verb *develop*, then crossed it out and replaced it with *define*, then crossed that out and settled on *defend* as his action verb. With this metaphor for combat in place, he exhorted, "if we are going to defend successfully . . . things like independence of speech and thought, honesty and courage of public life, dignity and quiet and serenity of the home and family . . . we had better start arming ourselves right now intellectually and morally for what is coming: for some pretty unpleasant and tough fighting." One wonders how his listeners conceptualized this intellectual and moral combat. When Kennan used such military metaphors in 1946–47 in warning about the Kremlin, Americans, to his later consternation, thought in terms of armies and atomic bombs.[233]

A few weeks after sending his tentative letter of resignation, he received a request for a major "interpretive analysis."[234] Kennan later dramatized the invitation. "Here was a case where nothing but the whole truth would do. They had asked for it. Now, by God, they would have it."[235] The "whole truth" of the long telegram actually invoked a fantastic scenario in which leaders of the Soviet Union appeared as an inhuman force, without morality, beyond the appeal of reason, unable to appreciate objective fact or truth, and compelled to destroy almost every decent aspect of life in the West. Kennan put front and center what had infuriated him since Stalin's crackdown on personal contact after 1934. The "most disquieting feature of diplomacy in Moscow" remained the isolation from Soviet policymakers, whom one cannot "see and cannot influence."[236]

At the end of the long telegram, Kennan assured his readers that the Soviet Union did not want war, stood weaker than the United States, and could be contained without war if the United States and Western Europe took the necessary steps. Yet it was his emotionalized depiction of the Soviet threat and his militarized language that grabbed attention. He described the Kremlin as "impervious to [the] logic of reason and ... highly sensitive to [the] logic of force. The United States should apply such logic of force with "political general staff work ... approached with [the] same thoroughness and care as [the] solution of [a] major strategic problem in war."[237] Not surprisingly, many readers concluded that containment required a massive American military buildup.

Kennan's narrow ideological focus nearly omitted World War II and the alliance that had won it. Totally unmentioned were even the words "Big Three," "ally," or "alliance." Stalin, whom Churchill at Fulton saluted as "my wartime comrade," appeared in the long telegram only as a shadowy figure, haranguing an audience in 1927 about the "battle" between capitalism and socialism. With graphic language, the long telegram drove home the argument that the Kremlin's rigid ideology, coupled with its "neurotic view of world affairs" and the need for a foreign enemy to justify domestic repression, locked Mos-

10.3. In this photograph of Kennan sitting at his desk in Moscow, the calendar is open to the 22nd of the month, the day in February 1946 when he dictated the long telegram. (Courtesy of the Seeley G. Mudd Manuscript Library, Princeton University.)

cow into unrelenting aggression against the West. The hostile premises of Soviet ideology were "simply not true," Kennan argued. To the contrary, the "coexistence of capitalist and socialist states is entirely possible."[238] (He was knocking down a straw man. Precisely a month before the long telegram, Stalin had assured Kennan's boss that Washington and Moscow could pursue divergent ideologies at home while finding "common ground" in foreign affairs.)[239]

Kennan depicted the rival not as people but rather as a collection of impersonal forces: the "steady advance of uneasy Russian nationalism," the "instinctive urges of Russian rulers," and the "official propaganda machine." The telegram included the names of only two persons: Lenin, who was mentioned once in passing, and Stalin, who was quoted once and mentioned twice. The intensive use of the passive voice also conveyed the sense of impersonal attack. The monster of the long telegram was so scary and such an unlikely negotiating partner because it was not a person who, however, cruel and ambitious, was nevertheless human and able to compromise, but a soulless "machine" or relentless "force."[240]

In one of the most widely quoted sentences of the long telegram, Kennan wrote: "In summary, we have here a political force committed fanatically to the belief that with [the] US there can be no permanent *modus vivendi*, that it is desirable and necessary that the internal harmony of our society be disrupted, our traditional way of life be destroyed, the international authority of our state be broken, if Soviet power is to be secure." Because the agent here was an abstract "political force" and because much of the sentence was in the passive voice and the archaic subjunctive, it was difficult to challenge its underlying premises by asking whether Soviet leaders had such designs, how capable they were of achieving them, and how Kennan came to know of them. The prospects for resistance appeared particularly grim because the reader could glean little idea of how the United States would "be disrupted" and "be destroyed." The missive had many sentences with similar construction: "Poor will be set against rich, black against white, young against old."[241] The repetition of passive sentences—all with an archaic tone and all conveying the message of unlimited action by an evil force—suggested a religious text or a fairy tale.

Throughout the document, the Soviet leadership, whether portrayed as a machine, a force, or as persons, engaged in the driving, aggressive behavior conventionally associated with masculinity. Kennan underscored this association by repeating the word "penetration" five times in reference to the Soviets' insistent, unwanted intrusion. He represented the Communist objective as splitting open Western societies that were already too divided. "Efforts will be made . . . to disrupt national self-confidence . . . to stimulate all forms of disunity." Juxtaposed to this image of the Soviet government as a masculine rapist was the representation of the West as dangerously accessible through "a wide variety of national associations or bodies which can be dominated or influenced by such penetration."[242] Kennan was such an effective prose stylist that readers of this phantasmagorical document praised its "realism."[243]

Perhaps the most striking aspect of the long telegram was that after demonizing the Soviet Union, Kennan shifted focus in recommending responses to this awful threat. The most decisive arena lay, not in foreign lands, but in the United States: "Every courageous and incisive measure to solve [the] internal problems of our own society is a diplomatic victory over Moscow." He concluded his analysis with five suggestions on "how to deal with Russia": appraise the problem with objectivity rather than emotion, launch a government program to educate the public, guide Western Europe, abstain from Soviet methods, and "solve [the] internal problems of our own society with "improve[d] self-confidence, discipline, morale and community spirit." Four of these suggestions required actions at home, the fifth touched on Western Europe, and none directly involved the Soviet Union. Despite his genuine alarm at Soviet expansion, Kennan exaggerated the danger in order to grab the attention of American officialdom.[244]

His timing was perfect. The long telegram was embraced by officials already sounding the alarm with less effective rhetoric. U.S. diplomats in Europe became "very excited" by the "new line."[245] Harriman passed the cable to Forrestal, who found the authoritative explanation he had been seeking. The navy secretary sent copies to Truman, the Cabinet, newspapers, and people in Congress and in business. He made it compulsory reading for navy officers. Moscow's spies studied it. Paraphrasing the document, Lippmann depicted the Soviet Union as "primitive, acquisitive, and morbidly self-centered."[246]

The manifesto also appealed as an argument against those calling for a hot war. Byrnes confided that "he has had men come in into his office with eyes gleaming, asking: 'How soon are we going to fight Russia?' as if they were just dying for a fight." He feared it "quite possible that war would come"; the situation was "very similar to the one that existed between the United States and Japan prior to Pearl Harbor."[247] Churchill stoked fears of imminent crisis by warning that the fate of the United Nations organization "may be determined before the end of this month."[248]

When Wallace and others protested the slide toward hostility, Kennan, reading the American press from Moscow, pushed back with even more extreme arguments. Why should Americans even try to negotiate with Soviet leaders suffering "a psychosis which permeates and determines [their] behavior"? In astounding contrast to the limited aims Stalin had enunciated to Harriman and would soon repeat to Smith, the diplomat insisted that "complete disarmament, delivery of our air and naval forces to Russia, and resigning of powers of government to American Communists would [not] even dent" Soviet hostility. "This is not facetious," he added in this official cable to the Department of State.[249]

Despite the absurdity of some of his assertions, Kennan rode the rising tide. "My reputation was made," he later recalled. "My voice now carried."[250] Brought home from Moscow in April, he would give some thirty State Department–sponsored lectures across the nation. To audiences of businessmen, university faculty, and women's groups he knocked down the idea that Big Three cooperation was still possible. He sought to "instill into our public appreciation for basic realities"—realities that echoed the long telegram and the societal criticism he had espoused for years.[251] Kennan also lectured to U.S. military and civilian officials after his appointment to the National War College in August 1946. He would become the first director of the State Department's Policy Planning Staff in 1947.

Americans anxious about the souring peace looked to those with firsthand authority. Just back from Moscow, the journalist Eddy Gilmore marveled that he could book speaking engagements for a "minimum $200 a night. I never imagined the enormous interest in Russia." All the "big city theaters and college gyms have been packed." He preached "a lot of Harriman gospel."[252] Harriman himself was warning popular audiences about "the depth and width of the ideological chasm between America and the Soviet Union." He peddled the dangerous thesis that "wherever a stand was made [Russia] would retreat."[253] Dodd echoed Harriman, asserting that the Russians "will probably back down—they always do when their bluff is called." As it would turn out, the Soviets would often back down, but not to the point of giving up their hard-won strategic gains in Eastern Europe, their political and economic ideology, or their pride. Regarding Red Army troops, a disgusted Dodd wrote that "the sight of them raises my blood pressure. . . . They are beasts and worse."[254]

Agitated public opinion achieved critical mass. Alarmed at the war talk, a State Department spokesman stressed to a *Washington Post* reporter "the conciliatory moves" made by Moscow. The newspaper, however, printed the story "unobtrusively on an inside page." The British Embassy observed that U.S. newspaper and magazine editors were even "revising despatches from Europe which happen to be of a reassuring rather than of an alarming character" so as to emphasize "sensational" stories that would spur sales. Similarly, the press gave greater coverage to a speech by Eisenhower calling for military preparedness than to another talk of his urging "patience and persistence" in dealing with the Soviets.[255] Forrestal, who had backed Harriman in attacking Roosevelt's policy and who had disseminated Kennan's long telegram, was cheered by the threatening international situation. "It is only when things look too bright that one needs to worry," he asserted.[256]

After helping to incite such furor, Stalin, Churchill, and Kennan each later implicitly acknowledged that he had exaggerated to the point of distortion. Though the risky consequences of their pronouncements continued to proliferate, they each seemed to make amends. Weeks after a speech that some U.S. leaders had likened to a "Declaration of World War III," Stalin spoke warmly to Ambassador Smith about the "accomplishments of the American Army" in winning the war. He appeared "very willing" to discuss "a mutual reduction of armaments" while affirming his commitment to peace and to the UN. He explained at length why U.S. and Soviet political ideologies were "not incompatible." Indeed, their national differences were like those "between brothers," and with patience and good will "would be reconciled."[257] Churchill continued to sound the tocsin for meeting the Soviet threat with a renewed Anglo-American alliance. Yet he, too, would eventually reconsider his demonizing of the Soviets. In the late 1940s and early 1950s, Churchill repeatedly advocated reviving Big Three diplomacy to ease or end the Cold War.[258]

The most dramatic revision, however, came from the author of the most uncompromising manifesto. In December 1946, Kennan, asked at the last minute to talk to a War College audience that included spouses and guests, allowed himself to speak, apparently, from the heart. His astonishing lecture revealed how inner concerns could fuel international struggles. The talk underscored Kennan's identification with the Russian people, his longing for intimacy with them, his ability to have them ventriloquize his agenda, and his tendency to slip into conjecture and even fantasy when explaining what was "really" going on in Russia. Asserting that he could "see" the United States "through Russian eyes," he projected into the Russians' "heart of hearts" his fervent desire since the 1930s to reform U.S. society. "If they have been ready to destroy us it was in reality for our failure to eradicate the weaknesses of our own society, for our failure to be what they thought we should be, to bring out the best they felt was in us."

In terms of the historiographical debate over whether the United States faced an implacable foe in the Cold War, the author of the long telegram and the subsequent containment doctrine, offered a stunning assessment: "The Russians, I can assure you, have never been a menace to us except as we have been a menace to ourselves." He explained, "The real threat to our society, the threat which has lain behind the Soviet armies" could only be met by actions at home, by "purg[ing] ourselves of some of our prejudices, our hypocrisies, and our lack of civic discipline."[259]

Lippmann also warned about the coalescing Cold War. Though not immune to Kennan's powerful language, he understood that in escalating rhetoric and emotions, leaders resembled "little boys playing with matches." The more serious the threats, "the greater the reason for not dealing with them verbally, rhetorically, dramatically, and grandiloquently."[260] He also saw the impact of the change since April 12, 1945. "The fact of the matter is that since the death of President Roosevelt . . . Soviet-American relations have been at arm's length, not directly and firmly in the hands of the men who alone can determine the issues."[261]

Truman's decision in early October 1945 not to reach out directly to Stalin chalks the outer bounds of plausible conjecture about what FDR might have done differently had he lived. Although Roosevelt's successor would make several momentous decisions—notably to inaugurate the Truman Doctrine, Marshall Plan, and NATO; build the hydrogen bomb; and enter the Korean War—an equally pivotal step was gambling on an atomic arms race rather than on a deal with Russia. That decision was heavily influenced by Truman's tunnel vision and blind faith in American exceptionalism. Also crucial was the Missourian's tendency, like most U.S. officials with the notable exception of Roosevelt, to allow cultural and ethnic sympathies for the Germans to influence policy. Unlike Truman, Roosevelt was willing to sacrifice the living standards of the Germans to bolster the postwar recovery of the Soviets and others who had suffered from Nazi invasion.

Postwar political and ideological rivalries with the Kremlin were probably inevitable. A militarized confrontation, however, was not. Atomic tensions and conflict over Germany smoldered and nearly ignited throughout the Cold War. Nuclear stockpiles and proliferation still loom. Perhaps the Cold War and nuclear weapons proliferation would have developed anyway. We shall never know. But a direct approach to the Russians offering to share scientific information might have led to a safer world. As Stalin acknowledged, the Grand Alliance needed a unifying project after victory. Even had Truman pushed Stimson's proposal, the Soviets would probably have insisted on a bomb of their own. Atomic parity, then, might have developed in an international regime impelled by agreement rather than by Armageddon. The United States and the Soviet Union did eventually arrive at a de facto nuclear understanding. But that achievement came only after the near-miss holocaust of the Cuban missile crisis and at the psychic costs of embracing the terror of mutual assured destruction.

The last word on the emotional and personal impetus to the Cold War belongs to Kennan. In 1975, he commented on the lasting trauma of the crackdowns, by Stalin and the U.S. State Department, on the freewheeling exuberance of Bullitt's "boys" in the Moscow embassy. He met up with Durbrow, his friend from those days whose girlfriend, Vera, had suffered exile. Kennan concluded that "Durby," still a Cold Warrior, appeared "locked into views that are more 40-year-old emotional states than rational opinions."[262]

Conclusion and Epilogue

"We took it more to heart than they did," Molotov insisted, when recalling how Americans had reacted to Roosevelt's death. In 1983, long after the wellspring of Bolshevik ideology had gone dry in the Soviet Union, Stalin's henchman, then ninety-two, still clung to the faith. His mind flitted back to 1945, to his sitting in a Pullman dining car crowded with Americans as he traveled to the San Francisco conference. A news flash: Roosevelt had died. "No one paid attention. No reaction at all. . . . Can you imagine how we felt?"[1]

A serious loss, ideological and cultural rigidity, and old age had conspired to construct this fantasy about Roosevelt's death. Molotov was in fact in Moscow on April 12, 1945. Appearing shaken, he had hurried to Spaso House at 3:00 a.m. to offer his condolences. Tens of millions of Americans had indeed mourned Roosevelt's passing. Many lined the track of his funeral train from Warm Springs, Georgia, to Hyde Park, New York.[2] But in the polarized universe of the Cold War, Russians' trauma at losing a trusted interlocutor meant, ipso facto, Americans' indifference. Within a Cold War mind set, even grief could become competitive. The former negotiator, whose seemingly emotionless obduracy had earned him such sobriquets as "Stone Ass," explained the supposedly cold reaction with the comment that "Americans are thick-skinned that way."[3] Just as emotional beliefs on each side magnified the political quarrels resulting in the Cold War, so, too, would each side subsequently accuse its opponent of a deficiency in normal human feeling. The most revealing nugget about the distorted "memory" was the Kremlin's apparent proprietary investment in Roosevelt, an ownership that surfaced in Molotov's plaintive query: "Can you imagine how *we* felt?"

As Stalin and Molotov affirmed many times in 1945–46, Roosevelt had functioned as the fulcrum of the alliance. Indeed, the Soviets tended to excuse their own overreaching by attributing the resulting furor to his departure. Nevertheless, it remains unfortunate that Roosevelt died and that Harriman, Kennan, and company came to the fore at such a critical juncture between war and peace.

The squire of Hyde Park aimed for a stable peace based on Big Three (or Four) cooperation. More than Churchill, he regarded wartime and postwar collaboration with the Soviets as indispensable. He expected a transition, perhaps lasting decades, to a stable, more multilateral world. In the meantime, the big powers would collectively discipline Germany and Japan while tamping down disputes among smaller nations. Roosevelt accepted Russian domination of Eastern Europe while hoping to moderate it. He intended to align with Stalin in promoting gradual decolonization, a process he expected the British to resist, especially if Churchill or someone like-minded held power. The partly "Asiatic" Soviet Union might also help head off a future "race war." FDR reinforced his diplomacy, especially with the difficult Soviets, by cultivating personal ties, playing to emotional dispositions, minimizing ideological and cultural differences, and restraining explosive emotions.

Like the other two leaders, Roosevelt also hedged his bets on postwar cooperation. He kept up his sleeve two aces: control over the atomic bomb and postwar economic aid. A proven master at timing, he doubtless hoped to play these cards at the opportune moment. Whether he would have won the hand, or the game, remains an unanswerable question. Truman exceeded Roosevelt in his fondness for cards and poker analogies. Although Henry Stimson's proposal for negotiating an atomic deal directly with the Soviets won the support of a majority in the Cabinet, Truman gambled that America's scientific lead and exceptionalist heritage made an atomic monopoly followed by an arms race the safer bet. Playing to, rather than challenging, Americans' confidence in their specialness also seemed to Truman the surest wager in domestic and legislative politics. Churchill, worried that Britain could be squeezed between the two rising powers, worked instead for an Anglo-American special relationship. By March 1946, Truman and most of his advisers were receptive to Churchill's thinking.

As Walter Lippmann remarked, Roosevelt was not naive about Stalin's beneficence but instead cynical in believing he could manipulate the Russians, as he had succeeded in doing with so many others. Corcoran added that FDR "had imagination, courage, and the guile to bring both to bear on seemingly insoluble problems."[4] The president trusted that postwar collaboration would not be insoluble, because Stalin's primary postwar aim was not revolution, but rather security against further German and Japanese aggression.[5]

As Clark Kerr's successor in Moscow affirmed, Stalin aimed for "a general bargain which would really divide the world into three."[6] With a partitioning of war spoils, the United States and Britain would legitimate the Soviet Union's preinvasion borders, its predominance in Eastern Europe, and the restoration of its pre-1905 position in the Far East. Most of the rest of the globe would fall into the British or the American spheres. The Big Three would prevent renewed aggression by the former Axis nations. That was the underlying deal at Tehran and Yalta—and what Stalin believed Moscow had earned from its blood sacrifice. Ironically, the international regime of the Cold War would sustain key aspects of this division, as well as the containment of German and Japanese military power. Regulating this international system, however, would not be the cautious collaboration envisioned by the Big Three, but rather an all-out militarized competition checked only by the threat of nuclear annihilation.

For a year after Roosevelt's death, reasons of national interest impelled the Soviets to try to sustain at least some elements of the wartime alliance. In early 1946, vice foreign minister Andrey Vyshinsky acknowledged that the Soviets "could not hope for the pacification of Europe, which they wanted, unless they could work with" London and Washington.[7] Stalin also sought a large loan from America and reparations from western Germany. Generally amicable ties with the Western allies would also encourage a falling out between Washington and London, or so Marxist dogma predicted. Stalin expected that left-leaning tendencies in the postwar world and prestige from vanquishing the Wehrmacht would foster a congenial environment for the USSR. With regard to Marxism's eventual triumph, however, the old Bolshevik had patience. As Roosevelt realized, millennial projects tended to fade over time. Stalin also pushed for a union of Slavic nations. He never let go of the option of militant Marxist-Leninist ideology and unrestrained rivalry with the more powerful Americans. He would warn his new Communist lackeys in Eastern Europe about the perfidy of all capitalists. Though Stalin would end up playing the Cold War card when Roosevelt died and the Grand Alliance folded, it was not his first choice.[8]

So much depended on Roosevelt. Despite the loss of his personal alliance partners, especially LeHand and Hopkins, he soldiered on. He changed his lifestyle so as to defy his heart disease. The subarachnoid aneurysm that finally burst could have killed him at any time. FDR was wrong in not taking Truman into his confidence. He was foolish in not recruiting new aides of the same caliber as LeHand, Hopkins, Welles, or Corcoran. Assuming he was indispensable, he believed he could meet the challenge of the postwar transition, as he had done with the Depression and the war. Hubris prompted him to boast about his fourth term, "I know who got me elected—it was FDR and the Lord."[9] Tragically, that team shifted its playing field at a perilous moment. Even Corcoran, the calculator, "didn't expect [Roosevelt] to die" so suddenly, he later remembered. "I thought that once the war was over, he would resign the Presidency in order to head up . . . the United Nations, and chair the world."[10]

The period from April 1945 to March 1946 stands out as a critical juncture in world history—like the months before and after August 1914, November 1989, and September 2001. At such turning points, the otherwise immovable elements of strategic imperative, political ambition, cultural habit, economic interest, and geographic location suddenly loosen their grip, and, like the ground in a massive earthquake, temporarily become plastic.[11] Roosevelt insisted that the postwar transition would be such a time of flux, with consequent danger and opportunity. Especially because of Stalin's suspicious, touchy nature, safe passage to peacetime collaboration required a U.S. leader with the emotional intelligence, elasticity, charm, and confidence of a

Franklin Roosevelt rather than the personality of a Harry Truman. As in 1914, 1989, and 2001, the particular leaders in charge made a decisive and lasting difference. Contingencies of personality, health, feelings, and cultural assumptions propelled massive events with dangerous, or positive, momentum.

With Roosevelt replaced by Truman, differences that might have been eased or papered over during the postwar transition would instead blow up into an ideologically fueled, tit-for-tat conflict. Once the emotional, exaggerated warnings by Harriman, Churchill, and Kennan about Soviet aggression became public knowledge, the kind of quiet deals formerly reached by the Big Three became unworkable in the glare of domestic politics. Rhetoric about the Soviet threat and the vicious spiral of fear and disrespect aggravated Stalin's suspicions and xenophobia, and opened the way for far-right anticommunists who within a few years were labeling even Truman an appeaser.

Though warped, Molotov's memory was rooted in the solid conviction that he and Stalin in 1943–45 had achieved significant understanding with Roosevelt. The former foreign minister acknowledged that the president, like all capitalists, "believed in dollars." Yet he also drew a distinction: It was "not that [Roosevelt] believed in nothing else."[12] Even as he granted the difference, Molotov remained fixated on matters of pride and respect, the emotion-suffused political concerns that impelled him and Stalin to act, especially after victory, with such self-righteous, counterproductive arrogance. He believed that Roosevelt had expected the Russians to grovel for postwar aid. (Each side's unwillingness to "grovel" in 1945–46 would be interpreted by the other side as brusque ingratitude.) When another veteran of Stalin's wartime clique, Nikita S. Khrushchev, was asked in 1960 whom he, as first secretary of the Soviet Communist Party, preferred in the election pitting John F. Kennedy against Richard M. Nixon, he tellingly replied, "Roosevelt!"[13] FDR was idealized in Soviet iconography as the "good president." Truman, in contrast, according to Molotov's memory, "had an openly hostile attitude."[14]

The sterile ideological and cultural rigidity that led Molotov to blot out Americans' mourning for FDR also, more tragically, shuttered Stalin's perspective. The authoritarian cultures of the Dzhugashvili family, semitribal Georgia, czarist Russia, the Orthodox seminary, and the Bolshevik Party intersected with a personality excessively eager to discipline and punish others. A clear-eyed realist on some matters, Stalin refused to guard against the dangers of antagonizing U.S. and British public opinion. He allowed the isolation of foreign diplomats, journalists, and military liaison officers—the very people who shaped the outside world's views of the Soviet Union. He no doubt worried that openness to the outside world would undermine his rule. The dictator also ignored Roosevelt's pleas for the fig leaf of segregated, Mississippi-style "elections" to mitigate the public uproar over annexing the Baltic states and imposing "friendly" governments in Eastern Europe.

The brutality of Soviet domination wracked U.S. officials. Harriman and former assistant secretary of war McCloy later reminisced about a celebration in Budapest they had witnessed in July 1945, soon after non-Communists had won the Hungarian election. Harriman said to his former colleague, "My heart sank because I knew god damned well we couldn't do a damn thing in the world for them. You recall the same emotions that I did?" And McCloy responded, "Oh, yes. Here these people were surging up to you. Here was the hope of the world, the American flag."[15]

In 1946, Harriman worried that the pacific traditions of that flag would trump the more militant ones. He feared that after winning the war the American people wanted not to confront Moscow but rather "go to the movies and drink coke."[16] As it would turn out, however, Americans would both contest the Kremlin and create a vibrant consumer culture. The ability to buy an automobile and the freedom to choose a specific brand of toothpaste would become emblematic of other economic, cultural, and political liberties. Hollywood movies and Coca-Cola went global in terms of their cultural influence. Both also became major export earners, helping the United States pay for the overseas political, economic, and military ventures that Harriman and other Cold Warriors promoted. Consumer products also became powerful elements of Western "soft power." Through radio, television, and increased travel, consumer cultures adapted to local preferences penetrated the empire Stalin had built in 1945–48 as well as the Soviet

Union itself. The popular quest for progress and glamor undermined the appeal of Molotov's, Khrushchev's, and even Mikhail Gorbachev's applications of Communist ideology.[17]

It was coincidental but nonetheless fitting that Molotov and Harriman both died in 1986, the year that Gorbachev and Ronald Reagan knit at their Reykjavik summit the personal ties that would enable the political breakthroughs ending the Cold War. As Roosevelt had understood in trying to "get-at" Stalin, engaging the Soviets, even on their terms, could ultimately redound to U.S. benefit. Even after the Soviet Union fractured in 1991 along the fissures of nationality that Stalin in his February 1946 "election" speech had tried to cement over with ideology, Russians acted quite differently from Americans or Britons. Whether it was before, during, or after the Cold War, ideology remained only one element along a spectrum of national cultural differences.[18] Moreover, the Cold War obscured the parallels in U.S. and Soviet ideologies, despite their differences. Both sets of beliefs rested on universalist assumptions and messianic aspirations. Each promised a sure path to material progress and modernity.

Like the gap between the actual and the imagined in Molotov's distorted memory, emotional experiences could expose underlying cultural prejudices that fostered the Cold War. One such experience occurred in the fall of 1945 at Schwechat airfield in Austria. In adjusting the four-power zonal borders in Austria, a Royal Air Force unit under Wing Commander G. H. Keat took over Schwechat from the Soviets. Keat reported to London that the move stood out as "one of the most disgusting experiences of my life. . . . Feces were everywhere. From baths to cupboards; from the Flying Control Tower to the chairs in the Officers' Mess; and the Russians, both Officers and men, were working and feeding in these surroundings. Lavatory pans were filled, the seats put down and the seats themselves piled high. The Officers' Mess in particular. . . . Bugs too were everywhere." Riding or trudging from battle to battle over the years, Red Army soldiers had little incentive to dig proper latrines. Most peasant recruits had no experience with flush toilets. Probably also impelling were feelings of revenge against the Germans who had built the base, and spite against the British who would inherit it.

Keat reacted with disgust and contempt at this apparent lack of civilized restraint.[19] Unlike Kollontay, Maisky, or Clark Kerr, he did not suggest immaturity as a mitigating factor. While describing Red Army soldiers as "filthy" and "stupid," Keat stressed that his contact with them had remained friendly. He believed that the Soviets, much like native peoples in the British Empire, required "a firm hand" and "stern justice." He concluded that "if a firm demand is made, a respectful acquiescence almost inevitably follows. Any attempt to ingratiate oneself, however, is met with a contemptuous refusal."[20]

Like Bullitt, Kennan, Harriman, Bohlen, Durbrow, Rossbach, Birse, Winterton, and many others appalled and angry at Soviet behavior, Keat reached beyond the evidence of a riveting personal experience to arrive at a dangerous emotional belief, a conviction that packed political dynamite: "This is no time, I have found, for appeasement."[21] A policy successfully smeared as "appeasement" was doomed. Because appeasing the Nazis had proven disastrous, the argument ran, compromising with the Soviets would only incite Hitler-like aggression. Russian experts in the Foreign Office declared Keat's reasoning "admirable." Thomas Brimelow, who had learned diplomatic drafting from Clark Kerr, remarked, ruefully, that on the "diplomatic level, nothing seems to command 'respectful acquiescence.'" To which Christopher Warner expostulated, "Perhaps because we have been insufficiently firm!"[22] Acting with sufficient firmness would become the first principle of their "Russia Committee," assembled to chart strategy in the emerging Cold War.[23]

While British and American officials habitually saw the Soviets as less advanced, Kremlin leaders, despite their pride, sometimes tacitly concurred. In January 1946, former ambassador Cripps spoke with Vyshinsky. Despite his gruesome record as prosecutor in the late 1930s purge trials, the voluble redhead had a sense of humor and delighted in debating foreigners. Invited to "say all he felt about" London's attitude, Vyshinsky poured out twenty-four complaints. The first focused on a key cultural difference. "[Soviet] ideas of freedom (i.e. of press, political views, etc.) were quite different to [Britain's]. Perhaps in 50–100 years they would have reached the state when they could hold our views. They could understand what our views were but they could not share them or practice them." Striking here was Vyshinsky's apparent admission that Western ideas of freedom were more advanced, that is, they constituted a legitimate future goal.

Vyshinsky focused on Germany. Why did the British want to maintain "German Armies" in their zone? He also emphasized matters of pride and respect. British army officers were "hostile to Soviet Russia in word and action." London's consulting first with Washington "put [the Soviets] into a position of inferiority. They wanted to be treated as equals." The British still considered themselves "a superior breed." Vyshinsky mentioned, with a hint of blackmail, that if the Soviets "had really wanted to make trouble, they would have done so in India." Cripps concluded that the Soviets "still feel in an unfair position and this greatly hurts their pride." Warner dismissed the complaints about status as "special pleading of the stock line."[24]

Nevertheless, when Molotov and Stalin were asked to explain postwar tensions, they replied that "the whole trouble lay in the refusal of the United States of America and Britain to treat the Soviet Union as an equal." Roberts judged that "however ridiculous" the complaint seemed, "it represents a genuine conviction."[25] This exchange was yet another echo of Maisky's plaint to Clark Kerr in July 1943. Throughout the Cold War the Soviets would reiterate their preference for sitting down with the United States on a basis of equality. Washington, convinced of its material and moral superiority and anxious to keep the "free world" lined up in an anti-Soviet row, would not grant such status. Nevertheless, as Roosevelt had demonstrated by journeying all the way to Tehran and Yalta to meet Stalin, bestowing respect could prove a smart bargain for a confident leader and nation.

By early 1946, however, "gloom and morbid defeatism" in the United States was displacing the confidence arising from victory, observed Joseph F. Barnes, foreign editor of the *New York Herald Tribune*. Barnes marveled that Americans seemed "the most defeated-minded nation . . . that had ever won a great war." Anxiety abounded because of the atomic bomb, tensions with Russia, strikes, and inflation. "We have got to have someone to blame. . . . [S]o far it is the Russians who are that someone."[26] A few weeks later, Kennan in his long telegram would argue that the Soviets needed a foreign enemy to justify their repression. Such psychological explanations for the Cold War remain inherently unprovable. What seems certain, however, is that emotional beliefs and cultural presumptions, in which ideology figured importantly but not exclusively, made political issues appear more intractable and compromise less desirable.

The Soviets under Stalin did do terrible things. Harriman and others were justified in their anger and disgust at the isolation, at the rape and pillage by Red Army soldiers, at the arrogance toward the Allies, at Stalin's shared responsibility for the crushing of the Warsaw uprising, at the callousness toward the liberated POWs, at the clumsy pressure on Iran and Turkey, at the grabbing in Manchuria and Germany, and at the oppression of Eastern Europe. Nevertheless, personally and morally satisfying expressions of anger and frustration produced a rhetoric in which measured, judicious strategic thinking was, tragically, blinkered.

Despite the egregiousness of Soviet actions, these actions—and the jabs and counterjabs that followed—did not justify the Cold War. The costs of that conflict proved far higher: deadly proxy wars, the atomic arms race (the full price of which we perhaps have not yet paid), the militarizing of U.S. society, and, probably, the deepening and prolonging of Soviet oppression. The Cold War may have prevented World War III, as some scholars have maintained. The conflict arguably also prevented the establishment of a genuinely peaceful, less anxiety-ridden world order in which atomic weaponry and U.S.-Soviet rivalry might have been contained at minimal levels not requiring the Russian-roulette risks of an ever-possible Armageddon.

Still another cost was the suppression of memory of how the Grand Alliance might have endured. Discerning as ever, Clark Kerr in mid-1945 warned a friend, "Policy is going to change." The alliance was "going to come apart." It was time for him to move on, because the British government did not "want anyone in Moscow who remembers what was said and done. That would just be an embarrassment."[27]

Like Clark Kerr, Kennan and Harriman had first arrived in Moscow excited about developing close personal and political relations with the Russians. Isolation from the Soviet people embittered the latter two. Personal frustration jaundiced their political analysis and advice. Harriman told an insecure Harry Truman that FDR's policy was based on fear of the Russians. Kennan and Harriman both expected the Soviets to yield to pressure, if not immediately, then eventually.

Ironically, decades before Russia did open up, Kennan and Harriman each reversed his tough stance to advocate reengaging with Moscow. Though irked at "revisionist" histories of the origins of the Cold War, they also tacitly revised their alarmist analysis of 1945–46. Kennan, dismayed by the "stupidity and primitivism" of the Soviets in invading Czechoslovakia in 1968, went so far as to write: "There are times when I could wish that Stalin was back in the saddle."[28]

It was Harriman, who had worked most tirelessly to distort and undo Roosevelt's vision, who later paid the most poignant testimony to his wartime boss. What Eden had confided to Sherwood in 1946, Harriman would confirm to Schlesinger two decades later. "FDR was basically right in thinking he could make progress by personal relations with Stalin. . . . The Russians were utterly convinced that the change came as a result of the shift from Roosevelt to Truman." Harriman added, "If Roosevelt had lived with full vigor, it's very hard to say what could happen because—Roosevelt could lead the world."[29]

Acknowledgments

This book evolved over a long time. Whether the development also evidences intelligent design, readers will have to decide. My study of how the Grand Alliance formed, functioned, and then collapsed started out as the projected first chapter of a book on how acculturation and emotional thinking shaped the Western alliance. Along the way, however, I became captivated by the achievements and the aborted promise of the wartime coalition. Compared with the post-1945 alliance, the structure of wartime diplomacy was more challenging, because here the two principal partners, the United States and the Soviet Union, nearly matched each other in power, whereas they diverged in ideology and in other aspects of culture. I discovered that although scholars have written shelves of books on the Big Three alliance and on the origins of the Cold War, they have neglected crucial aspects of the personal/political relations among the top leaders. Moreover, none of the many biographies of Roosevelt have focused on the tragedy that ensued from this president's depending on his closest aides while also making their lives so difficult. Rendering these topics all the more exciting was my finding untapped or underutilized primary sources.

The writing of this book was bracketed by residencies at two extraordinary havens for scholars, the Norwegian Nobel Institute in Oslo and the Institute for Advanced Study in Princeton, New Jersey. I am indebted to Geir Lundestad, Olav Njolstad, and Odd Arne Westad for creating such a stimulating and congenial place for study. Staff members Anne Kjelling, Grete Haram, and Torill Johansen smoothed the way with all things Norwegian. I benefited from discussions with other fellows, especially Christian Ostermann, who also introduced me to the theory and practice of afternoon shakes. My stay at the

Institute for Advanced Study was generously supported by funds from the National Endowment for the Humanities and the Andrew W. Mellon Foundation. At the IAS, Peter Goddard, Avishai Margalit, Nicola Di Cosmo, Caroline Walker Bynum, Irving Lavin, and Marilyn Aronberg Lavin were extraordinarily hospitable and helpful. I also learned much from talking with Michael Lurie, Ruth Bielfeldt, Thomas Hegghammer, Sandy Isenstadt, Emma Dillon, Thomas Laqueur, Frances Nethercott, Igor Khristoforov, Don Wyatt, Siobhan Roberts, Peter Katzenstein, Judith Pfeiffer, and Fa-Ti Fan. Staff support was superb in every way. Indeed, my year at the Institute ranks as one of the best in my life. I was also privileged to spend a year at the University of Connecticut Humanities Institute, where Christopher Clark and the late Susan Porter Benson provided stimulating conversation and good cheer. UCHI director and History Department colleague Dick Brown offered pointed questions at a critical stage in the writing. My work on this book was supported also by a fellowship from the Guggenheim Foundation, funds from the University of Connecticut Research Foundation, and sabbaticals from the University of Rhode Island and the University of Connecticut.

I was exceptionally fortunate in the readers chosen by Princeton University Press: Tim Borstelmann, Richard Immerman, and Melvyn P. Leffler. Each offered smart criticism and helpful suggestions. I especially appreciate the page-by-page suggestions of Mel Leffler, my close friend since we met in the archives four decades ago. Richard was extremely generous with his time and effort as I did final revisions. Other friends—Andy Rotter, Emily Rosenberg, and Bob Dean—read the entire manuscript and offered discerning advice. I have learned not only from the comments of these six readers but also from their pathbreaking scholarship. I was helped also by the suggestions of David Engerman, Kristin Hoganson, and Robert Nye on a draft of chapter 1. Geoffrey C. Ward and Steve Lomazow shared their insights on FDR. Roger Petersen offered a valuable reading from a political science perspective. I appreciate Bob Hannigan's help with the copy editing.

Gabriel Gorodetsky generously allowed me to use some selections from his forthcoming publication of Ivan Maisky's diary. June Hopkins was very thoughtful in sending me the unpublished biography of her grandfather, Harry Hopkins, written by James Halsted. Harry's daughter, Diana Hopkins, recounted fascinating aspects of her life in the Roosevelt White House. Geoffrey Wilson shared reminiscences of Archibald Clark Kerr. Andrew Preston and Geoffrey Roberts were kind enough to let me see their forthcoming books. Jeffrey Burds and Theodore A. Wilson graciously enabled me to benefit from their respective research projects. I am greatly indebted to Thomas Parrish for sharing interviews, done by the late Rudy Abramson, of Averell Harriman and his associates. Anand Toprani, Matthew Hinds, and Arthur Scott Mobley Jr. were generous with their unpublished work. Sherry Zane helped with research and allowed me to profit from her insightful work on FDR's early career. Michael Donoghue and Tom Westerman offered valuable research assistance.

J. Garry Clifford opened to me his trove of FDR documents—while also doing much more to make this book possible. Our drives to Hyde Park developed into rolling seminars on Franklin Roosevelt. A superb editor, Garry was sometimes more adept than I in expressing my ideas. I would send him a chapter late at night and find a marked-up version in my inbox by 8:00 the next morning. Another good friend and gifted wordsmith, Robert Gross, was also generous with his time and suggestions. My understanding of FDR was expanded by the careful reading and sound advice of that dean of Roosevelt scholars, Warren F. Kimball. Lloyd C. Gardner also offered good counsel.

For more than four decades, Walter LaFeber has stood out for me as an inspiration. He has achieved an extraordinary career as conscientious scholar, concerned public intellectual, and committed teacher—all the while remaining an eminently decent person. I treasure the long lunches with him and Sandy.

This book has gained much from the feedback of audiences at the University of Connecticut, Vassar College, Temple University, the University of Wisconsin at Madison, Ohio State University, the University of Oxford, and the Lone Star Forum, as well as my colleagues in the Society for Historians of American Foreign Relations. My research was aided by the superb staff at Connecticut's Homer Babbidge Library, the Olin Library at Cornell University, the Library of Congress, the National Archives at Kew, the National Archives in College Park, Maryland, and particularly by Dan Linke and Adriane Hanson at

Princeton University's Mudd Library. At the FDR Library, I received skilled assistance from Robert Clark, Mark Renovitch, and Virginia Lewick. I owe a special thanks to archivist extraordinaire David Langbart. For help with the illustrations I am indebted to Sarah Craig, Doug Snyder, Annessa Stagner, and James Graham Wilson. My colleague at the Nobel Institute, Irina Bystrova, did research for me in Russian archives. Documents were also translated by Alla Kok. My Connecticut colleagues Larry Langer and Emma Gilligan pitched in with some spot translations, as did Denis Kozlov. I appreciate the support from Arnie Offner, Mark Stoler, David Foglesong, Vladimir Pechatnov, and Ann Douglas. Jeremi Suri offered encouragement at a crucial point. Joanne Meyerowitz clarified an important detail.

Editor Brigitta van Rheinberg has sustained her faith in this project while providing direction at critical points in its development. It has been a pleasure working with her. Sarah Wolf, Kathleen Cioffi, and Beth Gianfagna expertly shepherded this book through production at Princeton University Press.

Others have extended crucial support, including department chairs Mike Honhart at the University of Rhode Island and Altina Waller and Shirley Roe at the University of Connecticut, as well as Deans Ross Mackinnon and Jeremy Teitelbaum at UConn. Molly Hite offered generous help at critical stages in the writing. My friends Joel Cohen, Lester Marion, and Carole Masters have learned not to ask if the book was yet done. Mike Berkowitz has inspired me to always try for waiter's waiter. Also in my corner have been my mother, Nancy Costigliola, who has blossomed intellectually in her late eighties; my daughters Mali Cox-Hite and Jennifer Nancy Costigliola, the latter now a scientist/scholar in her own right; fellow writer Josh Tarsky; my granddaughter, Aviva Tarsky; and Charles and Martha Costigliola. My father, the late Umberto Costigliola, would have enjoyed reading this book. I value the bond with my fellow lover of history, Frank Bertucci.

This book is dedicated to Diann Bertucci, who fills my life with love, joy, and satisfaction. At her side I look forward to years that will be fun and productive as I try to moderate my tendencies toward three-ish excess.

Bibliographical Note

Part of the strength of history as a discipline is that no matter how exhausted a topic might seem, scholars can almost always find fresh sources or interpret old ones in new ways. *Roosevelt's Lost Alliances* takes an original approach to a wide range of U.S. and British archives and to Russian documents. The book draws also on the unpublished papers of authors who, in the 1960s through the 1980s, wrote on FDR, the Grand Alliance, or the origins of the Cold War. Those were the years when leading figures of the wartime era—most notably Eleanor Roosevelt, Winston Churchill, and Averell Harriman—passed away. Former close associates now talked more freely with interviewers about the departed great ones. Although decades-old memories are notoriously unreliable with regard to specific facts or chronology, they can provide valuable evidence about poignant feelings, moods, and relationships of the past.

Much of my understanding of the intimate lives of Franklin and Eleanor Roosevelt comes from unpublished interviews done by Joseph P. Lash, the First Lady's friend and biographer. After Eleanor died in 1962, Lash interviewed many people who had known the Roosevelts since the 1910s. He then discovered, to his dismay, that the children of the former First Family insisted on passing judgment on what he published about their parents.[1] That censorship limited what Lash could include in his books. The rich material in the interviews conducted in the 1980s by Rudy Abramson, W. Averell Harriman's biographer, remained underutilized for a different reason. As a journalist writing about a figure whose varied career spanned nearly a century, Abramson could not develop, and perhaps did not fully realize, the full implications of what Harriman, his family, and his associates were telling him about personal and political relations during the wartime era.

Another well of untapped sources are the records and comments of women. Though not particularly close to Eleanor in his last years, FDR, who liked to relax in the company of women, did share with female confidantes his concerns about health, evaluations of Churchill and Stalin, and thoughts about the future. As the Roosevelt biographer Geoffrey C. Ward demonstrated in an edited volume of her diary, Margaret "Daisy" Suckley, a Dutchess County neighbor, remained FDR's closest companion until the day he died. Another listener was Dorothy Schiff, the heiress and liberal publisher of the *New York Post*, whom Roosevelt invited to spend weekends, without her husband, at Hyde Park. Schiff wrote contemporary memoranda and, later, reminiscences. Belle Willard Roosevelt was a White House visitor who jotted in her journal what FDR had told her. Courtney Letts de Espil, the American-born wife of the Argentine ambassador, recorded in her detailed diary FDR's behavior and the impact of the war on the diplomatic community in Washington. A gifted diplomat in her own right, de Espil managed to remain close friends with the wives of both Sumner Welles and his arch-enemy, Cordell Hull. The diary of Harold L. Ickes, only a small portion of which has been published, remains a treasure trove of information gleaned from the women and men that Harold and his wife, Jane Ickes, had befriended. FDR's daughter, Anna Roosevelt Boettiger, kept a Yalta diary that is invaluable for understanding the personal context in which her father was conducting political negotiations. Fears that his wife, Louise Macy, was unfaithful prompted former "Assistant President" Harry L. Hopkins to have the FBI tap his home telephone. After Roosevelt died, the transcripts of Louise's conversations revealed her husband's surprising response to the death of the "Boss," as well as his support of the Truman administration's shift in policy toward the Russians.

The rise and fall of the Grand Alliance took place at a historical moment when top leaders talked knowingly about emotions. Despite their cultural and personal differences, the Big Three were alike in referring to their own feelings. They believed that the affect, attitude, and mood of an official could signal that person's underlying political intent. The perceived need to read the personality of and influence other powerful men impelled Roosevelt, Churchill, and Stalin to endure the discomfort and risks of meeting in faraway places.

According to the current scholarly consensus, human thought is integrated rather than neatly separable into emotional thinking and rational thinking. Nevertheless, the assumption of a polarity between emotion and reason was so pervasive among historical actors, and this belief remains so alive in popular discourses, that scholars today are justified in considering the "emotions" as a category of historical analysis. Claims by historical actors about their own feelings or about the emotions of others can offer valuable evidence. Of course such claims must, like other assertions, be evaluated and interpreted. In analyzing such emotions it remains important not to overlook individual or cultural variation.

Historians can also tap for evidence the emotional tenor and impact of conversations, such as Harriman's briefings of Truman and his advisers in April 1945, or of statements, such as the ideological manifestos delivered by Stalin, Kennan, and Churchill in February and March 1946. Staged events, such as Roosevelt's laborious walk along the deck of the *Prince of Wales* during the Atlantic Conference or his journeying to Tehran and Yalta to meet Stalin, also packed emotional significance that can be decoded by historians. So can unscripted exchanges, such as Churchill's stormy sessions with Stalin in August 1942 or Truman's conversation about guilt with atomic scientist Robert Oppenheimer. A close reading of such sources reveals that emotions often influenced how leaders approached, assigned value to, reasoned about, and acted on issues.

Notes

Abbreviations

Abramson collection Rudy Abramson collection, privately held

Acheson papers Dean Acheson papers, Sterling Library, Yale University, New Haven, CT

Armstrong papers Hamilton Fish Armstrong papers, Mudd Library, Princeton University, Princeton, NJ

Barnes papers Joseph F. Barnes papers, Butler Library, Columbia University, New York, NY

Bassow papers Whitman Bassow papers, Library of Congress, Washington, DC

Boettiger papers John Boettiger papers, FDRL

Bohlen papers Charles E. Bohlen papers, Library of Congress, Washington, DC

Bruenn papers Howard G. Bruenn papers, Small Collections, FDRL

Bullitt papers William C. Bullitt papers, Sterling Library, Yale University, New Haven, CT

Childs papers Marquis W. Childs papers, Wisconsin Historical Society, Madison, WI

Clapper papers Raymond Clapper papers, Library of Congress, Washington, DC

Clark Kerr papers Lord Inverchapel [Archibald Clark Kerr] papers, Bodleian Library, University of Oxford, Oxford, UK

Corcoran papers Thomas G. Corcoran papers, Library of Congress, Washington, DC

Council on Foreign Relations papers Council on Foreign Relations papers, Mudd Library, Princeton University, Princeton, NJ

Cox papers Oscar Cox papers, FDRL

Cripps papers Stafford Cripps papers, Bodleian Library, University of Oxford, Oxford, UK

CUOHRC Columbia University Oral History Research Office Collection

CWIHP Cold War International History Project, Woodrow Wilson Center, Washington, DC

Davies papers Joseph E. Davies papers, Library of Congress, Washington, DC

de Espil diary Courtney Letts de Espil diary, Library of Congress, Washington, DC

FDRL Franklin D. Roosevelt Library, Hyde Park, NY

FRUS U.S. State Department, *Foreign Relations of the United States*

Graff papers Robert D. Graff papers, FDRL

Averell Harriman papers W. Averell Harriman papers, Library of Congress, Washington, DC

Pamela Churchill Harriman papers Pamela Churchill Harriman papers, Library of Congress, Washington, DC

Hersey papers John Hersey papers, Beinecke Library, Yale University, New Haven, CT

Hill papers George A. Hill papers, Hoover Institution, Stanford University, Palo Alto, CA

Hopkins papers, FDRL Harry L. Hopkins papers, FDRL

Hopkins papers, Georgetown Harry L. Hopkins papers, Lauinger Library, Georgetown University, Washington, DC

Louise Hopkins transcripts Louise Hopkins, FBI transcript of telephone conversations, J. Edgar Hoover Official and Confidential File, reel 13, University Publications of America

HSTL Harry S. Truman Library, Independence, MO

Ickes papers Harold L. Ickes papers, Library of Congress, Washington, DC

Kennan papers George F. Kennan papers, Mudd Library, Princeton University, Princeton, NJ

Lash papers Joseph P. Lash papers, FDRL

Lindley papers Ernest K. Lindley papers, University of Kansas Library, Lawrence, KS

Lippmann papers Walter Lippmann papers, Sterling Library, Yale University, New Haven, CT

Meiklejohn diary Robert K. Meiklejohn diary, box 211, W. Averell Harriman papers, Library of Congress, Washington, DC

Moore papers R. Walton Moore papers, FDRL

NA, UK National Archives, Kew, UK

NA, US National Archives, College Park, MD

Pearson papers Drew Pearson papers, Lyndon B. Johnson Library, Austin, TX

Anna Roosevelt Halsted papers Anna Roosevelt (Boettiger) Halsted papers, FDRL

Belle Willard Roosevelt diary Belle Willard Roosevelt diary, Kermit Roosevelt papers, Library of Congress, Washington, DC

Roosevelt, MR Franklin D. Roosevelt, Map Room Files, FDRL

Roosevelt, PSF Franklin D. Roosevelt, President's Secretary's File, FDRL

Scandrett papers Richard B. Scandrett papers, Kroch Library, Cornell University, Ithaca, NY

Schiff papers Dorothy Schiff papers, New York Public Library, New York, NY

Schlesinger seminar "Off the Record Discussion of the Origins of the Cold War," May 31, 1967, box 869, W. Averell Harriman papers, Library of Congress, Washington, DC

Sherwood papers Robert E. Sherwood papers, Houghton Library, Harvard University, Cambridge, MA

Stettinius papers   Edward R. Stettinius Jr. papers, Small Library, University of Virginia, Charlottesville, VA

Stiles papers   Leila Stiles papers, FDRL

Stimson papers   Henry L. Stimson papers, Sterling Library, Yale University, New Haven, CT

Thayer papers   Charles W. Thayer papers, HSTL

Truman, PSF   Harry S. Truman, President's Secretary's Files, HSTL

Yeaton papers   Ivan D. Yeaton papers, Hoover Institution, Stanford University, Palo Alto, CA

Introduction

1. Robert E. Sherwood, *Roosevelt and Hopkins, an Intimate History* (New York: Harper, 1948).

2. Robert Sherwood, "Notes on Meeting with Anthony Eden in Mr. Churchill's Offices, House of Parliament, Tuesday, August 27, 1946," Sherwood papers.

3. Vladislav Zubok and Constantine Pleshakov, *Inside the Kremlin's Cold War* (Cambridge, MA: Harvard University Press, 1996), 7.

4. David Reynolds, "The Erosion of British Influence," in *World War II in Europe: The Final Year*, ed. Charles Browers (New York: St. Martin's, 1998), 40.

5. For an introduction to Roosevelt as diplomat, see Warren F. Kimball, *The Juggler: Franklin Roosevelt as Wartime Statesman* (Princeton, NJ: Princeton University Press, 1991); Robert Dallek, *Franklin D. Roosevelt and American Foreign Policy, 1932–1945* (New York: Oxford University Press, 1979). For an overview of recent scholarship, see David B. Woolner, Warren F. Kimball, and David Reynolds, eds., *FDR's World: War, Peace, and Legacies* (New York: Palgrave Macmillan, 2008). Still the most perceptive, if incomplete, biography is Geoffrey C. Ward, *First-Class Temperament: The Emergence of Franklin Roosevelt* (New York: Harper & Row, 1989).

6. Churchill quoted in John Hersey to Patch [his wife], October 18, 1944, box 7, John Hersey papers.

7. Stalin quoted in Geoffrey Roberts, *Stalin's Wars* (New Haven, CT: Yale University Press, 2006), 235.

8. John Balfour, December 18, 1945, Record of Groups, vol. 16, Council on Foreign Relations papers.

9. Clark Clifford, interview with Rudy Abramson, August 12, 1988, Rudy Abramson collection. I am indebted to Thomas Parrish for sharing with me the interviews Abramson did to research his book, *Spanning the Century: The Life of W. Averell Harriman 1891–1986* (New York: William Morrow, 1992).

10. Lord Moran, *Churchill at War 1940–45* (New York: Carroll & Graf, 2002), 73.

11. Psychologists who have given test subjects oxytocin, a hormone that stimulates feelings of warmth toward others, report that those subjects became readier to risk trusting those around them. See Jonathan Mercer, "Emotional Beliefs," *International Organization* 64 (Winter 2010): 6.

12. Warren F. Kimball, "The Sheriffs: FDR's Postwar World," in *FDR's World: War, Peace, and Legacies* (New York: Palgrave Macmillan, 2008), 98.

13. Harriman press conference, February 4, 1944, box 748, Averell Harriman papers.

14. Frankfurter to Stettinius, April 18, 1949, box 877, Stettinius papers.

15. Bohlen to Stettinius, March 26, 1949, box 877, Stettinius papers.

16. This was the thesis of the most significant study of wartime diplomacy published in the 1950s, Herbert Feis's *Roosevelt Churchill Stalin* (Princeton, NJ: Princeton University Press, 1957). Feis acknowledged that he was "encouraged and aided" by Harriman, who had made available his voluminous, otherwise closed-for-research papers and who sat for interviews. Kennan also opened his papers to Feis. See ibid., v–vi.

17. The publication of Alperovitz's *Atomic Diplomacy* (New York: Simon and Schuster, 1965) touched off an intense debate that would rage for decades and in 1995 reach the public in the controversy over the Hiroshima exhibit at the Smithsonian Institution. It appears that the Truman administration saw the bomb's diplomatic impact on Moscow as useful but subsidiary to securing the quick surrender of Tokyo without a bloody invasion of the home islands. See Michael D. Gordin, *Red Cloud at Dawn* (New York: Farrar, Straus and Giroux, 2009); Andrew J. Rotter, *Hiroshima: The World's Bomb* (New York: Oxford University Press, 2008); Campbell Craig and Sergey Radchenko, *The Atomic Bomb and the Origins of the Cold War* (New Haven, CT: Yale University Press, 2008); Sean L. Malloy, *Atomic Tragedy* (Ithaca, NY: Cornell University Press, 2008); Wilson D. Miscamble, *From Roosevelt to Truman* (New York: Cambridge University Press, 2007); Tsuyoshi Hasegawa, *Racing the Enemy* (Cambridge, MA: Harvard University Press, 2005); J. Samuel Walker, *Prompt and Utter Destruction* (Chapel Hill: University of North Carolina Press, 1997); Michael J. Hogan, ed., *Hiroshima in History and Memory* (New York: Cambridge University Press, 1996).

18. Schlesinger seminar, 1967. Other participants were Hamilton Fish Armstrong, Philip Mosely, John J. McCloy, and Chester Cooper.

19. Kai Bird, *John J. McCloy, the Making of the American Establishment* (New York: Simon and Schuster, 1992).

20. Schlesinger seminar, 1967.

21. Arthur Schlesinger Jr., "The Origins of the Cold War," in *The Origins of the Cold War*, ed. Lloyd C. Gardner, Arthur Schlesinger Jr., and Hans J. Morgenthau (Waltham, MA: Ginn and Co., 1970), 73.

22. John Lewis Gaddis, "The Emerging Post-Revisionist Synthesis on the Origins of the Cold War," *Diplomatic History* 7 (Summer 1983): 176, 181.

23. Lloyd C. Gardner, "Response," ibid., 191–93; Warren F. Kimball, "Response," ibid., 198–200, 198 for the quotation.

24. Deborah Welch Larson, *Origins of Containment: A Psychological Explanation* (Princeton, NJ: Princeton University Press, 1985).

25. Robert Service, *Stalin* (London: Macmillan, 2004); Simon Sebag Montefiore, *Stalin: The Court of the Red Tsar* (New York: Knopf, 2004); Hiroaki Kuromiya, *Stalin* (Harlow, UK: Pearson Longman, 2005).

26. Vojtech Mastny, *The Cold War and Soviet Insecurity* (New York: Oxford University Press, 1996), 11–12, 194.

27. John Lewis Gaddis, *We Now Know* (New York: Oxford University Press, 1997), 25.

28. Ibid., 8, 21.

29. Ibid., 22, 15, 23. In his presidential address to the Society for Historians of American Foreign Relations in 1992, Gaddis depicted Stalin as so "psychologically disturbed" that, in the arena of postwar diplomacy, the dictator and the nation he had shaped "were incapable of functioning within the framework of mutual cooperation, indeed mutual coexistence." John Lewis Gaddis, "The Tragedy of Cold War History," *Diplomatic History* 17 (January 1993): 6, 11.

30. Zubok and Pleshakov, *Inside the Kremlin's Cold War*, 19.

31. Vladislav Zubok, *A Failed Empire: The Soviet Union in the Cold War from Stalin to Gorbachev* (Chapel Hill: University of North Carolina Press, 2007), 13–14.

32. Odd Arne Westad, *The Global Cold War: Third World Interventions and the Making of Our Times* (New York: Cambridge University Press, 2005).

33. Melvyn P. Leffler, *For the Soul of Mankind: The United States, the Soviet Union, and the Cold War* (New York: Hill and Wang, 2007), 34–36.

34. Roberts, *Stalin's Wars*, xi.

35. Miscamble, *From Roosevelt to Truman.*

36. Jonathan Haslam, *Russia's Cold War* (New Haven, CT: Yale University Press, 2011).

37. Jochen Laufer, *Pax Sovietica: Stalin die Westmächte und die deutsche Frage 1941–1945* (Cologne: Böhlau Verlag, 2009).

38. Norman M. Naimark, *Stalin's Genocides* (Princeton, NJ: Princeton University Press, 2010), 35, 50.

39. Timothy Snyder, *Bloodlands: Europe between Hitler and Stalin* (New York: Basic Books, 2010), 389.

40. Regarding emotions and diplomacy: In foreign relations, "reason" rules: both scholars and practitioners generally view policy as resulting from "rational" calculations by actors "realistically" appraising "objective" national interests. The assumption of a clear-cut opposition between the rational and the emotional says more, however, about traditional Western concepts about the division of mind and body than it does about the actual nature of thought. The emerging consensus among both humanists and scientists holds that emotion and cognition are not contrasting modes of thought but rather intertwined processes. Thought integrates cognition and emotion through constant feedback between the brain, bodily states, and culturally conditioned perceptions. The brain does not distinguish between cognitive and emotional thought, between concluding that Wednesday follows Tuesday or that rape is repugnant. Emotion is necessary to rational decision making. Emotions affect the intensity of what someone wants, believes, and does. In charging events and experiences with value, emotions help form and strengthen beliefs.

Although the polarity between the rational and the emotional is a construction that does not accurately represent how thought actually occurs, that polarity was nevertheless a basic premise of foreign policy makers as they discussed what they believed they and others were analyzing, feeling, and doing. Therefore it remains necessary to refer at times to emotion and reason as if they were easily separable modes of thinking. See Jerome Kagan, *What Is Emotion?* (New Haven, CT: Yale University Press, 2007). On using emotion as a category of historical analysis, see, for instance, William M. Reddy, *The Navigation of Feeling* (New York: Cambridge University Press, 2001); Barbara H. Rosenwein, *Emotional Communities in the Early Middle Ages* (Ithaca, NY: Cornell University Press, 2006). On psychological concepts held in the United States in the first half of the twentieth century, see Joel Pfister and Nancy Schnog, eds., *Inventing the Psychological* (New Haven, CT: Yale University Press, 1997); Karen Horney, *The Neurotic Personality of Our Time* (New York: W. W. Norton, 1937).

41. Mercer, "Emotional Beliefs," 1–31. See also Mercer, "Rationality and Psychology in International Politics," *International Organization* 59 (Winter 2005): 77–106; Robert Jervis, "Understanding Beliefs," *Political Psychology* 27 (2006): 641–63.

42. George F. Kennan, *Memoirs, 1925–1950* (Boston: Houghton Mifflin, 1967), 261.

43. Culture encompasses beliefs, values, practices, and attitudes; the analytical categories of race, class, and gender; and ideas and practices relating to religion, time, space, rituals, games, and so forth. Culture reflects and reinforces the meanings that we attach to experiences and developments.

44. Christopher F. A. Warner, memorandum of conversation with M. Koukin, May 19, 1945, F. O. 371/47854, National Archives, Kew, United Kingdom.

45. Norman M. Naimark, *The Russians in Germany* (Cambridge, MA: Harvard University Press, 1995), 69–140.

46. Stafford Cripps diary, November 7, 1940, Stafford Cripps papers.

47. Joseph E. Davies, "Discussion of Vatican with Molotov," May 28, 1943, box 13, Joseph E. Davies papers.

48. Andrew H. Kydd, *Trust and Mistrust in International Relations* (Princeton, NJ: Princeton University Press, 2005), 3–27.

49. Churchill quoted in James Forrestal diary, March 10, 1946, copy in box 186, Averell Harriman papers.

50. Naimark, *Stalin's Genocides*, 88–92; Snyder, *Bloodlands*, 119–54.

51. On Maisky's importance in Moscow, see Fraser J. Harbutt, *Yalta 1945* (New York: Cambridge University Press, 2010), 106–9.

52. Clark Kerr to Christopher Warner, August 10, 1943, F. O. 800/301/104-05, NA, UK.

53. Ibid. (emphasis in original).

Chapter 1. A Portrait of the Allies as Young Men: Franklin, Winston, and Koba

1. Elliott Roosevelt, ed., *FDR: His Personal Letters, 1905–1928* (New York: Duell, Sloan and Pearce, 1948), 11.

2. Robert Service, *Stalin* (London: Macmillan, 2004), 34, 44.

3. Ibid., 65–66, 74–75.

4. Simon Sebag Montefiore, *Young Stalin* (New York: Alfred A. Knopf, 2007), 176.

5. Randolph S. Churchill, *Winston S. Churchill: Young Statesman* (Boston: Houghton Mifflin, 1968), 190; Geoffrey C. Ward, *Before the Trumpet: Young Franklin Roosevelt, 1882–1905* (New York: Harper & Row, 1985), 229–30.

6. Alan Woods, *Bolshevism: The Road to Revolution* (London: Wellred Publications, 1999), 302–4.

7. Louis Adamic, *Dinner at the White House* (New York: Harper & Brothers, 1946), 68.

8. Peregrine Churchill and Julian Mitchell, *Jennie* (London: Collins, 1974), 68. With dark skin and purportedly Iroquois ancestry, Clara was nicknamed "Sitting Bull" by Randolph (ibid., 14). See also John Pearson, *The Private Lives of Winston Churchill* (New York: Simon & Schuster, 1991), 35–51.

9. Courtney Letts de Espil, October 1942, box 10, de Espil diary. Courtney Letts de Espil, an American, was married to Felipe de Espil, Argentine ambassador to Washington.

10. Sara Delano Roosevelt, *My Boy Franklin* (New York: R. Long and R. R. Smith, 1933), 43.

11. Jean Edward Smith, *FDR* (New York: Random House, 2007), 30.

12. Ibid., xvi.

13. Belle Willard Roosevelt diary, June 13, 1942, box 136.

14. Sara Delano Roosevelt, *My Boy Franklin*, 15.

15. Ibid.

16. Ward, *Before the Trumpet*, 158–63.

17. Paul Johnson, *Churchill* (New York: Viking, 2009), 26.

18. Jon Meacham, *Franklin and Winston* (New York: Random House, 2003), 11.

19. Martin Gilbert, *Churchill, a Life*, 8.

20. Ibid., 6.

21. Ibid., 9, 20–21.

22. Mary S. Lovell, *The Churchills in Love and War* (New York: W. W. Norton, 2011), 113, 579–80.

23. Winston S. Churchill, *My Early Life* (London: Butterworth, 1930), 46, 40.

24. Gilbert, *Churchill, a Life*, 38.

25. Lord Moran, *Churchill at War 1940–45* (New York: Carroll & Graf, 2002), 204. See also Lovell, *Churchills*, 267.

26. Johnson, *Churchill*, 7.

27. Churchill, *My Early Life*, 4.

28. Johnson, *Churchill*, 11–12.

29. Churchill, *My Early Life*, 46.

30. Gilbert, *Churchill, a Life*, 13.

31. Anthony Storr, "The Man," in *Churchill Revised*, ed. A.J.P. Taylor (New York: Dial, 1969), 251.

32. Randolph S. Churchill, ed., *Winston S. Churchill Companion Volume* (Boston: Houghton Mifflin, 1967), vol. 1, pt. 2, 815.

33. Ibid., 828.

34. Winston S. Churchill, *Savrola* (London: Longmans, 1900), 156–57.

35. Ibid., 108.

36. Norman Rose, *Churchill: The Unruly Giant* (New York: Free Press, 1995), 254.

37. Ibid., 71–73. See also Lovell, *Churchills*, 207–8.

38. Simon Sebag Montefiore, *Stalin: The Court of the Red Tsar* (New York: Knopf, 2004), 25–27; Service, *Stalin*, 17–25; Hiroaki Kuromiya, *Stalin* (Harlow, UK: Pearson Longman, 2005), 3.

39. Montefiore, *Stalin*, 182.

40. Service, *Stalin*, 30–31.

41. Service, *Stalin*, 25; Montefiore, *Stalin*, 152.

42. Johnson, *Churchill*, 3.

43. Ward, *Before the Trumpet*, 215; Smith, *FDR*, 28.

44. Churchill, *My Early Life*, 12.

45. Ibid., 18–21.

46. Johnson, *Churchill*, 10–11.

47. Montefiore, *Young Stalin*, 55–56.

48. Ibid., 60–62.

49. Kuromiya, *Stalin*, 7.

50. Montefiore, *Young Stalin*, 56.

51. Alfred J. Rieber, "Stalin, Man of the Borderlands," *American Historical Review* 106 (December 2001): 1668.

52. Montefiore, *Young Stalin*, 301.

53. Ibid., 286.

54. Kuromiya, *Stalin*, 20.

55. Service, *Stalin*, 232.

56. Kuromiya, *Stalin*, 7.

57. Montefiore, *Young Stalin*, 74–75.

58. Andrew Preston, *Sword of the Spirit, Shield of Faith: Religion in American War and Diplomacy* (New York: Knopf, forthcoming), 489–90.

59. Kim Townsend, *Manhood at Harvard* (New York: W. W. Norton, 1996), 17, 256–80; Sarah Watts, *Rough Rider in the White House* (Chicago: University of Chicago Press, 2003), 195–235.

60. Geoffrey C. Ward, *A First Class Temperament: The Emergence of Franklin Roosevelt* (New York: Harper & Row, 1989), 88.

61. Ibid., 86–88; Ward, *Before the Trumpet*, 195.

62. Smith, *FDR*, 28.

63. Watts, *Rough Rider in the White House*, 4; Townsend, *Manhood at Harvard*, 259.

64. Gore Vidal, "Theodore Roosevelt: An American Sissy," in *United States: Essays 1952–1992*, ed. Gore Vidal (New York: Random House, 1993), 733, 723–37.

65. Smith, *FDR*, 6.

66. Smith, *FDR*, 653.

67. Smith, *FDR*, 48.

68. Mark Bonham Carter and Mark Pottle, eds., *Lantern Slides: The Diaries and Letters of Violet Bonham Carter* (London: Weidenfeld and Nicolson, 1996), 356 (emphasis in original).

69. Watts, *Rough Rider in the White House*, 164. Though undoubtedly brave on the battlefield, TR also exaggerated the story of his famous charge up San Juan Hill (ibid., 164–65). On gender relations and the war, see Kristin Hoganson, *Fighting for American Manhood: How Gender Politics Provoked the Spanish-American and Philippine-American Wars* (New Haven, CT: Yale University Press, 1998).

70. Randolph S. Churchill, ed., *Churchill Companion Volume*, vol. 1, pt. 2, 793.

71. Ibid., 839.

72. Churchill, *My Early Life*, 1, 77.

73. Ibid., 129.

74. Randolph S. Churchill, ed., *Churchill Companion Volume*, vol. 1, pt. 2, 791.

75. Ibid., 792.

76. Richard Holmes, *In the Footsteps of Churchill* (New York: Basic Books, 2005), 57.

77. Mark Pottle, ed., *Champion Redoubtable: The Diaries and Letters of Violet Bonham Carter* (London: Weidenfeld and Nicolson, 1998), 25 (emphasis in original).

78. Ward, *First-Class Temperament*, 241–42.

79. Ibid., 301.

80. Frank Freidel, *Franklin D. Roosevelt: The Apprenticeship* (Boston: Little, Brown, 1952), 337–72.

81. Ward, *First-Class Temperament*, 346.

82. FDR's eldest son remembered his father as not eager to fight. James Roosevelt, *My Parents* (Chicago: Playboy Press, 1976), 44.

83. Freidel, *Franklin D. Roosevelt: The Apprenticeship*, 337.

84. Ibid., 346–48.

85. Montefiore, *Young Stalin*, 35, 46, 302.

86. Montefiore, *Stalin*, 456–58.

87. Service, *Stalin*, 164.

88. Jonathan Haslam, *Russia's Cold War* (New Haven, CT: Yale University Press, 2011), vi.

89. Service, *Stalin*, 83, 131, 139, 163–74; Montefiore, *Young Stalin*, 316.

90. Montefiore, *Young Stalin*, 57.

91. Service, *Stalin*, 39. For the overlap with his Marxist period, see Rieber, "Stalin," 1667.

92. Kuromiya, *Stalin*, 5.

93. Montefiore, *Young Stalin*, 200.

94. Ibid., 60.

95. Ibid.

96. Ward, *First-Class Temperament*, 54, 679–82; 682 for the quotation.

97. Violet Bonham Carter, *Winston Churchill: An Intimate Portrait* (New York: Harcourt, Brace & World, 1965), 7.

98. Montefiore, *Stalin*, 48.

99. Sergo Beria, *Beria, My Father* (London: Duckworth, 2001), 143–44.

100. Montefiore, *Stalin*, 178.

101. Ibid., 50.

102. Beria, *Beria*, 142.

103. Ibid., 134.

104. Montefiore, *Stalin*, 5.

105. Ward, *First-Class Temperament*, 771 (emphasis in original).

106. Ibid., 750.

107. John Gunther, *Roosevelt in Retrospect* (New York: Harper, 1950), 34.

108. Henry Kannee, interview with Graff, [1962], box 4, Graff papers.

109. Ward, *First-Class Temperament*, 222, 699.

110. Gunther, *Roosevelt*, 62.

111. Adamic, *Dinner at the White House*, 85.

112. Gunther, *Roosevelt*, 22–23 (emphasis in original).

113. Martin Gilbert, ed., *The Churchill War Papers* (New York: W. W. Norton, 1993), 3:1709.

114. Holmes, *In the Footsteps of Churchill*, 23.

115. Bonham Carter, *Churchill*, 9.

116. Ibid., 7.

117. Moran, *Churchill at War*, 301.

118. Bonham Carter, *Churchill*, 114.

119. Randall S. Churchill, ed., *Churchill Companion Volume*, vol. 1, pt. 2, 816–21.

120. Joseph P. Lash diary, January 1, 1942, box 31, Lash papers.

121. Ward, *Before the Trumpet*, 253 (emphasis in original).

122. Anna Rosenberg, interview with Joseph Lash, November 10, 1969, box 44, Lash papers.

123. Leila Stiles to mother, January 31, 1935, box 10, Stiles papers.

124. Stiles to mother, February 2, 1937, box 10, Stiles papers.

125. Moran, *Churchill at War*, 324.

126. Mary Soames, *Clementine Churchill* (Boston: Houghton Mifflin, 2003), 298–99.

127. Montefiore, *Young Stalin*, 241.

128. Montefiore, *Stalin*, 15–16.

129. Kuromiya, *Stalin*, 16–18.

130. Montefiore, *Stalin*, 15–16; Feliks Chuev, *Molotov Remembers* (Chicago: Ivan R. Dee, 1993), 174. To such men of power, keeping score with regard to women remained important, even amid the demands of wartime leadership. Following up his round-the-world tour, former Republican presidential candidate Wendell Willkie, who always kept his eye open for attractive women, reported on the "harem" of Stalin. "He likes them middle aged, fat, and frowsy." This was news that White House aides thought merited reporting to FDR "in great confidence." Marvin H. McIntyre to the president, October 22, 1943, box 173, Roosevelt, PSF.

131. Montefiore, *Stalin*, 46.

132. Montefiore, *Young Stalin*, 262.

133. Montefiore, *Stalin*, 87–88.

134. Reminiscences of Marquis Childs (1959), CUOHRC, 109–10. On androgyny, see Kari Weil, *Androgyny and the Denial of Difference* (Charlottesville: University of Virginia Press, 1992); Carolyn Heilbrun, *Toward a Recognition of Androgyny* (New York: Knopf, 1973).

135. Ward, *First-Class Temperament*, 551.

136. Josephus Daniels, interview with Frank Freidel, May 29, 1947, Small Collections, Oral History Interviews, FDRL.

137. Gunther, *Roosevelt*, 36, 72, 120, 164–65. Columnist Arthur Krock recalled that "Roosevelt had a strong feminine side." Reminiscences of Arthur Krock (1950), CUOHRC, 64.

138. Ibid., 62.

139. Ward, *Before the Trumpet*, 204–5.

140. Perceptions of FDR as feminine or as androgynous invite several layers of analysis. First, such depictions highlight the arbitrariness, in all constructions of gender, of trying neatly to separate out masculine and feminine traits. Second, the perceptions point up how certain gender stereotypes worked in his time. Women were supposedly more likely than men to rely on emotions, seduction, and subterfuge. Third, mixed messages could be sexy.

141. While quick to acknowledge Roosevelt's essential masculinity, observers also tried to account for why he appealed so intensely to men as well as to women. Lacking a vocabulary for what the feminist and queer theorist Eve Kosofsky Sedgwick has analyzed as "homosocial" feeling, some of FDR's contemporaries labeled as "feminine" an allure that a later generation, more attuned to gender bending, could interpret as flowing from a generic sexuality. Androgyny is often associated with glamor and charm. Charm, particularly when distilled into charisma, can be sexy even if the eroticism remains implicit. As the saying goes, power is an aphrodisiac. But explicitly sexual attraction is only one way by which power seduces. Sedgwick, *Between Men* (New York: Columbia University Press, 1985).

142. Reminiscences of Frances Perkins (1955), CUOHRC, 4:457.

143. Ward, *First-Class Temperament*, 183.

144. Belle Willard Roosevelt diary, June 13, 1942, box 136.

145. On the perceived association between disability and femininity, see Rosemarie Garland Thomson, *Extraordinary Bodies* (New York: Columbia University Press, 1997), 19–29; Catherine J. Kudlick, "Disability History: Why We Need Another 'Other,'" *American Historical Review* 108 (June 2003): 108.

146. Gunther, *Roosevelt*, 24.

147. Paul K. Longmore and Lauri Umansky, eds., *The New Disability History* (New York: New York University Press, 2001); "Disability and History," special issue of *Radical History* 94 (Winter 2006).

148. Frank Costigliola, "Broken Circle: The Isolation of Franklin D. Roosevelt in World War II," *Diplomatic History* 32 (November 2008): 686–87.

149. Pottle, *Champion Redoubtable*, 318.

150. Alex Danchev and Daniel Todman, eds., *War Diaries 1939–1945: Field Marshal Lord Alanbrooke* (Berkeley: University of California Press, 2001), 450.

151. Rose, *Churchill*, 248.

152. Holmes, *In the Footsteps of Churchill*, 20–21.

153. Johnson, *Churchill*, 113.

154. See chapter 5.

155. Churchill met other "powerful men . . . in his boudoir or in various stages of deshabille." Richard Holmes, *Churchill's Bunker* (New Haven, CT: Yale University Press, 2009), 97.

156. Andrew Schlesinger and Stephen Schlesinger, eds., *Journals 1952–2000: Arthur M. Schlesinger, Jr.* (New York: Penguin, 2007), 575.

157. Rose, *Churchill*, 240. For suggestions of familiarity with various drugs, see Churchill, *Savrola*, 124, 235.

158. Johnson, *Churchill*, 70–71.

159. Hopkins had the U.S. Navy analyze the pills. John Harper to Hopkins, December 8, 1941, Sherwood papers.

160. Reminiscences of Perkins (1955), CUOHRC, 8:640.

161. Montefiore, *Stalin*, 6.

162. Service, *Stalin*, 365.

163. Ibid., 226.

164. Rieber, "Stalin," 1669.

165. James Roosevelt and Sidney Shalett, *Affectionately, F.D.R.* (New York: Harcourt, Brace, 1959), 59–60.

166. Frank Freidel, *Roosevelt: The Ordeal* (Boston: Little, Brown, 1954), 30–31.

167. Churchill, *Savrola*, 109–10, 216.

168. Martin Gilbert, ed., *Churchill Companion Volume* (Boston: Houghton Mifflin, 1978), vol. 4, pt. 2, 921.

169. Rose, *Churchill*, 176–83.

170. While Churchill was in Moscow for the 1944 TOLSTOY conference, aides were startled by a bellowing from his bathroom. Responding to "Come in, Goddamit!" a diplomat found "the naked great Churchill bulk sitting in 3/4 of an inch of water. 'Bloody hell,' Churchill was roaring, 'Bloody goddam hell. Water stopped. Do something, man. No bloody Russian water.'" John Hersey to Patch, October 13, 1944, box 7, Hersey papers.

171. Rose, *Churchill*, 245, 250–51.

172. Pottle, *Champion Redoubtable*, 252.

173. Rose, *Churchill*, 179.

174. Ibid., 185.

175. Holmes, *In the Footsteps of Churchill*, 183.

176. Service, *Stalin*, 92–101; Rieber, "Stalin," 1651–91.

177. Service, *Stalin*, 341–42 (emphasis in original).

178. Montefiore, *Stalin*, 308.

179. Ibid., 139.

180. Rose, *Churchill*, 244.

181. Joseph P. Lash diary, June 8, 1941, box 31, Lash papers.

182. Schlesinger and Schlesinger, *Journals*, 575.

183. Dorothy Schiff, memorandum, November 23, 1981; interview with Jeffrey Potter, December 29, 1972; memorandum, October 9, 1943, all in box 258, Schiff papers.

184. Geoffrey W. Ward, ed., *Closest Companion* (Boston: Houghton Mifflin, 1995), 423 (emphasis in original).

185. For a rosier view of their friendship, see Meacham, *Franklin and Winston*.

186. Lord Moran, *Churchill Taken from the Diaries of Lord Moran* (Boston: Houghton Mifflin, 1966), 322. In his magisterial, six-volume history of the war written between 1948 and 1953, Churchill would burnish the memory of his friendship with Roosevelt. He appreciated both FDR's help during the war and the lucrative market in America for books that told a grand story. See David Reynolds, *In Command of History* (London: Penguin, 2004).

187. Geoffrey M. Wilson to Archibald Clark Kerr, May 15, 1944, F. O. 800/302/73, NA, UK.

188. Schlesinger and Schlesinger, *Journals*, 575.

Chapter 2. From Missy to Molotov: The Women and Men Who Sustained the Big Three

1. Reminiscences of Samuel I. Rosenman (1959), CUOHRC, 110.

2. Joseph P. Lash, ed., *From the Diaries of Felix Frankfurter* (New York: W. W. Norton, 1975), 162.

3. Bernard Asbell, *The F. D. R. Memoirs* (Garden City, NY: Doubleday), 249.

4. Harold L. Ickes diary, September 9, 1939, Harold L. Ickes papers. An ambitious, crotchety, self-styled "curmudgeon," Ickes was nonetheless scrupulous in recording in his diary his opinions and what people told him. He stayed in touch with leading figures in politics and journalism and was friends with Anna Roosevelt Boettiger, who in turn received regular letters from her mother's secretary.

5. "Missy," August 2, 1944, *Washington Post*, copy in box 23, Steve Early papers, FDRL.

6. Lash, *From the Diaries of Felix Frankfurter*, 162.

7. Ernest Cuneo, "Hopkins: Method of Operation," box 112, Ernest Cuneo papers, FDRL.

8. Ickes diary, April 7, 1945.

9. "Disability" is not an essential or natural marking, but rather a socially constructed category of differentiation, much like gender and class. Regarding a characteristic as a disability, whether it be difficulty in walking without crutches or seeing without corrective lenses, is one of the ways that a society determines its hierarchies. Disability means not inability but rather differently able. See Catherine J. Kudlick, "Disability History: Why We Need Another 'Other,'" *American Historical Review* 108 (June 2003): 764–65; Hugh Gregory Gallagher, *FDR's Splendid Deception* (New York: Dodd, Mead, 1985).

10. Samuel I. Rosenman, interview with Joseph P. Lash, December 3, 1969, box 44, Lash papers.

11. Abe Fortas, interview with Graff, [1962], box 4, Graff papers.

12. Dorothy Schiff, interview with Jeffrey Potter, December 29, 1972, box 258, Schiff papers.

13. Ickes diary, July 12, 1941.

14. Robert H. Ferrell, *The Dying President* (Columbia: University of Missouri Press, 1998), 168.

15. [Jay Carter Franklin], *The New Dealers* (New York: Literary Guild, 1934), 233.

16. Earl Miller to Miriam Abelow, August 23, 1966, Miriam Abelow papers, Small Collections, FDRL.

17. Eliot Janeway diary, May 24, 1941, Eliot Janeway papers, Library of Congress, Washington, DC.

18. Miller to Abelow, August 23, 1966, Miriam Abelow papers, Small Collections, FDRL.

19. Thomas G. Corcoran, interview with Philip Kopper, [1979], box 587, Corcoran papers.

20. Julie Gilbert, *Opposite Attraction: The Lives of Erich Maria Remarque and Paulette Goddard* (New York: Pantheon Books, 1995), 269.

21. Schiff, interview with Potter, January 13, 1973 and December 29, 1972, box 258, Schiff papers.

22. Katherine Hepburn, *Me* (New York: Knopf, 1992), 165.

23. Alfred B. Rollins, *Roosevelt and Howe* (New York: Knopf, 1962), 67–69.

24. Lela Stiles, *The Man behind Roosevelt* (Cleveland: World Publishing, 1954), 161. Stiles worked in the White House for Howe and Roosevelt.

25. R. H. Camalier, interview with Frank Freidel, May 28, 1948, Freidel interviews, Small Collections, FDRL.

26. Eleanor Roosevelt, *This I Remember* (New York: Harper & Brothers, 1949), 167.

27. Doris Faber, *The Life of Lorena Hickok* (New York: Morrow, 1980), 221.

28. Rowley, *Franklin and Eleanor* (New York: Farrar, Straus and Giroux, 2010), 260–61.

29. Stiles, *Man behind Roosevelt*, 279.

30. Corcoran, interview with Kopper, November 26, 1979, box 587, Corcoran papers; Joseph P. Lash, *Dealers and Dreamers* (New York: Doubleday, 1988), 230–32.

31. Corcoran, interview with Kopper, July 17, 1979, box 587, Corcoran papers.

32. Ibid. In response to Kopper's question, Corcoran remained discreet about "how indiscreet."

33. Corcoran, interview with Graff, [1962], box 4, Graff papers.

34. Amanda Smith, ed., *The Letters of Joseph P. Kennedy* (New York: Viking, 2001), 155–56.

35. Corcoran, interview with Kopper, July 17, 1979, box 587, Corcoran papers. The "Commies" comment may have been at the July 1935 gathering or at a

similar Roosevelt party at Kennedy's estate. Decades later, Corcoran attributed the comment to "George" and said that FDR "probably laughed."

36. David McKean, *Peddling Influence: Thomas "Tommy the Cork" Corcoran and the Birth of Modern Lobbying* (Hanover, NH: Steerforth Press, 2004) 104–12.

37. Michael Janeway, *The Fall of the House of Roosevelt* (New York: Columbia University Press, 2004), 14.

38. Philip Kopper, interview with author, July 17, 2007, phone conversation.

39. Ickes diary, July 16, 19, 1938.

40. Reminiscences of Marquis Childs (1958), CUOHRC, 106. Childs said that Baruch had told him the story. In the transcript, Childs deleted the name of the person who had accompanied Eleanor to Baruch's apartment. Even in 1958, Corcoran remained a person dangerous to offend.

41. Ickes diary, January 10, 1937. After their father died, James and FDR Jr. tried to get Frank Capra to direct a picture based on FDR's life. They consulted with Hopkins, who afterward observed, "They seem to have some pretty ambitious notions as to how much money can be made out of it." Hopkins to David Hopkins, December 18, 1945, series 1, box 1, Hopkins papers, Georgetown.

42. Ickes diary, October 9, 1937. The report came from Hopkins.

43. Ickes diary, April 1, 1939.

44. Reminiscences of Childs (1958), CUOHRC, 119.

45. Ickes diary, July 16, 1938.

46. Janeway, *Fall of the House of Roosevelt*, 22; McKean, *Peddling Influence*, 187–88.

47. Corcoran, "Rendezvous with Democracy," unpublished autobiography (written with Philip Kopper), chap. 10, pp. 15–16, box 587, Corcoran papers.

48. Ibid., p. 18.

49. Ibid., p. 19.

50. Ibid.

51. Asbell, *F. D. R. Memoirs*, 244.

52. Ibid., 241.

53. Doris Kearns Goodwin, *No Ordinary Time* (New York: Simon & Schuster, 1994), 117–19.

54. John Gunther, *Roosevelt in Retrospect* (New York: Harper, 1950), 73.

55. Lillian Rogers Parks, *The Roosevelts* (Englewood Cliffs, NJ: Prentice-Hall, 1981), 177, 82.

56. Unofficial Observer [John Franklin Carter], *The New Dealers* (New York: Simon & Schuster, 1934), 231–32.

57. Parks, *Roosevelts*, 177.

58. Elliott Roosevelt and James Brough, *An Untold Story* (G. P. Putnam's Sons, 1973); James Roosevelt, *My Parents* (Chicago: Playboy Press, 1976), 104–9.

59. Franklin D. Roosevelt Jr., interview with Lash, August 7, 1969, box 44, Lash papers.

60. Anna Roosevelt Halsted, interview with Lash [1966 or 1967], box 44, Lash papers.

61. Rosenman, interview with Lash, December 3, 1969, box 44, Lash papers.

62. Goodwin, *No Ordinary Time*; Gallagher, *Splendid Deception.*

63. Park, *Roosevelts*, 195–96.

64. Schiff memorandum, May 12, 1971, box 64, Schiff papers.

65. My thanks to Joanne Meyerowitz for clarifying this point via e-mail.

66. Corcoran, "Rendezvous with Democracy," chap. 5, p. 36.

67. She concluded the letter, "my love to you—much more of it than I like to confess." LeHand to Bullitt, January 17, 1934, box 49, Bullitt papers. On Bullitt, see Kenneth Weisbrode, *The Atlantic Century* (Cambridge, MA: Da Capo, 2009), 36–38

68. LeHand to Bullitt, March 9, no year, box 49, Bullitt papers.

69. LeHand to Bullitt, no date, box 49, Bullitt papers.

70. LeHand to Bullitt, February 8, no year, box 49, Bullitt papers.

71. LeHand to Bullitt, April 23, no year; May 5 no year, box 49, Bullitt papers.

72. Ernest Lindley, "Marguerite LeHand," August 1, 1933, box 62, Lindley papers.

73. Parks, *Roosevelts*, 180.

74. Stiles to her mother, August 9, 1935, box 10, Stiles papers. LeHand and Kennedy were friends. In a chatty note from London, the ambassador confided that after dinner at Windsor Castle, he had "got 'stinking' with the Queen. You know me. She is great. I'd even let her join our club. Boy, I miss you. Love, Joe" (Kennedy to LeHand, April 10, 1938, box 10, Grace Tully Archive, FDRL).

75. Diana Hopkins Halsted, interview with author, March 11, 2008, phone conversation.

76. Parks, *Roosevelts*, 184.

77. LeHand to Bullitt, Thursday [1934], January 25 [1935 or 1936], March, no year, box 49, Bullitt papers.

78. LeHand to Bullitt, January 25, 1940, box 49, Bullitt papers.

79. LeHand to Roosevelt, December 4, 1936, box 21, Roosevelt Family Papers Donated by the Children, FDRL.

80. LeHand to Roosevelts, Christmas 1936, file 3737, President's Personal File, FDRL.

81. LeHand to FDR, July 29, [1930s], box 31, Roosevelt Family Papers Donated by the Children, FDRL.

82. LeHand to Bullitt, May 21, 1935, box 49, Bullitt papers.

83. "Missy," August 2, 1944, *Washington Post*, copy in box 23, Steve Early papers, FDRL.

84. Corcoran, "Rendezvous with Democracy," chap. 5, p. 36.

85. Ickes diary, July 7, 1936.

86. Ibid., January 1, 1939.

87. Ibid., September 30, 1939.

88. Ibid., April 20, 1941.

89. Ibid., April 26, 1941.

90. In January 1941, the Norwegian king told Hopkins that "he was disturbed" about the "very nervous" behavior of Princess Martha, who was trying too hard

"to act as an emissary of good will." The king may have been obliquely advising that his married daughter's friendship with FDR was becoming embarrassing (Hopkins diary, January 30, 1941, reel 19, FDRL).

91. Goodwin, *No Ordinary Time*, 153.

92. Parks, *Roosevelts*, 200.

93. Walter Trohan, *Political Animals* (Garden City, NY: Doubleday, 1975), 136–37.

94. Parks, *Roosevelts*, 199–200.

95. Rowley, *Franklin and Eleanor*, 254.

96. Schiff, interview with Lash, September 18, 1968, box 44, Lash papers.

97. Bullitt to LeHand, May 29, 1940, box 10, Grace Tully Archive, FDRL.

98. Ickes diary, June 29 and August 3, 22, 1940, Ickes papers; Bullitt to Le-Hand, May 29, 1940; Carmel Offie to LeHand, August 9, 1939, box 10, Grace Tully Archive, FDRL.

99. Offie to LeHand, April 28, 1939, box 10, Grace Tully Archive, FDRL.

100. Ickes diary, February 11, 1940; Bullitt to LeHand, May 29, 1940; Offie to LeHand, November 15, 1939, box 10, Grace Tully Archive, FDRL. Will Brownell and Richard N. Billings, *So Close to Greatness* (New York: Macmillan, 1987), 53–62.

101. Benjamin Welles, *Sumner Welles: FDR's Global Strategist* (New York: St. Martin's Press, 1997), 275.

102. "Statement made by Mr. Luther Thomas, in charge of the Southern Railway Police on November 25th, 1940," box 210, Bullitt papers. See also Irwin F. Gellman, *Secret Affairs: FDR, Cordell Hull, and Sumner Welles* (New York: Enigma Books, 2002).

103. Orville H. Bullitt, ed., *For the President* (Boston: Houghton Mifflin, 1972), 513–14.

104. Ickes diary, September 20, 1941.

105. Bullitt, *For the President*, 553.

106. Ickes diary, March 29, 1942; Brownell and Billings, *So Close to Greatness*, 298–300.

107. Harriman, interview, November 16, 1953, box 872, Averell Harriman papers.

108. Franklin D. Roosevelt Jr., interview with Lash, August 7, 1969, box 44, Lash papers; Corcoran, interview with Philip Kopper, [1979], box 587, Corcoran papers.

109. Bernard Asbell, ed., *Mother & Daughter: The Letters of Eleanor and Anna Roosevelt* (New York: Coward, McCane & Geoghegan, 1982), 132.

110. Drew Pearson, notes, no date, file G247, Pearson papers.

111. Ickes diary, May 7, 1941.

112. Asbell, *Mother & Daughter*, 132.

113. June 5, 1941, FDR Day by Day—The Pare Lorentz Chronology, FDRL.

114. The Hopkins Medical Chart, June 1941, box 6, Ross T. McIntire papers, FDRL.

115. Parks, *Roosevelts*, 187.

116. June 21, 1941, FDR: Day by Day—The Pare Lorentz Chronology, FDRL.

117. Asbell, *The F. D. R. Memoirs*, 403.

118. Ickes diary, July 16, 1938.

119. Asbell, *The F. D. R. Memoirs*, 403.

120. Rosenman, interview with Lash, December 3, 1969, box 44, Lash papers. At the Franklin D. Roosevelt Library only a meager residue attests to her twenty-year relationship with "Effdee." Even the 2010 addition of the LeHand files in the Grace Tully Archive fails to document Missy's important role. Probably the best record of her activity in policy matters are snippets from the Harold Ickes diary. Ironically, Bullitt did save Missy's intimate letters, though he, too, cast her away emotionally.

121. Dr. Winfred Overholser to Roosevelt, August 28, 1941, file 3737, President's Personal File, FDRL.

122. Malvina Thompson to Anna Roosevelt Boettiger, September 29, 1941, box 75, Anna Roosevelt Halsted papers.

123. The Hopkins Medical Chart, 1942, box 6, Ross T. McIntire papers, FDRL.

124. Samuel I. Rosenman, *Working with Roosevelt* (New York: Harper & Brothers, 1952), 460.

125. Bullitt, interview with John Gunther, [1949], box 58, John Gunther papers, Regenstein Library, University of Chicago.

126. Pearson, notes, undated, file F169, Pearson papers.

127. Ickes diary, May 7, 1941.

128. Ibid., April 12, 1941.

129. Corcoran, "Rendezvous with Democracy," chap. 10, p. 13.

130. Robert E. Sherwood, *Roosevelt and Hopkins, an Intimate History* (New York: Harper, 1948), 2.

131. Cuneo, "Hopkins—Method of Operation," box 112, Ernest Cuneo papers, FDRL.

132. Goodwin, *No Ordinary Time*, 31.

133. Clare Boothe Luce, "The White House," July 25, 1940, box 56, Clare Boothe Luce papers, Library of Congress, Washington, DC.

134. Franklin D. Roosevelt Jr., interview with Diana Halsted and James Halsted, no date, FDRL.

135. Ibid.

136. The precise diagnosis remains uncertain. Chapter 8 of Dr. James Halsted's unpublished biography of Harry Hopkins discusses the possibilities. Manuscript in possession of June Hopkins.

137. Belle Willard Roosevelt diary, June 13, 1942, box 136.

138. Ickes diary, November 14, 1945.

139. Reminiscences of Perkins (1955), CUOHRC, 7:561.

140. Franklin D. Roosevelt Jr., interview with Diana Halsted and James Halsted, no date, FDRL.

141. Reminiscences of Perkins (1955), CUOHRC, 7:534.

142. Larry I. Bland, ed., *George C. Marshall Interviews and Reminiscences for Forrest C. Pogue* (Lexington, Va.: George C. Marshall Research Foundation,

1991), 433; Andrew Roberts, *Masters and Commanders* (New York: Harper, 2009), 27.

143. Forrest C. Pogue, *George C. Marshall: Ordeal and Hope* (New York: Viking, 1966), 25.

144. James Halsted, interview with Ernest Lindley, July 30, 1976, box 62, Lindley papers. I am indebted to J. Garry Clifford for sharing this document. Halsted, who had been Anna Roosevelt's husband when she died in 1975, subsequently married Harry Hopkins's daughter, Diana.

145. Malvina Thompson to Anna Roosevelt Boettiger, June 6, 1941, box 75, Anna Roosevelt Halsted papers.

146. Bland, *George C. Marshall Interviews*, 581.

147. Ibid., 434.

148. Memorandum by Raymond Clapper, January 3, 1942, box 23, Clapper papers.

149. Ickes diary, May 23, 1943.

150. Reminiscences of Perkins (1955), CUOHRC, 7:547–48.

151. For Hopkins and Hale, see Ickes diary, July 9, October 9, October 22, 1938; September 15, 1940; January 23, 1943.

152. FDR suggested she use the same architect and contractor he had chosen for Top Cottage. "I think we would both save money," he assured her. FDR to Schiff, April 5, 1938, box 64, Schiff papers. Schiff later remembered that when she hesitated, Sam Rosenman and presidential adviser Anna Rosenberg warned, "when the President asks you to do something, you do it" (Schiff memorandum, December 30, 1985, box 64, Schiff papers).

153. Schiff, interview with Potter, [1973], box 257, Schiff papers.

154. Hopkins's associate, Aubrey Williams, quoted in Halsted, unpublished biography of Hopkins, chap. 12. Corcoran later said that Hopkins had enlisted him and Baruch to minimize press reports of Harry's past relations with the dead woman. David McKean, *Peddling Influence*, 114.

155. Merle Miller, *Lyndon: An Oral Biography* (New York: G. P. Putnam's Sons, 1980), 70. Hopkins's interpreter in the Soviet Union was "an attractive-looking Russian woman." Sherwood, *Roosevelt and Hopkins*, 325–26.

156. Reminiscences of Perkins (1955), CUOHRC, 7:547–48.

157. Ickes diary, May 7, 1941.

158. Ibid.

159. Reminiscences of Perkins (1955), CUOHRC, 7:553.

160. Geoffrey W. Ward, ed., *Closest Companion* (Boston: Houghton Mifflin, 1995), 353.

161. Schiff, interviews with Potter, December 10, 29, 1972, box 258, Schiff papers.

162. Franklin D. Roosevelt Jr., interview with Diana Halsted and James Halsted, no date, FDRL.

163. "Profile," *New Yorker*, August 7, 1943, 3.

164. Thomas Parrish, *To Keep the British Isles Afloat* (New York: HarperCollins, 2009), 274.

165. Other problems detracted from the glitter of White House living. Meals prepared under head cook Henrietta Nesbitt were so bad that savvy dinner guests ate before arriving, and FDR relished food brought in by friends. One dinner guest observed "an army of cockroaches running around . . . climbing on chairs and even on one of our backs" (de Espil diary, April 1941, box 10). See also Laura Shapiro, "The First Kitchen: Eleanor Roosevelt's Depression-era Fare," *New Yorker*, November 22, 2010, 74–80.

166. Malvina Thompson to Anna Roosevelt Boettiger, July 18, 1942, box 74, Anna Roosevelt Halsted papers.

167. Diana Hopkins Halsted, interview with Emily Williams, 1979, FDRL.

168. Rosenman, interview with Lash, December 3, 1969, box 44, Lash papers.

169. Diana Hopkins Halsted, interview with Williams, 1979, FDRL.

170. Rosenman, interview with Lash, December 3, 1969, box 44, Lash papers.

171. James Halsted, unpublished biography of Harry Hopkins, chap. 12.

172. Ibid. The Pearson column appeared on August 6, 1943.

173. Francis Biddle, interview with Graff, [1962], box 4, Graff papers.

174. John Colville, *Fringes of Power: 10 Downing Street Diaries* (New York: W. W. Norton, 1985), 108, 132, 122, 143. For Colville's relationship with Churchill, see Roy Jenkins, *Churchill* (New York: Farrar, Straus and Giroux, 2001), 593.

175. Richard Holmes, *Churchill's Bunker* (New Haven, CT: Yale University Press, 2009), 98–102.

176. Jenkins, *Churchill*, 611, 621.

177. Martin Gilbert, *In Search of Churchill* (New York: John Wiley & Sons, 1994), 178, 164.

178. Kenneth Young, ed., *The Diaries of Sir Robert Bruce Lockhart 1939–1965* (London: Macmillan, 1980), 102; Andrew Roberts, *Masters and Commanders* (New York: HarperCollins, 2009), 17.

179. Young, *Diaries of Sir Robert Bruce Lockhart*, 177.

180. Ibid., 308.

181. Ibid., 186.

182. Ibid.

183. Colville, *Fringes of Power*, 130.

184. Lord Moran, *Churchill at War 1940–45* (New York: Carroll & Graf, 2002), 235–36.

185. Alex Danchev and Daniel Todman, eds., *War Diaries 1939–1945: Field Marshal Lord Alanbrooke* (Berkeley: University of California Press, 2001), 207.

186. Ibid., 678.

187. Moran, *Churchill at War*, 139.

188. Kathleen Harriman Mortimer, interview with Rudy Abramson, June 24, 1987, Rudy Abramson collection. My thanks to Thomas Parrish for allowing me to see the Abramson collection.

189. Danchev and Todman, *War Diaries 1939–1945: Field Marshal Lord Alan-brooke*, 676–77, 667–68.

190. Colville, *Fringes of Power*, 126–27.

191. Young, *Diaries of Sir Robert Bruce Lockhart*, 533.

192. Jenkins, *Churchill*, 639.

193. Ibid., 593.

194. Danchev and Todman, *War Diaries 1939–1945: Field Marshal Lord Alan-brooke*, 161.

195. Ibid., 445–46.

196. Roberts, *Masters and Commanders*, 58.

197. Danchev and Todman, *War Diaries 1939–1945: Field Marshal Lord Alan-brooke*, 459.

198. Young, *Diaries of Sir Robert Bruce Lockhart*, 533.

199. Ibid., 147.

200. Ibid., 524.

201. Ibid., 245.

202. Jenkins, *Churchill*, 731.

203. Young, *Diaries of Sir Robert Bruce Lockhart*, 307.

204. Ibid., 326.

205. Danchev and Todman, *War Diaries 1939–1945: Field Marshal Lord Alan-brooke*, 581.

206. Mark Bonham Carter and Mark Pottle, eds., *Lantern Slides: The Diaries and Letters of Violet Bonham Carter* (London: Weidenfeld and Nicolson, 1996), 318.

207. Danchev and Todman, *War Diaries 1939–1945: Field Marshal Lord Alan-brooke*, 647.

208. Young, *Diaries of Sir Robert Bruce Lockhart*, 563.

209. Norman M. Naimark, *Stalin's Genocides* (Princeton, NJ: Princeton University Press, 2010), 70–79, 99–120; Timothy Snyder, *Bloodlands: Europe between Hitler and Stalin* (New York: Basic Books, 2010), 21–87; Hiroaki Kuromiya, *Stalin* (Harlow, UK: Pearson Longman, 2005), 124–25.

210. Robert C. Tucker, *Stalin in Power: The Revolution from Above* (New York: Norton, 1990); Edvard Radzinsky, *Stalin* (New York: Doubleday, 1996); David L. Hoffman, *Stalinist Values* (Ithaca, NY: Cornell University Press, 2003); Stephane Courtois, et al., *The Black Book of Communism: Crimes, Terror, Repression* (Cambridge, MA: Harvard University Press, 1999). For the perspective of an American priest residing in Moscow, see G. M. Hamburg, ed., *In Lubianka's Shadow* (Notre Dame, IN: University of Notre Dame Press, 2006).

211. Oleg V. Khlevniuk, *Master of the House: Stalin and His Inner Circle* (New Haven, CT: Yale University Press, 2009), 217.

212. Sergo Beria, *Beria, My Father* (London: Duckworth, 2001), 144–45.

213. Strobe Talbott, ed., *Khrushchev Remembers* (Boston: Little, Brown, 1970), 154.

214. Kuromiya, *Stalin*, 123.

215. Snyder, *Bloodlands*, vii–xix.

216. Kuromiya, *Stalin*, 119.

217. Ibid., 127.

218. Ibid., 126.

219. Miklós Kun, *Stalin: An Unknown Portrait* (New York: Central European University Press, 2003), 332.

220. Kuromiya, *Stalin*, 148 (emphasis in original).

221. Khlevniuk, *Master of the House*, 216.

222. Svetlana Alliluyeva, *Twenty Letters to a Friend* (New York: Harper & Row, 1967), 190.

223. Milovan Djilas, *Conversations with Stalin* (New York: Harcourt, Brace & World, 1962), 76–77.

224. Kun, *Stalin*, 335.

225. Robert Service, *Stalin* (London: Macmillan, 2004), 436–37.

226. Kun, *Stalin*, 333.

227. Simon Sebag Montefiore, *Stalin: The Court of the Red Tsar* (New York: Knopf, 2004), 184.

228. Talbott, *Khrushchev Remembers*, 301.

229. See chapter 8.

230. Montefiore, *Stalin*, 522 for the quotation. See also 512–31; Talbott, *Khrushchev Remembers*, 297–305.

231. Alliluyeva, *Twenty Letters to a Friend*, 193.

232. Montefiore, *Stalin*, 105, 585.

233. Roberts, *Masters and Commanders*, 65.

Chapter 3. The Personal Touch: Forming the Alliance, January–August 1941

1. John Colville, *Fringes of Power: 10 Downing Street Diaries* (New York: W. W. Norton, 1985), 166–67.

2. Martin Gilbert, *Winston S. Churchill* (London: Heinemann, 1983), 6:972; Thomas Parrish, *To Keep the British Isles Afloat* (New York: HarperCollins, 2009), 150–207.

3. Lynne Olson, *Citizens of London* (New York: Random House, 2010), 10.

4. Churchill's decision to sink the French fleet off Oran in July 1940 had indicated to FDR that the PM was serious about the war. Roosevelt then proceeded with the destroyers-for-bases deal.

5. Robert E. Sherwood, *Roosevelt and Hopkins, an Intimate History* (New York: Harper, 1948), 238.

6. Pamela Churchill, interview with Christopher Ogden, unprocessed, Pamela Churchill Harriman papers.

7. Ibid.

8. Kathleen Harriman Mortimer, interview with Rudy Abramson, no. 2, no date but between 1983 and 1987, Abramson collection.

9. David Stafford, *Roosevelt and Churchill: Men of Secrets* (Woodstock, NY: Overlook Press, 2000), xxiii.

10. Averell Harriman, interview with Abramson, October 15, 1982, Abramson collection.

11. Sherwood, *Roosevelt and Hopkins*, 236.

12. Ibid., 238–39.

13. Colville, *Fringes of Power*, 141.

14. Oliver Lyttelton Chandos, *The Memoirs of Lord Chandos* (New York: New American Library, 1963), 158–59; Sherwood, *Roosevelt and Hopkins*, 242.

15. George T. McJimsey, *Harry Hopkins* (Cambridge, MA: Harvard University Press, 1987), 141.

16. Sherwood, *Roosevelt and Hopkins*, 244 (emphasis in original).

17. Mary Soames, interview with Verne Newton, video cassette, FDRL.

18. Sherwood, *Roosevelt and Hopkins*, 246.

19. Pamela Churchill Harriman, interview with Verne Newton, video cassette, FDRL.

20. Sherwood, *Roosevelt and Hopkins*, 254–55.

21. Pamela Churchill Harriman, interview with Verne Newton, video cassette, FDRL.

22. Lord Ismay, interview with Robert Sherwood; John G. Winant, interview with Sherwood, 13 September 1946, Houghton Library, Harvard University.

23. McJimsey, *Harry Hopkins*, 144.

24. Mary Soames, interview with Verne Newton, video cassette, FDRL.

25. Ruth 1:16.

26. Martin Gilbert, ed., *The Churchill War Papers* (New York: W. W. Norton, 1993) 3:91.

27. Kenneth Young, ed., *The Diaries of Sir Robert Bruce Lockhart 1939–1965* (London: Macmillan, 1980), 331.

28. Pamela Churchill Harriman, interview Verne Newton, video cassette, FDRL.

29. Gilbert, *Churchill War Papers*, 3:91.

30. J. Edgar Hoover to General Edwin M. Watson, February 12, 1941, box 304, Hopkins papers, FDRL; Sherwood, *Roosevelt and Hopkins*, 248–49.

31. Sherwood, *Roosevelt and Hopkins*, 250.

32. Gilbert, *Churchill War Papers*, 3:165.

33. Harold L. Ickes, *The Secret Diary of Harold L. Ickes* (New York: Simon & Schuster, 1953), 3:429.

34. Pamela Churchill Harriman, interview with Verne Newton, video cassette, FDRL; Mary Soames, interview with Newton, ibid.

35. Pamela Churchill Harriman, interview with Verne Newton, video cassette, FDRL.

36. Sherwood, *Roosevelt and Hopkins*, 241.

37. Ickes diary, February 8, 1941; Mary Soames, interview with Abramson, no date.

38. W. Averell Harriman reminiscences, October 12, 1953, Abramson collection.

39. Harriman, "Memorandum of Conversation with the President," February 18, 1941, Abramson collection.

40. Harriman reminiscences, October 12, 1953, Abramson collection.

41. Averell Harriman, interview with Abramson, October 15, 1982.

42. Harriman, "Memorandum of Conversation with the President," February 18, 1941, Abramson collection.

43. Ibid., March 7, 1941.

44. Sally Bedell Smith, *Reflected Glory: The Life of Pamela Churchill Harriman* (New York: Simon & Schuster, 1996), 78–79.

45. Ibid.

46. John J. McCloy, interview with Abramson, May 13, 1983, Abramson collection.

47. Allen Grover, interview with Abramson, September 28, 1983, Abramson collection.

48. William S. Paley, interview with Abramson, May 4, 1983, Abramson collection.

49. Charles Collingwood, interview with Abramson, May 3, 1983, Abramson collection.

50. Waldeman Nielsen, interview with Abramson, May 2, 1983, Abramson collection.

51. Franklin D. Roosevelt Jr., interview with Abramson, May 31, 1983, Abramson collection.

52. Kathleen Harriman Mortimer, interview with Abramson, no. 2 [between 1983 and 1987], Abramson collection.

53. McCloy, interview with Abramson, May 13, 1983; Franklin D. Roosevelt Jr., interview with Abramson, May 31, 1983, Abramson collection.

54. Reminiscences of Eliot Janeway (2003), CUOHRC, 34.

55. Averell Harriman reminiscences, October 12, 1953, Abramson collection; Parrish, *To Keep the British Isles Afloat*, 200–253.

56. Harriman to Hopkins, June 10, 1941, Abramson collection.

57. Kathleen Harriman Mortimer, interview with Abramson, no. 3, June 24, 1987, Abramson collection.

58. Kathleen Harriman Mortimer, interview with Abramson, no. 1, May 12, 1983, Abramson collection.

59. John Colville, interview with Abramson, no date, Abramson collection

60. Averell Harriman reminiscences, October 12, 1953, Abramson collection.

61. Olson, *Citizens of London*, 91.

62. Mary Soames, interview with Abramson, no date, Abramson collection.

63. Kathleen Harriman Mortimer, interview with Abramson, no. 3, June 24, 1987.

64. Soames, interview with Abramson, no date.

65. Colville, interview with Abramson, no date; Kathleen Harriman Mortimer, interview with Abramson, no. 3, June 24, 1987, Abramson collection.

66. Averell Harriman reminiscences, October 12, 1953, Abramson collection.

67. Kathleen Harriman Mortimer, interview with Abramson, no. 2, between 1983 and 1987, Abramson collection.

68. Olson, *Citizens of London*, 77.

69. Colville, interview with Abramson, no date, Abramson collection.

70. Elizabeth Bumiller, "Pamela Harriman: The Remarkable Life of the Democrats' Improbable Whirlwind," *Washington Post*, June 12, 1983, L5.

71. Kathleen Harriman Mortimer, interview with Abramson, no. 2, between 1983 and 1987, Abramson collection.

72. *Life*, January 6, 12, 20, 27; February 3, 17, 1941.

73. *Life*, February 17, 1941, 4.

74. Walter Isaacson and Evan Thomas, *The Wise Men* (New York: Simon & Schuster, 1986), 329.

75. Pamela Churchill Harriman, interview with Ogden, unprocessed, Pamela Churchill Harriman papers.

76. Colville, interview with Abramson, no date, Abramson collection.

77. Kathleen Harriman Mortimer, interview with Abramson, no. 2, between 1983 and 1987, Abramson collection.

78. Pamela Churchill to Averell Harriman, no date, unprocessed, Pamela Churchill Harriman papers.

79. Pamela Churchill Harriman, interview by Ogden, no date, unprocessed, Pamela Churchill Harriman papers.

80. Kathleen to Mary Harriman, May 30, 1941, unprocessed, Pamela Churchill Harriman papers.

81. Kathleen Harriman Mortimer, interview with Abramson, no. 3, June 24, 1987, Abramson collection.

82. Colville, interview with Abramson, no date, Abramson collection.

83. Kathleen Harriman Mortimer, interview with Abramson, no. 2, between 1983 and 1987, Abramson collection.

84. Christopher Ogden, *Life of the Party* (Boston: Little, Brown, 1994), 131.

85. Colville, interview with Abramson, no date but 1980s, Abramson collection.

86. Smith, *Reflected Glory*, 103.

87. Pamela Churchill to Franklin D. Roosevelt, July 1, 1942, unprocessed, Pamela Churchill Harriman papers.

88. Smith, *Reflected Glory*, 112.

89. Larry Lasueur, interview with Abramson, April 27, 1987, Abramson collection.

90. Pamela Churchill Harriman, interview with Ogden, unprocessed, Pamela Churchill Harriman papers.

91. Smith, *Reflected Glory*, 115.

92. Ogden, *Life of the Party*, 121–22. In 1942, Jock Whitney, one of Pamela Churchill's lovers, married FDR's former daughter-in-law, Betsey Cushing Roosevelt, whom Hopkins had also dated. Months later, Hopkins wed Whitney's former girlfriend, Louise Macy. Letters hand-carried by Hopkins helped FDR Jr. romance Kathleen Harriman. Kathleen apparently also dated Anderson's deputy, air general Ira Eaker. Randolph Churchill boasted to Harriman about his sexual escapades in Egypt. Averell's wife back in the States, Marie, had her own lover, the band leader Eddy Duchin. Year later, after Duchin's early death from leukemia,

Marie and Averell would help raise his son, Peter. Though most in this crowd knew or suspected who was sleeping with whom, discretion remained mandatory. Jealousy intruded, but it was overridden by the sense that total war suspended ordinary rules. The journalist Chris Hedges observed, "there is in wartime a nearly universal preoccupation with sexual liaisons." With "the currency of life and death cheap, eroticism races through all relationships." Chris Hedges, *War Is a Force That Gives Us Meaning* (New York: PublicAffairs, 2002), 100–102.

93. Harrison E. Salisbury, *A Journey for Our Times* (New York: Harper & Row, 1983), 183.

94. Portal to Pamela Churchill, February 1945, unprocessed, Pamela Churchill Harriman papers (emphasis in original).

95. Smith, *Reflected Glory*, 113.

96. Ogden, *Life of the Party*, 125.

97. Peter Duchin, interview with Abramson, May 11, 1983, Abramson collection.

98. Bumiller, "Pamela Harriman," L4.

99. Ibid.

100. Pamela Churchill to Kathleen Harriman, June 11, 1944, unprocessed, Pamela Churchill Harriman papers.

101. Pamela Churchill to Kathleen Harriman, January 6, 1944, unprocessed, Pamela Churchill Harriman papers.

102. Sherwood, *Roosevelt and Hopkins*, 270.

103. Fred L. Israel, ed., *The War Diary of Breckinridge Long* (Lincoln: University of Nebraska Press, 1966), 201, 203.

104. Waldo H. Heinrichs, *Threshold of War: Franklin D. Roosevelt and American Entry into World War II* (New York: Oxford University Press, 1988), 68–69.

105. *Complete Presidential Press Conferences of Franklin D. Roosevelt* (New York: Da Capo Press, 1972), 17:364.

106. Ickes diary, May 27, 1941.

107. There has been speculation that the blood loss resulted from radiation treatment for prostate cancer. See Steven Lomazow and Eric Fettmann, *FDR's Deadly Secret* (New York: PublicAffairs, 2009), 79–87.

108. Sherwood, *Roosevelt and Hopkins*, 293.

109. Ickes diary, June 8, 1941.

110. Adolf A Berle Jr. diary, May 26, 1941, reel 3, FDRL.

111. Entries in FDR: Day by Day—The Pare Lorentz Chronology, FDRL.

112. Belle Willard Roosevelt diary, June 13, 1942, box 136.

113. Hopkins diary, January 30, 1941, reel 19, Hopkins papers, FDRL.

114. Stiles to mother, June 16, 1941, box 10, Stiles papers.

115. Joseph E. Davies diary, June 23, 1941, box 12, Davies papers.

116. David C. Engerman, *Modernization from the Other Shore* (Cambridge, MA: Harvard University Press, 2003).

117. *FRUS 1941* (Washington, DC: Government Printing Office, 1958), 765.

118. Ibid.

119. Steinhardt to William C. Bullitt, June 16, 1941, box 78, Bullitt papers.

120. Reminiscences of Perkins (1955), CUOHRC, 8:315.

121. Henry L. Stimson diary, June 23, 1941, Stimson papers.

122. Yeaton quoted in J. Edgar Hoover to General George V. Strong, "The Influence of Brigadier General Philip R. Faymonville on Soviet-American Military Relations," July 26, 1943, box 3, Yeaton papers. For Yeaton's explanation of his sources, see unpublished Yeaton memoir, chap. 3, p. 25, box 1, Yeaton papers.

123. Stimson diary, June 30, 1941, Stimson papers. Though FDR blamed his lack of pep on the heat, he usually shrugged off the effects of Washington's semitropical climate.

124. Oumansky quoted in G. A. Arbatov et al., eds., *Sovetsko-amerikanskie otnosheniia vo vremia Velikoi otechestveoi voiny: 1941–1945* [Soviet-American Relations in the Time of the Great Patriotic War: 1941–1945] (Moscow, 1984), 77–79; Stimson diary, July 28–29, 1941, Stimson papers.

125. Stafford Cripps diary, July 10–11, 1941, Cripps papers.

126. David McKinley, "Flight to Archangel with Mr. Harry Hopkins—July/August 1941, reel 19, Hopkins papers, FDRL; David McKinley, interview with Verne Newton, video cassette, FDRL; John Alison, interview with Newton, ibid.

127. Sherwood, *Roosevelt and Hopkins*, 325–26.

128. Ibid., 326.

129. Valentin Berezhkov, interview with Verne Newton, video cassette, FDRL.

130. Ibid.

131. *FRUS 1941*, 1:803.

132. Archive of Foreign Policy of the Russian Federation, fond 06, opis. 3, papka 21, delo 288, list 5–9.

133. *FRUS 1941*, 1:804.

134. Archive of Foreign Policy of the Russian Federation, fond 06, opis. 3, papka 21, delo 288, list 10–15.

135. Sherwood, *Roosevelt and Hopkins*, 330 (emphasis in original).

136. *New York Herald Tribune*, October 22, 1938, 4.

137. Margaret Bourke-White, *Shooting the Russian War* (New York: Simon & Schuster, 1942), 217; Margaret Bourke-White, interview, May 15, 1963, in catalog of Margaret Bourke-White papers, Syracuse University, Syracuse, NY. Caldwell's broadcast transcripts are in box 8, Erskine Caldwell papers, Syracuse University, Syracuse, NY.

138. *FRUS 1941*, 1:806

139. Ibid., 813–14.

140. Ibid.

141. Yeaton to Colonel John A. Crane, July 9, 1940, box 1, Yeaton papers.

142. Yeaton to Captain Joseph A. Michela, June 15, 1940, box 1, Yeaton papers; Mary E. Glantz, *FDR and the Soviet Union* (Lawrence: University Press of Kansas, 2005), 49–52.

143. Minute by V. Cavendish-Bentinck, December 4, 1941, N708/122/38, F. O. 371/29501, NA, UK.

144. Unpublished Yeaton memoir, chap. 3, pp. 37–38, box 1; Yeaton to Thomas Julian, August 8, 1968, box 3, Yeaton papers (emphasis in original); Hopkins to Stimson, October 14, 1941, box 305, Hopkins papers, FDRL.

145. Yeaton to Thomas Julian, August 8, 1968; box 3; unpublished Yeaton memoir, chap. 3, pp. 37–38, box 1, both in Yeaton papers.

146. Harry Hopkins, "My Meeting with Stalin," *American Magazine* 132 (December 1941): 14–15, 114–17.

147. David McKinley, "Flight to Archangel with Mr. Harry Hopkins," reel 19, Hopkins papers, FDRL; David McKinley, interview with Verne Newton, video cassette, FDRL.

148. David Reynolds, "The Atlantic 'Flop': British Foreign Policy and the Churchill-Roosevelt Meeting of August 1941," in *The Atlantic Charter*, ed. Douglas Brinkley and David R. Facey-Crowther (New York: St. Martin's Press, 1994), 135.

149. David Reynolds, *In Command of History: Churchill Fighting and Writing the Second World War* (New York: Random House, 2005), 260.

150. Charles Peake to Oliver Harvey, August 1, 1941, piece no. 56402, Oliver Harvey papers, British Library, London.

151. Walter Henry Thompson, *Assignment: Churchill* (New York: Farrar, Straus and Young, 1955), 224.

152. H. V. Morton, *Atlantic Meeting* (London: Methuen, 1943), 30.

153. Ibid., 31, 64. For Churchill's siren suit, or "rompers," see David Dilks, ed., *The Diaries of Sir Alexander Cadogan 1938–1945* (New York: G. P. Putnam's Sons, 1972), 395.

154. Thompson, *Assignment*, 225.

155. Theodore A. Wilson, *The First Summit* (Lawrence: University Press of Kansas, 1991), 55.

156. Ian Jacob diary, August 5, 1941, Papers of Sir Ian Jacob, Churchill Archives Centre, Cambridge, UK.

157. Thompson, *Assignment*, 228–29.

158. Morton, *Atlantic Meeting*, 79–81; Dilks, *Diaries of Sir Alexander Cadogan*, 396.

159. W. Averell Harriman and Elie Abel, *Special Envoy to Churchill and Stalin 1941–1946* (New York: Random House, 1975), 75.

160. Hopkins, unpublished article on Atlantic Conference, October 1941, box 306, Hopkins papers, FDRL.

161. Sherwood, *Roosevelt and Hopkins*, 351.

162. FDR, "Memorandum of Trip to Meet Winston Churchill," August 23, 1941, box 1, Roosevelt, PSF (hereafter FDR, "Memorandum of Trip"); Geoffrey W. Ward, ed., *Closest Companion* (Boston: Houghton Mifflin, 1995), 140.

163. Ibid.

164. FDR, "Memorandum of Trip."

165. Elliott Roosevelt, *As He Saw It* (New York: Duell, Sloan and Pearce, 1946), 20.

166. Stimson diary, August 1, 4, 1941, Sterling Library, Yale University Library. The Germans got wind of the conference and broadcast the secret on August 6.

167. "Log of the President's Cruise on Board the U. S. S. Potomac and U. S. S. Augusta, August 3–16, 1941," box 1, PSF Safe file, FDRL (hereafter "Log of President's Cruise"); FDR, "Memorandum of Trip."

168. Regarding the public criticism, see de Espil diary, August 17, 1941, box 10.

169. Morton, *Atlantic Meeting*, 78.

170. Jacob diary, August 8, 1941.

171. Ibid., August 6, 1941.

172. Thompson, *Assignment*, 231; Dilks, *Diaries of Sir Alexander Cadogan*, 397.

173. Wilson, *First Summit*, 77.

174. Jacob diary, August 8, 1941.

175. Ibid., August 9, 1941.

176. Peake to Harvey, August 1, 1941, piece no. 56402, Harvey papers, British Library, London..

177. Elliott Roosevelt, *As He Saw It*, 22. Although the author seems to have exaggerated the vehemence of his father's statements, he probably captured FDR's overall perspective. For an appraisal of Elliott Roosevelt's veracity, see chapter 5, note 117.

178. Morton, *Atlantic Meeting*, 83.

179. Henry Harley Arnold diary, August 4, 1941, reel 2, Henry Harley Arnold papers, Library of Congress. Arnold mistakenly wrote "Bremer Pass."

180. Reynolds, "The Atlantic 'Flop,'" 140.

181. Hopkins, unpublished article on Atlantic Conference, October 1941, box 306, Hopkins papers, FDRL.

182. Henry Harley Arnold, *Global Mission* (New York: Harper, 1949), 254.

183. Wilson, *First Summit*, 77–79.

184. Ward, *Closest Companion*, 141.

185. Dilks, *Diaries of Sir Alexander Cadogan*, 397–98.

186. Wilson, *First Summit*, 93–95.

187. Arnold diary, August 9, 1941.

188. Elliott Roosevelt, *As He Saw It*, 29.

189. Wilson, *First Summit*, 94–95.

190. Arnold diary, August 10, 1941.

191. Jacob diary, August 19, 1941.

192. Wilson, *First Summit*, 95.

193. Roosevelt, *As He Saw It*, 30.

194. Dilks, *Diaries of Sir Alexander Cadogan*, 396.

195. Reynolds, "The Atlantic 'Flop,'" 143.

196. Wilson, *First Summit*, 149–75; Reynolds, "The Atlantic 'Flop,'" 129–46; Warren F. Kimball, *Forged in War* (New York: Morrow, 1997), 98–102.

197. Jacob diary, August 10, 1941.

198. Wilson, *First Summit*, 81.

199. Jacob diary, August 9, 1941; Wilson, *First Summit*, 91.

200. "Log of President's Cruise," 8.

201. Ibid., 10.

202. Reminiscences of Perkins (1955), CUOHRC, 8:24.

203. Ibid., 7:528–29.

204. Francis Biddle, interview with Graff, box 4, Graff papers.

205. John Martin, *Downing Street: The War Years* (London: Bloomsbury, 1991), 58.

206. Morton, *Atlantic Meeting*, 98.

207. Jacob diary, August 10, 1941.

208. Elizabeth Borgwardt, *A New Deal for the World* (Cambridge, MA: Harvard University Press), 1–45, 305.

209. Winston S. Churchill, *The Grand Alliance* (Boston: Houghton Mifflin, 1950), 431–32.

210. Morton, *Atlantic Meeting*, 102; Wilson, *First Summit*, 98–99; Jon Meacham, *Franklin and Winston* (New York: Random House, 2003), 114–16.

211. The moving pictures were taken by the British, who gave copies to the Americans. See, for example, newsreels #2011-1122:1-4; 2187-12:1-3, FDRL; Reminiscences of Perkins (1955), CUOHRC, 8:24.

212. Elliott Roosevelt, *As He Saw It*, 33 (emphasis in original). This quotation matches the navy log's account of what FDR said.

213. Jacob diary, August 12, 1941.

214. Harvey to Eden, August 24, 1941, piece no. 56402, Harvey papers, British Library, London.

215. J. Garry Clifford, "Both Ends of the Telescope: New Perspectives on FDR and American Entry into World War II," *Diplomatic History* 13 (Spring 1989): 213–30.

216. Jacob diary, August 11, 1941.

217. Philip Hamburger, "Talk of the Town," *New Yorker*, November 17, 1962.

218. Charles E. Bohlen, *Witness to History 1929–1969* (New York: W. W. Norton, 1973), 244.

219. Elie Abel, interview with Abramson, September 17, 1981, Abramson collection.

220. Olson, *Citizens of London*, 98.

Chapter 4. Transcending Differences: Eden Goes to Moscow and Churchill to Washington, December 1941

1. Frances Perkins, "Pearl Harbor Cabinet Meeting Memo," December 8, 1941, Speeches and Articles, Frances Perkins Coggeshall collection, Columbia University, New York, NY.

2. Doris Kearns Goodwin, *No Ordinary Time* (New York: Simon & Schuster, 1994), 292–93.

3. Simon Sebag Montefiore, *Stalin: The Court of the Red Tsar* (New York: Knopf, 2004), 374.

4. Ibid.

5. Joseph P. Lash diary, December 7, 1941, box 31, Lash papers.

6. Lela Stiles to mother, December 10, 1941, box 17, Stiles papers.

7. Thomas G. Corcoran, interview with Graff, [1962], box 4, Graff papers.

8. Huibertje Pruyn Hamlin, "Some Memories of Franklin Delano Roosevelt," Small Collections, FDRL.

9. Samuel I. Rosenman, *Working with Roosevelt* (New York: Harper & Brothers, 1952), 312.

10. Bernard Asbell, *The F. D. R. Memoirs* (Garden City, NY: Doubleday), 401.

11. Richard Overy, *Russia's War* (New York: TV Books, 1997), 102–3; Constantine Pleshakov, *Stalin's Folly* (Boston: Houghton Mifflin, 2005).

12. Gabriel Gorodetsky, *Grand Delusion* (New Haven, CT: Yale University Press, 1999); Geoffrey Roberts, *Stalin's Wars: From World War to Cold War, 1939–1953* (New Haven, CT: Yale University Press, 2006), 30–81.

13. Robert Service, *Stalin* (London: Macmillan, 2004), 410.

14. Montefiore, *Stalin*, 366.

15. Overy, *Russia's War*, 129–30.

16. Andrew Nagorski, *The Greatest Battle: The Fight for Moscow 1941–42* (New York: Simon & Schuster, 2008), 170, 168.

17. Nagorski, *Greatest Battle*, 174–75.

18. Rodric Braithwaite, *Moscow 1941* (London: Profile Books, 2006), 245–49.

19. Montefiore, *Stalin*, 399.

20. Ibid., 396.

21. Ibid.

22. Felix Chuev, ed., *Molotov Remembers* (Chicago: Ivan R. Dee, 1993), 208.

23. Montefiore, *Stalin*, 400.

24. Ibid., 400–403.

25. Braithwaite, *Moscow 1941*, 289; Montefiore, *Stalin*, 403.

26. Jonathan Haslam, *Russia's Cold War: From the October Revolution to the Fall of the Wall* (New Haven, CT: Yale University Press, 2011), 10–11.

27. John Harvey, ed., *The War Diaries of Oliver Harvey 1941–1945* (London: Collins, 1978), 57.

28. *Stalin's Correspondence with Churchill, Attlee, Roosevelt and Truman* (New York: Capricorn Books, 1958), 16, 19, 37 (hereafter *Stalin's Correspondence*).

29. Harvey, *War Diaries of Oliver Harvey*, 24.

30. *Stalin's Correspondence*, 33.

31. Stalin quoted in Eden to Cripps, November 20, 1941, F. O. 371/29471, NA, UK.

32. *Stalin's Correspondence*, 34–35; David Dilks, ed., *The Diaries of Sir Alexander Cadogan 1938–1945* (New York: G. P. Putnam's Sons, 1972), 413.

33. For an account that emphasizes F.O. planning for closer ties with the Soviets, see Fraser J. Harbutt, *Yalta 1945: Europe and America at the Crossroads* (New York: Cambridge University Press, 2010), 139–224.

34. Harvey, *War Diaries of Oliver Harvey*, 63.

35. Ibid., 31.

36. Ibid.

37. Dilks, *Diaries of Sir Alexander Cadogan*, 414.

38. Ibid., 418–19.

39. Harvey, *War Diaries of Oliver Harvey*, 72; Dilks, *Diaries of Sir Alexander Cadogan*, 419.

40. Harvey, *War Diaries of Oliver Harvey*, 73; Dilks, *Diaries of Sir Alexander Cadogan*, 420.

41. Dilks, *Diaries of Sir Alexander Cadogan*, 406, 412 (emphasis in original).

42. W. Averell Harriman and Elie Abel, *Special Envoy to Churchill and Stalin* (New York: Random House, 1975), 111.

43. Martin Gilbert, ed., *The Churchill War Papers* (New York: W. W. Norton, 1993) 3:1577.

44. Ibid., 3:1576.

45. David Reynolds, *In Command of History: Churchill Fighting and Writing the Second World War* (New York: Random House, 2005), 264. The published memoir discreetly toned down the joy.

46. Lord Moran, *Churchill at War 1940–45* (New York: Carroll & Graf, 2002), 9.

47. Harvey, *War Diaries of Oliver Harvey*, 70.

48. Moran, *Churchill at War*, 8.

49. Warren F. Kimball, ed., *Churchill & Roosevelt: The Complete Correspondence* (Princeton, NJ: Princeton University Press, 1984), 1:294–308; Mark M. Lowenthal, *Leadership and Indecision* (New York: Garland, 1988), 749–50.

50. Moran, *Churchill at War*, 10.

51. Dilks, *Diaries of Sir Alexander Cadogan*, 420; Anthony Eden, *The Reckoning* (Boston: Houghton Mifflin, 1965), 333.

52. Moran, *Churchill at War*, 10; Walter Henry Thompson, *Assignment: Churchill* (New York: Farrar, Straus and Young, 1955), 246.

53. Mary Soames, ed., *Winston and Clementine* (Boston: Houghton and Mifflin, 1999), 462.

54. Ian Jacob diary, January 1, 1942, Papers of Sir Ian Jacob, Churchill Archives Centre, Cambridge, UK.

55. Mark A. Stoler, *Allies and Adversaries* (Chapel Hill: University of North Carolina Press, 2000), 1–63; Lowenthal, *Leadership and Indecision*, 715–75.

56. Stoler, *Allies and Adversaries*, 64–69; Lowenthal, *Leadership and Indecision*, 748–75; Max Hastings, *Winston's War: Churchill 1940–1945* (New York: Alfred A. Knopf, 2010), 182–97.

57. Jacob diary, December 23–24, 1941, Papers of Sir Ian Jacob, Churchill Archives Centre, Cambridge, UK.

58. Ibid., and January 1, 1942.

59. David Irving, *Churchill's War* (London: Focal Point, 2001) 1:293.

60. Alex Danchev and Daniel Todman, eds., *War Diaries 1939–1945: Field Marshal Lord Alanbrooke* (Berkeley: University of California Press, 2001), 209.

61. Winston S. Churchill, The *Grand Alliance* (Boston: Houghton Mifflin, 1950), 662–63.

62. Moran, *Churchill at War*, 10.

63. Irving, *Churchill's War*, 2:281; Goodwin, *No Ordinary Time*, 309.

64. de Espil diary, December 26, 1941, box 4.

65. *Washington Post*, December 27, 1941.

66. Harold L. Ickes diary, December 26, 1941, Harold L. Ickes papers.

67. Irving, *Churchill's War*, 2:282; Claude R. Wickard diary, December 26, 1941, Claude R. Wickard papers, FDRL.

68. Moran, *Churchill at War*, 17–19.

69. Dilks, *Diaries of Sir Alexander Cadogan*, 468.

70. Irving, *Churchill's War*, 2:287.

71. Grace Tully, *F. D. R., My Boss* (New York: C. Scribner's Sons, 1949), 305.

72. Jacob diary, January 1, 1942.

73. Robert E. Sherwood, *Roosevelt and Hopkins, an Intimate History* (New York: Harper, 1948), 442.

74. Joseph P. Lash diary, January 1, 1942, box 31, Lash papers.

75. Geoffrey W. Ward, ed., *Closest Companion* (Boston: Houghton Mifflin, 1995), 384–85.

76. Gilbert, *Churchill War Papers*, 3:1676.

77. Thompson, *Assignment*, 248.

78. Moran, *Churchill at War*, 11.

79. Irving, *Churchill's War*, 2:292.

80. Record of meetings between Foreign Secretary Anthony Eden and M. Joseph Stalin, December 16–20, 1941, PREM3/394/3, NA, UK; Roberts, *Stalin's Wars*, 115.

81. Harvey, *War Diaries of Oliver Harvey*, 78.

82. Dilks, *Diaries of Sir Alexander Cadogan*, 423.

83. Harvey, *War Diaries of Oliver Harvey*, 78.

84. Eden, *Reckoning*, 350.

85. Chuev, *Molotov Remembers*, 50.

86. Harvey, *War Diaries of Oliver Harvey*, 79.

87. Eden, *Reckoning*, 351.

88. Harvey, *War Diaries of Oliver Harvey*, 79.

89. Ickes diary, March 20, 1943.

90. Harvey, *War Diaries of Oliver Harvey*, 75.

91. Ibid., 79.

92. Ben Pimlott, ed., *The Second World War Diary of Hugh Dalton 1940–45* (London: Cape, 1986), 349.

93. Dilks, *Diaries of Sir Alexander Cadogan*, 432.

94. Lowenthal, *Leadership and Indecision*, 754–55.

95. Ibid., 756–75; Stoler, *Allies and Adversaries*, 64–69.

96. Lash diary, December 26, 1941, box 31, Lash papers.

97. Thomas M. Campbell and George C. Herring, eds., *The Diaries of Edward R. Stettinius, Jr., 1943–1946* (New York: Franklin Watts, 1975), 215.

98. *Stalin's Correspondence*, 17–18.

99. Haslam, *Russia's Cold War*, 9.

100. Eleanor Roosevelt, interview, September 3, 1952, Small Collections, FDRL.

101. "Memorandum of a Fishing Trip with President Roosevelt, November 27, 1937–December 6, 1937," in Reminiscences of Robert Jackson (1952), CUOHRC, 583.

102. Lash diary, January 1, 1942, box 31, Lash papers.

103. Irving, *Churchill's War*, 2:303.

104. Ibid., 285–86.

105. Lash diary, January 1, 1942, box 31, Lash papers.

106. Eleanor Roosevelt, interview with Graff, January 1962, box 4, Graff papers.

107. Goodwin, *No Ordinary Time*, 311.

108. Louis Adamic, *Dinner at the White House* (New York, 1946), 33.

109. Huibertje Pruyn Hamlin diary, December 22, 1941, Small Collections, FDRL (capitals in original).

110. Moran, *Churchill's War*, 13.

111. Adamic, *Dinner at the White House*, 64–68.

112. Mike F. Reilly, *Reilly of the White House* (New York: Simon & Schuster, 1947), 124.

Chapter 5. Creating the "Family Circle": The Tortuous Path to Tehran, 1942–43

1. *FRUS: The Conferences at Washington, 1941–1942, and Casablanca, 1943* (Washington, DC: Government Printing Office, 1968), 506 (hereafter *FRUS: Casablanca*).

2. Henrietta Nesbitt, *White House Diary* (Garden City: Doubleday, 1948), 292; Geoffrey W. Ward, ed., *Closest Companion* (Boston: Houghton Mifflin, 1995), 201.

3. *FRUS: Casablanca*, 506–7.

4. *Stalin's Correspondence with Churchill, Attlee, Roosevelt and Truman* (New York: Capricorn Books, 1958), 50 (hereafter *Stalin's Correspondence*).

5. Henry Morgenthau Jr. diary, June 16, March 11, 1942, Henry Morgenthau, Jr. papers, FDRL.

6. Beatrice Bishop Berle and Travis Beal Jacobs, eds., *Navigating the Rapids* (New York: Harcourt Brace Jovanovich, 1973), 412.

7. Harvey to Eden, May 18, 1942, piece no. 56402, Oliver Harvey papers, British Library, London.

8. See Timothy Snyder, *Bloodlands: Europe between Hitler and Stalin* (New York: Basic Books, 2010), 298.

9. Harvey to Eden, May 18, 1942, piece no. 56402, Oliver Harvey papers, British Library, London.

10. William C. Bullitt, *The Great Globe Itself* (New York: C. Scribner's Sons, 1946), 2.

11. Warren F. Kimball, ed., *Churchill & Roosevelt: The Complete Correspondence* (Princeton, NJ: Princeton University Press, 1984), 1:421.

12. Maisky to Maxim Litvinov, February 27, 1942, in Gabriel Gorodetsky, ed., *The Diary of Ivan Maisky, Ambassador to London, 1932–1943* (New Haven, CT: Yale University Press, forthcoming). I am indebted to Professor Gorodetsky for sharing this document.

13. Harriman to the President, February 5, 1942, box 161, Averell Harriman papers.

14. *Stalin's Correspondence*, 23–24.

15. *FRUS: 1942* (Washington, DC: Government Printing Office, 1961), 3:553.

16. Oleg Rzheshevsky, ed., *War and Diplomacy: The Making of the Grand Alliance; Documents from Stalin's Archives* (Amsterdam: Harwood Academic Publishers, 1996), 67.

17. Ibid., 67–96; *FRUS: 1942*, 3:558.

18. Rzheshevsky, *War and Diplomacy*, 102, 104.

19. Ibid., 119, 122.

20. Ibid., 133; *FRUS: 1942*, 3:559–60.

21. Felix Chuev, ed., *Molotov Remembers* (Chicago: Ivan R. Dee, 1993), xv.

22. Ibid., xiii.

23. Ibid., 19.

24. John Harvey, ed., *The War Diaries of Oliver Harvey 1941–1945* (London: Collins, 1978), 125.

25. Rzheshevsky, *War and Diplomacy*, 190.

26. Hopkins, "Memorandum of Conversation," May 29, 1942, box 311, Hopkins papers, FDRL.

27. Robert E. Sherwood, *Roosevelt and Hopkins, an Intimate History* (New York: Harper, 1948), 561.

28. Ward, *Closest Companion*, 159 (emphasis in original). Like many of the women in FDR's life, Daisy Suckley loved him. After a drive together, she wrote in her diary: "The President is a MAN—*mentally, physically, & spiritually*—What more can I say?" (ibid., x, emphasis in original). He cared for her and even talked about their sharing his postpresidential years. Though they apparently once kissed on what she thereafter called "Our Hill," it does not appear that their physical intimacy proceeded further. During the war years, she was employed sorting papers at the newly established Franklin D. Roosevelt Library. Daisy kept a detailed diary as well as Roosevelt's letters to her. Both were discovered in a suitcase under her bed when she died in her hundredth year in 1991 (ibid., ix).

29. Samuel Cross memorandum, "Molotov Conversations," May 29, 1942, box 311, Hopkins papers, FDRL. Only portions of this memorandum were included in *FRUS: 1942*.

30. Chuev, *Molotov Remembers*, 48.

31. John M. Blum, ed., *The Price of Vision: The Diary of Henry A. Wallace, 1942–1946* (Boston: Houghton Mifflin, 1973), 146; Ward, *Closest Companion*, 162.

32. Hopkins, "Memorandum of Conversation," May 29, 1942, box 311, Hopkins papers, FDRL.

33. Rzheshevsky, *War and Diplomacy*, 135, 180.

34. Ibid., 186–87, 199.

35. *FRUS: 1942*, 3:577.

36. Rzheshevsky, *War and Diplomacy*, 206, 203.

37. Chuev, *Molotov Remembers*, 45–46.

38. *FRUS: 1942*, 3:569.

39. *FRUS: 1942*, 3:568–69; Lloyd C. Gardner, *Spheres of Influence* (Chicago: Ivan R. Dee, 1993).

40. Rzheshevsky, *War and Diplomacy*, 174, 194.

41. *FRUS: 1942*, 3:574.

42. Rzheshevsky, *War and Diplomacy*, 174, 194.

43. Ibid., 205.

44. Belle Willard Roosevelt diary, August 23, 1941, box 135.

45. *FRUS: 1942*, 3:580–81; Warren F. Kimball, *The Juggler: Franklin Roosevelt as Wartime Statesman* (Princeton, NJ: Princeton University Press, 1991), 135.

46. Hopkins to Winant, June 12, 1942, box 311, Hopkins papers, FDRL

47. Rzheshevsky, *War and Diplomacy*, 197.

48. Ibid., 195, 206, 216; *FRUS: 1942*, 3:586.

49. Blum, *Price of Vision*, 86.

50. Rzheshevsky, *War and Diplomacy*, 193; Sherwood, *Roosevelt and Hopkins*, 568.

51. Blum, *Price of Vision*, 210, 246. Precisely what Molotov did and whom he saw in New York remains uncertain. Although he might have met with Soviet agents or his brother-in-law, the Russian-American businessman Sam Carp, there is no mention of such contact in books on Soviet spying based on decrypted cables to Moscow. See Katherine A. S. Sibley, *Red Spies in America* (Lawrence: University Press of Kansas, 2004); John Earl Haynes and Harvey Klehr, *Venona* (New Haven, CT: Yale University Press, 1999); idem, *In Denial* (San Francisco: Encounter Books, 2003); Allen Weinstein and Alexander Vassiliev, *The Haunted Wood* (New York: Random House, 1999); Herbert Romerstein and Eric Breindel, *The Venona Secrets* (Washington: Regnery Publishing, 2000).

52. Chuev, *Molotov Remembers*, 51, 72.

53. Rzheshevsky, *War and Diplomacy*, 267, 281.

54. Ibid., 273, 282–83.

55. Memorandum of conversation between Molotov and Archibald Clark Kerr, June 17, 1942, Archive of Foreign Policy of the Russian Federation, Secretariat V. M. Molotov'a, op. [inventory] 4, por. [portfolio] 129, papka [folder] 14, list [pages] 31–37.

56. Dorothy Jones Brady, interview with Carol Fleisher, October 17, 1996, Small Collections, FDRL.

57. Lord Moran, *Churchill at War 1940–45* (New York: Carroll & Graf, 2002), 43.

58. Ward, *Closest Companion*, 162 (emphasis in original).

59. Moran, *Churchill at War*, 44. See also Warren F. Kimball, *Forged in War* (New York: Morrow, 1997), 150–52.

60. Gorodetsky, *Maisky Diary*, July 3, 1942, forthcoming.

61. Blum, *Price of Vision*, 100, 91.

62. Mary Soames, ed., *Winston and Clementine* (Boston: Houghton Mifflin, 1999), 466.

63. Harriman, "Personal Notes of 2nd Trip to Moscow, August 1942," box 162, Harriman papers; David Dilks, ed., *The Diaries of Sir Alexander Cadogan 1938–1945* (New York: G. P. Putnam's Sons, 1972), 472.

64. Record of Stalin's conversation with Churchill, August 12, 1942, Russian State Archive of Socio-Political History, Moscow, f. [collection] 558, op. [inventory] 11, d. [folder] 282, l. [pages] 27–31.

65. Meeting at the Kremlin on Wednesday, August 12, 1942, box 311, Hopkins papers, FDRL.

66. Harriman to the President, August 14, 1942, box 311, Hopkins papers, FDRL.

67. Meeting at the Kremlin on Wednesday, August 12, 1942, box 311, Hopkins papers, FDRL.

68. Moran, *Churchill at War*, 73.

69. Lord Tedder, *With Prejudice* (Boston: Little, Brown, 1966), 330.

70. Dilks, *Diaries of Sir Alexander Cadogan*, 471.

71. Clark Kerr diary, August 15, 1942, F. O. 800/300/132-33, NA, UK.

72. Chief Air Marshal Arthur Tedder relayed to the story to Joseph E. Davies. Davies diary, July 13, 1945, box 17, Davies papers.

73. Record of Stalin's conversation with Churchill, August 12, 1942, Russian State Archive of Socio-Political History, Moscow, f. [collection] 558, op. [inventory] 11, d. [folder] 282, l. [pages] 39–42.

74. Clark Kerr diary, August 15, 1942, F.O. 800/300/132-33, NA, UK.

75. Moran, *Churchill at War*, 71.

76. Prime Minister to War Cabinet, August 14, 1942, F. O. 800/300/96. Many histories have told the story of how Churchill defended British honor with such a torrent of oratory that the interpreters could not keep up. Stalin is quoted as saying: "I do not understand the words, but by God I like your spirit." But in his report to the War Cabinet, Churchill admitted that "whether [Stalin's praise] was in mockery or not, I could not tell." For historical accounts, see, for example, Dilk's editorial note in Dilks, *Diaries of Sir Alexander Cadogan*, 471.

77. Moran, *Churchill at War*, 72.

78. Clark Kerr diary, August 15, 1942, F. O. 800/300/139, National Archives, Kew.

79. Lord Tedder used this phrase in describing the scene. Davies diary, July 13, 1945, box 17, Davies papers.

80. Moran, *Churchill at War*, 75–76.

81. Churchill, *The Hinge of Fate* (Boston: Houghton Mifflin, 1950), 497.

82. Moran, *Churchill at War*, 76.

83. Clark Kerr diary, August 15, 1942, F. O. 800/300/139, National Archives, Kew; Ian Jacob diary, August 13, 1942, Papers of Sir Ian Jacob, Churchill Archives Centre, Cambridge, UK.

84. Geoffrey Roberts, *Vyacheslav Molotov* (Dulles, VA: Potomac Books, forthcoming), chap. 3.

85. W. Averell Harriman and Elie Abel, *Special Envoy to Churchill and Stalin, 1941–1946* (New York: Random House, 1975), 160.

86. Kimball, *Churchill & Roosevelt* 3:632.

87. Klaus Larres, *Churchill's Cold War* (New Haven, CT: Yale University Press, 2002).

88. Mike F. Reilly, *Reilly of the White House* (New York: Simon & Schuster, 1947), 161.

89. Sherwood, *Roosevelt and Hopkins*, 738.

90. Harriman and Abel, *Special Envoy*, 160.

91. *FRUS: Casablanca*, 495.

92. Ward, *Closest Companion*, 187.

93. *FRUS: Casablanca*, 499.

94. Moran, *Churchill at War*, 96 (both quotations).

95. *FRUS: Casablanca*, 559–60.

96. Alex Danchev and Daniel Todman, eds., *War Diaries 1939–1945: Field Marshal Lord Alanbrooke* (Berkeley: University of California Press, 2001), 364.

97. Mark A. Stoler, *Allies in War: Britain and America against the Axis Powers, 1940–1945* (London: Hodder Arnold, 2005), 91.

98. *Complete Presidential Press Conferences of Franklin D. Roosevelt* (hereafter *Press Conferences of FDR*) (New York: Da Capo Press, 1972), January 24, 1943, 21:88.

99. Ibid., 90.

100. Ibid., 87.

101. Charles Richardson, *From Churchill's Secret Circle to the BBC: The Biography of Lieutenant General Sir Ian Jacob* (London: Brassey's, 1991), 165.

102. Ibid., 155.

103. Belle Willard Roosevelt diary, [March 1943], box 136.

104. Elliott Roosevelt, *As He Saw It* (New York: Duell, Sloan and Pearce, 1946), 66.

105. Reilly, *Reilly of the White House*, 152.

106. Richardson, *From Churchill's Secret Circle to the BBC*, 156.

107. *FRUS: Casablanca*, 535.

108. Moran, *Churchill at War*, 99 (both quotations).

109. Stiles to mother, February 3, 1943, box 10, Stiles papers.

110. Kenneth Pendar, *Adventure in Diplomacy* (New York: Dodd, Mead, 1945), 149–50.

111. Harriman and Abel, *Special Envoy*, 191.

112. Pendar, *Adventure in Diplomacy*, 153.

113. Sherwood, *Roosevelt and Hopkins*, 694; Pendar, *Adventure in Diplomacy*, 154.

114. Pendar, *Adventure in Diplomacy*, 157. Churchill's opposition to independence for India antagonized many Americans. When FDR addressed Congress on relations with the Allies, British ambassador Lord Halifax noted with dismay "the paucity of the applause for Winston as compared with that for Stalin and Chiang Kai-Shek." Harold L. Ickes diary, January 9, 1943, Ickes papers. For the PM's perspective, see Richard Toye, *Churchill's Empire: The World That Made Him and the World He Made* (New York: Henry Holt, 2010) 195–262.

115. Ward, *Closest Companion*, 230 (emphasis in original).

116. Ibid., 197–98; *Press Conferences of FDR*, February 2, 1943, 21:106.

117. Roosevelt, *As He Saw It*, 115 (emphasis in original). Elliott's book on conversations with his father at wartime conferences presents a puzzle. He wrote the memoir between late 1945 and early 1946 to make money and to challenge the Truman administration's drift toward confrontation with Moscow. Elliott had the help of a collaborator who still remains unidentified. Although he claimed

that "I have depended more on my [wartime] notes than on my memory" (xviii), Elliott never gave such notes to his father's presidential library. Nor have the notes ever surfaced. Indeed, Elliott is the only child of Franklin and Eleanor not to have his own collection of papers at the FDRL. Perhaps marital strife—his five marriages set a record even among his siblings—was not conducive to preserving keepsakes. Despite the nonextant notes, the memoir is so accurate with dates, places, names, and topics of conversation that Elliott could not have simply fabricated it. The *FRUS* volumes on wartime conferences repeatedly cite the book as the only record for FDR's conversations with Churchill and others. It seems probable that Elliott, assisted by a professional writer, extrapolated lively dialogue from his notes and memory and from the official record. While historians should not rely on any particular quotation from the book, they can turn to it for a sense of FDR's opinions and concerns. See Kimball, *Juggler*, 217; David Reynolds, *In Command of History: Churchill Fighting and Writing the Second World War* (New York: Random House, 2005), 52–53.

118. Laura Delano, interview with Graff [1962], box 4, Graff papers.

119. *Press Conferences of FDR*, February 2, 1943, 21:106.

120. Pearson conversation with Charles McNary [1943], F169, Pearson papers.

121. Kimball, *Churchill and Roosevelt* 2:156–57.

122. Soames, *Winston and Clementine*, 478.

123. Harvey, *War Diaries of Oliver Harvey*, 227.

124. Sherwood, *Roosevelt and Hopkins*, 695.

125. *Press Conferences of FDR*, February 12, 1943, 21:141 (emphasis in original).

126. "Itinerary Washington, D. C. to Casablanca," no date, box 20, Secret Service Records, FDRL.

127. *Press Conferences of FDR*, February 2, 1943, 21:120; Ward, *Closest Companion*, 199.

128. Dorothy Schiff memorandum, November 23, 1981, box 64, Schiff papers.

129. Gorodetsky, *Maisky Diary*, January 1, 1943, forthcoming.

130. Belle Willard Roosevelt diary, July 13, 1943, box 136.

131. *Press Conferences of FDR*, February 12, 1943, 21:142.

132. Hopkins, interview with Clapper, March 30, 1943, box 23, Raymond Clapper papers.

133. *Press Conferences of FDR*, July 30, 1943, 22:50.

134. Ibid., September 7, 1943, 22:89–90.

135. Ibid.

136. Sumner Welles, interview with Louis Fisher, May 18, 1943, box 1, Louis Fisher papers, FDRL.

137. Reminiscences of Perkins (1955), CUOHRC, 7:561.

138. Patrick J. Hearden, *Architects of Globalism* (Fayetteville: University of Arkansas Press, 2002); Elizabeth Borgwardt, *A New Deal for the World* (Cambridge, MA: Harvard University Press); Mark A. Stoler, *Allies and Adversaries* (Chapel Hill: University of North Carolina Press, 2000; Kenneth Weisbrode,

"The Master, the Maverick, and the Machine: Three Wartime Promoters of Peace," *Journal of Policy History* 21, no. 4 (2009): 366–91.

139. Hopkins, interview with Clapper, February 11, 1943, box 23, Clapper papers.

140. Ibid.

141. Clapper memorandum, March 30, 1943, box 23, Clapper papers.

142. Ward, *Closest Companion*, 229.

143. de Espil diary, July 1941, box 4.

144. Former Undersecretary of State William R. Castle, quoted in Benjamin Welles, *Sumner Welles: FDR's Global Strategist* (New York: St. Martin's Press, 1997), 209.

145. Ibid., 324–40; Weisbrode, "The Master, the Maverick, and the Machine," 374, 378.

146. Ibid., 277–78.

147. Bullitt memorandum of conversation with Hull, December 22, 1942, box 40, Bullitt papers.

148. Eliot Janeway diary [May 1941], Eliot Janeway papers, Library of Congress.

149. Bullitt memorandum of conversation with Hull, December 22, 1942, box 40, Bullitt papers.

150. Ibid., January 15, 1943, box 210, Bullitt papers.

151. Ibid. Bullitt was incorrect about Welles's sojourning at Campobello and was also most likely wrong about any physical intimacy with Roosevelt.

152. de Espil diary, November 16, 1942, box 4.

153. Irwin F. Gellman, *Secret Affairs: Franklin Roosevelt, Cordell Hull, and Sumner Welles* (Baltimore: Johns Hopkins University Press, 1995), 310–12.

154. de Espil diary, May 27, 1941, box 4.

155. Ibid., February 12, 1942, box 4.

156. Ibid., February 24, 1943, August 1943, box 4 (emphasis in original).

157. Ibid., August 1943, box 11.

158. Bullitt memorandum of conversation with Hull, April 25, 1943, box 210, Bullitt papers.

159. Ibid., June 2, 1943, box 210, Bullitt papers.

160. Bullitt memorandum of conversation with the President, July 27, 1943, box 210, Bullitt papers.

161. Ward, *Closest Companion*, 227. The stenographer was Dorothy Brady.

162. Bullitt, interview with John Scott, March 30, 1943, box 12, Barnes papers.

163. Welles, *Sumner Welles*, 271–76.

164. Gellman, *Secret Affairs*, 318–31; Welles, *Sumner Welles*, 341–56.

165. D. M. Ladd to the Director, September 9, 1943, Carmel Offie FBI file. I am indebted to John Fox for obtaining this file for me.

166. John Russell to Armine Dew, February 9, 1943, F. O. 371/36954, National Archives, Kew.

167. Jonathan Haslam, *Russia's Cold War: From the October Revolution to the Fall of the Wall* (New Haven, CT: Yale University Press, 2011), 19.

168. Welles, interview with John Scott, March 29, 1943, box 12, Barnes papers.

169. Welles, interview with Louis Fisher, May 18, 1943, box 1, Louis Fisher papers, FDRL.

170. Raymond Clapper, "2nd Roosevelt Private Conference—October 20, 1943," box 23, Clapper papers.

171. John G. Winant, interview with Clapper, March 24, 1943, box 23, Clapper papers.

172. Hopkins, interview with Davies, April 30, 1943, box 13, Davies papers.

173. Eden minute on "The President at Home," December 20, 1943, F. O. 371/38516. Churchill seemed jealous that Roosevelt had confided in a lowly lieutenant. See Colville to Loxley, January 20, 1944, ibid.

174. Lt. Miles, "The President at Home," December 20, 1943, F. O. 371/38516. The visit ended on November 2, 1943.

175. Cordell Hull, *The Memoirs of Cordell Hull* (New York: Macmillan, 1948), 1247–64.

176. de Espil diary, [September 1943], box 4.

177. *FRUS: The Conferences at Cairo and Tehran 1943* (Washington, DC: Government Printing Office, 1961), 3–4 (hereafter *FRUS: Tehran*); Davies diary, April 29, 1943, box 13, Davies papers.

178. Davies, "Arrival in Washington and Report to the President," June 3, 1943, box 13, Davies papers.

179. Davies, "Conference with Stalin," May 26, 1943, box 13, Davies papers.

180. Davies, "Meetings with Stalin and Molotov," May 20, 1943, box 13, Davies papers.

181. Stoler, *Allies in War*, 121.

182. *FRUS: Tehran*, 18.

183. Ibid., 48.

184. Ibid., 54.

185. Eden to Cadogan, [August 1943], F. O. 371/36992. Eden paraphrased Hopkins.

186. Roosevelt, "Trip to Cairo and Teheran," November 13, 1943, box 64, OF [Office File], FDRL; for the Latin prize, see Geoffrey C. Ward, *Before the Trumpet: Young Franklin Roosevelt, 1882–1905* (New York: Harper & Row, 1985), 206.

187. Sergo Beria, *Beria: My Father* (London: Duckworth, 2001), 139.

188. Geoffrey Roberts, *Stalin's Wars: From World War to Cold War, 1939–1953* (New Haven, CT: Yale University Press, 2006), 177–80.

189. Harriman and Abel, *Special Envoy*, 248.

190. Hull, *Memoirs*, 1311.

191. Eden to Churchill, November 1, 1943; Churchill to Eden, November 1, 1943, both in CAB120/113, NA, UK.

192. Ward, *Closest Companion*, 253 (emphasis in original).

193. Moran, *Churchill at War*, 162.

194. Reminiscences of Walter Lippmann (1969), CUOHRC, 217.

195. Captain John L. McCrea, "History of the USS *Iowa*," box 11, John L. McCrea papers, Library of Congress.

196. Roosevelt, "Trip to Cairo and Teheran," November 27, 1943, box 64 OF (emphasis in original).

197. "List of Books in President's Library," William M. Rigdon papers, Small Collections, FDRL.

198. William M. Rigdon, *White House Sailor* (Garden City, NY: Doubleday, 1962), 180.

199. Reminiscences of Perkins (1955), CUOHRC, 8:312.

200. *FRUS: Tehran*: 461–63; Valentin Berezhkov, *History in the Making: Memoirs of World War II Diplomacy* (Moscow: Progress Publishers, 1982), 249–52; Reilly, *Reilly of the White House*, 175–78.

201. CNN interview with Sergo Beria [1996], http://www.cnn.com/SPECIALS/cold.war/episodes/01/interviews/beria (accessed January 27, 2008).

202. Danchev and Todman, *War Diaries*, 483.

203. Richard Park Jr., "Suggestions," no date, William M. Rigdon papers, Small Collections, FDRL (emphasis in original).

204. CNN interview with Sergo Beria.

205. *FRUS: Tehran*, 483; Reilly, *Reilly of the White House*, 179. In keeping with the usual discourse of diplomatic memoranda, Bohlen omitted mention of Stalin's smile and laugh. Such descriptions are, however, central to the genre of "tell-all" memoirs, like Reilly's, which he "told to" sportswriter William J. Slocum. Nevertheless, in view of Stalin's agenda and past behavior in similar settings, it seems likely that he did smile and laugh. (See Simon Sebag Montefiore, *Stalin: The Court of the Red Tsar* [New York: Knopf, 2004].) Moreover, even though memory is constructed and memory of details can blur, the moods and emotions of a riveting event are often what people retain.

206. *FRUS: Tehran*, 483.

207. Rigdon, *White House Sailor*, 81–82.

208. Film 3105-112-3, FDRL.

209. Charles E. Bohlen, *Witness to History, 1929–1969* (New York: W. W. Norton, 1973), 137.

210. *FRUS: Tehran*, 487, 497. For analysis of Tehran based largely on the Soviet record, see Roberts, *Stalin's Wars*, 180–91, 401–2. There does not seem to have been significant differences among the unpublished U.S., Soviet, and British transcripts of meetings.

211. *FRUS: Tehran*, 537.

212. "Record of Conversation between the Prime Minister and Marshal Stalin, 12:45 p.m., 30th November 1943," PREM3/136/8, National Archives.

213. Moran, *Churchill at War*, 164.

214. Films 3105-112-3; 3105-112-4; 71-8:62, FDRL.

215. Moran, *Churchill at War*, 173.

216. Dilks, *Diaries of Sir Alexander Cadogan*, 579.

217. Ibid., 580 (emphasis in original).

218. *FRUS: Tehran*: 511; Jochen Laufer, *Pax Sovietica: Stalin die Westmächte und die deutsche Frage 1941–1945* (Cologne: Böhlau Verlag, 2009), 372–78.

219. Bohlen, *Witness to History*, 147.

220. Moran, *Churchill at War*, 172.

221. Churchill, *Closing the Ring*, 373–74; Moran, *Churchill at War*, 173.

222. Moran, *Churchill at War*, 173.

223. Blum, *Price of Vision*, 180–81.

224. Henry A. Wallace diary, December 18, 1943, Henry A. Wallace papers, Butler Library, Columbia University, New York, NY.

225. *FRUS: Tehran*, 485–86. See also Toye, *Churchill's Empire*, 244–46.

226. Moran, *Churchill at War*, 159.

227. *FRUS: Tehran*, 570.

228. Wallace diary, December 17, 1943.

229. *FRUS: Tehran*, 532–33. For Stalin's interest in the four policemen approach, see also Vladimir O. Pechatnov, "The Soviet Union and the World," in *The Cambridge History of the Cold War*, ed. Melvyn P. Leffler and Odd Arne Westad (Cambridge, UK: Cambridge University Press, 2010), 94.

230. "President's Talk to a Group of MP's at His Villa in Cairo," [December 1943], Rigdon papers, FDRL.

231. "Record of a Conversation between Mr. Eden, M. Molotov and Mr. Harry Hopkins at His Majesty's Legation, Tehran, on 30th November, 1943," PREM3/136/8, National Archives.

232. *FRUS: Tehran*, 570.

233. "Record of a Conversation between Mr. Eden, M. Molotov and Mr. Harry Hopkins at His Majesty's Legation, Tehran, on 30th November, 1943," PREM3/136/8, NA, UK; *FRUS: Tehran*, 571.

234. Dilks, *Diaries of Sir Alexander Cadogan*, 581.

235. *FRUS: Tehran*, 594.

236. Bullitt memorandum of conversation with Otto von Habsburg, January 16, 1944, box 73, Bullitt papers. Von Habsburg talked with Bullitt immediately after seeing FDR.

237. Haslam, *Russia's Cold War*, 17.

238. *FRUS: Tehran*, 595.

239. *FRUS: Tehran*, 838.

240. Danchev and Todman, *War Diaries*, 482; Dilks, *Diaries of Sir Alexander Cadogan*, 578.

241. Moran, *Churchill at War*, 169, 171, 180.

242. Ward, *Closest Companion*, 252, 250.

243. Bohlen, *Witness to History*, 143–44; Kimball, *Forged in War*, 339–41.

244. Earl Miller, letter to Joseph Lash, [1968], box 44, Lash papers.

245. Captain John L. McCrea, "History of the *USS Iowa*," no date, but probably 1945, box 11, John L. McCrea papers, Library of Congress, Washington, DC.

246. McCrea, "History of the *USS Iowa*," box 11, John L. McCrea papers, Library of Congress, Washington, DC (emphasis in original).

247. Moran, *Churchill at War*, 177.

Chapter 6. "I've Worked It Out": Roosevelt's Plan to Win the Peace and Defy Death, 1944–45

1. *FRUS: 1945* (Washington, DC: Government Printing Office, 1967), 5:825–27.

2. Kathleen Harriman to Pamela Churchill, April 12, 1945, unprocessed, Pamela Churchill Harriman papers.

3. *FRUS: 1945*, 5:825–27.

4. Harriman to Eleanor Roosevelt, April 13, 1945, box 178, Averell Harriman papers.

5. Frank K. Roberts to Foreign Office, April 20, 1945 and minute, April 21, 1945, F. O. 371/47939, NA, UK.

6. Reminiscences of Elbridge Durbrow (1981), CUOHRC, 123.

7. Geoffrey W. Ward, ed., *Closest Companion* (Boston: Houghton Mifflin, 1995), 316.

8. *FRUS: The Conferences at Cairo and Tehran 1943* (Washington, DC: Government Printing Office, 1961), 487 (hereafter *FRUS: Tehran*).

9. John Harvey, ed., *The War Diaries of Oliver Harvey 1941–1945* (London: Collins, 1978), 335.

10. Marquis Childs, "Report of a Conversation with President Roosevelt on Friday, April 7, 1944," box 4, Marquis Childs papers. My thanks to Camille Torres for finding this document.

11. Rosenman interview with Joseph P. Lash, December 3, 1969, box 44, Lash papers.

12. Harry Hopkins to Robert Hopkins, February 2, 1944, ser. 3, box 5, Hopkins papers, Georgetown.

13. FDR to Hopkins, February 12, 1944, ser. 4, box 1; Harry Hopkins to Robert Hopkins, February 14, 1944, ser. 3, box 5, Hopkins papers, Georgetown.

14. James Halsted, unpublished biography of Harry Hopkins, chap. 15. Manuscript in possession of June Hopkins.

15. Harold L. Ickes diary, December 30, 1939; Ickes to Anna Roosevelt Boettiger, May 19, 1948, box 47, Ickes papers; Pamela Churchill Harriman, interview with Ogden, unprocessed, Pamela Churchill Harriman papers; Bascom N. Timmons, "John N. Garner's Story," *Saturday Evening Post*, March 6, 1948, 25; Robert E. Sherwood, *Roosevelt and Hopkins, an Intimate History* (New York: Harper, 1948), 91–99.

16. Corcoran, "Rendezvous with Democracy," unpublished autobiography ([written with Philip Kopper),] chap. 10, pp. 28–29, box 587, Corcoran papers; Ickes diary, December 11, 1943.

17. Belle Willard Roosevelt diary, [1943], box 136.

18. Halsted, unpublished biography of Hopkins, chap. 13.

19. Ibid.

20. Ward, *Closest Companion*, 299.

21. Reminiscences of Eliot Janeway, CUOHRC, 71.

22. Steven Lomazow and Eric Fettmann, *FDR's Deadly Secret* (New York: PublicAffairs, 2009), 152–53.

23. Ibid. Lomazow and Fettmann surmise he may also have suffered from prostate cancer.

24. Ibid., 94.

25. Ward, ed., *Closest Companion*, 272, 291, 295.

26. Robert H. Ferrell, *The Dying President* (Columbia: University of Missouri Press, 1998), 16.

27. Ward, ed., *Closest Companion*, 285.

28. Belle Willard diary, June 16, 1944, box 135.

29. Rose McDermott, *Presidential Leadership, Illness, and Decision Making* (New York: Cambridge University Press, 2008), 91, 96, 115.

30. Howard G. Bruenn, "Clinical Notes on the Illness and Death of President Franklin D. Roosevelt," April 23, 1944, Bruenn papers. Years later, Bruenn reworked and published a version of this medical diary. Unless otherwise noted, all citations here are to the unpublished version.

31. Lomazow and Fettmann, *FDR's Deadly Secret*, 149–59.

32. Howard G. Bruenn, "Clinical Notes," August 22, September 20, 1944, Bruenn papers.

33. FDR to Hopkins, May 18, 1944, in Halsted, unpublished biography of Hopkins, chap. 13.

34. Childs, "Report of a Conversation with President Roosevelt on Friday, April 7, 1944," box 4, Childs papers.

35. Ibid.

36. Bruenn, "Clinical Notes," September 20, 1944, Bruenn papers.

37. Ward, *Closest Companion*, 287; Joseph E. Persico, *Franklin & Lucy* (New York: Random House, 2008).

38. Russell D. Buhite and David W. Levy, eds., *FDR's Fireside Chats* (Norman: University of Oklahoma Press, 1992).

39. Miller Center of Public Affairs, University of Virginia, http://tapes.miller center.virginia.edu/clips/1940_0927_randolph (accessed June 5, 2008.)

40. Elizabeth Borgwardt, *A New Deal for the World* (Cambridge, MA: Harvard University Press), 304.

41. "Report of a Conversation with President Roosevelt on Friday, April 7, 1944," box 4, Childs papers.

42. Ibid.

43. Borgwardt, *A New Deal for the World*, 163–68; Fraser J. Harbutt, *Yalta 1945: Europe and America at the Crossroads* (New York: Cambridge University Press, 2010), 261–63.

44. Embassy to Foreign Secretary, May 29, 1944, F. O. 371/38544, NA, UK.

45. Reminiscences of Durbrow, CUOHRC, 109.

46. Forrest Davis, "What Really Happened at Teheran," *Saturday Evening Post*, May 20, 1944, 23.

47. *Complete Presidential Press Conferences of Franklin D. Roosevelt* (New York: Da Capo Press, 1972), May 24, 1944, 23:202–3 (hereafter *Press Conferences of FDR*).

48. Forrest Davis, "What Really Happened at Teheran," *Saturday Evening Post*, May 20, 1944, 22–23, 44, 46.

49. Ibid., 48.

50. Ward, *Closest Companion*, 316.

51. Harbutt, *Yalta 1945*, 108–9.

52. Vladimir O. Pechatnov, "The Big Three after World War II: New Documents on Soviet Thinking about Postwar Relations with the United States and Great Britain," Working Paper no. 13 (1995), 5, CWIHP, http://www.wilsoncenter.org/topics/pubs/ACF17F.PDF.

53. Ibid., 5, 17.

54. Ibid., 5.

55. Memorandum by Bernard Yarrow, June 26, 1944, box 26, entry 160, RG 226, NA, US.

56. Notes of Vassil Kolarov, meeting with J. Stalin, January 28, 1945, in "Stalin and the Cold War, 1945–1953: Cold War International History Project Document Reader," documents collected by the CWIHP and distributed at its conference, September 1999, 130 (hereafter "CWIHP Document Reader").

57. Eduard Mark, "Revolution by Degrees: Stalin's National-Front Strategy for Europe, 1941–1947," Working Paper no. 31 (2001), CWIHP, http://www.wilsoncenter.org/index.cfm?fuseaction=topics.publications&group_id=11901&topic_id=1409.

58. Ibid.; Pechatnov, "Big Three after World War II," 8.

59. Memorandum of conversation with Harriman, Stalin, and Molotov, February 2, 1944, box 80, Herbert Feis papers, Library of Congress, Washington, DC.

60. Schlesinger seminar.

61. Lynne Olson, *Citizens of London* (New York: Random House, 2010), 207–8.

62. George A. Hill, "Reminiscences of Four Years with the NKVD," unpublished memoir, p. 164, Hill papers.

63. Duncan McCallum to Eden, January 31, 1944, F. O. 954/20, NA, UK.

64. Owen O'Malley to Eden, January 22, 1944, F. O. 954/20, NA, UK.

65. Churchill to Clark Kerr, February 5, 1944, F. O. 954/20, NA, UK.

66. "Record of a Meeting Held at No. 10 Downing Street on 16th February 1944 at 5:30 p.m.," F. O. 954/20. See also "Record of a Meeting Held at No. 10 Downing Street on 6th February 1944 at 3 p.m."; O'Malley to Eden, February 13, 1944; Churchill to Eden, February 15, 1944, all in ibid.

67. Eden to Churchill, May 4, 1944, F. O. 954/20, NA, UK.

68. Churchill to Molotov (unsent), May 8, 1944, F. O. 954/20, NA, UK.

69. Churchill to Eden, May 8, 1944, F. O. 954/20, NA, UK.

70. See, for instance, Oscar Cox calendar, February 5, 1945; March 20, 1945; April 7, 1945; May 10, 1945; Walter Lippmann, "Today and Tomorrow," May 12, 1945, all in box 151, Cox papers.

71. Lippmann, "Today and Tomorrow," May 18, 1944.

72. Memorandum of Conversation with the President, October 21–November 19, 1944, box 175, Averell Harriman papers.

73. Anna M. Cienciala, "New Light on Oskar Lange as an Intermediary between Roosevelt and Stalin in Attempts to Create a New Polish Government (January–November 1944)," *Acta Poloniae Historica* 73 (1996): 125.

74. Record of a Conversation between I. V. Stalin and the Roman Catholic Priest St. Orlemanski, April 28, 1944, "CWIHP Document Reader," 1–4.

75. Record of a Conversation of Comrade I. V. Stalin and Comrade V. M. Molotov with the Polish Professor Lange, May 17, 1944, "CWIHP Document Reader," 7–19.

76. Ibid.

77. Notes of Stalin's Speech during a Reception at the Kremlin on June 23, 1944 to Celebrate ... the Polish Provisional Government of National Unity," "CWIHP Document Reader," 21.

78. Warren F. Kimball, ed., *Churchill & Roosevelt: The Complete Correspondence* (Princeton, NJ: Princeton University Press, 1984), 3:273.

79. Record of General de Gaulle's Meeting with Marshal Stalin, December 2, 1944, "CWIHP Document Reader," 88.

80. Conversation between General de Gaulle and Marshal Stalin, December 6, 1944, "CWIHP Document Reader," 96 (emphasis in original).

81. Władysław Gomułka memoirs, [March 1945], "CWIHP Document Reader," 121.

82. Harvey, *War Diaries of Oliver Harvey*, 350.

83. Timothy Snyder, *Bloodlands: Europe between Hitler and Stalin* (New York: Basic Books, 2010), 406.

84. Evan Mawdsley, *Thunder in the East: The Nazi-Soviet War, 1941–1945* (London: Hodder Arnold, 2005), 324–33; Anita J. Prazmowska, *Civil War in Poland, 1942–1948* (New York: Palgrave, 2004), 102–8. For British confirmation of the Soviet military setback, see Minute by Eden, August 8, 1944 in V. Cavendish-Bentinck to O. Sargent, August 7, 1944, F. O. 954/20, NA, UK.

85. *New York Times*, September 4, 1944, 13.

86. Irina Mukhina, "New Revelations from the Former Soviet Archives: The Kremlin, the Warsaw Uprising, and the Coming of the Cold War," *Cold War History* 6 (August 2006): 404; Prazmowska, *Civil War in Poland*, 69–93; Geoffrey Roberts, *Stalin's Wars: From World War to Cold War, 1939–1953* (New Haven, CT: Yale University Press, 2006), 203–17.

87. Mukhina, "New Revelations," 397–405; Stephane Courtois, et al., *The Black Book of Communism* (Cambridge, Mass.: Harvard University Press, 1999), 373–74.

88. Kimball, *Churchill & Roosevelt*, 3:461.

89. Mukhina, "New Revelations," 405–6, 410.

90. Charles Portal to Churchill, August 29, 1944, F. O. 954/20, NA, UK.

91. Kimball, *Churchill & Roosevelt* 3:282.

92. Lord Moran, *Churchill at War 1940–45* (New York: Carroll & Graf, 2002), 211.

93. Kathleen Harriman Mortimer, interview with Rudy Abramson no. 3, June 24, 1987, Rudy Abramson collection. The nephew was the son of Andre Poniatowski, a financier with ties to E. H. Harriman.

94. *FRUS: 1944*, 3:1389.

95. George F. Kennan diary, July 2, 1944, box 231, Kennan papers.

96. Kennan to Jeanette Hotchkiss, October 8, 1944, box 24, Kennan papers.

97. *New York Times*, October 9, 1944, 1; October 19, 1944, 12.

98. H. G. Nichols, ed., *Washington Dispatches 1941–1945* (Chicago: University of Chicago Press, 1981), 431.

99. Harvey, *War Diaries of Oliver Harvey*, 351.

100. *Stalin's Correspondence with Churchill, Attlee, Roosevelt and Truman* (New York: Capricorn Books, 1958), 156–57 (hereafter *Stalin's Correspondence*).

101. *Press Conferences of FDR*, October 3, 1944, 24:152.

102. Władysław Gomułka memoirs, [October 1944], "CWIHP Document Reader," 123.

103. J. V. Stalin Archive, http://www.marxists.org/reference/archive/stalin/works/1944/11/06.htm.

104. Ickes diary, June 24, 1944, Ickes papers.

105. Sherwood, *Roosevelt and Hopkins*, 813–14.

106. Clementine Churchill to children, September 18, 1944, read by Mary Soames in interview with Verne Newton, FDRL.

107. Mark A. Stoler, *Allies in War: Britain and America against the Axis Powers, 1940–1945* (London: Hodder Arnold, 2005), 168–70.

108. For a judicious overview, see Andrew J. Rotter, *Hiroshima: The World's Bomb* (New York: Oxford University Press, 2008).

109. Max Freedman, ed., *Roosevelt and Frankfurter* (Boston: Little, Brown, 1967), 723–35.

110. Jacques E. C. Hymans, "Britain and Hiroshima," *Journal of Strategic Studies* 32 (October 2009): 769–97, 781 for the quotation.

111. Martin J. Sherwin, *A World Destroyed* (New York: Vintage Books, 1977), appendix C, 284.

112. Henry L. Stimson diary, September 9, 1943. Stimson papers. Stimson later told him, "I knew they were spying on our work but they had not yet gotten any real knowledge of it." Stimson diary, December 31, 1944.

113. In 1943–45, U.S. officials filled Soviet Lend-Lease requests for four shipments consisting of 1,420 pounds of uranium oxide and uranium nitrate and 2.2 pounds of uranium metal. The Soviets had asked for more, explaining that it was for manufacturing weapons of steel. U.S. officials sought to "avoid arousing Soviet suspicions" by flatly turning down the requests. Joint Committee on Atomic Energy, *Soviet Atomic Espionage* (Washington, DC: GPO, 1951), 184–92; 188 for the quotation. There is no existing evidence that this uranium was used in the Soviet atomic bomb project. David Holloway, *Stalin and the Bomb* (New Haven, CT: Yale University Press, 1994), 101, 395n.6.

114. Michaela Hoenicke-Moore, *Know Your Enemy* (New York: Cambridge University Press, 2010), 297.

115. Ibid., 297–307.

116. George T. McJimsey, *Harry Hopkins* (Cambridge, MA: Harvard University Press, 1987), 343–47.

117. Ickes diary, August 6, 1944. In her last years, Missy lived with her sister, Anna Rochon, in Somerville, Massachusetts. Unlike Ickes, Bullitt, or Kennedy, Roosevelt had never visited. Resenting FDR's apparent indifference, Rochon informed him of her sister's anguish: Missy was "expecting you to call all Xmas Day." When no call came, Missy toasted him at dinner, "her eyes filled with tears." On New Year's Eve, "she started crying about 11:30, and we couldn't stop her." She "kept calling, 'F. D., come, please come to me, Oh, F. D.'—it really was the saddest thing you hope to see, we were all crying" (Ann Rochon to the President, [January 1943 or 1944], box 21, Roosevelt Family Papers Donated by the Children, FDRL). In early 1944, the Roosevelts twice put off her planned trip to the White House. Bullitt, her former lover, implored her to visit him instead, promising "better food than in the White House" and a "more comfortable bed" (Bullitt to LeHand, March 20, April, 6, 28, 1944, box 49, Bullitt papers). Rochon confided to Bullitt, "it just about killed her to have the [White House] trip postponed twice" (Rochon to Bullitt, [April 1944], ibid.).

118. Ward, *Closest Companion*, 363, 372, 377–80, 398–99, 405, 414.

119. Bruenn, "Clinical Notes," July 13–August 22, 1944, quotations from July 18, 27, 1944, Bruenn papers.

120. Ward, *Closest Companion*, 403.

121. Bruenn, "Clinical Notes," August 22, 1944, Bruenn papers; Lomazow and Fettmann, *FDR's Deadly Secret*, 132–33.

122. Hazel Rowley, *Franklin and Eleanor* (New York: Farrar, Straus and Giroux, 2010), 175.

123. Samuel I. Rosenman, *Working with Roosevelt* (New York: Harper, 1952), 458–59, 474–77.

124. *Press Conferences of FDR*, October 20, 1944, 24:187.

125. Julian E. Zelizer, *Arsenal of Democracy* (New York: Basic Books, 2010), 56–57.

126. Bruenn, "Clinical Notes," October 29, 1944, Bruenn papers.

127. Ferrell, *Dying President*, 85, 114.

128. Ward, *Closest Companion*, 343, 325, 352, 363–64, 346.

129. Schiff talked with FDR on October 9, 1943 and on Labor Day, 1944. Schiff memorandum, November 23, 1981; December 29, 1972; box 258, Schiff papers.

130. Clark Kerr to Foreign Secretary, September 25, 1944, PREM3/396/5, NA, UK.

131. Harvey, *War Diaries of Oliver Harvey*, 356; Moran, *Churchill at War*, 215.

132. W. Averell Harriman and Elie Abel, *Special Envoy to Churchill and Stalin, 1941–1946* (New York: Random House, 1975), 362.

133. Belle Willard Roosevelt diary, November 20, 1944, box 136.

134. Corcoran quoted what Roosevelt had reportedly told insider James Rowe. Corcoran, conversation with Philip Kopper (1979), box 587, Corcoran papers.

135. Reminiscences of Janeway, CUOHRC, 69.

136. Lippmann, "Today and Tomorrow," January 2, 1945.

137. Lippmann, "Today and Tomorrow," December 21, 1944.

138. Robert Rhodes James, ed., *Winston S. Churchill: His Complete Speeches* (New York: Chelsea House, 1974) 7:7071; "Churchill Misquotes Atlantic Charter," *New York Times*, December 16, 1944, 7.

139. *New York Times*, December 19, 1944, 20. By a three-to-one margin, Americans blamed the British rather than the Russians. Harbutt, *Yalta 1945*, 276.

140. Thomas M. Campbell and George C. Herring, eds., *The Diaries of Edward R. Stettinius, Jr., 1943–1946* (New York: Franklin Watts, 1975), 214.

141. *Press Conferences of FDR*, December 19, 1944, 24:266–70; December 22, 1944, 24:276–78

142. *Press Conferences of FDR*, January 2, 1945, 25: 8.

143. Belle Willard Roosevelt diary, June 16, 1944, box 136.

144. Kennan diary, [August 1944], box 231, Kennan papers.

145. *Press Conferences of FDR*, January 2, 1945, 25:8.

146. Sherwood, *Roosevelt and Hopkins*, 834.

147. Robert Dallek, *The Lost Peace: Leadership in a Time of Horror and Hope* (New York: Harper, 2010), 57.

148. Entries in FDR: Day by Day—The Pare Lorentz Chronology, FDRL.

149. Louise Hopkins transcripts.

150. Hugh DeSantis, *The Diplomacy of Silence* (Chicago: University of Chicago Press, 1980), 30.

151. Charles E. Bohlen, *Witness to History* (New York: W.W. Norton, 1973), 166.

152. Henry Hardy, ed., *Isaiah Berlin Letters, 1928–1946* (Cambridge: Cambridge University Press, 2004), 521.

153. Sherwood, *Roosevelt and Hopkins*, 843.

154. Belle Willard Roosevelt diary, November 20, 1944, box 136.

155. Hardy, *Berlin*, 521.

156. Lindley, interview with Halsted, July 30, 1976, box 62, Lindley papers.

157. *Press Conferences of FDR*, December 19, 1944, 24:263. On Dunn, see Kenneth Weisbrode, *Atlantic Century: Four Generations of Extraordinary Diplomats Who Forged America's Vital Alliance with Europe* (Cambridge, MA: Da Capo Press, 2009), 39–41.

158. Bohlen, interview with Sherwood, 1947, Sherwood papers.

159. Quoted in Halsted, unpublished biography of Hopkins, chap. 14.

160. Bohlen, *Witness to History*, 168.

161. Halsted, unpublished biography of Hopkins, chap. 14.

162. Helen Fitzpatrick Millbank, interview with Abramson, [1980s], Rudy Abramson collection.

163. Frances Perkins, *The Roosevelt I Knew* (New York: Viking Press, 1946), 393–94.

164. Ward, *Closest Companion*, 387.

165. Bruenn, "Clinical Notes," January 15, 21, 1945, Bruenn papers; Lomazow and Fettmann, *FDR's Deadly Secret*, 157. The authors claim the weight loss stemmed from the melanoma's having spread to his bowels.

166. Ward, *Closest Companion*, 390.

167. Anna Boettiger to John Boettiger, February 4, 1945, box 6, Boettiger papers.

168. David Dilks, ed., *The Diaries of Sir Alexander Cadogan 1938–1945* (New York: G. P. Putnam's Sons, 1972), 705.

169. Anna Roosevelt Boettiger, Yalta diary, February 1, 1945, box 84, Anna Roosevelt Halsted papers.

170. Boettiger, Yalta diary, February 2, 1945, box 84, Anna Roosevelt Halsted papers; Anna to John, February 4, 1945, box 6, Boettiger papers.

171. Jon Meacham, *Franklin and Winston* (New York: Random House, 2003), 316.

172. Wilson Brown, unpublished memoir, 154–55, box 1, Wilson Brown papers, FDRL.

173. Boettiger, Yalta diary, February 3, 1945, box 84, Anna Roosevelt Halsted papers.

174. Anthony Eden, *The Reckoning* (Boston: Houghton Mifflin, 1965), 592; Serhii Plokhy, *Yalta: The Price of Peace* (New York: Viking, 2010), 29–30.

175. Campbell and Herring, *Diaries of Edward R. Stettinius, Jr.*, 234–35.

176. Wilson Brown unpublished memoir, 183, Wilson Brown papers, FDRL.

177. Boettiger, Yalta diary, February 3, 1945, box 84, Anna Roosevelt Halsted papers; Plokhy, *Yalta*, 37–38.

178. Dilks, *Diaries of Sir Alexander Cadogan*, 704.

179. Bohlen, *Witness to History*, 172.

180. Valentin Berezhkov to Arthur Schlesinger Jr., no date, but probably 1970s, box 2, Miscellaneous Documents, Small Collections, FDRL.

181. Kathleen Harriman Mortimer, interview with Abramson no. 4, December 9, 1987, Rudy Abramson collection.

182. Bruenn, "Clinical Notes," February 8, 10, 1945, Bruenn papers.

183. Bruenn to Ross McIntire, August 1, 1946, Bruenn papers.

184. Ward, *Closest Companion*, 395.

185. Bruenn, "Clinical Notes," April 23, 1944; September 20, 1944; March 1, 1945, Bruenn papers.

186. Bruenn, "Clinical Notes," April 23, 1944; September 20, 1944; March 1, 1945, Bruenn papers; Lomazow and Fettmann, *FDR's Deadly Secret*, 154.

187. Ward, *Closest Companion*, 396.

188. Anna Boettiger to John Boettiger, February 5, 1945, box 6, Boettiger papers.

189. Anna Boettiger to John Boettiger, February 9, 1945, box 6, Boettiger papers.

190. Bohlen, interview with Sherwood, 1947, Sherwood papers.

191. Charles Portal to Pamela Churchill, February 1945, unprocessed, Pamela Churchill Harriman papers.

192. Anna Boettiger to John Boettiger, February 9, 1945, box 6, Boettiger papers.

193. Moran, *Churchill at War*, 281.

194. Ibid., 264–65.

195. Mary Soames, ed., *Winston and Clementine* (Boston: Houghton Mifflin, 1999), 511.

196. Moran, *Churchill at War*, 281.

197. Dilks, *Diaries of Sir Alexander Cadogan*, 706.

198. John Gunther, *Roosevelt in Retrospect* (New York: Harper, 1950), 18 (emphasis in original).

199. Stimson diary, March 13, 1945.

200. Sebag Montefiore, *Stalin: The Court of the Red Tsar* (New York: Knopf, 2004), 484.

201. Dilks, *Diaries of Sir Alexander Cadogan*, 706, 708–9 (emphasis in original).

202. Ibid., 704.

203. Ibid.

204. The Franklin D. Roosevelt Library has a collection of uncut movie footage. Alanbrooke commented on the disorder. Alex Danchev and Daniel Todman, eds., *War Diaries 1939–1945: Field Marshal Lord Alanbrooke* (Berkeley: University of California Press, 2001), 660.

205. Harriman to the President, October 12, 1944, box 174, Harriman papers.

206. Meacham, *Franklin and Winston*, 316.

207. Danchev and Todman, *War Diaries*, 653, 659.

208. Boettiger, Yalta diary, February 3, 1945, box 84, Anna Roosevelt Halsted papers (emphasis in original).

209. Harry N. Balkin, "Analysis of Harry L. Hopkins," December 29, 1934, ser. 4, box 1, Hopkins papers, Georgetown University.

210. Boettiger, Yalta diary, February 3, 1945, box 84, Halsted papers.

211. Moran, *Churchill at War*, 274–75.

212. Kathleen Harriman Mortimer, interview with Abramson no. 4, December 9, 1987, Rudy Abramson collection.

213. John R. Deane, *Strange Alliance: The Story of Our Efforts at Wartime Cooperation with Russia* (New York: Viking, 1947), 160.

214. Boettiger, Yalta diary, February 3, 1945, box 84, Anna Roosevelt Halsted papers; Plokhy, *Yalta*, 45.

215. Harriman and Abel, *Special Envoy*, 393.

216. Dilks, *Diaries of Sir Alexander Cadogan*, 706–7.

217. Plokhy, *Yalta*, 45–46.

218. Sergey. V. Iurchenko, *Grif Sekretnosti Sniat: Okhrana Ialtinskoi Konferentsii 1945 Goda* [Declassified: Guarding the Yalta Conference of 1945] (Sevastopol: Mia, 2003), 127.

219. Sergo Beria, *Beria: My Father* (London: Duckworth, 2001), 103–4.

220. Christopher Andrew and Vasilii Mitrokhin, *The Sword and the Shield: The Mitrokhin Archive and the Secret History of the KGB* (New York: Basic Books, 1999), 104–36; Plokhy, *Yalta*, 78–79.

221. Richard Park Jr., "Suggestions," no date, Rigdon papers, Small Collections, FDRL.

222. Anna Boettiger to John Boettiger, February 4, 1945, box 6, Boettiger papers; *FRUS: Malta and Yalta* (Washington, DC: Government Printing Office, 1955): 551.

223. Pesticide Action Network, http://www.panna.org/issues/persistent-poisons/the-ddt-story (accessed May 12, 2011).

224. Laurence S. Kuter, *Airman at Yalta* (New York: Duell, Sloan and Pearce, 1955), 122.

225. Sarah Churchill, *A Thread in the Tapestry* (New York: Dodd, Mead, 1967), 78.

226. Kuter, *Airman at Yalta*, 152.

227. Plokhy, *Yalta*, 331. Hiss was eventually convicted for perjury but not spying. Evidence from Soviet records indicates that although Hiss passed military information to his Soviet handlers, he was not asked to give them any political information. In fact at Yalta he advised Roosevelt to stand firm against the Soviets on several issues.

228. Boettiger, Yalta diary, February 3, 1945, box 84, Anna Roosevelt Halsted papers. Cadogan's tone also revealed condescension regarding "proper" food. "Of course [the Russians] have to be trained in the matter of breakfast. . . . We have now drilled them into giving us omelets and suchlike." Dilks, *Diaries of Sir Alexander Cadogan*, 706.

229. Moran, *Churchill at War*, 273.

230. Beria, *Beria*, 106.

231. Wilson Brown memoir, 186, Wilson Brown papers, FDRL.

232. Kathleen Harriman Mortimer, interview with Abramson no. 1, May 12, 1983, Rudy Abramson collection.

233. Moran, *Churchill at War*, 279.

234. Milovan Djilas, *Conversations with Stalin* (New York: Harcourt, Brace & World, 1962), 73. The full context this oft-quoted passage tilts even more against the British. Stalin railed against "English duplicity" in both world wars.

235. Montefiore, *Stalin*, 482, 486.

236. *FRUS: Malta and Yalta*, 571–73.

237. Stoler, *Allies in War*, 196.

238. Harbutt, *Yalta 1945*, 139–224, 307–8.

239. *FRUS: Malta and Yalta*, 798–99: Mary E. Glantz, *FDR and the Soviet Union* (Lawrence: University Press of Kansas, 2005), 159–60.

240. Roberts, *Stalin's Wars*, 241–42.

241. *FRUS: Malta and Yalta*, 766; Plokhy, *Yalta*, 216–28.

242. Plokhy, *Yalta*, 92–101; Jochen Laufer, *Pax Sovietica: Stalin die Westmächte und die deutsche Frage 1941–1945* (Cologne: Böhlau Verlag, 2009), 486–90.

243. Roberts, *Stalin's Wars*, 238–40; Plokhy, *Yalta*, 110–13.

244. *FRUS: Malta and Yalta*: 632, 622.

245. *Press Conferences of FDR*, February 5, 1944, 23:31.

246. Ward, *Closest Companion*, 291, 330.

247. *Press Conferences of FDR*, February 5, 1944, 23:33–34.

248. Walter LaFeber, "Roosevelt, Churchill, and Indochina," *American Historical Review* 80, no. 5 (December 1975): 1292; Patrick J. Hearden, *Architects of Globalism: Building a New World Order in World War II* (Fayetteville: University of Arkansas Press, 2002), 109–16.

249. LaFeber, "Roosevelt, Churchill, and Indochina," 1291.

250. Hearden, *Architects of Globalism*, 114–16.

251. *FRUS: Malta and Yalta*, 844; Warren F. Kimball, *The Juggler: Franklin Roosevelt as Wartime Statesman* (Princeton, NJ: Princeton University Press, 1991), 148–51; Richard Toye, *Churchill's Empire: The World That Made Him and the World He Made* (New York: Henry Holt, 2010), 253–54.

252. *FRUS: Malta and Yalta*, 844–45.

253. Felix Chuev, ed., *Molotov Remembers* (Chicago: Ivan R. Dee, 1993), 54.

254. Stoler, *Allies in War*, 194. See also Harbutt, *Yalta, 1945*; Plokhy, *Yalta*.

255. *Press Conferences of FDR*, November 21, 1944, 24:248.

256. *FRUS: Malta and Yalta*, 668–69.

257. Diane Shaver Clemens, *Yalta* (New York: Oxford University Press, 1970), 183, 188–90, 203–5; Plokhy, *Yalta*, 183–84.

258. *FRUS: Malta and Yalta*, 846, 851; Plokhy, *Yalta*, 152–80, 196–206.

259. *FRUS: Malta and Yalta*, 854; Plokhy, *Yalta*, 241–51.

260. Russell D. Buhite, *Decisions at Yalta* (Wilmington, DE: Scholarly Resources, 1986), 114–18; Harbutt, *Yalta 1945*, 313–20.

261. *FRUS: Malta and Yalta*, 848–49, 854.

262. Clemens, *Yalta*, 209.

263. Harbutt, *Yalta 1945*, 298–99; Borgwardt, *New Deal for the World*, 176.

264. *FRUS: Malta and Yalta*, 798.

265. Ibid., 920.

266. Roberts, *Stalin's Wars*, 243.

267. Moran, *Churchill at War*, 282; Soames, *Winston and Clementine*, 515.

268. Plokhy, *Yalta*, 231.

269. Dilks, *Diaries of Sir Alexander Cadogan*, 708.

270. Charles Portal to Pamela Churchill, [February 1945], unprocessed, Pamela Churchill Harriman papers (emphasis in original).

271. Beria, *Beria*, 106.

272. Robert Hopkins, *Witness to History* (Seattle: Castle Pacific Publishing, 2002), 153. See also Eric Alterman, *When Presidents Lie* (New York: Penguin, 2004), 23–44.

273. Plokhy, *Yalta*, 334.

274. *FRUS: Malta and Yalta*, 928.

275. Ibid., 923; Martin Gilbert, *Road to Victory 1941–1945* (Boston: Houghton Mifflin, 1986), 1208.

276. Harbutt, *Yalta 1945*, 353.

277. Ibid., 338.

278. Plokhy, *Yalta*, 347–49.

279. Harbutt, *Yalta 1945*, 343–44.

280. *New York Times*, February 14, 1945, 1, 10.

281. Wilson Brown memoir, 154, Wilson Brown papers, FDRL.

282. Doris Kearns Goodwin, *No Ordinary Time* (New York: Simon & Schuster, 1994), 583–84; Sherwood, *Roosevelt and Hopkins*, 873–74; McJimsey, *Hopkins*, 372; R. Hopkins, *Witness to History*, 170. Though Hopkins's principal biographers claim that this was their last meeting, Hopkins had lunch and dinner with Roosevelt on March 2, 1945. See the Pare Lorentz chronology, FDRL.

283. Samuel I. Rosenman oral history, Harry S. Truman Presidential Library, Independence, MO.

284. *Press Conferences of FDR*, February 23, 1945, 25:72–73.

285. It seems unlikely that, as Lomazow and Fettmann have argued, his departures from the prepared text stemmed from left hemianopia, a neurological condition caused by brain metastases from melanoma that would have resulted in an inability to read the left side of the page. Aside from the question of whether FDR did have melanoma, the ad-libs were lengthy and packed a consistent political message. See *FDR's Deadly Secret*, 1–8.

286. Lippmann, "Today and Tomorrow," March 3, 1945.

287. "Address of the President to the Joint Session of the Congress, March 1, 1945," box 86, Master Speech File, FDRL. On the drafting of the speech, see undated memorandum by Rosenman, "Yalta Speech," box 18, Rosenman papers, FDRL; Rosenman, *Working with Roosevelt*, 526–30.

288. Anna Boettiger to John Boettiger, February 14, 1945, box 6, Boettiger papers.

289. Ward, *Closest Companion*, 398.

290. Lippmann, "Today and Tomorrow," March 3, 1945.

291. Bruenn, "Clinical Notes," March 1, 1945, Bruenn papers.

292. Sumner Welles journal, January 11, 1933, box 265, Sumner Welles papers, FDRL.

293. Ruby Nell to Folks, February 14, 1938, Small Collections, FDRL.

294. Ickes diary, February 28, 1935.

295. Ibid., May 25, 1941.

296. Ibid., August 4, 1937.

297. Ibid., December 6, 1937.

298. Stiles to mother, February 28, 1945, box 17, Stiles papers.

299. Leon Henderson diary, March 13, 1945, box 36, Leon Henderson papers, FDRL. My thanks to Sherry Zane for sharing this document with me.

300. William Mackenzie King diary, March 13, 1945, Library and Archives Canada, http://www.collectionscanada.gc.ca/databases/king/index-e.html (accessed May 12, 2011).

301. On the negotiations, see Bradley F. Smith and Elena Agarossi, *Operation Sunrise* (New York: Basic Books, 1979); Peter Grose, *Gentleman Spy* (Boston: Houghton Mifflin, 1994), 226–56.

302. Stimson diary, March 13, 1945.

303. *Press Conferences of FDR*, March 13, 1945, 25:90–99.

304. William Mackenzie King diary, March 13, 1945, Library and Archives Canada, http://www.collectionscanada.gc.ca/databases/king/index-e.html (accessed May 12, 2011).

305. Stimson diary, March 14, 1945; Persico, *Franklin & Lucy*, 326.

306. Harriman and Abel, *Special Envoy*, 444.

307. Kimball, *Churchill & Roosevelt* 3:593–97.

308. Ibid., 3:588.

309. Ibid., 3:630; Glantz, *FDR and the Soviet Union*, 161–62.

310. Sherwin, *A World Destroyed*, appendix H, 290.

311. William Mackenzie King diary, March 9, 1945, Library and Archives Canada, http://www.collectionscanada.gc.ca/databases/king/index-e.html (accessed May 12, 2011).

312. Ibid. For the proto–Cold War struggle that ensued under Truman, see Tsuyoshi Hasegawa, *Racing the Enemy* (Cambridge, MA: Harvard University Press, 2005).

313. Bruenn, "Clinical Notes," March 16, 28, 1945, Bruenn papers.

314. Bruenn, "Clinical Notes," April 6, 1945, Bruenn papers.

315. Ward, *Closest Companion*, 418.

316. Ferrell, *Dying President*, 119.

317. The Internet Stroke Center, http://www.strokecenter.org/patients/sah.htm (accessed May 12, 2011). Years later, Bruenn explained that he had diagnosed the subarachnoid hemorrhage "by the usual things," especially "the rigid neck." Interview by Jan Kenneth Herman, January 31, 1990. My thanks to Robert Ferrell for sharing this document.

318. Plokhy, *Yalta*, 322–23.

Chapter 7. The Diplomacy of Trauma: Kennan and His Colleagues in Moscow, 1933–46

1. Orville H. Bullitt, ed., *For the President: Personal and Secret* (Boston: Houghton Mifflin, 1972), 66–69; Beatrice Farnsworth, *William C. Bullitt and the Soviet Union* (Bloomington: Indiana University Press, 1967), 214. See also Will Brownell and Richard N. Billings, *So Close to Greatness: A Biography of William C. Bullitt* (New York: Macmillan, 1987), 144.

2. John M. Blum, ed., *The Price of Vision: The Diary of Henry A. Wallace, 1942–1946* (Boston: Houghton Mifflin, 1973), 547–48.

3. Harold Balfour diary, "Moscow 1941," box 164, Averell Harriman papers. Balfour accompanied Harriman and Lord Beaverbrook on their October 1941 mission to Moscow.

4. "Marshal Stalin chaffs a Narkomindel interpreter," December 18, 1944, F. O. 371/4793, NA, UK.

5. See Frank Costigliola, "The 'Invisible Wall': Personal and Cultural Origins of the Cold War," *New England Journal of History* 64 (Fall 2007): 190–213; David S. Foglesong, *The American Mission and the "Evil Empire"* (New York: Cambridge University Press, 2007), 83–106.

6. Robert Meiklejohn diary, October 4, 1945, box 211.

7. Geoffrey J. A. Miles to John H. Godfrey, August 18, 1942, ADM223/249, NA, UK.

8. Kemp Tolley, *Caviar and Commissars* (Annapolis, MD: Naval Institute Press, 1983), 64.

9. Minute by Geoffrey Wilson, August 4, 1944, F. O. 371/43305, NA, UK.

10. "Survey of Contact," July 2, 1944, F. O. 371/43305, NA, UK.

11. Edgar Snow to President Roosevelt, December 28, 1944, box 49, Roosevelt, PSF.

12. Reminiscences of Elbridge Durbrow (1981), CUOHRC, 49, 64.

13. Samuel Spewack, *The Busy Busy People* (Boston: Houghton Mifflin, 1948), 144.

14. Schlesinger seminar.

15. Harrison Salisbury, interview with Whitman Bassow, July 6, 1985, box 3, Bassow papers.

16. Henry Shapiro, interview with Joseph Kauffman, [1977], copy in box 4, Bassow papers.

17. Salisbury, interview with Bassow, July 6, 1985, box 3, Bassow papers (capitalization in original). Upon discovering that his girlfriend had disappeared, Hill, the British SOE agent in Moscow, "walked slowly home. My thoughts were bitter. They had got my Luba. Luba whom I loved. Luba my comrade, mistress, and companion. I was going to miss her by day and night. What was happening to her, what corridors of fear was she passing through?" George A. Hill, "Reminiscences of Four Years with the NKVD," unpublished memoir, p. 213, Hill papers.

18. George F. Kennan, *Memoirs, 1950–1963* (Boston: Little, Brown, 1972), 126; "Fair Day, Adieu!," p. 18, box 240, Kennan papers; Kennan, *Memoirs, 1925–1950* (Boston: Little, Brown, 1967), 190; Kennan, "Flashbacks," in *At a Century's Ending* (New York: W. W. Norton, 1996), 31.

19. Robert W. Thurston, *Life and Terror in Stalin's Russia* (New Haven, CT: Yale University Press, 1996), 2.

20. Kennan, *Memoirs, 1925–1950*, 60; "Fair Day, Adieu!," p. 18, box 240, Kennan papers; Bullitt, *For the President*, 65; Kennan, "Flashbacks," 33, 34.

21. Kennan, *Memoirs, 1925–1950*, 62; Kennan to Charles Thayer, May 22, 1935, box 3, Thayer papers.

22. "Fair Day, Adieu!," pp. 7, 25, box 240, Kennan papers; Kennan to Thayer, May 22, 1935, box 3, Thayer papers; Charles Bohlen to Mother, April 15–May 15, 1934, box 36, Bohlen papers; Anders Stephanson, *Kennan and the Art of Foreign Policy* (Cambridge, MA: Harvard University Press), 215–17, 230–31; "Fair Day, Adieu!," p. 21, box 25, Kennan papers.

23. Bohlen to Mother, April 15–May 15, 1934, box 36, Bohlen papers; Thayer diary, April 13–May 20, 1934, box 6, Thayer papers; Bohlen to Mother, April 15–May 15, 1934, box 36, Bohlen papers.

24. Kennan to Thayer, May 22, 1935, box 3, Thayer papers.

25. "Fair Day, Adieu!," p. 22, box 240, Kennan papers; Kennan to John C. Wiley, February 4, 1935, box 7, John C. Wiley papers, FDRL; Ben C. Wright, "George F. Kennan, Scholar-Diplomat: 1926–1946," PhD diss. (University of Wisconsin at Madison, 1972), 61; Frieda Por to Whom it may concern, June 10, 1942, enclosed in Kennan to Secretary of State, July 13, 1942, 123K36/377, RG 59; NA, US; Fair Day, Adieu!," p. 22, box 240, Kennan papers.

26. Kennan, *Memoirs, 1925–1950*, 65; Bullitt, *For the President*, 83; George W. Bayer, ed., *A Question of Trust: The Memoirs of Loy W. Henderson* (Stanford, CA: Stanford University Press, 1986), 297.

27. Richard Stites, *The Women's Liberation Movement in Russia: Feminism, Nihilism and Bolshevism 1860–1930* (Princeton, NJ: Princeton University Press, 1978), 346–91.

28. Bullitt to Moore, May 14, 1934, box 3, Moore papers; Charles E. Bohlen, *Witness to History, 1929–1969* (New York: W. W. Norton, 1973), 20–21; see also Brownell and Billings, *So Close to Greatness*, 157.

29. Thayer diary, April 14–May 20, 1934, box 6, Thayer papers; Bohlen to Mother, April 15–May 15, 1934, box 36, Bohlen papers.

30. Ibid.; Bullitt to Moore, May 11, 1935, box 3, Moore papers; Thayer diary, April 14–May 20, 1934; Thayer papers; Bohlen, *Witness to History*, 22–23; Wiley to Robert F. Kelley, August 21, 1934, box 1, John C. Wiley papers, FDRL. See also David Mayers, *The Ambassadors and America's Soviet Policy* (New York: Oxford University Press, 1995), 112–13.

31. The emotional intensity within the embassy seems to have also encompassed homosocial feelings. The concept of the homosocial posits an emotional spectrum, that is, a continuum rather than an opposition or an equation, between male friendship and male homoerotic desire. This is not to say that homosociality necessarily entails homosexuality or behavior that is not conventionally masculine. Indeed, homosocial bonds are often fostered by the repudiation of overtly homosexual behavior. Homosocial emotions can arise when men focus on a common task, enemy, or object of desire—or when enemies focus on each other.

Even when such relations are not overtly erotic and do not involve physical contact, they may entail jealousy, anticipation, excitement, affection, seduction, allure, fascination, disappointment and bitterness—in other words, the very emotions that mark overtly erotic relations. Just as heterosexual attraction can raise the emotional charge of nonsexual relations between women and men, so can homosociality raise the emotional charge in relations among men. The commonly observed behaviors of "drinking buddies," sports fans, teammates, and brothers-in-arms suggest the ubiquity of emotions and behaviors that can be considered homosocial but that more often remain camouflaged or underanalyzed. As the ambiguity in the language "teammates" and "brothers-in-arms" suggests, homosocial emotions are both pervasive and ignored or denied. See Eve Kosofsky Sedgwick, *Between Men: English Literature and Male Homosocial Desire* (New York: Columbia University Press, 1985); Hazel V. Carby, *Race Men* (Cambridge, MA: Harvard University Press, 1998).

32. Bohlen, *Witness to History*, 35; Kennan, "Fair Day, Adieu!," p. 16, box 240, Kennan papers. See also Bayer, *A Question of Trust*, 265–97; *FRUS: The Soviet Union 1933–1939* (Washington: Government Printing Office, 1952), 398–400.

33. Bohlen to Mother, April 15–May 15, 1934, box 36, Bohlen papers; Thayer diary, April 13–May 20, 1934, box 6, Thayer papers.

34. Kennan, "Fair Day, Adieu!," p. 35, box 240, Kennan papers; *FRUS: The Soviet Union 1933–1939*, 399–400; Thayer to Sissy, August 18, 1937, box 5, Thayer papers; Kennan, *Memoirs, 1925–1950*, 70.

35. Bullitt to Wiley, January 7, 1935, box 2, John C. Wiley papers, FDRL; for the whistle-blowing, see Paul V. Harper, ed., *The Russia I Believe In: The Memoirs of Samuel N. Harper, 1902–1941* (Chicago: University of Chicago Press, 1945), 211; Bullitt to Moore, May 11, 1935, box 3, Moore papers; Bullitt to Moore, July 15, 1935, box 3, Moore papers.

36. Kennan, "Fair Day, Adieu!," pp. 71–73, box 240, Kennan papers.

37. J. Edgar Hoover to Edwin M. Watson, December 13, 1940, FBI Freedom of Information Act. "Pa" Watson was FDR's aide. I am indebted to Bruce Craig for sharing this document.

38. Yeaton, unpublished memoir, chap. 3, p. 26, box 1, Yeaton papers.

39. John Russell to A. J. Halpern, January 27, 1944, F. O. 371/43345, NA, UK.

40. J. Edgar Hoover to General George V. Strong, "The Influence of Brigadier General Philip R. Faymonville on Soviet-American Relations," July 26, 1943, box 29, Edwin M. Watson papers, University of Virginia, Charlottesville, VA.

41. Ibid.; FBI Reports, August 23, 27, 1943, in file Faymonville, Philip R., Hopkins papers, FDRL; Mary E. Glantz, *FDR and the Soviet Union* (Lawrence: University Press of Kansas, 2005), 128–38.

42. Charles W. Thayer, memorandum, May 23, 1941, enclosed in Steinhardt to Secretary of State, [May–June 1941], 861.00/11892, RG 59, NA, US.

43. Steinhardt to Secretary of State, [May–June 1941], 861.00/11892, RG 59, NA, US.

44. Reminiscences of Durbrow (1981), CUOHRC, 76, 78.

45. Ibid., 67, 132.

46. Arthur Herbert Birse, *Memoirs of an Interpreter* (London: Joseph, 1967), 75.

47. Ibid., 67–68.

48. Minute by Geoffrey Wilson, September 7, 1942, F. O. 371/32955; Bradley F. Smith, *Sharing Secrets with Stalin* (Lawrence: University Press of Kansas, 1996), 23–26, 37–44, 60, 180.

49. Birse, *Memoirs*, 67–68.

50. Ibid., 166–67.

51. Paul Winterton to Walter Layton, November 5, 1944, F. O. 371/43337, NA, UK.

52. Paul Winterton to Norman Cliff, September 14, 1944, F. O. 371/43337, NA, UK.

53. Clark Kerr to Foreign Office, July 17, 1944, F. O. 800/302/120, NA, UK.

54. Bullitt to R. Walton Moore, February 22, 1936, box 58, Bullitt papers.

55. Steinhardt to Henderson, March 16, 1940, box 79, Laurence Steinhardt papers, Library of Congress, Washington, DC.

56. Steinhardt to Frank C. Walker, February 1, 1940, box 78; Steinhardt to Colvin Brown, February 1, 1940, both in Laurence Steinhardt papers, Library of Congress, Washington, DC.

57. Steinhardt to John C. Wiley, September 21, 1939, box 78, Laurence Steinhardt papers, Library of Congress, Washington, DC.

58. Shapiro, interview with Kauffman, box 4, Bassow papers.

59. Kathleen Harriman Mortimer, interview with Rudy Abramson no. 3, June 24, 1987; no. 4, December 9, 1987, Abramson collection.

60. Yeaton to John A. Crane, July 9, 1940, box 1, Yeaton papers.

61. Yeaton to Joseph A. Michela, June 15, 1940, box 1, Yeaton papers.

62. Shapiro, interview with Kauffman, box 4, Bassow papers.

63. Yeaton to Truman Smith, September 13, 1949, box 3, Yeaton papers. An FBI investigator found Michela "moody. . . . He has little contact with Russian officials whom he really does not like." Hoover to Strong, Faymonville report, July 26, 1943, box 29, Edwin M. Watson papers, University of Virginia, Charlottesville, VA.

64. Joseph Michela to Department of War, June 2, 1941, 861.00/11903, RG 59, NA, US. (emphasis in original).

65. Final Report of the Naval Mission to Russia, 1943–45, [1945], ADM223/506, NA, UK.

66. "Political Instructions to Russian Seamen," Military Intelligence report, September 5, 1944, OSS document no. 97386, box 435, entry 21, RG 226, NA, US.

67. "Soviet Citizen Abroad: Be Worthy of Your Mission," [March 1945], copy in F. O. 371/47860, NA, UK.

68. British Military Mission, Rumania to W. O., January 3, 1945, F. O. 371/43662, NA, UK.

69. John Hersey to Patch, November 4, 1944, box 7.

70. Reported in William J. Donovan to Joint Chiefs of Staff, June 29, 1942, reel 104, M1642, RG 226, NA, US.

71. Quoted in "Reports from Casual Sources," February 13, 1945, F.O. 371/47934, NA, UK.

72. John Earl Haynes and Harvey Klehr, *Venona: Decoding Soviet Espionage in America* (New Haven, CT: Yale University Press, 1999); Allen Weinstein and Alexander Vassiliev, *The Haunted Wood: Soviet Espionage in America—the Stalin Era* (New York: Random House, 1999); John Earl Haynes, Harvey Klehr, Alexander Vassiliev, Philip Redko, and Stephen Shabad, *Spies: The Rise and Fall of the KGB in America* (New Haven, CT: Yale University Press, 2009); Katherine A. S. Sibley, *Red Spies in America* (Lawrence, KS: University Press of Kansas, 2004).

73. Alexander Vassiliev, Yellow Notebook #2, p. 15, CWIHP, http://www.wilsoncenter.org/topics/docs/Yellow_Notebook_No.2_Translated1.pdf.

74. Haynes, et al., *Spies*, 240.

75. Ibid., 241–48.

76. Richard Dunlop, *Donovan: America's Master Spy* (New York: Rand McNally, 1982).

77. See, for instance, Memorandum to Director, January 5, 1942, William D. Donovan file, Federal Bureau of Investigation, http://foia.fbi.gov/donovan/donovan2b.pdf.

78. Vassiliev, White Notebook #1, pp. 85–86, CWIHP, http://www.wilsoncenter.org/topics/docs/White_Notebook_No.1_Translated1.pdf; Harriman to Secretary of State, January 6, 1944, in J. Dane Hartgrove, ed., *The OSS-NKVD Relationship, 1943–1945* (New York: Garland, 1989), document 11. See also Douglas Waller, *Wild Bill Donovan* (New York: Free Press, 2011), 220–24.

79. Anthony Cave Brown, *The Last Hero: Wild Bill Donovan* (New York: Times Books, 1982), 420–21.

80. Vassiliev, White Notebook #1, pp. 85–86; Harriman to Secretary of State, January 6, 1944 in Hartgrove, *The OSS-NKVD Relationship*, document 11.

81. Kathleen Harriman Mortimer, interview with Rudy Abramson no. 3, June 24, 1987, Abramson collection.

82. Vassiliev, White Notebook #1, p. 86.

83. Harriman to the President, March 18, 1944, in Hartgrove, *OSS-NKVD Relationship*, document 27.

84. Ibid., documents 15, 16. For the ambitious efforts of British intelligence, see Thomas F. Troy, *Wild Bill and Intrepid: Donovan, Stephenson and the Origin of the CIA* (New Haven, CT: Yale University Press, 1996).

85. Roosevelt to Harriman, March 29, 1944, in Hartgrove, *The OSS-NKVD Relationship*, document 29.

86. Vassiliev, White Notebook #1, pp. 88, 92–93.

87. Haynes and Klehr, *Venona*, 104–7; Haynes, et al., *Spies*, 314–17; Lauren Kessler, *Clever Girl Elizabeth Bentley, the Spy Who Ushered in the McCarthy Era* (New York: HarperCollins, 2003), 82–83.

88. Hartgrove, *The OSS-NKVD Relationship*, document 27.

89. Vassiliev, White Notebook #1, p. 93.

90. Vassiliev, White Notebook #1, pp. 91, 96–100.

91. Vassiliev, White Notebook #1, p. 97.

92. Robert Meiklejohn, interview with Rudy Abramson, [1980s], Abramson collection.

93. Cave Brown, *Last Hero*, 755.

94. John R. Deane, *The Strange Alliance* (New York: Viking, 1947), 153.

95. Christopher Warner to Clark Kerr, July 13, 1944, F. O. 800/302/103; Clark Kerr to Foreign Office, July 27, 1944, F. O. 371/43306; Memorandum of Conversation with Harriman, Clark Kerr, and Stalin, September 23, 1944, F. O. 800/302/199, all NA, UK.

96. The tripartite committee could have fit under the umbrella of the proposed United Nations according to a modified version of Article 51 of the UN Charter, which would be approved in 1945. That would be the arrangement with several Western pacts set up in postwar years.

97. Snow to Roosevelt, December 28, 1944, box 49, PSF, FDRL.

98. Minute by Geoffrey Wilson, August 10, 1944; minute by J. G. Ward, August 15, 1944, F. O. 371/43306, NA, UK.

99. Minute by Geoffrey Wilson, August 10, 1944, F. O. 371/43306, NA, UK.

100. Alex Danchev and Daniel Todman, eds., *War Diaries 1939–1945: Field Marshal Lord Alanbrooke* (Berkeley: University of California Press, 2001), 575.

101. Minute by Geoffrey Wilson, August 10, 1944, F. O. 371/43306, NA, UK. Nearly all of Wilson's Foreign Office colleagues agreed. See minutes by Christopher Warner, August 11; J. G. Ward, August 15; M. Butler, August 16, 1944; draft minute for the Prime Minister from the Secretary of State, [October 1944]; Minute by Wilson, September 24, 1944, all in ibid. For Stalin's moles, see Richard J. Aldrich, *The Hidden Hand* (New York: Overlook Press, 2002), 19–121; Yuri Modin, *My Five Cambridge Friends* (New York: Farrar, Straus, Giroux, 1994).

102. Memorandum of Conversation with Harriman, Clark Kerr, and Stalin, September 23, 1944, F. O. 800/302/199, NA, UK.

103. Minute by Geoffrey Wilson, September 24, 1944, F. O. 371/43306, NA, UK.

104. Ismay to Eden, November 15, 1944; Warner minute, November 18, 1944, F. O. 371/43291, NA, UK.

105. Minute by Roberts, August 18, 1944, F. O. 371/43306, NA, UK.

106. Minute by Gladwyn Jebb, October 18, 1944, F. O. 371/43306, NA, UK.

107. Final Report of the Naval Mission to Russia, 1943–45 [1945], ADM223/506, NA, UK.

108. Thayer to Kennan, April 10, 1940, box 3, Thayer papers.

109. Robert D. Dean, *Imperial Brotherhood* (Amherst: University of Massachusetts Press, 2001), 100 (emphasis in original).

110. Ibid., 63–96; David K. Johnson, *The Lavender Scare* (Chicago: University of Chicago Press, 2004), 65–77; K. A. Cuordileone, *Manhood and American Political Culture in the Cold War* (New York: Routledge, 2005), 1–96.

111. Yeaton to Thomas Julian, [1968], box 3, Yeaton papers (emphasis in original).

112. Yeaton to Robert Wood, January 22, 1977, box 3, Yeaton papers (capitals in original).

113. Reminiscences of Durbrow (1981), CUOHRC, 108.

114. Bohlen to Walworth Barbour, November 19, 1951, box 5, Bohlen papers, RG 59, NA, US.

Chapter 8. Guns and Kisses in the Kremlin: Ambassadors Harriman and Clark Kerr Encounter Stalin, 1943–46

1. Alexander Werth, *Russia at War 1941–1945* (New York: Carroll & Graf, 1984), 753.

2. Ibid., 751–52.

3. Clark Kerr, "Stalin, an Obituary Appreciation," September 26, 1949, Clark Kerr papers. Clark Kerr wrote a number of such "obituaries" for the BBC. Ironically, he would die two years before Stalin.

4. Kathleen Harriman to Mary, November 9, 1943, box 170, Averell Harriman papers.

5. Ibid. Molotov had reason to feel uncertain. Also at the party was Bohlen, who found the uniforms "ridiculous" and the Soviets "inordinately proud" of them. The incident suggests how the Soviet quest for respect could backfire. Charles E. Bohlen, *Witness to History, 1929–1969* (New York: W. W. Norton, 1973) 130.

6. Clark Kerr to Eden, July 16, 1944, F. O. 800/302/111, NA, UK.

7. Clark Kerr to Eden, November 18, 1943, F. O. 800/301/250, NA, UK.

8. Kathleen Harriman to Mary, November 9, 1943, box 170, Averell Harriman papers.

9. Kathleen Harriman Mortimer, interview with Rudy Abramson no. 3 June 24, 1987, Abramson collection.

10. Clark Kerr to Eden, November 18, 1943, F. O. 800/301/250, NA, UK.

11. Ibid.

12. Kathleen Harriman to Mary, November 9, 1943, box 170, Averell Harriman papers; Werth, *Russia at War*, 753–54.

13. Kathleen Harriman to Mary, November 9, 1943, box 170, Averell Harriman papers. British naval officers at the party loyally recorded that Molotov had made "a concerted effort . . . to make our Ambassador drunk. Molotov himself did not come off best." "War Diary of the British Naval Mission, Moscow," November 7, 1943, enclosed in Richard D. Wyant to Warner, December 29, 1943, F. O. 371/43288, NA, UK.

14. John R. Deane, *The Strange Alliance* (New York: Viking, 1947), 84.

15. Thomas Brimelow to Donald Gillies, November 23, 1989, Donald Gillies collection, Bodleian Library, Oxford University, Oxford, UK.

16. Kathleen Harriman Mortimer, interview with Rudy Abramson no. 3, June 24, 1987, Abramson collection.

17. See Donald Gillies, *Radical Diplomat: The Life and Times of Archibald Clark Kerr Lord Inverchapel, 1882–1951* (London: I. B. Tauris, 1999).

18. Ben Pimlott ed., *The Second World War Diary of Hugh Dalton, 1940–1945* (London: Cape, 1986), 567–68.

19. Ibid.

20. Joseph Barnes to C. B. Omerod, October 22, 1946, box 14, Barnes papers.

21. Clark Kerr to Eden, August 31, 1944, F. O. 371/43336, NA, UK.

22. Clark Kerr to Eden, March 27, 1945, F. O. 371/47941, NA, UK. For approving minutes, see ibid., April 18, 19, 1945.

23. Walter Bell to Gillies, July 25, 1991, Donald Gillies collection, Bodleian Library, Oxford University, Oxford, UK.

24. John Tosh, *A Man's Place: Masculinity and the Middle-Class Home in Victorian England* (New Haven, CT: Yale University Press, 1999), 188–94.

25. Kathleen Harriman Mortimer, interview with Rudy Abramson no. 3, June 24, 1987, Abramson collection.

26. James Bertram, *The Shadow of a War* (London: Victor Gollancz, 1947), 87.

27. Meiklejohn diary, February 19, 1944, box 211, Averell Harriman papers.

28. Hersey to Patch [his wife], November 19, 1944, box 7, Hersey papers.

29. Hersey to Gillies, November 11, 1991, Donald Gillies collection, Bodleian Library, Oxford University, Oxford, UK.

30. Clark Kerr to Warner, July 30, 1943, F.O. 800/301/92, NA, UK; Gillies, *Radical Diplomat*, 125.

31. Clark Kerr to Christopher F. A. Warner, June 11, 1942, F. O. 800/300/24, NA, UK.

32. Clark Kerr to Eden, April 27, 1942, F. O. 800/300/-, NA, UK.

33. Gillies, *Radical Diplomat*, 156.

34. Frank Giles, "From Russia with Love," *Sunday Times* (London), March 6, 1980, 33.

35. Clark Kerr to Christopher Warner, June 11, 1942, F. O. 800/300/24; Clark Kerr to Eden, April 27, 1942, 800/300/-, NA, UK.

36. Ibid.

37. Ibid.

38. Clark Kerr to Christopher Warner, October 3, 1942, F. O. 800/300/198, NA, UK.

39. Kathleen Harriman Mortimer, interview with Rudy Abramson no. #1, May 12, 1983, Abramson collection.

40. John Melby oral history, Foreign Service History Program, Georgetown University, Washington, DC.

41. Meiklejohn, interview with Rudy Abramson [1980s], Abramson collection.

42. Harriman diary, October 21, 1943, box 170, Averell Harriman papers.

43. [Foreign Ministry of the USSR], *Sovetsko-Amerikanskie otnosheniia vo vremia velikoi otechestvennoi voiny 1941–1945* (Moscow, 1984), 386. My thanks to Olga Baeva for translating this document.

44. Harriman to the President, November 1, 1943, box 170, Averell Harriman papers.

45. "W. A. Harriman—Notes regarding meeting with Mr. Molotov at the Kremlin October 21, 1943," box 170, Averell Harriman papers.

46. Deane, *Strange Alliance*, 3.

47. Ibid., 25.

48. John Balfour to Christopher Warner, November 1, 1943, F.O. 800/300/235, NA, UK.

49. Harriman to the President and Acting Secretary of State, October 30, 1943, box 170, Averell Harriman papers.

50. Transcript of conversation held by Osipov and Fitin with Deane, February 19, 1944, Alexander Vassiliev, White Notebook #1, p. 87, CWIHP, http://www.wilsoncenter.org/topics/docs/White_Notebook_No.1_Translated1.pdf.

51. Kemp Tolley, *Caviar and Commissars* (Annapolis, MD: Naval Institute Press, 1983), 180.

52. *British Documents on Foreign Affairs* (London: Stationery Office, 1997), pt. 3, ser. A, 6:305.

53. David Mayers, *The Ambassadors and America's Soviet Policy* (New York: Oxford University Press, 1995), 149.

54. Harriman to the Secretary, November 1, 1943, box 170, Averell Harriman papers.

55. Arthur Scott Mobley Jr., "In Leahy's Hands: William Leahy, Franklin Roosevelt, and the Crafting of Coalition Strategy during World War II" (MA thesis, University of Wisconsin, 2010), 117.

56. Kennan, *Memoirs 1925–1950*, 210–11; William Larsh, "W. Averell Harriman and the Polish Question, December 1943–August 1944," *East European Politics and Societies* 7 (Fall 1993): 550. Decades later, when collaborating with Elie Abel in writing his memoir, *Special Envoy to Churchill and Stalin*, Averell disputed Abel's draft of a passage, based on a letter of Kathleen's, that he had been "about to collapse" from frustration during the Warsaw uprising. Harriman wanted to shape the published story so that it illustrated a key tenet of the Cold War: Americans responded with steely resolve to Russian challenges. He insisted

to Abel that "whatever my condition was, it was a sign of determination rather than weakness." He instructed that the offending passage "should be rewritten to make that clear" (Harriman to Abel, May 8, 1974, box 859, Averell Harriman papers). The published book reads that Harriman persevered despite his "beginning to show the strain" (Harriman and Abel, *Special Envoy*, 342). Kathleen's letter cannot be found in the Harriman papers.

57. Mark J. Conversino, *Fighting with the Soviets* (Lawrence: University Press of Kansas, 1997), 67.

58. Clark Kerr to Eden, July 16, 1944, F.O. 800/302/111, NA, UK.

59. Kathleen Harriman Mortimer, interview with Rudy Abramson no. 1, May 12, 1982, Abramson collection.

60. Deane, *Strange Alliance*, 119–20.

61. Frank Costigliola, "'I Had Come as a Friend': Emotion, Culture, and Ambiguity in the Formation of the Cold War, 1943–45," *Cold War History* 1 (August 2000): 116–17.

62. William R. Kaluta, *History of Eastern Command, U.S. Strategic Air Forces in Europe* (1945), Reel B5122/1473, p. 57, U.S. Air Force Historical Research Agency, Maxwell Air Force Base, Alabama. GI pranksters primed Russian soldiers to greet American officers with "Good morning, you lousy S.O.B." Ibid., 58.

63. Conversino, *Fighting with the Soviets*, 182.

64. Kaluta, *History of Eastern Command*, 66. Even as the practical utility of Poltava was declining, commanders worried that closing it "would deprive the United States Army of any base whatsoever on Russian soil." Deane to Spaatz, March 4, 1945, box 65, entry 311, RG 334, NA, US.

65. Tolley, *Caviar and Commissars*, 202.

66. Kaluta, *History of Eastern Command*, 146.

67. Ibid., 144.

68. See Jeffrey Burds, *Borderland Wars: Stalin's War against "Fifth Columnists" on the Soviet Periphery, 1937–1953*, forthcoming.

69. See Frank Costigliola, "'Like Animals or Worse': Narratives of Culture and Emotion by U.S. and British POWs and Airmen behind Soviet Lines, 1944–1945," *Diplomatic History* 28 (November 2004): 749–80.

70. Report in *Daily Herald*, [February 1945], W.O. 193/348, War Office, NA, UK.

71. Major John W. Dobson in "Statements of Liberated Ps/W," April 9, 1945, box 569, entry 43, RG 165, NA, US.

72. Testimony #22 from "Questionnaires received from U.S. Prisoners of War Recovered from Germany," enclosed in R. W. Berry to Commanding General, U.S. Military Mission, Moscow [General John R. Deane], April 21, 1945, box 22, entry 311, RG 334, NA, US (hereafter Questionnaires from U.S. POWs).

73. SOE memorandum, "Answers to Questions," no date but 1945, HS4/211, NA, UK.

74. Archer to Rushbrooke, April 16, 1945, ADM223/249, NA, UK.

75. Lt. Col. James D. Wilmeth, "Report on a Visit to Lublin, Poland February 27–March 28 1945," box 22, entry 319, RG 334, NA, US.

76. Deane, *Strange Alliance*, 182.

77. Report by Nelson, May 12, 1945, HS4/211, NA, UK.

78. "Report on Present Conditions in Poland by Corporal J. N. C. Davie," March 8, 1945, W. O. 208/1860, NA, UK.

79. Testimony #34, Questionnaires from U.S. POWs, April 21, 1945, box 22, entry 311, RG 334, NA, US.

80. Interrogation of Lt. R. Krohn, March 18, 1945, box 67, entry 311, RG 334, NA, US.

81. Interrogation of Lt. R. E. Beam, December 10, 1944, box 67, entry 311, RG 334, NA, US.

82. Interrogation of Lt. W. J. Bartlet, March 15, 1945, box 67, entry 311, RG 334, NA, US.

83. Interrogation of Lt. W. J. Sylvernal, March 15, 1945, box 67, entry 311, RG 334, NA, US.

84. Report by M/Sgt. Philip M. Mischenko, [December 1944], enclosed in General Edmund W. Hill to Harriman, December 28, 1944, box 67, entry 311, RG 334, NA, US.

85. Interrogation of Lt. Krohn, March 18, 1945, box 67, entry 311, RG 334, NA, US.

86. Kathleen Harriman to Mary, March 8, 1945, box 177, Averell Harriman papers.

87. Harriman to the President, March 8, 1945, box 34, Roosevelt, MR.

88. Harriman to the President, March 24, 1945, box 34, Roosevelt, MR.

89. Meiklejohn diary, February 23–25, 1945, box 211, Averell Harriman papers.

90. Ibid., March 17, 1945.

91. Ibid.

92. Ibid., March 25, 1945.

93. C. L. Sulzberger, *A Long Row of Candles, 1934–54* (New York: Macmillan, 1969), 258.

94. Harriman and Deane to Department of State, March 13, 1945; Harriman to Department of State, March 17, 1945, box 177, Averell Harriman papers.

95. Schlesinger seminar.

96. *Stalin's Correspondence with Churchill, Attlee, Roosevelt and Truman* (New York: Capricorn Books, 1958), 214.

97. Harriman to the President, April 12, 1945, box 178, Averell Harriman papers.

98. Roosevelt to Harriman, April 12, 1945, box 178, Averell Harriman papers.

99. Harriman to Secretary of State, unsent, April 10, 1945, box 178, Averell Harriman papers.

100. Pentagon generals, however, examined a list of similar complaints from Deane and judged them "irritating" but "of relatively minor moment." Diane Shaver Clemens, "From War to Cold War: The Role of Harriman, Deane, and the Joint Chiefs of Staff in the Reversal of Cooperation with the Soviet Union, April, 1945," *International History Review* 14 (May 1992): 280.

101. Alice Acheson, interview with Rudy Abramson, [1980s], Abramson collection.

Chapter 9. "Roosevelt's Death Has Changed Everything": Truman's First Days, April–June 1945

1. Meiklejohn diary, April 17–20, 1945, box 211.

2. Patrick Hurley to Harriman, May 15, 1945, box 179, Averell Harriman papers.

3. Meiklejohn diary, April 15–17, 1945, box 211.

4. Reminiscences of Durbrow (1981), CUOHRC, 65.

5. C. L. Sulzberger, *A Long Row of Candles, 1934–54* (New York: Macmillan, 1969), 255–56.

6. Meiklejohn diary, April 9, 1945, box 211.

7. Clark Kerr to Christopher Warner, June 21, 1945, F. O. 371/47862, NA, UK.

8. On the suddenness, see Theodore A. Wilson, "Endgames: V-E Day and War Termination," in *Victory in Europe 1945*, ed. Arnold A. Offner and Theodore A. Wilson (Lawrence: University Press of Kansas, 2000), 11–45.

9. For Truman's concerns about assuming the presidency and about the connection between height and presidential greatness, see Robert H. Ferrell, ed., *Off the Record: The Private Papers of Harry S. Truman* (New York: Harper & Row, 1980), 16; Margaret Truman, ed., *Where the Buck Stops* (New York: Warner Books, 1989), 77–79. On the activities of Harriman and Deane in Washington, see Diane Shaver Clemens, "From War to Cold War: The Role of Harriman, Deane, and the Joint Chiefs of Staff in the Reversal of Cooperation with the Soviet Union, April, 1945," *International History Review* 14 (May 1992): 293–303.

10. William E. Pemberton, *Harry S. Truman: Fair Dealer and Cold Warrior* (Boston: Twayne, 1989), 44.

11. Lord Moran, *Churchill at War 1940–45* (New York: Carroll & Graf, 2002), 326.

12. Reminiscences of Janeway (2003), CUOHRC, 81.

13. George C. Herring, *From Colony to Superpower: U.S. Foreign Relations since 1776* (New York: Oxford University Press, 2008), 600.

14. Pemberton, *Harry S. Truman*, 8.

15. George E. Mowry, "The Use of History by Recent Presidents," *Journal of American History* 53 (June 1966): 7. See also J. Garry Clifford, "President Truman and Peter the Great's Will," *Diplomatic History* 4 (October 1980): 371–86.

16. Pemberton, *Harry S. Truman*, 5, 8.

17. Lincoln ranked second and Washington third. Hadley Cantril, ed., *Public Opinion 1935–1946* (Princeton, NJ: Princeton University Press, 1951), 565.

18. John M. Blum, ed., *The Price of Vision: The Diary of Henry A. Wallace, 1942–1946* (Boston: Houghton Mifflin, 1973), 437.

19. Pemberton, *Harry S. Truman*, 6.

20. Robert H. Ferrell, ed., *Dear Bess* (New York: W. W. Norton, 1983), 254.

21. Ibid., 517.

22. Pemberton, *Harry S. Truman*, 40–41.

23. Henry L. Stimson diary, April 12, 1945, Stimson papers.

24. Pemberton, *Harry S. Truman*, 39.

25. Ferrell, *Dear Bess*, 471.

26. Department of State, *FRUS: 1945* (Washington, DC: Government Printing Office, 1967), 5:253. See also Elizabeth Edwards Spalding, *The First Cold Warrior* (Lexington: University of Kentucky Press, 2006), 24–35.

27. Eleanor Roosevelt to Harry Truman, May 14, 1945, in Allida Black, et al., eds., *The Eleanor Roosevelt Papers: Volume I The Human Rights Years, 1945–1948* (New York: Thomson Gale, 2007), 29.

28. Reminiscences of Frances Perkins (1955), CUOHRC, 8:815–16.

29. Louise Hopkins, FBI transcript of telephone conversation, April 14, 1945, The J. Edgar Hoover Official and Confidential File, reel 13, University Publications of America.

30. Melvyn P. Leffler, *For the Soul of Mankind: The United States, the Soviet Union, and the Cold War* (New York: Hill and Wang, 2007), 38.

31. Louise Hopkins, FBI transcript, April 14, 1945.

32. Ibid., April 23, 1945.

33. Ibid., April 12, 1945.

34. Ibid., April 13, 14, 15, 1945.

35. Ibid., April 14, 1945.

36. Henry Hardy, ed., *Isaiah Berlin Letters, 1928–1946* (Cambridge: Cambridge University Press, 2004), 553.

37. Louise Hopkins transcripts, April 14, 1945.

38. Ibid., April 16, 1945.

39. Schlesinger seminar.

40. Pearson memorandum, April 13, 1945, G 211, Pearson papers. This memorandum authoritatively cites secret telegrams exchanged among the Big Three before FDR's death. Pearson's informant appears to have been someone from the British Embassy.

41. Louise Hopkins, FBI transcript, April 14, 1945.

42. Elie Abel, interview with Rudy Abramson, September 17, 1981, Abramson collection.

43. Richard Helms, interview with Rudy Abramson [1980s], Abramson collection.

44. Lippmann to Hans Kohn, May 30, 1945, box 82, Lippmann papers.

45. Schlesinger seminar.

46. Elbridge Durbrow, interview with Rudy Abramson [1980s], Abramson collection.

47. Roberts, interview with Hoffman, June 24, 1968, box 15, Kennan papers; Roberts to Warner, March 14, 1945, F. O. 371/47934, NA, UK.

48. Davies diary, June 6, 1945, box 17, Davies papers. Though Joseph Davies sympathized with the Soviets, historians have not questioned the veracity of his diary. The entry cited here is an original, not one of the reworked passages that Davies did in the early 1950s. See also Melvyn P. Leffler, "Adherence to Agree-

ments: Yalta and the Experiences of the Early Cold War," *International Security* 11 (Summer 1986): 88–123; Eric Alterman, *When Presidents Lie* (New York: Penguin, 2004), 55–59.

49. Schlesinger seminar.

50. *FRUS: 1945,* 5:232.

51. Ibid.

52. Clemens, "From War to Cold War," 293–303.

53. Blum, *Price of Vision,* 451.

54. *FRUS: 1945,* 5:253.

55. Ibid., 5:253–55.

56. Davies conversation with Frankfurter in Davies journal, May 13, 1945, box 16, Davies papers.

57. Stimson diary, April 23, 1945.

58. *FRUS: 1945,* 5:253–55.

59. Ibid.; Charles E. Bohlen, *Witness to History, 1929–1969* (New York: W. W. Norton, 1973), 212–13.

60. Davies journal, April 23, 30, 1945, box 16, Davies papers.

61. Harry S. Truman, *Memoirs 1945: Year of Decisions* (Garden City, NY: Doubleday, 1955), 77.

62. Bohlen, *Witness to History,* 213.

63. Reminiscences of Durbrow (1981), CUOHRC, 70.

64. Davies journal, April 30, 1945, box 16, Davies papers. The quotation is from Davies's notes after his talk with Truman.

65. Hugh De Santis, *The Diplomacy of Silence: The American Foreign Service, the Soviet Union, and the Cold War, 1933–1947* (Chicago: University of Chicago Press, 1980), 139.

66. W. Averell Harriman and Elie Abel, *Special Envoy to Churchill and Stalin, 1941–1946* (New York: Random House, 1975), 454.

67. Bohlen, *Witness to History,* 213.

68. "Recollection of Mr. Harriman," October 23, 1953, box 872, Averell Harriman papers.

69. Vladislav Zubok, *A Failed Empire* (Chapel Hill: University of North Carolina Press, 2007), 15–16; Geoffrey Roberts, "Sexing up the Cold War: New Evidence on the Molotov-Truman Talks of April 1945," *Cold War History* 4, no. 3 (April 2004): 105–25, points up Truman's made-up punch line and then concludes that Truman was not particularly aggressive. He also argues that Molotov gave as good as he got, which is not borne out by either the U.S. or the Soviet transcripts. The latter is translated and reproduced in Roberts's article.

70. Felix Chuev, ed., *Molotov Remembers* (Chicago: Ivan R. Dee, 1993), 55.

71. Truman, *Memoirs,* 75.

72. Frank Roberts to Ernest Bevin, "Report on Leading Personalities in the Soviet Union," May 22, 1946, F. O. 371/56871, NA, UK.

73. Robert Sherwood to Hopkins, April 4, 1945, ser. 3, box 4, Hopkins papers, Georgetown.

74. Clark Kerr to Anthony Eden, August 31, 1944, F. O. 371/43336, NA, UK.

75. Sid Fine to Joseph Barnes, August 26, 1945, box 13, Barnes papers. See also Hersey to Patch, November 8, 1944, box 7, Hersey papers.

76. Kennan diary, July 27, 1944, box 231, Kennan papers.

77. Foreign Office officials worried that in the War Office referring to the Russians as "savages" was something "they nearly all do, more and more openly, starting from the very top." Geoffrey Wilson to Clark Kerr, October 3, 1944, F. O. 800/302/219; Warner to Clark Kerr, October 13, 1944, F. O. 800/302/236, NA, UK.

78. Frank Roberts to Foreign Office, October 19, 1945, F. O. 371/47807, NA, UK.

79. Arthur Herbert Birse, *Memoirs of an Interpreter* (London: Joseph, 1967), 209.

80. Ibid., 160.

81. Meiklejohn diary, July 12, 1944, box 211.

82. Reminiscences of Perkins (1955), CUOHRC, 8:315.

83. Fraser J. Harbutt, *Yalta 1945: Europe and America at the Crossroads* (New York: Cambridge University Press, 2010), 362.

84. Geoffrey Roberts, *Stalin's Wars* (New Haven, CT: Yale University Press, 2006), 331, 333.

85. Chuev, *Molotov Remembers*, 11, 19, 23, 44, 53, 55, 69, 77.

86. Ibid., 8, 52, 59, 65, 66, 73, 74.

87. Ibid., 53.

88. Ibid., 69.

89. Ibid., 47.

90. Zubok, *Failed Empire*, 15.

91. Roberts to Warner, March 14, 1945, F. O. 371/47934. An article in *Bolshevik* criticized a tendency of the British to describe as an "'enigma' anything which will not fit into their conception of things." D. Zaslavski, cited in minute by George Hill, April 18, 1945, F. O. 371/47853, NA, UK.

92. "Stalin Voices Aim for Amity and Aid of U.S. in the Peace," *New York Times*, October 1, 1945, copy in box 206, Averell Harriman papers.

93. Warner minute, May 19, 1945, F. O. 371/47854, NA, UK.

94. Minutes by Orme Sargent and Eden, May 21, 1945, F. O. 371/47854, NA, UK.

95. Wilson to Clark Kerr, March 19, 1944, F. O. 800/302/30, NA, UK.

96. Clark Kerr to Foreign Office, April 6, 1945, F. O. 371/47881, NA, UK. Harriman alluded to his talk with Kollontay in his unsent telegram of April 10, 1945, box 178, Averell Harriman papers.

97. Clark Kerr to Foreign Office, April 6, 1945, F. O. 371/47881; Roberts to Bevin, "Report on Leading Personalities in the Soviet Union," May 22, 1946, F. O. 371/56871, NA, UK.

98. Cadogan and Eden to Clark Kerr, April 8, 1945, F. O. 371/47881, NA, UK.

99. Memorandum by Sargent, April 2, 1945, F. O. 371/47881, NA, UK.

100. Minute by Cadogan, April 4, 1945, F. O. 371/47881, NA, UK.

101. Minute by Eden, April 8, 1945, F. O. 371/47881, NA, UK.

102. Roberts to Warner, April 25, 1945, F. O. 371/47882, NA, UK.

103. Clark Kerr, Discussion between the Prime Minister and the Soviet Ambassador at No. 10 Downing Street on May 18, 1945, PREM3/396, NA, UK.

104. Zubok, *Failed Empire*, 16.

105. Joint Planning Staff, "Operation 'Unthinkable,'" May 22, 1945, Churchill to Ismay, June 10, 1945, CAB 120/691, NA, UK. In the final draft of his memo to Ismay, Churchill changed the wording from "highly improbable event" to "purely hypothetical contingency."

106. Joseph Phillips to Harriman, May 28, 1945, box 179, Averell Harriman papers.

107. Anne O'Hare McCormick, "His 'Unfinished Business'—and Ours," *New York Times Magazine*, April 22, 1945, 5, 43–44.

108. Reminiscences of Lippmann (1969), CUOHRC, 220 (emphasis in original).

109. McCormick, "His 'Unfinished Business'—and Ours," 5, 43–44 (emphasis added).

110. Lippmann, "Today and Tomorrow," April 26, 1945.

111. McCormick, "His 'Unfinished Business'—and Ours," 5, 43–44.

112. Townsend Hoopes and Douglas Brinkley, *FDR and the Creation of the U.N.* (New Haven, CT: Yale University Press, 1997), 180–81.

113. McCormick, "His 'Unfinished Business'—and Ours," 5, 43–44.

114. Oscar Cox to Hugh Fulton, April 16, 1945, box 150, Cox papers. For a sense of Cox's extensive network, see his diary entries for May 1945, box 150, Cox papers.

115. Cox, "US-USSR Relationships," May 12, 1945, box 150, Cox papers.

116. Robert A. Divine, *Second Chance: The Triumph of Internationalism in America during World War II* (New York: Atheneum, 1967), 270–71; Stephen C. Schlesinger, *Act of Creation: The Founding of the United Nations* (Boulder, CO: Westview, 2003), 62–63.

117. Warren F. Kimball, "The Sheriffs: FDR's Postwar World" in *FDR's World: War, Peace, and Legacies* (New York: Palgrave Macmillan, 2008), 100.

118. Schlesinger seminar.

119. Barnes, "Wanted: A Guide to the Russians," *New York Herald Tribune*, May 11, 1945, copy in box 206, Averell Harriman papers.

120. Krystyna Kersten, *The Establishment of Communist Rule in Poland, 1943–1948* (Berkeley: University of California Press, 1991), 149–54; Anita J. Prazmowska, *Civil War in Poland, 1942–1948* (New York: Palgrave, 2004), 112, 116–17. Okulicki and Jankowski died in prison, perhaps murdered.

121. Anthony Eden, *The Reckoning* (Boston: Houghton Mifflin, 1965), 620.

122. Arthur H. Vandenberg Jr., ed., *The Private Papers of Senator Vandenberg* (Boston: Houghton Mifflin, 1952), 178.

123. Lippmann, "Today and Tomorrow," April 29, 1945.

124. Thomas M. Campbell and George C. Herring, eds., *The Diaries of Edward R. Stettinius, Jr., 1943–1946* (New York: Franklin Watts, 1975), 336–37.

125. Schlesinger, *Act of Creation*, 120.

126. "Recollections of Mr. Harriman," October 29, 1953, box 872, Averell Harriman papers.

127. Schlesinger, *Act of Creation*, 140; Campbell and Herring, *Stettinius Diaries*, 344.

128. Unsigned memorandum, "Harriman—Russia," May 2, 1945, enclosed in John Balfour to Christopher Warner, May 30, 1945, F. O. 371/47882, NA, UK.

129. Lippmann, "Today and Tomorrow," May 12, 1945. For the original conception of San Francisco, see Cox to White House aide Hugh Fulton, April 16, 1945, box 150, Cox papers.

130. Russell Porter, "Molotoff 'Charms' at Press Meetings," *New York Times*, May 8, 1945, 15.

131. Isaiah Bowman to George S. Franklin, June 24, 1946, records of groups, vol. 17, Council on Foreign Relations papers.

132. Porter, "Molotoff 'Charms' at Press Meetings," 15.

133. Bartley C. Crum to Joseph F. Barnes, June 12, 1945, box 26, Irita Van Doren papers, Library of Congress, Washington, DC.

134. Harriman, "Masaryk, Molotov, and the San Francisco Conference," December 30, 1953, box 872, Averell Harriman papers.

135. Robert Hopkins to Dad, May 14, 1945, ser. 3, box 5, Hopkins papers, Georgetown.

136. Schlesinger, *Act of Creation*, 154.

137. Lippmann, "Today and Tomorrow," May 3, 1945.

138. Schlesinger, *Act of Creation*, 143–57.

139. Clark Kerr sent a transcript of Harriman's briefing and the resulting exchange to the Foreign Office. Clark Kerr to Christopher Warner, June 21, 1945, F. O. 371/47862, NA, UK.

140. Unsigned memorandum, "Harriman—Russia," May 2, 1945, enclosed in Balfour to Warner, May 30, 1945, F. O. 371/47882, NA, UK.

141. Clark Kerr to Warner, June 21, 1945, F. O. 371/47862, NA, UK. (Capital letters in the original.)

142. James Clement Dunn, "Memorandum of Conversation," May 1, 1945, box 313, Stettinius papers.

143. Unsigned memorandum, "Harriman—Russia," May 2, 1945, enclosed in Balfour to Warner, May 30, 1945, F. O. 371/47882, NA, UK.

144. Blum, *Price of Vision*, 448.

145. Janeway to James Allen, September 8, 1945, Eliot Janeway papers, Library of Congress, Washington, DC.

146. Blum, *Price of Vision*, 447.

147. Dean Acheson to Mary Bundy, May 12, 1945, reel 4, Acheson papers.

148. Archibald MacLeish, "Our Policy toward Russia," May 22, 1945, 711.61/5-2245; MacLeish to Joseph Grew, May 26, 1945, 711.61/5-2645, RG 59, NA, US.

149. Acheson to Bundy, May 16, 1945, reel 4, Acheson papers.

150. "M'Leish Answers U.S., U.S.S.R. 'Fears,'" *New York Times*, May 19, 1945, 19.

151. Davies diary, May 21, 1945, box 17, Davies papers.

152. Sean L. Malloy, *Atomic Tragedy: Henry L. Stimson and the Decision to Use the Bomb against Japan* (Ithaca, NY: Cornell University Press, 2008), 93.

153. Andrew J. Rotter, *Hiroshima: The World's Bomb* (New York: Oxford University Press, 2008), 155.

154. Davies diary, May 13, 1945, box 16, Davies papers.

155. Ibid.

156. Memorandum of conversation with the President, Grew, Harriman, and Bohlen, May 15, 1945, box 179, Averell Harriman papers.

157. Davies diary, May 13, 21, 1945, boxes 16 and 17, Davies papers. Truman told Stimson that "he had postponed [the Big Three meeting] until the 15th of July on purpose to give us more time" to explode the first bomb. Stimson, "Memorandum of conversation with the President," June 6, 1945, reel 128, Stimson papers.

158. Schlesinger seminar.

159. Truman to Eleanor Roosevelt, May 10, 1945, in Black et al., *Eleanor Roosevelt Papers*, 1:28.

160. Davies diary, May 21, 1945, box 17, Davies papers.

161. Moran, *Churchill at War*, 306.

162. Davies diary, May 26, June 3, 1945, box 17, Davies papers; *FRUS: Conference of Berlin 1945* (Washington, DC: Government Printing Office, 1960) 1:64–78.

163. Ibid., 1:68.

164. Davies diary, May 26, June 3, 1945, box 17, Davies papers.

165. Davies diary, May 26, June 3, 1945, box 17, Davies papers; *FRUS: Conference of Berlin 1945*, 1:64–79.

166. Wilson D. Miscamble, *From Roosevelt to Truman* (New York: Cambridge University Press, 2007), 151.

167. Memorandum to Roger Allen, July 22, 1945, F. O. 371/47850, NA, UK.

168. Clark Kerr to Foreign Secretary, August 21, 1945, F. O. 800/303/169, NA, UK.

169. Schlesinger seminar.

170. *FRUS: Conference of Berlin*, 1:24–25.

171. Ibid., 1:58, 38.

172. Ibid., 1:27.

173. The figure was not much less than the 80 percent who favored continued cooperation with Britain. Schuyler Foster to Archibald MacLeish, May 24, 1945, 711.61/5-2445, RG 59, NA, US.

174. *FRUS: Conference of Berlin* 1:55.

175. Ibid., 1:39.

176. Meiklejohn diary, June 8, 1945, box 211.

177. *FRUS: Conference of Berlin*, 1:39.

178. Ibid., 1:55–56.

179. Ibid., 1:32–33, 35.

180. Ibid., 1:33.

181. Ibid., 1:39.

182. Ibid., 1:51.

183. Ibid., 1:29–30

184. Meiklejohn diary, June 5, 1945, box 211,.

185. Kennan to Jeanette Hotchkiss, June 6, 1945, box 24, Kennan papers.

186. Meiklejohn diary, June 5, 1945, box 211. For Kennan's ties with Bullitt, see Kennan diary, May 13, 1944, box 231, Kennan papers.

187. Kathleen Harriman to Mary, June 4, May 29, 1945, box 179, Averell Harriman papers; Meiklejohn diary, June 5, May 30, 1945, box 211.

188. *FRUS: Conference of Berlin*, 1:59–62; Arnold A. Offner, *Another Such Victory: President Truman and the Cold War* (Stanford, CA: Stanford University Press, 2002), 52–55.

189. Offner, *Another Such Victory*, 53.

190. Ferrell, *Off the Record*, 44.

191. Edward Page to F. F. Molochkov, May 29, 1945, box 179, Averell Harriman papers.

192. Louise Hopkins, FBI transcript, June 27, 28, 1945.

193. Ferrell, *Off the Record*, 45.

194. Louise Hopkins, FBI transcript, July 3, 1945.

195. Hopkins to Robert Hopkins, June 14, 1945, ser. 3, box 5, Hopkins papers, Georgetown.

196. Louise Hopkins, "We Flew across Europe," *Harper's Bazaar* (September 1945): 161.

197. Melvyn P. Leffler, *A Preponderance of Power: National Security, the Truman Administration, and the Cold War* (Stanford, CA: Stanford University Press, 1992), 5.

198. Reminiscences of Isador Lubin, (1957), CUOHRC, 78–84; Richard Scandrett to Otto Wanthey-Zorn, April 4, 1945, reel 6, Scandrett papers.

199. Reminiscences of Lubin, p. 86, CUOHRC.

200. Ibid., p. 85.

201. Edwin W. Pauley, "Washington and the World," chap. 6, p. 9, unpublished memoir, HSTL. My thanks to J. Garry Clifford for sharing this document.

202. Ibid., 4.

203. Richard Scandrett, interview with Walter LaFeber, 1966, Scandrett papers.

204. Scandrett, "Summary of Procedure of Allied Commission on Reparations," August 1945, reel 6, Scandrett papers.

205. Ibid.

206. Carolyn Eisenberg, *Drawing the Line* (New York: Cambridge University Press, 1996), 87–89.

207. Rotter, *Hiroshima*, 127–76; Malloy, *Atomic Tragedy*, 96–115.

208. Stimson, "Memorandum for Talk with the President," June 6, 1945; "Memorandum of Conference with the President," June 6, 1945, reel 128, Stimson papers.

209. Alex Danchev and Daniel Todman, eds., *War Diaries 1939–1945: Field Marshal Lord Alanbrooke* (Berkeley: University of California Press, 2001), 709.

210. David Halloway, *Stalin and the Bomb* (New Haven, CT: Yale University Press, 1994), 96–113.

211. *FRUS: Conference of Berlin*, 1:62.

212. Ferrell, *Off the Record*, 35 (emphasis in original).

213. Memorandum of conversation with Secretary Stettinius, J. D. Hickerson, L. E. Thompson, and Auguste de Schryver, June 12, 1945, box 313, Stettinius papers.

214. Ferrell, *Off the Record*, 44.

215. Davies journal, April 30, 1945, box 16, Davies papers.

216. Clark Kerr to F. O., May 28, 1945, F. O. 371/47882, NA, UK.

217. John W. Russell to Halifax, June 19, 1945, F. O. 371/47883, NA, UK.

Chapter 10. The Lost Alliance: Widespread Anxiety and Deepening Ideology, July 1945–March 1946

1. Robert H. Ferrell, ed., *Off the Record: The Private Papers of Harry S. Truman* (New York: Harper & Row, 1980), 50. Truman and his immediate entourage lived in Babelsberg, an undamaged suburb on a scenic lake between Berlin and Potsdam. Churchill was quartered two blocks away, with Stalin a mile distant, closer to the conference site, Cecilienhof. At Tehran and at Yalta, Stalin and Roosevelt had lived close enough for impromptu meetings.

2. Carolyn Eisenberg, *Drawing the Line* (New York: Cambridge University Press, 1996), 96.

3. Halifax to Foreign Office (Weekly Political Summary), February 17, 1946, F. O. 371/51606, NA, UK.

4. Ferrell, *Off the Record*, 51.

5. Ibid., 52–53.

6. William D. Leahy, *I Was There* (New York: Whittlesey House, 1950), 396. After seeing Berlin, Secretary of War Stimson commented, "I never saw anything as sad in my life." Stimson to Mabel Stimson, July 18, 1945, reel 11, Stimson papers. Two months later, Nuremberg prosecutor and subsequent U.S. Senator Thomas J. Dodd reported that the Russians "are beasts and worse." Meanwhile, "our people prefer the Germans to the English, French and all races in Europe." He added, "the Germans are an interesting people. They love flowers, for example." Christopher J. Dodd, ed., *Letters from Nuremberg* (New York: Crown Publishing, 2007), 129, 137. John Hersey, whose book *Hiroshima* would imprint on the American imagination the horror of atomic bombing, concluded after viewing the assiduous efforts by the Germans to kill Poles and Jews, "I'm positive that American readers simply will not believe those things" (Hersey to Patch, February 9, 1945, box 7, Hersey papers. For the political and cultural consequences of fraternization between U.S. soldiers and German women, see Petra Goedde, *GIs and Germans* (New Haven, CT: Yale University Press, 2003). On the destruction, see, for instance, William I. Hitchcock, *Liberation* (New York: Free Press, 2008); Richard Bessel, *Germany 1945* (New York: Harper, 2009).

7. Davies journal, July 17, 1945, box 17, Davies papers.

8. Meiklejohn diary, July 14, 20, 1945, box 211.

9. Mark Pottle, ed., *Champion Redoubtable: The Diaries and Letters of Violet Bonham Carter* (London: Weidenfeld and Nicolson, 1998), 363 (emphasis in original).

10. Leahy, *I Was There*, 395.

11. Ferrell, *Off the Record*, 52–53.

12. Davies journal, July 15, 16, 1945, box 17, Davies papers.

13. Robert H. Ferrell, ed., *Dear Bess* (New York: W. W. Norton, 1983), 515, 518.

14. Clark Kerr, "Harry S. Truman," November 12, 1950, Clark Kerr papers.

15. Ferrell, *Dear Bess*, 519–21.

16. Ibid., 522.

17. William E. Pemberton, *Harry S. Truman: Fair Dealer and Cold Warrior* (Boston: Twayne, 1989), 49.

18. Ferrell, *Off the Record*, 54.

19. Ibid., 519, 521, 522.

20. Ibid., 53; Ferrell, *Dear Bess*, 521.

21. Ferrell, *Off the Record*, 359. The remarks were in an unsent letter written on March 15, 1957, and addressed to Dean Acheson. Truman was five feet nine inches tall while Stalin was five feet six and Churchill five foot seven. Of course they, as well as ordinary mortals, shrank as they aged.

22. John J. McCloy diary, July 23–24, 1945, box DY1, John J. McCloy papers, Amherst College, Amherst, MA.

23. Michael D. Gordin, *Red Cloud at Dawn* (New York: Farrar, Straus and Giroux, 2009), 11.

24. David Holloway, *Stalin & the Bomb: The Soviet Union and Atomic Energy, 1939–1956* (New Haven: Yale University Press, 1994), 132.

25. Ibid.; Campbell Craig and Sergey Radchenko, *The Atomic Bomb and the Origins of the Cold War* (New Haven, CT: Yale University Press, 2008), 90–98.

26. Vladislav Zubok, *A Failed Empire* (Chapel Hill: University of North Carolina Press, 2007), 27.

27. Holloway, *Stalin & the Bomb*, 127.

28. Eisenberg, *Drawing the Line*, 104.

29. Hadley Cantril, ed., *Public Opinion 1935–1946* (Princeton, NJ: Princeton University Press, 1951), 491–92, 502.

30. Eisenberg, *Drawing the Line*, 99, 106.

31. Dennis Merrill, ed., *Documentary History of the Truman Administration* (Bethesda, MD: University Publications of America, 1995), 2:169.

32. Eisenberg, *Drawing the Line*, 99.

33. See Frank Costigliola, *Awkward Dominion: American Political, Economic, and Cultural Relations with Europe, 1919–1933* (Ithaca, NY: Cornell University Press, 2010).

34. Ferrell, *Dear Bess*, 520.

35. Ferrell, *Off the Record*, 348.

36. Ibid., 56.

37. "Address of Harry L. Hopkins," September 6, 1945, ser. 4, box 1, Hopkins papers, Georgetown.

38. Ferrell, *Dear Bess*, 522.

39. McCloy diary, July 16, 1945, box DY1, John J. McCloy papers, Amherst College, Amherst, MA.

40. Acheson to Frankfurter, August 9, 1945, reel 8, Acheson papers.

41. Kai Bird, *The Chairman: John J. McCloy and the Making of the American Establishment* (New York: Simon & Schuster, 1992), 261; McCloy, interview with Rudy Abramson, May 13, 1983, Abramson collection. Even before Hiroshima, Lord Cherwell had tried to alert Churchill to the dangers of "a race in this form of armament" unless the Anglo-Americans concluded with the Russians an atomic control agreement. Jacques E. C. Hymans, "Britain and Hiroshima," *Journal of Strategic Studies* 32 (October 2009): 776.

42. Sean L. Malloy, *Atomic Tragedy: Henry L. Stimson and the Decision to Use the Bomb against Japan* (Ithaca, NY: Cornell University Press, 2008).

43. Stimson to the President, September 11, 1945, Stimson diary, Stimson papers.

44. J. Edgar Hoover to Matthew Connelly, September 12, 1945, box 145, Truman, PSF. See also Holloway, *Stalin & the Bomb*, 82–95; Craig and Radchenko, *Atomic Bomb*, 34–61; Gordin, *Red Cloud at Dawn*, 25–132; Jonathan Haslam, *Russia's Cold War* (New Haven, CT: Yale University Press, 2011), 62.

45. Stimson to the President, September 11, 1945, Stimson diary, Stimson papers.

46. Stimson diary, September 4, 1945; Stimson to the President, September 11, 1945, Stimson papers.

47. Matthew Connelly, Cabinet meeting, September 7, 1945, box 173, Truman, PSF.

48. Stimson diary, Stimson to the President, September 11, 1945, Stimson papers.

49. Melvyn P. Leffler, *A Preponderance of Power: National Security, the Truman Administration, and the Cold War* (Stanford, CA: Stanford University Press, 1992), 26–30; Arnold A. Offner, *Another Such Victory: President Truman and the Cold War* (Stanford, CA: Stanford University Press, 1992), 2–21.

50. David E. Lilienthal, *Journals* (New York: Harper & Row, 1964), 2:7.

51. Henry Hardy, ed., *Isaiah Berlin, Letters, 1928–1946* (New York: Cambridge University Press, 2004), 553, 558.

52. Bird, *Chairman*, 263.

53. Thomas C. Campbell and George C. Herring, eds., *The Diaries of Edward R. Stettinius, Jr., 1943–1946* (New York: New Viewpoints, 1975), 429.

54. Ferrell, *Dear Bess*, 523.

55. Connelly, Cabinet meeting, September 21, 1945, box 173, HSTL.

56. Of the eighteen men in the room other than the president, ten concurred, three agreed but urged a six-month wait, four disagreed, and one was ambiguous.

57. Andrew J. Rotter, *Hiroshima: The World's Bomb* (New York: Oxford University Press, 2008).

58. Memorandum to the President, September 21, 1945, Forrestal diary, box 145, James V. Forrestal papers, Mudd Library, Princeton University, Princeton, NJ.

59. Connelly, Cabinet meeting, September 21, 1945, box 173, Truman, PSF; Forrestal diary, September 21, 1945, box 145, James V. Forrestal papers, Mudd Library, Princeton University, Princeton, NJ.

60. *New York Times*, September 22, 1945, 1.

61. Walter Millis, ed., *The Forrestal Diaries* (New York: Viking, 1951), 95.

62. Connelly, Cabinet meeting, September 21, 1945, box 173, Truman, PSF.

63. Forrestal to Admiral Edwards, Fleet Admiral King, Gates and Hensel, September 20, 1945, box 66, James V. Forrestal papers, Mudd Library, Princeton University, Princeton, NJ.

64. *New York Times*, September 22, 1945, 1.

65. Ibid.; *Los Angeles Times*, September 22, 1945.

66. Thomas P. Hughes, *American Genesis* (New York: Viking, 1989), 390.

67. *Los Angeles Times*, September 22, 1945.

68. *FRUS: 1945* (Washington, DC: Government Printing Office, 1967), 2:48–50; Ferrell, *Dear Bess*, 523.

69. Clinton P. Anderson to the President, September 25, 1945; Fred Vinson to the President, September 27, 1945, box 173, Truman, PSF.

70. Millis, *Forrestal Diaries*, 93.

71. Clinton P. Anderson to the President, September 25, 1945, box 173, Truman, PSF.

72. Henry A. Wallace to the President, September 24, 1945, box 173, Truman, PSF.

73. Margaret Truman, *Harry S. Truman* (New York: William Morrow, 1973), 260–61, 527.

74. Connelly, Cabinet meeting, August 31, 1945, box 173, Truman, PSF.

75. Cantril, *Public Opinion*, 21–25.

76. Hoover to Connelly, September 12, 1945, box 145, Truman, PSF.

77. Robert H. Ferrell, ed., *Truman in the White House: The Diary of Eben A. Ayers* (Columbia: University of Missouri Press, 1991), 83–84.

78. Hamilton Fish Armstrong memorandum of conversations with Cordell Hull and Lord Halifax, November 2, 1945, box 100, Armstrong papers.

79. Armstrong memorandum of conversation with Felix Frankfurter, November 7, 1945, box 100, Armstrong papers.

80. President's News Conference at Tiptonville, Tennessee, October 8, 1945, HSTL, http://www.trumanlibrary.org/publicpapers/index.php?pid=173&st=&st1=.

81. Kai Bird and Martin J. Sherwin, *American Prometheus: The Triumph and Tragedy of J. Robert Oppenheimer* (New York: Vintage, 2006), 331.

82. Gregg Herken, *The Winning Weapon: The Atomic Bomb in the Cold War, 1945–1950* (New York: Knopf, 1980), 39.

83. Richard E. Neustadt, "Truman in Action: A Retrospect," in *Modern Presidents and the Presidency*, ed. Marc Landy (Lexington, MA: D. C. Heath, 1985), 4.

84. Bird and Sherwin, *American Prometheus*, 332.

85. Robert H. Ferrell, "Harry S Truman: A 50th Anniversary Commemoration of His Presidency," Missouri State Archives, http://www.sos.mo.gov/archives/history/truman.asp (accessed February 11, 2011).

86. Roberts to Foreign Office, October 26, 1945, F. O. 371/47883, NA, UK.

87. *FRUS: 1945*, 2:884.

88. John M. Blum, ed., *The Price of Vision: The Diary of Henry A. Wallace, 1942–1946* (Boston: Houghton Mifflin, 1973), 504.

89. James L. Gormly, *From Potsdam to the Cold War* (Wilmington, DE: Scholarly Resources, 1990), 71–86.

90. Walter J. Brown diary, September 13, 1945, box 67, Walter J. Brown papers, Clemson University, Clemson, SC.

91. Herken, *Winning Weapon*, 53.

92. Vladimir O. Pechatnov, "The Allies Are Pressing on You to Break Your Will . . . ," Working Paper no. 26 (1999), 2, CWIHP, http://www.wilsoncenter.org/topics/pubs/ACFB29.PDF.

93. Gomulka's memorandum of a conversation with Stalin, November 14, 1945, Cold War International History Project, *Bulletin* 11 (Winter 1998): 135.

94. Dulles conversation with Armstrong, November 13, 1945, box 100, Armstrong papers.

95. Hull conversation with Armstrong, November 2, 1945, box 100, Armstrong papers.

96. Roberts to Foreign Office, October 26, 1945, F. O. 371/47883, NA, UK.

97. Pechatnov, "The Allies Are Pressing on You," 4.

98. Clark Kerr, "Conversation between the Secretary of State and M. Molotov on the 23rd September, 1945," F. O. 371/47883, NA, UK.

99. Pechatnov, "The Allies Are Pressing on You," 6–7; Zubok, *Failed Empire*, 32.

100. Pechatnov, "The Allies Are Pressing on You," 9.

101. Ibid., 11.

102. Ferrell, *Truman in the White House*, 95.

103. James L. Gormly, "The Washington Declaration and the 'Poor Relation': Anglo-American Atomic Diplomacy, 1945–46," *Diplomatic History* 8 (1984): 133–35.

104. Minute by John G. Ward, October 17, 1945, F. O. 371/50936, NA, UK.

105. *FRUS: 1946* (Washington, DC: Government Printing Office, 1972), 1:1235–37.

106. Among Britons, 46 percent replied that their feelings toward Americans remained unchanged; 54 percent had unchanged feelings toward the Soviets. George H. Gallup, ed., *The Gallup Poll: Public Opinion, 1935–1971* (New York: Random House, 1972), 1:542.

107. Simon Sebag Montefiore, *Stalin: The Court of the Red Tsar* (New York: Knopf, 2004), 532.

108. Ibid., 532–33; Robert Service, *Stalin* (London: Macmillan, 2004), 491.

109. Lippmann, "Today and Tomorrow," September 27, 1945.

110. "Recollections of Mr. Harriman," October 21, 1953, box 872, Averell Harriman papers.

111. Harriman to Secretary of State, October 26, 1945, 711.61/10-2645, RG 59, NA, US; Geoffrey Roberts, *Stalin's Wars* (New Haven, CT: Yale University Press, 2006), 301.

112. Roberts minute, October 28, 1945, F. O. 181/1008, NA, UK.

113. Harriman to Secretary of State, October 26, 1945, 711.61/10-2645, RG 59, NA, US.

114. Hopkins to Eleanor Roosevelt, November 23, 1945, Sherwood papers.

115. Roberts to Foreign Office, October 26, 1945, F. O. 371/47883, NA, UK.

116. Lippmann, "Today and Tomorrow," September 25, 1945.

117. John Foster Dulles conversation with Armstrong, November 13, 1945, box 100, Armstrong papers. Byrnes told Dulles.

118. President's News Conference, November 29, 1945, American Presidency Project, http://www.presidency.ucsb.edu/ws/index.php?pid=12276 (accessed February 11, 2011).

119. Gallup, *Gallup Poll*, 534–35. For the impact of domestic politics, see Campbell Craig and Fredrik Logevall, *America's Cold War* (Cambridge, MA: Harvard University Press, 2009).

120. Campbell and Herring, *Stettinius Diaries*, 431.

121. Daniel Yergin, *Shattered Peace* (Boston: Houghton Mifflin, 1977), 147.

122. *FRUS: 1945*, 5:922–24; Clark Kerr to Foreign Office, December 3, 1945, F. O. 371/50936, NA, UK.

123. Halifax to Foreign Office, November 29, 1945, F. O. 800/501/64; Halifax to Bevin, December 5, 1945, F. O. 800/501/73, NA, UK.

124. Lippmann, "Today and Tomorrow," November 7, 1945.

125. Clark Kerr to Foreign Office, November 30, 1945, F. O. 800/501/68, NA, UK.

126. Offner, *Another Such Victory*, 116.

127. Lippmann, "Today and Tomorrow," November 20, 1945.

128. Barnes to Connie and Mike, January 14, 1946, box 14, Barnes papers.

129. Robert L. Messer, *The End of an Alliance: James F. Byrnes, Roosevelt, Truman, and the Origins of the Cold War* (Chapel Hill: University of North Carolina Press, 1982), 143.

130. Ibid., 148.

131. Kennan diary, December 14, 1945, box 231, Kennan papers.

132. Yergin, *Shattered Peace*, 149.

133. *FRUS: 1945*, 2:757.

134. Herken, *Winning Weapon*, 77–86; James G. Hershberg, *James B. Conant* (New York: Knopf, 1993), 252–57.

135. Kennan diary, December 8, 14, 1945, box 231, Kennan papers.

136. Ibid., November 26, 24, 1945.

137. Ibid., December 19, 21, 1945.

138. Roger Bullen and M. E. Pelly, eds., *Documents on British Policy Overseas* (London: Her Majesty's Stationery Office, 1985), ser. 1, 2:803–4.

139. Roberts to Foreign Office, January 2, 1946, F. O. 371/56763, NA, UK.

140. Roberts to Warner, December 27, 1945, Bullen and Pelly, *Documents on British Policy Overseas*, ser. 1, vol. 2, microfiche document no. 258i.

141. James F. Byrnes, *Speaking Frankly* (New York: Harper, 1947), 121.

142. Ferrell, *Truman in the White House*, 101.

143. Hardy, *Berlin Letters*, 621.

144. Offner, *Another Such Victory*, 127.

145. Ferrell, *Dear Bess*, 524.

146. Offner, *Another Such Victory*, 127.

147. Messer, *End of an Alliance*, 158.

148. Ibid., 162.

149. Zubok, *Failed Empire*, 41.

150. Ibid., 45.

151. Offner, *Another Such Victory*, 133.

152. Natalia Yegorova, "The 'Iran Crisis' of 1945–46: A View from the Russian Archives," Working Paper no. 15 (1996), 1–24, CWIHP, http://www.wilsoncenter.org/topics/pubs/ACFB51.pdf; Zubok, *Failed Empire*, 40–45.

153. Merrill, *Documentary History of the Truman Administration*, 7:130, 134.

154. Clark Kerr to Bevin, January 29, 1946, F. O. 800/501/27; Roberts to Foreign Office, January 26, 1946, F. O. 181/1022, NA, UK; Haslam, *Russia's Cold War*, 47–48.

155. Melvyn P. Leffler, "Strategy, Diplomacy, and the Cold War: The United States, Turkey, and NATO, 1945–1952," *Journal of American History* 71 (March 1985): 807–25, 813 for the quotation.

156. Marc Gallichio, *The Scramble for Asia* (Lanham, MD: Rowman & Littlefield, 2008), 109.

157. Harriman memorandum of conversation with General Douglas MacArthur, February 6, 1946, box 186, Averell Harriman papers.

158. Millis, *Forrestal Diaries*, 132.

159. Clark Kerr to Bevin, January 29, 1946, F. O. 800/501/27; Roberts to Foreign Office, January 26, 1946, F. O. 181/1022, NA, UK.

160. V. N. Pavlov diary, January 26, 1946, Russian State Archive of Socio-Political History, Moscow, f. [collection] 558, op. [inventory] 11, d. [folder] 284, l. [pages] 123–29.

161. Eduard Mark, "Revolution by Degrees: Stalin's National-Front Strategy for Europe, 1941–1947," Working Paper no. 31 (2001), CWIHP, http://www.wilsoncenter.org/index.cfm?fuseaction=topics.publications&group_id=11901&topic_id=1409; Zubok, *Failed Empire*, 21–27; Naimark, "The Sovietization of Eastern Europe, 1944–1953," in *Cambridge History of the Cold War*, ed. Melvyn P. Leffler and Odd Arne Westad (Cambridge: Cambridge University Press, 2010), 196–97.

162. "Notes on Talk by Ambassador to Officers and Attaches of Embassy, Moscow—January 22, 1946," box 186, Averell Harriman papers.

163. Offner, *Another Such Victory*, 130–32.

164. Zubok, *Failed Empire*, 51; Thomas G. Paterson, *Soviet-American Confrontation* (Baltimore: Johns Hopkins University Press, 1973), 120–43.

165. Campbell and Herring, *Stettinius Diaries*, 445.

166. Thomas G. Paterson, *On Every Front* (New York: W. W. Norton, 1992), ix.

167. Leffler, *Preponderance of Power*, 25–140.

168. Kennan, *Memoirs, 1925–1950* (Boston: Little, Brown, 1967), 292–93.

169. Kennan to Secretary of State, March 9, 1946, box 63, George M. Elsey papers, HSTL.

170. Memorandum of conversation between Stalin and Harriman, January 23, 1946, 711.61/1-2346, RG 59, NA, US.

171. Robert C. Tucker, "Interpretive Report on Soviet Policy Based on the Press for December 1945," January 15, 1946, box 186, Averell Harriman papers.

172. Alexander Werth, *Russia: The Post-War Years* (New York: Taplinger, 1971), 92.

173. Mikhail Kalinin, letter to electorate, February 9, 1946, *Soviet Monitor*, copy in F. O. 371/56725, NA, UK.

174. Molotov speech, February 6, 1946, *Soviet Monitor*, copy in F. O. 371/56725, NA, UK.

175. J. V. Stalin Archive, http://www.marxists.org/reference/archive/stalin/works/1946/02/09.htm.

176. Millis, *Forrestal Diaries*, 134; Leffler, *Preponderance of Power*, 103; Offner, *Another Such Victory*, 128–29.

177. Lippmann, "Today and Tomorrow," February 13, 1946. The previous day's column urged a major U.S. effort to develop the Middle East.

178. "Stalin Sets a Huge Output Near Ours in 5-Year Plan; Expects to Lead in Science," *New York Times*, February 10, 1946, 1.

179. J. V. Stalin Archive, http://www.marxists.org/reference/archive/stalin/works/1946/02/09.htm.

180. Minute by J. C. Donnelly on weekly political situation in the United States, February 21, 1946, F. O. 371/51606, NA, UK.

181. *New York Times*, February 17, 1946, 4E.

182. J. V. Stalin Archive, http://www.marxists.org/reference/archive/stalin/works/1946/02/09.htm.

183. Ibid.

184. Isaiah Berlin conversation with Armstrong, February 26, 1946, box 100, Armstrong papers.

185. Offner, *Another Such Victory*, 128; Matthew A. Evangelista, "Stalin's Postwar Army Reappraised," *International Security* 7 (Winter 1982/1983): 110–38.

186. Harriman conversation with Armstrong, March 11, 1946, box 100, Armstrong papers.

187. Ferrell, *Truman in the White House*, 139.

188. Lilienthal, *Journals* 2: 30.

189. *New York Times*, March 1, 1946, 10.

190. Patrick Wright, *Iron Curtain: From Stage to Cold War* (New York: Oxford University Press, 2007), 50.

191. Ferrell, *Truman in the White House*, 139.

192. Zubok, *Failed Empire*, 53.

193. Lord Moran, *Churchill Taken from the Diaries of Lord Moran* (Boston: Houghton Mifflin, 1966), 322.

194. Mary Soames, *Clementine Churchill: The Biography of a Marriage* (Boston: Houghton Mifflin, 1979), 429.

195. Moran, *Churchill*, 328.

196. David Reynolds, *From World War to Cold War* (New York: Oxford University Press, 2006), 255–63, 263 for the quotation. See also Barbara Leaming, *Churchill Defiant: Fighting On, 1945–1955* (New York: Harper, 2010), 45–71.

197. Moran, *Churchill*, 332.

198. Gallup, *Gallup Poll*, 530, 535, 561.

199. Davies diary, January 6, 1946, box 22, Davies papers.

200. Hardy, *Berlin Letters*, 622.

201. R.M.A. Hankey minute, May 20, 1946, F. O. 371/56840, NA, UK.

202. Fraser Harbutt, *The Iron Curtain: Churchill, America, and the Origins of the Cold War* (New York: Oxford University Press, 1986), 161.

203. Randolph Churchill, ed., *The Sinews of Peace* (Boston: Houghton Mifflin, 1948), 92.

204. Ibid., 106–10.

205. Cantril, *Public Opinion*, 274, 328. The first poll was done in June 1942, the second in March 1946.

206. *New York Times*, March 6, 1946.

207. Wright, *Iron Curtain*, 21–29.

208. Churchill, *Sinews of Peace*, 93–105; Wright, *Iron Curtain*, 21–29.

209. Churchill, *Sinews of Peace*, 93–105.

210. Leffler, *Preponderance of Power*, 55–140.

211. Churchill, *Sinews of Peace*, 93–105.

212. Evgeni Tarle, "In Connection with Churchill's Speech," *Izvestia*, March 12, 1946, *Soviet Monitor*, copy in F. O. 371/56781, NA, UK.

213. *FRUS: 1946*, 6:696.

214. Kaganovich speech, [February 1946], *Soviet Monitor*, copy in F. O. 371/56725, NA, UK.

215. Wright, *Iron Curtain*, 397.

216. Ibid., 35; Offner, *Another Such Victory*, 136–37.

217. Wright, *Iron Curtain*, 45.

218. Gallup, *Gallup Poll*, 567.

219. Pearson memorandum, [1946], F169, Pearson papers; Malvina Thompson to Anna Boettiger, March 11, 1946, box 75, Anna Roosevelt Halsted papers.

220. Blum, *Price of Vision*, 556–57.

221. Lippmann, "Today and Tomorrow," March 7, 1946.

222. Reminiscences of Lippmann (1969), CUOHRC, 225 (emphasis in original).

223. Moran, *Churchill*, 333.

224. Clark Kerr to Bevin, January 29, 1946, F. O. 800/501/127, NA, UK.

225. "Stalin on Churchill's Speech," *Tass* Agency Bulletin, March 13, 1946, copy in F. O. 371/56781, NA, UK.

226. Tarle, "In Connection with Churchill's Speech," *Izvestia*, March 12, 1946.

227. Merrill, *Documentary History of the Truman Presidency*, 7:132–34.

228. Roberts to Warner, March 18, 1946, F. O. 371/56782, NA, UK.

229. Barnes to E. Urner Goodman, March 15, 1946, box 15, Barnes papers.

230. Kennan to Durbrow, January 21, 1946, box 186, Averell Harriman papers.

231. Kennan to Bullitt, January 22, 1946, box 44, Bullitt papers. See also Kennan to Bullitt, April 4, 23, 1944; May 29, 1944, box 44, Bullitt papers.

232. George F. Kennan, *Sketches from a Life* (New York: Pantheon Books, 1989), 43.

233. Kennan, "Remarks to the Officer Staff of the Legation at Lisbon," June 1944, box 298, Kennan papers.

234. Matthews to Kennan, February 13, 1946, 861.00/2-1246, RG 59, NA, US.

235. Kennan, *Memoirs 1925–1950*, 292–93.

236. *FRUS: 1946*, 6:701.

237. Ibid., 707.

238. Ibid., 698–99.

239. Memorandum of conversation between Stalin and Harriman, January 23, 1946, 711.61/1-2346, RG 59, NA, US.

240. *FRUS 1946*, 6: 700, 698.

241. Ibid., 706, 705.

242. Ibid., 702, 704, 706, 705.

243. See Frank Costigliola, "'Unceasing Pressure for Penetration': Gender, Pathology, and Emotion in George Kennan's Formation of the Cold War," *Journal of American History* 82 (March 1997): 1309–39.

244. *FRUS: 1946*, 6:707–9.

245. Robert Murphy to Mathews, April 3, 1946, 861.00/4-346, RG 59, NA, US.

246. Lippmann, "Today and Tomorrow," March 9, 1946.

247. "Memorandum by John Metcalfe on session with Byrnes," March 14, 1946, box 14, Barnes papers.

248. Armstrong, Notes from dinner for Winston Churchill, March 18, 1946, box 100, Armstrong papers.

249. *FRUS: 1946*, 6:722–23.

250. Kennan, *Memoirs, 1925–1950*, 295.

251. Costigliola, "'Unceasing Pressure,'" 1337.

252. Eddy Gilmore to Harriman, July 22, 1946, box 186, Averell Harriman papers.

253. Frank E. Evans to F. O., March 11, 1946, F. O. 371/56840, NA, UK.

254. Dodd (ed.), *Letters from Nuremberg*, 129, 251.

255. Report from Washington to Foreign Office, [September 1946], F. O. 371/56842, NA, UK.

256. Forrestal to Harriman, May 14, 1946, box 213, Averell Harriman papers.

257. Merrill, *Documentary History of the Truman Presidency*, 7:135, 132.

258. Klaus Larres, *Churchill's Cold War* (New Haven, CT: Yale University Press, 2002).

259. Kennan, "The Background of Current Russian Diplomatic Moves," December 10, 1946, in *Measures Short of War*, ed. Giles D. Harlow and George C. Maerz (Washington, DC: National Defense University Press, 1990), 86–87.

260. Lippmann, "Today and Tomorrow," March 16, 1946.

261. Ibid., March 14, 1946.

262. Kennan diary, February 16, 1975, box 239, Kennan papers.

Conclusion and Epilogue

1. Felix Chuev, ed., *Molotov Remembers* (Chicago: Ivan R. Dee, 1993), 51.

2. Robert Klara, *FDR's Funeral Train* (New York: Palgrave, 2010).

3. Chuev, *Molotov Remembers*, 51.

4. Corcoran interview with Philip Kopper [1979], box 587, Corcoran papers.

5. Decades later, Harriman would acknowledge the seriousness of Soviet fears, and his own ambivalence, about that dynamic nation. "The strange thing was that Stalin was afraid of Germany, Khrushchev was afraid of Germany, the present people are afraid of Germany—and *I* am afraid of Germany" (Schlesinger seminar, emphasis in original).

6. Peterson to Bevin, May 28, 1946, F. O. 371/56784, NA, UK.

7. Memorandum by Cripps, February 13, 1946; minute by Warner, February 25, 1946, F. O. 371/56780, NA, UK.

8. Pechatnov, "Soviet Union and the World," in *The Cambridge History of the Cold War*, ed. Melvyn P. Leffler and Odd Arne Westad (Cambridge: Cambridge University Press, 2010), 93–95.

9. Frances Perkins memorandum, June 16, 1945, regarding conversation with Roosevelt on March 29, 1945, speeches and articles 1940–45 file, Frances Perkins (Coggeshall) papers, Butler Library, Columbia University, New York, NY.

10. Corcoran, "Rendezvous with Democracy," fragment, pp. 3–4, box 587, Corcoran papers.

11. For an introduction to the theory, see Giovanni Capoccia and R. Daniel Klemen, "The Study of Critical Junctures," *World Politics* 59 (April 2007): 341–69.

12. Chuev, *Molotov Remembers*, 46.

13. William Taubman, *Khrushchev* (New York: W. W. Norton, 2003), 484.

14. Chuev, *Molotov Remembers*, 51.

15. Schlesinger seminar.

16. "Notes on Talk by Ambassador to Officers and Attaches of Embassy, Moscow—January 22, 1946," box 186, Averell Harriman papers.

17. Emily S. Rosenberg, "Consumer Capitalism and the End of the Cold War," in *Cambridge History of the Cold War*, ed. Leffler and Westad, 489–512.

18. See David S. Foglesong, *The American Mission and the "Evil Empire"* (New York: Cambridge University Press, 2007).

19. One reason that stench and resulting disgust have such a powerful impact on thought is that sharp odors, unlike the stimuli of sight or sound, travel directly to the amygdala of the brain without any mediation or thinking by the cortex.

20. Officer Commanding, No. 173 Staging Post to Air Officer Commanding, 216 Group, R.A.F., October 1, 1945, F. O. 371/47954, NA, UK.

21. Ibid.

22. Minutes by Thomas E. Galsworthy, November 8, 1945; Thomas Brimelow, November 10, 1945; Christopher Warner, [November 1945], F. O. 371/47954, NA, UK.

23. For the Russia Committee, see Marc J. Selverstone, *Constructing the Monolith* (Cambridge, MA: Harvard University Press, 2009), 39–43.

24. Memorandum by Cripps, February 13, 1946; minute by Warner, February 25, 1946, F. O. 371/56780, NA, UK.

25. Roberts to Foreign Office, April 4, 1946, F. O. 371/56831, NA, UK.

26. Barnes to Connie and Mike, January 14, 1946, box 14, Barnes papers.

27. The journalist-friend remembered this conversation as "one of the most important" of his life. Harrison E. Salisbury, *A Journey for Our Times* (New York: Harper & Row, 1983), 245.

28. Kennan to Carl Kaysen, July 27, 1968, box 19, Faculty Files, Shelby White and Leon Levy Archives Center, Institute for Advanced Study, Princeton, NJ.

29. Schlesinger seminar; Andrew Schlesinger and Stephen Schlesinger, eds., *Journals 1952–2000: Arthur M. Schlesinger, Jr.* (New York: Penguin, 2007), 335–36.

Bibliographical Note

1. James Roosevelt, interview with Joseph Lash, May 6, 1966, box 44, Lash papers.

Index

Acheson, Alice, 311

Acheson, Dean, 311, 315, 345, 369, 371, 373–74, 400, 406–7

Acheson-Lilienthal plan, 400

Alanbrooke, Lord, 48, 87–90, 179, 196, 204, 238, 286

Alliluyeva, Nadya, 45–46, 95

Alliluyeva, Svetlana, 94–95, 176, 366

Alperovitz, Gar, 8

American embassy in Moscow: "fun" and backlash in, 267–70; homosociality in, 267, 270; "honeymoon" of, 259–60, 264–70; isolation and, 260–64; mental stress in, 273–76; and sexuality, 267–73

Anderson, Clinton P., 372, 374, 376

Anderson, General Frederick, 101, 116–17, 461n92

Anderson, John, 222–23

Arcadia conference (Washington), 151–55, 157–62

Archer, Admiral Ernest, 307

Argentina, 339, 341–43, 352

Armstrong, Hamilton Fish, 376

Arnold, General H. Henry "Hap," 131–33

Atlantic Charter: and Cold War, 323; cultural resonance of, 156; foreign office resistance to, 146; as negotiated at Atlantic conference, 134–35; Roosevelt's disparagement of, 228, 251; Roosevelt's effort to educate public about, 191, 210–12, 229, 252, 258, 338; Roosevelt's evolution away from, 169, 184–86, 191, 203, 206, 210; side-stepping of by big powers, 227, 233; and Stalin 156, 164, 166, 203, 382; the "Volga Charter" and, 146–47, 162; and Yalta, 248

Atlantic conference, 99, 124, 127–38

atom bomb: and Attlee, 380–81; and Bohr's warning, 222–23; and Churchill, 155, 222–23, 256, 337, 365, 376, 404–5; and Lend Lease uranium, 484n113; and London Foreign Ministers conference, 378; and Moscow Foreign Ministers conference (1945), 383–86; and potential arms race, 202, 256, 357–59, 369–78, 417, 427, 513n41; and public opinion, 375–76; and relations with Russia, 356–57, 359, 365–66; and Roosevelt, 73, 222–23, 255–56, 419; and Soviet spying, 223, 279, 370, 376, 384; and Stimson's proposal, 369–78, 419; and Truman, 14–15, 346–47, 359, 362, 365, 366–77, 400, 417, 419

Attlee, Clement, 364, 380–81, 407

Axis threat, 118–20, 131–32, 148

Barnes, Joseph F., 426

Baruch, Bernard, 66, 400–401, 451n40, 455n154

bathroom facilities: emotional valence of, 148, 168, 241, 278

Beaverbrook, Lord (Max Aitken), 84, 87, 90, 101, 106, 117–18, 145

Beria, Lavrenty, 42, 91–92, 239

Beria, Sergo, 42–43, 91–92, 194, 196, 240

Biddle, Francis, 136

Big Three approach, 169, 184–85, 191, 201–3, 229, 357–58, 378–79, 383, 391, 393, 419

Big Three military committee, 285–87

Birse, Arthur H., 273–74, 329, 425

Boettiger, Anna Roosevelt, 45, 60, 65, 69, 71, 77, 79, 81–82, 208, 222, 232–33, 235–36, 238, 240–41, 247, 251, 253, 344, 434, 455n144

Bohlen, Charles, E. (Chip): background of, 230; and Isaiah Berlin, 230; and Bullitt, 230–31; and Byrnes's diplomacy,

Bohlen, Charles, E. (Chip): (*cont.*)
385–86; and historiography on Cold War,
7–8; and Hopkins, 229–31, 251, 318,
327, 393–94; and Hopkins's mission to
Moscow (1945), 317, 347, 349–50, 354;
and "honeymoon" of 1933–34, 260,
266–70; and Kennan, 265; and Kremlin
"whoopee" parties, 289–90; and shift in
U.S. policy toward Moscow, 323–24,
363–27, 344–45, 406–7; and Stalin and
postwar cooperation, 347; and Yalta
agreement on Poland, 320–21
Bohr, Niels, 222–23
Bolshevik Revolution, 14, 51–54
Boothby, Robert, 97, 139
Bourke-White, Margaret, 125
Bracken, Brendan, 85, 87, 90
Brimelow, Thomas, 295–96, 425
British policy, growing impatience with
Soviets of, 333–37
Brown, Wilson, 232–33, 242, 251
Bruenn, Dr. Howard G., 208–9, 224–26,
232, 234, 236, 247, 253, 256
Bukharin, Nikolai, 91, 264, 268
Bullitt, William C., 6, 52, 202; and Bohlen,
230–31; and FDR, 74–77; and "fun" in
Moscow embassy, 267–70; and Kennan
264–65, 353, 409; and Lenin, 263; and
LeHand, 62, 70–76, 454n120, 485n117;
and Offie, 188, 190; and Stalin, 165,
185, 259–60, 264, 268–69; and Welles,
74–75, 120, 178, 187–90
Burrows, General Brocas, 286–87, 329
Byrnes, James F.: ambitions of, 210, 319;
atomic bomb and, 346, 357, 370, 378,
383–87; and London Foreign Ministers
conference, 378–79, 383; and Moscow
Foreign Ministers conference (1945),
383–87; and opposition from Harriman
and Kennan, 385–86; and opposition
from Truman, 388–89; and opposition in
Washington, 393; at Potsdam, 364; and
pressure for a hot war, 413; and reparations, 356, 368–69; and Soviet eagerness
to confer, 391; tougher stance of, 400–
401; and Truman, 319, 326; and Yalta,
236, 250, 322

Cadogan, Alexander, 133–34, 146–48, 150,
156–57, 162, 168, 174–76, 199, 202,
233, 236–37, 248, 333–34, 386,
489n228
Caldwell, Erskine, 125
Carter, Edward C., 378
Casablanca conference, 178–80
Casey, Richard, 406
Cherbakov, Aleksandr, 293
Chiang Kai-Shek. *See* Jiang Jieshi
Childs, Marquis, 209, 211, 235, 451n40
Churchill, Clementine, 31, 45, 48, 88, 99,
104, 106–7, 111, 115, 118, 150, 160,
174, 212, 222, 401
Churchill, Lady Randolph (née Jennie
Jerome), 23–31, 152
Churchill, Lord Randolph (Winston's
father), 23–24, 26–29
Churchill, Pamela (later Pamela Churchill
Harriman): and Anderson 116–17; and
Beaverbrook, 117; and Winston
Churchill, 117–18, 148; comparison of
Roosevelt and Churchill of, 49, 55, 57;
and FDR, 115–16; and Harriman, 101,
112–18, 140, 148, 236; and Hopkins,
100–101, 104–5, 107, 114, 116; network of sex and secrets of, 99–101,
112–18; photograph in *Life,* 113–14;
and Portal 236, 249
Churchill, Randolph (Winston's son), 99,
115, 118, 407, 461n92
Churchill, Sarah (Vickers): and Stalin, 330;
and Winant, 112
Churchill, Winston S.: and address to Congress, 152–53; and ambassador Winant,
111–12; and Atlantic Charter, 134–35,
227–28; at Atlantic conference, 127–39;
and atom bomb, 222–23, 256, 357, 365,
376, 513n41; attitudes toward sexuality
of, 30–31, 45; attitude toward money of,
26; attitude toward war of, 37–38, 83;
autobiographical novel of, 30–31; background of, 23–24, 26–30, 33; and the
Big Three, 53–57; and Bolshevik Revolution, 51–53; boyishness of, 3, 48, 129;
and British empire, 21–23, 55, 86, 89,
103, 135, 152, 161–62, 182, 200, 222,
245, 248, 403, 474n114; and British
navy, 86; at Casablanca conference,
178–82; and Lord Cherwell, 85; courage
of, 105; and Davies mission, 347–39; depression of, 28, 89, 401; and Eden, 1–2,

145, 147–48, 150, 155–57, 159;
emotions of, 5, 28, 88–89, 175, 233,
145, 348; exhibitionism of, 48–49, 153–
55, 176–77, 448n155; gender identity of,
3, 48; and Harriman visit, 110–18;
health problems of, 3, 89–90, 153, 183,
203, 226, 236–37; and Hopkins visit,
99–100, 102–7, 319, 394; and ideology,
16; "Iron Curtain" speech of, 393–94,
401–8; military strategy of, 89, 134,
149–50, 157–58, 171–74, 193; and
"mixing up" with Americans, 112; Moscow 1942 visit of, 173–77; nighttime
hours of, 86–87; "Operation Unthinkable" and, 336–37; oratorical ability of,
44, 86, 98, 133–34, 152–53, 402; and
Pearl Harbor, 148–49; and Poland, 216,
219, 221, 246, 249–50, 255, 320; possible Asperger's syndrome of, 44, 160–61;
and Potsdam conference, 359–69; post-
Pearl Harbor visit to Washington of,
142, 149–55; preference for Washington
over Moscow of, 20; relations with aides
of, 85–90; and relations with Russians,
18, 121, 175, 194–95, 335–36; relations
with Stalin of, 6, 49, 56–57, 145–46,
173, 242–43, 249, 330, 380, 407–8, 415,
473n76; and Eleanor Roosevelt, 161;
self-medicating of, 50, 87, 448n157;
"special relationships" of, 177; and summit conferences, 3, 6; and Tehran conference, 165, 198–204; tendency to monologue of, 42; and threatened German
invasion, 86; and Truman, 360, 365,
394, 420; and visit to Malta, 232–33;
writing of, 41–42; and Yalta conference,
236–49. See also Roosevelt, Franklin D.,
relations with Churchill

Clark, Tom, 372

Clark Kerr, Archibald: and atomic bomb,
383; background and personality of,
296–98; and Churchill, 175–76, 199,
250, 293; and cultural insecurity of Soviets, 19–20, 286, 293, 332–33, 335, 426;
and Deane, 304; and difference between
FDR and Truman, 363; and Eisenhower,
349; and Harriman, 303, 313; and homosocial encounters in Moscow, 95,
176–77, 295, 300; and isolation in Moscow, 299–300; and November 1943

party, 291–95; and Polish issue, 250,
320–21; and shaping narratives, 295–97;
and shift toward cold war, 427; and Stalin, 226, 286, 292–93, 298–99, 390–91,
407, 498n3; and Yalta, 236–37, 320

Clifford, Clark, 371

Cohen, Ben, 385

Collingwood, Charles, 109

Colville, John, 85, 87–89, 112–13, 115

Conant, James B., 385

Connally, Tom, 141, 338–39

Connelly, Matthew J., 371

contact, Soviet perspective on, 260–61,
276–78

Corcoran, Thomas G., 13, 46, 59–63,
65–68, 70, 72–73, 75–78, 84, 142, 188,
207–8, 210, 224, 236, 385, 420–21,
450–51n35, 451n40, 455n154

Cox, Oscar, 320, 339

Cripps, Stafford, 17, 123, 425–26

critical juncture, 1945–46 as, 2, 419,
421–22

Currie, Lauchlin, 279

Davies, Joseph E., 18, 52, 192, 317, 324–
26, 345–49, 359, 362, 366, 504n48

Davis, Forrest, 211–12

Deane, General John R., 6, 239, 272, 282,
285–86, 294, 302–4, 307, 309–10, 319,
323–24, 502n100

de Espil, Courtney Letts, 188–89, 443n9

de Gaulle, Charles, 179, 190, 218, 231

Dewey, Thomas E, 220, 235, 338

"disability," 43, 61, 63, 78, 254, 447n145,
449n9

Dodd, Thomas J., 414, 511n6

Donovan, William "Wild Bill," 281–85

Douglas, William O., 397

Duggan, Lawrence, 279–80

Dulles, John Foster, 338, 379, 383

Dunn, James, 231, 324, 327, 339

Durbrow, Elbridge, 205, 260–61, 263, 272–
73, 289, 312, 319–21, 326, 358, 417

Dzhugashvili, Joseph. See Stalin

Eden, Anthony, 1–2, 87, 89–90, 137, 142,
145–48, 150, 155–57, 159, 162, 167,
191, 194, 201–2, 216, 226, 233, 237–38,
250, 294, 299–300, 325, 333, 335,
340–41, 405, 407, 428

Eisenhower, General Dwight D., 349, 415
"election" speech of Stalin, 394–400
emotional beliefs, 12–13, 246, 289, 418, 425, 427, 439n11; of Churchill, 13–14; of Harriman, 15; of Kennan, 16; of Roosevelt, 13; of Stalin, 14; of Truman, 14–15
emotional dispositions, 17, 195, 328–29, 382, 419
emotional reactions: anger, 4, 6, 17, 49, 52, 88–89, 99, 146, 175, 204, 216, 225, 232, 255, 263–64, 273–74, 278, 288, 292–93, 297, 309–10, 319, 334, 339, 368, 381, 386, 389–90, 392, 407–8, 425, 427; anxiety, 5, 17–18, 36, 43, 71, 100, 195, 205, 207, 221, 238, 272, 278, 289, 312–13, 328–29, 334–35, 344, 350, 356, 358, 360, 362, 379, 382, 395, 404–5, 414, 426; condescension, 150, 162, 165, 215, 241, 292–93, 297, 333, 388, 489n228; contempt, 17, 88, 134, 241, 273, 276, 286–87, 293, 308, 330, 356, 390, 425; disgust, 17, 53, 175, 244, 293, 295, 310, 348, 354, 361, 414, 424, 427, 521n19; fear, 4–5, 14, 42, 56, 71, 91, 103, 121, 127, 145, 149, 151, 160, 164, 179–80, 184, 199, 216, 232–33, 254, 258, 260, 269, 280, 284, 286–87, 297, 310–11, 313, 315, 318, 322, 324–26, 328–29, 331, 333, 335–37, 344–45, 348, 351, 358, 366, 369, 375, 383–84, 395, 404, 406, 413, 422–23, 428, 493n17, 521n5; humiliation, 42, 68, 75, 91, 95, 109, 146, 164, 173–75, 187, 239, 276, 293, 297, 323, 330, 352, 381, 401, 406, 408; pride, 5, 15, 17, 25, 28, 63–64, 69, 100, 111, 114, 119, 147, 165, 176, 201, 230, 268, 277, 284, 288, 292–94, 315, 322, 328–29, 336, 359–62, 377, 383–84, 395, 397–98, 403–4, 414, 422, 425, 498n5; resentment, 6, 19, 55, 91, 126, 161, 164, 168, 175, 215, 220, 238, 240, 245, 255, 258, 260, 262, 268–69, 273, 286, 296–97, 307, 309, 317, 319, 328, 334, 368, 381, 386, 397–98, 485n117; respect, 2, 5, 18, 50, 59, 104, 123, 150, 152, 163, 165, 168, 170, 174–75, 181, 192, 195–97, 216, 219, 239, 242, 249, 271, 277, 286, 304, 324–25, 328, 330–31, 336, 348, 352–53, 362, 380, 385, 401, 405–7, 422, 425–26, 498n5

emotions and foreign relations, 435, 441–42n40
"exoticism" of Soviets, 331, 506n91

Faymonville, Brigadier General Philip, 271–72
Fitin, Pavel, 281, 284
Forrestal, James V., 325, 344, 372–74, 391, 397, 413, 415
Franck, James, 374
Frankfurter, Felix, 7, 58–59, 324, 346, 376
Fulton speech. See Iron Curtain speech of Churchill

Gaddis, John L., 9–11, 441n29
Gardner, Lloyd C., 8
gender identity, 3, 46, 97–98, 139, 152, 266, 329, 341–42, 355, 405, 412; of Churchill, 48–49, 153; of Clark Kerr, 298; of Roosevelt, 46–48, 324, 447n140, 447n141; of Stalin, 50–51, 127
Germany, postwar policy toward, 2, 12, 23, 122, 155, 169, 185, 199–201, 211, 213–14, 217–18, 221, 223–24, 230, 243–44, 246, 256, 258, 286, 353, 355–56, 365–69, 377, 392, 417, 419, 426, 521n5
Gildersleeve, Virginia, 338
Gilmore, Eddy, 414
Gomułka, Władysław, 218, 221
Gorbachev, Mikhail, 424
Gousev, Fedor, 335–36
Gouzenko spy case, 280, 384
Grew, Joseph C., 231
Gromyko, Andrei, 213–15, 237, 242, 331, 393
Groves, General Leslie R., 373–74
Gymnast, 157–73

Hale, Dorothy, 78, 81, 125
Halifax, Lord, 113, 120, 131, 155, 160, 222–23, 318, 376, 474n114
Harlow, Jean, 45
Harriman, W. Averell, 6–7; background and personality of, 15, 109, 303, 311; and Churchill family, 111–12; and Pamela Churchill, 113–18; and Churchill visit to Moscow, 174–78; and Clark Kerr, 293; and Cold War historiography, 9; and comparison of Stalin with Roosevelt and Churchill, 9; and confronting

Stalin, 220, 260, 313, 319–24, 326; and cooperation between OSS and NKVD, 282–84; death of and Molotov, 424; and disapproval of Byrne's diplomacy, 385–87; on dollar diplomacy toward Russia, 367, 393; and emotional disposition, 382; and evacuation of POWs, 309; and excluding Russians from Berne negotiations, 248, 310; and expectations in Moscow, 301–2; and FDR, 75, 108–12, 230, 236, 310–11; and FDR's death, 205; and Hopkins, 82–83, 109–10, 187, 231, 394; and impact on Truman, 319–24, 328, 344–45; and Kennan's long telegram, 413; and Kremlin banquet drinking, 291, 293–94; as Lend Lease "Expediter," 99–102, 108–12, 140; and Maisky, 166; and Moscow mission of Hopkins, 347–50, 352–54; and Pearl Harbor, 148–49; and Poland, 190, 215, 219–20; and public opinion, 393, 414, 423; and renewed faith in FDR, 428; and Schlesinger, 9, 428; and Stalin, 15, 309, 381–82, 391; and Warsaw uprising, 219, 500–501n56

Harriman, Kathleen, 101, 107, 109–12, 115, 118, 148, 205, 232, 234, 238–40, 242, 275, 282, 291–94, 296–97, 301, 304, 309, 354, 461n92, 500n56

Harrison, Salisbury, 117, 263–64, 304, 462n93, 493n15, 493n17, 522n27

Harvey, Oliver, 137, 145–49, 156–57, 162, 164, 218, 221

Haskell, John H. F., 281–82

Haslam, Jonathan, 12

Helms, Richard, 320

Henderson, Leon, 255

Henderson, Loy, 260, 266, 326,

Hersey, John, 278, 298, 511n6

Hill, George A., 215, 493n17

Hiss, Alger, 241, 279, 289, 489n227

Hitler, Adolf, 12, 14, 54, 86, 93, 98, 100, 104, 119, 121, 126–27, 131, 134, 139, 143, 159, 167, 173, 178, 219, 249, 273, 284, 316, 327, 334, 348, 353, 356, 361, 367, 372, 379, 392, 408

homosexuality: and McCarthyite accusations, 289–90; in Moscow embassy, 270–72

homosocial behavior: and Anglo-American special relations, 106; definition of,

447n141, 494n31; at Kremlin banquets, 95, 259–60, 295, 300–301; in Moscow embassy, 267–70, 290

Hoover, J. Edgar, 106, 190, 222, 270, 281, 283–84, 317

Hopkins, Diana, 71, 82–84, 318, 455n144

Hopkins, Harry L.: and Atlantic conference, 127, 132, 134; and Bohlen, 229–31, 327, 349–50, 394; and Bracken, 85; and Byrnes, 319, 355; and Casablanca conference, 180; and Churchill, 50, 83, 99, 102–4, 129, 160, 238–39, 319; and Churchill family, 106–7, 111; and Pamela Churchill, 101, 106–7, 113–14, 116; and communism, 160, 168, and Corcoran, 68; courage of, 128, 140; death of, 393–94; estrangement from FDR of, 62, 83–84, 206–7, 222, 230, 232, 236, 238, 245, 250–51, 258, 317–18; 490n282; and FBI telephone transcripts, 222, 317; and FDR's caution regarding war, 119–20; and FDR's circle, 61, 78–84, 222; FDR's reliance on, 79–82, 112; and FDR's religious faith, 136; and "getting at" Stalin, 55; girlfriends of, 78, 81, 100, 455n154, 455n155, 461n92; and Harriman, 109–10, 349; health problems of, 61, 79–81, 123–24, 127–28, 132, 204, 207, 232, 236, 318, 354, 454n136; and Le-Hand, 72, 78; marriage of, 83–84; and Marshall, 80–81; and mission to London, 99–107, 117; and mission to Moscow (1941), 121, 123–27, 132; and mission to Moscow (1945), 347, 349–54; and Molotov, 168; and Poland, 190, 349–54; and postwar planning, 186, 189, 244; and postwar policy, 368, 382; presidential ambitions of, 79, 207, 238–39; revived influence of, 229–30; and Eleanor Roosevelt, 82; and Roosevelt family, 67, 451n41; as secretary of commerce, 110; and Stalin, 124–27, 140, 248, 349–54; and Steinhardt, 125; and "strategic strong points," 201–2; and Tehran conference, 187, 193, 195, 198–99, 201–2, 204; and Truman, 317–19, 327, 349–51, 354; and "white man's burden," 170; and Yalta conference, 231–32, 236, 238–39, 245, 248, 251; and Yeaton, 126

Hopkins, Louise (Macy), 83–84, 178, 206, 230, 317–18, 327, 349, 354–55, 461n92
House, Edward M., 366
Howe, Louis M., 13, 47, 59–64
Hull, Cordell, 74, 111, 119, 134, 143, 171, 178, 186–92, 194, 227, 338, 341, 379
Hull, Frances, 188–89
Hyde Park agreement (Tube Alloys), 173, 222

Ickes, Harold L., 58, 61–62, 70, 72, 74, 78, 106, 119, 153, 222, 224, 318, 320, 449n4
Ickes, Jane, 82
ideological manifestos, 394–95; of Churchill, 401–5; of Kennan, 408–13; of Stalin, 395–400; and subsequent back-tracking, 415–16
ideology and culture, 16, 24, 52, 146–47, 164, 267–68, 291–92, 303, 330, 350–51, 376, 403, 422–23, 427
Iron Curtain speech of Churchill, 360, 395, 402–8
Ismay, Lord Hastings "Pug," 88–90, 105, 287
isolation of diplomats in Moscow, 6, 16, 19, 181, 260–63, 268, 270–71, 277–78, 280–81, 410

Jacob, Ian, 129–31, 135–36, 138, 151, 153–54, 177, 181
Jackson, Robert, 159
Japan, 52, 108, 260, 372, 391; and post-war world, 2, 14, 169–70, 180, 194, 201, 211, 213, 217, 252, 256, 258, 346, 378, 380–82, 385, 392, 419–20; as war-time enemy, 8, 89, 97, 102, 119, 125, 134, 140, 142–44, 147–48, 152, 158, 173, 177, 198, 223, 243, 256, 281, 284, 304, 312, 349, 353, 363, 366, 401, 413
Jebb, Cynthia, 296
Jebb, Gladwyn, 281, 296
Jiang Jieshi (Chiang Kai-Shek), 56, 148, 193, 195, 243, 297, 299, 385, 390–91, 474n117

Kaganovich, Lazar, 43, 91, 406
Kalinin, Mikhail, 91, 265, 396
Kamenev, Lev, 46, 91
Katyn massacre, 164, 199, 215

Keat, G. H., 424–25
Kennan, George F.: and Bullitt, 259, 265, 268, 409; and Byrnes's diplomacy, 385–86; and Cold War emotionalism, 417; emotional beliefs of, 15–16; and "honeymoon" of 1933–34, 260, 264–66, 270; and Hopkins, 353; increased influence of, 413–14; isolation of foreigners and, 16, 220, 260, 401, 410; and long telegram, 394, 408–13, 416; passion for Russia of, 16, 220, 264, 416, 427; and postwar Russia, 328, 396; and purges, 269–70; and Roberts, 335; and Roosevelt's policy, 229; and Stalin 310, 428; and threats to American society, 409–10, 412–13, 416; and Warsaw uprising, 304
Kennedy, John F., 262, 314, 314, 341, 422
Kennedy, Joseph P., 66, 70, 100, 103, 401, 452n74, 485n117
Kerr, Archibald Clark. See Clark Kerr, Archibald
Khlevniuk, Oleg, 91
Khrushchev, Nikita S., 91, 93, 95, 422, 521n5
Kipling, Rudyard, 374
King, William Mackenzie, 255–56, 491n300, 491n304, 492n311
Knox, Frank, 119
Kolko, Gabriel, 8
Kollontay, Alexandra, 332–33, 352, 506n96
Korneichuk, Aleksandr, 293–95
Koukin, Konstantin, 332
Kuromiya, Hiroaki, 10

LaFeber, Walter, 8
Lange, Oskar, 217
Larson, Deborah Welch, 10
Laufer, Jochen, 12
lavender scare, 289
Leahy, Admiral William D., 90, 180, 210, 224, 236–37, 241, 251, 255, 303, 317, 324, 326, 360–62, 364, 403
Lee, Duncan, 279, 283–84
Leffler, Melvyn P., 11
LeHand, Marguerite "Missy": background and personality of, 70–71; and Bullitt, 62, 70, 75, 452n67, 485n117; closeness with FDR of, 68–70; collapse of, 58, 75–77; and Corcoran, 65–66; death of,

59, 224; and FDR's coolness toward, 76, 143, 485n117; and FDR's demands on, 68, 76, 84; and FDR's dependence on, 13, 58–61, 63, 71–73, 77–78, 143, 208, 222, 224, 258, 454n120; and FDR's will, 77; and Hopkins, 78; "party politics" of, 66; problems of, 61, 75; records of, 77, 454n120

Lend-Lease, 17, 80, 99–100, 102, 105, 107–8, 111, 117, 120, 126–27, 134, 140, 169, 212, 222, 240, 243, 250, 271, 277–81, 306, 320, 328, 331, 346, 350, 352–53, 374, 377, 389, 392, 398, 484n113

Lindbergh, Anne Morrow, 98

Lindemann, Frederick (Lord Cherwell, also "the Prof"), 85, 90, 115, 222–23, 513n41

Lippmann, Walter, 195, 216–17, 227, 250, 252–53, 320, 338–39, 341–43, 381, 383–84, 397, 406–7, 413, 416, 420

Litvinov, Maxim, 51, 121, 203, 213, 259, 262, 285, 316, 384, 393

Lockhart, Robert Bruce, 86–87, 89

London Foreign Ministers conference, 378–80

London Polish government, 221, 252, 354

long telegram of Kennan, 273, 335, 386, 394, 397, 408–14

Longworth, Alice Roosevelt, 46

Lubin, Isador, 355–56

Lublin Committee, 217, 221, 247, 250, 252, 320, 322

Luce, Clare Boothe, 74, 78, 157

Luce, Henry, 74, 113, 116, 118

Maclean, Donald, 240, 337

MacLeish, Archibald, 320, 345

Maisky, Ivan, 19, 166, 173, 184, 213–14, 237, 248, 258, 333, 367, 392, 425–26

Malta conference, 232–33, 240

Marshall, General George C., 79–81, 90, 112, 131–32, 157–58, 161, 163, 169, 173, 179, 193, 198, 207, 272, 294, 320, 324, 357, 362, 371

Martha, Crown Princess of Norway, 63–64, 72–77, 83, 120, 130, 172, 452n90

Mastny, Vojtech, 10

Matthews, H. Freeman "Doc," 386

Maxwell, Elsa, 342–43

McCarthy, Joseph, 189, 289–90

McCloy, John J., 9, 109, 365, 369, 371, 423

McCluer, Franc "Bullet," 403

McCormick, Anne O'Hare, 337–38

McIntire, Ross, 60, 79, 120, 208

Meiklejohn, Robert K., 261, 284, 301, 309, 312, 317, 319, 343, 354, 361

Mercer, Lucy (Rutherfurd), 62, 72–75, 120, 208–9, 225, 255–56, 318

Messer, Robert, 389

Michela, Joseph A. "Mike," 271–72, 275–76, 496n63

Mikołajczyk, Stanisław, 216, 218, 221, 354

Mikoyan, Anastas, 91, 145, 293–94, 300

Miller, Earl, 62–63, 204

Miscamble, Wilson D., 11

Molotov, Vyacheslav: and Churchill, 172, 407; and Davies, 323–24; and "election" campaign, 396; and German invasion, 141, 143; and getting guests drunk, 156, 291, 293–94, 499n13; and Harriman, 301–2, 312, 320, 424; and Iran, 389; and London Foreign Ministers conference, 378–80; mission to London of, 165–68, 171–72; mission to Washington of, 168–71; and Moscow Foreign Ministers conference (October 1943), 194; and Moscow Foreign Ministers conference (December 1945), 385–86; and new uniforms, 292–93, 498n5; and New York City vacation, 171, 176, 472n51; and not being "fooled," 165, 330–31, 352; personality of, 167–68; and Poles, 245, 250; and policeman approach, 169–70; and Potsdam conference, 364; press conferences of, 342; and pride, 328, 331, 422, 426; and reparations, 367; and respect, 18; and Roosevelt, 168, 171, 422; and Roosevelt's death, 205, 324–25, 418–19; and San Francisco conference, 334, 339–42, 349; and second front, 169; and Stalin's early years, 34, 46; Stalin's scapegoating of, 157, 299, 327, 330, 380–81; and Stalin's terror, 93–94; and Stalin's "wife," 144; and "strategic strongpoints," 201–2; and Truman, 323, 325–27, 422, 505n69; wife of, 95

Montefiore, Simon Sebag, 10

Moran, Lord (Charles Wilson), 45, 56, 87, 149, 152–53, 155, 173, 176, 179, 182, 198–200, 203, 219, 236, 242, 407

Morgenthau, Henry, Jr., 224, 355

Moscow Foreign Ministers conference (October 1943), 194

Moscow Foreign Ministers conference (December 1945), 383–87

Mowry, George F., 314

Murrow, Edward R., 99, 101–2, 107, 116–17, 125

Naimark, Norman, M. 12

open door policy, 7, 134–35, 156, 171, 184, 194, 222, 260, 262, 281, 329, 363, 382, 428

"Operation Unthinkable," 336, 348, 407

Oppenheimer, J. Robert, 377

Orlemanski, Stanislaus, 216–17

Oumansky, Constantine, 122–23

Ovakimyan, Gaik, 281

Patterson, Robert, 371

Pauley, Edwin W., 356, 367

Pearl Harbor, 141–43, 148–49

Pendar, Kenneth, 181–82

Pepper, Claude, 377

Perkins, Frances, 47, 78–82, 136, 141, 186, 207, 232, 317

Poland, 4, 18, 164, 169–70, 190–92, 201–3, 211, 215–21, 230, 234, 243, 246–50, 252, 255, 273, 293, 306–9, 320–26, 335–37, 339–41, 346, 349–52, 354, 367, 369, 405

Pleshakov, Constantine, 11

Poltava airbase, 304–9, 501n64

Portal, Charles "Peter," 101, 117, 236, 249

Post-Hostilities Planning Staff, 286, 336–37

Potsdam conference, 3, 5, 360–69, 378, 390, 408, 511n1

Princess Martha. See Martha, Crown Princess of Norway

public opinion polls, 315, 350, 367, 375–76, 381, 383, 402–3, 406, 486n139, 503n17, 509n173, 515n106

purges by Stalin, 14, 40, 43, 46, 54, 91, 93–94, 123, 192, 213, 260, 269, 272, 280, 326, 348, 396, 425

Radek, Karl, 91, 268

Reagan, Ronald, 424

Reilly, Mike, 162, 196, 478n205

reparations, 23, 155, 172, 244, 352, 355–56, 361, 366–69, 420

respect and trust as cultural signifiers, 18

Rigdon, William M., 196–97

Roberts, Frank K., 287, 292, 322, 326, 333, 335, 343, 379, 382, 386–87, 400, 408, 426

Roberts, Geoffrey, 11

Rockefeller, Nelson, 339–40

Roosevelt, Eleanor, 21, 35, 37, 43, 60, 62–69, 72–73, 75, 77, 81–84, 142, 161, 170, 205, 208, 225–26, 316, 320, 344, 406, 451n40

Roosevelt, Elliott, 66–67, 69, 130–34, 137, 183, 465n177, 474n117

Roosevelt, Franklin D.: acting ability of, 42; anticolonialism of, 162, 170, 183, 200, 244–45; and Arcadia conference, 151–55, 157–62; and Atlantic Charter, 134–35, 169, 184–85, 228–29, 251; and Atlantic conference, 128–39; and atom bomb, 222–23, 256, 419; attitude toward war of, 35, 38–39, 183–84, 445n82; and Axis threat, 118–20, 131–32; background and personality of, 13, 23–26, 54; boyish behavior of, 130, 178–79; and Casablanca conference, 178–82; charisma of, 42–44; and Churchill, 21–22, 41–42, 50, 55–57, 86, 90, 100–104, 106–7, 128–39, 146–48, 151–55, 157–62, 172–73, 177–78, 193, 198, 222–23, 233–36; 449n186; and communications with public, 209–12, 229, 250–53, 258; and communism, 51–52, 160; contingent death of, 253–58, 492n317; and "disability," 61–130, 136, 139, 178; and "Wild Bill" Donovan, 281–83; and Eleanor, 21, 64–65, 82–83, 170; election of 1944 and, 225–26; emotions of, 4–5; and failure of Woodrow Wilson, 184; and fear of "race war," 158–59, 170; and fireside chats, 120; and the four policemen approach, 160, 169, 185, 201–2, 229, 419; gambling instinct of, 13, 159–60; gender identity of, 3, 46–48, 97–98, 447n140–41; health problems of, 120, 183–84, 207–9, 224–

26, 232, 253–54, 256, 462n107, 463n123, 491n285; honeymoon of, 21; impact of death of, 2, 4, 11, 205, 311, 313–14, 316–17, 320, 323, 325, 327, 337–39, 342–46, 349–53, 355–58, 360, 362–63, 368, 376, 378–79, 383, 392, 416–17, 419, 421–22; and Middle East, 182, 195; and military strategies, 133–39, 150, 157–62, 165–66, 173, 179–80; and Missy, 58–59, 68–78; mode of thinking of, 79–80; and Molotov, 168–72; and monarchy, 24–25; and Pearl Harbor, 141–42, 148–49; and Poland, 191, 202–3, 215, 217, 221, 246–48; postwar criticism of, 289; and postwar Germany, 199, 223–24, 244; postwar vision of, 6, 419; relations with aides, 2, 13, 58–96, 143, 222, 224, 236, 421; religion of, 35, 136–37; report on Yalta of, 250–53; and Theodore Roosevelt, 35–37, 39, 41, 108, 375; schooling of, 32–33; and second front, 169; and Soviet borders, 164, 185; and Stalin, 1–3, 22–23, 55–57, 122–23, 126, 157, 159, 163–66, 170, 177, 192–93, 195–204, 206, 239, 242, 249, 255–56, 310–11, 420, 426, 428, 478n205; and Tehran conference, 6, 165, 193, 204; and Truman, 15, 62, 195, 224, 227, 346–47, 363, 371, 421; and unconditional surrender, 179–81, 184; and U.S. Navy, 119; and Welles controversy, 186–90; and women, 45, 63, 69–70, 72–74, 81, 83; and Yalta, 232–50, 355. *See also* Hopkins, Harry L.

Roosevelt, James (FDR's father), 25, 37

Roosevelt, Sara Delano, 24, 26

Roosevelt, Theodore, 21, 35–39, 41, 108, 375, 445n69

Rosenman, Samuel I., 58, 62, 69, 77, 83–84, 142–43, 206, 210, 225, 251, 455n152

Ross, Charles G., 371

Rossbach, Richard, 309

San Francisco conference, 337–43, 358

Sargent, Orme G., 146, 334, 352

Savrola, 30, 44, 52, 402

Scandrett, Richard, 356

Schiff, Dorothy, 55–56, 62–63, 69, 74, 81–82, 455n152

Schlesinger, Arthur M., Jr., 9–10, 12, 428

Service, Robert, 10

Sherwood, Robert E., 1, 78, 118, 120, 155, 210, 328, 428

sex and secrets: in London, 113–18; in Moscow embassy, 261–62, 266–67, 289

Shoumatoff, Elizabeth, 256–57

Smith, Walter Bedell, 390

Soames, Mary, 104–6, 111

Soviet loan request, 393

Soviet officials, and pride in new uniforms, 194, 199, 292, 498n5

Soviet sense of inferiority, 18–20, 195, 333, 379–80, 383, 426

Soviet soldiers, apparently "savage" behavior of, 286–87, 309–10, 361, 424–25, 506n77

Soviet spying, 223, 240–41, 261, 278–84

Spaak, Paul Henri, 341

Special Operations Executive (SOE), 215, 219, 281, 307

Spewack, Sam, 263, 275

Stalin, Joseph: and abortive U.S. loan, 393; as actor, 43; and Alexander I (czar), 2; and alienation of Allies, 392–93; and Nadya Alliluyeva (second wife), 46, 95; and Svetlana Alliluyeva (daughter), 94–95, 176, 366; and attitude toward war, 24, 39–40; and atom bomb, 256, 366, 377–78, 383, 385, 417; background and personality of, 14, 22–23, 31–35; and Bolshevism, 53; and Bullitt, 259–60, 268–69; and Berne surrender negotiations, 255, 310; charisma of, 42; and China, 390–91; and Churchill visit of August 1942, 173–77; and Churchill visit of October 1944, 227, 229; and Clark Kerr, 298–300; collapse of, 141–44; as compared to Roosevelt and Churchill, 9, 237; crimes of, 12, 90–93, 427; and cultural differences with the West, 329–23, 340–43, 354; daily routine of, 94–95; and D-day, 285; and Eden visit of December 1941, 147–48, 155–57; "election" speech of, 395–400; emotions of, 5, 146, 174–77; gender identity of, 50, 127, 298–99; and German invasion, 18, 141–45, 155; and Harriman, 301–4, 309–10, 381–82; and Hopkins's 1941 visit, 123–28, 140; and

Stalin, Joseph: (*cont.*)
   Hopkins's 1945 visit, 349–54; and ideo-
      logical control, 291–92; and Iran, 389–
      90; and Kremlin banquets, 156–57; and
      London trip of 1907, 22, 24; and Marx-
      ist-Leninism, 391–92; and military strat-
      egy, 159; and Molotov's diplomacy, 165–
      72, 340–42, 378–80, 385–87; and
      physical problems of, 50, 125, 203, 381;
      and Poland, 19, 164, 191, 215, 217–18,
      220–21, 246–48, 322, 325, 349–54,
      367–69; and postwar aims, 155–56, 167,
      170, 204, 212–15, 226, 243–44, 353,
      382, 389–92, 420–21; and postwar Ger-
      many, 199; and prospective meeting with
      Roosevelt, 163, 189, 192–93; as reader,
      33; and references to international moral
      standards, 124–26; and relations with
      aides, 42–43, 90–96; and relations with
      Allies, 194–95; and reluctance to travel,
      195, 226; responsibility for Cold War of,
      7–12; and revolution, 200; and second
      front, 163, 169, 192–93, 198; as a semi-
      nary student, 33–34; supposed Asian
      background of, 22, 122, 158–59, 165;
      supposed madness of, 8–12; and Tehran
      conference, 193–203; and Turkey, 390;
      and turning "isolationist," 392; values
      of, 53–54; and women, 45–46, 446n130;
      as writer, 40–41; and Yalta conference,
      237, 242–49. *See also* Churchill, Win-
      ston S, relations with Stalin; Roosevelt,
      Franklin D., relations with Stalin
Stassen, Harold, 338
Steinhardt, Laurence, 121–23, 125–26,
   272–75
Stettinius, Edward R., Jr., 7–8, 227, 230–
   32, 236–37, 241, 324, 327, 339–43, 358,
   371, 379, 393
Suckley, Margaret "Daisy," 56, 130, 132,
   154, 168, 172, 178, 182, 186, 208, 212,
   225–26, 235, 253, 256, 318, 471n28
Svanidze, Ekaterina, 45–46
Swing, Raymond, 353, 345

Tehran conference, 193–204
Thayer, Charles W., 266–70, 272–73,
   288–89
Thompson, Llewellyn, 262

Thompson, Walter Henry, 129, 154
Tolstoy conference, 227, 448n170
Truman, Harry S: and American exceptionalism, 376–77, 417, 419–20; and atom
   bomb, 356, 359, 366, 370–71, 384, 400,
   417, 440n17, 509n157; and attitude toward Anglo-American-Canadian atomic
   summit, 380–81; and attitude toward
   summits with Soviets, 3, 6, 363–65, 383,
   392; background and personality of, 14–
   15, 314–16, 171, 387, 417; and Big
   Three approach, 357–58, 363; and Byrnes, 319, 368–69, 387–88, 400; and
   changing Roosevelt's approach to Russians, 1–3, 11–12, 220, 313, 316–17,
   319–27, 337–40, 344, 347, 349–60, 363,
   366–67, 376, 422, 428; and Churchill,
   177, 360, 394; and Churchill's Fulton
   speech, 402–6, 420; and Davies, 325,
   346–47; and defeated Germans, 360–61,
   367–69, 417; emotional beliefs of, 14–
   15; emotional reactions to Russia of, 5,
   328, 358, 388–89, 428; and Harriman,
   312–13, 319–23, 326, 361, 400; and
   Hopkins, 317–19, 349–54; and Iran crisis, 389–90; and Lubin, 356; and Molotov, 325–27, 505n69; and Oppenheimer,
   377; and Pauley, 356; and Potsdam conference, 347, 359, 363, 390, 511n1;
   presidential style of, 314–16; and pride
   in American military, 362; and reparations, 356, 366–68; and Roosevelt, 62,
   195, 224, 227, 346–47, 363, 371, 421;
   and San Francisco conference, 340–42;
   and Stalin, 359, 362, 365, 377–78,
   512n21; and Stimson, 370–71, 376; and
   Turkish crisis, 390–91, 401; as vice president, 15, 227
Tully, Grace, 153

unconditional surrender, 179–80, 184, 312,
   348
United Nations: General Assembly of, 211,
   227, 248, 393–40, 378, 383, 386, 389;
   organization of, 186, 201, 211, 244–45,
   339–40, 413, 421, 497n96; Security
   Council of, 211, 247–48, 255, 339–40,
   354, 358, 386, 401
United Nations Declaration, 154, 228

Vandenberg, Arthur, 215, 338–39, 341, 354, 384, 401
Vaughan, Harry, 371
Venona. *See* Soviet spying
Vinson, Fred, 372, 374–75
Voroshilov, Kliment, 91–92, 157, 268–69, 300
Vyshinsky, Andrey, 362, 420, 425–26

Wallace, Henry A., 171, 173, 315, 320, 323, 371–73, 406–7, 413
Warsaw uprising, 218–20, 282, 304, 321, 427, 500n56
Welles, Sumner: ability of, 74, 186; and Atlantic Charter, 134–35, 147; and Bullitt's attack on, 74–75, 120, 187–90; and Churchill's drinking, 100; drinking problem of, 60, 187; and FDR, 47, 59–60, 185–86, 190, 476n151; feud with Hull of, 187–89; and Poles, 190; sexuality of, 61, 74
Warner, Christopher, 287, 332, 425, 499n13, 506n77, 506n91
Werth, Alexander, 291, 366
Westad, Odd Arne, 11
White, Harry Dexter, 279

White House: cockroaches in, 456m165; LeHand and, 69, 71, 73, 75; Molotov's visit to, 168–69
Whitney, John Hay "Jock," 116, 118, 461n92
Williams, William A., 8
Willkie, Wendell, 225, 248, 299–300, 446n130
Wilson, Geoffrey, 262, 332, 506n77
Wilson, Woodrow, 13, 38–39, 51, 70, 119, 184–85, 190, 210, 226, 263, 337, 366
Wilsonian principles, 134, 146–47, 185, 296, 219, 212, 229, 250, 316, 354, 368, 382
Winant, John G., 89, 99, 103, 105, 107, 111–12, 148–49, 159, 167, 190, 226
Winterton, Paul, 274, 425

Yalta conference, 232–50
Yeaton, Ivan D., 122, 126, 271–72, 275–76, 289

Zhdanov, Andrei, 91, 94, 330, 401
Zhukov, Marshall Georgi, 144, 380
Zinoviev Grigori, 40, 91
Zubok, Vladislav, 11